MICHAEL BURLEIGH has taught at Oxford, [...] been a Visiting Professor at Rutgers, Washington and Lee, and Stanford universities. His work has been translated into fifteen languages, and his *Third Reich: A New History* won the Samuel Johnson Prize for Non-fiction. He has also won three major film awards for historical television documentaries, including the British Film Institute Award for Archival Achievement. He writes for several newspapers on religion, history and politics.

Visit www.AuthorTracker.co.uk for exclusive information
on your favourite HarperCollins authors.

From the reviews of *Earthly Powers*:

'Remarkable . . . Startling and thrilling'
JONATHAN MEADES, *Observer*

'A hugely informative and stimulating book, by one of the most original historians of the modern age'
NOEL MALCOLM, *Evening Standard*

'*Earthly Powers* is a superb book. Its conception is profound, its execution brilliant. Burleigh is not only formidably learned, he has the true historian's ability to marshal his knowledge to maximum effect'
EDWARD SKIDELSKY, *New Statesman*

'[An] encyclopedic account of religion and politics between the French revolution and the First World War, in which a vast range of material is handled in a deft, readable way . . . Excellent'   *Economist*

'Stimulating . . . Burleigh weaves together a rich miscellany of themes . . . A thought-provoking, deeply civilised book'
KENNETH O. MORGAN, *Independent*

'Tackling everyone from Robespierre to Marx and Dostoevsky, the book has a sweeping ambition that is matched by its learning'
ANDREW HOLGATE, *Sunday Times*

'A fascinating study . . . leavened with dry wit and trenchant opinions
DOMINIC SANDBROOK,
Books of the Year, *Evening Standard*

'A major achievement. Burleigh writes with learning, elegance and insight. He places the great political movements of the nineteenth century in a new and fruitful perspective'
GEOFFREY A. HOSKING, *TLS*

'Fascinating'
PAUL JOHNSON, *Literary Review*

'Enthralling, often brilliant . . . Burleigh unfolds his narrative with great elegance, weaving the central theme into a panoramic view of modern Europe underpinned by deep learning. Beguilingly written and alive with sharply observed themes . . . [A] gripping and original epic narrative'
CHRISTOPHER CLARK, *THES*

'Brilliant . . . highly original'
SIMON HEFFER, *Country Life*

'An enormous and hugely ambitious subject and Burleigh . . . soars masterfully and sometimes acerbically across its wide horizons, swooping periodically to pick apart incidents . . . Scintillating'
STEPHEN BATES, *BBC History* magazine

'Splendid and thought-provoking'
OWEN CHADWICK, *The Tablet*

'Breathtaking in its scope and depth. Never before has the influence of religion on the secular state been described so compellingly and readably'
ALAIN WOODROW, Books of the Year, *The Tablet*

'Magnificent'
DAVID TWISTON-DAVIES, *Catholic Herald*

'[Burleigh's] writing is rich in anecdote and vivid portraiture . . . His analysis of the interplay between religion and politics is well-informed and refreshingly provocative . . . *Earthly Powers* should be required reading for anyone who understands that religion and politics, even when separate, can never be divorced'
PAUL BAUMANN, *Chicago Tribune*

By the same author

Prussian Society and the German Order
Germany turns Eastwards
The Racial State: Germany 1933–1945
Death and Deliverance
(ed) *Confronting the Nazi Past*
Ethics and Extermination: Reflections on Nazi Genocide
The Third Reich: A New History
*Sacred Causes: Religion and Politics from the
European Dictators to Al Qaeda*

MICHAEL BURLEIGH

Earthly Powers

RELIGION AND POLITICS IN EUROPE
FROM THE ENLIGHTENMENT TO
THE GREAT WAR

HARPER PERENNIAL
London, New York, Toronto and Sydney

For Martin Ivens

Harper Perennial
An imprint of HarperCollins*Publishers*
77–85 Fulham Palace Road
Hammersmith
London, w6 8jb

www.harperperennial.co.uk

This edition published by Harper Perennial 2006

1

First published in Great Britain by HarperCollins*Publishers* 2005

A catalogue record for this book
is available from the British Library

ISBN-13 978-0-00-719573-2
ISBN-10 0-00-719573-7

Set in PostScript Linotype Minion with Janson and Trajan display by
Rowland Phototypesetting Ltd, Bury St Edmunds, Suffolk

Printed and bound in Great Britain by Clays Ltd, St Ives plc

'Certain men, the children of Belial, are gone out
from among you, and have withdrawn the
inhabitants of their city, saying, Let us go and serve
other gods, which ye have not known'

Deuteronomy Ch. 13, verse 13

'Carrier came down to the Loire and slew,
Till all the ways and the waves were red:
Bound and drowned, slaying two by two,
Maidens and young men, naked and wed'

Swinburne, *Les Noyades*

'People no longer believe in God. The new religion
is nationalism. Nations no longer go to church. They
go to national associations'

Joseph Roth, *The Radetzsky March* (1932)

CONTENTS

ACKNOWLEDGEMENTS

While completing a book on the Third Reich five years ago I realised that the areas where politics and religion intersect offered fresher, and subtler, imaginative challenges than the reiteration of ghastly events in greater Germany sixty years ago, about which there are so many books, and which are rehearsed on our television screens almost every night. Reconciled to working in an historical backwater, the mass murders on 11 September 2001, and the revival of a broad range of religious questions, lent this new project an unanticipated salience, although it was never intended as a contribution to what Michael Oakeshott memorably called 'practical pasts'.

Earthly Powers is an exploration of the politics of religion, and the religion of politics, broadly construed, in Europe from the Enlightenment to the Great War, although a second, entirely free-standing, volume will link these themes to the totalitarian political religions and beyond. Such an endeavour is necessarily both ambitious and selective. This book is largely about what are called 'political', 'secular' and 'civil' religions, and how these related to Christianity during a time of fitful rather than remorseless secularisation. It does not discuss Islam or Judaism, about which there are so many excellent studies – notably Roger Scruton's *The West and the Rest* and David Vital's *A People Apart* – that another seems superfluous and I am equipped to write neither. The eclectic approach straddles the histories of modern ideologies and politics, of European secularisation, and also of the major Christian denominations, although in no sense is the author either an ecclesiastical historian or theologian, and this is not a history of Christianity.

I have sought to treat the various creeds and traditions, including that of militant secularists, with imaginative sympathy in what is a history rather than polemic. Since there are dark eras in the history of European rationalism, including one genocide committed in the name of Reason, religious people could be less defensive in response to attacks from self-proclaimed rationalists than they currently are. As in most works of history, there are a few messages to the present here, but these have been left encoded, because on some of the issues, such as the desirability of civil religions in the fragmented and secularised societies that the novelist Michel Houellebecq evokes so well in *Atomised* or *Platform*, the author is only slightly less confused than most readers, whose responses will in turn partly depend on their countries' historical experiences. An Australian may see the benefits of citizenship rituals in a way that an equally 'freeborn' English subject of the Queen may not. 'Europe' is frequently traduced nowadays, both by Islamic militants and some Christian circles in the US, as a 'Godless zone'. Some European Christians doubtless feel the same. Part of the point of this book is to show that there are many intermediate conditions, with which we continue to live very well.

At HarperCollins Tim Duggan in New York and Michael Fishwick in London are the best publishers anyone could hope for, while Peter James has again proved to be a prince among editors. The immensely professional Wylie Agency, notably Andrew himself and Michal Shavit in London, enabled me to do what I most enjoy free of academic distraction. John McDade SJ and Lawrence Hemming at Heythrop College gave the initial stimulus to this book when they fast bowled me the Cardinal Basil Hume Memorial Lectures in 2002 on the theme of 'religion and social evil'.

Contacts between historians are international nowadays, which is probably just as well. The History Department at Stanford University provided ideal conditions in which to read, write (and teach) during the winter of 2003. Bob and Liddie Conquest, and Joseph and Marguerite Frank, made the evenings congenial. I am also grateful to Professors Gerhard Besier, Karl Dietrich Bracher, Klaus Hildebrand, Hans Maier, Horst Möller and Heinrich-August Winkler in Germany for their advice and support, and to Tzvetan Todorov for an occasional dialogue in the vicinity of the Jardin des Plantes.

Dr John Nicholls at the London City Mission in Bermondsey enabled me to study its remarkable archive of missionary activity across the nineteenth-century capital. The London Library provided access to any number of books relevant to these themes while the library staff have been unfailingly helpful. Professor Alwin Jackson advised novice reading on Irish history, while Max Likin and Cedric Meletta helped photocopy materials on the provincial French clergy. Adolf and Dawn Wood, Desmond King, Bruce Mauleverer, Sophie Blum and Harvey Starte helped with comments on a book whose themes intrigued them. My wonderful wife Linden has again survived the ordeal of being married to a writer with good grace (most of the time) and has helped with practical problems.

Michael Burleigh
London
November 2004

INTRODUCTION

The simplest way to explain the aims of this book is by describing how it was first conceived, so as to reveal some of the alternative architectures that initially underpinned its surface. The intention was to discuss some notorious 'political religions', notably the civic cults of the Jacobins during the French Revolution, and the no less bizarre festivals and spectacles of the Bolsheviks, Fascists and National Socialists. These were meant to forge a sentimental community – in which emotional plangency was the norm – by refashioning space and time to envelop 'the masses' within a dominant ideology. This would involve wider discussion of related utopian projects, based on the creation of a 'new man' or 'new woman' from the old Adam, an exercise that presumed that human personality is as malleable as wet clay.

Some of this initial structure has been retained, which is why the book starts with the Enlightenment, when many of these projects assumed secular guises – for the notion of a 'new man' is surely related to Christian rebirth through baptism. However, so many important questions arose that the discussion of twentieth-century totalitarianisms had to be relegated to a future volume. In the present book, the final chapter merely introduces two harbingers of what was to re-emerge after the Great War, in the form of the extreme rightists Charles Maurras and Paul Anton de Lagarde, nineteenth-century prophets of the twentieth century's stranger gods.

In the original scheme, the interval of more than a century between the French Revolution and modern totalitarianism would have been filled with some familiar ruminations on the symbolic world of nineteenth-century European nation states, their festivals, monuments, statues, myths and patriotic songs. In its thoroughness, this process of 'nation-building' echoed Europe's conversion to Christianity during the Dark Ages, or more particularly the battle for hearts and minds during

1

the Reformation and Counter-Reformation, when indelible religious identities were formed.

This starting point, traces of which are to be found throughout this book, was reached after extended reading of those who worked in these fields before most of us were born. They were writing under difficult circumstances about the totalitarian regimes that had ruined their lives. It seems appropriate to begin with a homage that also identifies our main concerns, and then to work backwards towards remoter harbingers of the less familiar periods that are at the heart of this book.

Two of the most compelling, and widespread, ways of analysing the dictatorships of the twentieth century have been to compare them as 'totalitarianisms' or as 'political religions'. An influential minority of scholars dislike the term 'totalitarian' for two reasons. They object that it makes the messy, fractious reality of power in these dictatorships too streamlined, as if they operated in accord with the technical drawings of a malign engineer. This commonplace criticism avoids the argument that Communism, Fascism and Nazism *aspired* to, and fantasised about, levels of control unprecedented in history's autocracies and tyrannies, but which are familiar from the world of religion with its concerns with minds and rites. Critics do not even address the ways in which the totalitarian movements resembled Churches, or how, by transcending the separation of Church and state, they represented a reversion to ancient and primitive times when deity and ruler were one. Secondly, being on the liberal left themselves, such critics feel that their own subscription to progressive ideals is sullied whenever Communism, an offshoot of the Enlightenment and French Revolution, is associated with the predatory nihilism of National Socialism. However, since the BBC, the *Guardian* and *New York Times* routinely and rightly use the term 'totalitarian', this may be said to be a battle that has been lost except within parts of the Academy.[1]

The term 'political religion' has a more complicated genesis, and has similarly met with scepticism from secular-minded academics, notably those who wish to evaporate the messianic features of early socialism and Marxism, roots they do not care to be reminded of.[2] The one licensed exception is the current fascination with the theatrical spaces of modern politics, a field which dovetails with many postmodern concerns with representations and symbols.[3] Again, judging by the increasing currency of the term 'political religion', this is a battle that the academic liberal left are losing, at least in continental Europe, where history is not so determinedly divorced from either philosophy or theology.[4]

The term 'political religion' has a more venerable history than many may imagine. It came into widespread use after 1917 to describe the regimes established by Lenin, Mussolini, Hitler and Stalin. The religious analogy was usually with orthodox or heterodox Christianity, although occasionally – as in the case of Bertrand Russell writing in 1920 about Bolshevism – it was with generic Islam.[5] We need not tarry over Russell's historically jejune ratiocinations. In the space of a single paragraph the Bolsheviks reminded him of anchorites in ancient Egypt and Cromwell's Puritans. In a letter to Lady Ottoline Morrell that revealed two of his silly prejudices, Russell also wrote that the Bolsheviks reminded him of 'Americanised Jews' and 'a mixture of Sidney Webb and Rufus Isaacs'. He omitted that bizarre observation from the *New Republic* articles that he reconfigured for his not entirely worthless instant book.[6]

A century earlier the aristocratic scholar Alexis de Tocqueville had made a similar comparison with Islam when he wrote about the Jacobins during the French Revolution, in what many regard as the greatest study of these events yet written. The idea came to him after reading Schiller's account of how early modern religious wars spilled across political boundaries, which reminded Tocqueville of the ideological struggle between Jacobins and counter-revolutionaries in late-eighteenth-century Europe. In a passage that reveals Tocqueville's shifting thoughts he wrote:

> Because the Revolution seemed to be striving for the regeneration of the human race even more than for the reform of France, it lit a passion which the most violent political revolutions have never before been able to produce. It inspired conversions and generated propaganda. Thus, in the end, it took on that appearance of a religious revolution which so astonished contemporaries. Or rather, it itself became a new kind of religion, an incomplete religion, it is true, without God, without ritual, and without life after death, but one which nevertheless, like Islam, flooded the earth with its soldiers, apostles, and martyrs.[7]

By the 1930s, the term 'political [or secular] religion' was adopted by several thinkers in various countries. One of the earliest was the Expressionist writer Frank Werfel, husband of Alma Mahler, who was strongly attracted to Roman Catholicism. In a series of lectures in Germany in 1932,

Werfel described Communism and Nazism as 'substitutes for religion' and as 'forms of beliefs that are anti-religious surrogates for religion and not merely political ideals'.[8] Many of the 1930s writers we admire nowadays worked in rented rooms and with their worldly goods crammed into a suitcase. That erratic, urgent, pared-down quality, based on memories of libraries they had lost, is what recommends such books, in addition to their authors' qualities of mind and imagination.

These thinkers include the Austrian historian Lucie Varga, the brilliant French sociologist Raymond Aron, the German Catholic journalist Fritz Gerlich, the Hungarian screenwriter René Fülöp-Miller, the Russian-Jewish exile Waldemar Gurian, and the Italian Catholic priest–politician Luigi Sturzo, who wrote astute critiques of the contemporary worship of class, state, race and nation. The American Protestant theologian Reinhold Niebuhr also produced influential analyses of the 'new religion' of Soviet Communism, suggesting that such an approach was an ecumenical one.[9]

For many of these people, 'political religions' were not merely academic. Gerlich, for example, was badly beaten in Munich's Stadelheim prison, and then murdered in Dachau during the 'Night of the Long Knives' in June 1934, because of his searing journalistic criticisms of Nazism. As the author of a path-breaking account of Communist millenarianism, he would have met the same fate in Stalin's Soviet paradise.

The most sustained use of the term 'political religion' was by a formidable scholar also writing with personal experience of one. As a young man, the Cologne-born scholar Eric Voegelin had published analyses of the erotic and violent dramas of Franz Wedekind. He won his first academic post in Vienna, on the eve of the 1938 Anschluss with Nazi Germany. This was inauspicious. He lost his job as a political science professor in the law department shortly afterwards, though he was neither Jewish nor a man of the left, as he later explained to perplexed American acquaintances. When the Gestapo began snooping around his private library, Voegelin suggested they confiscate Hitler's *Mein Kampf* along with the *Communist Manifesto* as suspect literature. He decided to flee abroad. Encountering too many spiritual totalitarians among the liberals in East Coast Ivy League universities, he settled for the Hoover Institution at Stanford, which houses his papers, and then a quiet life at the State University in Baton Rouge, Louisiana, where his collected works swelled to over thirty-four volumes.[10]

In 1930s Austria the austere Voegelin had become a marked man. An early book had condemned the dogmas of race, while his second major publication had argued that whereas the inter-war Catholic authoritarian state of Dollfuss and Schussnigg might have evolved into a democracy, there was no such possibility north of the border in Hitler's Germany.[11] A clear-eyed acknowledgement of evil as a real power in the world is one clue to Voegelin's thought:

> When considering National Socialism from a religious stand-point, one should be able to proceed on the assumption that there is evil in the world and, moreover, that evil is not only a deficient mode of being, a negative element, but also a real substance and force that is effective in the world. Resistance against a satanical substance that is not only morally but also religiously evil can only be derived from an equally strong, religiously good force. One cannot fight a satanical force with morality and humanity alone.

Voegelin is a complicated thinker – to whom most ancient and many modern languages were familiar – with an expanding contemporary circle of admirers in Europe and America. His thought is expressed in theological terms, although his lectures and essays adopt a clearer and more polemical style. That obscurantism does not invalidate his use of the concept of 'political religions'. Raymond Aron used the analogous term 'secular religions', without subscribing to Voegelin's cosmic perspective on human affairs, hostility to the Enlightenment or 'pre-Reformation Christian' pessimism about human affairs.

Voegelin's aim was to show that Communism, Fascism and National Socialism were not simply the product of 'the stupidities of a couple of intellectuals in the nineteenth and twentieth centuries ... [but] the cumulative effect of unsolved problems and shallow attempts at a solution over a millennium of Western history'.[12] In his initial stab at these problems, he ventured much further back in time. The crucial distinction he made in his short 1938 book *The Political Religions* was between 'world-transcendent' and 'world-immanent' religions, or in other words the false worship of earth-bound fragments of the former. It was the difference between a god and an idol. Voegelin embarked on a deep archaeological excavation. He burrowed down, so to speak, through Puritan Britain, to medieval Gnostic heresies, until he reached the Nile valley four thousand years ago.

The first 'world-immanent' religion was under pharaoh Amenotheps IV, who in about 1376 BC introduced a new sun religion, declaring himself the son of the sun god Aton. He adopted the name Akhenaton. The phase passed; things reverted to normal. Next, Voegelin turned to the modern era in which the divine basis of political power was rejected, and Church and state gradually separated, but which also witnessed the 'sacralisation' of such collectives as race, state and nation. Put differently, medieval Christendom had been superseded by sovereign nations that ceased referring to divine right, while man sought meaning in the world, attaining ultimate knowledge of it through science. However, these new collectivities of race, state and nation also perpetuated the symbolic language that once linked political life on earth with the next world, including such terms as hierarchy and order, the community as 'church', a sense of collective chosenness, mission and purpose, the struggle between good and evil transmuted into secular terms, and so forth. In secularised forms, medieval millenarian Gnostic heresies contributed a narrower set of pathologies that reappeared as totalitarian ideologies and parties. Voegelin's book ended, where it began, with Akhenaton modernised as the sun-lit 'Führer' bursting through the clouds over Greater Germany: 'The god speaks only to the Führer, and the people are informed of his will through the mediation of the Führer.' Although these ideas may seem preciously remote from the hard thud of the jackboot, and rely upon the alleged identity of 'essences' that are thousands of years apart, it is important to recall that Voegelin interspersed them with powerful accounts of the delirious mass excitations and intoxications, or what in German is called the *Rausch*, of Communism, Fascism and Nazism that he had witnessed first hand:

> The transition from rigid pride to merging into and flowing with fraternity is both active and passive; the soul wants to experience itself and does experience itself as an active element in breaking down resistance; and at the same time, it is driven and swept along by a flood, to which it only has to abandon itself. The soul is united with the fraternal flow of the world: 'And I was one. And the whole flowed' ... The soul becomes depersonalised in the course of finding and unification, it frees itself completely of the cold ring of its own self, and grows beyond its own chilling smallness to become 'good and great'. By losing its own self it ascends to the grander reality of the people: 'I lost myself and found the people, the Reich.'[13]

In American exile, after a war spent arguing that there was something inherently wrong with his fellow Germans, Voegelin returned to the theme of Gnostic heresies as the key to understanding totalitarianism. Their elite salvific doctrines corresponded with the ideological certitudes of the totalitarians of his time. He used the phrase, typical of his writings, 'radical immanentizing of the echaton' to describe how class, nation, state or race forged a sense of sentimental community, giving spurious meaning to the chaos of existence through the substitution of a dream-world for reality. As a seventeenth-century Puritan *Glimpse of Sion's Glory* (1641) promised the dispossessed: 'You see that the Saints have very little now in this world; now they are the poorest and meanest of all; but when the adoption of the Sons of God comes in its fullness, then the world shall be theirs . . . Not only heaven shall be your kingdom, but the world shall be theirs . . . Not only heaven shall be your kingdom, but this world bodily.'[14] Gnostic ideologies were also inherently violent, since there was nothing above or beyond them to limit their activities within the dream turned nightmare. There were no restraints. Voegelin wrote: 'In the Gnostic dream world . . . nonrecognition of reality is the first principle. As a consequence, types of action that in the real world would be considered as morally insane because of the real effects that they have will be considered moral in the dream world because they intended an entirely different effect.' Those dry, limpid observations encompassed the mass murders of Lenin and Stalin, and the Jewish Holocaust. The British scholar Norman Cohn and the French historian Alain Besançon would develop them in their respective studies of millenarian heretics and the Gnostic affinities of Leninism.[15]

The remarkable contribution of British intellectuals to the analysis of totalitarianism is routinely undervalued in favour of the wall-eyed many who worshipped ideas transformed into unadulterated power.[16] We know too much about, for example, Sidney and Beatrice Webb – the admirers of Stalin who co-founded the London School of Economics – and too little about people who combated totalitarian dictatorships with the pen and their lives.

The English Catholic intellectual Christopher Dawson was not afraid to stand up to Nazi bullies when he encountered them. In 1932 he joined among others the historian Daniel Halévy and Stefan Zweig at a conference on 'Europe' in Rome. Speaking to an audience that included Mussolini and Hermann Göring, Dawson said:

The relatively benign Nationalism of the early Romantics paved the way for the fanaticism of the modern pan-racial theorists who subordinate civilisation to skull-measurements and who infuse an element of racial hatred into the political and economic rivalries of European peoples ... If we were to subtract from German culture, for example, all the contributions made by men who were not of pure Nordic type, German culture would be incalculably impoverished.[17]

A few years later that process of racial excision and subtraction was German state policy. In his 1935 *Religion and Modern State*, Dawson traced the rise of the modern imperial state which sought to colonise areas of existence that 'the statesmen of the past would no more have dared meddle with than with the course of the seasons or the movements of the stars'. This applied, Dawson claimed, to the benignly soft totalitarianism of the modern bureaucratic welfare state, as well as to the malignly hard police states of Communists and National Socialists. Politics replicated the absolutist pretensions of religion, enveloping ever wider and deeper areas of life in the political, simultaneously constricting the private. Like a Church, such movements orchestrated hysterical enthusiasm and mass sentimentality, while dictating morality and taste, and defining life's ultimate meanings. Unlike Churches, they also tried to suppress religion itself, pushing Christianity into the hitherto unaccustomed role of defending democracy and pluralism. Using more accessible language than Voegelin, Dawson saw that:

> this determination to build Jerusalem, at once and on the spot, is the very force which is responsible for the intolerance and violence of the new political order ... if we believe that the Kingdom of Heaven can be established by political or economic measures – that it can be an earthly state – then we can hardly object to the claims of such a State to embrace the whole of life and to demand the total submission of the individual ... there is a fundamental error in all this. That error is the ignoring of Original Sin and its consequences or rather identification of the Fall with some defective political or economic arrangement. If we could destroy the Capitalist system or the power of bankers or that of the Jews, everything in the garden would be lovely.[18]

While in 1938 Voegelin was wrestling with Akhenaton and Hitler, an altogether more practical mind was collecting impressions of Nazism derived from a spell as Berlin correspondent of the *Manchester Guardian*. Frederick Voigt was an Anglo-German and Protestant graduate of Birkbeck College's German Department. He was also the journalist who exposed Trotsky's covert connivance with Weimar Germany's illegal rearmament with aircraft, poison gas and tanks. Transferred to Paris shortly before the advent of a Hitler government in 1933, he kept abreast of events in Germany with the help of clandestine correspondents, before returning to London as his paper's chief foreign correspondent in 1934. In that year, Voigt, who in the interim had become a Burkean neo-Tory, largely because he found the left's use of 'Fascism' flat, unimaginative and underwhelming, published a remarkable book called *Unto Caesar*. In one passage he compared totalitarianisms with religions:

> We have referred to Marxism and National Socialism as secular religions. They are not opposites, but are fundamentally akin, in a religious as well as a secular sense. Both are messianic and socialistic. Both reject the Christian knowledge that all are under sin and both see in good and evil principles of class or race. Both are despotic in their methods and their mentality. Both have enthroned the modern Caesar, collective man, the implacable enemy of the individual soul. Both would render unto this Caesar the things which are God's. Both would make man master of his own destiny, establish the Kingdom of Heaven in this world. Neither will hear of any Kingdom that is not of this world.[19]

If we reformulate some of these points, we can see that a simple study of such 'political religions' as Jacobinism, Bolshevism, Fascism and Nazism involves looking at the Christian world of representations that still informs much of our politics, and, in a wider sense, at the anthropological basis of the symbolic world of the nation state, the worker's movement, Bolshevism, Fascism and Nazism. This means going deeper than a superficial contemporary concern with President George W. Bush's or Prime Minister Tony Blair's use of 'evil' and various messianic turns of phrase, and indeed beyond the constitutional worries about Church and state that arise over 'faith schools', Muslim headscarves or prayer breakfasts in the White House. By now, all the major figures began to appear blocked out on the canvas: political religions, utopians, the 'new man', heresy and ideology, and so forth. At that point the equally important blank spaces between these figures began to become worrisome.

The notion of 'political religions' raises a further set of problems – specifically, the implicit assumption that they were surrogates for traditional religion in an age of increasing disbelief or doubt. Voegelin was certainly concerned to show that 'political religions' were a decadent product of secularisation, but he also believed they were an anthropological necessity, in which the religious 'instinct' would always out, merely with another content camouflaged in (symbolically related) guises. In short, he was updating the history of idolatry, in line with George Bernard Shaw's pithy comment that 'The savage bows down to idols of wood and stone; the civilised man to idols of flesh and blood.' In the land of Durkheim, the French sociologist Raymond Aron adopted a more functional approach, when he argued: 'I propose to call secular religions the doctrines that in the souls of contemporaries take the place of a vanished faith, and that locate humanity's salvation in this world, in the distant future, in the form of a social order that has to be created.'[20] This defines religion so broadly that it could encompass old graffiti about the pop star 'Eric Clapton is God' or fans' 'worship' of Manchester United football club. One of the most elusive subjects that this book all too briefly addresses is when, why and how such things as high art (or by implication mass sport) became sources of this-worldly redemption, offering spiritual consolation and refreshment in an age without God, within autonomous and segmented areas, of which religion has itself become a subdivision of 'new age' and psychotherapy in bookshops.[21]

This is why the history of European secularisation is carefully and repeatedly woven into this narrative. It was not a straightforward, linear process, resulting in the present age of nihilism, residually tepid Christianity and confused liberalism that works for many of us in Europe and on the two 'Blue' coasts of the USA. That is not to detract from the many virtues of the core 'Red' heartlands, which it is impossible to replicate in European conditions. This process came about in fits and starts, and for complex reasons, many stemming from liberalised religion rather than science, with significant regressions towards the 'great transcendencies' of the traditional society whose break-up begins this book. It happened at a different pace in each individual country, and the regions that comprised them.[22] It was not the ever receding tide imagined by Matthew Arnold in his poem 'Dover Beach', but a movement of complex currents washing over a craggy shore, where the rock pools have been constantly replenished.

For much of the time, people managed to juggle religious and secular values and views, much as nineteenth-century German socialist workers felt no incongruity in having images of their leader August Bebel and Field Marshal Moltke, the hero of the Franco-Prussian War, pinned to their walls. But there were subtle transformations. Educated people ceased to believe in the Day of Judgement and the fiery reality of hell, focusing on progress within a world whose end reached to infinity when the planet would disappear into the sun. That applies to many educated Christians too, who adopted what is called 'cultural Protestantism', combining a Christianity reduced to a code of ethics and stripped of allegedly implausible elements, together with miltant anti-Catholicism and a broad range of cultural interests that spoke to a certain religiosity. Friedrich Nietzsche described the Protestant bourgeoisie of his time in these terms: 'They feel themselves already fully occupied, these good people, be it by their business or by their pleasures, not to mention the "Fatherland" and the newspapers, and their "family duties"; it seems that they have no time whatever left for religion . . . they live too much apart and outside to feel even the necessity for a "for or against" in such matters.'[23]

In a parallel world, the more intellectual leaders of the European labour movement similarly abandoned their own Edenic vision of heaven on earth, of happy workers striding along the Yellowbrick road to the Red sun. Their uneducated followers continued to subscribe to a revolutionary Judgement Day, in which the rich and powerful would be doomed, and an egalitarian version of Christian ethics, before, confronted by the resilience of capitalism, they too abandoned such apocalyptic revolutionary illusions in favour of the pragmatic amelioration of life on earth. That is why there is a parallel discussion of both Christian and socialist abandonment of the apocalyptic big bang of last days, in favour of the communitarian ethics on which so many European Christians and socialists find so much common ground nowadays.[24]

If the great transcendencies have nowadays collapsed into the atomised and plural outlook of myriad individuals (which makes that condition sound more inviting than its reality), then could it be that 'political religions' represent some halfway stage in times when the symbolic world of Christianity was still a known reality, albeit challenged by secular creeds so untried that their dangers were not widely apparent? Few of us, after all, regard 'science' with the same uncritical esteem as people living on the other side of Auschwitz and Hiroshima, although neither (very different event) should be regarded as the ultimate index of the human experience.[25]

If the fitful, rather than inexorable, history of European secularisation is integral to this story, it also incorporates more classical concerns. These include the relationship between Church and state, the 'culture wars' fought between Christians, liberals and socialists, and how religious institutions, for better or worse, intervened or shaped political life. For much of the century or so discussed in this book, the latter involved a rearguard attempt to perpetuate the traditional alliance of 'throne and altar'. As Chapter 4 shows, this reached its doctrinal zenith with the reactionary ideologues of a Restoration that in turn succumbed to liberal revolutions. This period also saw the beginnings of Catholic and Protestant involvement in the 'Social Questions' engendered by industrialisation, and the emergence of various forms of Christian Socialism on the political left and right.[26] That is why there is a lengthy account of the Churches' accommodations with, and adjustments to, this new form of society, in which, it should be noted, they were clearly a force for good.

Turning from the modestly practical to the impossibly megalomaniac, the book also gives detailed attention to the utopian philosophical religions of the nineteenth century, from Saint-Simon, via Robert Owen, to Auguste Comte and Karl Marx. These projects mainly involved filling the void left by the decline in religion with the no less absolutist and totalising worship of humanity itself, although there was little 'humanity' evident when some of these ideas became a ghastly reality for hundreds of millions of people.[27] This necessitated a lengthy detour into the more outré fringes of sectarian terrorist violence in tsarist Russia. The Gadarene 'devils' so brilliantly evoked in fictional form by Dostoevsky, James and Conrad, whose insights are unrivalled, are still among and around us, even though the religious tradition that partly informs them is not our own. I am not a literary critic, and do not claim to have advanced this particular discussion beyond some excellent books by, among others, James Billington, Joseph Frank and Franco Venturi. Incredibly, what might have been regarded as an eccentric digression has assumed ghastly saliency in a world where religious fanatics crash hijacked aircraft into skyscrapers or saw off the heads of hostages in scenes too terrible to show on western television.[28]

If much of this book consists of a discussion of the politics of religion and the religion of politics, it also includes examples of civil religions, the area that is most potentially relevant to those who may think atomistic pluralism and multiculturalism have gone too far, which would include Germany, France and the Netherlands, and many people – outside the well-paid oligarchs of the race-relations industry – in the UK. We have actually been here before. It is very striking how talk of civil religions coincides with periods of intense crisis, of what Durkheim called 'effervescence' in a nation's affairs. The term gained widespread currency in the 1970s, following a 1967 essay by the distinguished American sociologist Robert Bellah. It was no coincidence that he wrote about American 'oneness', election and messianic purpose at the time of alternative cultures, student protests and the divisive passions of the Vietnam War.[29] What did Bellah mean by civil religion?

If the messianic vision of the 'city upon a hill' derived from displaced English Puritans, the concept was Jean-Jacques Rousseau's. In 1762 he notoriously advocated 'a purely civil profession of faith . . . social sentiments without which a man cannot be a good citizen or a faithful subject'. Bellah was also influenced by the French sociologist Emile Durkheim, who thought that any human group is forged into a community by religious belief, a line of thought that acquired urgency as the Dreyfus Affair bitterly divided Catholic and secular France.[30] Bellah argued that this civil religion existed parallel to the Churches and official religious bodies of the modern USA. Its essence was the idea of America as a chosen nation, with a mission to uphold certain God-given principles and values. It was present, he claimed, in the Declaration of Independence of 1776, and in John F. Kennedy's 1961 inaugural address: 'With a good conscience our only sure reward, with history the final judge of our deeds, let us go forth to lead the land we love, asking His blessing and His help, but knowing that here on earth God's work must truly be our own.'

According to Bellah, this civil religion, consisting of beliefs, rituals, sacred spaces and symbols, 'is concerned that America be a society as perfectly in accord with the will of God as [humans] can make it, and a light to all nations'. As the Great Seal of the United States proclaims: 'annuit coeptis, novus ordo seclorum' ('He [God] gave his approval to these beginnings, a new world order'). At the heart of Washington DC, the major elements of this civil religion have been mightily and movingly rendered in stone, nowhere more so than in Arlington National Cemetery, with an eternal flame commemorating Kennedy himself. The addition of the sheer black Vietnam War memorial or the federal government Holocaust Memorial Museum suggests the adaptability and flexibility of American genius. Even the high-technology Apollo moonlandings could be incorporated as 'one small step for mankind', the fate too of the disastrous Challenger mission that blew up in mid-air, prompting one of Ronald Reagan's greatest speeches.[31]

Civil religion means the incorporation into political culture of a minimal religious reference, especially in societies, such as the USA, where there is a constitutional separation of Church and state. It also includes the creation of a civil ideology – such as secular republicanism – in countries, such as France, that aggressively seek to exclude religion from political life altogether. A monarch who is head of the state Church complicates understanding of this concept in Britain, where the notion seems alien. It is worth noting that Bellah did not conceive of his 'civil religion' as a form of American nationalism. Nor was he connected with the conservative thinker Leo Strauss, or the necessary 'noble lies' that appeal to neo-conservatives and so shock film-makers from the BBC even as they blithely compare the former with Islamist terrorist fanatics.[32]

Bellah was certainly no conservative of any hue. He thought American civil religion obliged people to oppose the Vietnam War. At the end of his essay, he expressed the hope that what he described would become 'simply part of a new civil religion of the world . . . A world civil religion could be accepted as a fulfillment and not as a denial of American civil religion. Indeed, such an outcome has been the eschatological hope of American civil religion from the beginning. To deny such an outcome would be to deny the meaning of American itself.'[33]

The challenge represented by international Islamic terrorism, with which some members of European domestic minorities are in varying degrees of sympathy, has made civil religions particularly pertinent in Europe. According to immigration minister Rita Verdonk, The Dutch government plans to send would-be immigrants a video including tulips and windmills, a biography of William of Orange, topless women sunbathers, and a homosexual wedding to convey the 'essence' of modern Dutch life. Commentators and policymakers have been asking the following questions. Can any nation state survive without a consensus on values that transcend special interests, and which are non-negotiable in the sense of 'Here we stand'? Can a nation state survive that is only a legal and political shell, or a 'market state' for discrete ethnic or religious communities that share little by way of common values other than use of the same currency? Can a society survive that is not the object of commitments to its core values or a focus for the fundamental identities of all its members? Should the indigenous multi-ethnic population also be encouraged to learn something of the values that immigrants are being obliged to adopt before becoming citizens? Should this incipient civil religion ignore the fact that Britain and Europe have been overwhelmingly Christian cultures for the last two millennia, something that surely shapes who they are? How do monarchies with subjects incorporate notions of citizenship derived from more recent republics?

The recent battles over how to acknowledge this in the draft European constitution indicate the problems involved. Even Aleksander Kwasniew-ski, the atheist president of Poland, remarked: 'There is no excuse for making references to ancient Greece and Rome, and to the Enlightenment, without making reference to the Christian values which are so important to the development of Europe.'[34] The way in which history is taught is significant here. Perhaps we need less exposure to the Second World War, and more on such themes as how Christianity came to be the dominant creed, the Reformation and Counter-Reformation, relations between Church and state, and the deep causes of present-day secularity. Not least because, without any of this, entire reaches of our common culture will simply become inaccessible and there will be ghettos of the unassimilated many.[35]

The British government has recently instituted public ceremonies for new 'citizens' although the British are in fact 'subjects' and one shudders at the thought of what a Dutch-style video might contain. In local town halls, people swear an oath of allegiance to the Queen and pledge 'loyalty to the United Kingdom and to respect its rights and freedoms', before adding, 'I will uphold its democratic values. I will observe its laws faithfully and fulfil my duties and obligations as a British citizen.'[36] Strikingly, this very secular conception of the obligations of citizenship omits any reference to the constitutional position of the Queen as Defender of the Faith and Supreme Governor of the Church of England, a position her likely successor may modify in favour of 'Defender of the Faiths'. In a wider sense, new citizens will remain largely ignorant of the ways in which Christianity permeates our culture, whether in the streets named after such obscure saints as Elmo or Maur, or in house numbers that jump from 12a to 14. To take one example, the second-century

Syrian bishop Erasmus or Elmo was martyred by having his innards wound out on a windlass. For this reason he became the patron saint of mariners, giving his name to the phenomenon of 'St Elmo's fire', the electrical effects on the mastheads of ships.[37]

While many people are probably comfortable with the notion of civil religion, especially when, as in the US, it can reinvent itself in sensitive adaptation to non-Christian minorities, stereotypically through the substitution of 'the holidays' for Christmas, others wonder whether such a civil religion is necessary at all. In a detailed criticism of Bellah's ideas, the Princeton theologian Richard Fenn has argued:

> Secular societies have no need for an idol that reduces the uncertainty and complexity within or around itself. Such a society refuses to reduce its awareness of the stakes and the risks, of the opportunities and also of the dangers that come from existing in an open, pluralistic world of rival groups and ideals. Indeed, idolatry is the antithesis of the openness and flexibility that are required if societies are to encounter each other in a global field of influence and communication that remains open to suggestion from all quarters and open as well to the future.[38]

Readers may wonder whether, writing before 11 September 2001, Professor Fenn imagined that global communication would involve his pluralistic groups, in this case largely consisting of deracinated Saudi Arabians, crashing aircraft into tall buildings in the name of a pathological Wahhabist strain within one of the world's monotheistic religions. American readers may also baulk at the idea that their inclusively subtle civil religion has much to do with 'idolatry'. It is actually an immensely sophisticated way of integrating a society constantly replenished by immigration. It is one of the many lessons Europeans, who desperately need immigrants too to counteract their demographic extinction, could learn from America.

The main civil religions discussed in this book are not the evanescent cults of the Jacobins and Directory, whose sudden eruption into the traditional religious world still seem as disturbing, jarring and perplexing as when the quaint streets of Paris seemed to Charles Dickens indelibly stained with blood. Nor were they the idiosyncratic schemes of the major utopians, whose following never rose above the cranky and tweedy crowded into back-street Comtean Temples of Humanity. Rather they were the myths and monuments of the classical European nation states (and of Washington DC across the Atlantic) some of which – like Whitehall's Cenotaph – are still profoundly moving, others – such as the giant Hermann the German in the Teutoburger Forest or the Victor Emmanuel I monument in Rome – bombastic and pretentious to our cooler tastes. However, in some key respects even these stone temples of the modern nation state were under-freighted with ambition. They were not concerned with defining good or evil or the making and unmaking of humanity, even if they provided an altar upon which more sinister idols were set up. Like the official days of national self-celebration, they were never universally respected or admired. The nineteenth-century limited state lacked the coercive means to clear the public space of any dissenting alternatives that was so characteristic of the Communist, Fascist and National Socialist states that arose within them. There were no parallel subcultures under Hitler or Stalin.

This brief introduction has staked out some of the overly ambitious ground that this book seeks to cover. It remains to mention a few remote harbingers of the 1930s thinkers we began with. One of them enjoyed some esteem among leading Bolsheviks before the Revolution. The religious–socialist Maxim Gorki introduced the exiled Lenin to a utopian tract called *The City of the Sun* by Tommaso Campanella when Lenin visited the writer at his villa on Capri for two weeks in 1908.[39] The Italian original of this had begun circulating in manuscript from 1602 onwards, but only in 1623 had a Latin translation been published, to be followed by endless editions. Although hostile to religious mysticism, Lenin was apparently so taken with Campanella's vision of omnipresent slogans and visual propaganda (imagined by an author who had died in May 1639), that he wished to inscribe Campanella's name on the refashioned Romanov Tricentennial Obelisk in Moscow. The connection is tenuous, but it serves the purposes of our discussion. Who was this early modern inspiration?

Born in 1568, Tommaso Campanella was a swarthy, warty-faced Calabrian Dominican friar who spent twenty-seven years in the dungeons of the citadels that loom above the gay shoreline of the Bay of Naples. A portrait shows a grim-looking fellow, which Campanella had every reason to be. The worst eight years' confinement were spent chained up in a dank and slimy darkness, although the breaking point had been a continuous forty-hour session of appalling torture that involved a choice between dislocation of the arms and relaxing on to a chair covered in sharp spikes. He survived an ordeal designed to test whether he was simulating insanity, for if he was mad he would not be burned as a heretic. Because of these grievous injuries Campanella would never be able to sit on a horse again.

The thirty-year-old Campanella had daringly crossed two lines. He had fallen foul of his own order, which, because of his obsession with magic, had charged him with such things as communicating with a demon under one of his fingernails. In 1594 he was arrested and tortured by the Holy Office, partly because he had discussed the faith with a converted Jew. In 1595 he was detained and tortured again on charges of heresy, an experience repeated in 1597 when he was denounced by a condemned Calabrian bandit. Undeterred by these horrors, in 1598 Campanella made the gravest mistake of his life. Although the details are obscure, insurgent bandits and peasants allegedly made use of the millenarian prophecies of various radical Dominican friars like Campanella in their bid to overthrow the Church and Spanish monarchy with the treasonable assistance of the Turkish fleet. Campanella was arrested, although whether he should be tried for heresy or sedition was a judicial confusion that saved his life.[40]

Although such rich and powerful men as the Fuggers of Augsburg and the future emperor of Austria endeavoured to improve the conditions of Campanella's captivity, his extraordinary stream of writings were clearly produced in unimaginable circumstances whenever he could acquire pens, paper and the light of candle. He became Europe's first convict celebrity, an essential stop-over for intelligent tourists who could purchase tickets to visit the friar's cell.

Not the least bizarre aspect of this affair was that Campanella was a budding propagandist for both the papacy and the Spanish monarchy. He had written a tract called *Della monarchia di Spagna* shortly before his longest imprisonment. This was an elaborate blueprint for Spanish universal monarchy, including recommendations for the cultural 'hispanisation' of the world through the universalisation of 'honour'. Campanella was eventually released from the dungeons of Naples in 1626. After a month of liberty, he was rearrested and sent in chains by galley to Rome. He did not regain his freedom until 1629, by which time the opportunistic friar–sage had insinuated his way into the good offices of pope Urban VIII, who regarded him as an astrologer and poet. Campanella devised a magic room in the pope's palace, where aromas, candles and silks signified astrological forces that would alleviate his holiness's ailments. In 1633 Campanella learned that the authorities in Naples were seeking his extradition for his role in further conspiracies. Heavily disguised, he fled to Marseilles, and then on to Paris. As a cross between Rip Van Winkle and an intellectual celebrity, Campanella soon moved in august circles, especially when his labile loyalties coincided with war between France and Spain. He was warmly received by Louis XIII – who remarked 'Très bien venu' – and granted the friar a pension. The ever itinerant Richelieu usually contrived not to pay it, and had a desperate Campanella perpetually at his heels.

Campanella set up his one-man authorial factory in the Dominican convent of the Jacobins in the Rue St Honoré. By the mid-1630s, he had exchanged his enthusiasm for the universal monarchy of the Habsburgs for that of the French. France, he now wrote, was to be the long arm of the pope. So favoured was the Calabrian friar that in 1638 Richelieu summoned him to draw up the astrological charts for a naked royal infant: the future Louis XIV. In one of the most brazen acts of authorial self-interest ever recorded, Campanella hoped that the future Sun King would build his fabled City of the Sun. He died in 1639 and was buried in the convent of the Jacobins. His monument fell victim in the 1790s to the de-Christianising fury of those who turned the Paris convent into the headquarters of their eponymous political club.[41]

Campanella was the first individual to refer to 'political religions', primarily as a result of his ambivalent response to the writings of Machiavelli. The Florentine thinker simultaneously divested the art of politics of traditional moral or religious restraints, while continuing to regard religious belief as an indispensable social cement, even if this involved lying about whether the poultry used in auguries to decide whether to go into battle had really been seen to peck by the priest–poultrymen.[42] Machiavelli also contrasted the civic virtues which ancient cults encouraged with the Christianity of his own time:

> the old religion [paganism] did not beatify men unless they were replete with worldly glory: army commanders, for instance, and rulers of republics. Our religion has glorified humble and contemplative men, rather than men of action. It has assigned as man's highest good humility, abnegation, and contempt for mundane things, whereas the other identified it with magnanimity, bodily strength, and everything else that conduces to make men very bold. And if our religion demands that in you there be strength, what it asks for is strength to suffer rather than

strength to do bold things. This pattern of life, therefore, appears to have made the world weak, and to have handed it over as a prey to the wicked, who run it successfully and securely since they are well aware that the generality of men, with paradise for their goal, consider how best to bear, rather than how best to avenge, their injuries. But, though it looks as if the world were to become effeminate and as if heaven were powerless, this undoubtedly is due rather to the pusillanimity of those who have interpreted our religion in terms of laissez-faire, not in terms of virtù.[43]

While Campanella agreed with Machiavelli that religion had an important binding function in societies, he contrived to be appalled by the amoral world of the Prince, though he was pretty amoral himself. The results of political amorality were all too apparent. This was not simply a matter of unscrupulous rulers who, for example, would murder anyone who got in their way, but of German princes who changed their religion as if changing a cloak, or the avarice the Spanish unleashed on America in the name of God. The advent of vicious inter-confessional strife in the wake of the sixteenth-century Reformation had also led to a redefinition of the meaning of 'religion' as an external reality divorced from fear and love of God. In the works of Machiavelli politics had slipped its transcendental moorings too; the result was that religion had become a political convenience rather than an end in itself. Instead of using religion to direct men towards God, rulers were using religion to advance worldly goals.[44] By contrast with Machiavelli's ground-breaking assertion of the autonomy of the political, Campanella thought that the state should be absorbed into the universal theocracy of the Roman Church, with Spanish or French universal monarchy as its secular arm. The state should encourage ceremonies in which priests would inculcate Christianity as the public religion.

Then there was Campanella's fantasy city. In his utopian dialogue, *The City of the Sun*, written in 1602, ultimate power resided with a supreme priest called 'the Metaphysician' or 'Sun' who would make all important decisions and act as supreme judge. Three other high priests called Power, Wisdom and Love (or Pon, Sin and Mor) would assist the Metaphysician. The ideal city was constructed within seven ascending concentric walls that were a stone reflection of the seven planets. A vast round temple rose within the highest ring. There was a huge celestial globe on the sun-shaped altar. Every available wall space in the city was covered with depictions of the natural world, science and such moral exemplars as Moses, Alexander, Christ, Caesar and Mohamed.

Goods and life were held and lived in common. The adult inhabitants wore an overall which they could exchange for other costumes at various times of the year. Diet and sex were regulated, the latter performed in accordance with complex astrological calculations and the rules of stock-breeding since Campanella had once been impressed when he visited an aristocratic stud-farm. Homosexuality was proscribed. An initial warning to homosexuals involved being publicly paraded for two days with a shoe around the neck. Those who defaulted again faced death. Those who injured the republic, God or the ruling officials met a similar fate through burning or stoning. As Campanella had once confronted the stake, he thoughtfully provided the condemned with a package of gunpowder to shorten their ordeal.[45]

The City of the Sun, or Solaria, could be called a proto-totalitarian environment, with a state religious cult. Its creed was based on confession and sacrifice. The Metaphysician conducted the latter, which involved winching a worthy person up to the temple dome to fast and suffer for twenty or thirty days in expiation of the sins of the community. Twenty-four priests lived, prayed and studied in the dome, only descending for medicinal sex. The entire population spent the time after communal dinner in singing and prayer, followed by dancing. There were public festivals, as the sun entered Aries, Cancer, Libra and Capricorn, as well as when the moon was full or new. The content of the public religion was a conflation of astrology, astronomy and Christianity.

Although there were other important contributions, from among others Thomas Hobbes, the themes which Campanella identified acquired renewed urgency when Europe was convulsed by the French Revolution. Christoph Martin Wieland was an Enlightened German scholar and writer who edited a periodical then called *Teutschen Merkur*. He moved in the orbit of Goethe at Weimar. Along with many of his contemporaries, Wieland welcomed the French Revolution as an opportunity to translate the principles of the Enlightenment into practice. Disillusionment soon set in since an imperialist tyranny had eventuated from the unlimited sovereignty of the people. He realised that democratic sovereignty was a 'million-headed beast', his own preference being for an enlightened aristocracy or monarchy. As a man of the Enlightenment, Wieland regarded religion as a private matter, and not something that should be compelled by the state. He was especially appalled by what he called 'a type of new political religion', which was being 'preached by [French generals] at the head of their armies'. They worshipped the idols 'freedom and equality' with a degree of intolerance that reminded Wieland of 'Mohamed and the Theodosians': 'Whoever is not with them, is against them. Whoever fails to regard their concepts of freedom and equality as the only truths, is an enemy of the human race, or a reprehensible slave.' That, as we shall see, was characteristic of most utopian projects, as it would be of the totalitarian regimes with which we started. With Wieland we have reached the approximate chronological and thematic starting point of the book in the mid-eighteenth century. Rather than anticipate what it says, we turn first to the traditional society that the Revolution erupted within and to the implementation of visions that, looked at soberly, were no stranger than the imaginings of an imprisoned seventeenth-century Dominican friar. That involves going to eighteenth-century France.[46]

CHAPTER 1

Age of Reason, Age of Faith

I ELDEST DAUGHTER OF THE CHURCH

We begin with the illusory stability of a Church with venerable roots but whose spiritual dynamism arguably lay in the past too. Since the time of St Louis (1226–70) French kings have been 'the most Christian', a term extended to France itself. Since the reign of Philip the Fair (1285–1314), France was known as 'the eldest daughter of the Church' and the French as God's chosen people. The Church and the French monarchy were linked in a hierarchy that reached down from God in His heavenly kingdom. Throne and altar were inseparable, with senior clerics omnipresent at solemn public occasions well into the French Revolution.[1]

Higher clergy dominated the coronation ceremonies at Rheims. On the afternoon of 10 June 1774, Louis XVI attended vespers to prepare him for the following day's long proceedings. The cathedral had already filled at four in the morning for ceremonies that commenced at six a.m. Louis took several oaths, silently praying as he carefully emphasised each word in Latin. He promised to protect the Church and to extirpate heretics, dipping his voice for this part since it did not accord with the sentiments of the late eighteenth century. The regalia were blessed and Louis was girded with the sword of Charlemagne, with which he was obliged to protect the Church, widows and orphans. He prostrated himself on a square of violet velvet, while the litanies of the saints were said over him. Kneeling before the aged archbishop la Roche-Aymon, Louis was anointed with six unctions, his gloves and ring were blessed, and he was handed Charlemagne's sceptre. He could touch people for scrofula, which he did a few days later.

The coronation proper was attended by the massed peerage. As the crown was held just above Louis XVI's head, the archbishop proclaimed: 'May God crown you with the crown of glory and of justice . . . and you will come to the everlasting crown.' Sitting on his throne in his new blue robe with the fleur-de-lis, Louis was now the 'rex christianissimus', the most Christian King of the Church's 'eldest daughter' of France. The doors were opened to enable the people to see the new king. Birds were released and trumpets blew as the archbishop declaimed: 'Vivat rex in aeternum.' The ceremonies finished with a mass and the Te Deum.[2]

Clergy were very visible in eighteenth-century France, especially in the towns. To take one not untypical example, there were twelve hundred in Toulouse, a city of about fifty-three thousand people. In Angers, one in sixty of its thirty-four thousand inhabitants were clerics, not counting seminarians and the like. Clerics participated in all major public occasions, singing Te Deums to celebrate a royal birth or military victory; they interceded with God to avert man-made and natural disasters. Chaplains accompanied the fleets on dangerous voyages and administered the last rites to soldiers dying on the battlefields. Dedicated religious orders negotiated with pirates and Islamic rulers who had enslaved Christian captives. Unfortunates condemned to death received sacramental consolation even if they did not want it. Since we have been effectively deafened by ambient noise it is easy to forget that this was a sensitive auditory culture. The peal of church bells marked sacred days, invasions, fires and storms.[3] The feasts of the Church gave the year articulation and meaning. The French clergy were not like Lutheran pastors in Frederick the Great's Prussia, who had become little more than state officials, but they had various quasi-governmental functions.[4] In the countryside, priests relayed government pronouncements after the Sunday sermon, often literally interpreting the high French of officialdom into the low patois (or foreign languages such as German or Spanish) spoken by their parishioners. Priests recorded the most rudimentary information on the lives of the king's subjects. Religious orders virtually controlled education, with many future revolutionaries indebted to Jesuit or Oratorian schoolmasters for their easy Latinity and knowledge of the politics of Roman antiquity.

The clergy were responsible for setting the moral tone in society in general, with these functional merits of religion being blindingly obvious even to sceptics such as Voltaire. There was virtual unanimity on the need for Hell to stop the servants stealing the spoons: anyone who cast doubt on the reality of eternal torment was certain to experience it.[5] The clergy tried to enforce Sunday as a day of rest and prayer and the Lenten fast, fighting back the pernicious influence of village tavern-keepers who offered men rival consolations. They denounced games of chance, loose women and rotten literature. They had to walk a fine line between curbing practices that made the Church look ridiculous to smart opinion in an age so concerned with reconciling reason and revelation, and alienating their flocks by outlawing customs which made abstract belief meaningful and tangible to them.

Historians have made various attempts to test the depth of religious conviction, an exercise as precise as encountering warm and chilly areas while swimming in an ocean. There seems to have been an increase in bastards born to servants, judging by the numbers of foundlings left outside the church doors. This was probably more indicative of rising grain prices than what these servants believed. Likewise, more and more couples resorted to contraception, but this may have reflected an upward valuation of children. The diminution in testamentary demand for masses for the repose of one's soul may speak to changes in how people regarded their own deaths, with the Church failing to convince them of the imminence of hellfire. It has been equally well argued that, urban sophisticates apart, most people may have had a more intelligent and personal comprehension of their faith than at any time since the Middle Ages.[6]

The clerical Estate was self-administering and self-taxing. Its 130,000 members were exempt from taxation, instead voting 'free gifts', amounting to up to 12 per cent of their revenues, at its five-yearly General Assemblies to bellicose or spendthrift monarchs. Between 1715 and 1788 this gift amounted to 3,600,000 livres, rising to an annual average of 5,700,000 livres under Louis XVI. Land and tithes meant that the Church was immensely rich, although this wealth was so unevenly distributed as to cause widespread resentment. The incomes of the 135 bishops varied immensely, from ten thousand livres per annum to two hundred thousand. One bishop in 1789 was from a bourgeois background; the rest were aristocrats, 65 per cent of them from families whose nobility emerged in illustrious mists before the year 1400. Bishops from leading aristocratic dynasties started well up the income scale, making a couple of strategic leaps to achieve the big money on offer at Rheims or Strasbourg. They pursued a variety of vocations according to their class, inclinations and temperaments. A few, such as Bernis or Brienne, continued the tradition of Mazarin, Richelieu and Fleury as first-rate administrators, diplomats and politicians. Brienne was sufficiently indistinguishable from his enlightened friends that in 1781, when his candidacy for promotion was being canvassed, Louis XVI famously averred 'that it was necessary that an archbishop of Paris should at least believe in God'.

Most bishops were efficient administrators of their dioceses, keeping their clergy up to the mark, or improving the local infrastructure with canals and roads. A few had the stereotypical vices of their class, preferring feasting, hunting or loose women, the stock-in-trade of anticlerical jibes over the centuries. Some of them never condescended to visit their dioceses, with a fifteen years' absence being a record many thought scandalous, although that did not mean they were not profitably employed, just that they did not like life in the provincial boonies or sticks. However, the majority organised diocesan seminaries or clerical conferences and routinely visited their clergy with sufficient investigative rigour as to be widely resented. The remainder of the six thousand or so higher clergy consisted of cathedral canons. These were aristocratic oligarchies, of say fifty canons per cathedral, whose function was to ensure that worship there was appropriately magnificent. This left them with much time on their hands for such hobbies as antiquarianism, botany, charity or visiting relatives, which, taken together with combined incomes of, say, the 3,500,000 livres that ninety canons shared at Chartres, caused envy.

Half the French clergy were regulars, that is, monks or nuns, indeed 60 to 70 per cent of regulars were women. After 1768, monks had to be over twenty-one, nuns aged over eighteen. There was a decline in entrance to the traditional orders, some of whose houses were inhabited by fewer than ten monks. Across eighteenth-century Europe monarchs cast a beady eye over religious orders whose wealth might be used to extend the network of parishes, provide education, once the monks had been converted into teachers, or boost the state's revenues in general. In France a commission on the regulars led to the suppression of eight orders, and the closure of 458 monasteries out of the three thousand or so in the country. The very wealthy abbeys and convents of France represented a supplementary source of income for aristocratic bishops. The bishopric of Orléans brought in forty-two thousand livres per annum, but two abbeys added a further sixty-five thousand livres to the bishop's income.[7] Apart from being the source for bread doles to the indigent, abbeys and convents were useful places to beach an illegitimate daughter or a libertine uncle. Many monks had abandoned habits for coats, stockings and the pleasures of very well-laid tables. Monks and nuns came in for the special scorn of the philosophes, the incipient intelligentsia of their day, although the regular clergy were rationalised and reformed during the late eighteenth century. Much eighteenth-century pornography was set in abbeys and convents. Indeed in French slang 'abbaye' is still a synonym for whorehouse. Pornography could also simultaneously be philosophy; notably the novel *Thérèse philosophe* (1748) in which the heroine is so appalled by a lascivious Jesuit that she abandons her faith and embarks on a life of copulation and discussions of ontology with an equally libidinous philosophic count. The anticlerical philosophe–pornographers had less to say about pious women who led exceptional lives as nurses in non-conventual communities, without whose ministrations the lives of the blind, foundlings, orphans, the sick and the elderly would have been unfathomably wretched.[8]

The sixty thousand parish curates or curés and their insecure and often indigent vicars were the real clerical workhorses, exempt from the opprobrium that enlightened opinion heaped on their sybaritic superiors and idle regulars. Since every candidate for priestly ordination had to have a minimum of a hundred livres independent income, these men were usually the sons of affluent artisans, manufacturers or such professional people as lawyers and notaries. The curés admonished, advised and consoled their parishioners, and as learned men brought a little agricultural or medical knowledge to places bereft of it. They promoted vaccination for smallpox, or lightning conductors on their village's tallest structure. Dominique Chaix, a country cleric in the Gapençais who was too poor to own a horse, was an authority on alpine plants, which he sold to buy the occasional book. This background enabled him to practise herbal medicine. Almost imperceptibly the clergy's role shifted from the care of souls to improving the brutish manners of their parishioners, although the artistry involved working with, rather than against, the grain of the old Adam. From here it was but a short step to offering opinions on what to do about such social issues as begging. Keeping parish records often led to an interest in local history, as they livened up their registers with events and happenings. The clergy were part of the intellectual culture of their time. Twenty-nine per cent of elite Academicians were clerics; and so were seven hundred of the twenty thousand freemasons, whose lodges were often the hubs of local intellectual activity. By the eighteenth century many of them had quite considerable libraries, of a hundred books or more, the majority being liturgical manuals or collections of sermons rather than anything as unearthed as theology. Some of them were notorious drunkards or gluttons, although standards had markedly improved since the previous century, due to the institution of diocesan seminaries. Reports on pastoral visits and the records of diocesan courts in the seventeenth century revealed any number of drunken, brawling, whoring secular clerics; by 1720, the roll-call of such delinquents had fallen to 5 per cent of the total. In fact, most secular clergy had spent about sixteen months in a seminary, and took their Counter-Reformation inspired status as part of a strict hierarchy watched over by God-as-judge seriously.

The majority were overworked and underpaid, and were respected by many philosophes for their work with the poor, with whom the latter rarely made any acquaintance. Clerical incomes derived from tithes and ancillary sums from land or surplice fees. Where he did not hold tithing rights, the priest received a much more meagre handout from the bishop, chapter or monastery which did, called the 'portion congrue'. Reformers thought that fifteen hundred livres would represent a living commensurate with the dignity of the clerical office. While some received over four thousand livres, the majority had to make do with about eight hundred, and sometimes considerably less. Demands on their slender resources were constant. They had to maintain a housekeeper and a horse to reach outlying areas, to contribute to the pension of the previous incumbent, and to anyone seeking emergency sustenance. The number of ordinations fell, especially among young townsmen, the result being the creeping countrification of the parochial clergy. By 1770, some 70 per cent of the clergy were from villages or small country towns.[9]

II JESUITS, JANSENISTS AND PHILOSOPHES

We need to go back to the exalted heights where Church and state met. The French monarchy enjoyed a supremacy over the Church that was as real as that exercised by Henry VIII in England, but without the deeper social support that came with Protestant nationalist messianism. The French monarchy negotiated rather than seized these rights. Gallicanism, as it is known, was the complex of agreements and traditions that served to limit or repulse the papacy's pretensions to power in France, beginning with the Concordat of Bologna in 1516 that enabled Francis I to nominate appointments to the most senior ecclesiastical positions. His successors never looked back. This monarchical ascendancy characterised several other Catholic countries in the eighteenth century. The substantial spectre of Henry VIII haunted the papacy's increasingly fraught dealings with an exceptionally independent-minded array of eighteenth-century Roman Catholic sovereigns. The popes had nothing to say anywhere about who should be king, that being a matter of dynastic lottery. By contrast, the ambassadors and crown cardinals of the major European Catholic powers could frustrate the election of candidates to the throne of St Peter, if they were thought unsympathetic to their respective national interests. In extreme circumstances they could exercise their right of veto.[10] In France, the pope had no power to intervene between king and clergy, usually approving the appointment of abbots and bishops, who were routinely aristocratic beneficiaries of royal patronage. Publication of a papal bull on doctrinal questions was dependent upon royal approval.

The preceding two centuries had experienced terrible religious civil wars between Catholics and Protestants and international wars with a powerful religious dimension.[11] Memories of these conflicts haunted enlightened opinion, rather in the way that the ghosts of recent genocides help shape the contemporary imagination if not international conduct. As the Peace of Westphalia in 1648 brought major inter-state religious wars to an end, rulers still had to decide the fate of religious minorities within their own borders. In 1731 the archbishop of Salzburg scandalised Protestant Europe by giving all Protestants over twelve years of age eight days to pack up and go, which resulted in twenty thousand people being resettled by the Prussians.[12] The empress Maria Theresa also believed in confessional homogeneity and was prepared to deport Protestant 'heretics' to achieve it. But in England Christianity had ceased to be a compulsory society. Its state Church had a genius for accommodating a variety of opinions, while formal sanctions against religious dissenters were flouted with official connivance. This more tolerant atmosphere spread to what had been bastions of orthodoxy. Joseph II, Maria Theresa's heir, argued that 'with freedom of religion, one religion will remain, that of guiding all citizens alike to the welfare of the state. Without this approach we shall not save any greater number of souls, and we shall lose a great many more useful and essential people.' His

1781 Edict of Toleration allowed dissenters to worship privately, and Calvinists, Lutherans and Greek Orthodox Christians to have churches without steeples. Frederick the Great of Prussia thought that the best way of integrating his burgeoning territories and of enhancing their prosperity was to tolerate Jews, Catholics and Calvinist immigrants in his predominantly Lutheran polity, one of the reasons why there are so many French surnames in the Berlin telephone book.

In France the Roman Catholic Church enjoyed a monopoly of public worship, but there were Lutherans in Alsace and a croissant-shaped scattering of Calvinists, stretching southwards from Poitou towards the Languedoc and then upwards again into the Dauphiné. The wealth of Protestant bankers, shipbuilders and traders in cities such as Bordeaux, La Rochelle, Marseilles and Nîmes, and their utility to the crown in raising its improbable loans, militated in favour of grudging toleration, provided Protestants were not too ostentatious in practising their faith. Wealth and religious difference combined were powerful incentives to resentment. The Edict of Toleration in 1787 legitimised Protestant marriages, inheritance and burial in exclusive or mixed cemeteries, while forbidding Protestants to worship in public. France's small Jewish community of forty thousand people consisted of Sephardim in places like Bordeaux and Carpentras or Paris, who hankered after integration, and yiddish-speaking Ashkenazis in Alsace, who wished to retain their communal independence. Enlightened opinion about the Jews ranged from Voltaire, who saw Judaism as the source of religious backwardness and fanaticism, to the abbé Grégoire who sought to 'reform' the Jews by opening up to them a range of professions including farming in return for their abandonment of their particularisms.

Censorship, lax in practice but all the more resented in theory, as well as ferocious blasphemy and sacrilege laws, sought to compel orthodoxy. The philosophes tended to highlight the most extreme cases, often omitting crucial details that might have modified their starkly contrived contrasts. In 1765 the chevalier François-Jean de la Barre was arraigned for defacing a crucifix on the bridge at Abbeville and various other instances of blasphemy and sacrilege, such as not doffing his hat to passing Capuchin friars on the ground that it was raining. The first charge did not stick, but that he had worn his hat in the presence of the sacrament, mocked priestly practices and had illicit books was proven. After the parlement of Paris confirmed his sentence, executioners spent twelve hours tormenting La Barre before striking off his head. In fact, individual malice by a lay legal official had led to his prosecution, with the parlement of Paris going the whole way in order to counter the reputation for anticlericalism it had accrued from its vindictive pursuit of the Jesuits. Senior clerics had actually intervened to commute La Barre's sentence; the Assembly of French clergy requested clemency, and the papal nuncio said a year in jail would have sufficed.[13]

The Gallican Church faced several threats. They were live or latent, from within as well as from without. Across Europe Catholic rulers in the Holy Roman Empire, Spain, Portugal and Tuscany were bent on conforming 'their' respective Churches to their enlightened definitions of national interest. A sort of Reformation from above took place, driven by reason rather than Protestant theology. Under the emperor Joseph II, half the monasteries in Austria were suppressed, with the financial dividend passing to a central fund designed to increase and upgrade the secular clergy and to boost popular education. Joseph's brother Leopold carried out an equally sweeping reform programme in Tuscany, crushing the Inquisition and turning hospitals over to laymen.[14]

Despite the absence of a successful Protestant Reformation, the French Catholic Church experienced something similar in spirit. In response to the challenge of Protestantism, Catholic reformers, many of them Jesuits, had re-emphasised the efficacy of good works and priestly intercession. The Jesuits' mission was in the world, to which they brought an optimistic faith that could find a solution to any spiritual crisis. They were adaptable and modern. But to many people the Jesuits were suspect on several levels and not only in Protestant countries where they had long acquired quasi-demonic status as crafty, fanatical conspirators. Since a high proportion of French Jesuits were from Normandy, this image dovetailed with the Normans' proverbial reputation among Frenchmen for a certain guileful shiftiness. As is implicit in what follows, some of the paranoia that attaches to Jews and freemasons was also evident in the case of the Jesuits.

As the Counter-Reformation Church's most militant representatives, the Jesuits epitomised papal interference in national affairs. They were easy to portray as meddlesome foreigners, as when in his famed fifth *Provincial Letter* the seventeenth-century Jansenist mathematician and philosopher Blaise Pascal has his imaginary Jesuit interlocutor reel off the names of theologians he used to confound the Church Fathers. '"They are very able and famous men," he said. "There is Villabos, Coninck, Llamas, Achoker, Dealkozer, Dellacruz, Vera-Cruz, Ugolin,

Tambourin, Fernandez, Martinez, Suarez, Henriquez, Vasquez, Lopez, Gomez, Sanchez, de Vechis, de Grassis, de Grassilis, de Pitigianis, de Graeis, Squilanti, Bizozeri, Barcola, de Bobadilla, Simancha, Perez de Lara, Aldretta, Lorca, de Scaria, Quaranta, Scophra, Pedrezza, Cabrezza, Bisbe, Dias, de Clavasio, Villagut, Adam a Manden, Iribarne Binsfeld, Volfangi a Vorberg, Vosthery, Strevesdorf." "Oh Father!" I said, quite alarmed, "were all of these men Christians?"' Of course, there was not a name readily identifiable as being French among them, a trick that would also be used by antisemites in subsequent centuries.[15]

As Pascal showed, the Jesuits' fabled casuistry seemed like a convenience designed to exculpate the sins of the rich, who could leave the confessional for a masked ball without over-straining their consciences. The philosophes of the Enlightenment refined Pascal's sceptical position on this issue. In his fifty-seventh *Persian Letter* Montesquieu has a confessor 'dervish' explain to an Usbek: 'I am telling you the secrets of a trade in which I have spent my life, and explaining its finer points. There is a way of presenting everything, even things which seem the least promising.'[16] Pornographers, such as the author of *Thérèse philosophe*, gave this a sexual twist, in the sense that the Jesuit villain of the story uses the Cartesian dichotomy of body and spirit to persuade a young woman to indulge his sadistic fantasies in order to liberate her spirit from the body he is flogging. The Jesuits were also too keen to educate the elites, in such collèges as Louis-le-Grand in Paris that had queues of bourgeois applicants keen to follow in the footsteps of Voltaire. The educational establishment in the hidebound universities did not like them. For all but six years between 1604 and 1764 the Jesuits provided all the confessors to the kings of France. Some of these men, like Louis XIV's confessor, a Norman called Michel Le Tellier, actually looked sinister, or as someone remarked: 'you'd have been scared if you met him in the corner of a wood.' This tendency to haunt the corridors of power suggested untoward political influence. Physical proximity to power became ominous once disparate, and rather routine, Jesuit writings by the Italian Bellarmine and the Spaniards Suarez and Mariana justifying tyrannicide in the case of heretical rulers were said to have guided the hands of French assassins – from Ravaillac, who killed Henry IV, to Damiens whose knife went three inches into Louis XV, for which crime Damiens died an excruciatingly painful and protracted death.[17]

The Jesuits tried to prove that the servant Damiens had been motivated by quasi-republican ideas he had ingested in the houses of Jansenist magistrates for whom he had worked; the magistrates responded by highlighting Damiens' two years as a servant at Louis-le-Grand, where the Jesuits had indoctrinated him for a mission designed to discredit their enemies in the parlements. If the Jesuits were accused of expanding their influence at home, overseas they were thought to be running their own satrapies. Happenings in exotic places further tarnished the image of the order in Europe. In China, Jesuit missionaries tried to incorporate as much Confucianism as possible to smooth the path of conversions. This outraged less doctrinally elastic missionaries, notably their old foes the Dominicans, and fuelled the Jesuits' European reputation for amoral expediency.

In faraway Paraguay, the Jesuits seemed to have created their own proto-totalitarian state, although the reality was that they were trying to subtract the indigenous Indians from the oppressions of their Creole masters. The local bishops were aggrieved since their writ did not run in these Reductions, which rumour claimed were an excuse secretly to mine precious metals. A 1750 treaty altering the borders between Spanish and Portuguese colonies in Latin America involved shifting some of the Indian settlements. They rebelled and the Jesuits were associated with their defiance. The Jesuits did not help their cause by calling the devastating 1755 Lisbon earthquake divine retribution upon the king of Portugal. An attempt to shoot king Joseph I in 1759 provided the Portuguese state with a pretext for outright war. The ruthless reforming ministry of the marquis of Pombal struck at the Jesuits in Portugal, deporting over a thousand Jesuits to the Papal States. The French Jesuits were the next to suffer when they were deemed corporately liable for debts accruing from ill-judged trading operations in the West Indies by a maverick member of the order. Thousands more French Jesuits joined their Portuguese brethren in exile. In Spain, the Jesuits were used as a scapegoat for riots against Charles III's attempts to force the Spanish to look like Frenchmen by wearing wigs under three-cornered hats. More shiploads of disconsolate Jesuits headed for Civita Vecchia, where the Pope refused to accommodate them. Further expulsions followed from Naples and the little duchy of Parma. Clement XIII baulked at the clergy being pushed around by this upstart midget. Parma's decrees were declared null and void and its officials excommunicated. Bourbon armies occupied papal territories in response. They also engineered the election of a new pope, Clement XIV, whom they then prevailed upon to abolish the Jesuit order. Whenever the pope prevaricated in this course, a tough Spanish ambassador reminded him that 'Toothache can only be cured by extraction.' On 21 July 1773 Clement XIV signed the brief *Dominus ac Redemptor* suppressing the order. Anticipating Stalin's dictum by nearly two centuries, an English commentator observed that 'The Pope has no fleet to support his Jesuits.' Paradoxically, the only monarchs to extend a welcoming hand to the Jesuits were the Protestant Frederick the Great of Prussia and the Orthodox Catherine the Great of Russia, who valued the Jesuits' role as teachers, or at least the part they might play in pacifying their Roman Catholic minorities.

These multiplying animosities, culminating in Catholic monarchs press-ganging the pope to suppress the order, explain why the Jansenists, the Jesuits' main theological opponents within the Catholic Church, were regarded sympathetically. The seventeenth-century cardinal Giovanni Bona once described Jansenists as Catholics who disliked Jesuits. The future Benedict XIV thought that Jansenism was a ghost invented by the Jesuits. Jansenism began as a theological tendency and ended up as a quasi-political programme.

Jansenists were followers of the seventeenth-century Flemish divine Cornelius Jansen, who from 1636 until his death four years later was bishop of Ypres. He has been well described as a Catholic Lutheran. Jansen's Augustinian views on predetermined damnation or salvation echoed the teachings of Calvin, but from within the Roman Catholic Church itself. Jansenists were like puritans within the Catholic fold, exclusive and severe people. Jansenism was an austere, rigorous creed that stressed individual study of the scriptures in the vernacular, the need for sincere contrition rather than mere fear of eternal damnation, the infrequency of Communion, and the remoteness of God from a concupiscent humanity. This set Jansenism on a collision course with baroquely lax Catholicism in which the Jesuits could allegedly finesse everything this way or that. Jansenism also mutated into a theory of Church government when it subsumed the ecclesiology of Edmund Richer, who regarded councils as the highest authority in the universal Church and argued that clerical synods should elect bishops. Christ had seventy-two disciples and not just the twelve apostles. Two writers, G. N. Maultrot and Henri Reymond, were responsible for developing Richerism into a coherent body of teaching on the dignity and rights of the lower clergy, whose essence was that a more democratic Church would be a more spiritually effective Church.[18]

Inevitably, these obscure theological issues attracted lay supporters so that Jansenism acquired political overtones, both because it was popular among some of the lawyers in the parlements and because Jesuit and papal attempts to crush it could be construed as an assault on the historic rights of the Gallican Church. Jansenism in France was propagated by the devouts Saint-Cyran and Antoine Arnaud, whose family had a history of battling with St Ignatius' foot soldiers. Disconcertingly, Jansenism attracted many people of immense talent, some of whom abandoned glittering secular careers to practise its solitary rigours, like the lawyer Antoine Le Maître. Jansenist genius included the mathematician Pascal, the playwright Racine and the painter Philippe de Champaigne. A decade-long vacancy in the Paris see and then an archbishop who sat on the fence enabled these doctrines to flourish among the Parisian clergy. Skilful Jansenist propaganda, notably Pascal's *Provincial Letters*, in which he poured mounting scorn on Jansenism's Jesuit opponents, was the jewel in a slew of polemics.[19] Later, the formidable Jansenist propaganda machine was augmented by the newspaper *Nouvelles Ecclésiastiques* (Ecclesiastical News), a mine of dirt on the Jesuits. Of course, those characteristics that led intellectuals like Pascal to live on water and vegetables while wearing a spiked belt next to his skin may also have repelled lesser mortals by making the achievement of salvation seem hopeless.

The Jansenists' independence of mind and ramified network within sections of society preternaturally inclined to defend their privileges eventually galvanised Louis XIV into taking action against them. In 1709 the aged nuns of the austerely fashionable suburban convent of Port-Royal, to which many eminent people had repaired to read and garden, were dispersed for refusing to abjure Jansenism. In 1711 the convent itself was obliterated and the bones of its three thousand former denizens disinterred and reburied in common graves to extinguish all memory of its existence. In 1713 Louis persuaded pope Clement XI to issue the bull *Unigenitus*, a comprehensive condemnation of 101 erroneous or heretical Jansenist propositions unearthed in the writings of Pasquier Quesnel. This simultaneously touched the nerve of Gallican autonomy, the zealously guarded prerogatives of the parlements and indeed the sympathies of plain people. The pronouncedly ascetic and intellectual faith of Jansenism had also begun to inspire popular convulsionaries who sought miraculous healing while shaking near the bones of François de Pâris, a devout Jansenist buried in the cemetery of Saint-Médard in a grim Parisian suburb. Some convulsionaries took things further, having thin nails repeatedly driven through their hands and feet. The cemetery was forcibly closed in 1732. These convulsionaries put the established Church in an awkward position vis-à-vis the philosophes, for how would it manage to discredit 'heretical' miracles without discrediting miracles in general?

Between 1614 and 1789 France had no national representative institution capable of challenging the monarchy. However, densely meshed local, sectional and regional privileged bodies could obstruct it. The parlements were appeal courts staffed by venal office-holders that were somewhat less than parliaments and something more than mere courts of law as a modern Briton might understand them. Responsible for scrutinising royal legislation, they could remonstrate if they found it incompatible with existing law, until the king overrode their opposition in a ceremony called 'the bed of justice'. Clashes with the Crown were like an exquisite pas de deux passing from respectful remonstrances all the way to the ritual expulsion and temporary exile of the offending magistrates.[20]

The parlements objected to the manner in which the bull *Unigenitus* had been forced upon the Church in violation of its Gallican privileges and procedures. They also suspected orthodox bishops of trying to exclude the parlements from any say in the affairs of the Church. Hence lay magistrates aggressively supported those Jansenist clerics who appealed against *Unigenitus*. In 1730 the government tried to force obedience by declaring *Unigenitus* a law of the state that all clergy were compelled to accept by taking an oath. Clergy who refused were to be denied the sacraments, while dying laymen had to produce a certificate of orthodoxy from the last priest from whom they had received absolution. The parlements took up the torch on behalf of those facing eternal damnation, forbidding parish priests to withhold the sacraments. The faith itself had become a matter of dispute between rival clerical factions that were attached to rival political camps.

A religious dispute had become highly political; an exceptionally austere creed was on the way to becoming the religion of opposition lawyers, although there would be a mere three Jansenists in the National Assembly. Louis XIV associated Jansenism with sedition, much as his English predecessors had done with Puritanism in a Protestant context. It was no coincidence that during these conflicts leading Jansenist lawyers claimed that these parlements were actually 'parliaments', allegedly coeval with the monarchy. This was historically fanciful since such institutions were unknown in the times of Clovis or Charlemagne. It was but a short step to claiming that the parlements were the guardians, indeed the incarnation, of the nation's 'fundamental laws' which the monarchy had flouted, despite the fact that the guardian–magistrates had themselves purchased their own offices and were hardly paragons of virtue.

These religious quarrels, which dragged on for over a century with varying degrees of intensity, undermined the claim that the Bourbon monarchy had imposed religious peace after decades of confessional warfare. They were not as lucky as their English fellow monarchs in having a Church with enough rooms to contain a broad range of clerical opinion, while finding ways of exempting Nonconformists from the theoretical rigours of legislation. Although by 1789 these were dying quarrels, Jansenist ideas persisted, albeit transformed into ostensibly secular ideologies, into the Revolution. There had been no internally generated reform of the French Church. Now it would come from outside like a whirlwind.

III DARING TO KNOW

This more serious challenge to the Church coalesced from several existing tendencies and novel developments that are known as the Enlightenment. At the height of the parlements' battles with the Jesuits, the philosophe d'Alembert had the temerity to claim credit for their destruction. This outraged Jansenists, one of whom observed: 'What is a true Jesuit if not a disguised philosophe, and what is a philosophe if not a disguised Jesuit?' Actually, the Jansenists and philosophes had more in common than this suggests. There was not a great gulf between Jansenists who believed that God had turned away from a corrupt world and philosophical Deists who claimed that, in the absence of providential intervention after the initial act of creation, the natural world functioned like a clock according to laws which science might uncover.

By the 1740s an identifiable family of thinkers had emerged across Europe and North America. Modern secular intellectuals like to trace their lineage to its luminaries, although as Carl Becker implied in 1932 that may be to overlook the former's limitless credulity towards irrational creeds, not to speak of that of the philosophes of the eighteenth century who may have been less secular-minded than we or they imagine.

Up to the early eighteenth century writers either had another source of income, as aristocrats, clerics or men of affairs, or depended upon a wealthy patron if their means were modest. Voltaire had silk- and watch-manufacturing operations on his estate at Ferney in Lorraine and lent money at interest to individuals and governments. His cadaverous, toothless face also enabled him to take out multiple life annuities at favourable rates even though – to the chagrin of his actuaries – he lived to eighty-three.[21]

Neither of these types disappeared, but their ranks were swelled by people who lived by the pen, whether compiling entries for dictionaries and encyclopaedias, or journalism and translation. Literary contracts could be enforced at law, ensuring that pirate editions would not appear so freely. The business of writing became professional. While censorship still existed, it was not thought prudent to exercise it too heavy-handedly, and books could always be printed and smuggled in from Britain or the Netherlands after having been written by authors who lived anywhere and everywhere. Only the advent of the internet and 'bloggers' has released such subversive potential upon complacent oligarchies.

The controversy and esteem these writers enjoyed presupposed something called public opinion, semi-detached from, and poorly controlled by, the traditional sources of cultural and intellectual authority, such as the Court, the Church and the universities. Eventually, public opinion, figuratively depicted as enthroned and dispensing laurel leaves, would displace the actual authority of the person occupying the throne.[22] Fame, the opinion of posterity, displaced the judgement of God. As Diderot wrote: 'Posterity is to the philosopher what the next world is to the religious man.' Academies, cafés, lodges and salons were where the intellectual action was, breeding grounds for a sort of lateral intellectual solidarity detached from the hierarchy represented by the Court. The authorities could, and did, try to meet like with like by hiring their own propagandists, but these had to compete in a market of rival ideas. Of course, the literary world had its own pecking order. Beneath the cosmopolitan and successful luminaries of the Enlightenment lay a subterranean world of literary journalists and hack writers, who vulgarised the ideas of the former, just as the major figures were very often doing no more than popularising the thought of their seventeenth-century British or Dutch precursors. Below them was an underworld of purveyors of outright libels and salacious gossip who may have done much to discredit established authority through smears, smut and scandal, which resurfaced as a mania to cleanse, persecute and purify during the Revolution, that singular accomplishment of moralising lawyers, renegade priests and hack journalists.[23]

The Enlightenment was described by Immanuel Kant as man's coming of age, a freeing of the mind from external controls. *Sapere aude* or 'dare to know' is as good a definition as any. It meant a belief in man's natural goodness, an optimistic faith in reason and a confidence in empirical research, whose enemies were political tyranny, religious fanaticism, moral hypocrisy and prejudice. Notwithstanding the existence of a Catholic Enlightenment, which was ready to reform abuses within the Church and to condemn superstition also with the aid of reason, it is undoubtedly the case that the philosophes often combined anti-clericalism (itself no invention of the eighteenth century) with Deism, materialism or in some cases atheism. While the clergy might have been at one with the philosophes on the need to extirpate popular superstition or to reform ecclesiastical institution, they could not easily accommodate the mocking tone and outright scepticism that Voltaire and others brought to their fundamental beliefs. This was difficult for Catholic apologists who often lacked the fervour and moralising self-righteousness that characterised opponents gripped by the belief that the winds of change were with them. One could try to rewrite a 'reasonable' Christianity, one of the central preoccupations of the age, but where did enlightened insistence on the natural goodness of mankind leave original sin, or science the Christian miracles? Comparative religion, as we would call it, also brought other dangers.

Most modern readers will find little shocking in the entry 'Abraham' in Voltaire's 1764 pocket *Philosophical Dictionary*: 'Abraham is one of the names famous in Asia Minor and in Arabia, like Thoth among the Egyptians, the first Zoroaster in Persia, Hercules in Greece, Orpheus in Thrace, Odin among the northern nations, and so many others whose fame is greater than the authenticity of their history.'[24] Actually, that flourish of anthropological erudition is deadly enough, before it delivers the sting in its tail by juxtaposing legend with 'history'.

As the products of recent centuries during which pagan antiquity was 'rediscovered', and of a fine classical education at the hands of Jesuit or Oratorian clerics, the philosophes were keen on those parts of the classical heritage that Christianity had discarded as surplus to doctrinal requirements.[25] Regarding nothing as being beyond rational scrutiny, except their own deepest prejudices, the philosophes were interested in the construction and social functioning of religion. Several classical authors had taken an instrumental, utilitarian view of religion, merely going through the motions of cults, whose primary function was to integrate conquered peoples and to keep their own lower orders quiescent. As Gibbon put it: 'The various modes of worship which prevailed in the Roman world were all considered by the people as equally true, by the philosopher as equally false, and by the magistrate as equally useful. And thus toleration produced not only mutual indulgence, but even religious concord.'[26]

The Scots philosopher David Hume devoted his *Natural History of Religion*, published in 1757, to the social and psychological exploration of the origins of religious belief. It is worth reiterating what he had to say in this elegantly learned essay. Arguing that primitive polytheism preceded sophisticated monotheism, Hume claimed that 'the first ideas of religion arose not from a contemplation of the works of nature, but from a concern with regard to the events of life, and from the incessant hopes and fears, which actuate the human mind'. These 'gross apprehensions' included:

> the anxious concern for happiness, the dread of future misery, the terror of death, the thirst of revenge, the appetite for food and other necessaries. Agitated by hopes and fears of this nature ... men scrutinize, with a trembling curiosity, the course of future causes, and examine the various and contrary events of human life. And in this disordered scene, with eyes still more disordered and astonished, they see the first obscure traces of divinity.

There were gods for everything, as each new event demanded a separate supernatural explanation. Some of these gods were allegorical personifications of vice and virtue; others the apotheosis of once living kings and heroes. Having no scriptures, ancient religions could cope with inconsistency, and were fundamentally tolerant. The emergence of one dominant ruler in human society was echoed by the elevation of one god above the host of lesser divinities who were in any case all too human. A remote God, supported by scriptural authority, encouraged the abasements of monks and persecutory intolerance. Hume did not see this as a simple progression. Since everything is 'a flux and reflux', the remoteness of this sole divinity from human concerns in turn led to worship of lesser gods: 'The Virgin Mary, ere checked by the reformation, had proceeded, from being merely a good woman, to usurp many attributes of the Almighty: God and St Nicholas go hand in hand, in all the prayers and petitions of the Muscovites.' All Gods, including the Judaeo-Christian God, combined mixed moral characteristics – here Hume cites a Catholic author who traduced Protestants by comparing them with anthropomorphising pagans: 'The grosser pagans contented themselves with divinising lust, incest, and adultery; but the predestinarian doctors have divinised cruelty, wrath, fury, vengeance, and all the blackest vices.' Likewise, formal religious zeal may not be incompatible with the grossest cruelty: 'it is justly regarded as unsafe to draw any certain inference in favour of man's morals, from the fervour or strictness of his religious exercises, even though he himself believe them sincere'. Family or friendship engender one set of moral obligations; some then add more austere virtues 'such as public spirit, filial duty, temperance, or integrity'. Religion is irrelevant to this: 'a riddle, an enigma, an inexplicable mystery'. Hume 'happily' made his escape 'into the calm, though obscure, regions of philosophy'.[27]

Enlightened thought was haunted by the bloodshed of the Wars of Religion (1569–94). The desire, fanatically pursued, to eradicate the infamy of fanaticism was a reflection of these collective memories. Voltaire, who awoke from his sleep in a feverish state every anniversary of the massacre of St Bartholomew's Day, constantly contrasted what he imagined to be the reasonableness and toleration of Roman antiquity with the bloodshed and irrationalism of the succeeding Christian centuries. Here he is on the subject of 'martyrs':

> Thinking to make the ancient Romans odious they made themselves ridiculous. Do you want good, well-attested barbarities; good, well-authenticated massacres; rivers of blood that really ran; fathers, mothers, husbands, women, children at the breast really butchered and piled up on each other? Persecuting monsters, seek these truths only in your annals: you will find them in the crusades against the Albigensians, in the massacres of Mérindol and Cabrières, in the appalling day of saint Bartholomew, in the Irish massacres, in the valleys of the Waldenses. It well becomes you, barbarians that you are, to impute extravagant cruelties to the best of emperors, you who have inundated Europe with blood, and covered it with dying bodies, to prove that it is possible to be in a thousand places at once, and that the pope can sell indulgences! Stop slandering the Romans, who gave you

your laws, and ask God's forgiveness for the abominations of your fathers.[28]

The Revolution simplified these battle lines, in ways that were not especially typical of how sinuous Catholic apologists had reacted to the philosophes during the eighteenth century. One could argue by using the techniques of empirical scholarship to support biblical truths, or one could vacate that terrain, where the philosophes excelled, falling back instead to arguments based on faith, revelation and tradition.[29] Others of a less serene disposition pummelled the philosophes in their own books and tracts, in some respects providing the conceptual building blocks for what after 1789 would be the ideology of the conservative counter-revolution. Decades before the Revolution, anti-philosophes indiscriminately bundled their enemies together, accusing them of conspiring to subvert throne and altar and of undermining public morality. Some of these writers prophesied the onset of anarchy, and congratulated themselves when it duly reared its monstrous head. The anglomania of many leading philosophes, such as Voltaire, and their deference towards such British progenitors as Locke enabled their opponents to draw upon the poisoned well of Counter-Reformation anti-Protestant polemics, for example, when they portrayed the philosophes as a fanaticised cabal or sect of conspirators, a discourse easily adapted to antisemitism.[30]

What the religious of the time found impossible was to explore what the philosophes owed to the Christian tradition without being conscious of it. Like the Christians, the philosophes ransacked the past to illustrate a story whose outcome they knew in advance. Christianity, with its Garden of Eden, the Fall and Judgement Day, replicated each man's individual passage from innocent infancy, via the vale of tears of middle years, and on to the uplands of resigned old age. Judgement Day would finally right real wrongs and the rich man would not easily pass through the eye of a needle. The philosophes made large claims to the empirical nature of their philosophical history. But in reality they transposed their own Garden of Eden on to the classical Golden Age, from which a mankind haunted by priests and demons was then expelled into the long night of the Middle Ages. Like the Christians they also wanted a happy ending, but could not believe in a transcendental heaven. In the new religion of humanity, heaven would be the perfect future state that a regenerated mankind would create through his own volition. The ultimate arbiter would no longer be a divine judge, but rather future generations of happier mankind vaguely defined as 'posterity'. Self-fulfilment became a form of atonement, love of humanity a substitute for love of God.[31]

Conservative contemporaries were so traumatised by the French Revolution and its repercussions that they thought more about its relationship with the antecedent Enlightenment than they did about what the latter may have owed to religious modes of thinking. Because the Enlightenment preceded the Revolution, it was tempting to ascribe paternity. Counter-revolutionaries, such as the abbé Barruel, were quick to think along those lines, combining divine punishment of a decadent France with dark conspiracies by philosophes in the classical temples of the freemasons. Edmund Burke gave this literature a peculiarly British emphasis, though he shared many of the local assumptions of French counter-revolutionaries. Burke was not an unqualified supporter of the French ancien régime; he approved of the reforms it had undergone in 1787–8 and thought it had equipped itself for peaceful constitutional progress. After 1789 his key insight was to realise that 'a theory concerning government may become as much a cause of fanaticism as a dogma in religion'.[32] Here Burke's thoughts drifted to an earlier English historical analogy. He drew upon an Anglican discourse about 'enthusiasm' as applied to the dissenting sectarians of the mid-seventeenth century. Although the following extract from Burke is, superficially speaking, a routine denunciation of the philosophes (in other circumstances Burke might have been one himself), it also draws upon the vocabulary of High Anglican disdain for the religious precursors of modern ideological 'fanatics':

> The literary cabal had some years ago formed something like a regular plan for the destruction of the Christian religion. This object they pursued with a degree of zeal which hitherto had been discovered only in the propagators of some system of piety. They were possessed with a spirit of proselytism in the most fanatical degree; and from thence, by an easy progress, with spirit of persecution according to their means. What was not to be done towards their great end by any direct or immediate act, might be wrought by a longer process through the medium of opinion. To command that opinion, the first step is to establish dominion over those who direct it. They contrived to possess themselves, with great method and perseverance, of all the

avenues to literary fame ... These Atheistical fathers have a bigotry of their own; and they have learnt to talk against monks with the spirit of a monk. But in some things they are men of the world. The resources of intrigue are called in to supply the defects of argument and wit. To this system of literary monopoly was joined an unremitting industry to blacken and discredit in every way, and by every means, all those who did not hold to their faction. To those who have observed the spirit of their conduct, it has long been clear that nothing was wanted but the power of carrying the intolerance of the tongue and of the pen into a persecution which would strike at property, liberty, and life.[33]

Writing from beyond the Revolution, its greatest historian Alexis de Tocqueville was similarly appalled by the dangerous hubris of the secular intelligentsia:

> Every public passion was thus wrapped up in philosophy; political life was violently driven back into literature, and writers, taking in hand the direction of opinion, found themselves for a moment taking the place that party leaders usually hold in free countries ... Above the real society ... there was slowly built an imaginary society in which everything seemed simple and coordinated, uniform, equitable, and in accord with reason. Gradually the imagination of the crowd deserted the former to concentrate on the latter. One lost interest in what was, in order to think about what could be, and finally one lived mentally in that ideal city the writers had built.[34]

He added: 'What is merit in a writer is sometimes vice in a statesman, and the same things which have often made lovely books can lead to great revolutions.'

This may have been to exaggerate the lines of division and the importance of the philosophes. To begin with, revolutionaries and counter-revolutionaries, clergy and laity shared a taste for the same authors. In 1778 Marie Antoinette attended the opening night of Voltaire's last play, doubtless disappointing the gaggle of clerical demonstrators. Her consort, Louis XVI, read Montesquieu and Voltaire, along with Corneille and La Fontaine, in the Temple where he was imprisoned. Clerics were avid readers of the philosophes, and mixed easily in the provincial academies and masonic lodges, which, together with salons, were the institutional hubs of enlightenment. The Jesuit monthly *Journal de Trévoux* included admiring and intelligent reviews of Diderot's *Encyclopédie*, archly indicating which entries had been lifted from a Jesuit encyclopaedia and a Jesuit philosopher without appropriate acknowledgement. Counter-Englightenment authors were not slow to adopt Rousseau when it came to challenging the icy supremacy of reason over faith and feeling.

Any political movement, including those that seek to abolish the past, sooner or later seeks to fabricate a lineage. The French Revolution was no exception. The Revolution adopted Voltaire and Rousseau as its intellectual parents, translating their earthly remains to the Pantheon, in 1791 and 1794 respectively, with elaborate ceremonies that echoed religious processions. One can see this crude appropriation in low-grade revolutionary catechisms:

Question: Who are the men who by their writings prepared the revolution?
Answer: Helvétius, Mably, J. J. Rousseau, Voltaire, and Franklin.
Question: What do you call these great men?
Answer: Philosophers.
Question: What does that word mean?
Answer: Sage, friend of humanity.[35]

In politics, the philosophes were interested in enlightened reform rather than violent revolution. Since Voltaire, friend of monarchs, had written supporting chancellor Maupeou's 1771 'coup' against the parlements, and was contemptuous of literary hacks, it is improbable he would have viewed the brief rise to power of the pockmarked gargoyle Marat with equanimity. He had a very exclusive view of who might be safely enlightened. Writing to Frederick the Great he argued: 'Your Majesty will do the human race an eternal service in extirpating this infamous superstition [he meant Christianity] I do not say among the rabble, who are not worthy of being enlightened and who are apt for every yoke; I say among the well-bred, among those who wish to think.'[36] The philosophes wanted rulers to see the world as they saw it and to act accordingly although their role was as unimpressive as that of most intellectuals in politics. Anne-Robert Turgot, the only physiocrat, the economist sub-species of philosophe, briefly to exercise political power, triggered so-called flour wars after the institution of a free market in grain led to massive price rises.[37]

In a sense, the philosophes were the beneficiaries of those Calvinists and Jansenists who had propelled an infinitely good God further away from this corrupt world. The latter became autonomous, observable and potentially malleable, its links with the celestial hierarchy attenuated to invisibility.[38] Some philosophes thought that their ideas could only be implemented in small city-state republics, others by enlightened rulers, or on the vast blank canvas of North America. The philosophes were divided about whether it would be best to constrain monarchical power to lessen the likelihood of despotism and tyranny, or to increase it so as to brush aside vested interests, such as the aristocracy, Church or guilds, that frustrated their modernising reforms. Only two issues brought complete unanimity and promised worthwhile reforms: the need for religious toleration, and the need for a less barbaric criminal law not reliant upon judicial torture or cruel and unnecessary punishments.

The assault on the Church served to undermine one of the essential supports of monarchical authority, namely the supernatural element we began with. Incessant criticism, some of it well below the belt, led to gradual disenchantment with both throne and altar. Louis XIV had filled France with a huge sun-lit cloud of power. Neither Louis XV nor Louis XVI could occupy that space. A family monarchy in which children were slow to appear, while the king required sexual counselling by the Austrian emperor to connect penetration with ejaculation, was a contradiction in terms. A pornographer's delight too, for where did the Austrian queen satisfy her allegedly voracious carnal appetites? Over time, the very language of political debate shifted, so that notions like 'the nation' came to be contested between a patriotic family monarchy (the alternative to Louis XIV's cosmic display of power) and patriotic opinion as embodied in the embattled parlements, vying to be that nation's sole incarnation.

These were the incipient battle lines as a bankrupt monarchy was forced to resort to an Estates General after the failure of short-term solutions and a 175-year interval. Almost effortlessly, much of the Gallican Church switched tracks, like a train gliding over points, aligning itself with the moderate constitutional revolution. But the irreconcilable residue was permanently identified with counter-revolution, an identification which led to spoliation and persecution as moderation ceased to be the Revolution's watchword. Even those clergy who sought to collaborate with the Revolution were eventually persecuted too. As the Revolution embarked upon building a secular republic as the prelude to the messianic regeneration of mankind, a Church whose own history provided the only known exemplars for the compulsory imposition of a creed posited upon 'rebirth' was almost destroyed. This remarkable turn of events will occupy the following two chapters. The first looks at the Church during the opening phases of the Revolution; the second at the attempt to convert the Revolution itself into a form of religion. The results were disastrous, leaving the Church deeply hostile to any future invocations of equality, liberty, nation or people.

CHAPTER 2

The Church and the Revolution

The Estates General opened on a bright May morning in 1789. The event was preceded by a procession to the church of Saint-Louis, with each Estate ranged in ascending order towards the royal party at the rear. Nearest the king, the bishops and clergy of the First Estate were themselves separated, to the obvious chagrin of the curés, by a troupe of musicians.

The painter Couder captured the opening session. Louis XVI, his queen and the princes of the blood were seated on the upper steps of a raised dais. According to an American visitor, every gesture they made or word they uttered was keenly scrutinised for its possible meanings. The clerical First Estate, with a scarlet-robed cardinal marking their position, and the aristocratic Second Estate in their cloaks, white stockings and fine shoes, were physically separated by an ocean of gold and magenta carpet from the ranks of the sombrely dressed Third Estate.

The precise number of those present is hard to establish, since deputies were still arriving from remote regions in June. Survivors of hurricanes and shipwrecks only straggled in from the colonies in February 1791. There were about thirteen hundred deputies in total, with twice as many from the Third as the other two Estates combined. Although the deputies were not bereft of administrative, judicial or political hinterlands, after a gap of 175 years the Estates General was a learning process in how to exercise power for all concerned. Each deputy was subject to the magnetic forces of group and regional interests, patriotism and public opinion on this new national stage. Right from the start their role was ambiguous. So was the notion of a constitution. This could simply mean how best to redistribute power between the executive, legislature and judiciary. But it could also signify a much deeper attempt to 'regenerate public order', a potentially limitless root-and-branch reform of society and its institutions in accordance with utopian imaginings.

Once the opening ceremonies were concluded, questions of naked power arose. The king wanted the deputies' credentials verified according to their separate orders; the Third Estate challenged this attempt to divide and rule, taking the momentous step on 12 June of verifying its deputies' own credentials.

Clerical and noble defections from the First and Second Estates thwarted the king's desire for each Estate to deliberate and vote separately. Each accession of the higher orders to the Third Estate was greeted with emotional scenes of recognition and rejoicing. The lower clergy were the first to break ranks, presuming an identity of aims, background and outlook with the men of the Third Estate.[1] About 150 clergy crossed over from the Salle des Cent-Suisses to the Third Estate's Menu-Plaisirs. On 17 June the combined delegates went with abbé Sieyès' call to dub themselves the National Assembly, swearing three days later in the Tennis Court Oath not to disperse until they had given France a new constitution. In the painter David's rendition of what was an intensely fraternal moment, clerics were very prominent, for as yet there had been no breach, and abbé Grégoire was central to the emotional occasion David depicted.[2]

Let's go behind the scenes and look at the deputies in more detail. Under a ruling in late January 1789, bishops and curés were given a single vote in the election of the First Estate. Over two hundred parish priests were returned, together with about fifty bishops under the presidency of cardinal La Rochefoucauld, the amiable and respected archbishop of Rouen. Hierarchy and a desire for a more collegial, Richerist, reform of the Church were thus uneasily combined within the clergy's representation. Some noble bishops regarded the large number of curés as little more than clod-hopping peasants; the curés muttered about the haughtiness of bishops whom they refused to call 'Monseigneur'. Only 3 per cent of the clergy were regulars, which immediately presaged their vulnerability, should both the laity and the seculars decide to gang up on them in order to suppress what both had come to regard as the uselessness of contemplation.[3]

The lower clergy had managed to stamp their views on the general cahiers of grievances that they and the other Estates drew up during elections to the Estates General. Essentially they sought a more collegial management of the Church, and an episcopacy that led by moral example rather than by virtue of birth. In this their aims overlapped with those of the Third Estate, as expressed in their cahiers, there being little disagreement, for the moment, on such fundamentals as the need to preserve and reform the Gallican Church or Roman Catholicism as the predominant faith of France. This alliance against privilege would prove evanescent.[4]

The lay estates were also not free of inner tensions. Aristocratic sophisticates in the capital or Versailles were sometimes snooty towards their rough-mannered and unkempt noble country cousins. Bourgeois deputies were simultaneously repelled and tantalised by aristocratic soldiers whose idea of a rational debate was to draw swords from their scabbards in a combustible mix of anger and outraged honour. Since sword rage was an upper-class vice, a number of intra-aristocratic duels added the colour of blood to the weeks of the Estates General. Noblemen who regarded themselves literally as a separate 'race' did not contribute to smooth relations between the Second and Third Estates. Actually, aristocratic hauteur doubly rankled because one in twelve of the Third Estate deputies were from recently ennobled families, with a few from commensurately grand lineages. Otherwise, many of the bourgeois flushed with pride to find themselves in close proximity to the grandest noble names in the kingdom, writing gossipy letters back to their wives and friends in the provinces.[5]

The sessions of the Estates General did not occur in a void, although at times there was a vacuum of authority. Some noble deputies deplored a minority of their liberal fellows who seemed to be making common cause with the Third Estate for opportunistic reasons. As noblemen they had direct access to the king, which could be construed as the exercise of undue influence. By contrast, when a deputation from the Third Estate tried to breach etiquette in order to render their condolences for the death on 4 June of the child dauphin, they were turned away.[6] Then there were the crowds of ordinary people who hung upon the deputies' every word. Heckling from the galleries of the Assembly was occasionally backed up with violence towards unpopular deputies, as when archbishop de Juigné, who had advised the king to dismiss the Estates General, was dragged from his coach and would have been killed, had not deputies of the Third Estate intervened to protect him. Some deputies developed demagogic talents, and confused enthusiastic Parisian crowds with the national will, while others persisted in identifying mass democracy with tyranny.[7]

The loyalty of French troops came under strain as their orders conflicted with the crowd's exhortations to side with the self-styled patriots. Each hostile movement of foreign soldiers in or around Paris generated increased trepidation. The governor of the Bastille and the chief magistrate of Paris were hacked to pieces and decapitated, followed by the city's intendant and his father-in-law. Across the country revolutionary committees and citizen militias came into being to contain worsening urban food riots. The 'Great Fear' swept the countryside as people there construed grain shortages as part of an aristocratic plot to starve them into submission. These 'plots' took a more sinister turn as indigent gangs, and the armed bands of farmers tracking them, were themselves mythologised as invading aristocratic armies.

Villagers turned on the 'source' of the conspiracy, partly continuing a long tradition of rural uprisings, partly using the new political vocabulary of 'people power'. They raided the châteaux, burning the written traces of their subjection, and such symbols of noble privilege as dovecots, wine presses and weathervanes. In Alsace the Great Fear took the form of attacks on Ashkenazi Jewish money-lenders in about seventy places. Taxes and tithes ceased to be paid. Both rural uprisings and urban mob violence terrified the National Assembly and the classes they represented. Some deputies literally had their ears to the ground, in terrified anticipation of the mob's trampling footfalls heading towards them.

Thoughtful people felt they were being dragged along by events whose outcome they dreaded. Writing to an English aristocrat, the bishop of Chartres revealed: 'I find myself in the way, without having sought it, of playing a role myself [in the Revolution] ... At present therefore, the torrent pulls me along like everyone else because it would be too dangerous to oppose it. But I give way with repugnance and with a disquiet too well founded that all this excess may force us back to the other extreme.'[8] Hitherto uncommitted clerical deputies, like the diarist Rouph de Varicourt, curé of Gex, began to take exception to the secular mentality that appeared to dominate their Third Estate colleagues, and hence turned cool towards the Revolution.[9]

Anticlericalism began to emerge in the Assembly over the issue of renouncing feudal privileges. To regain mastery over a country slipping out of control, without using an army that might defect, the deputies decided to renounce their own privileges in a sort of orgy of self-repudiation. Spokesmen of every corporate interest vied to sacrifice their historic privileges. The bishops surrendered their feudal dues, the curés the casual fees they received from their parishioners. The annates which each new bishop owed to Rome were abrogated. There was also a tit-for-tat element. When the bishop of Chartres suggested abolition of hunting rights, an angry duc de Châtelet responded by calling for the end of the tithe, adding, 'I'm going to take something from him too.'[10] Although only one in ten of the cahiers of the Third Estate had called for the abolition of tithes, these were abolished without much thought to an alternative system to replace them.

The modalities of abolition were announced on 11 August when it was declared: 'The National Assembly entirely destroys the feudal regime.' In fact, along with dovecots and hunting rights, much of what was abolished was not 'feudal' at all, but the venal office-holding which a cash-strapped monarchy had encouraged since the early seventeenth century. The tithe was abolished, although it would continue to be collected pending the introduction of some new mechanism for supporting the clergy. These were momentous decisions, wiping out a host of intermediary bodies that made the ancien régime what it was.[11]

A once zealously defended clerical interest suffered implicit derogation as the Declaration of the Rights of Man, promulgated on 26 August, located the origin and source of all authority in the French nation. The idea of societies functioning without the aid of religion, or of a separation of Church and state, would have struck almost everyone as absurd. The social utility of religion was recognised in Articles 16 and 17, but Article 18 did not entirely reassure the clergy: 'No one can be disturbed for his opinions, even religious ones, provided that their expression does not infringe the public order declared by the law.' The idea of including explicit recognition of the predominance of the Roman Catholic Church into the opening of the Declaration was rejected. Exemption of 'bad books' from the article on freedom of the press did not quite compensate for this glaring omission.

The lands of the Church were one major casualty of the radicalisation of the public mood. Archbishop Boisgelin of Aix vainly offered a major loan that would have forestalled outright confiscation. While the national-isation of Church property to liquidate the national debt had been canvassed many times before, paradoxically it was one of the staunchest erstwhile defenders of the privileges of the clerical Estate who proposed it.

Charles Maurice de Talleyrand came from one of the grandest noble dynasties in France. A clubfoot excluded him from following the family tradition of a military career. He may have resented having to pursue a priestly vocation, for which his long-standing liaison with the comtesse de Flahaut suggested he had little aptitude. Family connections ensured a rapid rise up the clerical hierarchy. He served for five years as agent-general of the Assembly of the Clergy, distinguishing himself as a dogged defender of clerical privileges against the Crown, before becoming bishop of Autun at the relatively young age of thirty-five. Since he was a new-comer to Autun, the clergy lacked any personal grounds not to elect him as a delegate to the Estates General; lavish fish banquets cooked by his personal chef for the local clergy further inclined them to vote for him. The fact that Talleyrand had intimate connections to a declining faction at Louis XVI's Court may have led him into liberal–patriotic political circles. Talleyrand challenged the received view of the nature of clerical property: 'It is evident that the clergy is not a proprietor in the same sense that others are, since the goods of which they have the use and of which they cannot dispose were given to them not for their personal benefit, but for use in the performance of their functions.'[12]

In other words, the wealth of the Church was not property in the normal sense, but something the Church had been given with which to do good works. Since the state would now assume responsibility for the poor, the assets of the Church should be transferred to the state, which would henceforth pay clerics a salary in payment for their activities in morally educating the public. The clergy strenuously argued against this view. Their lands had been assembled incrementally through pious donations of great antiquity. Some clergy used a more utilitarian line of reasoning. Their predecessors had toiled for centuries to turn remote and unpromising lands into fertile fields and vineyards. They were part of their communities, sharing in the ups and downs of living by or from the land. They were no more immune to hailstones, fire and flood than anyone else. If they became state-supported salaried functionaries (and salaries in this society bore a certain stigma signifying lack of inde-pendence) these bonds would dissolve. Sequestration would result in an unseemly speculative orgy conducted by businessmen and Jews. The abbé Maury warned that it was rash to speculate about the origins of property rights.

A cash-strapped Assembly first identified four hundred million livres of Church property which it then sold in order to back the new paper assignats it was printing. On 2 November 1789 the Assembly voted 568 to 346 to sequestrate ecclesiastical property, in a decision that dwarfed the more modest depredations of Henry VIII. The bishops decided not to respond. As one explained to the pope: 'Our silence demonstrated how we were inaccessible, personally, to all the temporal interests whose possession had drawn on us hatred and envy.'[13] Henceforth bishops were to receive not less than twelve thousand livres per annum (and not more than fifty thousand livres), while the curés would be paid not less than twelve hundred livres per annum plus their lodgings and gardens. An immediate fiscal crisis had led the Assembly to lay hands on the resources of the Church. It was logical that the Assembly should next seek to eradicate any remaining fat. A popular engraving showed the desired way forward. The pencil-thin black-garbed abbé of today was contrasted with the pantophagous abbé of yesteryear.[14] Since the state was now responsible for clerical salaries, all sources of alleged excess had to disappear. On 13 February 1790 a decree abolished all but hospital and teaching orders. In the course of these debates Bonal, bishop of Clermont, muttered that the Assembly was exceeding its competence, ineluctably trespassing into what the clergy believed to be spiritual matters. Contrary to the widespread view that monks were idlers, Bonal argued that the monastic state was 'the most fitting for the support of the nation, because of the influence of prayer on the success of human affairs'.[15]

Self-abnegation was not high among the virtues celebrated by either the philosophes or those who had ingested their disdain for the regular orders, a disdain shared by many regular clerics. In his novel *La Religieuse* (not published until 1795), Diderot had highlighted the problem of coerced religious vocations and the psychological and sexual deviations resulting from the monotonous intensity of the celibate cloistered life. The novel is also a rather daring piece of soft-core pornography, abounding with flagellation, undone habits, fondling and Richter-scale orgasms. This distracts from the novel's more serious point. A young illegitimate girl called Suzanne Simonin is despatched to a convent to enable her parents to concentrate their slender resources upon the dowries of two older daughters. Suzanne is subjected to the close attentions of a scatterbrained lesbian mother superior and is raped by a Benedictine confessor who facilitates her escape from the former.[16] While Diderot concentrated on the malign psychological environment of single-sex religious communities, others took a more economistic view, although Diderot does allude to the ex-nun Suzanne's complete unemployability save as either laundress or prostitute. Modern man was supposed to engage productively and usefully with the world, and that included what some regarded as 'his' national duty to have children. During the discussions in the Assembly, Barnave (who was from a Protestant family) articulated the dominant view, skilfully locking the deputies in the logic of their own idealism:

> I do not believe it is necessary to demonstrate that the religious orders are incompatible with the rights of man. A profession that deprives men of the rights you have recognised is incompatible with those rights. Obliged to undertake duties that are not prescribed by Nature, which Nature reproves, are they not by Nature herself condemned to violate them?[17]

At a stroke in February 1790, monasteries and convents not engaged in useful work were dissolved and forbidden to accept novices. Monks and nuns were relieved of their vows and offered a pension if they left their houses. Those who refused were concentrated in fewer institutions, where having to rub shoulders with men from a variety of orders soon inclined them to pack up and leave the monastic life. Barbers and tailors did a roaring trade with those who had abandoned the habit. It is safe to assume that monks and nuns living in dysfunctional houses were the first to pack up and leave, along with those whose vocations were tepid or who were young enough to contemplate a different career. Some former monks became prominent revolutionary terrorists. Made anxious by these developments, the bishop of Nancy asked for confirmation that Roman Catholicism was the state religion. No confirmation came.

The pope grudgingly acknowledged these measures, as he had earlier accepted Joseph II's dissolution of the Austrian monasteries in order to expand useful education. But the potential for a major clash over the right of the temporal power, in this case 'the people', to interfere in a quintessentially spiritual matter, had obviously increased. Yet it would be untrue to claim that most clerics were appalled by these measures. On the contrary, they could just as easily regard them as a return to the apostolic simplicities of the early Church, and as a salutary renunciation of sources of potential corruption and temptation. Optimists might almost have said that the National Assembly was doing the work of a reforming Church council. There were also clerics prepared to take this line to its logical conclusion by advocating a sort of national religion posited on the union of an egalitarian national Church and a democratised nation. The great religious truths had found their social expression through the Revolution.

The abbé Claude Fauchet, author of *De la religion nationale*, and proud owner of a soutane rent by shot during the storming of the Bastille, was one of the most fervent advocates of this fusion of radicalised religion and radical politics. Originally from the central Nièvre, Fauchet was a brilliant preacher and author of *Life of Jesus, Man of the People*, in which he blamed 'aristocrats' for the crucifixion. He wanted such things as restrictions on wealth, including reform of inheritance laws, and state promotion of egalitarianism through encouragement of marriages between different social classes. Vice was to be suppressed, freedom of the press curbed, and the theatre given over to moral instruction: 'Thus will legislation conform to the spirit of the Gospels, to the inherent morality of brotherly love, which is the basis and the crowning glory of the public weal in a nation which is wisely governed for the happiness of all its citizens.' Subsequently as constitutional bishop of Calvados, Fauchet signed himself 'Claude Fauchet, by the grace of God and the will of the people, in the communion of the holy apostolic see and in the charity of the human race, bishop of Calvados'.

The prospects for a national religion, centred upon Christian egalitarianism, as advocated by Fauchet or the abbé Grégoire, faded while old animosities were reactivated, or unexpected solidarities arose when the room for manoeuvre diminished.

In some regions sectarian tensions lay just beneath the surface. Majority Catholic resentments were triggered wherever already economically powerful Protestant manufacturers and merchants assumed the reins of local political power. Savage communal sectarian violence broke out in Montauban or Nîmes, whose Protestant dominated National Guard shot down over three hundred Catholics during the bitterly contested departmental elections.[18] Intelligent aristocratic counter-revolutionaries began to espy a potential mass constituency among those who were starting to associate the Revolution with Protestantism, irreligion or the return of religious persecution, views being put about abroad by clerical–intellectual members of the emigration.

By some irony, the National Assembly inadvertently managed the considerable feat of transforming the staunchly Gallican Church into what would emerge as one of the most fiercely ultramontane Churches in nineteenth-century Europe. For it continued to be much less tentative in its reform of relations between Church and state than it had so far been in its handling of the problem of the increasingly marginalised but symbolically important king. How amity developed into schism brought about by the Civil Constitution of the Clergy will occupy the rest of this chapter. The schism lasted for nearly two hundred years.[19]

II OATHS

As the embodiment of the nation, the Constituent Assembly felt itself responsible for issuing constitutions regarding local government, the armed forces and so forth. In keeping with this, it issued a 'Civil Constitution' of the clergy; that is, a constitution governing those aspects of the Church that came within the ambit of the secular power. The Assembly could claim, with some justification if one thinks of Joseph II, that it was not 'innovating' in its policies towards Church affairs, but merely continuing what Catholic monarchs had done virtually every-where else in eighteenth-century Europe. In August 1789 it established its own fifteen-man Ecclesiastical Committee, consisting of two bishops, Mercy of Luçon and its chairman Bonal of Clermont, three curés and ten laymen. The bishops managed to quash the madder recommenda-tions. But by February 1790, aggressively Gallican lawyers on the Com-mittee cleverly argued that its numbers were not adequate to its daunting tasks. Fifteen laymen of a more radical disposition were then co-opted to ensure that proposals went ahead by majority vote. On 29 May 1790 the Committee presented a draft Civil Constitution of the Clergy to the Assembly, although there was little 'civil' about it since in the eyes of many it was a presbyterian diktat regarding issues that were ultimately spiritual.

It proposed to abolish more than fifty sees, while conforming the rest to the boundaries of the new departments of France, of which there were eighty-three. This meant that the large diocese of Le Mans was divided into sees at Laval, Avranches and Lisieux, the inhabitants of Saint-Malo, Dol, Tréguier and Saint-Pol-de-Léon in Brittany found themselves without bishops. Parishes would also be rationalised to con-form with the shifting realities of population densities, a measure that annoyed those who now had to travel long distances to their new parish. About four thousand parishes were simply abolished. Clergy who had no pastoral function, such as cathedral canons, would follow the regulars into oblivion. By stipulating that bishops should have served fifteen years in the parishes, and thus emphasising their common ministerial vocation, the Assembly drastically reduced the gulf between prelates and priests – a point underlined by the introduction of a more collegial style of diocesan administration, in which bishops were obliged to pay heed to the views of ten or twelve of their diocesan clerics. The salaries of priests were raised on a scale between twelve hundred and six thousand livres, according to the size of their flocks, while bishops had to make do with between twelve and twenty thousand livres rather than the stratospheric six-figure incomes the richest had hitherto enjoyed. Henceforth, the laity were to elect both their bishops at departmental level and priests within the parish district. Since citizenship overrode everything else, these lay electors would include non-Catholics, and not just Protestants but also Jews, who after protracted debates concerning the assimilated Sephardim in the Bordelais and the 'foreign' eastern European Ashkenazim of Alsace and Lorraine, had been successively granted citizenship by late September 1791.[20]

So far we have hardly mentioned the papacy, whose international profile was far more modest in the eighteenth century than it was in the nineteenth or than it is now. Not only were the eighteenth-century popes undistinguished, but the Papal States were a byword for governmental corruption. Joseph II had unilaterally abolished the monasteries, while the enlightened Russian tsarina Catherine the Great had rearranged the diocesan boundaries in Russian Poland. Pilgrimages to Rome declined because the enlightened ruler of Tuscany would not let them traverse his territories. The Civil Constitution went one stage further in forbidding newly elected French bishops from seeking confirmation of their election from the pope.

Pius VI maintained a public silence towards the Revolution's handling of the Gallican Church although he was privately condemnatory of the Declaration of the Rights of Man, the sacred text of the Revolution. In August 1790 he formed a congregation of twenty cardinals to advise him about events in France. Although some cardinals counselled moderation over such matters as reshaping the diocesan boundaries, most took a dim view of the subversion of ecclesiastical hierarchy. Papal silence became an impossible stance as supporters of the Revolution in the papal enclaves of Avignon and the Comtat Venaissin insisted upon incorporation by France. On the day after Louis XVI assented to the Civil Constitution, he received a letter from Pius VI condemning it.

Opinion about the Civil Constitution had begun to polarise both within and beyond the National Assembly. The bishops were the first to sound alarm bells about the fact that the Civil Constitution raised issues of spiritual authority in what was still a constituent branch of the universal Roman Catholic Church. The politicians of one country could not simply legislate changes for a universal institution. Nor for that matter could they fiddle around with diocesan boundaries, or with how bishops and priests were appointed, nor dispense monks and nuns from vows of the highest solemnity. Clerics were more than 'public functionaries'. These issues were set forth in a cool and collected manner by Boisgelin of Aix in his *Exposition des principes sur la Constitution civile du clergé*, to which thirty bishops signed up.[21]

These clerical objections were countered by claims that the Assembly was merely restoring the Church to its ancient pristine condition, or simply continuing the traditional tough supervision that the French monarchs had formally exercised. If that past royal regimen had been legitimate, who could gainsay a new authority based on the will of the entire French people? So what if Protestants and Jews were now entitled to elect priests; was this any worse than bishops who owed their appointment to the machinations of a royal bastard or mistress? By depicting the Church as a remnant from the ancien régime, while simultaneously seeking to perpetuate that regime's tight rein on the Gallican Church, the Assembly was blending innovation with tradition. One deputy, Camus, warned the clergy: 'The Church is part of the state. The state is not part of the Church.' In other words, canon law was not going to override popular sovereignty.

The Assembly rejected all clerical attempts to summon a national ecclesiastical council, since even determining the form of this would drag on into infinity, while it would also signify a return to hated corporate bodies. Since the national council was a non-starter, even prominent clerical reformers now turned expectantly towards the papacy. Throughout the summer Pius VI prevaricated, leaving the clergy and the Assembly to enjoy a prolongation of their false dawn.

In the summer of 1790, these were just faint stirrings of discontent. Talleyrand and other clerics took prominent parts in the celebration of the Festival of the Federation on 14 July 1790. Draped in red, white and blue, Talleyrand celebrated the mass on the 'Altar of the Fatherland' set up on the Champs de Mars. All over the country, clerics were similarly generously represented at the various regional festivals. Very few clergy refused to participate.

On 12 July the National Assembly approved the Civil Constitution of the Clergy. It received the royal assent on 24 August, partly because Louis XVI was worried that he would be deposed in favour of his son, brother or cousin if he refused it. The pope had so far not formally spoken. Tempers started to fray when clergy followed the logic of approval or disapproval of the Civil Constitution. When a leading clerical reformer in the Assembly was elected bishop of Quimper, the bishop of Rouen refused him canonical institution.[22] Some deputies on the police committee thought there should be a more explicit test of clerical acceptance of the new dispensation. Religion, in other words, was an aspect of public order. In some departments an oath was already being used to test whether clergy accepted the new order; if they refused to take it, like the bishop of Soissons, they were deposed. On 26 November 1790 the National Assembly debated such measures. Clergy were to be given eight days to swear an oath to 'be faithful to the Nation, the law and the King', and to 'maintain with all their power the Constitution decreed by the National Assembly and accepted by the King'. Those who refused to take this oath were deemed to have resigned their offices. The Assembly voted to impose the oath on 27 November 1790 and it was promulgated with royal approval a month later.

The Civil Constitution of the Clergy was too radical to be reconciled with orthodox Catholicism, and too traditional to assuage revolutionary idealists who sought a civic religion which would serve the interests of the revolutionary state. By denying the clergy any collective response to policies that touched on spiritual questions, the Assembly managed to bring about a dangerous religious schism, providing the disparate and incoherent forces of counter-revolution with an issue around which they could gather a genuine mass following. They managed to turn a myth into a menacing reality. A counter-revolution hitherto perhaps too facilely identified with the defence of mere privilege could thenceforth claim, with reason, to be about fundamental issues of conscience. Finally, once the refractory clergy had become identified with counter-revolution, there was always the danger that the more radical revolutionaries would apply this identification to the clergy in general, including the Constitutionals who had taken the oath, despite the latter's porosity towards the ideas of the Revolution. This was precisely what happened and it resulted in a split between the religion and politics of the country that took two centuries to repair.[23]

On the afternoon of 4 January 1791 the clerical members of the Assembly were called upon to take the oath to the Civil Constitution. Attempts to prevaricate by separating its purely civil from its wider spiritual content were brushed aside by deputies who were in no mood to compromise. With the exception of Talleyrand, Brienne and two others, all forty-four bishops in the Assembly refused to take the oath. They were followed by the entire French episcopate. This gave a lead to their humbler colleagues, who, now that parasitic canons and monks were no more, rediscovered a common clerical identity with their bishops. Of the lower clergy present, only 107 swore the oath, leaving two-thirds in the dissident camp. Attempts to coerce them by calling upon each individual in a roll-call failed to intimidate – although the presence in the gallery of a baying mob already intimated that refusal to take the oath was construed as treasonable.

Oath-taking was repeated on a national scale through the remainder of January 1791. Some regions revealed a high proportion of so-called juring priests, who took the oath, especially in the capital and the Paris basin, Berry, Champagne, Dauphiné, Picardy, Poitou and Provence. Dissent was most evident in Alsace, Anjou, Artois, Brittany, Flanders, Languedoc and Lower Normandy, which all included large numbers of refractories (as those who refused to take the oath were called). In Strasbourg, a non-juring priest refused to leave the cathedral and hit the new juring bishop. The previous incumbent, Rohan, excommunicated his successor from the safety of exile in Germany. It is difficult to generalise about the areas in either the juring or non-juring camps. Dense concentrations of clerics in urban centres ensured solidarity in numbers for those who refused to swear the oath. By contrast, isolated country clergy were easy to put pressure on. It may be the case that the clergy's parishioners determined their stance. Where popular piety was intense, no more so than in the maritime west, clergy did not swear the oath. Here, many of them were scions of the better-off land-holding peasantry, who were both well-to-do and serious, in a Tridentine sort of way, about their religious vocations. Others, whom one might call 'demi-jurors', tried to hedge the oath with reservations or purely verbal protestations of loyalty to the Revolution.[24]

The reasons why individuals took the oath cannot simply be reduced to their need for a salary overriding their principles, a stance neatly expressed by the curé who said: 'In order to live, I'd gladly take as many oaths as there are threads in my wig.' Some lower clergy sincerely identified the Civil Constitution with the more presbyterian forms of Church government they had advocated for years. Like Fauchet they believed that a synthesis of reformed (or regenerated) Christianity and revolutionary politics was possible. In fact, many juring or Constitutional clergy may have had respectable theological reasons for taking the oath. A drawing of a Constitutional cleric celebrating mass shows him simply attired as a cloud of mitres and croziers fly away from him, the caption being 'Vanity of vanities, all nothing but vanity'. Others went with the local flow, listening to the arguments of family, friends and neighbours who supported the Revolution. A few took the oath to spite ambitious subordinates eyeing up their benefice, like the priest who took the oath, telling his ambitious juring vicaire: 'Ah, canaille, you think you'll get my parish. But you won't!'[25]

The bishops who refused to swear the oath had to be replaced by others. Elections took place between January and May 1791. Many of these elections were poorly attended, as at Rennes where only 60 per cent of eligible electors voted for bishop Claude Le Coz. The papacy was forced to abandon its hitherto cautious public response to these events when Talleyrand, who had resigned his see on 13 January 1791 to pursue an administrative career, was recalled to consecrate two so-called constitutional bishops in Paris. That opened the way for the creation of a parallel hierarchy, and what amounted to a schismatic Church consisting of priests willing to take the oath of the Civil Constitution. On 18 April the king made his sympathies explicit when he and the queen vainly sought to reach Saint-Cloud in order to take communion from a non-juring priest, a gesture which resulted in them being confined in their coach for over two hours by a hostile mob.[26]

By omitting the obligatory oath of fidelity to the pope from the consecration, Talleyrand made a confrontation with the papacy virtually inevitable. The deputy Camus added another layer of provocation when he referred to the pope as 'a minister of Christ like the others'. This was a challenge to its right of investiture that the papacy could not ignore. On 10 March 1791 Pius VI issued a brief that gave juring priests forty days to recant the oath they had taken. This was followed up by a declaration that the Civil Constitution was heretical, sacrilegious and schismatical. Elections of the new bishops were null and void. By the end of the month, Pius had broken off diplomatic relations with France, after an effigy representing 'the ogre on the Tiber' had been burned in the garden of the Palais-Royal. The pope figured in any number of revolutionary caricatures. One image showed Pius VI being turned away by St Peter at the gates of heaven; another had the pope blowing bulls, in the manner of a child's bubbles, towards a figure of France who repelled them. Cruder images showed a revolutionary wiping his arse with the papal letter.[27] Ironically, the pope's firm stance coincided with a newfound spirit of compromise in the Assembly. Fundamentally, the problem was that a coerced oath sat uneasily with the guarantees of liberty contained in the Declaration of the Rights of Man. Despite their refusal to swear the oath, non-juring clergy remained as members of the National Assembly. Attempts were made to fudge the graver consequences of dissent by separating disqualification of non-juring priests from public office from performance of their religious functions. On 7 May the Assembly decreed that non-juring priests could still conduct masses in what had become Constitutional churches, provided the laymen who rented the building for the occasion had sought prior official permission.

This spirit of compromise was not reflected in the new Legislative Assembly that met for the first time in October 1791. The greatly diminished clerical component now consisted of twenty-eight oath-taking clergy, while the number of radicals had increased dramatically in comparison with its Constituent predecessor, whose members had disqualified themselves from the successor chamber. The new Assembly included twenty-eight physicians, twenty-eight clergy, including two Protestants, about a hundred businessmen and landowners, some professors and journalists, and four hundred lawyers. On 9 October this more radical Assembly heard a report about the westernmost departments. Insofar as there were any Constitutional clergy, they were having a hard time of it. They were being ostracised by their parishioners who continued to respect the old priests. Those who attended the churches of the former were called 'patriots'; those who went to non-juring clergy were dubbed 'aristocrats'. Juring clergy found that bell-ropes were smeared with malodorous materials or that distressed cats sprang out of chests and cupboards. Supporters of both sides depicted the other's clergy with comically elongated noses, and as more or less bound straight for hell.

In October 1791 the new Assembly passed a decree declaring non-juring clergy 'suspects'. France's deteriorating international position, culminating in war with Austria and reverses on the battlefield in the summer of 1792, further radicalised the mood of the Assembly, as did the urban radicals who repeatedly intimidated it. By a decree dated 27 May 1792, refractory priests who were denounced by a minimum of twenty active citizens (those wealthy enough to vote) were liable to deportation without prior judicial proceedings. Priests caught hiding faced a minimum of ten years' imprisonment, and those who aided and abetted them had to defray the costs of these search-and-arrest operations themselves. The suspension, on 10 August, of the king from all his functions served to radicalise the Assembly still more. No one knows the name of the deputy who proposed an oath for all public functionaries and pensioners, a measure that applied to the salaried Constitutionals and the pensioned-off refractories alike. On 14 August all clergy were compelled to take the oath: 'I swear to be faithful to the Nation, to maintain with all my power liberty, equality, the security of persons and property, and to die if necessary for the execution of the laws.' Non-jurors were given a fortnight to leave metropolitan France or face deportation to New Guinea. If they returned to metropolitan France they faced ten years' imprisonment. Only the ailing or elderly were exempted from these draconian measures, and they had to be concentrated in departmental capitals for close observation. Finally, on 20 September, in its final session, the Assembly laicised the state and sanctioned civil divorce.[28]

In late September 1792 the Prussian army captured the frontier fortress of Longwy and threatened Verdun too, the last line of defence before Paris. Fearing a fifth column, many non-juring clergy were incarcerated, until the prisons were so overcrowded that ad-hoc jails were established in abbeys and convents. Panic then spread among the Parisian plain-dressed popular militants or sans-culottes that 'counter-revolutionary' detainees were planning simultaneous uprisings. Violent mobs fell upon these places of incarceration, knifing the detainees to death. Between two and three thousand prisoners were murdered, including three bishops and 220 priests.[29]

The Constitutional clergy were left between the rock and hard place of revolutionaries whose anticlericalism had developed into calls to 'de-Christianise' France and a refractory clergy that was falling into the embrace of various counter-revolutionary forces. The Constitutional clergy were effectively state officials, although such functions as registering the rites of passage had been hived off from them to civil servants in September 1792. Inevitably, with something like half of the clergy refusing to swear the oath and hence expelled from their livings, there was a vast amount of movement within the clergy, with new faces popping up in unfamiliar settings. A manpower shortage ensured that many Constitutional or juring priests were former monks needing an income and housing.

Whereas large parts of the clergy had been on hand to bless secular political events, by 1791–2, the newly elected Constitutional bishops sometimes needed an armed escort even to enter their sees, leading bishop Pouderous of Béziers to be known as 'Bishop of the Bayonets'. Despite the fact that many of these men were highly talented, and not cynical opportunists like Talleyrand, they often met a rough reception in their dioceses. Thus bishop Minée of Nantes was met by jeering women who shouted, 'Minée, you're a mouse, you're a mouse!' Bishops and priests whose election and installation owed much to respectively the vote-rigging skills of the local Jacobin clubs and the bayonets of the National Guard lived a lonely life amid their hostile parishioners. They were 'intrus' (intruders) who were installed in ceremonies usually dominated by republican guards and functionaries, where the curé might be the only cleric present. Installation was the easy part. Life among villagers who detested them was tough on the Constitutionals. Guns were discharged outside their windows late at night; dead cats, excrement or in some cases coffins were left on the rectory doorstep. They discovered that the pool of lay goodwill necessary for the upkeep of their churches had abruptly emptied as bell-ropes or the keys to the door or treasure literally vanished. In some parishes people would not even sell them life's necessities or perform routine repairs.[30]

So far from revolutionary radicals resting content with the complete subordination of Church to state that the Civil Constitution signified, the new Convention, which replaced the National Assembly in September 1792, introduced measures which began to affect clerics in general rather than just those who refused the oath. Citizens could henceforth choose their own names, while only one bronze bell per parish was spared the state's crucibles. From February 1793 onwards, the Convention introduced measures that encouraged clerics to marry, not least by punishing those bishops who might try to stop them. These measures affected Constitutionals and refractories alike. Between 4,500 and 6,000 clergy married, often formalising earlier arrangements with their long-standing partners. Nuns faced an especially grim time after being forced out of their convents, since unlike monks they could not easily find work as administrators, soldiers or teachers. Of those who married, about a quarter married former priests. A few claimed to have been influenced by 'philosophic persons' or by the temptation of being 'a Jacobine, a worldly girl, frequenting balls and societies'.[31]

Many clergy were coerced or fell eagerly into apostasy, adopting 'natural religion' and abjuring 'priestcraft'. Nearly half of the Constitutional clergy simply gave up their vocations, with some of them volunteering for the Republic's armies or turning to secular school teaching. It amounted to a process of 'civic baptism'. As a priest from Hérault announced: 'Now that the state of priesthood contravenes the happiness of the people, and hinders the progress of the Revolution, I abdicate from it and throw myself into the arms of society.' By 1794, only 150 of France's 40,000 pre-Revolution parishes were openly celebrating mass.

We turn next to the fate of the refractories and attempts to make the revolution itself a religion. For about the necessity for a religion there was little or no doubt. A Jacobin writer a little conversant with history wondered:

> How was the Christian religion established? By the preaching of the apostles of the Gospel. How can we firmly establish the Constitution? By the mission of the apostles of liberty and equality. Each society should take charge of the neighbouring country districts ... It is enough to send an enlightened and zealous patriot with instructions which he will adapt to the locality: he should also provide himself with a copy of the Declaration of Rights, the Constitution, the Almanack du Père Gérard [by Collot d'Herbois], a good tract against fanaticism, a good journal and a good model of a pike.

Armed missionaries were despatched into France profonde as well as across the length and breadth of Europe to propagate the new tidings as Reason militant went on the march.[32]

CHAPTER 3

Puritans Thinking They are Spartans Run Amok in Eighteenth-Century Paris

I TWO PAINTERS

The cultural history of the Revolution enables us to get closer to the minds of those who made or opposed it, to explore their fears and longings, for intense emotions were abroad. We might as well start with an opponent, so as to bring the Revolution's self-understanding into sharper relief. Johan Zauffalÿ was born in 1733 near Frankfurt am Main. He moved to London in 1760 after training in Italy as an artist. As Johan Zoffany, he enjoyed success as a painter of conversation pieces and portraits. Many of the latter had religious accents since Zoffany, although nominally Anglican, remained a closet Roman Catholic. The highpoint of his career was his depiction of the Tribuna in Florence's Uffizi in which he detailed the contents of this inner sanctum of artistic excellence on behalf of queen Charlotte. Six years' exile in British India was designed to make his fortune among the colonial nouveaux riches; he returned a sick man subject to paralysis. By the early 1790s, Zoffany's once promising career was stalled. How many allusively clever self-portraits could an artist of his abilities churn out? At this juncture he tried, and to some extent managed to achieve, something strikingly different.

In 1794 Zoffany painted two large canvases devoted to scenes from two consecutive days during the French Revolution – 10 and 12 August 1792. These two paintings are remarkable on several grounds. Unlike most counter-revolutionary art, they do not focus on the intimate tribulations of Louis XVI and his family in their months of confinement in

67

the Temple. Nor do they bother with recording what was an intense military engagement in the purlieus of the Tuileries Palace. Instead, Zoffany depicted the brutal aftermath of battle, with images derived from the more ephemeral media of cartoon or print as used by Gillray, Hogarth or Rowlandson. Zoffany's greater contemporary, Goya, would have more ruthlessly edited, and hence focused, the horror. Zoffany's canvases are so febrile that they divert the view into too many separate horrors at once, thereby lessening the overall impact, even if the ideological message he wished to convey comes across starkly. This message was derived from Edmund Burke's highly prescient account of where events in Revolutionary France tended, and of the base and bestial motives that had been unleashed once the speculations of the philosophes had been evangelised among the lower orders, a commonplace too in British anti-Jacobin novels of the 1790s.[1]

Zoffany's paintings are titled *Plundering the King's Wine Cellar* and *Celebrating over the Bodies of the Swiss Soldiers* on respectively 10 and 12 August 1792. Nominally the paintings depict scenes that followed the murderous assault by Parisian sans-culottes on the Tuileries Palace shortly after Austria and Prussia had issued the Brunswick Manifesto that promised savage reprisals against the capital if the king and queen were injured. In the course of this assault, Swiss mercenaries opened fire on the interlopers. Ordered by an equivocating, or humane, Louis XVI to lay down their arms, the Swiss and Louis' noble bodyguards were themselves slaughtered by the insurgents. The mob then plundered the palace. Since Zoffany did not witness the events he depicted, he relied heavily on contemporary British and French caricatures of the Revolution, at its bloodthirsty terroristic zenith, incorporating themes that occurred months and years after the specific events he chronicled in these pictures. His two canvases are a distillation of his view of the Revolution in general.

The first painting is of a bacchanalian mob of trouserless men (for in contemporary British mythology 'sans culottes' meant being bare-arsed rather than wearing baggy trousers instead of knee breeches) and décolletée women helping themselves to bottles of wine from huge wicker baskets. That is the first scene the eye alights on before it notices more shocking images. A glassy-eyed black boy has vomited the wine he has drunk; a Jew purchases the mob's loot. A man pours wine into the gaping mouth of a dead Swiss soldier. A plebeian hag plunges a knife into a prone well-to-do woman whose watch she is simultaneously removing. A priest hangs inertly from the iron rail of a lantern. In obvious allusion to Christ and the two thieves, two severed heads are held aloft on pikes beside another bearing the revolutionary red bonnet, and various people, including a priest about to be laid low with a sabre, are being done to death in the foreground.

The action takes place within and beyond a massive stone arch, evocative of medieval renditions of the gaping mouth of hell. Various statues adorn the arch, notably Hercules slaying Hydra, a mythological figure that the Revolution itself employed, but which Zoffany here reappropriated for the royalist cause. Hydra was the mob; Hercules represented order. Women figure prominently in Zoffany's second canvas, beginning with a sans-culottiste standing, knife in hand, on a pile of corpses. She is simultaneously a grotesque parody of the figure of 'Liberty' and a hag that has strayed from depictions of witches' sabbaths. Both this figure and the insane, naked female scuttling about on all fours in the foreground anticipate the nightmarish images of Goya's 'Black Paintings' by about thirty years. Although violent women dominate the painting, Zoffany manages to incorporate the duc d'Orléans, Philippe Egalité, in the left-hand corner, thereby insinuating that these scenes of carnage had sinister conspiratorial origins. The duke's own eventual fate (he was executed in 1793) is symbolised by the knife that a sans-culotte holds poised above his aristocratic head.[2]

While Zoffany's talent fell some way short of the major historical events he transformed into paint, the Revolution itself had at least one artistic talent of genius at its disposal – a sort of 'Robespierre of the brush'. David enables us to get close to the Revolution's own religious self-understanding. For the artist was a high-ranking Jacobin; he shared their vision of the world.

Jacques-Louis David was born in Paris in 1748, the son of a merchant and tax officer who was killed in a duel when David was nine. Two architect uncles supported his quest to become an artist. In 1774 David won the Prix de Rome at the third attempt, and in the following year set out for what would be almost a five-year sojourn among the classical ruins of that city. Sketchbook after sketchbook was filled with his impressions of ancient bas-reliefs, cameos, sarcophagi, statues and utensils, genre scenes and landscapes, as well as copies of Caravaggio, Guido Reni, Michelangelo and Raphael. If a Dionysian Rubens had inspired many of the greatest eighteenth-century French painters, such as Boucher, Fragonard and Watteau, David's spiritual progenitor was that austere Apollonian seventeenth-century classicist Nicholas Poussin.

News of David's great talent preceded his return to Paris where work he exhibited at the 1781 Salon led to Louis XVI granting him rent-free living quarters and a massive studio in the Louvre. He was a fashionable and rich artist, whom the well-born queued up to support. Gratitude was not his strong suit. In August 1783 he became a member of the exclusive and hierarchical Royal Academy, an institution which he, as a man who knew how to nurse a grudge over the long haul, would shortly contrive to have abolished as a sort of artistic Bastille. Probably in order to escape his burgeoning army of students, in the following year David returned to Rome, where for nearly a year he worked on the *Oath of the Horatii* – up to that point his greatest masterpiece. Between 1787 and 1789 he produced two further representations of antique virtues, namely *The Death of Socrates* and *The Lictors Returning to Brutus the Bodies of his Sons*, a canvas that was deemed so politically inflammatory in 1789, because of the implicit contrast between Brutus' moral fortitude and the failure of Louis XVI to dispose of 'wicked' advisers, that the authorities sought to remove it from the Salon. Popular clamour ensured that the canvas remained. In February 1790 David joined the Jacobins.[3]

A hard and single-minded man, who clearly did not suffer fools gladly, David was fully aware of his own historical importance at a crucial juncture in history. In late 1789 he oversaw the painting of over sixty portraits of illustrious Frenchmen from both the seventeenth and eighteenth centuries, commissioned by king Stanislaus-Augustus of Poland, suggestively including a self-portrait in the first consignment to Cracow. Given his famous *Oath of the Horatii*, which he had painted in 1784–5, David was the logical choice to depict one of the most significant moments in the Revolution, the 20 June 1789 taking of the Tennis Court Oath. The oath both resonated with ancient archetypes, like the three Horatii with their extended right arms, and signified a contract with the future.[4] As David explained:

Artists used to lack subjects and needed to repeat themselves, now subjects will lack artists. No history of any people offers me anything as great or as sublime as the Oath of the Tennis Court which I must paint. No, I will not have to invoke the gods of the myths to inspire my genius. French Nation! I wish to propagate your glory. People of the universe, present and future, I wish to teach you this great lesson. Holy humanity, I wish to remind you of your rights, through a unique example in the annals of history. Oh, woe to the artist whose spirit will not be inflamed when embraced by such powerful causes![5]

The Oath of the Tennis Court was supposed to be paid for by public subscription. Interest waned and, besides, David had constantly to obliterate from the huge canvas once prominent deputies who had subsequently lapsed into disfavour and been executed. Perhaps he turned with relief from this Herculean labour of hundreds of figures and portraits crowded on to twenty-six feet of canvas to the more focused subject matter of individual revolutionary martyrs, to whom he devoted three major commemorative portraits (although he called them history paintings) in 1793–4. These three paintings include one work of indisputable genius.

The three subjects were the Convention's educational expert and former nobleman Le Peletier de Saint-Fargeau, assassinated by one of Louis XVI's guards on 20 January 1793, after Le Peletier, like deputy David himself, had voted for the execution of the king. This painting was destroyed in 1826 by Le Peletier's daughter, who disapproved of her father's regicide vote. It survives in drawings. The second, and most famous, painting was The Death of Marat, which commemorated the former physician and radical journalist who had been assassinated by Charlotte Corday, a sympathiser of the Girondin faction who were mainly from south-western France. And the final image, The Death of Joseph Bara, which can be found in Avignon's splendid Musée Calvet, shows the boy martyr expiring in the open countryside, allegedly after being stabbed by Vendéan royalist brigands for crying 'Long live the Republic!' instead of 'Long live the King!' These last two images were destined to hang behind the president's chair in the National Assembly to inspire the nation to greater things. Prints of the boy martyr Bara were also to be distributed to primary schools.

The paintings were the permanent legacy of otherwise ephemeral commemorative ceremonies that David masterminded, in conjunction with the poet André Chénier, beginning with the funeral rites themselves. Le Peletier's body was to be exhibited on an elaborate deathbed to be placed upon the pedestal of the demolished statue of Louis XIV on the Place Vendôme. David next proposed that this scene be turned into a more permanent marble statue. He also set to work on a painting, which only survives as a drawing and a slightly different, and damaged, engraving. Here a sword of Damocles hangs over the reclining and semi-naked martyr, piercing a piece of paper that reads, 'I vote for the death of the tyrant.' Blood drips from the sword point. David offered the painting to the National Convention in late March 1793. He explained its didactic purpose:

> I will have accomplished my task if one day I impel an elderly father surrounded by his large family to say: Come, my children, come see one of your representatives who was the first to die to give you liberty. See how serene his features are – that's because when one dies for one's country one has nothing to reproach oneself with. Do you see this sword suspended above his head which is only held up by a hair? Well, my children, this indicates what courage it took for Michel Le Peletier, as well as his generous colleagues, to condemn to death the infamous tyrant who had oppressed us for such a long time, because at the slightest movement this hair broke and they were all inhumanely immolated.

The Death of Marat is the greatest work of the three, one of the finest examples of political art of all time, and surely the painting most personal to David himself. Its Roman nobility bore little relationship to the squalid life of its subject. Born in 1743, Marat moved to England in 1767 where he practised medicine before and after buying a degree from the University of St Andrews. He combined this with parallel aspirations as a man of letters and natural scientist. Voltaire's dismissive review of his very first book alighted upon Marat's main flaw: 'One should not indulge one's contempt for others and one's regard for one's self to an extent that revolts every reader.' Unsurprisingly, Marat's subsequent 'scientific' attempts to harness the power of hailstorms or to disprove the usefulness of lightning conductors were not taken seriously by such authorities as Condorcet or Franklin. Nor was he successful – after having been rebuffed – in rebranding himself as the most suitable candidate for secretary of a new academy in Madrid with the remit to defend the faith against the materialist philosophes. The Revolution enabled Marat to find his true vocation as a rabidly self-righteous journalist, with his own paper *L'Ami du Peuple*. He combined megalomania with murderousness, convinced that he embodied the all-seeing eye that brought denunciation and execution to the people's hidden enemies. In September 1790, looking back to July 1789, Marat claimed it would have been better had five hundred enemies of the people been killed, for now it was necessary to kill ten thousand. By the autumn of 1791 the deaths of between two and three hundred thousand were deemed necessary to safeguard the Revolution.[6]

David sat, alongside Danton, Marat and Robespierre, as a Jacobin deputy in the Convention. The artist called on Marat the day before his assassination, finding him hard at work propped up in a cold bath, with a vinegar-soaked turban wrapped around his head, both measures designed to meliorate his psoriasis on a close July day. Meanwhile, his assassin had arrived in Paris. Charlotte Corday was from a Norman aristocratic family, and a descendant of Corneille. Having fallen out with her father over her support for the Revolution, Corday had moved in with a spinster aunt in Caen. There, in 1792, she witnessed an incident when National Guardsmen who had failed to find refractory priests in a nearby village took out their frustrations on a chapel which they sacked, and on fifty women whom they bound, branded and sheared before forcing them to march to Caen. Three of these women died and all were severely distressed by this treatment. Corday identified Marat's strident journalism as the source of such 'derailments' of the original Revolution.[7] The day after David's visit to the necrotic demagogue, the twenty-five-year-old Corday purchased a butcher's knife with a six-inch blade and made her first, failed attempt to gain access to Marat's lodgings. Rebuffed a second time, she returned to her hotel, and wrote to Marat denouncing Girondins in her native Caen. This nefarious act stoked his interest. When she returned to his lodgings in the evening, this denunciation secured her access to the bathing revolutionary. Corday found Marat in his tub, writing with the aid of a board placed across the bath. She told him the names of Girondins involved in an uprising in Caen. He reassured her that they would soon be guillotined. She rammed the knife into his chest. He died instantly. David organised a rather modest night-time funeral for Marat (whose corpse was rapidly decomposing in the summer heat) in the grounds of the chapel of the Cordeliers which had become an annexe to the political club. Marat was interred in a cave in a mound of rocks surmounted by the inscription 'friend of the people'. His heart was suspended in an urn from the roof of the Cordeliers, a club on the Parisian left bank with a strong working-class following. These attenuated arrangements suited Robespierre, who was cool towards this improbable martyr.

Meanwhile, in the Convention, a distraught David was told, 'There is one more painting for you to do.' Another deputy added: 'Return Marat to us whole again.' David erased everything that characterised Marat's austere abode, whether the pistols on a shelf, the shoe-shaped bath or the printed wallpaper. The result is extreme simplicity, although the painting had a propaganda point to make. A great sheet of darkness covers half the painting, its shadows extend downwards across the dying revolutionary's chest and on either side of his wooden writing box simply inscribed 'À Marat. David. L'An II'. Marat's necrotic body has become part antique torso, part dying Christ. The face was drawn from Marat's death mask. By tilting Marat's head, David ensured that the viewer would find it uncomfortable to scrutinise the texture of that face too closely. David also obliterated Charlotte Corday, but not without managing to insinuate a highly selective version of her character that is contrasted with the simple nobility of her victim.

What the viewer can see without cricking of necks are two letters. One is to Marat from Corday; the other is from Marat about an unknown patriotic widow to whom he is sending charity. Corday's letter to 'citoyen Marat' reads: 'It is enough that I should be quite wretched to have a right to your benevolence.' Marat's letter reads: 'You will give this assignat to this mother of 5 children and whose husband died defending his country.' Since we have Corday's actual letter to Marat, which was longer, we know that David chose one sentence where she used the educated subjunctive and substituted the fancy term 'benevolence' for her more straightforward request for his 'protection'. The intention was to convey the childless Corday's educated guile, in marked contrast to the simple charity Marat expressed towards the 'child rich' patriotic widow. In fact, Marat's last moments were spent clutching Corday's list of names of Girondins, who in his last breath he said would go to the guillotine. What David did was to take Charlotte Corday's own last request that her remaining monies go to the victims of men like Marat and insert this in the form of a letter from him as his last conscious activity.[8] When David delivered the finished canvas to the Convention, he called for Marat's 'pantheonisation'. He added:

> Hurry up everyone! The mother, the widow, the orphan, the oppressed soldier, all of you whom he defended in peril of his own life, approach and contemplate your friend; he who watched over you is gone. His pen, the terror of traitors, his pen falls from his hands. Oh despair! Our indefatigable one is dead ... he has died without even having the means for his own burial. Posterity, you will avenge him, you will tell our nephews

the extent to which he could have been rich if he had not preferred virtue to wealth. Humanity, you will tell those who called him bloodthirsty that Marat, your cherished child, never caused you to weep.

David turned to a real 'cherished child' for another painting of a revolutionary martyr. The fourteen-year-old Joseph Bara's transformation into a republican exemplar for other children began when the general commanding a division fighting Vendéan insurgents reported to the Convention the death of this apprentice hussar, allegedly for refusing to surrender two horses he was guarding, in order to secure Bara's grieving mother a government pension. General Desmarres' despatch made no mention of Bara's refusal to cry 'Long live the King,' the alleged motive for his death at the hands of the insurgents. This embellishment was added by Robespierre in a speech to the Convention about ten days after the general's report, in which he charged David with organising a festival to mark the 'pantheonisation' of Bara, soon to be joined by another child martyr, Agricole Viala, who took a bullet in the head from anti Parisian Federalist forces in the Midi. Although elaborate plans for this festival existed, it never took place because Robespierre, its guiding spirit, was himself executed on 9th Thermidor.

David's painting may have been intended to play a part in this festival, since plans for it remark that columns of marchers were to bear images of the two boy victims. Because the painting of Bara was to be engraved and sent to every primary school, all traces of violence were omitted, lest the gory details distract from the didactic message. The painting is of the utmost simplicity; indeed, it has a deliberately unfinished quality, probably to reflect a life cut short before its time by the forces of tyranny whose presence is restricted to a ghostly banner in the left-hand corner. The painting is effectively of a sculpted figure against an ethereal landscape. An adolescent boy has evidently dragged himself as far as he can before expiring. Bara's legs are already lifeless, but he has started to raise his upper body and curly-haired head in a final gesture of moral and spiritual defiance over mortality. His hands clutch a revolutionary cockade and an illegible letter, which unlike the portrait of Marat provides no clues to help us. Maybe the unfinished quality of the picture, and the innocence of the boy hero, is all David wished to communicate. This was not exactly in concordance with the historical truth, for Bara was not some insipid pre-Raphaelite youth, but a tough little tike. General

Desmares had sent a second letter to the Convention, detailing Bara's last moments: 'I think Bara should be shown as he was when he received the final blows, on foot, holding two horses by the reins, surrounded by brigands, and replying to the men who had come forward to try and make him give up the horses: "You fucking brigand, give you the horses, the commander's horses, and mine? Certainly not." '[9]

David also masterminded several of the Revolution's major public festivals, acting as the 'pageant-master of the Revolution'. The great nineteenth-century republican historian Michelet described these festivities as an attempt to abolish natural boundaries, to leap over the natural barriers of hills, mountain ranges and rivers, as well as myriad local and regional dialects in an orgy of membership, recognition and unity. According to Michelet, attending one of these 'love-ins' was like existing in a different dimension: 'Time and space, those material conditions to which life is subject, are no more. A strange *vita nuova*, one eminently spiritual, and making her whole Revolution a sort of dream, at one time delightful, at another terrible, is now beginning for France. It knew neither time nor space.' They became so frequent that people wrote of 'festomania'.[10]

These festivals of federation began when National Guard militias were encouraged to make contact with their confrères in other cities or regions as a warning to aristocrats, brigands and peasants who had gone on the rampage that the days of disorder were numbered and that the Revolution had its defenders. The giant festival on the Champ de Mars on 14 July 1790 was supposed to be the capstone of this process, culminating in an oath and a mass that would be synchronised throughout the provinces. While it certainly exploited popular enthusiasm and mass sentiment, the festival was designed to demobilise passions, signifying that the Revolution was over, a goal that proved as chimerical as the desire to make it perpetual.

The federated National Guard delegates to the capital were selected on the basis of ascending election, while the army contingent was chosen by length of service. People unused to travelling very far undertook the journey of their lives, chanting the urgent rhythms of *Ça ira* to pass the march away. A huge volunteer workforce laboured to convert the plain of the Champ de Mars into a valley between two hills on which the spectators stood. As Michelet grandiosely commented: 'France was determined; and the thing was done.'

Fifty thousand Guardsmen and soldiers marched across the amphitheatre, albeit in rainy 'aristocratic weather', past an altar of the fatherland and three hundred thousand spectators. Talleyrand and three hundred priests celebrated mass; Lafayette administered the oath 'to be faithful for ever to the nation, the law and the king', who himself mumbled an oath to uphold the constitution. The delegates cum pilgrims returned laden with sacred mementoes, and via interminable celebratory suppers, exhausted but exhilarated to their home towns. The provincial analogues of the festival were characterised by fun, imagination and spontaneity.[11]

Later revolutionary festivals were more choreographed than this, especially after David took charge, and they often reflected the political message of rival revolutionary factions. To take an obvious example, those who celebrated the freeing from the galleys of the mutinous Swiss soldiers of Châteauvieux in the 15 April 1792 Festival of Liberty were not those who on 3 June of that year turned out for the Festival of Law to commemorate Jacques Simmoneau, the mayor of Étampes, who had been lynched that March for refusing to put a ceiling on grain prices.[12]

All such occasions ultimately derived from Rousseau's belief that such civic festivals would counteract Christian deprecation of earthly affairs and detachment from secular governance. Rousseau argued for a minimal civil religion that would integrate communities more effectively than had been the case under a divisive and intolerant Christianity. Rousseau discussed festivals and civil religion in his 1758 Letter to d'Alembert, in Book Four, chapter 8 of his 1762 *The Social Contract*, and in his 1772 *Considerations on the Government of Poland*; his response to proposed reforms in Poland.

The Letter to d'Alembert arose in response to the playwright Voltaire's campaign to encourage the Genevan authorities to rescind their prohibition of theatre, something he pursued via a long paragraph advocating such a course, which he had slipped into the general entry on Geneva (otherwise written by d'Alembert), in the *Encyclopédie*. Towards the end of Rousseau's spirited polemic, his nostalgia for the simplicities of the Geneva of his youth led him to advocate Spartan-style open-air games and festivals as the most natural form of recreation for republics:

> But let us not adopt these exclusive entertainments which close
> up a small number of people in melancholy fashion in a gloomy

cavern, which keeps them fearful and immobile in silence and inaction ... No, happy peoples, these are not your festivals. It is in the open air, under the sky, that you ought to gather and give yourselves to the sweet sentiment of your happiness. Let your pleasures not be effeminate or mercenary; let nothing that has an odor of constraint and selfishness poison them; let them be free and generous like you are, let the sun illuminate your innocent entertainments; you will constitute one yourselves, the worthiest it can illuminate.

As to the character of these festivals, Rousseau added:

What will be shown in them? Nothing if you please. With liberty, wherever abundance reigns, well-being also reigns. Plant a stake crowned with flowers in the middle of a square; gather the people together there, and you will have a festival. Do better yet; let the spectators become an entertainment to themselves; make them actors themselves; do it so that each sees and loves himself in the others so that all will be better united.[13]

There could not be a better description of what thoughts informed the revolutionary festivals. In his more extended political writings, Rousseau discussed what he dubbed 'civil religion'. He revealed himself more admiring of Islam's blurring of the sacred and temporal than of Christianity. He sought to transcend the potentially divisive duality of spiritual and secular powers inherent in Christianity (with hindsight its major saving grace), by separating each citizen's right to an individual opinion on the afterlife from his duties as a citizen and moral actor in society. The latter was to have as much weight as the former. The resulting 'civil religion' was to consist of belief in a God and an afterlife, the happiness of the just, the punishment of the wicked, the sanctity of the social contract and the laws, and the prohibition of intolerance. This did not extend to those who rejected or reneged upon this compact. The sovereign was empowered to banish unsociable unbelievers, and to execute those who committed what amounted to secular apostasy by their failure to live according to these precepts.[14] In his *Considerations on the Government of Poland*, Rousseau took three ancient and biblical lawmakers, Moses, Lycurgus and Numa, as examples of how to bind unpromising humanity both together and to their 'fatherland' through morals, laws, rites and festivals:

All of them [ancient lawgivers] sought bonds that might attach the Citizens to the fatherland and to one another, and they found them in distinctive practices, in religious ceremonies which by their very nature were always exclusive and national, in games which kept the citizens frequently assembled, in exercises which increased their pride and self-esteem together with their vigour and strength, in spectacles which by reminding them of the history of their ancestors, their misfortunes, their virtues, stirred their hearts, fired them with a lively spirit of emulation, and strongly attached them to the fatherland with which they were being kept constantly occupied.[15]

Rousseau aired his considerable animus against princely courts, the opera and theatres, as enclosed places riddled with corruption, falsity and intrigue, and which in the last two cases involved paying to gain access. He cited Spanish bullfighting as an example of how an entire people retained something of its primordial vigour in this quintessentially Spanish ritual. Turning to Poland, Rousseau advised that public games and spectacles, perhaps involving feats of horsemanship, would foster body and soul together, while earthing the elite among the many in a common enthusiasm, thereby inculcating an essential unity without compromising hierarchy.[16]

We can take a closer look at one of the more elaborate festivals, that of the Unity and Indivisibility of the Republic held on 10 August 1793 against a background of civil and international strife. This was designed to commemorate the fall of the monarchy and the promulgation of the new Constitution. Equipped with a budget about a fifth of what he had sought, David had the festival run through certain key sites, or processional stations, beginning before dawn and ending on the Champ de Mars sixteen hours later. Political clubs bearing a banner adorned with the all-seeing eye of revolutionary surveillance led the procession. Next came members of the Convention, themselves members of the same clubs, with a cedarwood ark containing the new Constitution. The rear was taken up by representatives of the people interspersed with floats and tableaux honouring such groups as the aged, the blind, soldiers and workers. The procession, which David kept on cue with a signalling system, commenced with the rising of the sun at the site of the former Bastille, whose scattered stones were inscribed with literal reminders of the dark past such as 'this stone was never illuminated', not to speak of 'my faithful spider was crushed before my eyes' (this cryptic inscription being a reference to the mental torments of solitary confinement, where only an eight-legged creature kept the prisoner company).

An imposing Egyptoid statue of Nature disbursed water from her multiple breasts into a cup held aloft by the president of the Convention. He then passed this cup to eighty-six elderly men representing the departments, who drank, kissed and uttered patriotic sentiments. Moving on to the Boulevard des Poissonnières, the president embraced a group of women seated upon gun carriages beneath a triumphal arch in commemoration of their role in fighting during early October 1789. The third site was the Place de la Révolution, where a statue of Liberty had been erected on the spot usually occupied by the guillotine. The president put a torch to a great bonfire of heraldic symbols, sceptres, thrones and so forth, as three thousand birds were released skywards. But Liberty was now a thing of the past. At the Invalides, a statue of the French people as Hercules had been set up, with this colossus holding on to the fasces symbolising the united departments, in order to club the hydra of Federalism writhing at his feet that much harder. The spectators had nothing to do here, except marvel at themselves crushing the forces of disunity.[17] David intended to turn this figure into a statue of the People, some fifteen metres in height, and adorned with such words as 'Enlightenment', 'Strength' and 'Work' on its various parts. Finally, the column entered the Champ de Mars, bowing before a stone-mason's level suspended from tricolour ribbons attached to two pillars. The president climbed an altar cum mountain from which he promulgated the Constitution. He was handed pikes symbolising the departments, which he bound together with a red, blue and white ribbon. Finally the spectators, or rather participants, settled down to a picnic on the grass, to watch tableaux of the major events of the Revolution, including one of the procession they had just witnessed.

The priestly presence at the centre of the July 1790 Festival of the Federation had vanished from the Festival of the Unity and Indivisibility of the Republic three years later, replaced by a vaguely pantheistic celebration of Nature. Bastille Day celebrations in the provinces revealed a similar attenuation of the Christian element, with the fraction of Provençal communes that included a mass in the commemorations declining from three-quarters to one-fifth. This was symptomatic of the next stage in the radicalisation of the Convention, its armies and emissaries, as well as local de-Christianising zealots. The attempted fusion of Church and Revolution through the Constitutional Church had been a divisive failure.[18] So why not elevate the Revolution itself into the religion? After all, it had its creeds, liturgies and sacred texts, its own vocabulary of virtues and vices, and, last but not least, the ambition of regenerating mankind itself, even if it denied divine intervention or the afterlife. The result was a series of deified abstractions worshipped through the denatured language and liturgy of Christianity.

The discourse of the Revolution was saturated with religious terminology. Words like catechism, credo, fanatical, gospel, martyr, missionary, propaganda, sacrament, sermon, zealot, were transferred from a religious to a political context.[19] In 1792 Mirabeau wrote that 'the Declaration of the Rights of Man has become a political Gospel and the French Constitution a religion for which people are prepared to die'. A year later, the poet Marie-Joseph Chénier asked the Convention to 'Wrest the sons of the Republic from the yoke of theocracy which still weighs upon them . . . You will know how to found on the ruins of dethroned superstition, the single universal religion . . . which has neither sects nor mysteries . . . of which our law-makers are the preachers, the magistrates the pontiffs, and in which the human family burns its incense only at the altar of the Patrie, common mother and divinity.'[20] Ironically, many of the symbols employed in this process were derived (non-exclusively) from the Christian tradition, whether the Liberty Tree, the masonic triangle cum Trinity, and the Mountain from which the virtues of the Republic were supposed to radiate like the decalogue of Moses. One of the meanings of 'regeneration' was derived from the transformation that a Catholic was supposed to undergo with baptism, that is, entry into a new spiritual world. The other was the quasi-miraculous manner in which human tissue heals after suffering a wound. Festivals were intended morally to regenerate all those Frenchmen who had evaded the guillotine. A declaration by the Committee of Public Safety – interestingly the French for 'safety' also means 'salvation' – established in April 1793 acknowledged this:

> We will show this Fatherland to the citizen ceaselessly, in his laws, in his games, in his home, in his loves, in his festivities. We will never leave him to himself alone. We will by this continual coercion awaken ardent love for the Fatherland. We will direct his inclination toward this single passion. It is in this way that

the Frenchman will acquire a national physiognomy; it is in this way that, by identifying him so to speak with the happiness in his country, we will bring about this vitally necessary transformation of the monarchical spirit into a republican spirit.[21]

Rejecting the Christian concept of original sin, the Jacobins subscribed to the infinite malleability of the human race. The new-born baby could be shaped this way or that, or as one Jacobin catechism had it: 'we think he is a soft wax capable of receiving whatever imprint one wishes'. Long before a child started to learn to read and write, toys could be used as allegories. Not just the do-it-yourself Bastilles, or the toy guillotines, but bubbles signifying the ephemerality of aristocratic conspiracy, card castles that fell with one puff of breath, kites that flew free and high like the new Rights of Man, and ninepins representing the coalition of hostile powers.[22] A new range of 'bonbons patriotiques' would have wrappers printed with hortatory Jacobin slogans. Pre-school education was supposed to address such issues as the humanity of the king. A story book for small children had a child hero called Emilien who, after watching the king make a grand entrance, asked his mother: 'But does the King go pee-pee?' To which his mother responded: 'Yes, my dear, just like you.' Although not much of the Jacobin educational programme was implemented, even basic alphabets and grammars were loaded with political content. Older children were to be taught through manuals modelled on catechisms:

Question: What is Baptism?
Answer: It is the regeneration of the French begun on 14 July 1789, and soon supported by the entire French nation.

. . .

Question: What is Communion?
Answer: It is the association proposed to all peoples by the French Republic henceforth to form on earth only one family of brothers who no longer recognise or worship any idol or tyrant.

Question: What is Penitence?
Answer: Today it is the wandering existence of traitors to their Fatherland. It is the banishment of all those monsters who, unworthy to inhabit the land of Liberty and to share the benefits which their villainy has only delayed, will soon be driven out of every corner of the globe, and, having become an abomination

to all life, will have no refuge except in the bowels of the earth which they have overly polluted with their crimes.

Biographies of revolutionary heroes, like young Bara, were intended to be exemplary. So too were new history books that demonstrated the inherent superiority of republics over monarchies, oligarchies and tyrannies. Books of republican manners and morals were designed to fashion a new man. He was to be no slouch, always walking in a brisk, upright fashion, never kissing ladies' hands, and calling everyone 'citizen' with a peremptory bark. An ambitious programme of buildings and public works would include both baths, fountains, swimming pools and public lavatories, but also imposing structures designed to enforce community or to inculcate the desired virtues. Sitting on their egalitarian rows of benches, from which everyone present was visible, the citizenry would sing revolutionary hymns, listen to civic homilies, hear the Rights of Man declaimed, witness public oaths and join in honouring some exemplary man or woman.[23]

While many of the buildings never left the drawing board, there was a series of attempts to obliterate the preceding eighteen centuries of throne and altar that were tantamount to a 'cultural revolution', although that term was never used by anyone before the late twentieth century. The eighteenth century preferred 'regeneration'.[24] The Revolution inaugurated modern gesture politics, anticipating all those grim public-housing projects named after Nelson Mandela or whatever the municipal commissars dream up in our own day as an alternative to doing much about educational failure or inner-city deprivation. The Convention sought to eradicate all symbolic reminders of the old order, by removing the word 'saint' from, say, the Rue Saint-Jacques or transforming Bourg-la-Reine into Bourg-Egalité or Mont-Saint-Michel into Mont-Libre, not to speak of eradicating all those Bar-le-Ducs in favour of Bar-sur-Ornain. One hundred and eighty-one communes restyled themselves Liberté, forty Égalité and seventeen Fraternité. The abbé Grégoire was responsible for 'defanaticising' Parisian addresses, so that Rue de la Constitution led into Rue du Bonheur. In the provinces, entire communes, although only a fraction of the total, underwent a process of 'débaptisation', adopting such names as Liberty, Equality, Fraternity, or Bara, Brutus or Marat, as when the little port of Le Havre briefly became Havre Marat or Saint-Maximin became Marathon, in twofold obeisance to the ancient battlefield and the revolutionary martyr.

A few enthusiasts, or conformists, took the opportunity to rename themselves or to name their children after classical heroes, usually Brutus, Gracchus or Scipio. Take François-Noël-Toussaint Niçaisse, who became Camillus Caius Gracchus Babeuf:

> I had the moral purpose, in taking as my patron saints, the most honorable men, in my opinion, of the Roman republic ... To erase the traces of royalism, of aristocracy, and of fanaticism we have given republican names to our districts, cities, streets, and to everything that bore the imprint of these three types of tyranny ... Why wish to force me always to preserve 'St Joseph' as my patron saint and model? I want nothing of the virtues of that fine fellow ... In the midst of free opinion, it is repugnant to me still to bear the second name of 'Toussaint'. And 'Nicaisse', the third and last happy saint whom my beloved sponsor gave me for imitation, has a tone which I do not like at all; and if some day my head falls, I have no intention of walking about carrying it in my hands. I should rather die outright like the Gracchi, whose life also pleases me, and under whose tutelage I henceforth place myself exclusively.[25]

The fact that only 62 of 593 children born in Poitiers or 26 born in Besançon in Year II received such names suggests the limited appeal of becoming Régénéré Anatole Pierre Lycurgue Combert rather than plain old Pierre, François or Jean.[26] Indeed, in the rural Limousin, 95 per cent of the population stayed with Léonard and Antoine, Marie and Marguerite. People whose occupations bore the mark of Satan quickly changed them. In February 1794, for example, the *Régisseurs des poudres et salpêtres* requested a name change – to national agency of gunpowders. The *milice* mutated into the *garde*, while such terms as *impôt* were replaced by the more voluntaristic-sounding *contribution* to designate taxes. Advocates became *hommes de loi* and physicians *officiers de santé*. Following up the suggestion of Mlle de Kéralio, an aristocratic republican lady and writer, that citizens should use a universal second person singular (*tu*) rather than the formal (*vous*), this practice enjoyed a brief vogue until formality returned, at least in the Convention, in Year III. Fashionable too was the habit of prefixing the 'one-time' or 'former' before someone or something left over by the old regime, as in the 'ci-devant comte de la Touche' or the 'ci-devant châteaux'.[27]

Wherever a local fanaticised minority was emboldened by larger outside forces, either the regime's roving representatives (significantly called 'missionaires') or its fanaticised soldiery, a much cruder de-Christianisation occurred. The constant search for precious metals to finance armies, and for baser metals to munition them, meant an orgy of despoliation of the churches, which dovetailed felicitously with a desire to remove anything essential to Christian worship. Such plundering was bad enough, but it was sometimes accompanied by actions and rhetoric whose power to shock has not been diminished by the intervening centuries. Priests were held up to obloquy as crafty, idle seducers of allegedly credulous women: 'and you, you bloody bitches, you are their whores [the priests'], particularly those who attend their bloody masses, and listen to their mumbo-jumbo'. Others, emulating Dark Age pagans, dared divine retribution by pouring wine from holy chalices down their parched throats, 'saying that Jesus Christ was a bastard, a useless bugger, a man with no power, who, by consorting with the Magdalene, had hit the jackpot, that the Virgin was a whore, Christ a bastard and Saint Joseph a bloody cuckold, adding that if there was a bloody God, he only had to show his power by crushing him'. Among those appalled by these blasphemous revels were Danton and Robespierre, the latter alive to the dangers of needlessly multiplying the Revolution's enemies by treading on people's sensitivities or making an enemy of Christianity itself.[28]

While drunken hobbledehoys mocked the clergy, sober rationalists set about eradicating the ways in which Christianity had imposed itself on people's most unconscious daily rhythms. A desire to impose uniformity on a bewildering array of local weights and measurements, many of feudal origin, through a universal decimal system was accompanied by a more dubious attempt to reorder the passage of time with a new revolutionary calendar. Confusion was the calendar's midwife. Before the Revolution, attempts to devise a new 'moral' calendar had been condemned as blasphemous. After the Revolution, patriots had taken to appending the phrase 'First Year of Liberty' to mark the fall of the Bastille on 14 July 1789. This raised the question of whether that year ended on 31 December 1789 or on 13 July 1790, the eve of that event's anniversary. In 1792 the Legislative Assembly resolved the matter by designating 1 January 1792 as the first day of the Fourth Year of Liberty. The execution of the king and the declaration of a republic further complicated the issue, so that 1 January 1792 was retroactively designated as the first day of Year I of the French Republic even though that event occurred on 22 September.

The related question of how to reconcile years designated by numbers ascending from Year I with the traditional Gregorian calendar was hived off to the Committee of Public Instruction. Its leading light was the highly numerate Auvernat deputy Gilbert Romme. He proposed beginning the year on 22 September, when there had been a coincidence of the autumn equinox and the proclamation of the Republic. The twelve months would consist of three décades of ten days, primidi, duodi, tridi and so forth, each divided into decimalised parts. These months were to receive 'moral' names such as Bastille, Liberty or Equality. The five days left over due to the solar year were to be devoted to games, with the extra day on leap year called 'franciade'.

The Convention rejected the 'moral' names, preferring simple numbers. Since this would have led to such unwieldy dating as 'tenth day of the fifth month of Year III' another commission, which included the painter David, was charged with devising a better nomenclature. Demented obsessives got to work. This commission came up with the famous revolutionary calendar that began in autumn and ended in high summer instead of January and December. The months were Vendémiaire (vintage), Brumaire (fog), Frimaire (cold), Nivôse (snow), Pluviôse (rain), Ventôse (wind), Germinal (budding), Floréal (flowers), Prairial (meadows), Messidor (harvest), Thermidor (heat) and Fructidor (fruit). This calendar was clearly designed to enable people to harmonise their spirits with the rhythms of nature: the winter months ended with a sad 'o' sound; spring with a bright and upbeat 'a'.[29] Each of these months was subdivided into three ten-day weeks, which therefore abolished Sundays along with Christ's birthday and all saints' days, with the five or six surplus days at the end of the year provocatively called 'sans-culottides'. On the recommendation of Fabre d'Eglantine festivals on these special days were to be called Virtue, Genius, Labour, Recompenses and Opinion.[30]

The new calendar was formally adopted on 4 Frimaire (24 November) Year II, but only for civil usage. This meant that bureaucrats and judges went on to a nine-day working week, with the total of their days off reduced from fifty-two to thirty-six per annum. Attempts to impose this system on workers in government industries led to strikes. It was often ignored in the countryside, where Sundays were not just for church, but also for courting, drinking, gossiping and so forth. Of course, the old maxim about the Devil making work for idle hands applied just as much to the new décades as to the old Sundays. This problem was compounded by serial slackers who decided to take not only the traditional seventh day off, but the new tenth day too.

These novel days of rest were an open invitation to those seeking to supplant Christianity with revolutionary cults of their own devising. Since that was a highly provocative step, it inevitably disturbed those on the ruling Committee of Public Safety, notably Robespierre, whose primary concern was with using terror to concentrate national energies against advancing foreign armies without blithely multiplying the Revolution's domestic enemies.

The abjuration of the priesthood by Gobel, bishop of Paris, and four hundred Parisian priests in early November 1793 provided radicals with the pretext to transform the venerable cathedral of Notre-Dame into a 'Temple of Reason', dedicated 'to philosophy'. A makeshift Mountain, topped off with a temple, was set up inside. Mlle Maillard, a noted opera singer and beauty, was dressed as the goddess of Liberty. She was used to distinguish obeisance to abstract virtues from common or garden idolatry: 'this living woman, despite all the charms that embellished her, could not be deified by the ignorant, as would a statue of stone', The dancing of the carmagnole and the trumpet blasts and laughter scandalised not only traditionalists. After the ceremony, the goddess (by now become Reason) was carried to the Convention where she received a fraternal kiss from the president. In the provinces, the conversion of churches into similar 'temples of reason' was accompanied by anticlerical outrages and the desecration of sacred furnishings. The really reasonable obviously deplored all this.

These excesses appalled Robespierre, an orthodox Deist, who realised that revolutionary irreligion was a major recruiting sergeant for massed counter-revolution. Provoking and punishing the religious was self-defeating: 'They are the ill who must be prepared for healing by reassuring them; one makes them fanatics by forcing a cure on them.'[31] Worse, he began to suspect that the 'ultras' whose hand he detected behind de-Christianisation and the temples of reason were agents of counter-revolution whose covert intention was to discredit the Revolution, a suspicion that suggests mounting paranoia. Writing to a roving representative of the Revolution in the Somme, Robespierre explained: 'We must be careful not to give hypocritical counter-revolutionists, who seek to light the flame of civil war, any pretext that seems to justify their calumnies. No opportunity must be presented to them for saying that the freedom of worship is violated or that war is made on religion itself . . .

In regions where patriotism is lukewarm or sluggish, the violent remedies necessary in rebellious and counter-revolutionary regions must not be applied.' How he sought to placate both those seeking new cults and those who regarded traditional religion as a source of moral order became bound up with his downfall.[32]

II GOODNESS AND VIRTUE

So far we have been concerned with the externals of cults that sought to rival Christianity. However, the calendar, classical names, the plundering of churches, David's martyrs, the festivals and the new choral music were merely symptoms of a Jacobin state of mind and emotion. While this was a product of its own time, it owed much, in spirit at least, to romanticised recollections of ancient Sparta, Rome and Cromwell's Puritans. By imaginatively conflating these things, one comes up with beings somewhat like the Jacobins. Gentler exemplars, whether the American Republic, Britain's constitutional monarchy or indeed the more hedonistic periods of Athenian antiquity, fell by the wayside along with the heads of those who still proposed them, in contrast to the puritanical longing for the militarised austerities of ancient Sparta.

Although the Jacobins fractured into a bewildering array of sub-factions, alternately named after prominent individuals or imputed characteristics, they were the motor-force of the Revolution, progressively comprising the dominant grouping in its successive legislative assemblies, and in the executive Committee of Public Safety, the regime that emerged once it was realised that an assembly could not be a viable wartime executive. They were also vulnerable, in a guilt-ridden sort of way, to the unpredictable sans-culotte oligarchies of radicalised democrats that dominated the urban district sections and the Paris Commune as well as the streets of the capital. The Jacobins' invocations of 'the People' as an abstraction were perpetually menaced by 'the Street', a tiger that could be manipulated by demagogic oratory but that was never entirely controllable by anyone reluctant to shoot it down. This simple description conceals very complex political developments whereby former friends would cluster in rival factions where the animosities were as personal as they were political, and abruptly despatch each other to the guillotine, but the details of these developments, which will not detain us, need not obscure either some striking generic characteristics or underlying pathologies, for there is surely something mad about all-consuming political passions. It was entirely consonant with the type that their headquarters was in the former headquarters of the Dominican friars in Paris.[33]

Jacobins were respectable, middling people, deeply embedded in local society. They were overwhelmingly middle-aged too, the average being about forty years old.[34] Club members often knew one another through charitable activity, masonic lodges or reading and smoking societies as well as from such professional contexts as the provincial bar. Actually, priests, rather than lawyers, were the most over-represented profession among the Jacobins, making up 6 per cent of the total membership but only half of 1 per cent of the population, but this is the sort of prosopographical detail that we can pass over in our quest for a typology.[35]

The thousands of affiliated Jacobin clubs were structured with committees and rules, and characterised by a fraternal form of civility in which, after 1793, the intimate 'tu' became mandatory just as the title 'Monsieur' was abolished. The more zealous clubs had no heating in winter so as to discourage all but the most high-minded. Often meeting in former churches, the Jacobins' rhetoric and rituals were as much indebted to Christian prototypes as to recollections of their classical schooling. Decorum was everything, adultery, drunkenness and gluttony disdained. Foul language was formally prohibited. Their oratory oscillated between a studied coldness and torrents of romantic rhetoric, in which the speaker frequently threatened to kill himself in the antique mode, if his wishes, often reflexively confused with those of the People, were thwarted. This oratorical gambit usually worked, unless his audience had decided that the speaker had to be executed to restore the mythical harmony he and his faction had subverted. Victims of the Revolutionary Tribunal endeavoured to prove their innocence through the intensity of their final pleas; their judges invariably remained true to their inner selves by discounting 'false pity'. They were sincere and therefore virtuous; the condemned were insincere monsters of no moral worth.

Although accounts of the Jacobins routinely stress Reason, in fact there was an equal intensity of emotion, and a tearful sentimentalism whenever the People were invoked. A sceptical Mme Necker once remarked of the constant, insincere evocation of feeling: 'Love of country, humanity – vague terms empty of meaning that men invented to hide their insensitivity under the very veil of sentiment.[36] Individual virtue within the virtuous elite was established through public confessions, inquisitions and periodic purges. Where once there had been free discussion, a terrible unanimity prevailed.

But, before one's thoughts stray to Russia in the 1930s, it is important to remember that the Jacobins defy facile alignment with the ideological illusions of a modern era that has now passed. They were not simply Lenin's distant French grandparents. On the one hand, Jacobins believed in the family, private property, individual entrepreneurship and the virtues of charity, education and hard work; on the other, class struggle and economic collectivism were anathema to them. Yet, before we rush to view them as little more than small-town conservative Rotarians, we should remember that they were not keen on banks, bankrupts, credit or speculation, and they were not above imposing punitive taxation upon rich people or wage controls on poor people in times of national emergency. Given their advocacy of the moral equality of mankind and their guilt-ridden sentimental porosity to radical democrats to the left of them, there was always a potential slippage towards more literal forms of egalitarianism – for, once invoked, the latter was difficult to confine to the sphere of abstract political rights.[37]

So far we have evaded the well-springs of the terroristic violence that they unleashed upon their enemies and their own kind. Following Burke, many commentators have identified a fateful infatuation with an abstract ought-world to which mere human beings in all their complexity necessarily failed to conform. Frustration led to their reluctant elimination, although, clearly, not a few Jacobins were tantalised by the flashing fall of what they called 'la fenêtre nationale' (the national window) or more literally 'le rasoir national' (the national razor). The earthier sansculottes, who literally butchered their victims in order to skewer the choice bits and pieces on stakes, seem not to have heard of the onset of the age of Enlightened criminology.[38]

Assuming power at the most critical moment in the Republic's history, the Jacobins were trapped in time between the corporate, Court society of an ancien régime that they believed was rotten to the core and a society based on antagonistic social classes, both forms of divisiveness that threatened their abstract vision of community, harmony and national unity. Indeed, they may have flown swiftly towards that abstract realm precisely because of the impossibility of doing much about those material inequalities: a sort of 'flight forwards' into moral imperialism. They believed that once the burden of superstition and tyranny had been overthrown, the latent goodness of the people would become apparent, to the degree that the people would seem as if they had been reborn, disburdened of tyranny's corrupting weight – for the ancien régime, in the form of Louis-the-last, the pig-king, was literally over-weight. Released from the burden of the past, lean and muscular new men would stand straight again.

The cardinal trope in their rhetoric was the moralising antimony. Here is Robespierre on 17 February 1794 discussing the moral principles that should guide the Republic's domestic administration:

> In our country we want to substitute ethics for egotism, integrity for honour, principles for habits, duties for protocol, the empire of reason for the tyranny of changing taste, scorn of vice for the scorn of misfortune, pride for insolence, elevation of soul for vanity, the love of glory for the love of money, good men for amusing companions, merit for intrigue, genius for cleverness, truth for wit, the charm of happiness for the boredom of sensualism, the greatness of man for the pettiness of 'the great', a magnanimous, strong, happy people for an amiable, frivolous miserable people, that is to say all the virtues and all the miracles of the republic for the vices and all the absurdities of the monarchy.[39]

Openness versus Hypocrisy, Virtue versus Vice, Good versus Evil, Light versus Darkness: this was a Manichaean view of the world, heavily indebted to monotheistic religion. Any form of dissent or opposition, real or imagined, bore the taint of moral leprosy, something to be amputated or excised from an otherwise healthy body. This resulted in an all-pervasive suspicion, a perpetual raking and rooting around in the opponents' deeper motives, until this climate was enshrined on 17 September 1793 in the Law of Suspects that instituted universal suspicion.[40]

The idea that the Revolution was a 'political religion' (a term first used by the utopian Campanella in the seventeenth century to describe the political use of religious belief) was current at the time of the event. The enlightened German poet and writer Christoph Martin Wieland edited a cultural journal called Der Teutsche Merkur from Goethe's Weimar. Like many of his European contemporaries, Wieland initially welcomed the Revolution as an opportunity to implement the principles of the Enlightenment in the sense of liberating people from arbitrary despotic abuse. By 1793, however, he was no longer so sure. Freedom and Equality had been perverted into idols, and those who refused them worship were being persecuted by Terror. A 'new political religion' was being preached by French generals at the head of revolutionary armies; they were as intolerant as 'Mohammed or the Theodosians'. Wieland continued: 'Whoever does not recognize their notions of Freedom and Equality as the sole truth, is an enemy of the human race, or a despicable slave, who, bowed down by the narrow-chested prejudices of the old political idolatry, bends his knee before self-made idols.'[41]

Such thoughts were taken up by Alexis de Tocqueville, possibly the greatest writer on the Revolution in terms of pure application of mind to the events. Since he probably knew nothing of Wieland, Tocqueville developed the idea after reading Burke on 'armed doctrine' and Friedrich Schiller's *History of the Thirty Years War*. The latter impressed on him how confessional passions could remould conventional political allegiances, rending seventeenth-century Europe into antagonistic religious blocs. Tocqueville claimed that, while Robespierre was personally against exporting the Revolution with 'armed missionaries', he and his colleagues proselytised their views in the manner of a militant religion, declaring a holy war on the unregenerate regimes of Europe. As in the religious wars of the early modern period, merely local allegiances were dissolved by confessional conflicts that spanned Europe:

> Because the Revolution seemed to be striving for the regeneration of the human race even more than for the reform of France, it lit a passion which the most violent political revolutions had never before been able to produce. It inspired conversions and generated propaganda. Thus, in the end, it took on that appearance of a religious revolution that so astonished its contemporaries. Or rather, it itself became a new kind of religion, an incomplete religion, it is true, without God, without ritual, and without life after death, but one which nevertheless, like Islam, flooded the earth with its soldiers, apostles, and martyrs.[42]

But to paraphrase a remark of the revolutionary calendar-maker Romme, who stabbed himself to death to avoid the guillotine, eighteen centuries did not disappear from men's characters just by declaring it to be Year II. Those who bore the weight of the past did not simply unbend and stand up straight, like the naked male holding aloft the Declaration of the Rights of Man as lightning strikes symbols of the ancien régime in one of many allegorical visual renditions of regeneration. The psychological legacy of the ancien régime did not simply vanish along with the bonfires of feudal charters, pigeon lofts and weathervanes, or the execution of the king and queen. The Jacobins' moralising intolerance and Manichaean division of politics (which was now everything) into good and evil were derived and distilled from religious discourse, as mediated and secularised by the intellectual intolerance of the Enlightenment.[43] Their resort to exemplary sanctions against opponents, real and imagined, marked them as children of the ancien régime that had preceded them, however much they strained to deny it. But there was something else too. They pioneered the very modern idea of regarding people as empty glass vessels, which could be filled almost with the content of their choice. The following story, whose details are superficially simple, illustrates some of these themes.

In the early hours of 23 May 1793 a middle-aged civil servant called L'Amiral was apprehended after a gunfight in a house in the Rue Favart. Having failed to kill Robespierre, his victim of preference, L'Amiral had gone for Collot d'Herbois, a failed actor and plawright who also belonged to the Committee of Public Safety, and who lived in the same building. During the mêlée of L'Amiral's arrest it became apparent that a man called Geffroy, a local locksmith and father of three, had been critically wounded by a stray shot. The following day, a twenty-year-old woman, Cécile Renault, was detained after trying to see Robespierre and was found to have two knives about her person.[44]

In fevered sessions the Convention, of which Collot was a deputy, imposed its own meanings upon a failed assassination bid that was quickly construed as a British-inspired plot to kill the nation's representatives. It became a pretext for intensification of the Terror: 'Our enemies are like those venomous plants that proliferate as soon as the cultivator forgets to root them up completely. We must resume this task with the most extreme fervour.' But it also became an opportunity to demonstrate that the hand of Providence hovered over the lives of the nation's representatives: 'since justice and virtue have been made the order of the day, since we have proclaimed with all nature the existence of the Supreme Being and the immortality of the soul, Providence protects the nation's representatives ... Freedom is a gift from heaven that heaven does not withdraw from virtuous men: the human race needs this example, for the Supreme Being, whom the corrupt have so outraged, arranged for Collot d'Herbois to be saved.' The humble locksmith Geffroy was Providence's tool. Since the defunct monarchy had gone in for regular health bulletins every time Louis XVI had a cold, the Convention demanded up-to-date information on how scar tissue was regenerating the locksmith's gunshot wounds. There were twenty such medical bulletins, whose shocking descriptions of haemorrhages and purulent pus led the radical sections and the Committee of Public Safety to compete in their desire to root out and destroy those responsible for Geffroy's suffering. Fifty-four people were guillotined along with the assassins L'Amiral and Renault after a batch-style show trial that swept in Renault's innocent relatives.

Clubs and sections vied to transfigure Citizen Geffroy's wounds into a multi-layered metaphor for how the Republic would eradicate its enemies to achieve mankind's regeneration: 'Continue, Legislators, make the Republic triumph completely to avenge this sacrifice! May domestic enemies fall under the sword of the law; our surveillance will help you discover them.' In countless provincial attestations, Geffroy was transformed into the new regenerated man: 'Receive, brave martyr, the pure homage of a regenerated people who in the midst of corruption, for centuries bent under the harness of degradation and opprobrium, could, in the image of your example, resume its rights, break the chains of slavery and be reborn to happiness under the aegis of the Supreme Being.'

Geffroy became a Christ-like figure at what was tantamount to a revolutionary Day of Judgement in which the righteous virtuous would be separated from the incorrigibly corrupt like a vast ocean perpetually churning and ejecting detritus, dirty foam and flotsam and jetsam:

What a day of terror for the wicked when, Legislators, you recalled man to his primal dignity, to a new life, that day when you interested Divinity itself in the cause of freedom! What a day of dread for the corrupt when martyrs rise up by the thousands to make a rampart of their bodies against the blows of assassins. They do not know that the reign of the virtuous has created millions of Geffroys in the Republic! Our regeneration will be sublime, it will consume the old man to form the new man: it will annihilate kings and priests. In their place it will offer a God, virtue, law; it will present a great country of thinking beings, free, happy. Yes! A people who recognize the Supreme Being, a people ready to sacrifice itself wholly for law, is a virtuous people, and a virtuous people never perishes: it has the right to immortality of the soul.

Well on the way to recovery, the martyr Geffroy appeared in person, with his family, to receive the plaudits of the Convention and the grant of a lifelong pension. The man whose life he saved, Collot d'Herbois, returned him from the exceptional to the typical:

Yes, citizens, there are millions of families in the Republic who think and who act in the same way. There are in the Republic millions of virtuous and revolutionary families. For, Citizen Representatives, you have brought about such a state of things, that revolution is nothing but the simple and daily practice of austere and fruitful virtues. And the heart of the millions of Geffroys who people our Republic is an inexhaustible source of virtues that regenerate the human race and prepare the felicity of future generations.[45]

III 'VERTICAL DEPORTATION INTO THE NATIONAL BATHTUB':
LIBERTY, EQUALITY, FRATERNITY AND GENOCIDE

While the new political priesthood celebrated its utopian rites, the lot of the clergy deteriorated. During the winter of 1792–3 as many as a third of the French lower clergy and three-quarters of the bishops went into exile, between twenty-five and thirty thousand priests. Seven thousand of them found refuge (via the Channel Islands) in Protestant England, whose domestic complement of Catholic clergy was a mere three hundred. Attempts to maintain a domestic hierarchy quickly broke down, as bishops were special targets for revolutionary zealotry. Leadership was imperfectly exercised from the corners of Europe to which senior clergy fled.

The position of non-juring priests marooned within France resembled that of recusant clergy in Elizabethan England, that is, a life in disguise, hiding and on the run. For except in regions of widespread rebellion, the refractory Church had, of necessity, to become a clandestine Church, with priests holding services in farm buildings or in the open air. With priests scarce, parents took over the catechetical instruction of the young, while laymen began holding services in which a priest would normally have presided. Schoolmasters and sacristans usually officiated at these 'messes blanches', since, having seconded the priest, they generally knew the service from memory. This was a double-edged development. Of course nothing is as smooth as it can be described. The simultaneous presence of Constitutional and refractory clergy in a place could be bitterly divisive. The two clerical camps did their best to undermine each other, like the rector of Saint-Jacques-de-la-Lande, who said of the Constitutional bishop Le Coz of Rennes: 'the current bishop of Rennes is no more a bishop than his dog'.[46] The refractories spread rumours that baptisms and marriages celebrated by Constitutionals were invalid, or that those who attended their masses were liable to be excommunicated. Marriages became highly fractious when the wife worshipped with the refractory while the husband opted for conformity. Parents and children also fell out, although the Lyons father who backed up his demand that his adolescent daughter abandon the refractory for his juring priest, by knocking her down and standing on her windpipe, was probably exceptional.[47] The Revolution accelerated religious sexual dimorphism. A core of highly religious women distinguished themselves in resisting organised male irreligion. Since the authorities persisted in regarding women as prone to hysteria, and hence less responsible than their 'fanatic' menfolk, women tended to take the lead in resisting de-Christianising iconoclasm. Male officials recoiled in embarrassment at some of the more earthy antics of women protesting at the removal of church bells or sacred paraphernalia.[48]

There was one part of France where the refractory clergy could function more or less openly, namely where what has been called the 'guerre franco-française' had its origins. In spring 1793 large-scale anti-revolutionary popular uprisings broke out in western France which encompassed not just the Vendée, but the adjacent departments of Loire-Inférieure, Maine et Loire, and Deux-Sèvres. Aristocratic conspiracy was a reality in this part of France, but it had little or no connection with revolts whose primary impulse was profound hostility to the de-Christianising thrust of the new order. Over 60 per cent of the rebels were small, medium and well-to-do farmers or their servants and labourers, and a further 34 per cent were village artisans, shopkeepers and rural silk weavers. This was a revolt of the People (primitive rebels if you will) against the so-called People's Revolution, a bottom-up affair rather than a matter of innocent rustic dupes of malign clerical and noble conspirators. Not surprisingly, republican historians have always regarded the revolt as 'inexplicable', especially since a quarter of a million people perished during the revolt's brutal suppression by 'fanatics' who even resorted to technologies of mass extermination. This was the first occasion in history when an 'anticlerical' and self-styled 'non-religious' state embarked on a programme of mass murder that anticipated many twentieth-century horrors. The secular state was just as capable of unimaginable barbarity as any inspired by religion, eclipsing such limited atrocities as the Inquisition or the Massacre of St Bartholomew's Day, a modest affair when set alongside rampaging mobs of sans-culottes, in what was tantamount to genocide.[49]

The causes of anti-republican revolt in this large rectangle of hedged and wooded bocage bounded by the Atlantic to the west, the Loire to the north and the rivers Lay, Layon and Thouet to the east were both contingent and partly attributable to the unique way of life in this region. Persecution of the refractory clergy in these intensely Catholic western parts of the country aggravated other grievances over conscription for revolutionary armies that could no longer draw upon enthusiasm, or taxation that seemed to fall unfairly upon the shoulders of tenant producers who, in contrast to rich Jacobin townsmen, had failed to benefit from the Revolution's landed sale of the century. Since these multiple ills seemed to stem from town-based revolutionary cadres based in Angers or Saumur, the rural populations of the west had a clear focus for their hostility. The outlawing of a local clergy that was tightly bound into the local social scene, and the importation of Constitutional clergy who had little or no connection with their parishioners, was the trigger for armed revolt.

The uprising in the Vendée began on 12 March 1793, shortly after the call for conscripts to make up a levy of three hundred thousand soldiers. By the end of March disparate bands of rebels (or loyalists) had coalesced into the 'Catholic and Royal Army' of the Vendée, bearing images of the Virgin Mary and singing hymns as they criss-crossed the countryside.

Although conservatives have a tendency to become dewy-eyed about these 'White' religious rebels, they were sometimes as bloodthirsty as their 'Blue' republican opponents. The decision of one 'White' rebel band to massacre republican prisoners in the market town of Machecoul inaugurated a spiral of reciprocal violence. The Convention called for the summary execution of any rebel caught bearing arms, and despatched three revolutionary armies to suppress the rising. That they failed in this objective was due to the simultaneity of the localised Vendéan rising with the more widespread Federalist revolt, that is, the response of moderate provincial republicans to the Montagnard coup against the Girondin deputies in Paris, and of the provincial bourgeoisie to the untoward influence of sans-culotte mobs in the capital. Royalist counter-revolutionaries managed to attach themselves to what amounted to the first serious challenge to the hegemony of Paris in the events we have been considering. Since the Federalist revolt assumed menacing proportions in such geographically widely cast cities as Bordeaux, Lyons, Marseilles, Toulouse and Toulon, this gave the harassed Vendéans time to regroup.

As experienced huntsmen the rebels were formidable sharpshooters, but as unpaid family men they had multiple obligations and were reluctant to undertake military operations too far from home. The opposite problem afflicted the forces put together by 'representatives of the people' (the high-powered emissaries of the Committee of Public Safety) since government troops were less liable to desert as they moved away from their homes, but were more likely to behave like barbarian marauders as they drew away from the familiar, something that would repeat itself on Russia's plains and in the jungles of Vietnam in the twentieth century. The suppression of the Federalist revolt was followed by terrible reprisals against the erstwhile centres of insurgency. Lyons was renamed 'Liberated Town' or Ville-Affranchie and Toulon became 'Mountain-Port' or Port-de-la-Montagne. The former actor and theatre manager Collot d'Herbois (an early example of why posturing 'artistes' should be disbarred from politics) and the quondam professor of physics Joseph Fouché set to work in Lyons. An attempt literally to demolish the city stone by stone and brick by brick proved over ambitious. After briefly entertaining the idea of deporting the 'good' half of Lyons' population so as to concentrate their attentions on the 'evil' half who remained, Collot and Fouché cobbled together a local Temporary Commission of Jacobin loyalists and awaited the arrival of a Revolutionary Army. The playwright Ronsin who commanded this force recorded its ominous entry into the Rhône city:

> Terror was painted on every face. The deep silence that I took
> care to recommend to our brave troops made their march even

more menacing and terrible. Most of the shops were closed. A few women stood along our way. In their faces could be read more indignation than fear. The men stayed hidden in those same dens from which, during the siege, they came out to murder the true friends of liberty. The guillotine and the fusillade have done justice to more than four hundred rebels. But a new revolutionary commission has just been established, composed of true sans-culottes. My colleague Parein is president, and in a few days grapeshot, launched by our cannoneers, will have delivered us in a single instant of more than four thousand conspirators. It is time to shorten the forms.

While the guillotine fell so frenziedly that the execution site became a health hazard, the terrorists took up Ronsin's idea of using cannonfire to gun down large batches of prisoners, with swordsmen finishing off those left half dead by rounds of grapeshot. By April 1794 nearly two thousand people had been executed in Lyons. In a New Year message to the Convention, Fouché anticipated most of the arguments later used by totalitarian mass murderers to justify his actions:

Our mission here is difficult and painful. Only an ardent love of country can console and reward the man who, renouncing all the affections which nature and gentle habits have made dear to his heart, surrendering his own sensibility and his own existence, thinks, acts and lives only in the people and with the people, and shutting his eyes to everything about him, sees nothing but the Republic that will rise in posterity on the graves of conspirators and the broken swords of tyranny.

If the Vendéan rebels had benefited from the distractions of the Federalist revolt, the latter's suppression, together with the enforced domestic redeployment of a revolutionary army defeated at Mainz (or Mayence), sealed the rebels' fate. Four revolutionary columns criss-crossed the Vendée for four months in early 1794, primed with instructions from the Committee of Public Safety:

Kill the bandits instead of burning the farms, get the runaways and the cowards punished and totally crush this horrible Vendee . . . Plan with general Turreau the most assured means to exterminate all in this race of bandits.

Orders to troops were no less explicit countenancing the loss of the loyal few among the rebrobate many.

> Comrades, we enter the insurgent region. I order you to burn down everything that can be burned and to spear with your bayonets all the inhabitants you encounter along the way. I know there may be a few patriots in this region – it matters not, we must sacrifice all.

Writing on paper headed 'Liberty, Fraternity, Equality or Death', general Turreau instructed his soldiers[50]

> All the brigands found with weapons in hand, or suspected of having carried them, will be speared with the bayonet. We will act equally with women, girls and children ... Even people only suspected will not be spared any longer. All the villages, towns, hamlets, and all that can be burned will be put to the flames.

These troops included Joseph-Léopold-Sigisbert or rather 'Brutus' Hugo, father of the novelist Victor, a twenty-two-year-old army officer whose troops wiped out entire villages and massacred church congregations. The process of turning the Vendée into a 'sad desert' was captured in letters which the perpetrators wrote to their relatives. Writing to his sister in January 1794, a captain in the Liberty battalion said:

> wherever we pass by, we bring flames and death. Neither age or sex are respected. Here, one of our detachments burns a village. A volunteer kills three women with his own hands. It's horrific but the health of the Republic is an urgent imperative. What a war! We haven't seen a single individual without shooting them. Everywhere is strewn with corpses; everywhere the flames bring their ravages.

After losing a pitched battle at Cholet, the rebel remnant marched towards Granville, in the ill-coordinated hope of linking up with British and émigré forces that were supposed to have landed. Since this port was still in republican hands, the rebels fell back to Le Mans, where three thousand of them were caught by the forces of Kléber, Marceau and Westermann. Another nine thousand perished as they fell back towards Nantes. Mass shootings of thousands of people took place in Angers and Laval. Ironically, this headlong rebel retreat triggered panic among the Jacobins of Nantes, who perpetrated one of the most notorious massacres of the Terror.[51]

Representative Jean-Baptiste Carrier had installed himself in the villa of a former slave-trader where he entertained the local Nantais prostitutes, although his official mistress was the aunt of Victor Hugo's mother. He reserved the guillotine for aristocrats, priests and the wealthy bourgeoisie, but then decided to economise on musket balls and powder when he needed to thin out overcrowded prisons. Batches of bound prisoners were taken out on to the choppy waters of the Loire in barges that were then scuttled with the aid of specially designed hatches. Those prisoners who tried to clamber on to boats brought along to salvage the barge's crews, rather than what Carrier called their 'cargoes', in another premonition of the age of Hitler and Stalin, had their hands hacked away by drunken revolutionary soldiers armed with sabres. Revolutionaries added a few amusements, such as stripping male and female prisoners naked, tying them together, and then throwing them overboard in what they called 'republican marriages'. Priests were prominent among the eighteen hundred victims of these 'noyades', which were allegedly a humane response to epidemics and overcrowding in Nantais prisons. That they were also called 'vertical deportations into the national bathtub' or 'patriotic baptisms' suggests that the main motive was hardly public hygiene.[52] As a result of these atrocities, which involved such scenes as young women stretched upside down on trees and cut almost in half, up to a third of the population perished, a statistic roughly equivalent to the horrors of twentieth-century Cambodia.

There was a parallel revolt – of the Chouans, their name derived from the local word for owl, whose warning hoots were imitated by the region's smugglers. The nickname 'Chouan' was adopted by Jean Cottereau, a salt smuggler turned guerrilla leader, and from him it spread to the rebels as a whole. The Church was central to life in these parts of the west, for it was the only institution that gave isolated small villages a sense of community. The intrusion of Constitutional clergy, who were often outsiders, really rankled in these areas. So did republican military conscription and grain requisitions. In the eyes of many Bretons the term 'citizen' was one of abuse; republicans were almost a separate species of being who allegedly smelled as well as spoke differently. The Chouans were royalists and Christians, nostalgic for a unified rural world, in which royal government had hardly impinged at all under the ancien régime.[53] The Chouannerie was hard to combat since it consisted of ad-hoc guerrilla bands operating across ten western departments. Their attacks took the form of ambushes of grain convoys, and the assassination of Constitutional priests and republican officials. In a single fortnight in Fougères they killed twenty-three municipal officials and republicans. These bands were crushed only by the deployment of overwhelming government forces in the person of General Lazare Hoche and a new 140,000-man Army of the Coasts and the Ocean. Hoche's flying columns swept through the bocage day and night, preventing the Chouans from moving around with impunity. The latter were also poorly armed – often with hunting guns if they had a gun at all – and they were running low on powder. Eventually the Chouans had little choice but to surrender their weapons to the government's forces.[54]

The suppression of large-scale regional revolts ran parallel with the escalation of revolutionary Terror, that combination of delation, kangaroo courts and paranoia in which many of the most notable figures in the Revolution perished themselves as the ruling Committee of Public Safety struck at radical democratic extremists and moderates, by implicating them in conspiracies whose 'cross-party' permutations became progressively improbable. Something had gone seriously awry in a polity that scythed down Lavoisier, its most distinguished scientist, as well as Romme, who had designed its calendar. The Terror cut down so many of the political class in such an apparently indiscriminate fashion that strange alliances of self-preservation came into being, primed to strike at the individuals they held most responsible for months of escalating bloodshed. Hatred focused on Robespierre, whose moralising self-righteousness and virtuous superiority had cast a sinister shadow over too many compromised consciences, especially since he had employed considerable deceit and deviousness to bring about the deaths of his own political opponents, warm praise from him routinely being prefatory to cold-steeled extinction.

Paradoxically, it was Robespierre's most concerted attempt to draw a line under de-Christianisation through what he intended as the definitive and ultimate revolutionary cult that finally brought about his downfall. As a severe Deist, Robespierre had been appalled by the blasphemous antics of the Cult of Reason. The cult of the Supreme Being was celebrated in the gardens of the Tuileries on 20 Prairial Year II (8 June 1794). Commencing at 8 a.m., columns of men, women and youths from the Parisian sections converged on the Tuileries. The men carried branches of oak leaves, the women bouquets of roses, and girls baskets of flowers.

It was a bright and beautiful summer day. Robespierre had a light breakfast while he watched these scenes, remarking, 'Behold, the most interesting part of humanity.' At noon he and the rest of the Convention appeared on a balcony, with Robespierre's dark marine coat distinguishing him from deputies dressed in cornflower blue. His sermon in two parts outlined the purpose of the festival: 'O people, let us deliver ourselves today, under his auspices, to the just transports of a pure festivity. Tomorrow we shall return to the combat with vice and tyrants. We shall give the world the example of republican virtue.' France's providential mission was to 'purify the earth they have soiled.'[55]

Artists from the Opéra sang a hymn by Desorgues to a setting by Gossec:

> Père de l'Univers, suprême intelligence,
> Bienfaiteur ignoré des aveugles mortels,
> Tu révélas ton être à la reconnaissance
> Qui seul éleva tes autels.
>
> Ton temple, est sur les monts, dans les airs, sur les ondes
> Tu n'as point de passé, tu n'as point d'avenir:
> Et sans les occuper, tu remplis tous les mondes
> Qui ne peuvent te contenir.
>
> (Father of the Universe, supreme intelligence,
> Benefactor unknown to blinded mortals,
> You revealed your being to thankfulness
> Only to who built your altars.
> Your temple is on the mountain tops, in the air, in the waves
> You have no past, you have no future
> And without occupying them, you fill all the worlds
> Which cannot contain you.)

Robespierre took a flaming torch from the artist David, and set fire to a cardboard statue of Atheism, in a deliberate riposte to those who – in the name of materialism – had burned ecclesiastical images and vestments. A smoke-damaged image of Wisdom emerged from the collapsing remnant of Atheism and its confederates Ambition, Egoism,

Discord and False Modesty, figures collectively dubbed 'Sole Foreign Hope'. Robespierre resumed his sermon:

> Let us be grave and discreet in our deliberations, as men who determine the interests of the world. Let us be ardent and stubborn in our wrath against the confederated tyrants; imperturbable in danger, terrible in adversity, modest and vigilant in success. Let us be generous toward the good, compassionate toward the unfortunate, inexorable toward men of evil, just towards all.[56]

After the speeches a procession set off for the Champs de Réunion, with cavalry troopers, drummer boys and cannoneers in the van. The Parisian sections were represented too. The Lepeletier Section, named after the assassinated educationalist martyr, included a chariot of blind children, bearing aloft a crowned portrait of the locksmith hero Geffroy who had saved the life of Collot d'Herbois. The entire Convention followed, the whole group bound by a tricolour ribbon, and with president Robespierre in the lead. His enemies deviously accentuated the impression that it was his show by falling significantly behind him. Arrived at the Champs de Réunion, Robespierre led the deputies up a steep mock mountain, to the accompaniment of artillery salvoes, hymns and cries of 'Long live the Republic'. There were 2,400 choristers alone. The male choristers sang the revolutionary song Marseillaise (which only became the national anthem in 1879), with the male spectators chiming in. Women and girls took over for the second verse, with everyone joining in for the finale. Mothers held babies aloft, girls tossed bouquets in the air, and boys drew sabres while their fathers blessed their heads.

A week later, Marc Vadier, one of Robespierre's opponents on the lesser Committee of General Security, entertained the Convention with police intelligence on a harmless elderly mystic called Catherine Théot, who claimed that she was about to give birth to a divine being. Snide remarks about religion in an audience including many dedicated anticlericals clearly had a political purpose. Implacably opposed to Robespierre's purely tactical toleration of Catholicism, his enemies sought to forge evidence showing that Robespierre had tried to induce Catherine Théot to declare him the son of God. In the following days, Robespierre made the fundamental mistake of remaining aloof from the bureaucratic structures on which his power depended, isolating himself in solipsistic agony while he brooded on Socrates, hemlock cups and the like.

Over-estimating the significance of his supporters in the Commune and at the Jacobin club, on 8 Thermidor Robespierre spoke in the Convention. His speech was a long, rambling exercise in self-justification, in which he introduced the thought that revolutionary government would have to be permanent, a view his auditors took as the harbinger of personal dictatorship. The next day, he and four others were arrested in the Convention and conveyed to various Parisian jails. Troops of the Convention pre-empted an inept attempt to free them by some of the radical sections. Robespierre botched an attempt to shoot himself. He and his colleagues were guillotined the following day, with his paralysed ally Couthon screaming as he was straightened up for the plank, while Robespierre howled with pain as paper bandages were ripped from his gunshot-shattered jaw. The bureaucratic apparatus of terrorism was dismantled by the newly ascendant Dantonists, Girondins and former terrorists who reasserted the rule of the Convention over the committees. The Jacobin clubs were forbidden to correspond with one another, preparatory to being closed altogether. Poor persons were excluded from the National Guard and the power of the sections was diminished.

Theatres, cafés and ballrooms did well and something like plurality of opinion returned to the newspapers. Women began to wear clothes of their own choosing. The Jacobin cultural revolution was virtually over before it had started, although its stirring mythology would reverberate almost to our own time.

IV A NEW START

The Convention that established a new constitution consisted of men known as 'Toads of the Marsh', the centrist remnant left after Thermidor. Between 1795 and 1799 France was ruled by a five-man Directory, aptly described as 'a government of regicides who feared the return of the king and a government of the bourgeoisie who feared the demands of the people'.[57] Initially, they professed toleration of the bitterly divided Catholic Church, provided it kept out of politics and operated under considerable restrictions. Church and state were separated on 21 February 1795. Constitutional and refractory clergy could compete for 'market share', along with Protestants and Jews, but a regime which included so many vociferous anticlericals was not going to use state power (or money) to prevent any of these groups from going to the liquidators. While most people did not want a return to Tridentine Catholicism, they did want a Church concerned with parish life, centred on church services and the rites of Christian passage. The fortunes of the Catholic clergy waxed and waned as the Directory veered towards left or right with election results overturned by military force, in ways that gave ambitious generals something to think about. In September 1797 the 'Fructidor' coup brought anticlericals back into power, who insisted on a new clerical oath demanding 'hatred of royalty', with deportation to New Guinea as the price for those who refused it. The ascendancy of the left meant a ban on the wearing of clerical dress in public, religious processions and open-air worship, and on bells and images that could be heard or seen by the general public. Observance of the republican décades was enforced and Catholic practices were obstructed by such petty measures as a ban on the sale of fish on Fridays. The Constitutional Church, which was based on the idea that Catholics could also be republicans, fared no better under a regime that tended to regard all clergy as the same.

The Directory tried to perpetuate republican festivals, but these were progressively passionless affairs in which most of those who participated did so in compulsory groups. It took three years, from 1795 to 1798, even to get the seven major festivals off the drawing board. Although the Deistic cult of 'theophilanthropy', dreamed up by a masonic republican librarian, highlighted the connection between religion and morality, the cult itself was too desiccated to attract any significant following beyond its nineteen Parisian temples. None of the civic cults of the Revolution had managed to engender much of a popular response; reluctant acknowledgement of that failure would pave the way for a new religious settlement under Napoleon, who had a much keener sense of the value of spiritual power.

Any fitful signs of a rapprochement between Catholics prepared to detach themselves from reflexive royalism and realists in the regime who saw the tactical advantages of ending nearly a decade of estrangement between the state and Catholicism were shattered by the fourth obligatory loyalty oath for all clergy. This included the unnecessary phrase 'hatred of royalty' rather than a simple profession of submission to the Constitution or existing government. Furthermore, any faint indications that the papacy was softening its stance towards the Revolution were dispelled by the invasion in 1798 by French troops of the Papal States, followed by the exile and captivity of Pius VI. When Pius died a year later at Valence, the municipal registrar recorded: 'Jean Ange Braschi, exercising the profession of pontiff'. Although casuistry enabled some clerics to take the new oath, those who refused to swear faced deportation to New Guinea, a measure that particularly affected those who were too aged or infirm to evade its consequences. Many of the deportees never reached West Africa. They were interned for years in deplorable circumstances on ships anchored off Bordeaux or Rochefort. Of the 762 priests who boarded these 'floating Bastilles', some 527 died of disease aggravated by scurvy, with the survivors being released in late 1796.[58]

Since the state consciously allowed the Constitutional Church to wither, and actively persecuted the refractory clergy who refused to take their loyalty oaths, the survival of Catholicism in France was largely due to the dedication of the laity, and, in particular, to the piety of women. They defied the cruder manifestations of republican anticlerical provocation and took over many of the traditionally masculine functions of the clergy.[59]

If the survival of the refractory Church can be attributed to the tenacious traditionalism of the laity, the remarkable persistence of the Constitutional Church was a reflection of the skill of its leadership. Its survival was no mean thing, since its clergy faced the combined hostility of anticlerical republicans and of Catholic royalists. Its congregations may have melted away, but it remained a presence in French life, claiming the mantle of historic Gallicanism. While the ranks of its bishops declined from eighty-three to twenty-five between 1792 and 1795, and its priests to around six thousand, deft reorganization by its republican (and regicide) leader, Henri Grégoire, bishop of Blois, meant that it had to be considered in any final religious settlement. This came under the consular regime of Napoleon Bonaparte after 18 Brumaire (November 1799).

Although Bonaparte had a substratum of Catholicism that waxed and waned whenever his thoughts were diverted by something other than himself, his attitudes to religion were both pragmatic and strategic. As he remarked in 1800: 'It was by making myself a Catholic that I won the war in the Vendée, by making myself a Moslem that I established myself in Egypt, by making myself an ultramontane that I turned men's hearts towards me in Italy. If I were to govern a nation of Jews I would rebuild the Temple of Solomon.'[60] As Mme de Remusat remarked, the immortality of his name was of another order of importance than that

of his soul. Napoleon's mind was not poisoned by the anticlerical obses-
sions of the preceding regimes; the clergy were just another 'asset' whose
effectiveness could be quantified like that of soldiers – the pope was
the equivalent of two hundred thousand troops on a battlefield. What
he correctly took to be signs of a religious revival would be useful in
guaranteeing his own power and social stability in general.[61] As he put
it: 'When a man is dying of hunger beside another who is stuffing
himself, he cannot accept this difference if there is not an authority
who tells him: "God wishes it so".'[62] Before the end of 1799 Napoleon
had made several conciliatory gestures towards the moderate refractory
clergy, allowing them use of those churches that had not been sold off,
rescinding the Directory's literally hate-filled oath, and according Pius
VI an elaborate funeral. Although the revolutionary calendar lingered
for a few more years, until 1806 in fact, the décades lapsed in favour of
the traditional Sunday.

Bonaparte chose abbé Etienne Bernier, who in January 1800 had negotiated the peace of Montfaucon that ended the war in the Vendée, to
parley on his behalf, one of his aims being to break the hold on the
Church in France of 'fifty émigré bishops in English pay' by invoking
the authority of the papacy. The new pontiff Pius VII had already
signalled that the survival of Catholicism in France was not automatically
bound up with the restoration of the Bourbon monarchy. Pius had been
elected in Venice. At fifty-nine he was relatively spritely, and as 'citizen–
cardinal' of Imola (within the Cisalpine Republic) had preached that
democracy and the Gospels were not necessarily incompatible, although
in no meaningful sense was Pius VII a liberal.

On his return to France after the battle of Marengo in 1800, Bonaparte
indicated to Pius VII that both men might profit from an end to religious
schism. Bonaparte regarded the pope as a useful means of disciplining
the Church, especially if he could tell his holiness what to do. That
would be achieved by leaving the pope enough territory to be ranked as
monarch, but small enough to require Bonaparte's perpetual 'protection'.
As for Pius, he stood to reassert his authority over the Church, particularly over the Constitutional Church of France, which was picking up
support after the relaxation of religious persecution. These various objectives produced the 1801 Concordat. The weight of the issues involved,
such as the fate of the Constitutional Church, of the revolutionary
expropriation of the Church, of married priests, not to speak of religious
toleration, civil marriage and divorce, led to tense negotiations lasting

almost a year. Although Napoleon and his ministers (none of whom wanted a Concordat) tried to hoodwink the Vatican, the fact that a furious Napoleon threw the eighth draft concordat into the fire indicates that the pope's plenipotentiaries had negotiating skills of a high order. It was indicative of the sensitivity of the issues that the Concordat was not even called so by name but rather 'Convention between the French Government and his Holiness Pius VII' to avoid reminding either clerics or republicans of the agreement of 1516 whose memory was disagreeable to both sides.[63] When the Concordat was celebrated with a Te Deum in Paris, a republican general opined: 'all that is missing are those hundreds of thousands of Frenchmen who died to get rid of this'. He was not alone in this view.

The Church in France effectively became a department of state, with a ministry of cults under Portalis who liaised via bishop Bernier with the pope's representative cardinal Caprara. The Church acknowledged that its former lands were irrevocably lost to their new owners; the state would pay the clergy a salary. The clergy would add the words 'Domine salvam fac republicam, salvos fac consules' to the conclusion of the mass. Catholicism was recognised as 'the religion of the vast majority of French citizens', a formula which preserved the recently won rights of Protestants and Jews, but fell well short of it being proclaimed 'the religion of the State'. The new episcopate would be chosen, after the existing bishops had all resigned, from a consolidated pool of former Constitutional and refractory clerics. This meant not only that the pope had to swallow the legality of ordinations in the Constitutional Church, but that he had to force thirty-eight refractory bishops to resign. This would have produced apoplexy in the Gallican Church of the ancien régime. Twelve former Constitutional bishops were subsequently nominated to the new bench of bishops. Like the lower clergy they were obliged to make a declaration of loyalty to the government and to pray for the health of the Consulate at the end of every mass. The position of priests who had married, sometimes to avoid persecution, was regularised by laicising them, although Pius drew the line at Talleyrand, the married former bishop of Autun, whose vow of chastity he refused to relieve, while refusing him (retroactive) permission to marry. There was no mention of religious orders, although Bonaparte tolerated a few for men, especially missionary orders that would support imperialist ventures, and two hundred communities of women that would be useful as nurses and teachers.

The details of Church and state relations were managed by a series of 'Organic Articles', or rather administrative regulations for they were not organic at all, which effectively slipped in Gallican controls of the Church by the back door. As in the old days, laws and texts of the Holy See had to have prior French government approval before being disseminated in France. Bishops could not leave their dioceses or establish a chapter or seminary without government permission. It was illegal for a priest to marry couples without prior civil ceremonies. Clergy were obliged to denounce crimes to the authorities and to preach obedience to the state. The replacement of the Feast of the Assumption on 15 August by St Napoleon's Day was an unnecessary reminder of where power now lay. Ironically, it was now anticlerical republicans who felt the fingers of authority on their cuffs whenever their pens were poised to strike. The minister of police was instructed to prevent journalists from attacking either the clergy or religion, a remarkable reversal of the habits of more than a decade, even if it hardly signalled the end of intellectual anticlericalism. Pius VII was given a limited role in the coronation ceremonies of 2 December 1804. He was brought to Paris to anoint rather than crown the emperor and his consort, whose marriage he had celebrated the night before. The pope was obscured by the platform from which the emperor read out his coronation oath, placing the imperial crown on his own head.

Several things had changed, irrevocably, in relations between Church and state since the Revolution. The Church had ceased to be the First Estate, and laymen could relax in their enjoyment of its once extensive lands. A once rich monastic culture had all but disappeared. The lawyerly Gallican tradition of zealous autonomy vis-à-vis the papacy had vanished along with the monarchy and the parlements of the ancien régime. The Concordat quietly interred the decentred and popular refractory Church, with its enhanced role for the laity, in favour of clawing back a shadow of the Church's traditional power.[64] Religious affiliation was no longer integral to citizenship. As revolutionary and Napoleonic armies criss-crossed Europe, they obliterated the power both of enlightened despots, whose political cardinals had rigged papal elections, and of once mighty ecclesiastical principalities. Ineluctably, the papacy assumed a solitary dignity in a drastically simplified landscape, and ultramontanism, or overarching loyalty to the pope, grew among the clergy as a defence mechanism against those who paid their salaries and who could therefore dismiss them for dissidence. Bonaparte may have ended up abducting

Pius VII too, when he refused to sanction the former's European 'new order', but, as a by-product of such tribulations, ultramontane sentiments grew among the faithful too. The first sustained attempts to create secular civic cults, rivalling traditional Christianity, had failed miserably. The hatreds which that vain and genocidal campaign engendered poisoned domestic French politics for a century or more. Its symbols, not withstanding the facts that underpinned them, still had remaining currency, at least among those ignorant of the Vendée, which did not include the Russian novelist Alexander Solzhenitsyn, who made a point of visiting there after he landed in France shortly after his expulsion from the Soviet Union, skipping audiences with French intellectuals.[65]

CHAPTER 4

The Alliance of Throne and Altar in Restoration Europe

I THE SETTING IN 1814–1815

The Revolution antagonised the Catholic Church, although reform-minded members of the French clergy had initially welcomed it. The ensuing conflict degenerated into a genocidal franco-French war in which exponents of the new secular creed tried to exterminate determined adherents of the old. When revolutionary and Napoleonic armies and administrators exported blasphemy and sacrilege, the result was the fusion, whether in Spain, Germany or Russia, of counter-revolution, nationalism and religion, although to use these concepts is neatly to divide what was probably perceived as a whole. Whatever the subtle realities of Napoleon's attempts to use the Concordat Church to perpetuate both his dynasty and his regime, the perception grew that the arrival of French troops, under the command of the Corsican Anti-Christ, meant the draining of communion wine, the host snaffled by horses, soldiers larking about in clerical garb, their whores writhing on altars, pipes lit from holy lights, and the raucous chorus of revolutionary song where more lofty tones had prevailed. General count Hugo, as he had become under Napoleon, was responsible for perpetuating some of the grisly scenes in Spain depicted by Goya in his *Disasters of War* engravings, and was especially proud of his display of severed 'bandit' heads, which he sometimes arranged above the portals of churches. This was difficult to reconcile with his son's claim that 'That Army [Napoleon's army in Spain] carried the *Encyclopédie* in its knapsack.' Reading that work evidently made scant impact on a father who shot up the tomb of El Cid, tried to blow up Burgos cathedral, and looted every Goya, Murillo and Velásquez he could lay his grubby hands on when it was time for the French to retreat.[1]

Across Europe statues of saints allegedly averted their gaze, bled, wept and threatened to depart, to avoid the impieties that so offended humble folk that tens of thousands of them were prepared to take up arms and fight the French. In Spain, patriots drew upon centuries of Christian resistance to the Moors, literally exchanging the latter's robes and turbans for the Jacobins' blue coats and red caps, as happened during an 1808 procession in Cadiz that celebrated the feast day of St James. True Christians and Spaniards became synonymous. Icons and incense were similarly heavily present whenever the Russian tsar's armies went into battle with Napoleon's polyglot legions. Napoleon's aide de camp watched before Borodino how icons were paraded before the Russian host: 'This solemn spectacle, the exhortations of the officers, the benedictions of the priests, finally aroused the courage of the spectators to a fanatical heat. Down to the simplest soldier, they believed themselves consecrated by God to the defence of Heaven and the sacred soil of Russia.'[2]

Events seemed to gust with the violence of solar storms. Writing to a friend in 1819, the philosopher Hegel confessed: 'I am just fifty years old, and have lived most of my life in these eternally restless times of fear and hope, and I have hoped that sometime these fears and hopes might cease. But now I must see that they will go on for ever, indeed in moments of depression I think they will grow worse.' As a young man he had sympathised with the Revolution, writing 'Vive la liberté' in his private album, and had regarded Napoleon as 'the world soul on horseback', despite having his meagre possessions pillaged by French troops as they swept through Frankfurt. Aptly enough, a philosopher who was adept in the eddies and currents of world history, philosophy and religion also had a nose for which way the wind blew in accordance with his self-interest. After publishing an essay that poured cold water on the desirability of constitutions, in 1817 Hegel was appointed to a professorship of philosophy in Berlin, virtually becoming Prussia's official state philosopher, although his style was so opaque that, as his soi-disant pupil Ludwig Feuerbach (and Karl Marx) proved, Hegel's thought could run in many directions.[3]

In the circles that regained power in 1814–15, the political ideals of the Enlightenment were discredited by a Revolution whose possibilities had narrowed to either anarchy and terror or continental military dictatorship, notwithstanding the brief parenthesis of the Directory. Statesmen, of whom the greatest was the Austrian foreign minister and chancellor Metternich, might privately have held enlightened views, but felt it inexpedient to espouse them publicly. In England and Wales, where senior clerics were not usually given to either lurid imaginings or political pronouncements, Anglican bishops followed the abbé Barruel in regarding the Revolution as a conspiracy and the rise of Napoleon as the advent of the reign of Anti-Christ. They joined the Tory John Wesley in offering to raise militias to combat domestic radicals and foreign invasion.[4]

Across Europe where there had been hope there was disillusionment, as the biographies of innumerable Romantic artists, musicians, poets, thinkers and writers witness. The British poets Coleridge, Southey and Wordsworth were among those who progressed from a naive enthusiasm for the French Revolution to more conservative opinions, putting away, as Coleridge had it, his 'squeaking baby trumpet of sedition' after French forces invaded his beloved Switzerland.[5] The future poet laureate Southey took longer to outgrow the political equivalent of juvenile acne, but the implacability of his mature views, when juxtaposed with his youthful enthusiasms for the Jacobins or the medieval peasant leader Wat Tyler, ensured the enmity of the genius Byron and the professionally snide Hazlitt.[6] The ideal of individual cultivation, coupled with political conservatism, took the place of a youthful fixation with liberty as these erstwhile romantics turned greyly prudent.[7] Many prominent continental thinkers, such as Clemens Brentano, Chateaubriand and Joseph Görres, discovered harmony, hierarchy, history and order in what one might call cultural Roman Catholicism, appreciating the faith for its aesthetic qualities rather than for its spiritual truth. A Breton nobleman, once memorably described as looking like 'a hunchback without the hump', Chateaubriand had lost his brother in the Terror. The death of his pious mother triggered the exile's religious crisis – 'I confess that I did not undergo any great supernatural illumination. My conviction came from my heart. I wept and believed' – which he resolved in his *Le Génie du Christianisme*. This was an extended and nostalgic paean to Christianity as the supreme cultural value on the part of a man who did not hesitate to bring his mistress when he was appointed secretary to the French embassy to the Holy See.[8] Not a few Protestant thinkers, such as Adam Müller in 1805 or Friedrich Schlegel in 1808, converted to Rome, although the general trend was otherwise, in their search for certainty and order in a chaotic world. The politics of creative artists too did not move in an entirely synchronised manner from left to right, for in France Victor Hugo and Alphonse de Lamartine would transfer their sympathies from throne-and-altar conservatism to enthusiasm for the liberal 1830 July Revolution.

Throughout Europe monarchs adopted local versions of 'God Save the King' and flags based on the Union flag's crosses rather than threatening bands of three colours. Everywhere religion restored seemed a compelling alternative to reason rampant, since the logic of the latter seemed to have culminated in the Terror and genocide in the Vendée. Men developed a new respect for infinity, perhaps best reflected in the diminutive and solitary figures wandering, their backs invariably turned towards us, amid the fog, forests, waters and wastes of Caspar David Friedrich's numinous landscapes.[9] They also rediscovered the imagined harmonies of organic rural communities and hierarchy stretching from earth to heaven. A Romantic enthusiasm for the Middle Ages, imagined as an 'Age of Faith', in which peace prevailed in Christendom while war was externalised against Arab and Turk, or a kind of epic narcissism based on the cult of the original genius, supplanted the austerities of neoclassicism and the fluent whimsicality of the rococo. The (Protestant) poet Novalis, the pen name of Friedrich von Hardenberg, gave eloquent expression to this Romantic longing for unity in an essay called *Christendom or Europe* written at the height of the French Revolutionary Wars. He exalted the Middle Ages and condemned the Reformation for dividing the indivisible Church and confining religion within political frontiers. Although the French Revolution was the distant progeny of the Reformation, Novalis nonetheless regarded it as the purifying moment at which Europe could renew its fundamental Christian spiritual unity with Jerusalem as the capital of the world.[10]

The view was widespread that any assault on religion led logically to the subversion of governmental authority, and with it morality, it making little odds if that authority was not even Christian. Just to demonstrate how pervasive this view was, let's briefly visit the outer edges of Christendom. In 1798 the Greek Orthodox patriarch Anthimos warned against 'the fiend [who] tries us with newly appearing types of constitution and government, allegedly more desirable and more beneficial . . . resolutely give your obedience to the civil government, which grants you that which alone is necessary to the present life, and what is more valuable than anything, does not present any obstacle or damage to your spiritual salvation'. He meant, of course, the Muslim Ottoman authorities, to whom he guaranteed the loyalty of the Orthodox population, in return, it should be noted, for more religious toleration than existed in much of Christian Europe.[11]

That view was as common in Anglican Britain, which included Ireland, as it was among continental Roman Catholics and Protestants. It was a theme that could unite the bishops of the Protestant Church of Ireland and the Irish Catholic prelates. Despite being one of the few Whig bishops and, initially, a supporter of the Revolution, bishop Richard Watson of Llandaff wrote: 'when religion shall have lost its hold on men's consciences, government will lose its authority over their persons, and a state of barbarous anarchy will ensue'.[12] Religion was a guarantor of political freedom: its rejection the gateway to anarchy and tyranny. That is why a self-consciously and sometimes aggressively Protestant England provided state as well as Church support between 1792 and 1820 to exiled French Catholic clergy.

In his 1831 'Catechism on Revolution' pope Gregory XVI asked: 'Does the Holy Law of God permit rebellion against the legitimate temporal sovereign?' He answered: 'No, never, because the temporal power comes from God.'[13] The following year he issued the encyclical *Mirari vos* that said:

> We have learned that certain teachings are being spread among the common people in writings which attack the trust and submission due to princes; the torches of treason are being lit everywhere ... both divine and human laws cry out against those who strive by treason and sedition to drive the people from confidence in their princes and from their government.

A French bishop, monsignor Le Groing de la Romagère, was prepared to take that even further when he called upon his flock 'to continue to obey in the civil order whoever derives sovereign power from above, however evil his morals, whatever his religious beliefs, whatever the abuses, apparent or real, of his government, and however impious and tyrannical the laws he enacts in order to pervert you'.[14]

Throne and altar in alliance was to be the foundation of legitimate authority. The revolutionary notion that the state rested upon a contract with the nation was rejected in favour of the restoration of princely dynasties ruling sovereign states, many of which were empires consisting of multiple ethnicities speaking several non-standardised languages. The necessity for a Genoese–Italian dictionary in 1851 highlights the problem, even if many more Italians understood the high version of the language than either spoke or wrote it.[15] It was also regarded as natural that, say, the king of England ruled German Hanover too, or that Habsburg princes and viceroys held power in northern Italian Lombardy and the Veneto. Metternich notoriously denied the existence of such a thing as 'Italy' (as opposed to seven sovereign states) except as a 'geographical expression' and he dismissed the desire for 'Germany' (as distinct from thirty-nine states and sovereign cities) as a daydream 'incapable of realization by any operation of human ingenuity'.[16]

What was Restoration Europe like and was it more than a brief conservative parenthesis between two ages of revolution? French remained the language of diplomacy and high politics, but its distinguishing idiom was the languid aristocratic drawl of statesmen, many of who combined hard-headedness and exquisite sensuality, rather than the vehement bawling about virtue and morality by aroused fishwives and radicalised lawyers in marketplaces and revolutionary tribunals. Some returning émigrés had spent so long abroad that they sounded like foreigners. After seven years' exile in England, Chateaubriand counted in English and expressed spontaneous emotion too in that language, for some while after he returned to France in 1800 to serve Napoleon. The duc de Richelieu, who in 1815 became Louis XVIII's chief minister, and who had spent so long governing southern Russia from Odessa (where he installed the famous steps) that he spoke French with a Slavic accent, was known to wits as 'The Frenchman with the best knowledge of the Crimea'. The ubiquitous Talleyrand still slithered through the corridors of power: 'his unprepossessing figure, clad in an old-fashioned coat of the Directory, stooping, heavily advancing on crooked legs . . . An enormous mouth filled with rotten teeth above a high collar, small deep-set grey eyes without any expression in them, a face striking in its insignificance, cold and calm, incapable of blushing or revealing any emotions . . . a real Mephistopheles'.[17]

The aims of the Great Powers, Austria, Britain, Russia and Prussia, had been given limited definition by the 1814 Treaty of Chaumont, although the desire to defeat Napoleon bulked larger than any plans for a peacetime 'new order', a notion they were mercifully ignorant of except in the most mystical formulations. This relatively simple objective was complicated by the need simultaneously to restore and restrain a monarchical France, in order to prevent 'a Calmuk prince', that is the Russian tsar, exploiting the threat of further revolution as a pretext for becoming the ultimate arbiter of Europe.[18] The other powers wanted the Cossacks to disappear back into the steppes. France was restrained by bringing Russia further into Poland, while Prussia filched part of Saxony, Westphalia and the left bank of the Rhine. Austria took Lombardy–Venetia, the Netherlands acquired Belgium, and the kingdom of Piedmont–Sardinia was extended to include Genoa. What the people thought was irrelevant to all concerned.

This inner alliance dominated the Congress of Vienna, which convened from the autumn of 1814 onwards, an interlocking series of informal meetings between sovereigns and their principals; specialist committees to discuss specific problems; and sessions where smaller powers were presented with the decisions of the major players. The victors treated Bourbon France with moderation, allowing Talleyrand into their midst better to restrain Russia, but their mood hardened after the hundred-day interlude when Napoleon escaped Elba. The French king taxed the patience of allies whose armies had restored him to his throne. At a dinner in the Tuileries Palace, attended by the king of Prussia and the Russian tsar, Louis XVIII went in first, and then exploded 'To me first, to me first!' when a valet served the exquisitely polite Alexander first.[19] The big four powers concluded a Quadruple Alliance and agreed to meet periodically in concert to ensure maintenance of agreements that they regarded as the best bet for equilibrium and peace in Europe. France was subjected to occupation and reparations. At Aix-la-Chapelle Bourbon France was admitted to a Quintuple Alliance 'consecrated to protect the arts of peace, to increase the internal prosperity of the various states, and to awaken those sentiments of religion and morality which the misfortunes of the time had weakened'.

The Congress System was designed to crush any recrudescence of the spirit of 1789 and to resolve differences between the Great Powers through diplomacy. That these congresses fell somewhat short of a permanent 'system' to impose order was largely due to British suspicions of unlimited obligations towards reactionary continental monarchies seeking to repress liberal or nationalist reforms and revolutions which captured the imagination of political romantics across Europe. However, with or without Britain, the other Great Powers successfully crushed revolutions at either end of the Italian peninsula and in Portugal and Spain in 1820–1, with only the 1821–31 Orthodox Greek revolt against the Muslim Ottoman Turks complicating the matter of their sympathies.[20]

In 1815 Metternich arrived for a supper with tsar Alexander I. He found four places laid at table. This perplexed him. Apart from himself and the tsar, the only other guest present was a Baltic German woman whose mind seemed unfocused. When Metternich inquired as to the identity of the absent fourth guest, the tsar explained that the place was set for Jesus.[21] The Restoration saw fitful attempts to reconstitute the divine basis of political authority. Mystical fervour, hard to recapture even in our era of White House prayer breakfasts and magic crystals in Downing Street, was evident in the most explicit attempt to bolster monarchical government through religion. Tsar Alexander had a fervent interest in mysticism due to the influence of two friends – 'brothers in Christ' – prince Alexander Golitsyn and Rodion Koshlev. The former was the procurator of the Holy Synod, which made him head of the Orthodox Church, while Koshlev kept Alexander au courant with every new mystical publication in Europe. Over a decade, Golitsyn dined with Alexander 3,635 times, or virtually every day. There was also the lady we have already encountered.

Baroness Juliane von Krüdener had left her Russian diplomat husband to take up with a younger French officer in Paris. Reconciled to her husband, the baroness went to Riga in 1804 where she was 'converted' to her millenarian faith by a Moravian cobbler. Clearly receptive to the prophetic enthusiasms of the lower classes, in Prussia she was persuaded by a peasant that a man would emerge 'from the north . . . from the rising of the sun' to destroy the Corsican Anti-Christ. In mid-1815 she secured a lengthy interview with Alexander as he passed the summer in the quiet backwater of Heilbrunn, away from the balls and receptions that this tortured soul had ceased to enjoy. At precisely the moment when Alexander was thinking of seeking her out, the baroness appeared at the Rauch'sche Palais.

The baroness was already a known quantity to the tsar. Inspired by a presence she dubbed 'the Voice', she (habitually dressed in a religious habit) preached at the weeping tsar for three hours: 'Be filled with divine creation! Let the life of Christ permeate morally your spiritual body.' Alexander declared he had found inner peace, although this was premature since he would subsequently seek out all manner of religious counsel. On 11 September 1815 the baroness played a prominent role in a military parade on the Plain of Vertus held to celebrate the feast of the tsar's patron saint Alexander Nevsky. The baroness and the tsar processed past seven altars symbolising the mystic number of the Apocalypse.[22]

Though the tsar would disentangle himself from the clutches of this ageing religious maniac, a rupture that was final when she besought his blessing for the Greek Revolution, Alexander wanted to make religion the cornerstone of international order. He provocatively issued a 'Declaration of the Rights of God' as part of the Holy Alliance which was signed by Francis I of Austria, Frederick William III of Prussia and the tsar himself on 26 September 1815. There was little 'traditional' about this project since Europe's monarchies, whether Catholic or Protestant, had spent the previous five hundred years defying such universal pretensions.[23] The Holy Alliance licensed the suppression of liberal and nationalist revolutionaries, and sanctioned open-ended breaches of state sovereignty. It was a reactionary anticipation of what many liberal human rights moralists (and their neo-Jacobin conservative analogues) seek to impose on a world sceptical of their faiths today.

British statesmen refused to sign up to what Castlereagh famously dismissed as 'sublime mysticism and nonsense', while the German conservative thinker Friedrich von Gentz dismissed it as 'a monument to human and princely eccentricity'. Pope Pius VII excused himself from a compact with schismatic Orthodox Russians and heretical Protestant Prussians, which to him smacked of 'indifferentism' and 'syncretism'. He added: 'from time immemorial the papacy has been in possession of Christian truth and needed no new interpretation of it'. As Muslims, the Ottoman Turks were excluded. Metternich, who identified Protestantism with anarchy, but who, as a rational aristocratic Catholic, also despised the fervour of theocrats, confided to his diary: 'Abstract ideas count for very little. We take things as they are, and look for those factors that may save us from becoming prisoners of illusions about the real world.'[24]

At a time when even conservatives say that 'true' conservatism has become an American phenomenon, it is useful to remember 'old' Europe's (and especially France's) contribution to a tradition that involves more than rich garagistes seeking to pay no taxes and a tendency to throw one's weight around internationally in the name of 'world order'. Several thinkers attempted to supply a more comprehensive justification for the restoration of monarchy and religion in an alliance of throne and altar, the apex of a hierarchy resting upon strong aristocratic intermediary authorities, religion and the patriarchal family. This was hypocritical since it had been the absolutist monarchs of ancien régime Europe whose enlightened reforms had cleared away the dense entanglements of localised rights, while reforming and subordinating the Church, thereby not only performing much of the work of the Revolution for it but creating an appetite for further reform. It was also ironic that Europe's absolute monarchs had been compelled to mobilise precisely those nationally conscious elements to fight Napoleon that after 1815 they were so concerned to suppress once they had performed this limited objective. They had unleashed forces that they would never be able fully to control, although it would take the rest of the century for that aspect of democracy to become evident.[25]

III A PECULIARLY DIFFERENT ENGLAND

Many continental ideologists of the Restoration were heavily indebted to the genius of the Irish Whig Edmund Burke. The nub of Burke's political philosophy was to favour experience, history, prejudice and tradition, with changes happening by increment, and each living generation conscious of what it owed to the dead as well as the unborn. Burke was also an admirer of dogma, meaning the beliefs, values and state of mind into which one is born. Religion underpinned domestic social hierarchy and in the form of international law provided the 'great ligament of mankind'.

> We know, and, what is better, we feel inwardly, that religion is the basis of civil society, and the source of all good, and of all comfort. In England we are so convinced of this, that there is no rust of superstition, with which the accumulated absurdity of the human mind might have crusted it over in the course of ages, that ninety-nine in a hundred of the people of England would not prefer to impiety.

Burke detested the idea of separating Church and state, regarding disestablishment as almost as pernicious as the French Revolution's 'Atheism by Establishment'. He was also hostile to the very notion of 'alliance' between throne and altar – commonplace in most Restoration conservative thinking – for 'an alliance is between two things that are in their nature distinct and independent such as between two sovereign states. But in a Christian commonwealth the Church and State are one and the same thing, being different integral parts of the same whole.'[26] The political function of religion was not simply to keep the lower orders quiescent, as has been tiresomely argued by generations of Marxists, but also to impress upon those who had power that they were here today and gone tomorrow, and responsible to those below and Him above: 'All persons possessing any portion of power ought to be strongly and awfully impressed with an idea that they act in trust, and that they are to account for their conduct in that trust to the one great Master, Author, and Founder of society.'

By the time these doctrines were enunciated, both English society and English religion were undergoing great transformations. By the mid-eighteenth century the Anglican Church, whatever its problems, seemed to have seen off any rivals. It was ensconced in the post-Reformation remnants of a medieval Catholic Church that since the Venerable Bede had helped define the essence of Englishness. It benefited from its identification with the English state, and a sense of Protestant providential purpose that steered a moderate path between popish fanaticism and Puritan zealousness. Its competitors were in poor shape. Old Dissent had lost many of its higher-ranking adherents, who were reabsorbed into Anglicanism, which in turn diminished its purchase on the lower classes. New Dissent was merely an Evangelical minority tendency within the Church of England. The defection of upper-class Catholics, chafing at their legalised marginality, similarly halved the number of English Catholics in the fifty years before 1740, before their ranks were increased by Irish immigration.

Yet the ground was shifting beneath the Anglican Church's ramparts, its monopolistic position being challenged in an era of profound social and economic upheaval, which has reminded some of the ways in which the Roman Catholic Church establishment is being eclipsed nowadays by Pentecostalism in the teeming cities of Latin America. Religious voluntarism, which the Anglican Church partially encouraged, might either revivify the Church or develop, as Methodism eventually did, into a powerful secessionist competitor, captivating and capturing classes that Anglicanism failed to greet. Large-scale Irish migration would give an enormous fillip to Catholicism, again partly because of an ethnic and social coincidence between priest and people. By contrast, in the 1830s the Anglican Church was in danger of becoming a minority establishment. Because it lacked internal machinery for reform, between 1717 and 1852 its Convocations were prorogued, and the state set about reforming it, thereby giving further impetus to the secularisation of the originally indivisible establishment. How had things reached this pass?

It would be relatively easy to paint a picture of eighteenth- or early-nineteenth-century clergy whose sermons contained more Cicero than Christ, or who regarded practice of their religion as a bothersome distraction from chasing foxes. They were hardly unique in that, because in 1819 the bishop of Kildare and Leighlin in Ireland forbade his Roman Catholic clergy to deal in land or to hunt, they being more familiar with 'ejaculating "Tally Ho!" than *Dominus Vobiscum*', as the bishop pithily had it.[27] In a nutshell, the Anglican Church was like any old-fashioned corporate monopoly faced with energetic competition from rivals who had a more flexible and imaginative understanding of existing or potential markets within a wider context characterised by tentative religious toleration.

Anglican assurance about the stability of the alliance not only between throne and altar, but between parson and squire (so interlinked as to be known as the 'squarson') mistook conditions in the arable heartlands of lowland England for Britain as a whole, where parish structure, settlement patterns, tenurial arrangements and new ways of making a livelihood all militated against the dependence and deference that ensue from settlement. In the century 1741 to 1841 the population of England and Wales rose by 165 per cent from six to nearly sixteen millions. The population of classical agricultural counties doubled, while that of those where industry or commerce predominated tripled or quadrupled. This latter growth was in regions where the parochial net was broad rather than fine, and where the inhabitants neither lived in compact villages nor were constrained by a resident squirarchy, whose presence or absence was as important as that of clerics.

Methodism, and successive Nonconformist denominations, reached out to those whom John Wesley dubbed 'low, insignificant people', providing them with an associational, communal and recreational focus, as well as a theology and moral code that complemented and reinforced their own social and economic aspirations. It was never simply a creed designed to discipline an industrial workforce, a charge routinely made by modern British academic apologists for a political religion that preferred to discipline workers by means of Arctic concentration camps, but it did separate large numbers of ambitious artisans and the like from the more hedonistic culture of the popular classes in previous centuries, a sort of extended parenthesis before they sank back into a more debased version of it in the late twentieth century. Methodism sought people out wherever they were, whereas, as the bishop of Lichfield explained to a curate in 1837: 'If the inhabitants will not take the trouble to come . . . to hear your sermons, and much more to hear the beautiful prayers of our Liturgy, which are superior to any sermons that were ever written, I am sure they do not deserve to have them brought to their doors.' Moreover, as the Anglican establishment became more and more enmeshed in the preservation of an unreformed political order, so people turned to evangelical Nonconformity partly to register their newfound independence of a social order that had little relevance to them. That was implicit in the duchess of Buckingham's condemnation of Methodist doctrines as 'strongly tinctured with impertinence and disrespect . . . towards superiors, in perpetually endeavouring to level all ranks, and do away with all distinctions'. The duchess was appalled to 'be told that you have a heart as sinful as the common wretches that crawl on the earth', a powerful challenge to a society hitherto based on hierarchy and inherited landed wealth but gradually being exposed to other values.[28]

IV PAPERING OVER THE CRACKS

Since French experience of the Revolution was most sustained and visceral, it is unsurprising that thinkers with knowledge of France were the most intransigent exponents of what might be called the palaeo-conservative position during the Restoration. Maistre and Bonald sought to bury the optimistic assumptions of the Enlightenment about man and society and to restore the Church to the position from whence the Revolution had expelled it. Paradoxically they used a highly sophisticated application of reason to advocate the irrational, and, though intellectuals themselves, despised those whose intellectual conceit lacked grounding in reality. Both of them came to the rather odd conclusion that it would be better if fewer books and ideas were in general circulation, not the first instance where their thought battered every assumption of modernity including claims that more knowledge is better. What is one to make of Maistre's observation: 'I dare say that what we ought not to know is more important than what we ought to know'? These men wanted to restore the power of throne and altar; they were neither 'freaks' as one member of the British Marxist academic Establishment has claimed, nor part of the long genealogy of Fascism, a quirky charge once levelled by Isaiah Berlin, which has been dismissed by Robert Paxton, a leading American historian of Fascism who has spent a lifetime studying the actuality of that phenomenon.[29]

Joseph de Maistre was an ennobled Savoyard lawyer. Savoy was a province of Piedmont–Sardinia, whose king ruled from across the Alps in Turin. Maistre was both a devout Catholic and an enthusiastic free-mason. Masonry was fashionable and philanthropic, which could no longer be said of the old-style lay religious confraternities. An admirer of the British constitution, Maistre also approved of the American Revolution, writing, 'Liberty, insulted in Europe, has taken flight to another hemisphere,' and he regarded the initial stages of the French Revolution with equanimity. He was an advocate of the separation of powers, with the judiciary advising monarchy, and religion holding society together like cement. The Declaration of the Rights of Man and a reading in September 1791 of Burke's *Reflections*, whose author's intelligent rage articulated the Savoyard's own, represented a turning point, as did the behaviour of his fellow countrymen after Savoy had been annexed by revolutionary France. Bitter experience affected the tone of his writing, which in fluent radicality went far to the right of Burke.

Accompanied by his expectant wife and two small children Maistre fled to Aosta, returning only briefly to Chambéry to establish how awful rule by revolutionaries could be. Years later he recalled: 'Savoy . . . was invaded in the midst of the great paroxysm; one had to see churches closed, priests chased out, the king's portrait paraded in public and stabbed; one had to listen to the Marseillaise sung at the elevation (I heard it); my heart was not strong enough to put up with all that.'[30] In 1793 Maistre moved to Lausanne, where he combined counter-revolutionary pamphleteering with running a Savoyard intelligence net-work whose findings he reported back to the government in Turin. Clearly feeling undervalued by his own monarch, he would complain that 'I was the knight errant of a power that wanted nothing to do with me.'[31]

In 1797 Maistre published *Considerations on France*, his providential reading of the multiple shortcomings of the ancien régime and the divine punishment represented by the Revolution. He intended to enhance royalist fortunes in the French elections in March that year as well as to reassure people (in a France he visited for the first time in 1817) that counter-revolution would not entail punitive confiscation of lands stolen from their rightful owners or a vengeful bloodbath. Despite this moderate mission, his relative Lamartine described it as 'thought out by an exterminating mind and written in blood'.

Thereafter Maistre's hopes of preferment as a major ideologue of counter-revolution were dashed as the storms of revolution gusted into each city and state he sought refuge in. It was like being stalked by a typhoon. Dragging his family of young children across Europe, Maistre was reduced to selling the silver. During bouts of enforced leisure he read intelligently and voraciously, for he was a great lover of books. In July 1799 he was appointed regent in Sardinia, an unhappy posting for Maistre was bored with both law and public administration, and he clashed badly with the soldier viceroy.

In 1803 he was designated Sardinian ambassador to St Petersburg, for after Bonaparte's annexation of Piedmont in 1800 the island was all that was left of Victor Emmanuel I's north Italian kingdom. The man who confidently and wrongly predicted that no capital could ever be built on the swamps of the Potomac found himself posted to Peter the Great's northerly pastiche of Venice. Through sheer presence Maistre gained influence at the Russian Court, for he was the representative of an impoverished kingdom that had been reduced to an island outpost, and the exiled monarch in Rome was dependent upon subsidies from Maistre's present Russian hosts and the British.

A contemporary described him in St Petersburg:

> I believe I can still see before me that noble old man, walking with his head high, crowned by hair whitened by both nature and the caprice of fashion. His large forehead, his pale face stamped with features as striking as his thoughts, marked too by the misfortunes of his life, his blue eyes half dimmed by deep and laborious studies; and finally the accomplished elegance of his costume, the urbanity of his language and manners – all that forms in my mind a certain original and suave whole.

His jokes were also good, in a characteristically dark sort of way. In a letter from St Petersburg to a young relative he told the story of a mass baptism around a hole in the ice of the River Neva. When the presiding Orthodox archbishop accidentally let slip an infant who disappeared into the dark waters below, he remarked 'davai drugoi' (give me another one) and continued as if nothing had happened.[32]

Apart from his official duties, Maistre acted as an adviser to Louis XVIII and to Alexander I, whom he thought slightly mad. He read deeply and took copious notes from great tomes in English, German, Italian and, of course, French, Latin and ancient Greek. He had a special admiration for the English, and knew people like Edward Gibbon whom he had met in Switzerland. Maistre would have been content to live out his days in Russia, but the ever closer identification of Russian patriotism with Orthodoxy (though he denied it the name) ensured that this articulate, proselytising Catholic became persona non grata. The atmosphere became positively hostile once the tsar expelled the Jesuits in 1816, perhaps because their exclusive allegiance to the pope clashed with the role of saviour of Europe that he derived from the Holy Alliance. In February 1816 Maistre had a rather intimidating interview with Alexander: 'The emperor advances with twenty-six million men in his pockets (one sees them clearly), he presses you at close quarters, and even, since his hearing is poor, brings his head close to yours. His eye interrogates, his eyebrows are suspicious, and power comes out of his pores.' Maistre left Russia in the spring of 1817, spending six weeks in Paris where he met Louis XVIII, who perversely avoided any mention of the writings of one of the major apologists of the Bourbon cause. On his return to Sardinia, Maistre was appointed a minister of state until his death a few years later. Having alienated the Sardinian royal house by appearing too francophile, he had managed to antagonise the restored Bourbons by describing their politique 1814 constitutional Charter as 'a soapbubble'.[33]

In the course of the *Considerations*, Maistre confessed, 'I am a perfect stranger to France, which I have never seen, and I expect nothing from her King, whom I shall never know.' The *Considerations* opens with a rejection of Rousseau's dictum that 'man is born free, and everywhere he is in chains'. Maistre countered: 'We are all attached to the throne of the Supreme Being by a supple chain that restrains us without enslaving us.' He viewed the Revolution as 'a whirlwind carrying along like light straw everything that human force has opposed to it; no one has hindered its course with impunity'. The leaders, whom he dismissed as 'criminals', 'mediocrities', 'monsters' and 'rascals', were in reality merely the led. Politics had no autonomy from the divine drama and anyone who thought they were willing events to happen was utterly self-deluded since everything was in God's hands. Using concepts, like purification, that paradoxically enough were permeated by Jacobin concerns, Maistre saw Providence at work in even the Revolution's most bloody phases:

The great purification must be accomplished and eyes must be opened; the metal of France, freed from its sour and impure dross, must emerge cleaner and more malleable into the hands of a future king. Doubtless, Providence does not have to punish in this life in order to be justified, but in our epoch, coming down to our level, Providence punishes like a human tribunal. (c. 14)

For each blow and setback was part of a providential scheme, in which terrible punishments were accompanied by quasi-miracles on the battlefields of Europe that expanded French power. Under a different dispensation, this power might be used to good effect, namely a French-led 'moral revolution' in Europe. His mode of argument could be typified by the claim that even the exile in Protestant England of large numbers of Catholic clerics had contributed to a greater spirit of tolerance on the part of the Church of England, for God works in such mysterious ways. Mere events were of secondary significance, as when Maistre dismissed 9 Thermidor as being the day when 'a few scoundrels killed a few scoundrels'.[34] The only power capable of restoring order was absolute monarchy, uncontrolled by anything other than the monarch's conscience and God. However, here he radically departed from the Gallican tradition, by arguing that the monarch must be subject to God's vicar on earth, that is the pope, who embodied the only institution with a continuous eighteen hundred years' existence.

Maistre saw the Revolution as so 'radically bad' that its evil bordered on the 'satanic'. It was an unnatural event, something out of joint, season or sequence, such as the miracle of a tree fructifying in January. Its leading lights, and the philosophers who had inspired them, were guilty of the heaven-storming pride of Prometheus. He did not believe in social contracts and he thought written constitutions worthless. He divined a 'fight to the death between Christianity and philosophism'. Refusing to believe in the 'fecundity of nothingness', he heaped scorn on the civic cults of the Revolution, on the incapacity of men invested with immense power and prodigious resources 'to organize a simple holiday'. His attitude to the Rights of 'Man' was as follows: 'there is no such thing as man in the world. In my lifetime I have seen Frenchmen, Italians, Russians, etc; thanks to Montesquieu, I even know that one can be Persian. But as for man, I declare that I have never in my life met him; if he exists, he is unknown to me.'[35]

He mocked the incessant deliberations of successive French assemblies, counting the 15,479 laws passed in six years. He doubted that three successive royal dynasties had legislated so much. Revolutionary irreligion struck at his deepest conception of political order: 'Either every imaginable institution is founded on a religious concept or it is only a passing phenomenon. Institutions are strong and durable to the degree that they are, so to speak, deified. Not only is human reason, or what is ignorantly called philosophy, incapable of supplying these foundations, which with equal ignorance are called superstitious, but philosophy is, on the contrary, an essentially disruptive force.'[36]

Where the philosophes simply wanted to conform human society to laws putatively operating in the natural world, Maistre saw that nature consisted of infinite murder, in which every creature lives from whatever is weaker. Man was the greatest murderer of all. Murder took the form of war, which in the sacrifice of the innocent propitiated God for the sins of mankind: 'The whole earth, perpetually steeped in blood, is nothing but a vast altar, upon which all that is living must be sacrificed without end, without measure, without pause, until the consummation of things, until evil is extinct, until the death of death.'[37] Modern liberals will never forgive his alighting upon society's ultimate pariah – the executioner – as the force capable of keeping the flimsy hut of human society above the raging waters which perpetually threaten to engulf it. He described the sinister movements of such figures with all too apparent relish, as the hangman–pariah parted a gawping, shuddering crowd to smash human bones deliberately with iron bars, the pre-guillotine mode of public execution.[38] They will also be inherently antagonistic to his bestselling ultramontane work *Du Pape*, overlooking the fact that Maistre regarded the papacy as an essential check on the untrammelled exercise of state power:

> By virtue of a divine law, there is always by the side of every sovereignty some power or other that acts as a check. It may be a law, a custom, conscience, a pope, a dagger, but there is always some curb ... Now, the authority of the Popes was the power chosen and constituted by the Middle Ages to balance the temporal power and make it bearable for men ... In the Middle Ages, nations had within themselves only worthless or despised laws and corrupt customs. This indispensable check had therefore to be sought from without. It was found, and could only be found, in papal authority.[39]

Maistre's main rival Louis de Bonald came from a noble family in Millau in the Rouergue. Born under the ancien régime, his life spanned the Revolution, exile, the glory of France under Napoleon, political office under the Restoration and, finally, disillusionment in the last decade of his life, when like Job he admitted that his pilgrimage had been short and hopeless.

After a short stint as a royal musketeer, Bonald became mayor of Millau in 1785, where he introduced free primary school education. So long as the Revolution consisted of provincial noble reassertion against central power, he was prepared to work within it, becoming a member of the departmental Council of Aveyron in 1790. A loyal Gallican with Jansenist leanings, he believed in reforming the Church. But he resigned from public office rather than enforce an oath to the Civil Constitution of the Clergy. In late 1791 he joined the emigration in the Rhineland. He eventually settled in Heidelberg, where he wrote his three-volume *Théorie du pouvoir politique et religieux dans la société civile*. In 1797 he slipped back to Paris where he spent two years in hiding, during which time he read prodigiously, before emerging in the sunlight of Napoleon, who treated him as a minor amusement.

Bonald's thought was more sociologically and less theologically inclined than Maistre's, and his cast of mind was more scientific than Chateaubriand's aesthetic appreciation of religion. Although Bonald moved in the same social circles, he regarded Chateaubriand as an intellectual lightweight who eschewed dogma in favour of flummery and nostalgia. His relations with Maistre were duplicitous, although in later life he discovered a similar capacity to outrage liberal opinion.

Bonald was one of the godfathers of modern sociology, whose concerns with status, hierarchy, ritual, integration, control and order reflect a conservative preoccupation with the atomised consequences of Enlightenment individualism. They were interested in what are called statics rather than dynamics, and in facts rather than ideal values.[40] Bonald thought in terms of power and structures, the latter like formulae in algebra or figures in geometry: 'power; force; will' or 'power; minister; subject' being typical of his way of understanding society in groups of three concepts. Everything came in threes: 'In cosmology God is the cause, movement the means, body the effect. In a State the government is the cause, the minister the means, the subject the effect. In a family, the father is the cause, the mother the means, the child the effect.' Men of power, or leaders, constituted society, for without them a multitude of men would amount to a scattering of dust. Government was not based on contract; rather, those who governed should be separated from the governed by an impassable gulf of birth or wealth. Whereas Burke thought in terms of hereditary privilege as a means of checking royal absolutism, Bonald followed the Jacobins in believing in the desirability of unitary power. The nobility, who were central to all his writings, existed to implement the will of the monarch, with the rest of mankind functionally divided into those who pray, trade, work and so forth. The nobility were to be educated as a national caste, in special schools, and identified by a special gold ring. They would man virtually every significant office in the administration, the army, the judiciary and so on. Bonald was clearly influenced too by Rousseau's views on the importance of civic cults, this being unusual in the wake of such experiments during the Revolution. Unlike other counter-revolutionaries who contented themselves with attempts to revitalise the Church, Bonald proposed a sort of hybrid medieval chivalric order with the visual symbols that the Revolution had appropriated from freemasonry. This must have made theocrats uneasy.

Society would be given symbolic focus by a pyramidal Temple of Providence in the geographic centre of France. Ringed by a vast circle and by statues of great men, this Temple would be the site for national rituals and the place where the heir to the throne and the most exemplary nobles lived. The function of Christianity (which played less of a role in his thought than in Maistre's) was to symbolise the social hierarchy and to inculcate such values as sacrifice or respect. Here Bonald came very close to articulating a conservative civil religion:

> Government is a real religion: it has its dogmas, its mysteries, its ministry; to annihilate or to submit it to discussion by every individual, amounts to the same . . . it lives only by the strength of the national reason, that is to say of political faith . . . The first need of man is that his emerging reason should be curbed by a double yoke, that is to say that it annihilates itself, that is to say that it merges with and becomes lost in the national reason, in order that it changes its individual existence into another common existence, like a river precipitating itself into the Ocean.[41]

In subsequent works, Bonald elaborated his view that the individual had only duties rather than rights, duties towards human nature, society and to God. He emphasised the family as the basis of society, with the professions and professional corporations higher up his social pyramid, until one encounters 'power' at the apex. A leading opponent of legalised divorce, he regarded the modern family as the breeding ground for such dangerous notions as equality. When married couples separated, he thought that the woman was to be confined in a convent; the man was to forfeit public office; and both were to deliver their children to the state. He envisaged the state determining who should be allowed to marry; and compounded his hostility to Protestantism with the view that Jews (whom he regarded as both alien and divisive) should be discouraged from bearing children by curtailing their ability to marry.

Bonald advocated a vast extension of state regulation, whether in relation to how people dressed (people were to be attired according to their functions) or in relation to what they were allowed to read, for he thought that far too many indifferent books were being published. People had to have a licence to possess weapons; how much more so should new books require official sanction. He thought there should be a national catechism, for 'dogmas make nations'. The Académie Française was to be the regulative analogue of the Catholic Church in the greatly reduced field of letters. He was an enthusiast for censorship. As he grew older his detestation of the money-mad urban bourgeoisie and love for rural self-sufficiency increased, until in self-imposed isolation he duly turned on the regime whose propagandist he had tried to become.[42]

The Restoration was initially far more pragmatic in temper than the thought of these men suggests. In France the restored Bourbon monarch Louis XVIII sought to fuse the tradition he represented with the new spirit of the times. Dissimulation was probably inevitable, though it is apocryphal that as he blew kisses to a crowd he muttered 'scoundrels, Jacobins, monsters'. He may have insisted on referring to 1814 as the nineteenth year of 'our reign', but he also called for collective amnesia regarding who had done what to whom in the recent past, a surprisingly modern and sophisticated approach to legacies of hatred. After a short moderate interlude, the implacable ultras regained the ascendancy when in early 1820 a Bonapartist saddler called Pierre Louvel killed the duc de Berry. Given impotence in high places, Berry was the de-facto heir to the throne. Although the widowed duchess would give birth to a 'miracle' son, the conservative ultras spoke darkly of the assassin's knife as a 'liberal idea'. Under the Villèle ministry the ultras would be in power for the following six years.

The ultras immediately sought to restore the influence of the clergy. The latter were integral to the cult of Bourbon pathos that enveloped the memory of the martyr king Louis XVI, Marie Antoinette and other members of their family circle. The anniversary of that great crime on 21 January became a day of national expiation, although the price was that the centuries of Bourbon symbolism were jettisoned in favour of an imagery that derived from, at most, two decades of counter-revolutionary conservatism. It seemed pallid next to the rising romantic counter-mythology of the moody Minotaur on St Helena.

Clerics re-emerged where they were not welcome. Napoleon had centralised all higher and secondary education through the Sorbonne University. The ultramontane cleric Lamennais, whom we will shortly encounter, wanted the whole shop shut down:

> I have no hesitation in saying that, of all Bonaparte's concep-tions, the most appalling to every considering man, the most profoundly anti-social, in a word the most characteristic of its author, is the University. When the tyrant thought he had made sure by so many horrible laws of the misery of the present generation, he raised this monstrous edifice as a monument of his hatred for future generations; it was as though he wanted to rob the human race even of hope.[43]

The centralised Napoleonic university was replaced by seventeen sep-arate institutions under the Royal Council of Public Instruction. In 1821 this system was scrapped in turn, and Frayssinous, bishop of Hermopolis, was appointed grand master of the revived centralised system. A circular to the faculty opined: 'He who has the misfortune to live without religion or not to be devoted to the reigning House cannot but feel that he is in some measure unsuited to be an instructor of youth.' Eleven professors were dismissed and the lectures of the brilliant Protestant historian Guizot deleted. Two years later Frayssinous became head of a combined ministry of education and ecclesiastical affairs. Guizot commented: 'This is a declaration of war by a considerable part of the Catholic Church in France upon French society as it is.' There were concerted attempts to swamp entire swathes of France with Christian missionaries. Missions descended on areas that had few priests of their own because of the Revo-lution's murderous assaults or natural wastage. Carnivals and dances were prohibited; church services were elaborated with massed outdoor sermons, communions, military parades and penitential processions.[44]

In September 1824 the Voltairean roué Louis XVIII was succeeded by his brother Charles X, the new king being an over-earnest reformed rake. His coronation was an opportunity to rehearse rituals of an archaic kind that Louis had avoided. The rood loft was decorated with France and Religion supporting the Crown in literal symbolism of the union of throne and altar. The flask containing the holy oil brought by a dove for the anointing of Clovis may have been smashed in the Revolution, but it was claimed that sufficient globules had adhered to the fragments for smearing on the new king's brow. Anticlericals had a field day with this mumbo-jumbo, and especially with Charles X's prostration before the altar, a gesture that must have seemed pathetic when juxtaposed with the Corsican emperor's auto-coronation. The satirist Béranger did six months in jail for a piece entitled 'The Coronation of Charles the Simple':

> In belt of Charlemagne arrayed,
> As though just such a roistering blade,
> Charles in the dust now prostrate lies;
> 'Rise up, Sir King,' a soldier cries.
> 'No,' quoth the Bishop, 'and by St Peter,
> The Church crowns you; with bounty treat her!
> Heaven sends, but 'tis the priests who give;
> Long may legitimacy live!'[45]

Clumsy financial schemes were introduced to compensate former émigrés – many of whom had borne arms against France – while nothing was done for peasants in the Vendée whose farms had been torched. Liberal sensibilities were inflamed by a draconian sacrilege law, under which malefactors would have a hand chopped off before their head followed. Bonald blandly claimed that 'by a sentence of death you are sending [the criminal] before his natural judge', which only incensed enlightened liberal opinion further even if the sentence was never once imposed. Next, the ministry tried to reclericalise education. Primary schooling was placed in the hands of local bishops and in the senior schools lay teachers were replaced with priests. Seminaries were opened to youths with no priestly vocation in the hope that their minds might be moulded in a more conservative direction. In a disastrous development, Bonald was appointed chief censor. Moderate legitimists, such as Chateaubriand, began to draw closer to the liberal opposition, effectively signifying the drift of French Romanticism from right to left.[46] Liberal opponents of these rather limited attempts to undo the Revolution were quick to alight upon conspiracy to explain their failure to do well in the intense competition for very few government jobs. An amorphous network called the Congregation had been founded in 1801 by a former Jesuit to encourage upper-class Catholics to live devoutly and to undertake charity. Its illustrious membership partially overlapped with a more secretive organisation called the Knights of Faith whose objectives were more political. The illegal presence of five hundred Jesuits in France added further layers of suspicion, especially since it was rumoured that Charles X himself belonged to the Society. Conservative Gallicans and Liberals credulously lapped up the conspiracy theories of a quixotic aristocrat, the comte de Montlosier who claimed that France was being run by an ultramontane conspiracy. It was said that the Jesuit house at Montrouge contained fifty thousand priests, who were learning how to use firearms rather than studying the writings of Ignatius Loyola. In fact, there were 108 Jesuit priests at the time in the whole of France. When Villèle lost the 1827 election, Charles attempted another tack with the comparatively restrained Martignac ministry. A year later he reversed course by appointing the ultra-reactionary Polignac, who in his pious conceit imagined that the Virgin had appointed him saviour of France. In the July Ordinances, Charles dissolved the Chamber, reduced the electorate from one hundred thousand to twenty-five thousand, and subjected all publications to government licence. The absence of the army in Algeria enabled disgruntled Bonapartist workers to dominate the streets as the liberal bourgeoisie looked on aghast. In the absence of a Bonaparte, Guizot, Lafayette and Thiers effectively made the duc d'Orléans king Louis Philippe. His coronation was a civil affair in which he swore to uphold the revised Charter, signing it in triplicate. Catholicism was described merely as 'the religion of the majority of Frenchmen'. In France at least, the era of Restoration was over, along with the Bourbon dynasty. The rule of 'middlingness' took over.

The papacy owed the restoration of its temporal possessions to the Great Powers. Time and again, and not just in the conclaves where popes were chosen, they were popes by the grace of Metternich who prevented them being swept away by liberal revolutionaries. By this time, Pius VII was a very old and sick man, who went about his chambers attached to the walls by a cord because periodic paralysis and vertigo would otherwise have deposited him on the floor. Under these circumstances, what amounted to a provisional government under Agostino Rivarola was not encouraging: archaeological excavations in the city, gas lighting and vaccination were all prohibited, while the Jews were returned to the ghetto and the Inquisition revived. These measures were partly rescinded under the energetic secretary of state Ercole Consalvi, who displaced clerics from functions for which they had no competence, abolished onerous taxes and prohibited torture in a revised judicial system. The spirit behind these reforms was evanescent.

Leo XII excommunicated members of the secret societies on the ground that their rites were blasphemous, while his short-lived successor Pius VIII imposed the death penalty on those subversives his police force detected. Conditions in the Papal States were so bad that by May 1831 a conference of the ambassadors of the five major powers presented pope Gregory XVI with a memorandum that spelled out the changes he needed to make to his temporal government, such as financial reform and an enhanced role for laymen. A flurry of edicts resulted, to minimal effect. The papacy may have been pragmatic in its dealings with newly independent republics in Latin America, but in Europe it was a bastion of monarchical legitimism. It supported the status quo on the Italian peninsula, calling upon the Austrians whenever the Papal States were threatened, and it opposed liberal or nationalist revolution everywhere except Ireland. This included revolutions where Roman Catholics played a major part, notably in Poland and Belgium. Gregory XVI, an elderly former Camoldolese monk, whose knowledge of the world was very limited, endorsed the repression that tsar Nicholas I inflicted on Poland after the abortive November Rising, including measures that struck at the Church's own privileges. In an 1832 encyclical to the Polish bishops, admittedly toned up under Metternich's influence, the pope reminded them of the need to obey temporal authority and condemned the Polish revolutionary movement.

V LAMENNAIS AND BELGIUM'S MOMENT

Not all Catholic thinkers responded to the challenge of liberal and nationalist revolution by retreating behind the slogan 'throne and altar'. Some recognised that the legitimist game was up, or regarded the altar as the more enduring part of this duopoly than the 'here today, gone tomorrow' occupants of earthly thrones. What if state power was actually crushing the Church, like a corpse locked in rigor mortis around someone still breathing? To explain this we need to venture into the history of Belgium, while relating this to the extraordinary life of one of the most remarkable figures in nineteenth-century Europe.

In 1814 the Great Powers assigned the former Austrian Netherlands and Liège (what we now know as Belgium) to the Calvinist William I of what became the United Kingdom of the Netherlands. William's reign got off to an inauspicious start when he used 'Dutch arithmetic' (a euphemism for jiggery-pokery) to nullify the votes of the Belgian parliamentary deputies who refused to approve the new constitution. Those who abstained or voted no were counted as having voted yes. The ascendancy of what in the combined kingdom was the minority language of Dutch, and of Dutch-speakers in public office, so antagonised Belgian opinion that no amount of economic prosperity would persuade them of the virtues of Dutch rule. Uniquely, William I managed to create an alliance, or Union, of Catholics and Liberals by forcing candidates for the priesthood to take philosophy at what until 1835 was the state university of Louvain, while simultaneously imprisoning liberal journal editors. In the autumn of 1830 the Dutch regime was overthrown and an independent Belgian kingdom proclaimed under the Lutheran Leopold I. The February 1831 Constitution separated Church and state. It also granted the Church freedoms that it enjoyed nowhere else in Catholic Europe. These included autonomous control over the appointment of bishops, freedom to publish what it liked and unimpeded communication with the Catholic hierarchy in Rome.[47]

A young Breton cleric, Félicité de La Mennais, later known as Lamennais, was important in forging this improbable rapprochement between Catholics and liberals.[48] Improbable because the papacy was in the vanguard of opposing freedom of opinion, while liberalism (especially in France) was often synonymous with anticlericalism, partly because liberals perceived the Church to be the weakest element in the marriage of throne and altar, and partly because clerics were easily identifiable at a time when other defenders of the status quo dressed much the same as their liberal opponents.

Lamennais had begun his meteoric career as an impassioned advocate of the limitless expansion of papal power so as to liberate the Church from state interference and the otherwise supine tyranny of the Gallican French bishops. The immediate pretext was Napoleon's attempt in 1809 to circumvent the necessity of persuading the (imprisoned) pope to invest bishops canonically whom Napoleon had effectively appointed.

Lamennais and his brother co-authored an enormous three-volume defence of the rights of the pope that was so unambiguous that Lamennais fled France during the Hundred Days. On his return, he published a major critique of the view that the truth of a religious doctrine is a matter of indifference, and hence that ethics can be detached from dogma and conduct from belief. When he went to Rome in 1824 pope Leo XII granted him private audiences, even if he was merely recognising a literary talent whose defences of the Church were winning wide admiration, rather than sanctioning the young priest's opinions.

Lamennais' critique of the superficial deference paid by the Restoration state to the Church came in a two-part work called *De la religion considérée dans ses rapports avec l'ordre politique et civil* (1825–6). It resulted in him being fined for attacking the king and the Gallican Articles. The book was banned. Lamennais argued that the Restoration had not 'restored' ancient arrangements, but had subordinated the Church to the state to the extent that it was no different from an art gallery, stud-farm or theatre. Politics separated from religion was nothing more than 'force directed by interest'. Religion alone ensured that politics was something more than the satisfaction of material self-interest. As Lamennais pithily wrote: 'A bazaar is not at all the same thing as a city.' Gallicanism effectively dispensed rulers from any sense of obligation to the spiritual power and identified the Church too closely with national interests. Only the papacy could prevent rulers from 'crushing all freedom, both in church and in state', since it alone was external to all national interests. Lamennais' logic was no pope, no church. No church, no Christianity. No Christianity, no religion. No religion, no society. The Church should abandon its compact with the state, coming to terms with the forces that claimed to represent the People. Only the pope could guarantee man's freedom from state power, as well as the peace between peoples that the madcap Holy Alliance aspired to.[49]

Lamennais became the hub of a circle of talented admirers at his family estate at La Chênaie. He founded his own order, the Congregation of St Peter, which enabled regular clergy to live communally in an atmosphere of study, journalism and prayer. Although he was personally unprepossessing, Lamennais had some impressive disciples; they included Auguste Comte, Victor Hugo, Alphonse de Lamartine, Alfred de Vigny and Sainte-Beuve. Lamennais became convinced that the Bourbon monarchy was doomed and that the Church should not go down with it any more than lifeboats should sink with a ship. In contrast to the stuffy French ecclesiastical hierarchy, Lamennais welcomed the July 1830 Revolution that brought Louis Philippe to the throne. One of his disciples posed the apposite question of the defunct regime: 'Did the Son of God die eighteen hundred years ago on a gibbet in order to re-establish the Bourbons on the throne?'[50]

In *L'Avenir* – the first Catholic daily paper in Europe – Lamennais suggested that, instead of supporting unpopular monarchies, the Church should make common cause with the most reasonable of the 'progressive' causes of the age, namely moderate liberalism, thereby freeing it to reshape society in a more Christian direction under the general guidance of the papacy. The causes the paper advocated ensured the hostility of the new monarchy (which Lamennais regarded as so much flim-flam in a regime where the people were sovereign) and the French hierarchy whose salaries he proposed to abolish: 'The scraps of bread thrown to the clergy are the title deeds of her subjection . . . It was not with a cheque drawn on Caesar's bank that Jesus sent his Apostles out into the world.'[51] In *L'Avenir* Lamennais and his associates advocated the complete separation of Church and state, including the suppression of clerical state salaries; freedom for parents to educate their children as they chose; freedom of association and of the press; universal suffrage; and enhanced local autonomy and self-government. Lamennais also founded a General Agency for the Defence of Religious Liberty, the first lay organisation of its kind, which sprang into action whenever the state encroached on the freedom the Church had won. The 'Mennaisians', that is his followers, also took a keen interest in the fortunes of Catholic peoples elsewhere, hoping to form a liberal Catholic international. Their paper followed events in Belgium, Ireland, Poland, Portugal and Spain, where they were often sympathetic to rebellion, proving inconsistent only in denouncing as 'anarchists' and 'Jacobins' those who presumed to trouble the temporal rule of the pope. If in this respect they were out of step with Europe's liberals, in another they were ahead of them. In a prescient piece, one of Lamennais' associates wrote:

> The debates in our parliament or in the international conference, the delimitation of the frontiers of Belgium [at the London Conference], the fall of a dynasty, parliamentary reform, these are questions of no importance by comparison with the leprosy of pauperism which is ravaging Europe. But like the astrologer who was so busy looking at the stars that he did not see the

abyss that was open before him, we fix our attention on the lofty regions of the political world, as if the interests that are canvassed there must be a permanent influence on the fate of our country. If we want to know about that, we must look much lower down – into the midst of the multitudes who are called 'the people' when they are needed and otherwise 'the populace'.[52]

Lamennais always claimed, perhaps disingenuously, that he had never changed his views; they had merely evolved from an initial ultramontanism resembling that of his friend Maistre. This was partially true. He simply substituted 'democracy' for 'throne' in a refashioned alliance with 'altar', and when he used the slogan 'God and Liberty' he meant the collective emancipation of Ireland or Poland rather than the freedom of individuals.[53] After *L'Avenir*, whose readers were mainly younger priests, folded – there were more supporters than subscribers – he and his core supporters decided to appeal directly to the pope to win him over to the liberal-catholic ideas they espoused. Convinced that the corrupt Gallican hierarchy was preventing his message from reaching Gregory XVI, Lamennais and two younger sympathisers, Lacordaire and Montalembert, set off for Rome in December 1831 to persuade the aged pope that he should abandon his support for reaction. Since the papacy had admired his earlier fervent ultramontanism, he supposed he might persuade the pope to drink at liberalism's well too. He expected him to come round to his view that the French Revolution was not just the judgement of God on a sinful world, but an opportunity for the Church and mankind as a whole. His enemies, the most important of whom were the French hierarchy, Metternich and the ambassador of the Russian tsar, managed to derail him before he had even spoken with the pope.

The Breton cleric underestimated the capacity of the papacy to kill off his kind of prophetic excitement simply by doing nothing. The winter weather in Rome was leaden and Lamennais' opinions of the temporal regime of the pope that he had recently defended against anarchic Jacobins turned sour. In February he wrote to a friend:

I hope ... I shall not have to stay in Rome much longer, and one of the happiest days of my life will be that on which I get out of this great tomb where there is nothing but worms and bones, Oh! How thankful I am for the decision I took, some years ago, to settle elsewhere ... In this moral desert I should have led a useless life, wearing myself out in boredom and vexation. This was no place for me. I need air and movement and faith and love and everything that one vainly seeks amid these ancient ruins over which like filthy reptiles, in the shade and in the silence, the vilest human passions creep.

The pope is pious and means well; but he knows nothing about the world or about the state of the church and the state of society; motionless in the thick darkness by which he is surrounded, he weeps and prays; his role, his mission is to prepare and hasten the final convulsions which must precede the regeneration of society; that is why God has delivered him into the hands of the basest kind of men; ambitious, greedy, corrupt; frenzied idiots who call upon the Tartars to re-establish in Europe what they call order, and who adore the saviour of the church in the Nero of Poland, in the crowned Robespierre who is carrying through, at this very moment, his imperial '93 . . . Another twenty years of this kind of thing, and Catholicism would be dead; God will save it through the peoples: what else matters to me? For me, politics means the triumph of Christ, legitimacy means his law; my fatherland is the human race which he has redeemed with his blood.[54]

After a wait of two months, Lamennais' party were finally granted an audience with 'the only authority in the world I want to obey'. This lasted fifteen minutes, with desultory talk of Lamennais' brother, of Geneva and of a silver statuette by Michelangelo, which the pope had to search for. In conclusion, the 'only authority' offered them snuff and blessed their rosaries before bidding them a courteous farewell.

On 15 August 1832 Gregory XVI issued his first encyclical *Mirari vos*: 'Depravity exults; science is impudent; liberty, dissolute.' In many respects anticipating the strident antimodernism of Pius IX, it lambasted freedom of conscience and freedom of the press ('hateful'), religious indifferentism, the notion of just revolution, and Lamennais' hobby-horse, separation of Church and state: 'Nor can we predict happier times for religion and government from the plans of those who desire vehemently to separate the Church from the state, and to break the mutual concord between temporal authority and the priesthood. It is certain that concord which always was favourable and beneficial for the sacred and the civil order is feared by the shameless lovers of liberty.' The encyclical did not mention Lamennais, as a cardinal explained in a covering letter, but various passages clearly had the French priest in mind. He received a copy of the encyclical on a silver platter at a banquet in his honour in Munich given by among others Görres and Schlegel.

In a letter to a friend Lamennais wrote of the papacy: 'Its ideas are like the swaddling bands that wrap up Egyptian mummies. It talks of a world that does not exist any more. Its sound is like those remote rumbles that are heard in the consecrated tombs of Memphis.' Less charitably, he described Gregory XVI as a 'cowardly old imbecile'.[55]

Whatever his not so private views, Lamennais appeared to submit to papal discipline in his initial responses to *Mirari vos*. Publication of *L'Avenir* was suspended, and the Agency closed down. However, one of these submissions included the qualification that 'I have a duty to affirm that while Christians have only to hear and obey in the realm of religion, they remain entirely free in their opinions and words and acts in the sphere that is purely temporal.' Some verses which he appended to a book that the poet Adam Mickiewicz wrote to strengthen the resolve of Polish exiles did not help, because, as we shall see in the next chapter, the pope had condemned the Poles' rebellion against their Russian rulers. Worse, in April 1834 Lamennais published the controversial *Paroles d'un croyant* (Words of a Believer). People queued to read what the London *Times* described as 'a fireship launched in the midst of the moral world' and others more sensationally called the work of 'Robespierre in a surplice' or a 'Jacobin red bonnet planted on a Cross'. Lamennais argued that the oppressed should seek salvation in Christ from unjust laws and tyrannical governments whom an apocalypse would soon sweep away. The monarchs of the Holy Alliance were arraigned alongside the great biblical tyrants in a manner that must have seemed shocking at the time. Not surprisingly they did not let this go unopposed. Metternich was quick to denounce Lamennais as 'an anarchist' who had gone mad, adding rather darkly: 'the practice of burning heretics and their works has been abandoned: that is a matter for regret in the present instance'. The pope, who was 'always happy to know your opinion which he likes best of all to know', described Lamennais' book as 'the work of the most shameful and wild impiety, as the profession of faith of a complete revolutionary'. The pope duly issued a second encyclical, *Singulari nos*, which did name Lamennais and condemned a book 'little in size but vast in perversity'. Lamennais abandoned the Church in the autumn of 1834 in disgust with the papacy for having missed its chance to align itself with the new spirit of the times. Contemporaries saw him scurrying about in civilian clothes, but with the haunted, preoccupied look of a Graham Greene priest. He had spent a lifetime promoting a highly elevated view of the papacy's function only to be undermined by forces that had little or nothing to do with Christianity, at least as he understood it. He eventually settled on a philanthropic religion of humanity that was indistinguishable from several others on offer from the left. Lamennais died largely forgotten in February 1854, refusing to have a cross on his grave.[56]

We began by considering contemporary endeavours to provide a conceptual basis for the restoration of the alliance of throne and altar, even though the ideas concerned often subconsciously reflected the impact of the Revolution that these writers professed to despise. In the case of Lamennais, this gave rise to doubts that plunged him into a profound personal crisis. If Maistre saw the Revolution as a satanically inspired project, Lamennais wondered whether such a momentous event might be more than a scourge sent to afflict sinful humanity. Perhaps it contained the divine spark itself? Perhaps it was an unprecedented opportunity? He had become alienated from both the Gallican Church, which he regarded as a self-serving racket, and the Bourbon regime, which he viewed as moribund whatever its outward air of piety. Revolt against these might not be impiety at all. Indeed, revolt might itself denote a quest for deeper truths beyond the nostrums of the day, and hence provide an opportunity for Christianity to flood back into an appetent society through the breaches in the edifice of throne and altar, Church and state, that had bound the Church too tightly with the merely temporal. Perhaps the People themselves were God? In the next chapter we can turn to the nineteenth-century world of 'chosen peoples', to the nation as a form of religion.

CHAPTER 5

Chosen Peoples: Political Messianism and Nationalism

I SPRINGTIME OF THE NATIONS

Christianity left its imprint on the political ideologies that stirred mankind in the modern era, most notably nationalism, the concern of this chapter, and socialism which is discussed in the following one. That both influenced how man imagined God, for in changing times God did not remain the celestial equivalent of a terrestrial absolute monarch, will also be developed in these two chapters.

Nationalism, the belief that the nation state represents the best arrangement to fulfil a human need for intense belonging, has so far proved to be the most potent of these ideologies, although it has been constantly challenged by doctrines (including Catholicism and socialism) that set greater store upon shared humanity. That does not mean that nationalism was antagonistic to the universal; indeed many early nationalists were highly cosmopolitan in outlook, and regarded the nations as like an ensemble of colourful flowers in a garden.

Nationalism was not simply a surrogate for Christianity, the religion of the overwhelming majority of Europeans a couple of centuries ago. These relationships were subtler than surrogacy suggests. The nineteenth-century creed of nationalism, as many of its apostles and disciples called it without any sense of irony, did not simply rise like a new building on the waste land to which secularisation had allegedly levelled traditional religious faith, for its history runs parallel with periods of de-Christianisation and re-Christianisation during that period.[1] Nationalism effortlessly incorporated some of the major themes of the Judaeo-

Christian tradition, including the notion of divine election, or the belief that a people had been chosen to fulfil a providential purpose, a notion that is alive and well in the universal values pursued by the United States, and for that matter in the allegedly gentler, less strident role which some Europeans view as their continent's post-imperial mission: the repository of softer values, after earlier nationalisms had eventuated in two disastrous wars and the Holocaust.[2]

While nationalism did not disturb the traditional religious beliefs of many people, for the elite minorities of nationalists their patriotic faith became analogous, depending on the depth and intensity of their commitment, to membership of an alternative Church, or in extreme cases worship of the nation as a God. The boundaries between these two forms of devotion could easily become blurred; the worst outcome was merely anticipated by intelligent commentators like Tocqueville or Burckhardt in the nineteenth century, before becoming all too luridly apparent in the twentieth century.

Nationalists would claim that intimations of nationhood, as of Christ, are always latent within us, but it took time for nationalist elites, using the power of the state, which replicated that earlier deployed by the Church, to diffuse their views among fellow citizens, or subjects, whose own views are largely a matter of guesswork. The latter's sense of belonging was probably either more parochial (the fate of most people) or, at the highest levels, among those with a sense of aristocratic caste, resistant to such narrow frontiers. In a process of education that in its enormous ambition and scope rivalled Europe's conversion to Christianity both in the Dark Ages and in the vernacular missions of the Reformation and Counter-Reformation, nationalists adapted religious exemplars, ranging from secular catechisms to images of St Joan of Arc, or sought to invest secular historical events and personalities, such as Garibaldi, with a vicarious sacredness that would have made the man himself whirr in his grave. The analogy with the missions of the Counter-Reformation clergy to eradicate popular paganism and superstition was explicit at the beginning of this process of nation-building during the French Revolution. As a Girondin put it in 1791: 'What the impostors did in the name of God and the King, so as to enslave minds and captivate men, you must do in the name of liberty and the patrie.' Why, another revolutionary asked in 1792, 'should we not do in the name of truth and freedom what [the priests] so often did in the name of error and slavery?'[3]

Attempts during the French Revolution to eradicate Catholicism in favour of a series of rationalist tableaux morts in primary colours were a failure. Yet the notion that states should have a common and unique religion remained pervasive, with Hegel, among others, arguing that such a religion 'expresses the innermost being of all people, so that all external and diffuse matters aside, they can find a common focus and, despite inequality and transformations in other spheres and conditions, are still able to trust and rely on each other'. Hegel is often traduced for saying that 'man must . . . venerate the state as a secular deity', whereas he had a high regard for codified laws, corporations and written constitutions.[4]

Among German nationalists, to whom we turn first, the search for a national religion was important, for, with the example of the biblical Jews in mind, many of them believed that such an ethno-religion gave a people cohesion, stamina and transcendental purpose. While there were always a few Teutomanes, who felt that the 'altars of Germany will only become truly German altars again when they are consecrated to Thor and Woden instead of the religion of the Cross, and when the Nordic Edda has replaced the Gospel', in practice that national religion was Protestantism rather than Wodenism, the henotheistic fetish of fanaticised individuals.

This does not mean that there were no Catholic nationalists, but rather that they were comparatively few on the ground in a country where being German increasingly meant being Protestant, and whose next step was for non-Christians to call themselves Protestants largely by dint of their liberal anti-Catholicism and a certain type of cultural affiliation.[5] Clearly there have been Catholic nationalists, but, as the examples of Ireland or Poland suggest, this is invariably a matter of religion being used as a useful auxiliary in their battle for national self-assertion.[6]

Christian universalism, like belief in the value of such supranational institutions as the papacy or Holy Roman Reich, was more apparent in Roman Catholicism than in its historic Protestant rivals, whose raison d'être was bound up with local defiance of the claims of the papacy and its lay supporters. Since Roman Catholics were primarily attached to the universal Church, they had difficulties in regarding the nation as the highest form of human community that God had established, something which they had in common with an Enlightenment belief in human universality, however much they may have despised and feared other aspects of that variegated project. German Protestant nationalists also sometimes traduced the Roman Catholic Church, which used Latin in worship, as being 'Jewish', in the sense of being an imitation of the 'state of the high priests', thereby revealing their own ambivalence towards the Jews as being exemplary in their Old Testament form but alien in the present. Like the Jews, Catholics were routinely suspected of dual allegiances, when they were not simply regarded as tools of Rome. The German chancellor Bismarck numbered Catholics as among the enemies of the German Reich, a 'black international' only marginally less menacing that the 'red international' of the socialists. Benefiting from the financial advice of a Jewish banker, he reserved his snideness towards the 'gold' international to private company. That such suspicions towards Catholics were not confined to Germany, or to the right of the political spectrum, can be seen from the French left-Republican Léon Gambetta's outburst: 'It is rare indeed for a Catholic to be a patriot,' sentiments that Bismarck would have been comfortable with, even as they would have seemed insane in Ireland or Poland.[7]

Since the popes were absolute rulers themselves, and supporters of absolutism elsewhere, they were hostile to a liberalism synonymous with belief in the absolute sovereignty of the people, equating both with a whole range of phenomena they deplored in the modern world. This was expressed at its most strident in Pius IX's December 1864 encyclical *Quanta Cura* and the accompanying *Syllabus* or Catalogue of Errors, although it is often overlooked that 'statism' was condemned among the beliefs that liberals professed. Modernity hit back with a rather unthinking triumphalism. Shortly after the new Italian nation state had captured Rome in 1870, a liberal newspaper crowed: 'The medieval world has fallen; the modern age stands resplendent on the ruins of the theocracy.'[8] The widely varying impact of industrialisation enabled liberal Protestants to identify themselves with material and scientific progress and Catholicism with atavistic backwardness, a constant feature of German dealings with the Poles, of British relations with Ireland, or indeed, within the Catholic camp, of northern Italian liberal attitudes towards the Mezzogiorno.[9]

Nationalisms do not have tidy starting points, as asserted by the late Elie Kedourie, in apparent ignorance of much medieval or early modern European history.[10] Nationalisms were rarely invented out of thin air, as those who wish to transcend them routinely claim, but were *constructed*, from a selection of pre-existing components, such as institutions, landscapes, language, law and, not least, local experience of the coming of

Christianity, as well as the more rehearsed areas of myth and memory, that compose peoples' historical identities. As Ernest Gellner argued, countries whose high culture and state formation had taken place at a relatively early date (such as Anglo-Saxon England, France or Spain) had highly developed national consciousnesses long before the anomie of the modern industrial world allegedly required integration through nationalism. A sense of English ethnic chosenness goes back to the time of the historian Bede and King Alfred in the eighth century, resurfacing in Protestant form during the Reformation, when a future bishop of London could confidently assert that 'God is English.' England's Celtic neighbours elaborated their own separate identities on the basis of lost daughters of the pharaoh or their unique experience of conversion to Christianity.[11] Elsewhere, where there was no such historic coincidence between culture and state, nationalists relied upon notions of dormition, to explain why an attachment they believed to be latent and universal in mankind was only awakened – a favourite nationalist image – after they themselves had kissed the national sleeping beauty or, rather, shaken her into sentience with a burst of nationalistic art, music, history and literature.

The emergence of a German nation was retarded by the fact that power was contested by, on the one hand, princely dynasts and high aristocrats, who regarded themselves as the embodiment of such a thing and, on the other hand, the longevity of the supranational Holy Roman Empire that straddled two continents. The Reformation and Counter-Reformation superimposed further deep confessional divisions. Patriotic sentiment was largely centrifugal, and focused upon individual dynastic territories, or such cities as Hamburg. The wars of Frederick the Great of Prussia, which devastated parts of Germany, stimulated a nationwide debate among educated people who began to realise that their 'national interests' were not necessarily synonymous with those of their princely rulers. An incipient national public emerged that read about national issues in publications whose titles invariably included the word 'German'. Quick to shed tears about the plight of Germany in the late eighteenth century, this public lacked clear political objectives, and was ignored by the rulers of Austria and Prussia, who in partitioning Poland made their polities less, rather than more, ethnically 'German'.[12] Parallel with these social and political developments were shifts in the religious sphere that also played a part in the emergence of German nationalism.

Seventeenth-century German Pietism influenced the Romantic cults of the self and of God being present in nature. Pietism meant a faith based on love of Christ rather than intellectual subscription to a creed. It was about the heart rather than the head.[13] Sweeping like a series of waves across the whole of northern Europe, including both Britain and Scandinavia, it was a reaction to the dusty dogmatism that had settled upon orthodox Lutheranism and the cold, rationalistic clockwork religion of the Deists. Its emphasis on emotion would hence make Germany very receptive to Romanticism. Pietism was democratic in that it celebrated the simple virtues of the common man and was resistant to any signs of social status, such as separate pews for the wellborn, in churches. Some Pietists withdrew into communities where they practised mystical community with God, removed from a sinful world; others engaged with that world through education and charity, the former indispensable to spreading an ability to read the Scriptures in the vernacular.

Pietism involved not just the individual's direct experience of God, but acknowledgement of God's presence in wider fellowships and communities. These included the family, church and nation, the units within which it was really possible for human beings to know each other. A sermon delivered in 1815 sentimentalised this intense feeling of belonging:

> When a man speaks of the fatherland, he includes in this idea everything he loves on earth: the bosom of his parents, his circle of brothers and sisters, the family altar, his childhood playgrounds, the dreams of his youth, the places of his education, his field of work, and those thousand bonds that link him with his fellow citizens, the same language, the same customs, the same nationality, the same common life, common names, common possessions, common renown, common welfare, common sorrows.[14]

This implicitly challenged the emptiness of the philosophes' concern with universal humanity. Pietism did not cease to be concerned with humanity as a whole, but it redefined how one might best serve it. 'To serve mankind is noble. But this is possible only when one is convinced of the value of one's own people.'[15] These were the words of the most influential Protestant theologian since Luther or Calvin. Friedrich Schleiermacher combined the Pietist emotionalism of his youth with intellectual powers of a very high order. He argued that 'The usual conception of God as one single being outside of the world and behind the world is not the beginning and the end of religion ... The true nature of religion is neither this idea nor any other, but immediate consciousness of the Deity as He is found in ourselves and in the world.' Religion is antecedent to beliefs and dogmas, rather consisting of 'a sense and taste for the Infinite', that is the underlying unity of the universe as a whole. By emphasising the disposition towards rather than the content of faith, Schleiermacher gave a sophisticated theological underpinning to a diffuse religiosity that was relevant wherever a people experienced a deep sense of community. But there was also a more explicitly political message.

States, he argued, were natural entities whose borders should be contiguous with that of the nation as a whole. Nations possessed both distinctive characters and common destines; immoderate immigration was undesirable: 'every nation, my friends, which has developed to a certain height is degraded by receiving into it a foreign element, even though that may be good in itself'.[16] This intense desire for belonging encountered a parallel process of arousing the dormant Volk against an erstwhile liberator turned oppressor.

Pietism contributed to a spiritual climate in which such collectives as the nation became vehicles of intensified worship, but it was hardly the sole source of nationalist ideology. Acute conflict and latent resentment helped define a sense of national difference, which had independent moorings, in this case specifically the 'German' Protestant Reformation, around which it might cluster, rather in the way that Shakespeare's brand of Elizabethan patriotism had a hundred years of Anglo-French conflict to work with.

Decades before revolutionary or Napoleonic armies embarked on their democratically despotic rampage, French cultural hegemony was resented, although this did not entail demands for the replacement of the dynastic patchwork with a modern unitary nation state. Nowadays the French are to the fore in protesting about the deleterious impact of 'Anglo-Saxon' globalisation upon francophone culture. Two hundred years ago French culture was the object of burning resentment on the part of provincial literati whose route to fame and fortune was blocked by a cosmopolitan, francophone, elite that dominated both the ancien régime courts and the major metropolitan centres, from whence its influence leeched into the provinces. The French language, like English today, seemed disturbingly pervasive: 'This language, used in diplomacy, spoken in many German towns, in Italy, in the Low Countries, in part of the country around Liège, in Luxembourg, in Switzerland, even in Canada and on the banks of the Mississippi, by what mischance is it still unknown to a very large number of the French?'[17]

French had strong support at the most august levels. When in 1743 Frederick the Great restored the Berlin Academy, as the Académie Royale des Sciences et Belles-Lettres de Prusse, he appointed the French mathematician Maupertius as its first president, and when he died replaced him with the French philosopher d'Alembert. The Academy's proceedings and publications were in French. When in 1777 the comte de Montmorency-Laval told the king of his keenness to learn German, the Prussian monarch told him not to bother since nothing of any consequence had been published in that language. Famously he used German only to talk to servants.[18] The ascendancy of French beyond France had its ludicrous aspects. A Pietist preacher recommended how to address young noblemen who had been to France for their education, the italicised words liberally sprinkled amid German being the pretentious borrowings from French: 'Monsieur, als ein braver Cavalier thu mir doch die plaisir, und visitir mich auf meinem Logier; ich will ihn mit Poculieren nicht importunieren, sondern ihn dimittieren, sobald er mirs wird imperiren.'[19] The early nationalist ideologue Ernst Moritz Arndt recalled German farmers conversing in Pomeranian backwaters:

> Scraps of French were thrown in, too, every now and then, and I remember my amusement when I began to learn the language, at recognizing the 'fladrun' (flacon) as Fraulein B— used to call her water bottle, and the Wun Schur (bonjour) and à la Wundor (à la bonne heure!) and similar flourishes with which on their rides, the huntsmen and farmers used to greet one another when they wished to be particularly elegant.[20]

One consequence of such cultural resentments was the cosmopolitan nationalism of the Lutheran clergyman and philosopher Johann Gottfried Herder, himself deeply influenced by Pietism and Rousseau. Herder thought that religion could dispense with reason and be reconstructed on the basis of feeling. Knowledge of God could be attained through consciousness of belonging to the whole. Most of the great German late-eighteenth-century writers and philosophers, including Goethe, Kant, Lessing and Schiller, were cosmopolitans who found nationalism narrowly vulgar and unattractive.

Herder was a cosmopolitan too, but for him the route to the general good of humanity lay through the intensely local rather than vapid subscription to universal principles. Herder doubted whether the whole of human history had been simply anticipatory of the wit of Voltaire, the epitome of all that was shallowly sparkling, rather than profoundly slow-burning, in the French Enlightenment. In his revulsion for the desiccated rationalism and superficial wit of the philosophes, Herder became an exponent of luxuriant diversity, with each people, regardless of its stage of development, important in the eyes of a God who had separated each nation by immutable laws planted in each human heart. An Eskimo or Mongol was as worthy of respect as the most sophisticated Parisian. Echoing Pietism's enthusiasm for the common man, Herder claimed that a nation's authentic culture was not that of the deracinated cosmopolitan elites, but that of plain people as reflected in their indigenous folksongs which he collected. These vernacular songs were important because language was God-given, 'the organ of our soul-forces', and expressed a nation's character, again something he had probably picked up from Rousseau, who had campaigned on behalf of earthy Italian operas against the formal classicism of the French court composer Rameau. In a profound sense, individual languages were untranslatable since they encapsulated each nation's spirit. Herder's views were hardly chauvinistic, because in rejecting the Cartesian rationalism inherent in use of French he indirectly enabled Germans to appreciate the merits of, say, Cervantes and Shakespeare, geniuses largely ignored by the French.[21] Herder's disciple Wilhelm Heinrich Wackenröder also helped promote recognition of the authentic beauties of early music or such gothic masterpieces as Bamberg and Naumburg cathedrals.

There was a political aspect to Herder's cultural ruminations. As the ideal medium between individual and humanity, nations were the means whereby the individual achieved fulfilment, their flourishing the route by which humanity would achieve perfection too. The different peoples were like flowers in a vast garden:

> We should rejoice, like Sultan Suleiman, that there are such varied flowers and peoples on the great meadow of this earth, that such different blossoms can bloom on both sides of the alps, and that such varied fruits can ripen. Let us rejoice that Time, the great mother of all things, throws now these and now other gifts from her horn of plenty and slowly builds up mankind in all its different component parts.

According to Herder, each people had a creative soul whose mission was to fulfil itself as a self-aware nation, the blossoming profusion of these individual plants being the fulfilment of God's plan.[22]

Unlike philosophers, and before the age of the schoolmaster, clergymen had a virtual monopoly on large gatherings where they could mobilise patriotic fervour through their sermons. If incipient nationalisms seem suffused with religion this was often because pastors (and, in Catholic Europe, priests) played a vital role in their transmission, giving them moral and spiritual accents that resonated at a time when Christianity seemed under attack by the militant Jacobin godless. For what had begun as a widely admired experiment in regarding the nation as the ultimate source of sovereignty, had degenerated into terror and foreign conquest, followed by a military despotism that skilfully exploited the new notion of nationhood in order to pursue classical dynastic imperial ambitions.[23]

This reaction was as evident in Roman Catholic countries occupied by the French as in Protestant northern Europe. The ways in which religion assumed a distinctly nationalistic edge were evident in a Spanish 'Civil Catechism' that was so potent that the erratic Romantic dramatist Heinrich von Kleist produced a German version. The prototype appeared in 1808, the handiwork of Catholic clergy who played a prominent part in the guerrilla war that Spanish people of all stripes and classes waged against the French usurper Joseph and his local francophile clients:

Q. 'Tell me, child, who art thou?'
A. 'A Spaniard.'
Q. 'What does that mean? A Spaniard?'
A. 'An honest man.'
Q. 'How many duties hath such a man?'
A. 'Three: he must be a Catholic Christian, he must defend his religion, his fatherland and its laws and die, rather than allow himself to be oppressed.'
Q. 'Who is our King?'
A. 'Ferdinand the Seventh.'
Q. 'By what manner of love shall we be bound to him?'
A. 'By the love that his virtue and his misfortune deserve.'
Q. 'Who is the enemy of our happiness?'
A. 'The Emperor of the French.'
Q. 'Who, then, is he?'

A. 'A new, infinitely bloodthirsty and rapacious monarch, the beginning of all evil, the end of all good: the essence of all vice and malice.'

Q. 'How many natures hath he?'

A. 'Two: a satanic and a human nature.'

Q. 'Who are the French?'

A. 'Former Christians and present heretics.'

Q. 'What hath led them into their new servitude?'

A. 'False philosophy and the licence of their corrupted morals . . .'

Q. 'Shall this unrighteous regime soon pass away?'

A. 'The opinion of those sages who understand politics is that its fall is close at hand.'[24]

Napoleon's conquests similarly gave a spur to the nationalisation of religion in Germany where Protestantism was swept by the great wave of Pietist subjectivism, one aspect of which was to ascribe divine attributes to the nation. Rather than competing, or succeeding one another, Protestant clergy and nationalist tribunes met halfway, when they were not one and the same persons, for the politicisation of religion paralleled the sacralisation of politics, and the pastors and theologians themselves played an important role as tribunes of the people.[25]

The circumstances that saw stirrings of German national consciousness could not have been less propitious, perhaps most starkly symbolised by the execution by the French of a Nuremberg bookseller for purveying a pamphlet entitled *Germany in its Deepest Humiliation*. Napoleon annexed large tracts of north-western Germany and reduced the states of central Germany to clients and satellites. Austria and Prussia suffered humiliating defeats. Napoleonic hegemony provoked different responses among German patriots: a conservative, Christian and anti-Enlightenment patriotism that sought to restore the status quo, and a no less anti-French but reformist patriotism that sought to modernise the German states along French lines, and to mobilise the population in the manner that the French themselves had so successfully pioneered. Under the influence of prominent reformers, both Austria and Prussia attempted to mobilise popular resistance to the Corsican Prometheus with appeals to German patriotism, although these forces were potentially liable to detach themselves from loyalties to dynastic states that were nervous of popular forces or subject to the enormous pressure that

Napoleon could bring to bear. There was a popular anti-French, and anti-Bavarian, rising in the Tyrol. A German legion wrought havoc across northern Germany and then went to fight against Napoleon in Spain. And finally, disappointed with the paralysed inanition of the Prussian king, leading generals and reformers, including Boyen, Clausewitz, Gneisenau and Stein, defected to the Russians in 1812 to form a further anti-Napoleonic German Legion. Following the failure of Napoleon's 1812 invasion of Russia, German patriots rose up against French occupation, a rising that the reluctant Prussian monarch eventually endorsed. Frederick William III had few alternatives since even marshal Blücher, the nemesis of Napoleon at Waterloo, warned that if the princes opposed an armed national uprising, 'they should be hunted away together with Bonaparte'.[26] Not the least of the accomplishments of the clear-eyed Austrian conservative Metternich was to see that this patriotic movement was keener on domestic constitutional reform than on creating a unified Germany, and hence that the sooner the struggle against Napoleon reverted to being a conventional cabinet conflict the better for the dynasties concerned.

Although the contribution of patriotic forces to the outcome of the wars against Napoleon was marginal, the impetus these wars gave to nationalism in Germany was unmistakable, not least in providing the first patriotic martyrs and a founding example of how future patriots should ideally conduct themselves. There was a religious dimension to this that deserves not to be overlooked. Clergy and theologians played a significant part in investing the nation with sacred properties. Schleiermacher espoused the view that the individual only attained his highest ethical potential through the nation, although it took many disillusioning experiences for him to identify the latter with Germany rather than with Prussia. What seemed like rather academic concerns in his earliest writings became somewhat more visceral under the impact of grim personal experience. In October 1806 the young university chaplain was caught up in fighting between French and Prussian troops to control the main bridge over the Saale in Halle. He was robbed of his paltry savings, his shirts and his watch by French troops who crashed into his lodgings; when the French closed the university, he was plunged into abject poverty.[27]

In sermons delivered in November 1806 Schleiermacher explained to his worried auditors in French-occupied Halle that God directed the destinies of nations, allowing misfortunes to happen so that the nation might achieve a higher goal. Schleiermacher himself joined a nationalist secret society, the Charlottenburger Verein, even acting as a secret courier in 1808 to tsar Alexander I so as to glean intelligence on whether the latter was about to renew his war with France. He used a code for correspondence in which Napoleon figured as 'the dear man'.

Other Protestant clergy similarly endeavoured to give catastrophic defeat higher meaning by blaming the victims of foreign aggression. As clergymen they were irresistibly drawn to the theme of the moral laxity of the defeated rather than to the superiority of French generals and soldiers. Since depravity invariably meant excessive individualism and selfishness, the answer was to rediscover a community that they construed in moral, national and religious terms, with the caveat that national could as easily be focused on one particular state, such as Prussia, as on the German nation as a whole.

History was scoured for instances where something positive had resulted from utterly unpropitious circumstances; natural occurrences could also be pressed into their reading of events. A large comet that passed over northern Europe in the autumn of 1812 heralded the annus mirabilis of Napoleon's retreat from Russia that winter and the Allied victory outside Leipzig the following summer. The ebb and flow of fortunes on the battlefield were directed by a higher power who in the hands of Arndt became the 'German God' battling the 'French Devil':

> But God looked down from
> His heavenly height into the crush of battle
> He spoke the judgement of vengeance
> Today fall, false dragon!
> Prevail today, cause righteous!
> Rejoice today, German victory!
> The French fell,
> the false, the disloyal . . .
> and the poisonous serpent fled'.[28]

God had even summoned the inclement weather:

> The Lord who does wonders commanded and violent cold took hold of the tormentor of nations with his hapless hirelings. Hunger and sickness wasted his innumerable troops just as the angel of death did to the troops of Sennacherib, just as flame

destroys dry grass. He was delivered like a defenceless piece of booty into the hands of the enemy pursuing him with righteous vengeance.

If God had sent the snows and icy winds in late 1812, reducing Napoleon's mighty invasion force to a battered remnant, He had blessed Germany with such an abundant harvest in 1813 that it had sustained huge Allied armies long enough to inflict a crushing defeat on the Corsican. Moreover, God had miraculously fostered unity among Napoleon's enemies as well as public spirit among their hitherto apathetic, quiescent and selfish peoples. The nation began to override lesser loyalties, to dynasty, family, region, town and so forth: 'Lift up your eyes and behold an invisible inward power that drives your youth to the weapons. The lament of the mother cannot hold back the only son, or the supplications of the bride the betrothed. The voice of the heart calls them into the tumult of battle to fulfil the scripture, "Whoever loves father or mother more than me is not worthy of me".' The individual was to dedicate himself to the national community, ready, if need be, to make the ultimate sacrifice – martyrdom on the altar of the fatherland. As the poet Körner put it: 'Drauf, wackres Volk! ... Was kümmern dich die Hügel deiner Leichen?' (Onwards and upwards, brave nation! ... Why do the mounds of your dead perturb you?).

Once it was accepted that nations were as essential to the divine plan as the family or monarchy, a view encouraged by belief in divine immanence, then the rather glaring contradiction between love of one's own kind and the universal love of the Gospels became more apparent than real. One could only appreciate the virtues of other peoples once certain of the virtues of one's own Volk. As Schleiermacher explained:

> Would we charge the failings of the lovers to the weakness of love itself? Let us rather all the more affirm that the person who is not filled with the worth of his own people and clings to it with love, will not appreciate these things in another ... And the person who is not enlightened with the calling of his own people knows not the mission characteristic of other peoples.[29]

If 'nationhood' was hard to discover in the Gospels, the Old Testament was scoured for analogies between ancient Israel and the German Chosen People of the present, a practice that in England and elsewhere had been common a thousand years before. Nationalist prophets, many conscious of the parallel implicit in that epithet, interpreted the past and present of a nation, defined in terms of culture, language and religion within that Old Testament template.[30] This did not resolve the problem of exactly where the German nation was. The poet Schenkendorf saw it everywhere and nowhere, in church spires, fields, hills, woods and so forth. Goethe, who despised the nationalist (and Romantic) enthusiasms of other writers, gave this his own gloss when he wrote that 'the fatherland is nowhere and everywhere'. Arndt tried geography and then switched to putative national characteristics within a Manichaean framework:

> What is the German's Fatherland?
> Is it Prussia? Is it Swabia?
> Is it where the vine flourishes in the Rhineland? . . .
> O no, no!
> His Fatherland must be greater!

> What is the German's Fatherland?
> Where a handshake seals an oath,
> when loyalty shines from bright eyes,
> and love sits warmly in hearts –
> That shall be it!
> That, valiant German, call your own.

> That is the German Fatherland
> Where wrath destroys Latin frivolity,
> Where every Frenchman is called foe
> Where every German is called friend –
> That shall it be!
> The whole of Germany shall it be.

> The whole of Germany shall it be!
> O heavenly God look below
> and give us true German courage
> that we love it truly and well
> That shall it be!
> The whole of Germany shall it be![31]

Schleiermacher may have insisted that patriotism was distinguishable from chauvinism, but the passions of the age sometimes made this distinction difficult for others to sustain. Arndt devised a political catechism based on hate: 'I hate all the French without exception in the name of God and my people . . . I teach my son this hatred. I will work to the end of my days to ensure that this deprecation and hatred strikes the deepest roots in German hearts.'[32] The wars of liberation ceased to be about specific military objectives, becoming instead a crusade or holy war, fought by men with iron crosses on their caps, against the powers of darkness.

Cartoonists depicted Napoleon as the devil. In one cartoon, Napoleon and three marshals arrive in hell, where the welcoming devil invites the emperor to ascend a throne made up of the bones of Napoleon's victims. In another, entitled 'This is my dear son in whom I am most pleased', the Devil cradles a child–man who is unmistakably Napoleon and whose swaddling clothes consist of the tricolour.[33] Patriotic songwriters invested the war with eschatological purpose:

> Then this war is certainly
> like no other war:
> Here light battles darkness,
> Truth struggles with lies;
> Here God himself appears
> to tie down the Devil;
> That's what the war means
> which we fight at the moment.

One feature of the wars against Napoleon across Europe was the role played by irregulars and volunteers. In Germany this involved twenty-five thousand men, of whom a mere 5 per cent were students. Their military contribution was immaterial to battles fought by hundreds of thousands of professional soldiers whose motivation was less frothy. Romanticised by the raucous chorus of pastors and professors of the time and by their successors, the popular contribution to the wars of liberation assumed a life of its own, just as the poetry, songs and slogans that urged 'the German nation' into battle endured beyond the immediate struggle against Napoleon. These were not sentiments that rulers could turn on and off at will; indeed they would return throughout the century to haunt those who imagined they could easily be exploited.

In addition to giving full throttle to his hatred of the French, sentiments which were neither exclusive to Germans nor especially novel, Arndt let slip the advanced conviction that:

To be a nation, to have one feeling for one cause, to come together with the bloody sword of revenge, is the religion of our times. Leave all the little religions and perform the great duty to the single highest, and unite yourselves in it to one belief high above the Pope or Luther. That is the ultimate religion, to hold the Fatherland more dearly than lords and princes, than father and mother, than wives and children.

Others agreed even if they regarded this outpouring of patriotic devotion in a rather different light from Arndt. Reporting to Louis XVIII on events in Germany, Talleyrand said that for young people the unification of Germany had become 'their cry, their doctrine, their religion, carried even to fanaticism'.[34] Of course, while Arndt urged the Germans to transcend their confessional differences, thereby implicitly reducing the importance of their respective Churches, he was not suggesting they substitute nationalism for Christianity. But, once minds turned to fleshing out how such a national religion might look, some swam dangerously into the orbit of the French revolutionary civic cults. One ended up advocating worship of flags and cannons.

The Berlin philosopher Fichte had welcomed the French Revolution for its enthronement of the rights of the individual. Paralleling the evolutions of Rousseau, he began to regard civil, or collective, freedom as more valuable, arguing that no German could be free until all Germans had achieved their national liberation by forming a self-sufficient nation state liberated from international commerce and in which foreign travel would be the preserve of the few.[35]

Fichte also envisaged a future national Church consisting of an ever growing number of 'general Christians' whose 'fourth denomination' would eventually be a requirement for citizenship in any future German state:

> On Sunday morning ... when all parishioners have arrived, the church doors are thrown open and amid soft music the congregation enters ... When all are seated the great curtains at the altar are drawn aside, revealing the cannon, muskets, and other weapons which constitute the parish armoury. For every German youth from his twentieth birthday to his death is a soldier. Then there appears before the congregation the justice of the peace, who unfurls the flag ...[36]

The idea of nationhood had to be propagated beyond the elites who were its initial supporters, at a time when multinational dynastic states were inherently conservative, and hostile to a creed that was largely coterminous with liberalism or Jacobin radicalism. The ruling dynasties were not the only conservatives who failed to be attracted to these novel doctrines. When in 1846 Polish noblemen essayed a nationalist uprising in Austrian Galicia, they were tracked down and killed by peasants who doggedly considered themselves to be 'Austrian' or 'imperial' subjects, the only 'Poles' being the feudal landlords whom they murdered. In other words, a doctrine that was racy with the notion of 'the people' generally represented but a narrow segment of them. That was the nub of the problem.[37]

Nationalism was heavily reliant upon self-dramatisation, or at least the willingness of people to confuse what they felt in the present with artistic renditions of selected highlights from the past. But, away from the art gallery, historical novel and the operatic stage, it was customarily propagated in contexts where the only drama was the occasional cough or polite interjection. Clubs and societies (where shared curiosity and common commitment played a greater role than distinctions of class) were where national consciousness and enthusiasm were forged and propagated. They provided the institutional focus that Christianity derived from Churches, although the Churches themselves were vehicles for the propagation of nationalist doctrines. Some of these associations were professional organisations that brought together booksellers, farmers, doctors, Germanists and scientists from across the cultural nation. Only radical students provided an added frisson of radical subversion and the conceit that these ideas represented 'the future'.

In medieval universities students had been grouped in nations that were broader than any categories that would seem coherent to us today. The first 'Burschenschaft' for students from all regional backgrounds was founded at the University of Jena in June 1815: 'the students are as one: they all belong to a single region, that of Germany'. Student societies rapidly proliferated, constituting a nationwide student state, although no more than a fifth of students ever belonged to them, and students from Catholic regions were significantly under-represented. Many of the societies excluded unbaptised Jews who formed their own societies. Politically, the societies espoused the values of 'honour, freedom and fatherland', adopting as their colours the red, black and gold flag of the Lützow volunteers during the wars of liberation. A more radical fringe at the universities of Giessen and Jena was prepared to countenance violence and terror to achieve their objectives. This resulted in the assassination of an official and a much hated writer, August Kotzebue, who reported on student activists to the Russian government, providing Metternich with a welcome pretext to clamp down on the universities.[38]

Patriotic festivals provided an opportunity for nationalists to inflate the scale of their support in a very public manner. In mid-October 1817 the Jena Burschenschaft brought together 468 students at the Wartburg fortress to celebrate the tercentenary of the Reformation and the recent victory over Napoleon at Leipzig. No invitations were sent to Catholic student societies, so as to spare their sensitivities regarding the heretical Luther, but 4 per cent of the participants were Catholics. Festival participants commemorated the Reformation not for correcting ecclesiastical abuses, but as the beginning of intellectual and spiritual freedom, which was the precondition for the contemporary political uprising against Napoleon, the result of a religious patriotism that had united Germans into the nation as Church. Patriotic piety had been transformed into religious patriotism, with the nation itself elevated into something sacred. Prior to the opening of the festivities, the students indulged in burning symbols of reaction and, indeed, so-called reactionary books. A Catholic priest remonstrated with them: 'The founder of the Christian religion obviously did not intend a national but a universal religion which embraces all people, empires, states and individuals.'[39] Where that national religion might tend was all too evident in a speech by Jakob Friedrich Fries with his wild cries of 'One God, a German sword, a German spirit for honour and justice!' In private Fries doubted whether that religion would be Christianity, whose emphasis on peace and penance was hard to reconcile with his desire for a religion that would be 'intolerant and addicted to conversion in the highest degree, as soon as it gains a feeling of its strength'.[40] No wonder that Jewish observers of the Wartburg festival, including those whose books the students had burned, thought that Protestantism came second best to Catholicism in terms of cosmopolitanism and openness to universal education.[41]

In addition to student societies, there were other forms of association for people of a nationalist persuasion, although membership was rarely incompatible with social self-aggrandisement. Unlike Catholicism where worshippers uttered spoken responses to a priest who mediated God's presence, Protestant worship revolved around communal hymn-singing. Choral societies sang the patriotic anthems of the wars of liberation.

Sharp-shooting clubs enabled men to hone their military skills while providing a forum in which to talk and drink beer or wine. Finally, gymnastic associations fostered a military esprit de corps among young men, whose co-ordinated wholesomeness was supposed to be emblematic of the emergent nation. A more cosmopolitan utopian version of this survives in the Olympic Games.[42]

The pietist teacher 'Turnvater' Jahn took his pupils twice a week to fields and woods in Berlin. He selected a core group, who from 1811 onwards began to meet regularly on the city's Hasenheide to use a range of rudimentary gymnastic equipment such as a vaulting horse that looked more like a cow. Jahn played a prominent role in opposition to Napoleon, helping to form – and becoming an officer of – the Lützow volunteer corps. He was instrumental in establishing both the student societies and the Wartburg festival. Jahn's pupils helped form gymnastic societies in other parts of the country. There were around twelve thousand gymnasts organised throughout Germany when gymnastics were banned in the wake of Kotzebue's murder. Jahn himself was arrested in June 1819; after several years' confinement in various fortresses, he was forbidden even to set foot in towns with a university.[43]

II SECRET SOCIETIES

Burgeoning associational life provided a framework for incipient nationalist enthusiasm not just in Germany. The Italian states had been transformed during the Revolutionary and Napoleonic Wars. Between 1809 and 1814 their political geography was drastically simplified: the French annexed the north-west and centre; the north-east became an Italian kingdom and the south was subsumed into a kingdom of Naples. The earlier work of Italian enlightened despots was continued and extended by the introduction of moderate representative governments, something the French never achieved at home. When the old order was restored, those Italians who had benefited from the rule of Napoleon or his Italian clients were edged aside by restored or returned adherents of the old regime, regardless of whether they lacked the former's merits or talents. These resentments were compounded by the fact that the regimes of Restoration Italy depended on Austrian military power to suppress domestic liberals.

Opposition political activity was confined to secret societies that had mutated out of the various strands of freemasonry, to the extent that they were no longer necessarily synonymous with anticlericalism. This was almost certainly wise since the various popular anti-Jacobin revolts in Italy had partly been inspired by Catholic revulsion towards the impiety of the French and their bourgeois Jacobin collaborators. The most serious of these revolts, that of the Sanfedisti in Italy's Deep South, had been led by a cardinal. Secret societies of a politically liberal hue were the handiwork of disillusioned Jacobins or young army officers disgruntled by the despotism of Napoleon. The name of the largest sect became generic: the Carbonari or charcoal burners.[44]

Their inspiration derived from French officers already familiar with such societies in the Jura, which met in forests because virtue had allegedly a better chance of being preserved there than in the towns and cities. The transforming powers of heat and light on wood were central to their rituals, as were such Christian symbols as the crown of thorns, the path of Calvary, and – for those who attained the highest grades – symbolic crucifixion and receipt of the stigmata. The initiates belonged to cells, arranged in a pyramidal structure that could constitute a parallel government.

The earliest secret society was that of Naples, founded before 1810, followed by others in Bologna, Lombardy and Piedmont. Members included doctors, lawyers, students, small property-owners, and civil servants and officers who had served the Napoleonic regime but who now lacked a job. They had no common programme, for in Rome the Carbonari sought to introduce rule by laymen; in Sicily they wanted to expel the ruling Neapolitans; in the north the Piedmontese wanted a liberal constitution; some of the conspirators were liberal monarchists; others militant republicans. When they and a wider penumbra of constitutional liberals essayed revolutions in Naples and Piedmont in 1820–1, without either international or popular support, these were crushed by Austria.[45]

Only where cultural affinity and religion complicated the sympathies of the major powers and educated opinion did secret societies stand much chance of success. Greece was a case in point for Orthodox Christianity bound Greece to Russia, while even the most conservative statesmen, otherwise not inclined to sympathise with revolution against legitimate sovereigns, had had a classical and Christian education. Metternich was the conspicuous exception, wishing that the Greek revolt would 'burn itself out beyond the pale of European civilisation'.

Eighteenth-century Greece was part of the Ottoman Empire; its elites – including the senior Orthodox clergy – were deeply embedded in the corruption that typified Ottoman rule. Greek patriots identified two factors that inhibited Greek nationhood: 'the two reasons, o my dear Greeks, why up to now we are bound with the fetters of tyranny, are the ignorant priesthood and the absence abroad of the best of our fellow countrymen'. There were two important figures in late-eighteenth-century Greek nationalism, both of whom spent years exiled abroad. The classical scholar Adhamántios Koraís sought to strip the Greek language of Byzantine (meaning Orthodox) and Ottoman accretions so as to regenerate the ancient Greeks allegedly lurking within the hoary bandits and wily traders of his present; a Hellenised Vlach, Rigas Velestinlis, became the first major modern Greek martyr when in 1798 another Greek betrayed this would-be revolutionary tyro of the Balkans to the ruling Turks, who murdered him. One of his songs, 'Thourios', became a Greek revolutionary anthem.

Beyond the mainland and its thousands of islands, Greece consisted of a large mercantile diaspora operating in the Balkans, Mediterranean, Black Sea and as far afield as India. Greek merchants and shipowners thrived during the Revolutionary Wars, sending their sons to universities in western Europe, where they imbibed the ideas of the Enlightenment, French Revolution and romantic nationalism. What Ernest Gellner dubbed these 'heresies within Christendom' gave an ideological edge to what otherwise constituted an attempt to replace the Ottoman Empire with a neo-Byzantium, or, less fancily, a traditional revolt on the part of peripheral bandits and tribesmen.[46]

In 1814 three minor Greek merchants in Odessa founded a pan-Greek association, the Philiki Etairia, or Friendly Society, whose object was to liberate Greece and the rest of the Balkan peoples. For a secret society, modelled on freemasonry, its inner workings are remarkably well known. Membership was by co-option. Postulants were obliged to take oaths of successive nationalist specificity before a priest and then over a holy icon. The Great Oath included the following passages:

> I swear that I will nourish in my heart undying hatred towards the tyrants of my country, their followers and those who think like them, I want to carry out in all ways damage towards them and, when circumstances permit, their complete ruination . . .
> I swear to you, O holy and wretched Motherland! I swear by

your long years of suffering. I swear by the bitter tears which your wretched children have shed for such centuries! By my own tears, which flow at this minute! To the future freedom of my compatriots I dedicate all myself to you! In the future you will be the cause and object of my thoughts, your name the guide of my actions and your happiness the reward of my efforts! Let divine justice empty over my head all the thunderbolts of its justice, let my name be held in contempt and myself be the object of the curse of anathema of my compatriots, if I should forget for one moment their misfortunes and if I do not fulfil my duty and let death be the inevitable punishment for my sin, so as not to defile the sanctity of the Society with my participation.

The Society had a catechism which was used to initiate differing grades of member. The lowest grade, who like most Greeks were illiterate, were called the Brothers. One rung higher up were the Associates who could read and write. Next up were the Priests, who could recruit to their own or a lower level, and then the Shepherds, who were distinguished by exceptional learning or wealth. The highest level were called the Invisible Directorate (the arkhi). As the name suggests, they were unknown to anyone else and were designated by letter codes such as AB, AD, AG, AH and so on. All members were expected to make financial contributions. They included members of the professions, merchants, students, clergy and a smattering of artisans.[47]

The opportunity for revolt came when the Turks were diverted by the defection of the Albanian Ali Pasha of Janina, a warlord in the Napoleonic mode, who ruled most of mainland Greece on behalf of the Ottomans. This gave the Greeks their chance. In line with mythical expectations that deliverance would come from the north, military leadership devolved upon an ethnic Greek, Alexander Ypsilantis, a one-armed former Russian army general who began by trying to provoke a general Balkan revolt. This ran into difficulties when the Bulgars, Romanians and Serbs, who were ruled by Greek hospodars, showed no inclination to make common cause with compatriots of their own overlords. There was a further problem. The tsar's concern for Orthodox Christians under Ottoman rule was counterbalanced by his fear of revolution which had come dangerously close to home in the shape of the Decembrist Rising. Metternich ensured that the latter concern proved dominant, obliging the tsar to disown Ypsilantis, who on fleeing the Balkans fell into Austrian hands. He died seven years later shortly after being released from jail. Another national hero was born.[48]

A more extensive Greek uprising occurred in the Morea, that is Greece south of the Corinth isthmus, which resulted in the massacre of thousands of Turks. Rumours abounded of nefarious plots to cause mayhem in Istanbul itself. The Ottomans reacted with savagery, hanging the Greek Orthodox patriarch Grigorios V outside the patriarchate gates on Easter Sunday 1821. This took time since the ascetic patriarch was not a heavy man. His body was left hanging as an obstruction in the doorway, before, by way of further insult, Jews were co-opted to drag his body through the blood and offal of a marketplace before tossing him into the Bosphorus. Sailors retrieved the patriarch's corpse so that he eventually received a more dignified interment in Odessa. Ironically, the patriarchs had denounced rebellion against the Ottomans in the most unambiguous terms, using 'political verse' to inculcate the need for obedience to the secular power, whosoever that might be. Despite anathemas, Grigorios V had not been able to make his own bishops and clergy toe the traditional line, which meant that as far as the Ottomans were concerned the patriarch had broken a solemn contract – toleration in return for submission – and hence his life was automatically forfeit. On 18 April the preceding patriarch and eight other clergy were executed in Adrianople. In May 1821 the Cypriot prelates were all hanged while the hundred-year-old bishop of Mirioupolis was beheaded, followed by all the remaining bishops of Constantinople. Up to ten thousand clerics and monks were murdered during the ten-year war of independence, while innumerable churches were destroyed and great libraries pillaged.[49]

These actions appalled opinion throughout Europe, Russia and the United States of America, some of whose educated classes temporarily mistook the gnarled Greeks for the marble busts that had survived Periclean Athens. So-called Greek committees, including some in the United States, provided the Greeks with the material wherewithal to fight, while Philhellenic volunteers, including the poets Byron and Pushkin, endeavoured to support the Greeks on the ground. Among those peoples who had not achieved nationhood themselves, such as the Germans, Irish, Italians, Poles and Scots, the struggles by the Greeks for freedom were a surrogate war fought while they awaited their own deliverance.[50]

In 1821 and 1822 the Greeks scored several victories on land and sea, their own less than savoury way with captives, amply demonstrated at the siege of Tripolis, being eclipsed by such Turkish enormities as the massacre on Chios that the artist Delacroix turned into an icon of the travails of national liberation struggles. By January 1822 a national assembly had proclaimed Greek independence. Three years later the Ottoman sultan Mahmud II was forced to rely upon the armies of the Egyptian usurper Mehmet Ali and his son Ibrahim Pasha, who from his base on Crete reconquered the islands and then the mainland Morea. One of the last places to fall to Ibrahim's army was the fortress of Missolonghi, where, following the failure of a massed breakout, the besieged Greeks blew themselves up. The Turkish habit of consigning captives to slavery, and the rumour that Ibrahim Pasha was planning to exterminate the Greeks and replace them with Muslim colonists from North Africa, prompted Britain, France and Russia to bring matters to a head by insisting that the Ottomans cede Greece a large measure of autonomy. Although the three powers wanted to mediate rather than intervene, in October 1827 an Allied force under a British admiral sank the Egyptian–Turkish fleet at Navarino, killing four thousand men in what was the last major battle fought by ships under sail. While the new Prime Minister Wellington apologised for the inadvertence of this occurrence, tsar Nicholas I pressed ahead with a war against the Turks that was nominally designed to force them to a settlement with the Greeks. By late 1829 Russian armies were ensconced in the Balkans and on the peripheries of Constantinople. At a conference in London in early 1830, England, France and Russia guaranteed what was recognised as an independent Greek kingdom, although it took three goes before a seventeen-year-old Bavarian prince ascended the throne as Otto I. The majority of Greeks, however, remained under Ottoman rule, for the British had insisted on a truncated and weak polity, to minimise its strategic utility to its Russian patron. Their first president, Ioannis Kapodistrias, was assassinated in October 1831 after trying to impose some semblance of order upon factions that had coalesced only to overthrow the Turks.

If the Greek struggle for independence bore fruit in 1831, both Poland and Ireland were the paradigmatic martyr nations, seemingly eternally denied self-realisation by their respective grim masters, who in Poland's case were three rather than one. Following the last partition of Poland by Austria, Prussia and Russia in 1795, independent Polish statehood ceased to exist. This alone inclined many Poles towards revolutionary France as their saviour from foreign absolutist monarchies. Napoleon, for whom so many Poles loyally fought, created a Grand Duchy of Warsaw from what had mostly been Prussian Poland. After 1815 the Great Powers were prepared to tolerate the westward expansion of Russia, provided tsar Alexander I ceded a degree of autonomy and freedom to what was known as the Congress Kingdom of Poland. This preserved Napoleon's reforms while adding a constitution, a bicameral diet, a Polish army and a separate Crown. Even radicals began to hope that tsar Alexander might actually increase the size of the Congress Kingdom at the expense of Lithuania. Of course, the relative liberality of Congress Poland bitterly annoyed progressive Russians who hankered after a similar dispensation.

The fact of foreign domination engendered any number of responses in the Poles. Some of these are not as well known as the Romantic insurrectionism that figures so prominently in the literature. There were Polish loyalists who were 'loyal' to the partitioning power, although few probably took things as far as Stanisław Potocki in recommending: 'Poles should abandon all memory of their fatherland; I am a Russian for ever.' Others, anticipating what the twentieth-century Polish poet Czesław Milosz called 'ketman', combined external displays of loyalty with a sentimental patriotism regarding Polish culture, history and traditions. If these dilemmas were not enough, Roman Catholicism further encouraged the heightened moral awareness of many Poles, for the pragmatic conduct of the Roman Catholic Church in Poland often belied the nationalist image of Poland as the martyred 'Christ among nations'. Clergy sometimes demanded far more severe punishments for members of secret societies than lay judges. Article 11 of the constitution of Congress Poland conceded that:

> The Catholic religion is the religion of the majority of the population in the Kingdom of Poland, and it stands under the

special protection of the government; without exception other religions are free to practise their beliefs and their freedom will not be curtailed. Membership of the various Christian denominations is not grounds for any form of discrimination with regard to political or civil rights.

This explains why the deeply traditionalist Polish Catholic clergy kept their distance from political conspiracy on the part of lay elites who were children of the Enlightenment when they were not overtly irreligious. When revolt came, the pope was completely condemnatory.[51]

Insofar as they were not Loyalists, the Church could be numbered among the Conciliators who sought to reconcile the fact of partition by foreign powers with the widespread desire for some acknowledgement of indigenous traditions to be reflected in Polish institutions. To the left of this important swathe of opinion were those who practised either inner or foreign emigration, with the former abstracting themselves from public life and the latter leaving the country, and, finally, those who went in for active or passive forms of resistance, which Romantic artists and poets succeeded in making synonymous with Polish identity.[52]

The hub of Polish disaffection from the partitioning powers was within the army, which included many men who had fought under Napoleon across Europe and Russia. Just as many Russian officers had been exposed to new experiences and ideas while fighting in western Europe or during the occupation of France after 1815, so Polish soldiers resented the narrow-mindedness of the Russians who were placed in charge of them. They especially disliked being subjected to the obsession with military drill of Alexander's brother Constantine who acted as viceroy in the Congress Kingdom. Experienced warriors chafed at being treated like lead soldiers. A Polish general berated for marching less than perfectly by Constantine, responded: 'I would remind Your Imperial Highness that it was nevertheless with this step that I marched into Moscow in 1812.' Soldiers formed secret societies, modelled on the Carbonari, which in 1821 coalesced into a Patriotic Society whose object was Polish independence. It was not effective since by the late 1820s most of the leadership had been arrested, a fate that had similarly befallen the nationalist student society called the Philomathians at Lithuania's University of Vilna in mid-decade. By this time Alexander I had been succeeded by Nicholas I, the commencement of whose reign coincided with the Decembrist Revolt in Russia. Never possessed of a hope of success, this episode merely set Nicholas on a path of unrelenting reaction.

In late 1830 the next more impetuous echelon of Polish soldier–nationalists essayed a rising in Warsaw, while Russian attention was diverted by revolution in Belgium and France. Although they managed to secure control of the capital, grand duke Constantine and most of the Russian garrison escaped, preferring to leave Polish loyalists to sort things out rather than deploying the massive forces he had at his disposal. The rebels endeavoured to win both elite and popular backing for the rising, with Warsaw's poets working furiously to produce verses calculated to rouse a populace who on the whole preferred to stay at home behind locked doors. The elite Administrative Council appointed general Jan Chlopicki as a virtual dictator in Warsaw while sending prince Adam Czartoryski to placate Nicholas I, who promised generous terms once the rising was suppressed. Neither of these measures dissuaded the Warsaw revolutionaries from their illusory belief that the Russians would not fight, that the revolt would spread, or that 'Europe' would come to their assistance. The parliament then provoked a final breach when it formally deposed the Russian tsar from his Polish throne. It managed to minimise its own support by refusing to contemplate agrarian reform that might have roused the peasantry to support the rebel side. In February the rebels marched out of Warsaw to engage Russian forces, achieving some notable early victories. Despite this, and the ravages of cholera, by the autumn the Russian army had encircled the Polish capital. The arrival of French, German, Italian and Swiss volunteers to assist the Poles did not affect the outcome of the wider struggle. The Russians launched a major assault on Warsaw from the west. This forced its defenders to surrender on 7 September. About fifty-five thousand Polish troops and six thousand civilians were allowed to slip away on what became a long exodus. The property of the insurgents was confiscated. In the Organic Statute of February 1832 Nicholas abrogated the Polish constitution, abolished both the independent army and the parliament or Sejm, and appointed ethnic Russians to all key posts in the administration.

At first Józef Bem, the commander of the tens of thousands of exiled Polish troops, fantasised that they could either move around Europe as a cohesive, free-floating force, or be taken en masse into Prussian or Belgian service for a possible war with Russia, or with a newly independent Belgium against William of Holland. Eventually, many of the common soldiers returned to Poland following Nicholas I's offer of an amnesty, but a hard core of eight thousand officers lived to fight another day in the host cities of the Polish emigration. Paris was the centre of Polish exile politics, for it was there that Adam Czartoryski decamped in the wake of the November 1830 rising.

The vast majority of the Polish rebels were Roman Catholics. They included many priests. Some bishops explicitly supported the rising. While a rebel emissary tried to win the support of Gregory XVI, the tsar's man in Rome, prince Gagarin, sought to conflate the Polish rebels with the Italian secret societies. Since liberal Catholics like Lamennais fervently supported the Poles, it was unsurprising on whose side the pope's sympathies lay. The pope wrote to the Polish bishops recommending that they preach 'obedience and submission as advocated by St Paul'. This letter was deemed too mild by the Russians, who, with Metternich's aid, contrived a much more censorious communication which condemned 'those authors of lying and trickery who, under cover of religion, defy the legitimate power of princes, break all the ties of submission imposed by duty and plunge their country into misfortune and mourning'. This document caused outrage throughout liberal Europe, although in fairness to the pope no mention was made of a parallel letter to the tsar which denounced the 'wicked chicanery' of the Russian regime in Poland.

Romantic Polish literature provided a grand narrative for these events, events which it invariably treated in an imagery and language saturated with religious allegory. In this respect one Polish poet stood out from the rest. Adam Mickiewicz was born in late 1798, the son of a minor lawyer in Zaosie, Lithuania. His most vivid childhood memories were of the conquests of Napoleon upon whom Polish patriots set such store: 'God is with Napoleon, Napoleon is with us' went their refrain. In 1815 Mickiewicz entered the University of Vilno where he co-founded the Philomathian student society. After graduating in 1819 he became a schoolmaster in Kovno. Having begun to write at university, his poetry derived inspiration from the beguiling Lithuanian countryside and from Lithuania's illustrious medieval history. In mid-1823 this idyll came to an abrupt end when the poet was arrested in a general Russian clampdown upon schools and colleges. He was imprisoned in the Basilian convent until April 1824 when he was released pending the tsar's decision upon his sentence. That autumn he was banished to Russia. He spent the next five years living in Moscow, Odessa and St Petersburg under the eye of the tsarist police. Despite the surveillance that he and other

Poles endured, Mickiewicz became close friends with leading Russian poets such as Pushkin. These friends ensured that he was not banished to the back of beyond but rather circulated in liberal salons in major cities. It must have been an odd kind of exile since, in between the dances and soirées, he was given permission to tour the Crimea, whose beauties inspired a sequence of vivid sonnets.

While in Moscow Mickiewicz produced *Konrad Wallenrod* (1828), set during the wars that the Teutonic Knights waged against the heathen Lithuanians. The eponymous hero was a brooding mysterious figure who by virtue of his military prowess became grand master of the order. Gradually, a series of dramatic devices intimates that Konrad was in fact a Lithuanian boy who had been brought up in German captivity. After escaping the Knights' clutches, he decides, having become a young man, to forsake his bride, friends and family, returning to join the Knights, solely in order to lead them to disaster in the Lithuanian wilderness. After the onset of winter, and still led by Konrad, although he had betrayed them, the Knights straggled back to Prussia. Konrad evaded a grisly death by swallowing poison. The term 'Wallenrodism' entered the Polish political lexicon as a synonym for a lifetime of purposeful deception. Eventually, the Russian authorities deciphered the political message and revoked Mickiewicz's passport. This was not done with sufficient alacrity, enabling him to flee to Germany. He travelled southwards, meeting August Schlegel in Bonn, Goethe and Lessing in Weimar, and Hegel and Mendelssohn in Berlin, before continuing on to Rome, which made an abiding impression on him. On learning of the November 1830 Rising, Mickiewicz hastened to join it, but by the time he reached Posen in Prussian Poland the Russians had triumphed.

In the spring of 1832, the poet settled in Dresden. The city was awash with exiles from the November Rising. A rush of inspiration compelled him to work day and night on the third part of a great dramatic poem called *Forefathers' Eve* whose earlier parts he had written in Russian exile. In this intensely mystical poem, containing passages that bordered on blasphemy, Mickiewicz dissolves into the nation while the nation is transfigured into the Passion of Christ:

> Now is my soul incarnate in my country
> And in my body dwells her soul;
> My fatherland and I and are one great whole.
> My name is million, because I love as millions:

Their pain and suffering I feel;
I gaze upon my country fallen on days
Of torment, as a son would gaze
Upon his father broken on the wheel.
I feel within myself my country's massacre
Even as the mother feels within her womb
The travail of the children whom
She bears.[53]

Mickiewicz returned to this theme in *Books of the Polish Nation and of the Pilgrimage of Poland* (1832). The Poles were not exiles or refugees, but pilgrims en route to the Holy Land of liberty regained. The poet became an oracle interpreting the mysterious workings of divine Providence to his fellow countrymen. Mickiewicz provided an account of what had happened to Poland that gave its tribulations meaning and purpose, combining this with various precepts as to how the pilgrims should conduct themselves in order to sustain their national consciousness. Providence had scattered the Poles throughout the world so that they might disseminate the heightened values engendered by their suffering. They were God's Chosen People whose mission was to bring freedom and brotherly love to the whole of Europe:

And the Kings, renouncing Christ, made new idols which they set up in the sight of the people, and made them bow down . . . And the nations forgot that they had sprung from one Father. Finally in idolatrous Europe, there arose three rulers, a satanic Trinity – Frederick whose name signifieth 'Friend of Peace', and Catherine, which in Greek signifieth 'Woman of Purity', and Maria Theresa, who bore the name of the immaculate Mother of our Saviour. Their names were thus three blasphemies, their lives three crimes, their memories three curses. And this Trinity fashioned a new idol, unknown to the ancients, and they called it POLITICAL INTEREST . . .

But the Polish nation alone did not bow down . . . And Poland said, 'Whatsoever will come to me shall be free and equal for I am FREEDOM.' But the Kings, when they heard it, were frightened in their hearts, and they crucified the Polish nation, and laid it in its grave, crying out 'We have slain and buried Freedom.' But they cried out foolishly . . .

For the Polish Nation did not die. Its Body lieth in the grave;

but its spirit has descended into the abyss, that is into the private lives of people who suffer slavery in their own country . . . For on the Third Day, the Soul shall return again to the Body; and the Nation shall arise, and free all the peoples of Europe from slavery.

Mickiewicz urged the Poles to transcend the rancour of exile, and not to dwell upon the sins of commission and omission in the past. He suggested that former soldiers should continue to wear their national uniform. He thought they should celebrate key national feasts and the anniversary of the November Rising. On that day they should go to church, fast all day, and donate the money saved to patriotic causes.

Following work on his vast epic poem *Thaddeus*, Mickiewicz effectively abandoned poetry for good. In 1834 he married Celina Szymanowska, their life together in Paris being blighted by dire poverty and her recurrent bouts of mental illness. From 1840 onwards Mickiewicz occupied the chair of Slavonic literature at the Collège de France, where he lectured to audiences that included Chopin, Czartoryski, George Sand, Michelet, Quinet and the liberal Catholic Montalembert. His own mental health buckled along with that of his wife, especially since his lectures became unscripted outpourings of patriotic fervor whose impromptu nature took a toll on his nerves. The cure proved more deadly than the disease. In the summer of 1841 a Lithuanian mystic called Andrzej Towianski appeared at his Paris lodgings, claiming to be on a mission of national moment. When Mickiewicz expressed surprise on learning that Towianski was God's chosen instrument for the deliverance of Poland and the entire human race, Towianski offered proof in the form of a cure for Celina, Mickiewicz's wife. This he achieved simply by whispering something in Celina's ear. Thenceforth, Mickiewicz referred to Towianski as the 'Master', and fell under the spell of a bizarre mishmash of ideas, not the least strange of which was that Towianski was in communion with the spirit of Napoleon, whom he regarded as the greatest man since Christ. Mickiewicz joined one of the seven-man cells that made up what Towianski dubbed the Circle devoted to the heterodox Cause that he extolled. These involvements alienated Mickiewicz's more orthodox compatriots. He began to burn his poetry, while his lectures at the Collège became outpourings of his mystical faith. From Belgium, to where the French authorities had deported him, Towianski dictated the increasingly febrile content of Mickiewicz's lectures. In March 1844 Mickiewicz told his listeners, who included members of the Circle, that he possessed a higher truth: 'The joy that I have felt, and which will not be taken away from me, the joy that I have felt to be commissioned to tell you of, will be the joy of all my life, and of all my lives; and as I do not speak from books, as I do not expose a system to you, I proclaim myself before Heaven the living witness of the new revelation.'

When he prefaced his lectures by handing out small images of Napoleon and then inveighed against the ruling Orléans monarchy he was dismissed from his post. Mickiewicz immersed himself in working for the Circle, although in the succeeding years relations between him and the 'Master' cooled. In 1848 he tried to organise a Polish Legion in Rome who would liberate their fellow countrymen in the year of European revolutions. This grandiose-sounding enterprise, with its echoes of Kosciuszko, eventually consisted of twelve art students. In 1855 Mickiewicz went to Turkey to organise a similar project among Poles serving in the Ottoman army, but there he contracted cholera and died.[54]

While the papacy was condemnatory of the failed rising in Poland, it was also forced to deal with governments that were the product of successful liberal revolutions. In the Constitution *Sollicitudo Ecclesiarum* of August 1831, Gregory XVI declared that 'the Roman pontiffs would enter into diplomatic relations with those who were de facto in power'. This enabled the pope to condemn revolutionary movements, while accepting those that succeeded in their goals. Of course, in reality, things were not as clear cut as this suggests. While Gregory cautiously recognised the new Belgian regime, in the Iberian peninsula his sympathies were clearly with the ultra-Catholic 'wicked uncles' Don Miguel in Portugal and Don Carlos in Spain, who sought to displace their relatively liberal nieces who had become queens. In both countries, this meant that liberals became aggressively anticlerical, although only in Madrid did this result in actual violence, with the Puerta del Sol echoing to cries of 'Down with Christ! Long live Satan!' as churches were burned and clergy murdered.

The question of papal sympathies was more straightforward when the cause of Catholicism was virtually identical with the national movement, only veering towards coolness when that movement complicated its wider diplomatic gambits, or engaged in outright hostility when religious nationalism usurped Catholicism. In late-eighteenth-century Ireland the Catholic Church had been hostile to the attempts of the largely northern

Protestant leadership of the United Irishmen to transcend confessional differences in favour of a secular and democratic Irish republic modelled along the lines of American and French exemplars. The catechism of the United Irishmen made these influences explicit:

> Question: What have you got in your hand?
> Answer: A green bough.
> Question: Where did it first grow?
> Answer: In America.
> Question: Where did it bud?
> Answer: In France.
> Question: Where are you going to plant it?
> Answer: In the crown of Great Britain.[55]

But within a few decades the Irish Catholic Church became so integral to the popular political struggle led by the radical lawyer Daniel O'Connell that nationalism and Catholicism became progressively synonymous, in what, moreover, was the sole early-nineteenth-century European nationalist movement to enjoy support from the peasant masses. By contrast, the dominant role of Protestant Dissenters in the opening stages of Irish nationalism was replaced by the identification of the 1801 Act of Union with a beleaguered Protestantism and the blurring of the considerable gulf between militant Orangemen and the genteel world of the Church of Ireland.[56] These were never games that only Irishmen played. The British Whigs and Tories who governed Ireland through the apparatus at Dublin Castle were divided on whether concessions to the Catholics would bring the entire edifice of a uni-confessional Church and state crashing down (by and large the Tory position), or whether timely concessions to the enemies of the Protestant Constitution might preserve it (the view put forward by the Whigs and the 'trimming' Tories). The Holy See was also flexible in dealing with these issues. Like the Catholic Church in England it saw no difficulty in a deal over Emancipation, conceding a British government veto over episcopal appointments, and at least entertaining the idea of state salaries for the Catholic clergy.

O'Connell was born in 1775 into a wealthy Kerry family which had found ways of circumventing the various penal laws that theoretically afflicted all Catholics. He received a first-rate education at religious academies in St Omer and Douai that served him well in his chosen careers as a lawyer and popular tribune. His juvenile religious scepticism was replaced by an increasingly fervid Catholicism, while direct experience of the French Revolution, when he had to flee France as an 'English' schoolboy, made him a lifelong foe of political violence. This view was cemented by a career in a profession dependent upon the rule of law for its very existence. Much later in life – when he was sixty-nine and indicted on a charge of seditious conspiracy – O'Connell crisply stated his political philosophy:

> From the day when I first entered the arena of politics until the present hour, I have never neglected an opportunity of impressing upon the minds of my fellow countrymen the fact, that I was an apostle of that political sect who held that liberty was only to be attained under such agencies as were strictly consistent with the law and the constitution – that freedom was to be attained, not by the effusion of human blood, but by the constitutional combination of good and wise men; by perseverance in the courses of tranquillity and good order, and by an utter abhorrence of violence and bloodshed.[57]

O'Connell encouraged the British government to deploy more troops to suppress such agrarian terrorist gangs as the 'Whiteboys', 'Molly Maguires' and 'Ribbonmen'. He was also socially conservative: 'I desire no social revolution, no social change. In short, salutary restoration without revolution, an Irish parliament, British connexion, one King, two legislatures.'[58] As a Benthamite liberal he wanted less rather than more government, albeit with power redistributed towards the Catholic middle classes and away from the aristocratic Protestants of the Ascendancy. He was opposed to trade unions. His generosity of mind and sense of injustice also made him a lifelong opponent of slavery (which annoyed his American supporters) and advocate of such causes as Latin American independence (his son tried to fight for that other 'Liberator' Simon Bolivar) and the right of British Jews to become members of parliament. The obverse side of his considerable generosity was a rebarbative 'Billingsgate' (London's main fish market) vulgarity towards opponents and, until the intercessions of his wife prevented him from fighting Robert Peel in a duel, a quick resort to the trigger. His relationship with Irish cultural nationalism was contradictory. He grew up speaking Irish – thanks to the herdsmen among whom he was fostered – but then averred: 'the superior utility of the English tongue, as the medium of all modern communication, is so great, that I can witness without a sigh the gradual

Trees were planted to symbolise the advent of liberty for all
eternity; liberty was imposed in France and exported
elsewhere with the bayonets of revolutionary armies.

The British artist Zoffany represented the counter-revolutionary view of events in France as an opportunity for the mob to unleash its basest instincts.

Jacques-Louis David was called the 'pageant-master' of the Revolution, and less charitably the 'Robespierre of the brush'. He largely supplied the Revolution's self-image.

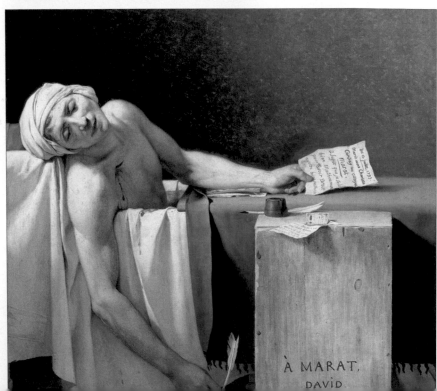

The death of the boy martyr was to play an important pedagogic function, although Bara himself [*see inset*] was less epicene than David's picture suggests.

Opposite page: David's subtle idealisation of the journalist as terrorist is one of the greatest examples of politicised art.

The Jacobins were influenced by Jean-Jacques Rousseau's writings on civic religion and created symbolic alternatives to the traditional imagery of throne and altar.

The triumph of Reason unleashed waves of iconoclastic destruction in which nothing was regarded as sacred.

The guillotine operated too slowly for the liking of some Jacobin terrorists so they used mass drownings to kill 'enemies of the Revolution' instead. The British poet Swinburne subsequently commemorated the dead in *les Noyades*.

In countries occupied by his armies Napoleon was regarded as the Devil incarnate as in this German example of counter-revolutionary propaganda in which the Devil is 'well pleased' with his offspring.

During the Restoration many artists, writers and thinkers rediscovered religion as a source of social stability and order, reminding man that he was not the centre of the universe as this painting by the German artist Friedrich shows.

disuse of the Irish'. Yet as he became a successful demagogue he was not above adopting all the symbolic trappings of capacious cloaks, green suits, harps and shamrocks once he realised their electrical potency among his simpler constituents. Leaving aside the fact that the shamrock 'has no objective existence' in nature, many of these ancient 'national' symbols, like the ubiquitous round towers and shaggy wolfhounds, were of recent provenance (wolfhounds had almost become extinct by the early nineteenth century and had to be re-created by crossing whatever mongrelised stock remained with Scottish deerhounds), the discovery of enthusiastic antiquaries whose findings were taken up by equally enthusiastic nationalists. The harp owed its ubiquity to its having been adopted in 1862 as a trademark of the (Protestant) Guinness Brewery. In the early 1840s, the artist Henry MacManus and the Young Ireland activist Charles Gavan Duffy designed an 'Irish' hat. It had stiff sides resembling a crown, with a 'jellybag' tasselled centre. The green velvet version, embroidered with gold shamrocks, was presented to O'Connell. The common or garden version, made from grey shoddy, was said to bear 'an awkward and fatal resemblance to a nightcap'.[59]

The progression from lawyer to populist politician was spectacular, although O'Connell did not single-handedly conjure forth the already politicised constituency that supported him. O'Connell traversed a court circuit in the south-west of Ireland, earning ever larger fees that always lagged behind the cost of an increasing family. Carefully chosen and symbolically charged cases enabled him to build a local following. Although O'Connell was the most talented lawyer of his day, his religion disbarred him from taking silk or judicial office. He began by controlling the various boards and committees that represented Catholic interests and opinion in the shadow of the 1793 Convention Act that periodically suppressed them. He played a leading role in the founding of the Irish Catholic Association in April 1823 which used the courts to contest various generic grievances affecting Catholics, before launching its full-scale campaign to rescind those sections of the 1793 Catholic Relief Act which, despite a number of important concessions, still prevented Catholics from being members of parliament or enjoying the highest offices. That may explain elite Catholic support, but so dry an issue could hardly account for the mass support that the issue generated.

O'Connell recognised the sheer weight of demographic facts in a country where, outside Ulster, Catholics were in the vast majority. While the one-guinea-a-year subscription for full membership of the

Association was prohibitive, associate status was offered through a 'Catholic Rent' of a penny a month which dramatically boosted the number of supporters. The commitment shown during collections was as important as the prodigious sums collected, which were then used to finance test cases, a burgeoning Catholic press, petitions and schools. The Catholic clergy, whose membership dues were waived, played a key role in collecting money at chapel doors (for Catholics were not allowed to have 'churches') and in organising the committees that appointed collectors for out-of-the-way places.[60] A proselytising 'Second Reformation' launched by some of the island's Protestants, in addition to a more pervasive desire to follow as well as lead their flocks, helped foster their commitment.[61] When the Association was suppressed, along with the Orange lodges in 1825, O'Connell established a New Catholic Association, whose remit included everything not explicitly forbidden in the Suppression Act that had done away with its predecessor. This was the extra-parliamentary arm of a campaign that, thanks to the commitment to emancipation of British Whigs, liberal and radical, was constantly kept before successive governments, regardless of whether the king (despite O'Connell's extravagant professions of loyalty) and the House of Lords opposed it.[62]

In 1826 the stakes rose when what seemed like highly advanced Catholic organisational methods were deployed, by the political priest Rev. J. Sheehan and O'Connell's associate Thomas Wyse, to unseat Lord George Beresford in his Waterford electoral fiefdom. The bishop of Waterford was encouraged to conduct a religious census of his diocese whose effect was to highlight the slightness of the Protestant Ascendancy in the county: in Ardmore parish there were 7,800 Catholics to 39 Protestants, in Kilgobbin 3,799 to 4 and so on.[63] The Association carefully studied how people were likely to vote, and provided finance and housing when Beresford had obstreperous tenants evicted. It brought in and housed people from outlying areas so that they could vote. In other words, the Association severed the historic linkages between property and power in Ireland. Beresford called off the contest when the scale of his impending defeat by Villiers Stuart, a liberal Protestant landlord whom the Catholic Association backed, became obvious. This success was repeated in several other county constituencies.[64] The Association also threatened to oppose the candidacy of every supporter of the new Wellington administration that had come to office in January 1828. This occurred almost immediately when Vesey Fitzgerald, the pro-Emancipationist liberal Tory president of the Board of Trade in Wellington's cabinet, was obliged to seek re-election in Clare, and O'Connell himself was persuaded to stand against him, even though as a Catholic he was disbarred from taking up a seat in parliament since he refused to take the oath of allegiance with its negations of his own religion. As a sour commentator remarked of this election: 'Every altar became a tribune.' Priests warned those who were contemplating voting for O'Connell's opponent: 'Men, are ye going to betray your God and your country?' O'Connell won the election by 2,057 votes to 982, going on to make a triumphal introitus upon a chariot when he went to Dublin after the victory in Clare.

The strength of Catholic mobilisation indirectly played upon British fears that use of force to suppress it would result in catastrophe, an apocalyptic scenario indirectly confirmed by the mushrooming of ultra-Protestant Brunswick Clubs to support the endangered Protestant Ascendancy. Fear of some seventy Catholic MPs being returned to a parliament they could not join without swearing the oath proved greater. Wellington therefore prevailed upon an extremely reluctant George IV as well as such opponents of Emancipation as Robert Peel to swallow the bitter pill in return for the disfranchisement of the 40-shillings freeholders who had been the Catholic Association's electoral mainstay, the suppression of the Association itself, and the exclusion of Catholics from the office of lord chancellor.

After Catholic Emancipation, O'Connell turned his attention to the cause of 'Justice for Ireland' in the form of the abolition of institutional disadvantages under which Catholics laboured, backed up by the Damoclean sword of a campaign to Repeal the Act of Union. In 1835 he entered into a gentlemen's agreement, the Litchfield House Compact, with the Whig administration, which in any case had its own reforming agenda for Ireland, as evidenced by the 1833 Irish Church Temporalities Act that rationalised the Church of Ireland. One product of this alliance was the reform of municipal corporations, which by the by resulted in O'Connell's appointment as lord mayor of Dublin. When Peel's Tory administration came to power in 1841, O'Connell switched to campaigning for Repeal, using many of the organisational techniques that had earlier been used to achieve Emancipation. One novel development was the use of massed outdoor rallies – with one at Tara in Meath attracting perhaps between a half and three-quarters of a million people – which were part fair, part revivalist theatre.[65] Charles Gavan Duffy jotted down his impressions of that August afternoon:

Each town was preceded by its band in the national uniform of green and white, and by banners with suitable inscriptions. They were mustered by mounted marshals, distinguished by badges, horsemen four deep, footmen six deep, and the men of each parish marched, O'Connell afterwards declared, 'as if they were in battalions'. Three miles from the hill the vehicles had to be abandoned; from the immensity of the attendance there was space only for footmen ... The procession however was but as a river discharging itself into an ocean. The whole district was covered with men ... It was impossible from any one point to see the entire meeting; the hill rose almost perpendicular out of the level plain, and hill and plain were covered with a multitude 'countless as the bearded grain'.[66]

Another was the creation of a co-operative bank and a network of 'arbitration courts' designed to enable supporters of Repeal to bypass the official court system. The government began reinforcing the number of troops across the water. In 1843 the mother of monster rallies was supposed to take place at Clontarf as the climax of the Repeal campaign. This was banned on the ground that loose talk beforehand by among others O'Connell indicated that it might have had a paramilitary dimension. O'Connell acquiesced, which did not prevent an absurd trial in Dublin for the crime of seditious conspiracy, before a jury from which Catholics had been removed.

Much to the outrage of his English supporters, who held a banquet attended by a thousand people in Covent Garden at which the great man appeared, O'Connell was sentenced to a year's imprisonment in a fine suite of rooms with ladies in attendance. When his conviction was overturned by a writ of error in the House of Lords, O'Connell was released. He was taken in a triumphal car, replete with aged harpist and his grandchildren decked out in green velvet and white-feathered caps, on a procession through Dublin with huge crowds of supporters lining the streets. The triumph was evanescent since younger, more radical men were snapping at his heels. After his release O'Connell flirted with those advocating a federal solution to the Irish Question, the retention of one imperial parliament and the creation of two subordinate legislatures for Great Britain and Ireland dealing with domestic issues. This served to antagonise younger radicals connected to the *Nation* newspaper, who since O'Connell's climbdown at Clontarf had begun to regard him as a spent force.

Young Ireland was the Irish manifestation of the Romantic cultural nationalism in Germany. Like the Repeal movement, its adherents included both Catholics and Protestants. Its leading light was Thomas Davis, a young Irish Protestant of Welsh ancestry, who sought to transcend the facts of Ireland's ethnic strata and sectarian divisions by emphasising the impact of environment, history, literature and above all language.[67] This required education through the medium of books and newspapers, to be made available through the network of Repeal reading-rooms. The *Nation* newspaper, whose motto was 'to create and foster public opinion in Ireland and to make it racy of the soil', together with the cheap books produced by the Library of Ireland, ransacked Ireland's incredibly rich history and then reforged it through stories of ancient derring-do, ballads, songs and poetry into a master-narrative in which 'the history of Ireland may be written as English crimes'. Their contents abounded with the hearts of patriots beating strongly, green banners unfurled, while the legs of warrior chieftains were wrapped in 'cold clay'. Davis was especially keen to use the visual arts to raise national consciousness: 'When we speak of high art, we mean art used to instruct and ennoble men; to teach them great deeds; whether historical, religious, or romantic; to awaken their piety, their pride, their justice, and their valour; to paint the hero, the martyr, the rescuer, the lover, the patriot, the friend, the saint, and the Saviour.'

Paintings with a nationalist content were to be commissioned, from such obliging friends as Frederic Burton, himself as it happened a staunch Unionist but the most talented Irish artist of the early nineteenth century. Like virtually every Irish painter, he lived and worked in London, and it is unclear to what extent their paintings of medieval or rustic scenes were 'nationalist' or part of a general appetite for the Middle Ages and life in the wind- and rain-swept outer fringes of Europe. The subjects favoured by Davis included 'The Landing of the Milesians', 'Tone, Emmett, and Keogh in the Rathfarnam Garden', 'Father Mathew Administering the Pledge in a Munster County', 'Conciliation: Orange and Green' and 'The Lifting of the Irish Flags of a National Army and Fleet'. Competitions would counter the lack of patronage. As another founder of the journal remarked: 'Passion and imagination have won victories which reason and self-interest would have attempted in vain, and it was upon these subtle forces the young men mainly counted.' They did not amount to much, but what they left in the property cupboard could be ransacked in turn by others with a far greater grasp of the realities of the Irish than these rather sickly young men had themselves.[68]

Under the skilful leadership of O'Connell's old foe Peel, the British government began to see the utility of appeasing the Catholic Church in order to divide and rule the Repeal movement. A series of bland-sounding laws were the chosen weapon. Peel's opening gambit was the Charitable Donations and Bequests Act of 1844 which persuaded a significant number of Catholic bishops to ignore O'Connell's advice not to take part in administering bequests to the Catholic clergy. The following year Peel trebled the annual grant to the Catholic seminary at Maynooth, adding a further £30,000 for building work. Maynooth had been established under Pitt to encourage the Catholic clergy in a more conservative direction, for many of its instructors were French exiles from the Jacobins. This scheme backfired as the Seminary engendered solidarities among the priests themselves and between them and the people they came from. The Academical Institutions (Ireland) Bill was designed to make up for the huge disparity between higher education in Ireland vis-à-vis Scotland by creating four non-denominational 'Queen's Colleges'. While the Belfast Presbyterians welcomed what became Queen's University Belfast, the issue split those Catholic laity who could see the colleges' advantages from the Catholic hierarchy (and the papacy) who condemned them as 'infidel' institutions. It also underlined the rift between O'Connell, who supported the hierarchy's view, and the supporters of Young Ireland, who welcomed the new colleges as part of their crusade for more education. Finally, on the diplomatic front, the British government persuaded the pope to issue a rescript reproving clergy who meddled in politics, in response to which the bishops divided into those who stuck with O'Connell, those who retreated into neutrality and those who were prepared to work with the British government. The effect of Peel's measures was both to highlight and to divide a 'clerical' interest that may have had O'Connell's support but was increasingly at odds with the firebrands of Young Ireland who smelled priestly tyranny. There was also the matter of political violence, to which all that gushing celebration of mythic militarism inevitably led. Relations between O'Connell and Young Ireland broke down when in a November 1845 editorial in the *Nation*, in response to a British commentary on how railways would expedite troop movements on the island, John Mitchel wrote:

it might be useful to promulgate through the country, to be read by all Repeal Wardens in their parishes, a few short and easy rules, as to the mode of dealing with railways in case of any enemy daring to make a hostile use of them . . . to lift a mile of rail, to fill a perch or two of any cutting or tunnel, to break down a piece of embankment, seem obvious and easy enough . . . Hofer and his Tyroliens [sic] could hardly desire a deadlier ambush than the brinks of a deep cutting upon a railway.

Backed by the Catholic Church, which eschewed violence, O'Connell used this article for a showdown with Young Ireland, forcing them to choose between forswearing physical violence and seceding from 'his' Association. Those who would not submit left, to form a separate Irish Confederation. They included Mitchel, who even before the Young Irishmen launched what was contemptuously called the 'cabbage garden revolution' – for the denouement was in a cottage garden – had been tried for treason and deported. A myth had been born, despite the fact that, as one of his colleagues remarked, 'the people of Munster knew as little of Mitchel as of Mahomet', and despite his subsequent support for slavery (he fought for the Confederacy) and opposition to Jewish emancipation. O'Connell's last months were spent trying to repair these multiple tears in the fabric of the Repeal movement, against the descending darkness of a famine that killed a million people. Desperately ill, he spent his final weeks on a pilgrimage to Rome. He never made it, dying at Genoa on 17 May 1847, although his heart, inappropriately enough, was sent on to Rome's Irish College and his body returned to Dublin.

IV MAZZINI THE MARTYR

Genoa was the birthplace of the most dedicated exponent of what one might call a religion of cosmopolitan Romantic nationalism. Giuseppe Mazzini was far from being theologically literate, but rarely can someone have so thoroughly confused religion with politics, to the point where his political writings were like (idiosyncratic) religious utterances. Mazzini was born in French-ruled Genoa, the son of a doctor with

Jacobin sympathies, who like many long-suffering parents of Italian exiles would support him throughout his indigent peregrinations. Mazzini experienced his political epiphany while walking with his mother along Genoa's Strada Nuova. They were approached by a man collecting for veterans of the 1820 revolutions who were moving through the port en route to exile: 'That was the first day of my life in which I sensed, perhaps confusedly, not the ideals of Homeland and Liberty, but the thought that one could, and that therefore one should, fight for the liberty of one's homeland.'

After graduating in law, Mazzini combined legal practice with the literary journalism that was his true métier. In 1827 he joined a Genoese cell of the Carbonari, travelling the following year to Tuscany to establish affiliated societies that Mazzini compared with the Greek Etairia. He was arrested and, after a brief spell in prison, chose expatriation over internal banishment to a remote region.

Mazzini based himself in Marseilles, whence sailors could smuggle subversive materials into Genoa. It did not take long to decide to remain aloof from that ancient mariner of the Revolution, Filippo Buonarroti, whose Paris-focused communist insurrectionism did not appeal to the younger Mazzini. The latter thought it was not up to France to give other revolutions the red or green signal. He also decided to break with the format of secret societies, which he claimed bore the marks of the original sin of dependency upon (anti-Napoleonic) Italian monarchs.[69]

In the summer of 1831 Mazzini and thirty others founded Young Italy, the name reflecting the desire to restrict membership to the under forties, even though the rules were bent in favour of the 'young in spirit'. There were initiation rites and recognition procedures that owed much to the heritage of the secret societies. When two 'Cousins' met they must have seemed like windmills. As one crossed his arms with palms flat on his chest, the other tried the trickier manoeuvre of crossing the arms with the palms upwards to signify an open heart. The question 'what is the time?' was meant to elicit the response 'time for the struggle'.

Young Italy's programme was a declaration of faith:

> The one thing wanting to twenty millions of Italians, desirous of emancipating themselves, is not power, but faith.
> Young Italy will endeavour to inspire this faith – first by its teachings, and afterwards by an energetic initiative.

Breaking with the French Revolution's insistence upon abstract rights, Young Italy stressed both a national 'mission' and the moral duty incumbent upon Italians to fulfil it:

> Right is the faith of the individual; duty is a collective faith. Right can only organize resistance, it can destroy but not lay foundations. Duty builds and creates collaboration ... Right undermines sacrifice and eliminates martyrdom from the world. In any theory of individual rights interests alone predominate and martyrdom becomes an absurdity. No interests could survive one's death. Nevertheless, it is martyrdom which frequently serves as the baptism of a new world and the initiation of progress.[70]

Young Italy was republican, for this was Italy's 'historic' form of government and monarchs had always betrayed the national cause. It was 'unitarian' because federalism would only promote the autonomy sought by such places as Sicily with its separate culture, history and institutions. It was self-reliant in the sense that dependence upon external events or sympathetic foreign powers would mean that these alone determined the tempo of events. Above all, Young Italy combined a political programme with a regenerative moral mission, something it had in common with most national liberation movements:

> Both initiators and initiated must never forget that the moral application of every principle is the first and the most essential; that without morality there is no true citizen; that the first step towards the achievement of a holy enterprise is the purification of the soul by virtue; that, where the daily life of the individual is not in harmony with the principles he preaches, the inculcation of those principles is an infamous profanation and hypocrisy; that it is only by virtue that the members of Young Italy can win over others to their belief; that if we do not show ourselves far superior to those who deny our principles, we are but miserable sectarians; and that Young Italy must be neither a sect nor a party, but a faith and an apostolate. As the precursors of Italian regeneration, it is our duty to lay the first stone of its religion.[71]

At least in theory, Young Italy was characterised by high moral tone; criminals, drunks and womanisers were unwelcome. The mission of its 'apostles' was to convert into a 'popolo' (people) the unregenerate 'gente' (mob) who populated the intensely fissiparous and provincial regions of Italy. In other words, the revolution was moral before it was political, and it had to be for the people rather than by the people, who were as yet unformed.[72]

Young Italy's manifesto was saturated with words like apostolate, belief, creed, crusade, enthusiasm, faith, incarnation, martyrs, mission, purification, regeneration, religion, sacred, sacrifice, salvation, and punctuated with sentences such as 'Our religion of today is still that of martyrdom; tomorrow it will be the religion of victory.' The password members used to identify one another was 'Martyrdom' to which the correct reply was 'Resurrection'. Mazzini once said of himself: 'I am not a Christian, or rather I am a Christian plus something more.'[73]

It is difficult to extrapolate a coherent set of religious beliefs from Mazzini's writings. By fostering internal and external fraternity, the nation was a divinely inspired Church, through which humanity would appreciate the essential truths within each major religion. The nation was the ideal intermediary between man and God, for it was there that individuals invested with rights could realise their higher selves through association, brotherhood and patriotic duty.[74] Each nation had a God-given mission and it was the duty of each and every Italian to contribute to its fulfilment. Nationalism was a more spiritual alternative to communism or utilitarian liberalism, which Mazzini rightly regarded as excessively materialistic and overly focused on either the collective or the individual. While he was no anticlerical or freethinker, he thought that because it had supported absolutism the papacy should be replaced by a general council which could then deliberate the merits of all major religions. This Third Rome would then inspire humanity as the Rome of the Caesars and popes had done in the past.[75]

Mazzini was important less for anything he achieved, although he sometimes upset others' plans in a decisive way, than for the iron commitment to the national cause that his life represented, a life of promiscuous wordage (his collected outpourings comprise over a hundred volumes) spewed forth from the modest rented rooms that were his lot in exile. He was belief incarnate. His unshakeable faith in divine Providence and that 'national forces' were the 'ruling principle of the future' suggests how belief in God, History and Progress enabled him and his followers to account for, and surmount, any temporary obstacles. That may have been one of the chief functional effects of treating politics as a religion. Portentous talk about seeing the finger of God in the pages of a nation's history enabled Mazzini, who has been described as an 'autocratic democrat', to ignore those occasions when the will of the People was manifestly not with him.[76]

Mazzini was often the long hand behind various abortive coups and revolts in various parts of Italy; in the wake of one such failure – to topple king Charles Albert of Piedmont–Sardinia – a close friend committed suicide in prison. After being expelled from France in 1833, Mazzini spent the ensuing three years in Switzerland. From there he organised and participated in an attempt by a polyglot volunteer army of revolutionaries to seize power in Savoy, whose inhabitants would then be presented with the choice of remaining within Piedmont–Sardinia or joining the Swiss Confederation. The military operation was an ill-co-ordinated fiasco. Mazzini had to go into hiding as the French and Piedmontese lobbied for his expulsion from Switzerland. While in Berne, he formed Young Europe in 1834 as a 'holy alliance of Peoples who are constituted as great single aggregates according to the dominant moral and material attributes that determine their particular national mission'.[77]

Just as Young Italy had sought to co-ordinate general Italian support for local revolutionary episodes on the peninsula, so Young Europe was designed to give wider European aid to any nation involved in insurrection. Mazzini outlined the heady synthesis of politics and religion that guided the new foundation:

> We fell as a political party; we must rise again as a religious party.
> When, at Young Europe's dawn, all the altars of the old world have fallen, two altars shall be raised upon this soil that the divine Word has made fruitful; and the finger of the herald-people shall inscribe upon one Fatherland, and upon the other Humanity.
> Like sons of the same mother, like brothers who will not be parted, the people shall gather around these two altars and offer sacrifice in peace and love. And the incense of the sacrifice shall ascend to heaven in two columns that shall draw near each other as they mount, until they are confounded in one point, which is God.[78]

Mazzini's involvement in Young Europe underscores the fact that his nationalism lacked xenophobic tendencies, indeed, he tended to use the word 'nationalism' in a rather negative manner, preferring to describe himself as a 'patriot'. Nationhood would enable individuals to achieve a higher collective version of themselves, with the plurality of liberated nations realising this on behalf of humanity as a whole:

> We believe in the people, one and indivisible; recognising neither castes nor privileges, save those of genius and virtue; neither proletariat nor aristocracy; whether landed or financial; but simply an aggregate of faculties and forces consecrated to the well-being of all, to the administration of the common substance and possession – the territorial globe. We believe in the people, one and independent; so organized as to harmonize the individual faculties within the social idea; living by the fruits of its own labour. We believe in the people bound together in brotherhood by a common faith, tradition, the idea of love; striving towards the progressive fulfilment of its special mission; consecrated to the apostolate of duties; never forgetful of a truth once attained, but never sinking into inertia in consequence of its attainment.[79]

In mid-1836 the Swiss authorities bowed to international pressure by insisting that Mazzini leave a country he regarded with some affection. Early in 1837 he arrived in London, where he remained for much of the rest of his life. His modest income as a journalist and writer did not prove an obstacle to his being lionised by some of the great Englishmen and women of the day such as the Carlyles. In London, he wrote and thought, while refounding Young Italy with a younger generation of democratic revolutionaries.

In Italy itself, Mazzini's democratic insurrectionary nationalism faced competition from more moderate figures. There were those like the Piedmontese nobleman Cesare Balbo who argued that a solution to the Italian Question would come only from the interaction of the relatively powerful Piedmontese state within the international system. This proved prescient. In contrast to the rest of Italy, Piedmont had a constitution, a dynamic and liberalised economy and effective armed forces. Piedmont was not just the sole Italian state with an indigenous ruling dynasty, but also one whose existence was regarded as an indispensable check to the extension of French power. This meant it might undertake adventures for whose failure it would not have to pay a territorial price. These adventures were invariably conceived in terms of an extension of Piedmontese power in northern Italy rather than in order to unite the peninsula, a utopian goal that Piedmont's moderate conservative leaders associated with Mazzinian republicans whom they regarded as dangerous and despicable in equal measure.

If some realists began to bank on Piedmontese power, others transferred their utopian longings from the exiled Mazzinian conspirators to the improbable figure of the pope. In his *Of the Moral and Civil Primacy of the Italians*, which appeared in 1843, the Piedmontese priest Vincenzo Gioberti argued that both the papacy and Roman Catholicism were the glories of an Italian civilisation that was superior to all the rest. Rejecting the idea of unification as chimerical, Gioberti called for a federation of independent Italian states under the presidency of the pope whose moral leadership would be bolstered by the military might of Piedmont–Sardinia. Such a scheme would reconcile liberals, nationalists and Catholics. This proposal was dubbed 'neo-Guelphism', in a conscious echo of the party that had supported the popes in their power struggles with the 'Ghibellines' who had backed the medieval German emperors. If there was not much prospect of recruiting that ailing octogenarian Gregory XVI to the cause of reconciling Catholicism, liberalism and nationalism, there were (slight) grounds for thinking that his fifty-four-year-old successor, Pius IX, might put these fraught relationships on a fresh footing. Unlike his Luddite predecessor, who had prohibited the introduction of railways to the Papal States, Pius IX even travelled in a train.[80] But appearances of modernity were illusory. Pius may have begun his pontificate with a conventional flurry of reforms in the Papal States, but he was also ultra-orthodox on theological issues and from the beginning made it clear that he condemned the intellectual and political legacies of the Enlightenment and the French Revolution. His first encyclical, *Qui pluribus*, issued on 9 November 1846, condemned moral and philosophical liberalism, execrated the secret societies 'which have emerged from darkness for the ruin of religion and of States', described the notion of progress as 'sacrilege' and condemned 'the execrable teachings of communism, which can establish itself only by destroying the rights and true interests of all'.

The 1848 Italian revolutions exploded the false expectations that others had placed upon the new pontiff. He was in a dilemma: 'As an Italian I desire the nation's prosperity, and realise that the surest means of achieving it is a confederation of her several States. But as head of the Church I cannot declare war on a power [Austria] which has given me no cause to do so.[81] While the pope refused to declare war on faithful Austria, papal troops defected to the Piedmontese cause. When the latter suffered catastrophic defeat at Custoza, a vengeful mood spread in Rome towards all those who were less than wholeheartedly for the Revolution. The victims included Pellegrino Rossi whom Pius IX had chosen as prime minister with a view to stablising the Papal States at a time of general revolution. Rossi was killed in November 1848, by an assassin who plunged a knife into his carotid artery as he mounted the steps of the parliament. Rome was given over to mob rule. One of the pope's secretaries was killed by a stray shot as he stood next to the pontiff at a window in the Quirinal. In late November the pope slipped out of the city, disguised in a simple cassock, dark glasses and a muffler, taking up residence in Gaeta in the Bourbon kingdom of Naples, and leaving the French ambassador who was complicit in his escape talking to himself in an empty room.[82]

The new Roman Republic declared that the temporal powers of the papacy were at an end, together with Catholicism as the religion of state. Both Mazzini and the roving revolutionary Garibaldi descended upon this oasis of anarchy and freedom, while to the north the revolutionaries were being systematically routed by Radetsky's Habsburg troops. A French army under General Oudinot was despatched by Louis Napoleon, both to ingratiate his regime with domestic Catholic opinion and to forestall the prospect of the pope being restored solely by Austrian arms. From April 1850 when he returned to Rome – choosing to reside in the Vatican rather than the Quirinal to be safer from the urban mob – the pope's temporal power ultimately rested upon the presence of two alien armies: the Austrians and the French.

During the 1850s, prime minister Cavour sought to enhance the progressive reputation of Piedmont–Sardinia by reforming the Church in line with his dictum 'a free Church in a free State'. Since he thought the key to the wealth of Protestant states was based on their suppression of contemplative idlers, he suppressed all those monasteries that were not dedicated to socially useful activities. When in 1857 his government lost its majority, he blamed the increased vote for the right upon malign clerical influence. Charges of corruption involving clerics were used simply to unseat opposition candidates who had probably been fairly elected. It was at this time that a Catholic newspaper editor coined the phrase 'Nè eletti nè elettori' (Neither elected nor electors) to indicate Catholic suspicion of the representative character of the democratic process. The following year it was the turn of liberals to be legitimately outraged over the squalid saga of the kidnapping of Edgardo Mortara, a Jewish boy who had been secretly baptised by a family servant and who was then literally snatched away to be brought up as a Catholic, thereby scandalising much of European opinion.[83]

Meanwhile, the exiled Mazzini persisted in a conspiratorial insurrectionism that was designed to show the world that Italians could liberate themselves. One such expedition in 1856, led by the Neapolitan nobleman Carlo Pisacane, resulted in the liberators being killed as 'brigands' by troops and peasants in upper Calabria. Such madcap adventures were fitfully relevant to how the big players handled events, for, as a later Italian patriot remarked, it was Cavour's achievement to make the Italian Revolution the subject of European diplomacy.

In 1858 dissident associates of Mazzini's tried to assassinate Napoleon III by hurling grenades into his carriage. So great was the latter's fear of the lethality of Italian republicanism that six months later he was prepared to enter into the secret Plombières agreement with Cavour. France and Piedmont agreed to expel Austria from northern Italy, a move made possible by the weakening of Austria's diplomatic hand because of its equivocations during the Crimean War, the major cause of diplomatic instability in the mid-nineteenth century. The result would be four kingdoms within an Italian confederation under the honorary presidency of the pope. France would be rewarded with Savoy and Nice. When, following the bloody battles of Magenta and Solferino, Napoleon III unexpectedly concluded an armistice at Villafranca with Austria, the idea of a federal Italy was dropped. On 26 March 1860 Pius IX excommunicated those who had usurped his lands in the papal legations, the start of his implacable hostility to the emergent Italian state.

Mazzini then made a further providential intervention in events. Cavour had little interest in the Italian south, for many northerners thought 'Africa' began among the kasbah alleyways of Naples, a view succinctly expressed in a letter from Carlo Farini, who was its first chief administrator: 'But, my friend, what lands are these, Molise and the South! What barbarism! Some Italy! This is Africa; compared to these peasants the Bedouins are the pinnacle of civilisation. And what misdeeds!'

The involvement of Mazzini in persuading Garibaldi (who in disgust at the surrender of his homeland Nizza to the French had joined the service of the new Tuscan regime) to extend the war southwards by landing in support of a minor rising in Sicily was sufficient for Cavour to take up the goal of national unification while substituting monarchism for Mazzinian republicanism. Whereas Garibaldi thought that a negotiated union between north and south would concede Sicily a large degree of autonomy in recognition of its distinct traditions, Cavour decided upon outright annexation and enforced assimilation. Endemic divisions and different goals within the southern opposition to the Bourbons enabled him to win the peace after others had won the war.[84]

Garibaldi's 'Thousand' rapidly defeated superior numbers of Bourbon troops, partly thanks to the local knowledge of Francesco Crispi, the Sicilian nationalist given the task of stabilising the island in the wake of Garibaldi's conquests.[85] The Bourbon monarch Francis circled the wagons at Gaeta to fight another day. Garibaldi crossed over to Reggio Calabria, racing up the peninsula, in such a hurry that for his triumphal entry into Naples he took a train. Mazzini arrived in the great southern city, his agenda being not just rapidly to unify Italy, but to increase the likelihood of it becoming a republic. Mazzini urged Garibaldi to make a further dash to take Rome and then Venice, a strategy that would have ensured the intervention of Austria and France. But after defeating the Bourbons at Volturno on 1 October 1860, Garibaldi handed the former Kingdom of the Two Sicilies to Victor Emmanuel and retired to the island of Caprera. Victor Emmanuel became Italy's first king after a series of plebiscites had resulted in the annexation of Garibaldi's conquests. The encounter between liberal Piedmontese administrators (including the denatured southerners who accompanied them) and the Mezzogiorno was a rude one. Many of them reported that the south was figuratively or literally sick: 'in every way fusion with the Neapolitans frightens me; it's like going to bed with someone who has smallpox'. Instead of being welcomed as liberators, northern and southern liberals found themselves fighting a grim war against remnants of Garibaldian democrats, diehard adherents of the Bourbons and what they called 'bandits'. The solution was 'troops, troops and more troops', with two-thirds of the Italian army despatched southwards in the 1860s. The 'nation's' liberals rapidly accustomed themselves to martial law, the suppression of classical liberal freedoms, laying siege to villages and shooting captives in the head or the back.[86]

Looking back on these events from the vantage of 1868, Francesco Crispi reflected:

Italy was born eight years ago. It was born prematurely, and when no one was expecting it. It is we who conspired to make it. It needs to be strengthened and brought to manhood. Time is required to achieve this. We have destroyed the old governments; and we have linked up the various provinces: south to centre, centre to north. But this is no great achievement: it needs to be cemented. The stitches of our union are still visible: they must disappear, and the whole body made seamless.[87]

The chasm between the 'legal' Italy that had been created between 1860 and 1870 and the 'real' Italy of his own constituency in central Basilicata, in the arch between the heel and toe, was symbolised by the fact that on Crispi's rare visits from Turin or Florence, the seats of government until 1870, priests had to be a staple of every reception party since they alone could speak Italian, a language Cavour spoke haltingly. A fashionably biologistic cast of mind encouraged the view that, although nationhood was always latent, centuries of clericalism and despotism had resulted in a 'national' enfeeblement that could only be cured by regular doses of the 'national story'. Having originally espoused the small state and dense local government, along the lines of the British model, Italian liberals awoke to the educative potentialities of the state in a country utterly lacking any common history since classical antiquity. But there was more. In order to induce that sense of latent nationhood, the new masters of Italy turned to what they regarded as another innate human impulse: 'In man, religiosity is something innate, organic like sexuality, property, and the family ... No system will succeed in suppressing religiosity in the myriad forms in which this instinct manifests itself. It is the task of politicians simply to direct it towards good, and the maximum benefit of society.'[88]

The exemplary character of the lives of great men was recognised by the ancients, a practice that Christianity paralleled with its saints. Even while fighting continued, the leaders of the nationalist movement were subject to secular canonisation. When Garibaldi's red-shirted legions stormed into battle, courtesy of the smocks worn by butchers in Uruguay, they sang a hymn that described martyrs breaking out of their tombs to take up arms. When Garibaldi was wounded, as at Aspromonte in 1862, the wounds were depicted as stigmata on a man whom some peasants confused with Christ. His bullet-punctured boot and bloody sock became the relics of the age. Patriotic altars with his bust were surrounded by fetching displays of cannon balls and bayonets, in fulfilment of the patriotic religion envisaged by Fichte in Germany, who would doubtless have approved of a Lord's Prayer containing the verse: 'Give us today our daily cartridges'. There were ten patriotic commandments:

1. I am Giuseppe Garibaldi your General.
2. Thou shalt not be a soldier of the General's in vain.
3. Thou shalt remember to keep the National feast days.
4. Thou shalt honour thy Motherland.
5. Thou shalt not kill, except those who bear arms against Italy.
6. Thou shalt not fornicate, unless it be to harm the enemies of Italy.
7. Thou shalt not steal, other than St Peter's pence in order to use it for the redemption of Rome and Venice.
8. Thou shalt not bear false witness like the priests do in order to sustain their temporal power.
9. Thou shalt not wish to invade the motherland of others.
10. Thou shalt not dishonour thy Motherland.[89]

From these ad-hoc beginnings developed a much more knowing attempt to construct a communion of the faithful to the Fatherland, which was both modelled on the rituals of the Church and meant to supplant them:

We need to make this religion of the Fatherland, which must be our principal if not only religion, as solemn and as popular as possible. We all of us, servants of Progress, have gradually destroyed a faith that for centuries sufficed our people, precisely because through the ritualised forms of its displays it appealed to the visual senses, and through the visual senses to the minds of the masses, who are impressionable, imaginative, and artistic, eager for shapes, colours and sounds to feed their fantasies. What have we substituted for their faith? As far as the masses are concerned, nothing. We have closed our new Gods of Reason and Duty within ourselves, offering sacrifices to them, modestly in the course of our everyday lives, heroically in times of danger, but without adorning them with the external trappings of religion that still today, in the absence of an alternative, draw to church people who are nostalgic for beauty at a time when beauty is tending to disappear. We must address this, as the character of a people is not changed from one day to the next;

it is moulded not only by education but also by the natural surroundings in which it is condemned to live.[90]

Following the deaths of Victor Emmanuel in early 1878 and Garibaldi in 1882, both became central to the state-sponsored national cult. Elaborate ceremonies accompanied the body of Victor Emmanuel into Rome's Pantheon where, despite his equivocal attitude to unification during his lifetime, he was memorialised as the 'father of the fatherland'. From the mid-1880s, plans were afoot for the imposing, gleaming-white monument to Victor Emmanuel, which was eventually completed in 1911, the idea of incorporating the Italian parliament into the monument having been dropped. Garibaldi was already the subject of a cult in his own lifetime, as reflected in the number of institutions and streets named after him, not to speak of a profusion of hagiographical icons. That Garibaldi wanted his ashes interred on the remote island of Caprera was initially an obstacle to a major funerary monument in the capital.

As in united Germany, anniversaries, festivals, historical paintings and school history textbooks were other important ways of establishing the national canon. In 1886 a commission on the teaching of history at secondary level discovered that no textbook existed that met 'the needs of the present' or promoted the 'noble goal of national education'. Until 1867, the history curriculum stopped in 1815, partly to avoid the problem of the Risorgimento being taught by clerics who disapproved of its outcome for the Church. However, the recruitment of more lay teachers meant that in 1884 the modern history curriculum was extended to 1870. Apart from being used to educate people who were 'upright, peaceful, strong and sober', the content of history classes was also adjusted according to whether Mazzini or Cavour were 'in' or 'out'. Beyond the schoolroom, the equivalent of the Church's feasts and saints' days were picked out in the calendar, commemorating the deaths of Garibaldi, Mazzini and Victor Emmanuel, or such events as the taking of Rome or Palermo, celebrations which were attended by surviving veterans of these engagements. The dead were present too. In an emotional address in Palermo's Politeama theatre in 1885, Crispi began with a roll-call of the martyrs, anticipating the use of such evocatively plangent strategies by the dictatorships (and some of the democracies) of the following century, for by then public displays of hysterical emotion had become universal:

The ranks of the honoured phalanx have been thinned by death, and more than six hundred have not answered the call of the noble city.
The supreme captain: absent!
Giuseppe Sirtori, his learned and intrepid lieutenant: absent!
Nino Bixio, the modern Achilles: absent!
Giancinto Carini, the brilliant captain of the Calatafimi: absent!
Francesco Nullo, the soldier of humanity: absent!
Giuseppe La Masa, the daring rebel of 12 January 1848: absent!
Enrico Cairoli, the unsullied and fearless fighter: absent!

Similar roll-calls of the absent dead would echo in post-war Italy and Germany after 1918. The sentiments that Fascism would develop and exploit were already gathering around the altars of the nineteenth-century fatherlands, which for many people seemed too hierarchical, remote and impersonal, besides the more potent symbols of modern mass totalitarianisms. The British had things relatively easy with their medieval Westminster and eighteenth-century anthem 'God Save the King'. Other, newer, nations experienced an orgy of national symbol-making in the nineteenth century. Between 1870 and 1900 Germany, with which we began, was studded with new monuments. Some were dynastic, like the Deutsches Eck at the confluence of Rhine and Mosel in Koblenz, although Ludwig I of Bavaria built his Valhalla at Regensburg as a national monument. Others, notably the vast figures of Germania in the Niederwald or Hermann in the Teutoburger Forest, were the products of nationalist enthusiasm only ever partly satisfied by the Hohenzollern Reich, and which abandoned the notions of freedom and humanity that originally accompanied it. They dated terribly quickly. After the shock of the First World War expectations were abroad that required more than beribboned worthies gathered to celebrate anniversaries that lost their emotional force as the years passed, around monuments that did not transcend the era in which they were built, and which nowadays seem as if they had been put there by visitors from Mars. Before we trace the fate of those enthusiasms, we need to look at some powerful nineteenth-century creeds, some of which are still very much with us.

CHAPTER 6

Century of Faiths

I 'CHRISTIANS BY FEAR'

Nationalism was the most pervasive and potent Church to emerge during the nineteenth century, although for most people belonging to their nation was entirely compatible with Christian, Jewish or other devotions. Few followed the historian Jules Michelet in explicitly welcoming nationalism as a surrogate for Christianity: 'It is from you that I shall ask for help, my noble country, you must take the place of the God who escapes us, that you may fill within us the immeasurable abyss which extinct Christianity has left there.' But the intensity of commitment to the nation was already beginning to alarm such Roman Catholic commentators as archbishop Manning of Westminster, who with Italy, rather than Ireland, in mind in the 1860s denounced what he called the 'deification of the civil power' and the 'tyranny of modern nationalism', a view that was consistently held by the Roman Catholic Church whatever its politique dealings with individual governments.[1]

The nineteenth century was a great age of Christian faith that added drama and intensity to the phenomenon of 'honest doubt'. The chilly neo-gothic urban churches of the British present were once packed with worshippers, the reason many are deserted now being the over-capacity already evident in Victorian Britain as well as whatever alternative consolations the twenty-first century offers.[2] The rows of books on religion from the Victorian era that gather dust in the quiet corners of today's grander libraries once had avid readers who were theologically literate enough to enjoy them. Theology enjoyed a significant readership. In 1851 one-sixth of all the books published in German were on theology; in 1871 the figure was still one in eight.[3] As the Victorian critic and poet

Matthew Arnold discovered, *St Paul and Protestantism* or *Literature and Dogma* sold in ways that his *Culture and Anarchy* hadn't.[4] Dedicated missionaries took the faith to the 'darkest' continents where, despite the darkness having become the shade of pitch in the interim, many would say contemporary Christianity appears most dynamic.

But it was also an age of publicly aired religious doubt, often resulting from challenges from history, theology or science, and then reflected in literature which was like a thermometer of what constituted respectable conduct or opinion. The word respectable is important here, since most anguished Victorians retained respect for religion, and would have regarded today's philosophical or scientific 'anti-theists' as deeply uncouth and vulgar, their rationalism as arid and insensible. Take the novelist George Eliot, who at the age of twenty-two lost her severe Evangelical faith. Looking back in 1859 at the supervening period of aggressive agnosticism, Eliot wrote:

> I have no longer any antagonism towards any faith in which human sorrow and human longing for purity have expressed themselves; on the contrary, I have a sympathy with it that predominates over all argumentative tendencies. I have not returned to dogmatic Christianity – to the acceptance of any set of doctrines as a creed, and a superhuman revelation of the Unseen, but I see in it the highest expression of the religious sentiment that has yet found its place in the history of mankind, and I have the profoundest interest in the inward life of sincere Christians in all ages. Many things I should have argued against ten years ago, I now feel myself too ignorant and too limited in moral sensibility to speak of with confident disapprobation: on many points where I used to delight in expressing intellectual difference, I now delight in feeling an emotional agreement.[5]

The impossibility of believing in miracles in an age of science and scientific history occupied one of the most striking novels of the Victorian age. Mary Ward's 1888 three-volume *Robert Elsmere* was also one of the most commercially successful novels of the time. The author's life was so rich, and relevant to her writing, that it warrants some attention. Ward was the niece of Matthew Arnold and the aunt of Aldous Huxley, who did not much care for her. Her father, Thomas Arnold, tried farming in New Zealand, before becoming a schools' inspector in Tasmania where Mary was born in 1851. In the first of several somersaults, in 1856 Thomas

Arnold converted to Rome, resigned his post and went to teach in Dublin. In 1865 he rejoined the Anglican faith and settled in Oxford. His daughter Mary, the only child raised as an Anglican, joined her father after a long sojourn at her grandmother's house in Westmoreland. Left to her own devices by her self-preoccupied father, Ward developed a keen interest in medieval Hispanic studies, virtually unknown in Oxford at that time. In 1872 she married a lacklustre Brasenose don called Thomas Humphry Ward, who after duly resigning his bachelor fellowship attempted to support his family on the stipend of a lowly college tutor.

Ward's father had returned to Anglicanism in order to pursue a career at Oxford on the back of Arnold family connections. He gradually recovered respectability and a scholarly reputation. However, in 1876, on the eve of his becoming the £1,000-a-year Rawlinson professor of Anglo-Saxon, he announced his relapse towards Rome and his inability to accept the chair. Meanwhile both Wards chafed at the genteel poverty that was their lot in Oxford. She grew bored of researching entries on the Visigoths for *The Dictionary of Christian Biography*; Humphry wearied of the accidie and dulling grind of an Oxford teacher's life. They were like modern dons who dream of a Jaguar as they pootle about in their sputtering third-hand Volvos. In 1881 Humphry Ward abandoned academia to become a leader writer on *The Times*, where he would be at the centre of public affairs and under an invigorating nightly pressure. He also gambled on the art market by buying low and selling high. While he bought a 'Rembrandt' for a few shillings, he also paid £800 for a 'Velàsquez' that turned out to be a fake. Because of Humphry's art mania, life in their Russell Square household in Bloomsbury was tight. Mary Ward was under some pressure to become a successful popular writer, despite a number of recurrent ailments that made holding a pen or sitting an ordeal. The idea that she wrote her books to purchase, say, a dressing gown from Harvey Nicholls for her daughter is rather endearing.

Before we look at *Elsmere*, we should briefly mention Mary Ward's many subsequent accomplishments. She played a major role in founding Somerville, an Oxford college for women, establishing 'play centres' for children and successfully lobbying for special schools for the handicapped. President Theodore Roosevelt was a keen admirer, once cutting short an interview with kaiser Wilhelm II in order to converse with her. In the Great War she became the first woman journalist to visit the Western Front, partly to write (at Roosevelt's behest) a book that would bring the US into the war. Ireland made her a reform-minded conservative, although passages in *Elsmere* indicate an instinctual resistance to the dubious charm of the blarney. Since Ward equated feminists with Fenian terrorists (an uncle-in-law had been a hard-line chief secretary in Dublin) she became president of the Anti-Suffrage League, which campaigned against votes for women. Her own sex, she thought, should exercise discreet influence rather than overt economic or political power.[6]

Ward's masterpiece, published in 1888, displays an easy familiarity with the major theological issues of the day, an insider's grasp of donnish indolence and inertia, and a feeling for the land- and skyscapes of the Lake District. Parts of the novel are also stodgy and thin, reflecting drastic cutting as well as her poor characterisations, but the whole is as satisfying an experience as a snooze in a worn leather armchair. It is also a brilliant evocation of 'transition England', including the process of 'religion-making' as traditional Christianity appeared to wane.

The Wards' social calendar (including visits from the bailiffs), bouts of insomnia and writer's cramp make it remarkable that she could write a domestic shopping list as opposed to a three-volume novel. On 1 May 1886 the Gosses and Walter Pater came to dine; on the 26th Robert Browning; on 5 June Henry James; on the 29th dinner elsewhere with Thomas Hardy, among others.[7] She also fell out with her publishers Macmillan, who haggled about money, doubted her talent and saw little profit in the project. *Robert Elsmere* follows its protagonist, an idealistic Anglican cleric, from halcyon days in Victorian Oxford to the cloudy grandeur of the Lake District. There he meets his more fervid Evangelical wife Catherine, who faces the choice of marrying Elsmere or looking after her widowed mother and flightier younger sisters. She marries Robert and they move to a comfortable living at Murewell in Surrey.

Elsmere keeps up with his Oxford acquaintance. A don called Langham falls for Catherine's talented and vibrant musician sister. He eventually proposes marriage, only to run away from the flesh-and-blood young woman. An older don called Grey forges a synthesis of Christianity, rational scepticism and social action, which Elsmere eventually adopts. At Murewell, Elsmere, who has the conventional social compunctions of his time, takes up the cudgels on behalf of the poor labourers of an aloof and bleakly rationalist Squire Wendover, whose corrupt managing agent has allowed his villages to go to rack and ruin. Squire and cleric fall out when village waifs fall to diphtheria, and then, once the agent has been dismissed and the villages improved, become firm friends due to their common scholarly interests. Crates of expensive and obscure books on medieval history and German theology pass backwards and forwards between big house and rectory. Wendover constantly challenges Robert's faith, to the obvious discomfort of Catherine.[8] Robert Elsmere's faith breaks:

> 'Do I believe in God? Surely, surely! "Though He slay me yet will I trust in Him!"' Do I believe in Christ? Yes, – in the teacher, the martyr, the symbol to us Westerners of all things heavenly and abiding, the image and pledge of the invisible life of the spirit – with all my soul and all my mind!
>
> 'But in the Man-God, the Word from Eternity, – in a wonder-working Christ, in a risen and ascended Jesus, in the living Intercessor and Mediator for the lives of His doomed brethren?'
>
> He waited, conscious that it was the crisis of his history and there rose in him, as though articulated one by one by an audible voice, words of irrevocable meaning. 'Every human soul in which the voice of God makes itself felt, enjoys, equally with Jesus of Nazareth, the divine sonship, and miracles do not happen!' It was done.[9]

Rather than hypocritically mouth what he has ceased to believe, Elsmere decides to ruin Catherine's Thirty-Nine Articles complacencies (and family comfort) by resigning his clerical living: 'Christianity seems to me something small and local. Behind it, around it – including it – I see the great drama of the world, sweeping on – led by God – from change to change, from act to act. It is not that Christianity is false, but that it is only an imperfect human reflection of a part of truth. Truth has never been, can never be, contained in any one creed or system!'[10] With Catherine in tow, he follows the great tide of Victorian philanthropic concern debouching into working-class London. A cynical society hostess in the novel calls it 'East-Ending', and we shall see a lot of it in a later chapter.[11] Wandering around the historic churches of the City and East End, Elsmere perceives 'blank failure, or rather obvious want of success – as the devoted men now beating the void there were themselves the first to admit, with pain and patient submission to the inscrutable Will of God'.[12] He makes himself useful at a night-school, discussing religion with wiseacre artisan cynics and sceptics. He realises that 'Religion has been on the whole irrationally presented to him, and the result on his part has been an irrational breach with the whole moral and religious order of ideas.' He alights upon a working men's club in Elsgood Street, the local epicentre of anticlericalism and agnosticism. In a long, manly but rational address to the members of this club, for the men have had enough of fervid Evangelicals and epicene High Anglican priests, Elsmere wins many recruits to his 'New Brotherhood of Christ', a hybrid Deist temple and centre for social improvement. A rich friend, Flaxman, who subsequently marries Rose, helps convert warehouses into educational and social facilities for the upper-working class, for Mrs Ward retained a finely graded sense of distinction. Working men were represented on the Brotherhood's governing committees. Every member donated part of their earnings and a fixed amount of unpaid labour. The original meeting place became an austere temple, with the only articles of faith being:

> In Thee, O Eternal, have I put my trust;
> This do in remembrance of Me.

The names of members, past and present, were inscribed in wall recesses, while the walls themselves were decorated with copies of Giotto's Paduan Virtues. Ceremonies commenced with a simple affirmation of adoration 'essentially modern, expressing the modern spirit, answering to the modern need'. Elsmere would then expound on an aspect of the life of Christ as if it were 'a passage of Tacitus, historically and critically', before delivering an address designed to touch the hearts of his auditors. Psalms and hymns followed, which the artisans were supposed to sing at home too.[13] The Brotherhood thrives, we assume, although Elsmere sickens and takes a long time dying of TB. Ancillary characters are bade farewell through the device of 'Gain and Loss'; Squire Wendover dies a miserable death and Rose marries Elsmere's rich young patron Flaxman.

Robert Elsmere was a huge commercial success, partly because the serious critical responses were dilatory, cool and largely hostile. A ten-thousand-word review by Gladstone helped immeasurably, the former prime minister being so stirred by the book that he held two lengthy interviews with Mary Ward at Keble College, Oxford. Typically, Gladstone's notion of a 'similar' book one could not put down was Thucydides, although he profoundly disliked its protagonist's repudiation of Anglicanism and an Oxford that Ward associated with relative poverty and tedium. Pirate editions of the book did very well in the USA, although Mrs Ward was probably not gratified to learn that her book was being given away along with bars of Maine's Balsam Fir Soap.

Success in the USA was partly revenge for the popularity in Britain of *Uncle Tom's Cabin*. Since the British (along with other Europeans) liked to rub moralistic American noses in the dirt over slavery, US readers relished *Elsmere* because it seemed implicitly to criticise the Anglican Establishment, suggesting that Americans had achieved a much superior resolution of relations between Church and state in their estimable Constitution.[14]

Apart from 'honest doubt', one of the themes that Ward developed was that religion was essential to the maintenance of any moral and social order. The nineteenth century witnessed several attempts to reconcile religion with the dual imperatives of order and progress, through the medium of a new generation of secular religions, none of which had the state sanctions briefly available to the Jacobins as they sought to bring about a this-worldly utopia through mass murder.

Some of these faiths were merely eccentric, others more plausible; this one was confined to elite coteries, that one constituted the underlying assumption of entire generations. Some, like liberalism, are mercifully still with us, while others – such as scientism and Marxist socialism – have taken a battering, the last recamouflaged as left Eclecticism, largely confined in the western world nowadays to the universities, sardonically described by one major sceptic as 'a kind of heaven for concepts that have slipped their earthly moorings'.[15]

The nineteenth-century alternatives to Christianity were not the tranquilliser, shopping mall, soap opera and spectator sports that archbishops, moralists and pessimists worry about today, but a quest for a more plausibly up-to-date social religion without which, it was feared, societies would descend into anarchy, barbarism and immorality. The desire for such order often stemmed from the right, but the content increasingly hailed from the liberal and socialist left. So far from being aberrant products of the reaction to the French Revolution, the views of Burke, Bonald and Maistre on religion as a guarantor of social stability were widely held, often being adopted and adapted by those who wished to combine the new creed of Progress with retention of Order. Thinkers with more than life's fair share of eccentricity or insanity yearned for an end to anarchy and entropy. The wildest utopian speculations were often an attempt to restore harmony and stability as the aftershocks of the French Revolution continued to reverberate beneath Europe, while a way of life was turned upside down by rampant industrialisation.

The reality of anarchy became shockingly evident between 23 and

26 June 1848 in eastern Paris. Following the overthrow of the 'bourgeois' monarch Louis Philippe that February, the Parisian unemployed rose against the property-owners who dominated the Second Republic (1848–51) when the latter reneged on emergency measures to alleviate chronic mass unemployment. Viscount Victor Hugo, a former royalist ultra who had thrived under the July Monarchy after 1830 before becoming a deputy in the republican National Assembly, spent three days directing troops against the insurgents; another poet, Baudelaire, fought on the miserable side of the barricades.[16] The revolt of the 'smocks', that being the garb of the workers, was suppressed with great brutality. The novelist Gustave Flaubert, himself no friend of democracy, devoted several passages of his *Sentimental Education* – an attempt to gauge the moral climate of an age – to the ensuing bloodbath:

> By and large the National Guards were merciless. Those who had not taken part in the fighting wanted to distinguish themselves; and in an explosion of panic they took their revenge at one and the same time for the newspapers, the clubs, the demonstrations, the doctrines, for everything which had been infuriating them for the past six months. Despite their victory, equality – as if to punish its defenders and ridicule its enemies – asserted itself triumphantly: an equality of brute beasts, a common level of bloody atrocities; for the fanaticism of the rich counterbalanced the frenzy of the poor, the aristocracy shared the fury of the rabble, and the cotton nightcap was just as savage as the red bonnet. The public's reason was deranged as if by some great natural upheaval. Intelligent men lost their sanity for the rest of their lives.[17]

Fifteen hundred insurgents were summarily shot by the forces of the republican General Cavaignac, and a further eleven thousand were deported to Algeria.

During the Revolution of February 1848, priests had accompanied mayors to plant liberty trees, while a stray bullet killed the archbishop of Paris as he tried to mediate a ceasefire during the revolutionary June Days. A handful of clerics, like Lamennais and Frédéric Ozanam in their journal *L'Ere Nouvelle*, criticised industrialists who may have observed the Lord's day but whose factories sinned six days every week. But the majority of clergy, virtually none of whom came from the urban poor themselves, taught that social inequality was divinely decreed, that the charitable instinct ennobled both rich and poor, and that the affairs of this world did not matter anyway. This indifference was not evident in quotidian politics, where bourgeois fear of the insurgent unemployed presented the Catholic Church with an opportunity to reconcile itself with its sceptical opponents.

The Catholic Church abandoned the lost cause of Bourbon legitimism – it had never been keen on the anticlerical Louis Philippe, as it noted the increasing numbers of the erstwhile Voltairean bourgeoisie who had become 'Christians by fear'. These were fears that Voltaire himself would have appreciated, for had he not declared: 'I like my lawyer, my tailor, my servants and my wife to believe in God because I can then expect to find myself less often robbed and less often cuckolded'?[18]

Judging by the library left by a tax inspector who died in 1817, Voltaire was still highly influential, for of the inspector's 190 books 72 were by the wit of Verney while a further 37 were by Rousseau. Before 1848 indifference or outright hostility to religion was especially evident among the bourgeoisie, which at this time meant inhabitants of cities and bourgs (or small towns) who derived their income from the professions and renting land rather than industrialists. These people were routinely fingered by clerics for never venturing near a church. They deplored interruptions to the working week in the form of endless feast days, while their industrial counterparts ostentatiously kept their enterprises firing furiously on Sundays as an act of anticlerical provocation. They resented the Church's revived strictures on lending money at exorbitant interest. Their sons made any attempt to teach religion in the state and municipal secondary schools an impossibility.[19]

After 1848 the old alliance of throne and altar was replaced by the alliance of altar and strong-box (autel et coffre-fort). It was never as warm a relationship as that between Church and aristocracy or monarchy under the ancien régime because on both sides it was explicitly instrumental. In October 1848 a Parisian priest reported to the bishop of Autun a meeting with some industrialists and proprietors, in the course of which the priest had remarked that the only basis for private property was that the Commandments condemned theft, while rewards for the poor would be deferred to an afterlife. This had got the millionaires thinking. The priest continued:

> Since that time two of the company (including the industrialist)
> have come to find me, and have started discussions on religion,

from which I expect, with God's grace, the best results. That is how things are with the bourgeoisie: it will help us as a counter-weight to doctrines that it fears, and as a kind of spiritual police, called to obtain respect for the laws which benefit it. But that is the limit of its esteem and confidence in us.[20]

Following the 1848 Revolution the more well-to-do sections of the bourgeoisie alighted upon the Church as a means of keeping the lower classes in order, even though they sometimes maintained their Voltairean anticlericalism in private. Once the Church had left the Bourbons in the lurch, Catholicism became a means of reconciling otherwise rival conservative factions, Bonapartists, Bourbons and Orléanists, just as visceral anticlericalism would become what held the fissiparous liberal-left together. In other words, the Church became a mainstay of a new Party of Order while anticlericalism became a badge of the progressive liberal and radical left.

The Church campaigned furiously on behalf of the presidential candidacy of Louis Napoleon, the emperor's nephew, in the December 1848 election, for he promised to restore their influence in education and to support the pope against the Roman Republic. Louis Napoleon won by a landslide. The results revealed the link between religious observance and political conservatism that has characterised France ever since. This was repeated in elections in May 1849, where the Party of Order did well in the west and south-east of the Massif Central, while the republican left (known once more as the Mountain) scored better in the Limousin, Périgord, Allier, Cher and Nièvre where the Church had never recovered from the Revolution.[21]

Politicians hitherto cool in their attitudes to religion sang a different tune. Thus in January 1849 Adolphe Thiers told parliament: 'I want to make the influence of the clergy all-powerful. I ask that the role of curé be strengthened, made much more important than it is, because I count on him to propagate that sound philosophy which teaches man that he is here on earth to suffer, and not that other philosophy which on the contrary says to man: enjoy yourself.' Catholics who regarded liberalism with scepticism, such as the ultra-Catholic journalist Louis Veuillot, detected a certain cynicism: 'M. Thiers' aim these days is to reinforce the party of contented and satiated revolutionaries of which he is the leader with a body of gendarmes in cassocks, because of the evident inadequacy of the other lot.'

Notoriously anticlerical liberals, who had resisted the attempts of the Church to re-establish itself in education, endeavoured to restore clerical control, at least at the elementary level. Such people included Victor Hugo, subsequently rabid in his anticlericalism, who at this time supported the reclericalisation of education. 'What was a teacher?' asked Thiers. Nothing but a country boy who, having received a fancy education, returned to some remote village to preach resentment and sedition to peasant boys: 'The teachers are thirty-five thousand socialists and Communists. There is only one remedy; elementary education must be left entirely in the hands of the Church.' Only clerics were capable of the humility required. Such notions would resurface before and during Vichy.

Since the Church lacked the personnel to staff every elementary school, under the March 1850 Falloux Law teachers were to be nominated by local councils but supervised by mayors and priests. The procedures for opening secondary schools were liberalised so as to favour clerical establishments, of which 249 had been founded by 1854, while the clergy gained control of a further fifty municipal collèges. These developments had several fateful consequences. First, education became the preferred battleground in an endemic political conflict. Second, while the first generation of 'Christians by fear' combined public clericalism with private scepticism, the next generation tended to a more militant Catholicism, a development that undermines the notion of linear secularisation. Finally, the virtual identification of the clergy with the Party of Order in the state and the proprietors' interest, led opponents to detect a sinister 'clericalism' – that is the Church exercising untoward political power – to which the only response was an equally implacable anticlericalism. The immediate result of the Falloux Law took the form of 'Red' victories in by-elections (the left republicans had already notched up a respectable 250 seats in national elections in May 1849), to which the Party of Order responded by shaving off nearly three million voters in a new electoral law which introduced a covert property qualification.

Against this background, Louis Napoleon endeavoured to change the law so as to permit a further presidential term, while quietly slipping clients into key military positions for the eventuality of a coup. The cobblestones of Paris were smoothed with tarmac to facilitate the movement of cannons. Using the Assembly's refusal to restore universal suffrage as an excuse, on 2 December 1851 Bonaparte ordered the coup d'état codenamed Operation Rubicon. Victor Hugo scurried about trying to incite resistance:

Hugo: Follow my sash to the barricades.

A Worker: That's not going to put another forty sous in my pocket.

Hugo: You are a cur.

In Paris, a hundred leading opponents were quietly rounded up in dawn raids. They were followed by two hundred, mostly conservative, deputies, including Tocqueville, who had met in an underground version of the Assembly to depose Napoleon before he got rid of them. The following day, troops opened fire on a pathetic attempt to barricade the city centre, killing dozens of innocent bystanders in the process. Children and dogs were bayoneted or shot. A general joked with M. Sax (inventor of the saxophone) outside the Café Anglais, 'We're having our own little concert!'[22] Sporadic risings in the provinces, which were rejigged as a Red-inspired jacquerie, served as a pretext for twenty-five thousand arrests, the deportation of ten thousand to Algeria or Cayenne, and the enforced exile of two thousand more. A year after the coup Louis Napoleon became the emperor Napoleon III, the opening phase of his regime being an amalgam of economic reform and clericalism.[23]

The Second Empire reminded observers of 'a bawdy house blessed by the bishops', with the 'envoy of the Almighty' (Napoleon III) surrounded by 'crooks and pimps'. Tocqueville was especially scathing about the role of the Catholic Church: 'I am saddened and disturbed more than I ever have been before when I see in so many Catholics this aspiration toward tyranny, this attraction to servitude, this love of force, of the police, of the censor, of the gallows.'[24] The Church was advantaged. The budget devoted to religious worship rose from thirty-nine to forty-eight million francs. The Church enjoyed freedoms of the press and speech that were denied everywhere else. The number of regular clergy climbed, from a combined total of men and women of 37,300 in 1851 to 106,900 in 1861 to 157,200 by 1877. The number of priests rose from forty-six thousand to fifty-six thousand during Napoleon III's reign. Under Fortoul, the minister of education, the irreligious were weeded out of the university and up to fifteen hundred secondary school teachers were dismissed. Philosophy was narrowed to logic and mass was made compulsory in state schools on Thursdays and Sundays with confession once a term. Whereas the rule of Charles X had been sincerely Catholic, that of Napoleon III was ostentatiously clerical. Religion even crept into French foreign policy, as was evident in the going to war in the Crimea with Orthodox Russia in 1854–6, nominally over custodianship of the Holy

Places in Palestine. The French Catholic Church dubbed this ill-conceived and badly executed enterprise a crusade. War with ultra-Catholic Austria and support for Piedmontese expansionism in Italy put paid to that alliance since the pope, whose temporal possessions were threatened, soon informed the French ambassador: 'Your Emperor is nothing but a liar and rascal.'

While wealthier members of the bourgeoisie joined Napoleon III in acknowledging the social utility of Catholicism, slightly down the social scale, among academics, doctors, lawyers and middling businessmen, there was hostility to the Church, as being too complicit with a repressive and oligarchical regime, which censored the press and flouted individual liberties. Anticlerical republicanism attracted disproportionate numbers of Protestants and Jews, who regarded the Catholic Church as responsible for past slights and oppressions. Edgar Quinet and others were anxious to push republicans into Protestantism; while Jules Favre became one and George Sand had her granddaughters baptised by a pastor to protest against the Catholic Church. They were vastly outnumbered by people who had been brought up as Catholics but who rejected their childhood faith in favour of the ethical sociability of the masonic lodges. Under the Second Empire these became the main hubs of liberal and radical defence; under the Third Republic they would go on the offensive.

Since the republican tradition stemmed from a Revolution that had tried to eradicate the Church and Christianity, the pertinacity of hostility is perhaps unremarkable. Church and Republic had been briefly reconciled in February 1848, and then rent asunder in the summer over the June rising. The reliance of Napoleon III's democratic dictatorship on the Church meant a resurgence of that hostility. Exiles like Victor Hugo in the Channel Islands, Ledru-Rollin in London and Quinet in Switzerland hated Church and Empire with a passion. So did Tocqueville, who retired to write his great history of the ancien régime and Revolution. Although French republicans came second to none in their vehement anti-Catholicism, they were part of a much wider cooling of the educated liberal bourgeoisie towards religion, a phenomenon that was as evident in predominantly Protestant as in Catholic Europe. It had many sources, not least the Churches' close involvements with regimes that liberals were already hostile to, illustrated here at some length in the case of France, but which was equally true of conservative support for the reaction that set in across Germany in the wake of the 1848 Revolutions.

If anticlericalism fuelled the hostility of significant numbers of liberal and radical European bourgeois towards the Churches, that hostility also had many other sources. Paradoxically, one of these was Christianity itself, for opposition to the Churches could and did stem from people who thought they subscribed to a purer form of faith than established Churches compromised by their support for illiberal governments and an unjust social order. The Churches' apparent indifference to the 'social question', that is endemic indigence in industrialising societies, offended those with a social conscience, and not simply those who dubbed themselves Christian Socialists in the manner of Charles Kingsley, Frederick Maurice or John Malcolm Ludlow in Britain. The almost wilful obscurantism represented by the 1864 *Syllabus of Errors* and the 1870 declaration of papal infallibility offended those who had come to believe in the freedom of intellectual inquiry and the shibboleths of progress. The restoration of the Catholic Church in England to Europe with the reintroduction of a Catholic hierarchy in 1850 (roughly coinciding with the Trojan horse represented by Tractarianism within the Established Church) meant that the ultramontane threat had even penetrated Protestantism's island redoubt in the guise of the new Catholic archbishops of Westminster and Southwark.[25] The early Church had used dogma sparingly against heresies that threatened the fundamentals of Christian belief. In the nineteenth century dogmatic assertions seemed to rain down upon this or that uncongenial aspect of the modern world, while the merely eccentric were deemed heretics and elevated as martyrs.[26] John Colonso, Anglican bishop of Natal, used arithmetic to question the historical factuality of the Pentateuch, after, having learned Zulu, he entered into theological dialogue with a Zulu flock when a monologue was all that the Church desired. Faced with questions from the Zulus about how all the animals and their fodder had been accommodated within Noah's ark, the bishop was compelled to ask: 'Shall a man speak lies in the name of the LORD?' Deposed for heresy, Colonso was vindicated by a hearing in the Privy Council, only to be excommunicated when he returned triumphantly to South Africa. The critical spirit spread from the Zulus to the British timber merchant who gleefully informed bishop Walsham How that he had calculated the size and weight of Noah's ark and found it incredible. The prospect that such incredulity was leaching into the lower classes appalled Matthew Arnold, who condemned Colonso's book for unsettling the faith (and by implication the morality) of the lower classes, without offering anything by way of edification to stabilise it. Doubts about religious questions, which would be commonplace today, except to Catholic or Protestant literalists, almost automatically elided with matters of morality or politics.[27]

The ethical implications of Christianity were another area of dispute for they seemed to undermine the meliorist assumptions of the age. When environmental, hereditarian and psychological explanations of human conduct were gaining pace, ethically sensitive people regarded the divine lottery of who was predestined for heaven or hell with distaste, especially given the newfound emphasis upon reform rather than retribution in temporal punishment.[28] Societies that were humanising their judicial and penal systems found the idea of the damned being poked or roasted uncongenial. In his autobiography, Darwin gave voice to a moral critique of Christianity when he wrote: 'I can indeed hardly see how anyone ought to wish Christianity to be true; for if so, the plain language of the text seems to show that the men who do not believe, and this would include my Father, Brother and almost all my best friends, will be everlastingly punished. And this is a damnable doctrine.' His own researches into the cruelty and wastefulness of nature, and the deaths of the Darwins' children, compounded this view.[29] Others, including Charles Dickens and William Makepeace Thackeray, were appalled by the indiscriminate tribal mayhem of the Old Testament, with Thackeray noting, 'Murder them Jehu Smite smash run them through the body Kill 'em old and young,' as he read about the grisly fate of the priests of Baal.[30] Several prominent Victorian agnostics, including Matthew Arnold, George Eliot, J. A. Froude and F. W. Newman, turned to science or source criticism after they had already registered profound ethical objections to Christianity. Arnold penned the most famous lament for receding religious faith:

> The Sea of Faith,
> Was once, too, at the full, and round earth's shore
> Lay like the folds of a bright girdle furled.
> But now I hear
> Its melancholy, long, withdrawing roar,
> Retreating, to the breath
> Of the night-wind, down the vast edges drear
> And naked shingles of the world.

But his religious views were more complicated than this suggests. He despised the aesthetic impoverishment and provincialism of the British 'Puritan' tradition, updated as Dissent or Nonconformity, tellingly regarding them as 'prisoners of grievance', the progenitors of all sectarian victims-become-victimisers everywhere. That keen antipathy partly explains his corresponding warmth towards the Broad Church tradition within the Church of England. It eschewed dogma and enthusiasm while its state-supported breadth made it 'a great national society for the promotion of goodness'. Questions of taste were at work here too, as when Arnold endorsed the non-admission of Dissenting ministers to Anglican graveyards on the ground that their services lacked corresponding poetry. But there was something else at work in the thought of the Victorian poet and critic whose religious writings chipped and chivvied away at the biblical literalism of many of his British contemporaries. Like many Victorians, Arnold was concerned with working-class indifference to religion in an age when mass democracy was discernible to perceptive people. Culture would enable Christianity to reconnect with the most vital forces of the age, while supplanting religion as the main vehicle of ethical improvement since so much of that religion hardly seemed ethical at all. Potentially, Culture could become modern man's substitute for religious consolation, although since so much of that culture was of religious inspiration Arnold perhaps understimated a future in which the consumers of culture would gawp at their Piero della Francescas with headphones and captions filling in the great void in what passes for education.[31]

Many liberals (and socialists) were powerfully convinced by scientifically informed critiques of what were, sometimes erroneously, construed as essential Christian beliefs. Science enjoyed mounting prestige in an age of ceaseless discovery, in which mankind's comprehension of and control of the world advanced dramatically. It was the most obvious feature of a wider belief in indefinite material progress, which clashed with the Christian view that life on earth is subject to sudden, or wavelike, extra-temporal interventions, and that the end of the world was 'nigh'. Apart from sectarian minorities who continued to make proximate calculations for this event, the major Churches tended to treat it as a symbol, whose imminence was propelled into infinity. Apart from sectarians, the Christian Churches increasingly downplayed the eschatological aspects of their beliefs so as to accommodate themselves to the dominant secular creed of their time, namely that progress was occurring in the here and now. This provided them with common ground with a host of meliorists, while Christianity became a variant system of ethics.[32]

Scientists, and by extension physicians, like Flaubert's distinguished father, were the new heroes, whose authority eclipsed that of priests; indeed Darwin's first cousin Francis Galton wanted scientists to become a 'new priesthood'.[33] So did the distinguished German pathologist Rudolf Virschow, who in 1860 claimed that the natural sciences were taking the place of the Churches, and five years later that 'science has become a religion for us', claims rarely mentioned by today's anti-religious exponents of scientific hubris.[34] After the First World War, the sociologist Max Weber served up a more disenchanted version of this creed in a famous lecture entitled 'Science as a Vocation'.[35] Medical men, like Emile Zola's fictional *Docteur Pascal*, became secular saints wrestling with the forces of religious obscurantism. Religious explanations of, for example, epidemic diseases declined as a sober appreciation of sanitation rose, although in Victorian Britain national days of prayer to atone for cholera epidemics overlapped with campaigns to provide drains and sewers.

The reality of any battle is that it is confused and labile. Medical science edged aside miracles, but medical people informed by religion did not vacate the field: rather they regrouped to fight, as they still do, where the issues were primarily about human values.[36] There were other sensible shifts and accommodations that only religious fundamentalists or militant scientific reductionists find disagreeable. Gradually, by the late 1870s, even candidates for ordination in the Church of England who were agnostic about miracles or virgin births could find a bishop prepared to ordain them, provided they did not feel obliged to scandalise more traditional parishioners. Taste, if nothing else, ensured that many toed the official line, something inconceivable to today's aggrieved militant minorities.[37]

Few scientists were as fierce as their most enthusiastic promoters, who like Taine claimed: 'The growth of science is infinite. We can look forward to the time when it will reign supreme over the whole of thought and over all man's actions.' Many scientists failed to recognise any insuperable conflict between science and their own professions of faith. The two most eminent English geologists of their day were devout clergymen: the reverend professors William Buckland at Oxford and Adam Sedgwick at Cambridge. Neither had difficulty reconciling their discoveries with the existence of a divine creator.[38] The roll-call of scientific geniuses who were Christians would include such figures as Ampere, Faraday, Kelvin, Lister, Mendel and Pasteur to range no further, facts ignored by today's scientistic reductionists who seem wholly ignorant of their less two-dimensional predecessors.

Mention of battlegrounds (and in some countries the clash between Church and state spread from education into health and welfare) brings us to what was vulgarly construed as an epochal clash between science and religion. Evolution was not a new idea, and Christianity had got along untroubled by Anaximander of Miletus' claim that everything was descended from fishes. It had also gradually reconciled itself to geological evidence that earth was hundreds of millions of years old. The battle about Darwin commenced at the British Association meeting in the wet June of Oxford in 1860. Men and monkeys bulked larger in the debate than they did in *The Origin of Species*, where both are mentioned only once.[39] Barbs about apes and ladies' ancestors by the main protagonists T. H. Huxley and bishop 'Soapy Sam' Wilberforce, who famously locked horns on behalf of respectively science and religion, made good copy in an age that was easily scandalised.[40] The first leader in *The Times* newspaper on the bigger theme appeared in May 1864, to be followed in succeeding decades by such books as J. W. Draper's *A History of the Conflict between Science and Religion* (1875) and A. D. White's *The Warfare of Science with Theology* (1876). Such books traced the conflict back in time, thereby elevating such figures as Galileo or Giordano Bruno to the status of proto-martyrs.

For there were ideologues, publicists and zealots, some of them scientists, such as Haeckel, Huxley, Moleschott, Wallace and Vogt, who made extravagant claims on behalf of science regarding religious or philosophical questions to which, on sober reflection, 'science' offered few answers. In its more politicised formulations, such forms of scientific hubris raised the prospect of the modern 'expertocracy', consisting of rule by engineers or scientists, a fantasy that had already tantalised Henri Saint-Simon, but which by the late nineteenth century had become the nightmare of eugenics and Galton's scientific priesthood regulating the national gene pool. In Victorian England, clergymen gradually abandoned attempts to 'prove' that God had perversely planted fossils in rocks to test faith or recalculated Old Testament years into quarters so as to make the astonishing longevity of the patriarchs more plausible.[41] But they remained prepared to pounce on scientists when they opined on matters upon which their expertise was no greater than anyone else's, while at the same time cautiously accommodating scientific truths within their worldview. Some churchmen positively welcomed Darwin, judging by a sermon preached in 1879 by Stewart Headlam, in which he claimed that Christ was inspiring Lyell or Darwin and that 'it gives us far grander notions of God to think of him making the world by his Spirit through the ages, than to think of him making it in a few days'.

In 1882 Darwin was buried in Westminster Abbey with Christian obsequies, while the archbishops of Canterbury and York served on the committee of his memorial fund. *The Times* pronounced the 1860 clash between Huxley and Wilberforce 'ancient history', and clergymen competed to heap praise on a freethinking genius whose awareness of the sensibilities of those around him, a virtue rarely evident in strident Darwinians, had led him to keep militant secularists at arm's length.[42] Two years later, Frederick Temple, who in 1896 would become archbishop of Canterbury, delivered the prestigious Bampton Lectures on 'The Relations between Science and Religion' in which evolution was assumed to be axiomatic.[43]

That this conflict coincided with the most extravagantly dogmatic statements of the papacy facilitated caricature of the religious position, which was not identical with the most conservative wing of the Roman Catholic Church, but included liberal Protestants who did not need to defend every word in the Bible. In reality, many critics of the religious position had developed their animosity, for whatever personal reasons, long before Darwinian evolution or geology provided scientific support for it, conveniently overlooking the fact that much of the criticism of Darwinian 'speculations' hailed not from bishops like poor Wilberforce whose jibe about simian 'grandparents' Huxley turned back on him, but from other scientists, such as the anatomist Sir Richard Owen, who were not persuaded by the evidence Darwin had so compellingly marshalled.

While the work of geologists and palaeontologists had implications for the biblical computation of the world's antiquity, and that of physiologists and psychologists left the whereabouts of the soul uncertain, other religious verities appeared under parallel assault from biblical scholarship, philology and the comparative study of myths and religions by anthropologists. The nineteenth century did not invent vigorous interrogation of the scriptures; the preceding century had included Johann Salomo Semler, whose investigations into the historical evolution of the Bible had indicated a gulf between theology and religion.[44] The young theologian Hegel had written a *Life of Jesus* in which there was no mention of miracles.[45] Since educated people consumed far more popular works on religion than on science, this literature was arguably more subversive of faith than learned tomes about fossils, frogs, rocks and snails, especially when it made the ambiguous claim that the Gospels were neither fabricated nor true, but testimony to a religious reality concealed within myth and legend. Mrs Humphry Ward caught the subversive power of historical criticism in *Robert Elsmere*:

> He [Robert Elsmere] pored feverishly on one test point after another, on the Pentateuch, the Prophets, the relation of the New Testament to the thoughts and beliefs of its time, the Gospel of St. John, the intellectual and moral conditions surrounding the formation of the canon. His mind swayed hither and thither, driven from each resting place in turn by the pressure of some new difficulty. And – let it be said again – all through, the only constant element in the whole dismal process was his trained historical sense . . . the keen instrument he had sharpened so laboriously on indifferent material now ploughed its agonizing way, bit by bit, into the most intimate processes of thought and faith.[46]

Disbelief in miracles had little or nothing to do with contemporary science, but everything to do with what was afoot among theologians in the sleepy German university town of Tübingen who in turn were influenced by the study of collective myth. The word 'German' came to be synonymous with darknesses that inevitably strike us as innocent, but which were sinister by the lights of the Victorian era.[47]

Paradoxically, almost scandalous opinions were expressed where orthodoxy appeared to be most entrenched. This was Germany. The state had always been German Protestantism's 'natural ally' because of historical dependencies since the Reformation and because Protestantism lacked the external centre of authority represented by the papacy. During the Restoration these dependencies quickened, as Protestant churchmen saw the state as a bulwark against dangerous opinions, while the state regarded the Church as a bulwark against revolution. In 1822 king Frederick William III of Prussia merged the Reformed and Lutheran Churches into a Union, which was then closely integrated into the 'state machine'. He established structures that reflected his belief that he could command the Church in the same way he could the Prussian army. Following the accession of Frederick William IV in 1840, Prussia was proclaimed as the 'Christian state', one of whose bases was a Pietism that had always rejected rationalism and which in the meantime had calcified into being a Church. Intellectual support for this latest manifestation of the alliance of throne and altar was provided by, among others,

Friedrich Julius Stahl, a prominent conservative who at seventeen had converted to Protestantism from Judaism. Human sinfulness justified a strictly hierarchical and unchanging political order. The Gerlach brothers, Ernst Ludwig and Leopold, were at the centre of the conservative camarilla at the Prussian Court, and played a major role in the elaboration of the 'Christian state', which by 1854 meant that religion was the most important subject taught in schools, while the German classics were excluded in favour of whatever promoted the idea of a corporate Christian agrarian society.

After the 1848 revolutions, Protestant churchmen across Germany became the most articulate and fervent spokesmen of throne-and-altar reaction. They may have differed in their view of how relations between Church and state should operate, but they were as one in believing that the function of the Church was to legitimise the state, which in turn would enable them to proclaim the Gospel. That the National Assembly in Frankfurt am Main had dispensed with prayers at its opening session did not endear its memory to conservative Protestant clergy, who also congratulated themselves on the pious quiescence of the countryside, which had done more than government bureaucracies to quarantine urban revolution. Some of them, such as the Hessian theologian August Vilmar, eclipsed Pius IX in reactionary vehemence: 'Have we learned that democracy, with everything in any way associated with it, is nothing other than stupidity, scandal, dissoluteness, robbery, theft and murder?' The *Evangelische Kirchenzeitung* of Ernst Wilhelm Hengstenberg was the chief organ of ecclesiastical orthodoxy, one of its achievements being to campaign against rationalist theology professors, one of whom it successfully hounded from his post.[48] Hengstenberg recognised that the stakes were high when in 1836 he wrote: 'Infidelity will gradually divest itself of any remnants of faith, just as faith will purge the remnants of infidelity from itself.'[49] The Church was a bulwark against social disorder – sin being its explanation of both political discontent and poverty, preaching of the Gospel being its only solution. Fundamentalist Protestantism found no scriptural basis for liberal or democratic freedoms: 'Daily bread is in the Lord's prayer, but there is nothing there about political liberty.'[50]

In liberal circles this orthodox refusal to countenance the idea that heaven could ever be made on earth was gradually challenged by the idea of a religion of humanity. In 1835 the theologian David Friedrich Strauss published his *Life of Jesus. Critically Examined*. A Hegelian who had come to sit at the master's feet in Berlin only to find that he had died, Strauss thought that Christ was the incidental embodiment of an idea, namely of humanity moving towards perfection as the process of history was fulfilled. Strauss rejected both the orthodox view that everything, whether natural or supernatural, in the Gospels was true. He argued that the Gospels constituted not a legend – that is a story that proceeds from the facts – but a myth in which concepts or states of mind preceded the construction of the story. The Gospels were a mythopoeic rendition of the Jewish people's anticipation of a Messiah: the historical reality was contoured to conform to this expectation, which was why so many of the miracles of Jesus corresponded to those of Moses, Elisha and Elijah. Strauss did not deny that Christ was a historical person. Christ saw Himself as the Messiah, and such was the indelible impression that He made, the communal imaginings of His followers transformed Him into the divine and supernatural figure, with the aid of miraculous materials from the Old Testament that were projected on to Christ Himself. Employing a tone of ironic detachment, which in itself raised critics' hackles, Strauss asked whether the meaning and truth of the dogma of Christ depend on the historical reliability of the Gospel reports of the life of Jesus and His miraculous uniqueness. Were the Jesus of history and the Christ of faith identical? If the answer to these two questions was 'yes', Strauss thought he could demonstrate the collapse of the Christian case. His assurance that 'the supernatural birth of Christ, his miracles, his resurrection and ascension, remain eternal truths, whatever doubts may be cast on their reality as historical facts', did little to dispel widespread disquiet. The furore caused by Strauss's work took the form of a clash between the respective claims of philosophy and religious authority, which in turn involved the Prussian state.

While Strauss was politically conservative, the intense debates about his work resulted in the gradual coalescence of a group of 'Young Hegelians', one of whom, Bruno Bauer, rejected Hegel's own attempts to reconcile religion and philosophy. Christianity had separated, or alienated, man from the world, rendering him incapable of changing the world but reliant upon anti-rational miracles. In early 1842 Bauer was dismissed from his academic post for speaking on behalf of a prominent liberal editor. His acolytes and doctoral students would also have no hope of a university career, for such conformist circles routinely practised guilt by association. The guilty included Karl Marx, who abandoned hope of academic preferment and turned to journalism as editor of a Rhineland newspaper. Where this group was tending was made clear in a letter written by one of their Cologne supporters: 'If Marx, Bruno Bauer and Feuerbach come together to found a theological–philosophical review, God would do well to surround Himself with all His angels and indulge in self-pity, for these three will certainly drive Him out of His heaven . . . For Marx, at any rate, the Christian religion is one of the most immoral there is.' We will pick up this story later.[51]

Strauss's dense Hegelianism made few waves in Catholic Europe, but a far more accessible life of Jesus, by a lapsed Catholic seminarian, became the French bestseller of the century. Ernest Renan came from a modest Breton background and was destined for the clergy. An immensely gifted linguist (he was expert in the Semitic tongues), Renan decided to embark on 'the rational verification of Christianity'. By the autumn of 1845 he had abandoned the faith, leaving the security of the Church to become a scholar. In 1860 he went on an archaeological expedition to the Levant with his wife Cornélie and his beloved sister Henriette, both effectively rivals for his affections. He was moved by the living landscape of the Bible, the backdrop to his 1863 *Vie de Jésus*. This was written in the Lebanon in the company of Henriette after his wife had returned to Paris. Both siblings caught malaria, although it killed Henriette rather than Ernest. Lesser disasters followed. In 1861 Renan was appointed to the chair of Hebrew at the Collège de France, the post he most aspired to and for which he was eminently qualified. Despite having been warned to avoid controversial subjects, in his inaugural lecture he remarked that Jesus was 'an incomparable man', so great that he would not contradict those who, impressed by His remarkable achievements, called Him 'God'. This periphrastic denial of Christ's divinity did not deceive keen-eared Catholics and Protestants in the audience, and within a month the government had suspended the rest of his lectures.[52] More controversy came when he published his *Life of Jesus*, which within a year had sold fifty thousand copies and had appeared in most European languages.

Renan used a revealing analogy to explain his scepticism towards his sources. The Gospels were akin to the reminiscences of Napoleon's veterans: 'It is clear that their narratives would contain numerous errors and great discordances. One of them would place Wagram before Marengo; another would write without hesitation that Napoleon drove the government of Robespierre from the Tuileries; a third would omit expeditions of the highest importance.'[53] But, despite all these tricks of memory, the character of the hero would still emerge with clarity and truthfulness. The Gospels were legends with some basis in history, the legendary being the miraculous and supernatural elements introduced by memory passed down by oral tradition. Having decided that Christ had actually existed, Renan set about explaining how He had been enveloped by the legendary. It was largely a matter of projection and wish-fulfilment: 'the more people believed in him, the more he believed in himself', as if Christ was a prototype of Hitler or the actor Steve Berkoff. People had expected Jesus to work miracles, so He had gone along with this, up to the point of trickery, to ensure that His moral message got through, just as popular messianic expectations resulted in Christ's (self-)sacrifice. After Christ's crucifixion, the disciples scanned His life for earlier signs of the miraculous. Jesus had brought out mankind's God-making propensity and was Himself the highest form of the divine that the mind of men could conceive.

II GOLDEN AGES

These multiple challenges to Christian faith did not mean a wholesale adoption of atheism and militant scientific materialism. That was but one option in a century that also saw people interested in metaphysical religions based on individual spiritual growth, neo-paganism, occultism and exotic spiritualities.[54] The latter had the advantage of being known in their purest form, against which the failings of institutional religion in the west could be contrasted to ill-effect by people who knew little or nothing about the squalid social realities that went with eastern religions, whose wisdom was distilled into the dusty tomes of men like the Sanskrit scholar Max Müller.[55] Apart from general obeisance to the social utility of religion, especially as far as the masses were concerned, there was almost universal recognition that man is a fundamentally religious being, whether in terms of his awed response to nature or in terms of his solitary reflections on his individual destiny. The retreat from Christianity into irreligion (or rather infinite gradations between the two) was paralleled by a much larger retreat from Christianity into religion, as a religious instinct far older and more pervasive than any single religion, like water, discovered its own level. Whereas Maistre had looked back nostalgically to a vanished and largely imaginary world of Christian order, others, innocent of firing squads and gulags, declared that 'The golden age of the human species is not behind us, it is before us. It lies in the perfection of the social order. Our forefathers did not witness it, our offspring will attain it one day. It is up to us to clear the way for them.' Virtually all of the utopians, except the most successful, felt compelled to crown their creations with a religion.[56] Although some of them were amusingly idiosyncratic fellows, perceptive readers should be alert to one sinister tendency that is common to them all. They all thought that human nature was both good and a given, evil being the product of the social circumstances that distorted or suppressed what was inherently good in mankind. This was inherently despotic, since what would be the fate of people who rejected the transformations that would restore this innate goodness? A French writer asked, at the end of a pamphlet written in 1840, 'What if people do not want this?' To which he replied: 'What if the inmates of the Bicêtre [mad house] refuse to have baths?' Who would decide who were the mad and the sane? Who would police the keepers of the 'morally insane', the dark term for those immune to the lure of utopia? Who determined whether people were in or out of step with the world-historical trends the utopians claimed to detect?[57]

Under the Second Empire, when political opposition was not openly allowed, masonic lodges became important venues for political discussion. The roll-call of masons who became prominent political figures under the Third Republic was impressive: it included Bourgeois, Brisson, Buisson, Combes, Ferry and Gambetta. Masonry had originally incorporated belief in a supreme being; indeed affirmation of the existence of God had been explicitly incorporated into the 1849 constitution of France's Grand Orient lodge. By the 1870s masonry had become much more anticlerical and freethinking, as symbolised by the decision of the same lodge to delete the clause just referred to. The lodges were pressure groups for republican causes, rival charitable networks, and networks that were useful in rigging appointments and promotions while denying them to Roman Catholics. Many middle-class people also subscribed to something called Positivism, a creed that nowadays virtually everyone has forgotten, although its slogan 'Order and Progress' is still inscribed on the national flag of Brazil.

Positivism was the belief in the certain and distinctive kind of knowledge obtainable by science. Its immediate origins lay in the circle of Idéologues under the Directory who wanted to create a secular and scientific morality and an enlightened elite who would lead government and society, with productive enterprise as the great healer of the Revolution's legacy of acute social conflict.

The Directorial and Napoleonic Idéologues influenced comte Claude Henri de Rouvroy de Saint-Simon, or Saint-Simon for short, who had fought in the American War of Independence, had been to Mexico, where he proposed cutting the Isthmus with a canal, and had returned to France where he narrowly escaped execution during the Terror. He subsequently made, and lost, a deal of money, before embarking upon a career as an amiably crackbrained writer. In 1820 he was arrested for having said in a pamphlet that whereas the loss of fifty of the best artists, bankers, industrialists and scientists in each field would be catastrophic, France would not lament the loss of the thirty thousand people who made up its hierarchy, the monarchy, rentiers, clerics and so forth, for the benign comte could be quite casual with the lives of yesterday's men, a trait he shared with other utopians. This far from original thought coincided with the assassination of the duc de Berry, who had figured in the list of those who would 'not be missed'. Saint-Simon's trial and acquittal made him a celebrity.[58] In 1823, by which time the 'genius' was living in pitiful penury surrounded by books, papers, crusts of bread, dirty linen and a cranky entourage, he decided to kill himself. He loaded seven bullets into a gun, and took out his watch, so as to think about the reorganisation of society until the end. He fired six bullets at his head: the seventh missed, but, apart from one that extinguished an eye, the others only grazed his scalp. When a doctor found him bent over a basin into which the blood flowed, Saint-Simon greeted him: 'Explain this, my dear Sarlandière, a man with seven bullets in his head can still live and think.'

Saint-Simon thought he was a genius. His valet may have concurred, for each morning he woke his master with the words: 'Rise, M. le Comte – you have great things to achieve.' Saint-Simon's disordered and fragile mental state probably explains the obsession with order, planning and totalising theories – something even more exponential in the case of his renegade disciple Auguste Comte, who was madder than the maverick master.

Saint-Simon was the ur-guru of all future technocratic solutions to social problems and one of the early lights of European central socialist planning through which so much misery was inflicted on so many. Beyond that, he was the ancestor of those who seek global governance, world parliaments and world peace, the contemporary manifestation of the utopian legacy. Since he blamed bumptious lawyers for the French

Revolution and disdained their talk of liberty and rights, at least he can't be blamed for international courts of justice. While millionaire bankers posthumously published his collected works and paid to maintain his grave in the Père Lachaise cemetery, the Soviets erected an obelisk to his memory in Moscow. If the former liked his idea of 'an aristocracy of talent', the latter were keener on his division of humanity into productive worker bees and eliminable parasitic drones. Saint-Simon's 'socialism' rejected equality and welcomed profit. His doctrines left their mark (for he said that ideas were like the lingering smell of musk) on such projects as the Crédit Mobilier, the European railway networks and the Suez Canal of de Lesseps. Saint-Simon's local influence was most evident in the regime of Napoleon III.

Just as Saint-Simon was not fussy about which autocrat might implement his schemes, so his thinking was eclectic and open to surprising ideological influences, in the manner of twentieth-century postmodernists, who are at least theoretically open to the ideas of right as well as left, although they too have the herd-like mentality of academics everywhere. Saint-Simon took much from the ultra-reactionaries Bonald and Maistre, putting it at the service of the liberal bourgeoisie who detested the outmoded rule of aristocrats and clergy that these two had lauded.[59] Admirers say that Saint-Simon was a philanthropic aristocrat struggling to adapt to what he correctly saw as the coming age of science and industry – an extraordinarily prescient vision, as it turned out, for he wrote at a time when most of Europe's population were still subsistence farmers. Undeterred by the fact that what science he knew came from his practice of lavishly entertaining down-at-heel professors when he was in funds himself, Saint-Simon had boundless confidence in the future of science.

Scientists were the first group to whom he promised the earth, on the ground that their political advancement would benefit humanity as a whole, a proposition that is quite different from the fact that most of us prefer scientific medicine to magic or witchcraft when we are ill. From 1814 onwards he added bureaucrats, magistrates and merchants to the new elite, before transferring the leading role in transforming the world to the 'industriels', a term whose meaning shifted but which was always coterminous with 'productive elements' ranging from bankers to humble workers. An advocate of free trade, which he thought would inaugurate an age of peace, Saint-Simon wanted industrialists to take over administration of the state, which would be cut back to a few police functions since there would be no economic regulation. The state had developed partly to defend people against the Church; without the Church the state could wither away. Later he refined his focus to advocacy of rule by bankers alone, which probably explains his popularity with Messrs Lafitte and Péreire, the financial princes of their day. The world would become one giant multinational enterprise, linked together by the flows of international capital.

In its final elaborations, Saint-Simonian utopianism consisted of semi-corporatist 'Chambers'. Central planning of huge infrastructural projects was the responsibility of a Chamber of Invention, dominated by engineers, the new class, who fused the skills of businessmen and scientists, and whose future importance Saint-Simon was among the first to notice. He was obsessed with canals and roads, which would be punctuated with vast gardens, with museums displaying the natural and industrial products of any given locality. Culture would no longer be a luxury for the few, but something used to refine the mass of humanity, for Saint-Simon was the first 'engineer of human souls' to set to work on the creative arts. Other aspects of his thought also have the cabbage whiff of the east European people's palace circa 1950. Public festivities would exhort people to more work, and remind them of the perdition they had transcended. A Chamber of Review, consisting of hundreds of pure scientists, would 'review' the schemes of the Chamber of Inventions, and organise further festivals, celebrating men and women, boys and girls, mothers, fathers, children, managers and workers. A Chamber of Deputies, consisting entirely of industrialists, would be the executive, raise taxes and implement massive public projects. Striking a proto-Communist or proto-Fascist note, Saint-Simon warned: 'The role of the talkers is approaching its end, that of the doers will not be long delayed in making its appearance.'[60]

The Enlightenment had rejected the medieval and absolutist past, although it was fond of a dimly known republican antiquity. By contrast, Saint-Simon claimed that progress resulted from the dialectical interaction of 'organic' and 'critical' periods in history. Organic periods included classical Hellenic and medieval Christian civilisations when all ideas were in harmony and in the service of the common good; but critical periods – such as Saint-Simon's own – were equally necessary, for they dissolved the former while simultaneously giving birth to higher organic periods. He found virtue in surprising places, including the medieval Church which had held Europe together, civilising and pacifying wherever it could. One cannot imagine any Enlightenment thinker writing that up to the fifteenth century:

> the men of the Church were superior to the laity in their talents and virtues. It was the clergy that cleared land for cultivation, and drained unhealthy marshes; it was they who deciphered ancient manuscripts. They taught reading and writing to the lay population ... the clergy founded the first hospitals, and the first modern institutions of learning; they united the European nations in their resistance to the Saracens.[61]

Living in what he regarded as a time of critical dissolution, Saint-Simon could not resist the challenge of elevating social science into a new religion that would guarantee order together with progress. Like everyone who had lived through the Revolution, and many of those who hadn't, he had a fear of the guillotine and of being rabbled. This was where the downgraded savants came in. They were to be organised into an Academy of Reasoning and an Academy of Sentiment. The former would draft laws and regulations; the latter, consisting of artists, moralists, poets, painters and theologians, would paint images of the bright future. So far, this vision lacked any religion. Isaiah Berlin was wrong to claim that Saint-Simon was 'the first originator of what might be called secular religions', for the Jacobins had already passed that way.[62] But from 1821 onwards Saint-Simon began to elaborate what he called 'New Christianity', for, as he put it, 'The throne of the absolute could not remain untenanted.' There was also a social agenda, for he also wrote: 'Religion is the collection of applications of general science by means of which enlightened men rule the ignorant ... I believe in the necessity of a religion for the maintenance of the social order.' That was the beginning of the Orwellian double morality whereby the enlightened elite espoused one code of values while force-feeding the donkeys with another.[63] Arguing that one God must translate into one sublime commandment, Saint-Simon claimed that it was that men should behave as brothers. Both rich and poor would be morally improved if they acknowledged that it was incumbent on everyone to work on behalf of the poor. The heretical papacy had perverted this doctrine through its corrupt proximity to earthly powers. The Church had become a secular rather than a spiritual force. If the Catholic Church was 'Anti-Christian', the Reformation had hardly been an improvement, since Luther too had done little by way of 'public works' to benefit the poor. He had also replaced an institution that over time exhibited adaptability and flexibility with the rigidity of what was written in one book. If the new religion was capitalistic philanthropy, its priesthood consisted of artists and scientists – or priests retrained as such – while the messiah was none other than the prophet through whom God spoke: Saint-Simon himself.[64]

After his death, Saint-Simon's disciples Amand Bazard and Barthélemy Prosper Enfantin developed the master's doctrines in different ways in a series of evening lectures. Bazard wished to abolish private inheritance of property. Inheritances would go to a central bank which would reinvest in new productive enterprises, a project dimly perceived behind the realities of government investment in railways and the Crédit Mobilier.[65] Enfantin was more interested in founding a Saint-Simonian religious sect. This took the form of a commune at Ménilmontant on the outskirts of Paris, where the disciples lived according to a pseudo-monastic rule based on the injunction 'All men must work' and espoused brotherly love as the basic tenet. They wore a special uniform, whose vest could only be fastened from the back, a symbolic daily reminder of human interdependence. Raymond Bonheur painted the composer Félicien David wearing this outfit. Rumour had it that their constant talk of love was not confined to the sublimated variety, which guaranteed that the idly prurient flocked to witness the suburban cult in action. This resulted in a celebrated trial for causing a public scandal.[66] The reasons why Saint-Simonianism remained stuck at the stage of a sectarian cult were primarily to do with its lack of cosmic drama. Talleyrand put his finger on the limitations of all such secular cults when the creator of a new religion asked 'what would your Excellency recommend' regarding his failure to make many converts. 'I would recommend you to be crucified and rise again the third day' was the deadpan reply.[67]

Saint-Simon's later writings were so indebted to his disciples that it is not easy to determine whose thought was whose. His most illustrious disciple was Auguste Comte who became the great man's secretary in 1817, breaking with Saint-Simon in 1824, partly over this issue of authorship, and distancing himself from the religious sect that bore the guru's name. Saint-Simon, Comte wrote, was nothing but a 'depraved charlatan'.

Comte's lifelong obsession with numbers, systems and order was not unrelated to the squalor of his private life and his intermittent bouts of madness. In 1822 Comte wandered into a bookstore where he recognised behind the counter a prostitute with whom he had earlier consorted. Caroline Massin became his common-law wife; the fateful relationship between her former career and his enveloping paranoia ensured that beginning in 1826, as he began an important lecture series, Comte went insane. A long stay in an asylum was to small avail. On the return trip, his companions realised something was still amiss when Comte insisted that the Austerlitz bridge was the Golden Horn in Istanbul. He then hit the friend who tried to disabuse him. Returned home Comte imagined that he was a highlander in a Walter Scott novel, throwing knives at Caroline Massin while reciting verses from Homer. When his mother dined with him and Massin, a minor disagreement led him to slit his own throat at the table leaving his neck scarred for life. A little later, a gendarme narrowly prevented Comte from throwing himself from the Pont des Arts. A regime of 'cerebral hygiene', involving abstaining from reading newspapers, sex and meat enabled him to toil with great industry thereafter, even if increasingly the only works he read were his own. In 1844, by which time his academic career and marriage had disintegrated, Comte fell in love with a younger woman called Clothilde de Vaux whose husband had abandoned her. Her refusal to satisfy his sexual importunities, perhaps complicated by the fact that Comte was impotent, resulted in further bouts of insanity, until the death from tuberculosis of his 'incomparable angel' resolved things. Some claim that this was literally an epiphany, leading neatly to Comte's 'religion of humanity', in which worship of Clothilde (and the plush red chair she had sat on) figures prominently, but his definitive biographer disagrees.[68] At any rate, thereafter each morning Comte spent forty minutes in 'Commemorating' Clothilde, followed by twenty minutes of 'Effusions', kneeling before her dead flowers. Midday prayers involved reading the whole of her last letter to him, together with long passages of Virgil, Dante and Petrarch. Evening prayers were offered, 'in bed seated' and then 'lying down'. Apparently his psychoses abated as a result of this regimen.[69]

These rituals were accompanied by Herculean labours on books that few read then and which fewer read now. Even limiting each sentence to five lines, and each paragraph to seven sentences, did not promote clarity. One of the fathers of modern social 'science', who in 1839 coined the term 'sociology', Comte sought to establish the philosophical basis for the sciences and for the scientific ordering and reform of society, a formula calculated to appeal to the right as well as the left. In his six-volume *Course on Positivist Philosophy*, Comte showed how each of the sciences, maths, astronomy, physics, chemistry and biology, had become 'positive', that is based on empirically verifiable laws. Between 1851 and 1854 he published a four-volume work of sociology, which laid the basis for his Religion of Humanity. Positivism was supposed to be a third way between the outmoded theologically grounded world of the ancien régime and an abstract, critical rationalism that had become anarchic and incapable of creating anything. Positivism and its religious manifestation were based on a marriage of Maistre and Condorcet, and represented an attempt to synthesise progress and order.[70]

Comte's most famous idea was the law of three stages, whereby every area of thought passes through a theological (fictional), a metaphysical (abstract) and a scientific phase, this last being called 'positive'. This was true too of historical epochs, which in his view were governed by regnant ideas, with an early military and theological stage (from antiquity to the fourteenth century) giving way to an era of decay and renewal (from the fourteenth century to the French Revolution) and finally the industrial and scientific era that succeeded it in which mankind was menaced by rampant individualism just at the time the old beliefs had faded away.[71] Essentially Comte sought a new unifying social doctrine to replace theology and the Church.

The would-be Aristotle gradually metamorphosed into a would-be St Paul.[72] The essence of his Religion of Humanity was to redirect mankind's spiritual energies away from the transcendental and towards the creation of a happier and more moral life here on earth through the worship of the best in man himself. Even highly astute commentators have found this beguiling, for since Comte there have been much grimmer examples of 'sociolatry', that is the worship of human society.[73] The leading Catholic thinker Henri de Lubac was more reserved: 'one cannot take seriously the musings of a man who never understood a word of the Gospel and who sank deeper, every day, into a monstrous egocentricity; the crude and lachrymose "consolations" to which Comte innocently abandoned himself in his sanctuary cannot be taken for genuine spirituality'.[74]

British sceptics called Comte's Religion of Humanity 'Catholicism minus Christianity'. The Comtean religion fused elements from the civic cults of the French Revolution with transpositions from Roman Catholicism. While Comte rejected Chrisitianity on the grounds that it regarded women as the source of evil, labour as a 'divine curse' and benevolence as alien to our flawed natures, he also admired the separation of spiritual and temporal powers, the cult of the Blessed Virgin and the aesthetic achievements of medieval Catholicism. The detail was maniacal, the role of numerical permutations obsessive. The worship of 'le Grand Être' (echoes of the supreme being) had its dogmas and ceremonies, saints and sacraments, designed to merge public and private life. There were public saints, like Archimedes, Aristotle, Dante, Descartes, Frederick the Great and Gutenberg, after whom the lunar months were named in a calendar beginning in 1789; and private saints – or 'angels' cum 'domestic goddesses' – consisting of mothers, sisters, wives, servants and inevitably 'beloved women' dead or alive, for whom Clothilde de Vaux was the prototype. Comte became interested in future female parthenogenesis, that is reproduction without congress between the sexes, hoping that this would be an ennoblement of marriage equivalent to the epochal progression from polygamy to monogamy. The year was also punctuated by festivals celebrating fundamental social relations, whether of parent and child or master and servant; festivals which recognised earlier stages of religion, fetishism, polytheism, monotheism; and festivals which celebrated the social functions of capitalists, workers and women. There were nine sacraments: presentation of the infant, initiation at fourteen, admission at twenty-one, destination at twenty-eight, marriage before thirty-five (twenty-one for women), maturity at forty-two, retirement at sixty-two and, after death, the sacrament of transformation, whereby after a decent seven-year interval the subjective residue of a personality was consigned to immortality in the sacred grove next to the temple of humanity. The immortal's memory would become part of the Great Being. As Comte wrote: "To live in others is, in the truest sense of the word, life . . . To prolong our life indefinitely in the Past and Future, so as to make it more perfect in the Present, is abundant compensation for the illusions of our youth which have now passed away for ever.' By contrast, the condemned and suicides passed into oblivion while 'unworthy spouses' went to the Positivist's hell.

Comte's thought was cosmic, as well as comic, in ambition. He wished to replace the earth's elliptical path with a circular orbit to harmonise extremes of climate. In addition to wishing to convert first Europe and Russia, then the Middle East, India and Africa to Positivism, Comte had prescriptions for the government of human society. Existing states should be divided into small republics the size of Sardinia or Tuscany, so that France would become seventeen such units. Existing nations, such as England, France or Spain, were merely 'factitious aggregates without solid justification'.[75] The entire western world would be divided into five hundred such units, each with between one and three million inhabitants. An admirer of medieval theocracy and of the Jacobin Club, Comte wanted his 'sociocracy' to be based on the temporal rule of bankers and industrialists, with spiritual power in the hands (or rather minds) of the scientific contemplatives who had been winnowed out of the over-specialised 'pedantocracy'. This new priesthood would consist of people who had mastered every form of art and science, and who were responsible for the cure of souls and bodies. Like Maistre, Comte believed that the pope would be the moral arbiter between nations. The middle class would disappear, leaving 120 million proletarians ruled by two thousand patrician bankers. Comte rejected democracy of any kind, and his Positivistic religion was not open to critical discussion. Duties rather than a riot of rights were paramount. By transferring to man rights derived from God, Comte left individuals bereft of any autonomy regarding the new God of abstract humanity. Man was enclosed from cradle to beyond the grave in society with no external moorings other than himself.[76]

While few people went in for the sectarian version of Positivism, its underlying beliefs were attractive to many middle-class people, including such worthies as professors of history or mathematics at University College London and the Webbs, co-founders of the London School of Economics, with Sidney worshipping the ghastly Beatrice as well as the beastly Soviet Union. Such beliefs included a rather uncritical subscription to the benefits of scientific and technological progress; the conviction that human altruism was more worthy than individual salvation in an afterlife; and finally, since Positivism virtually wanted to abolish carnal relations between the sexes, an ability to repudiate the Catholic charge that abandonment of a transcendent God would result in mass immorality.

Positivism never appealed to more than a fraction of the population, albeit in France a fraction with considerable political power under the Third Republic. As a secular creed it was eclipsed by socialism, the only non-supernatural religion of humanity with mass currency. A few dotty dons shuffled in and out of Positivist temples inscribed with 'Live Openly' or 'Order and Progress'; marching masses followed the red banners.

European socialism had many roots, including utopianism and Christianity. Two examples will suffice to highlight the former here: the whimsies of an eccentric French clerk and the visions of a successful Welsh cotton spinner. The former, travelling salesman and commercial correspondence clerk Charles Fourier, became, with the aid of a modest legacy, an isolate in a Parisian garret, surrounded by cats and parrots. He covered reams of paper with cryptic ruminations on the ways in which contemporary institutions (notably the family) distorted human passions, while industrial progress turned gold into dross, increasing the boredom of the rich and the misery of the poor. The world of laissez-faire and mammon had liberated no one; yesterday's serf had more security than the workers crammed into attics, cellars and pestiferous courts. Fourier detested commerce. Why did an apple cost a hundred times more in Paris than in his native Besançon?[77] Apples set him thinking. In the history of the world there had been two evil apples, those of Adam and Paris (the apple of discord). There were also two good apples, that of Newton and now Fourier's own.

Fourier fused ideas on the organisation of production with rudimentary psychological criteria based on twelve common passions which, he calculated, resulted in 810 types of character. Instead of forcing people to be the same, why not acknowledge their enormous diversity of talents, wealth and personalities, channelling rather than repressing their differences in the interests of harmony? Disdaining the entire history of morals and philosophy, Fourier had three sources for his 'thought': strangers he encountered in his career as a salesman; newspapers; and introspection into his own fantasy world. The result was an extraordinary mixture of fitful insights into human nature and fantasies that suggest advanced megalomaniac derangement: 'It is a store clerk who is going to confound these libraries of politics and morals, the shameful fruit of ancient and modern charlatanism. Well! It is not the first time that God has used a lowly man to humble the great and has chosen an obscure man to bring to the world the most important message.'[78]

Fourier lived in anticipation of a patron who would help put his schemes into practice, returning to his lodgings each day at noon in the vain expectation that a Maecenas had called. If only there could be one experimental society along the lines he outlined, then everyone would rush to adopt it. Fourier had the sad salesman's dream of clinching everything with a brilliant three-minute pitch, whether to the king of France, the Russian tsar or the Rothschilds. Since he was planning to make Constantinople the capital of the world and to substitute sleepy Nevers for the Parisian metropolis, there was little chance of that. Unlike the Saint-Simonians who sought a revolution in human behaviour, Fourier believed in working with the grain of human nature by channelling man's passions. That was the point of his 'phalansteries' (communes designed for optimum living, free from external regulation and holding property in common which might be called 'phalanxes' in common English); they were meant to cater to the kaleidoscope of ambitions and longings that anyone might fantasise about in the course of a day. There is something rather poignant about his concern to minimise life's disappointments. For example, a rejected suitor would not be left wallowing in dejection, but would be wafted away by a special corps of 'fairies', who would soon cure him of his lovesickness.

Fourier imagined agricultural settlements, each of about five hundred acres in size, which because human nature was a constant were suited to every nation and society. If you multiplied the 810 types of character by two, and added a few dozen more people to promote variety, the ideal phalanx would have two thousand people. One day there would be six million of these phalansteries, encompassing the world's population, knitted together in spirit by teams of travelling artists, and loosely ruled by a world 'omniarch'. Napoleon declined the post when Fourier offered it to him. Subsequently Fourier opted for a world congress of phalansteries as the ultimate governing body. Projects of world-changing import would be performed by vast 'harmonious armies' consisting of 2 to 3 per cent of any country's population, together with an équipe of young women who would satisfy their sexual desires. Since the evils of the present system had adversely affected the environment and natural kingdom, the new social order would result in planetary change. This would include changes in climate, diversion of rivers, melting of glaciers, reforested mountains, habitable polar icecaps, lemonade instead of salt water in the world's seas, and benign 'anti-lions' and 'anti-whales' who would befriend man. Armies would also fight 'harmonious wars' along the lines of a game of chess, in which nobody was killed. Prisoners of war (of both sexes) could attenuate their confinement by volunteering to have sex with elderly partners. (Fourier was good on the loneliness of old age.)

Life in the phalansteries was to be a round of banquets, operas, parades and lovemaking in a rural setting, for Fourier was a Rabelaisian sort of character. Although individuals retained their private property and gradations of wealth, luxuries were so superabundant as to make these distinctions unnecessary. A bit more work bought variegated clothes.

The underlying big idea was to find optimum living arrangements to cater to every aspect of the individual, since the family was too circumscribed. In the phalansteries people would behave like butterflies, moving gaily from flower to flower. Anticipating an idyll that tantalised Marx, Fourier imagined that tasks would change on the hour, so that everyone would experience command and subordination, competition and harmony – the morning's cabbage-growing competition would become the afternoon's orchestral performance. Different age groups would be allotted tasks for which they were suited, so that young children, for example, could revel in shovelling excrement. Potential mass-murderers or Neros would be able to work off their psychotic propensities as butchers. All age-groups would have an equal opportunity to experience sexual bliss and the institution of marriage would wither away. Mention of the sexual needs of strangers brings us back to the lonely author. Should a figure like the real-life Fourier visit a phalanstery, he could consult the commune's psychological card registry to find a suitable partner for casual sex, for, like Marx, Fourier detested the licensed prostitution of bourgeois marriage.[79]

The Welsh social reformer Robert Owen was an altogether more austere personality, product of a puritanical society in which sex, our neighbours say, is synonymous with a hot-water bottle. By the age of ten, by which time Owen was helping to teach his peers, he had decided that all theologies were erroneous. He remained virulently anticlerical in adult life. His hatred of the established Church was based on its erroneous idea that the individual sinner was responsible for his or her own character and actions, rather than the social environment that produced these. As we shall see, he was hardly irreligious.

Moving to Manchester in 1788, the enterprising Owen (who aged twenty was earning £300 a year managing cotton mills) accumulated sufficient capital to buy himself into cotton mills at New Lanark on the Clyde owned by his future father-in-law David Dale. By 1816 the austerely grand New Lanark Mills were the largest water-powered cotton-manufacturing complex in Britain, employing between 1,400 and 1,500 people, two-thirds of them women. Owen built upon Dale's record as a paternalistic employer, who had augmented his labour force with abandoned children while providing housing for workers if they conformed. Owen still discovered depressing residual evidence of drunkenness and sloth. Not for long, for as Owen put it: 'habitual bacchanalians are now conspicuous for undeviating sobriety'.[80]

Under Owen the Lanark mills became renowned for their cotton, their profitability and the discipline of their employees. When exogenous economic forces during the Napoleonic Wars led to mass layoffs, he continued to pay his workers. His mill-hands, who included five hundred children over ten, toiled from 6 a.m. to 7 p.m. with half an hour for breakfast and three-quarters of an hour for supper. There was a 'silent monitor', consisting of a wooden block next to each employee, whose black, blue, yellow or white surfaces were rotated to show the conduct of the worker on the previous day. Each week a superintendent entered the tally of positive or negative colours in a 'book of character', which Owen read, so as to identify each individual employee's industry or idleness.[81]

New Lanark village was gradually refashioned into a model community, whose inhabitants were communally coerced into such virtues as cleanliness and sobriety, although decent whisky was available, at a price, in place of toxic homebrewed grog. There were 'Bug Monitors' to inspect household bedding. A school endeavoured to educate child-workers in the values of the community, for Owen was convinced that character was essentially malleable: 'The character of man is formed for him, not by him.' Since he also disdained notions like blame or punishment, as well as original sin, and advocated non-denominational education, he clashed with the Christian Churches, which became his most implacable opponents.[82] His desire to erase parental influence in favour of consciousness of community was reflected in the admission of pupils aged one, who gurgled contentedly unaware of the experiment whose subject they were.

The barrack-like regime at New Lanark won the admiration of many army and navy officers turned philanthropists, as the discipline and regimentation appealed to them.[83] Although a strand in Owenism has been co-opted into the mythology of British socialism, in reality, the early Owenites could, and did, cite the Tory poet Robert Southey with approval. Owenism initially attracted a number of Tory squires and Scots and Irish landowners, drawn to its pastoral paternalism and its emphasis upon community in an age of worrying social and economic upheaval. Working-class people, already sometimes organised in burial clubs, friendly societies and incipient trade unions (or Methodist chapels), also discovered in Owenism an echo of their developing collectivism.

If Owen's desire for a rational applied 'social science' represented the extension into the nineteenth century of the values of Condorcet and the Enlightenment, a powerful millennial current in Owenism appealed to religious sectarians on both sides of the Atlantic. The emphases upon arts and agriculture, and the primacy of the collective over the individual or family, found in Shaker communities in the US, had much in common with the ideal communities founded by Owen and his admirers. For Owenism had all the hallmarks of any religious sect. These characteristics included a rejection of the wider world, and especially the family, the Churches and the prevailing economic order. There was also an emphasis upon fellowship, a delusional insistence upon possession of the sole truth, a totalitarian desire to dominate individual members' lives, and an obligation to propagate the good news from a position of sectarian reclusion from the world. Like most sects, modest achievements went with grandiose titles: Association of All Classes of All Nations (1835) or Universal Society of Rational Religionists (1839). There was also the standard sectarian explanation for failure. Since most Owenite communities were built within existing communities, if they did not prove successful the classic millenarian and utopian defence could be deployed. The ideal world had already been corrupted by its antecedents and therefore had never been perfectly realised. In fact, the hundreds of Owenite communities in Britain and America foundered upon rocky soil, a lack of economic prudence and, last but not least, the unmalleability of mankind.

No ideal community is an island: the logic always tended towards the total transformation of human society, resulting in a 'new moral world'. On the back of the modest New Lanark experiment, Owen elaborated a number of utopian projects which reflected his conviction that environment determined character, as well as a less flighty concern that mechanisation was responsible for high levels of unemployment in the aftermath of the Napoleonic Wars. In 1817 Owen proposed ways of alleviating unemployment to a Select Committee of the House of Commons. He envisaged self-sustaining light industrial villages of between 500 and 1,500 people, which would grow or manufacture everything they might need. Costing £60,000 per village from the public purse, these would consist of a quadrangle, made up of public buildings and family apartments, ringed by manufacturing installations, and then a surrounding thousand-acre belt of farmland. In 1818, Owen vainly touted this plan to among others tsar Alexander I at the Congress of Aix-la-Chapelle. Undeterred, Owen next came up with proposals for a global system of co-operative socialism consisting of agro-industrial settlements in remote places where their philanthropist founders could modify the behaviour of their workers in almost laboratory conditions. Age was to be the chief organising principle, with responsibilities assigned according to how old a person was, so that both government, and relations between such settlements, were to be in the hands of a gerontocracy.

In 1825 Owen tried out such a scheme at New Harmony on the River Wabash in Indiana. He purchased the town for $125,000 and spent a further $75,000 transforming it. This bought him twenty thousand acres, a village, churches, four mills, a textile factory, distilleries and brewery, plus ancillary craft shops. The existing Rappites (a Shaker-style sect) moved out, and nine hundred Owenites, as well as drifters and free-loaders, moved in. The constitution of New Harmony was partly authored by a Kentucky Shaker, although it was changed six times in two years thereafter. There were communal laundries and kitchens, which did not appeal to territorially minded women. There was a community form of dress. Women wore a knee-length coat and pantaloons, men wide pantaloons buttoned over a boy's jacket and without collars, reminding the uncharitable of convicts awaiting execution, or of a capacious mat-tress tied tight in the middle when the male wearer of this mad garb was obese. American (and British) rugged individualists, who liked to drink alcohol or smoke, chafed at a theoretically democratic regime where the subscribers held all the cards. By 1827 the community had effectively fragmented and collapsed.[84] Part of the problem was that brotherly or sisterly love was harder to achieve in practice than in theory. 'Oh, if you could see some of the rough uncouth creatures here, I think you would find it rather hard to look upon them exactly in the light of brothers and sisters,' wrote a middle-class communitarian at New Harmony. At Nashoba near Memphis, Tennessee, the Owenites essayed a multiracial community that included donated or freed slaves. This lasted three years until the local inhabitants, on discovering that a white Owenite was cohabiting with a black woman, closed the settlement down as a 'brothel'. Every successive satellite community broke up too; perhaps the fractious inhabitants of Yellow Springs in Ohio were unaware that the name is synonymous with 'hell' in Chinese. Despite these small-scale failures, Owen's ideas grew to megalomaniac proportions: in 1829 he tried to purchase Coahuila province and Texas from the Mexican govern-ment. The bid was rejected, and Texas, at least, remains to this day a land of rather admirable rugged individualists.

Owen had greater success with both co-operative societies and the early trade union movement into which Owenism was briefly diverted. The early nineteenth century was a great time for co-operative societies, although most enjoyed only a brief existence because of lack of capital and expertise in running businesses.[85] One scheme that tantalised Owen was based upon the exchange of goods, whose value would be determined by the number of man hours expended in their production. To that end, in 1832 Owen established a National Equitable Labour Exchange, although this collapsed only two years later, partly because of internal disagreements, but also because the Exchange could not dictate prices and wages in the wider economy. The general idea was that a tailor who spent six hours using four shillings' worth of cloth making a waistcoat would receive a note for that amount, which he could then exchange for a pair of shoes, whose materials and labour costs were four shillings and six hours of the cobbler's time. Simultaneously, Owen sought to capitalise on his prestige in the trade union movement by seeking to transform unions into co-operatives and to break down their extreme local particularism. He seems to have subscribed to a non-violent syndicalism, in which a general strike would usher in union control of industry. In 1834 almost half of trade unions in Britain affiliated themselves to his Grand National Council of Trades Unions. Their attempts to support the Tolpuddle Martyrs by supporting striking workers led to the financial ruination of the federated trade unions and in 1838 the GNCTU broke up.[86] Only the chiliastic manner in which Owen propagated his vision can explain its extraordinary resonance with ordinary workers, whose imaginations were fired by visions of a more egalitarian and just society, precisely because this utopian world was so far removed from the grim dog-eat-dog realities of their lives.

Within a year a wave of strikes, to which employers responded with lockouts, resulted in the dissolution of the Grand National Council and the end of Owen's practical influence upon the organised labour movement. Undeterred, Owen reverted to his dreams of co-operative societies. In 1835, he founded the Universal Community Society of Rational Religionists (Rational Society for short) whose paper *New Moral World* propagated the old man's opinions. The first issue on 1 November 1834 revealed Owen's own secularised form of millenarian fervour. He wrote:

> The rubicon between the Old Immoral and the New Moral
> World is finally passed ... This ... is the great Advent of the

world, the second coming of Christ, – for Truth and Christ are one and the same. The first coming of Christ was a partial development of Truth to the few ... The second coming of Christ will make Truth known to the many ... The time is therefore arrived when the foretold millennium is about to commence.[87]

Sectarian millennial doctrines were effectively transformed into an ideology of social progress whose Advent would come not with the millennium described in Daniel or Revelation, but as a consequence of general subscription to the communitarian way of life. In 1839, the Society acquired land in Hampshire upon which to found a community called Queenswood, which was supposed to advertise the Owenite brand of socialism. The letters C. M. were inscribed on the vast main building, meaning 'Commencement of the Millennium'. There and at Owenite meetings everywhere, the *Book of the New Moral World* took the place of the Bible. There were also a Creed, Catechism and articles, as well as a book of 'Social Hymns':

> Community! The joyful sound
> That cheers the social band,
> And spreads a holy zeal around
> To dwell upon the land.
>
> Community is labour bless'd,
> Redemption from the fall;
> The good of all by each possess'd,
> The good of each by all ...
>
> Community doth wealth increase,
> Extends the years of life,
> Begins on earth the reign of peace,
> And ends the reign of strife.
>
> Community does all possess
> That can to man be given;
> Community is happiness,
> Community is heaven.[88]

Owen himself became the 'Social Father', performing 'namings' of infants and giving funeral orations for the Red dead. Between 1839 and 1841 some £32,000 was invested in Halls of Science in such cities as

Glasgow, Huddersfield, Macclesfield and Sheffield. These were a fusion of Mechanics Institute and Methodist chapel. They were supposed to afford members a foretaste of the New Moral World, in which dancing would go with free buns and lemonade. Owenite lecturers were known as social missionaries. Since artisans from the Midlands made poor farmers, Queenswood soon collapsed, dragging the Rational Society with it into bankruptcy. Owen's twilight years were spent lecturing in America, and attempting to commune with the spirit world, rather than with living humanity. While visiting an American medium in London, he heard raps on the table, from spirits wishing to contact him from beyond. He claimed to have spoken with the spirits of Franklin, Jefferson and the Duke of Kent, an eccentric fate for the founder of a Rational Society.

The collapse of Owen's schemes for social and economic reform was followed by concerted demands for political participation by working people as manifested in the 1837 People's Charter, the Mosaic tablet of the movement known as Chartism. The demand for working-class representation was the one platform that united what would otherwise have been severely localised agitations for such causes as a cheaper press or reform of the harsh Poor Laws that failed to discriminate between the culpable indigent and the honest who had fallen on hard times.

Most Anglican clergy, apart from a tiny minority, regarded Chartism as an ominous local reprise of the reversion to barbarism represented by Jacobinism, although some Tory bishops took the opportunity to blame working-class radicalism upon:

> modern liberalism ... the Devil's creed: a heartless steam-engine, un-Christian, low ... utilitarian creed which would put down all that is really great and high and noble: all old remembrances and customs: merely to let up what is low and multiply such miserable comforts as going very fast through the air on a railroad – and for this purpose it would overturn the Church; that is Christianity; and worship the very devil if his horns were gold and his tail was a steam-engine.

Chartism was not simply one of the forerunners of modern British socialism. In the (hostile) eyes of bishop Samuel Wilberforce of Oxford, whose condemnation of the social disintegration that liberalism had visited upon industrial England we have been listening to, Chartism was:

but the outgrown religious dissent of the preceding generations. What are they, but the moral history of those who have run through all sects, until, in the vexation of their weary spirits, they believe that all religion is sectarian; and who, therefore, having given up with Christianity the first principles which hold together family and social life, are now groping blindly after an impossible unity amidst the pollutions of a low and selfish sensuality.

In other words, Chartism was little more than a secularised form of Methodism.[89]

'Study the New Testament,' a Chartist newspaper enjoined, 'it contains the elements of Chartism.'[90] Chartist modes of agitation were heavily indebted to Methodism, whether in the form of classes in Chartist principles or mass open-air meetings that resembled revivalist gatherings and where the demagogues sounded very like preachers. The author of the People's Charter, William Lovett, was himself from a strict Methodist background, where the only movement permitted on Sundays was the three daily visits to chapel. Lovett's heavily moralised political beliefs – he led the 'moral force', as opposed to violent O'Connorite wing of the movement – reflected mounting disillusionment with the disparities between Christian principles, the Churches and social realities in Victorian Britain. So desperate were the Chartists for the endorsement of the Churches that, beginning with Stockport in 1839, they invaded and occupied them, demanding sermons that supported the rights of labour. Failing that, the Scottish Chartist habit of founding their own independent Chartist churches spread southwards to England. Following violent confrontations in Birmingham and Newport, the movement petered out in the spring drizzle of the capital in April 1848, beneath the unforgiving eyes of the massed guns of authority.

III 'SO COMRADES COME, RALLY / AND THE LAST FIGHT LET US FACE': MARXISM AS ESCHATOLOGY

In the 1840s, Communism was something that filled property-owners with dread rather than a real presence among Europe's minority of industrial workers, who were comprehensively outnumbered by rural and urban paupers. It is salutary to remember that in 1850 only 5 per cent of Europe's population lived in the forty-seven major cities, the vast majority of which were in Great Britain.[91] There really was no 'proletariat', it being the achievement of, among others, Marx and Engels to give it definition, consciousness and purpose as the force that would deliver mankind from self-alienation. A class that Marx and Engels discovered (and which hardly existed in their own time) became the motor force of human history.

The spirit of Communism, rather than the word itself, derived from the conspiracy 'of equals' which Gracchus Babeuf had launched in 1798 against the Directory, which was why 'Communism' was initially called 'Babouvism'. According to an account of the conspiracy written in 1828 by one of its participants, Filippo Buonarrotti, 'the perpetual cause of the enslavement of peoples is nothing but inequality, and as long as it exists the assertion of national rights will be illusory as far as the masses are concerned, sunk as they are beneath the level of human dignity'.[92] Equality of goods, to be achieved by distributing the property of the rich, would guarantee paradise on earth. That was the true natural order. During the July Monarchy, which was seen as a betrayal of the 1830 Revolution, the term Communism referred to those who believed in expropriating the rich as the aim of a successful revolution. Under the mildly repressive circumstances that these Communists experienced, one group went underground to plot uprisings, while another, associated with the utopianist Etienne Cabet, who was exiled to England, came under the influence of Robert Owen.

If Robert Owen was the first person to use the term 'socialism' in print, in 1827, the first documented use of the word 'Communism' was by a conservative German newspaper in March 1840 which darkly noted: 'The Communists have in view nothing less than a levelling of society, substituting for the presently existing order of things the absurd, immoral and impossible utopia of a community of goods.' Such people had existed in France for a decade, though there was nothing so formal as a 'Communist Party' as opposed to a halfway house for displaced intellectuals and exiled artisans.[93]

Communists emphasised equality and identified with the most drastic, Jacobin phase of the French Revolution. On these grounds Communism was distinct from utopian socialism, which had little time for equality, rejected violent revolution and was more concerned with how to achieve harmony than with how to capitalise upon human strife. What it could not ignore in socialism was that it had got there first in providing workers with rudimentary organisation. In a zoomorphic sense, Communists resembled those aggressive African bees that colonise and transform more placid hives.

Until recently the debt which Communism owed to religion has sometimes been under-emphasised by historians who are sympathetic to 'scientific' socialism and resistant to the rather separate notion that Marxism was a religiously inspired mythopoetic drama carefully camouflaged within various scientific-sounding accretions. An admixture of quasi-religious ideals encouraged acceptance of Communism among pious working people, and helped foster sectarian solidarities among the deracinated artisans and intellectuals who constituted the nucleus of the first Communist movements. Hence the desperate concern of early Communists to claim an identical etymological root between Communism and communion. The initial compatibility of what would be retroactively reworked as the quintessential atheist creed and an egalitarian version of Christianity can easily be demonstrated to the point of parody. This was a series of sects that burgeoned into a worldwide Church only fifty years after the sacred texts had been authored in the British Library rather than handed down on Mount Sinai.

In 1840 a twenty-year-old youth called John Goodwin Barmby went to Paris, armed with a letter of introduction from Robert Owen, to set up regular communication between British and French socialists. On 20 June he presented the prospectus for a proposed 'International Association for the Promotion of Mutual Intercourse among all Nations', which may well have been the first outline of an international Communist organisation, for he was much taken with the Communists whom he met at banquets in Paris. Back in England he founded a Communist Propaganda Society and a journal called *The Promethean or Communitarian Apostle*, soon renamed *Communist Chronicle*. Striking a Comtean note, Barmby described himself as the 'Pontifarch of the Communist Church' and Communism as the final religion of humanity: 'I believe . . . that the divine is communism, that the demoniac is individualism.' Based at his central 'communitarium' at Harnwell, he worked up a fourfold periodisation of history and the route to a Communist society, while instituting a new calendar and a new vegetarian diet. While living on the isles of Wight and Man, where he endeavoured to set up further communities, Barmby elaborated initiation rituals for Communist postulants, beginning with 'Frigidary', a cold bath, followed by 'Calidary', a hot one, then 'Tepidary', merely warm, and 'Frictionary', that is vigorous exercise. Oil and perfume would follow. Although it has been assiduously edited from memory, early Communism was saturated with religious symbolism. For example, *L'Atelier*, the first French journal exclusively produced by and for workers, carried an engraving called 'Christ preaching fraternity to the world' with Christ on top of the world holding a ribbon inscribed 'fraternity' and with the serpent of 'egoism' crushed under His feet. Religious themes were equally evident among the German socialists, some of whom had established a secret society in Paris called the League of the Just, the German word 'Bund' having religious associations.

In 1839 some of these exiled artisans and intellectuals relocated to London, where they founded a front organisation off the Tottenham Court Road called the German Workers Educational Association. Its meetings took the form of talks delivered in a room above a pub. A very great novelist cast a cool eye over such radicals in an unusual book that examines the clash between fineness of spirit and murderous resentments through a protagonist who, as the bastard son of an aristocrat and the dress-maker who murdered him, drifts between both worlds. In his 1886 *The Princess Casamassima* Henry James included descriptions of gatherings of radicals, his fictional setting being a room over the Sun and Moon public house in London's Bloomsbury, the area where Marx worked:

> They came oftener, this second winter, for the season was terribly hard; and as in that lower world one walked with one's ear nearer the ground, the deep perpetual groan of London misery seemed to swell and form the whole undertone of life. The filthy air came into the place in the damp coats of silent men, and hung there till it brewed to a nauseous warmth, and ugly, serious faces squared themselves through it, and strong-smelling pipes contributed their element in a fierce, dogged manner which appeared to say that it now had to stand for everything – for bread and meat and beer, for shoes and blankets and the poor things at the pawnbroker's and the smokeless chimney at home. Hyacinth's colleagues [Hyacinth Robinson being the novel's protagonist] seemed to him wiser then, and more permeated with intentions boding ill to the satisfied classes ... it was brought home to our hero on more than one occasion that

revolution was ripe at last. This was especially the case on the evening I began referring to, when Eustace Poupin [an exiled former Communard book-binder with whom Hyacinth works] squeezed in and announced, as if it were a great piece of news, that in the east of London, that night, there were forty thousand men out of work. He looked round the circle with his dilated foreign eye, as he took his place; he seemed to address the company individually as well as collectively, and to make each man responsible for hearing him. He owed his position at the 'Sun and Moon' to the brilliancy with which he represented the political exile, the magnanimous immaculate citizen wrenched out of his bed at dead of night, torn from his hearth-stone, his loved ones and his profession, and hurried across the frontier with only the coat on his back. Poupin had performed in this character now for many years, but he had never lost the bloom of the outraged proscript, and the passionate pictures he had often drawn of the bitterness of exile were moving even to those who knew with what success he had set up his household gods in Lisson Grove. He was recognised as suffering everything for his opinions; and his hearers in Bloomsbury – who, after all, even in their most concentrated hours, were very good-natured – appeared never to have made the subtle reflection, though they made many others, that there was a want of tact in his calling upon them to sympathise with him for being one of themselves.[94]

Naively idealistic, or bitterly resentful, artisans were relatively easy for so-called intellectuals to displace. The most influential theorist of the League of the Just was the tailor Wilhelm Weitling, who, as a translator of one of Lamennais' later works, espoused a revolutionary socialism heavily permeated by this-worldly Christianity. In 1837 Weitling had been mandated by the League to report on the feasibility of 'community of goods'. In his *Mankind as it is and as it ought to be* he argued that Money was literally the root of evil, since every aspect of the workers' lives was subjected to it. As a cure, he proposed the abolition of individual property ownership and rights of inheritance. The value of products was to be established by the number of hours of work put into them. Borrowing from Fourier, Weitling envisaged communities based on family associations with an elected Senate and a ruling executive directory to establish social priorities. An 'order of production', based on four estates, would include an industrial estate with a conscripted industrial army of fifteen- to eighteen-year-olds which would organise public utilities and heavy manufacturing. Work would be compulsory, but, like Fourier, Weitling wanted to see people alternating their tasks on a bi-hourly basis.[95] In his utopia, there would be no hatred or envy, no crime or evil desires. Universal brotherhood would prevail, and national languages would become obsolescent within three generations.[96]

The forging of links between these various socialist grouplets was the self-appointed task of a Brussels Communist Correspondence Committee that had been set up in early 1846 by Karl Marx and Friedrich Engels. Weitling put in an early appearance, dressed in an elegant coat and with a coquettishly trimmed beard, at what amounted to Dr Marx's seminar around a small green table. The abrasive Marx [to whom manners were immaterial] almost immediately asked: 'Tell us, Weitling, you who have made such a noise in Germany with your preaching: on what grounds do you justify your activity and what do you intend to base it on in the future?' Failing to rise to this challenge, Weitling stumbled through his speech, whose burden was the need to enlighten the workers regarding their misery and to promote their self-organisation. An angry Marx put a stop to Weitling's meanderings, claiming that 'to call to the workers without any strictly scientific ideas or constructive doctrine, especially in Germany, was equivalent to vain dishonest play at preaching which assumed on the one side an inspired prophet and on the other only gaping asses'. When Weitling alluded to his own organisational achievements and the support he had received, venturing even a criticism or two of 'armchair analysts', Marx thumped his fist on the table and said: 'Ignorance never yet helped anybody!'[97]

Back in London, Weitling was gradually marginalised by leaders of the League who did not subscribe to his views on the necessity for violent revolution and who thought that Communism would supersede his socialistic form of Christianity. By 1842 Weitling had himself abandoned his earlier religious enthusiasms.[98] The new leaders, Marx, Engels and Wilhelm Marr, were looking for a new doctrine, preferably combining moral passion and scientism into one eschatological romance, and someone was eager to supply it. Having identified a theoretical vacuum at the heart of an organisation involving up to a thousand 'workers', Marx and Engels decided to make their involvement with the League formal. A congress was held in June 1847 at which a Communist catechism was to be adumbrated and new statutes elaborated. The name was changed to League of Communists. Its slogan was no longer 'All men are Brothers', which still had a whiff of Christianity, but 'Proletarians of all Countries – Unite!' Engels took upon himself production of a 'Draft of the Communist Confession of Faith' that was to be the League's programme. A few months later Engels's proposals had become a new document called 'Principles of Communism'. Since he wished to include historical materials, he subsequently argued that the League drop the concepts of 'catechism' and 'principles', replacing them with the term 'manifesto'. He and Marx delivered the *Communist Manifesto* before 1 February 1848.[99]

The scion of a distinguished rabbinical family, whose father had converted to Protestantism to pursue a legal career, Marx had hoped to follow an academic path, before his involvements with the dissident Young Hegelians meant that journalism and writing became his lot in life, although he never abandoned his highly romantic view of the world-transforming powers of (his) philosophy. When the Prussian government suppressed the *Rheinische Zeitung* (which he edited) in early 1843, Marx and his bride Jenny moved to Paris where he worked on a new journal called the *Deutsch-französische Jahrbücher* (German–French Annals).

The Young Hegelians were a loose grouping of those who emphasised the subversive potentialities in the deceased Prussian philosopher's thought. Strauss's *Life of Jesus* was the immediate stimulus for these debates.[100] Marx, along with many others, was also influenced by the writings of Ludwig Feuerbach, a wealthy freelance scholar. The essence of Feuerbach's 'transformational criticism' was that 'A is nothing but B.'[101] His *Essence of Christianity* argued that religion was an alienated form of human consciousness, an acoustical effect derived from man's own voice. God was a projection of the needs of the human species; a consoling God simply reflected mankind's need for consolation. God did not will history as part of His self-realisation, rather man created God from his own self-knowledge: 'The personality of God is nothing else than the projected personality of man.' For, on closer inspection, God was a peculiar mixture of the metaphysical omniscience ascribed to Him by the theologians and the very human characteristics, such as grieving, loving, suffering and so on, of popular religious belief. God was nothing more than man contemplating his own image in an infinity of mirrors.[102]

Beneath Feuerbach's claims lay a desire to restore unity to human existence by redirecting man's focus from an otherworldly God to this world and his own kind. Men should cease being alienated 'candidates for the afterlife' but rather 'students of this life'.

Marx sharpened Feuerbach's reflections on human alienation by treating religion as the ideological manifestation of particular modes of production and the social order that accompanied them, culminating in a capitalist world where men had become shadows flitting amid mere things that had assumed greater substantiality even though many of them were abstractions such as money or credit. The fancy term for this process is reification, though we need not tarry over labyrinthine complexities that appeal only to a certain generation of academic.

Religion was 'the illusory sun turning around man as long as he does not yet turn around himself'. In an 1843 essay Marx notoriously described religion as 'the sigh of the oppressed creature, the heart of a heartless world, the soul of a soulless environment. It is the opium of the people.' This was not an especially new idea about religion, although the reference to the drug for which the British had gone to war in China between 1839 and 1842 gave it contemporary resonance. Whether or not religion was true or untrue had ceased to be important; what mattered was the social function it allegedly played in masking material existence in 'illusory bliss'. Its function was palliative; since religion did not address the underlying disease, it could not be a cure.[103] Of course, it could be argued that Feuerbach and Marx, like Comte, were simply substituting humanity for the Christian God. That was the thrust of the criticism made in 1844 by Max Stirner, a Young Hegelian atheist polemicist who wrote:

> the human religion is only the last metamorphosis of the Christian religion ... it separates my essence from me and sets it above me ... it exalts 'Man' to the same extent as any other religion does its God or idol ... it makes what is mine into something other worldly ... in short ... it sets me beneath Man, and thereby creates for me a vocation.

So as to suppress the idealistic and theological underpinnings of what was supposed to be a radical post-religious applied philosophy, Marx jettisoned ideas and morals as potencies in the world, substituting material forces and the class struggle. Frothy 'ideology' (the term used for ethics, metaphysics, religion and so forth) lost any independence from the deeper currents of material productive forces. Feuerbach had allegedly settled the religious question for ever. One questionable assertion followed hard upon another, none of them standing up to serious scientific scrutiny. The ultimate human and social reality became that of class struggle, which allegedly determined the entire historical process, culminating in the Promethean–proletarian proposition: 'I am nothing and I should be everything.' The fight was no longer against non-existent Gods, but against the idols of commodity fetishism.[104]

The rather academic question of what Marxism owed to German theological debates has to be set within the much broader context of Marxism's unconscious indebtedness to what Marx and his adherents dismissed as baseless religious narcotics. After all, Marx *claimed* to be unprejudiced by moral judgements and evaluations, but his entire oeuvre was permeated by both. Did all class antagonisms stem from exploitation? And isn't exploitation a moral judgement? Perhaps what Marx claimed to be scientific predictions were little more than messianic prophecies: giving both prophet and his disciples 'the assurance of things to be hoped for' even though the prophecies have virtually all turned out to be disastrously wrong. Since he and his followers claimed that ideologies were epiphenomenal manifestations of deeper, secret causes, what can be said about the deeper mythopoetic and prophetic currents that underlay Marx's supposedly scientific and empirically verifiable theses?

It is relatively easy to transpose some of the key terms from the Judaeo-Christian heritage to Marxism: 'consciousness' (soul), 'comrades' (faithful), 'capitalist' (sinner), 'devil' (counter-revolutionary), 'proletariat' (chosen people) and 'classless society' (paradise). The ruling classes were also going to face a revolutionary form of 'Last Judgement' (Weltgericht). But there were far deeper unacknowledged correspondences, including nostalgia for a lost oneness and the beliefs that time was linear (the ancients thought it was cyclical), that the achievement of higher consciousness brought salvation, and that history was progressing with its meaning and purpose evident to the discerning, knowledgeable vanguard.[105]

Although Marxists dispensed with a God capable of intervening in this world, their scheme of history replicated Judaeo-Christian eschatology, with what was good and perfect evident only at the beginning and at the end of the story. If the religious account of time concerned what occurred between the Fall of Adam and the Apocalypse, so for

Marxists time began with the Great Expropriation, when primitive communism was replaced by class society and man's alienation commenced, and it would end with a global revolution, which would restore man to an even higher version of his unalienated humanity: 'We know that the new form of social production, to achieve the good life, needs only new men.'[106] After the Apocalypse–Revolution this New Man would arise, based on the reintegration of hitherto alienated self-expression (or 'work') and thought, since the object of the Apocalypse–Revolution was to restore this lost harmony. There were other striking correspondences. For Christians and Jews biblical personalities are not just 'characters' but symbolic 'types' that perform or prefigure crucial functions within the divine scheme of things. Likewise, for Marxists, less developed societies are supposed to emulate the historical patterns already revealed in more advanced ones, even when this course seems catastrophic, while real historical individuals become transferable as 'Cromwells', 'Dantons' and so forth across historical eras. Communist regimes would do much the same with the slave leader Spartacus or the Anabaptist fanatic Thomas Müntzer, romanticised exemplars and precursors of their own unheroic realities.[107]

As in Christian eschatology, the unfolding of the Marxist scheme of history was not without contingencies and setbacks, although these were a result of resistance by the forces of reaction, which operated like the obstacles thrown in man's path by diabolic powers.

Of course, it could be objected that Christian emphasis upon the world to come, and upon the powerlessness of man vis-à-vis an all-powerful deity, makes these comparisons with Marxism, which aimed to understand and transform the world, at best pointless. In fact, Marxism managed to incorporate what Christianity since St Augustine has managed to push to the heterodox margins with the certainty of the orthodox version. Marxism combined the assurance that everything was operating according to the dispositions of secularised versions of higher powers with Gnostic sectarian belief that the messianic elect that had grasped these laws was morally entitled to destroy existing society (which was entirely without virtue) in order to achieve earthly paradise. Like medieval millenarians or early modern Protestant zealots, Communists took it upon themselves to realise heaven on earth through transforming violence: that exercise in regrettable but necessary killing which would murder eighty or a hundred million people in the twentieth century. Like Marxists, medieval millenarians believed they would be able to extricate man from a 'darkened level of being', successfully reintegrating him into the light. Perhaps appropriately enough, when Marx came to explain how the proletariat became the saviour class, he had recourse to the Gnostic concept of 'pneumatics' and talked mysteriously of 'that breath of spirit'. For it was otherwise hard to explain how, if the proletariat was history's creator–subject, it had emerged only in Marx's own century.

IV SECULARISATION AND SOCIETY

Many nineteenth-century thinkers believed that society was progressing from backward epochs when religion was pervasive to future times when religion would be regarded as an outmoded illusion, perhaps to be superseded by a 'rational' creed focused on humanity. This continues to be reflected in the views of prominent Marxist historians, who, convinced that the residual vitality of religion is 'archaic' or 'recessive', are enviably certain about when, where and why secularisation occurred, though this confidence eludes those who have spent a lifetime acquiring detailed knowledge of these questions.[108]

A number of nineteenth-century writers argued that religion was retreating from areas of existence where it had once been important, the metaphor of tides slipping away from a beach being a favourite after Matthew Arnold's 'Dover Beach', despite the fact that tides roll in and out. They coined new terms to express this process. Although the word 'secular' has a long history, 'secularism' was employed in 1851 by the English radical George Jacob Holyoake when a lawyer advised him that it might raise fewer hackles than 'atheism'. This enabled the resulting Secular Societies of the 1850s to avoid the widespread charge that disbelief in God resulted in immorality.[109]

'Secularisation' also acquired new meanings, beyond the expropriation of church properties during the Reformation and French Revolution, which was its original sense. William Lecky, author of an influential history of European rationalism, was among the first to use 'secularisation' to encapsulate his claim that religion had ceased to play a major role in international relations, notably as a reason why states went to war. He would have marvelled at the twenty-first century. Later, the academic sociologists Emile Durkheim and Max Weber argued that the multiple functions of the clergy were being usurped by a proliferating host of professionals, whose knowledge and skill confined religion to unanswerable metaphysical questions, while diminishing the importance of saints and miracles to mastery of the elements or life's contingencies. The advanced parts of the world were being 'disenchanted' by processes which made Christianity both implausible and irrelevant. How many Catholics called upon St Christopher any more when the tram or train broke down? Although people continued to have accidents, fall ill and die, they felt they possessed a mastery of the physical world by virtue of their own effort and intellect. Salvationism gave way to meliorism and, with it, an underlying optimism about a future in which material prosperity and scientific progress would banish poverty, scarcity and disease. In 1884 Sir James Stephen informed readers of the *Nineteenth Century*:

> If human life is in the course of being fully described by science, I do not see what materials there are for any religion, or indeed, what would be the use of one, or why it is wanted. We can get on very well without one, for though the view of life which science is opening to us gives us nothing to worship, it gives us an infinite number of things to enjoy ... The world seems to me a very good world, if it would only last. It is full of pleasant people and curious things, and I think that most men find no great difficulty in turning their minds away from its transient character.[110]

Secularisation was not a straight descent from a putative peak of faith, whose historical whereabouts were elusive. There were those in, for example, Hanoverian Britain who claimed that religion had become 'a principal subject of mirth and ridicule', shortly before the onset of Methodist revivalism. Secularisation was a congeries of intellectual and social trends, punctuated (and punctured) by resurgences of Christian fervour, or awareness that Christianity performed essential moral, political, charitable and social functions that it would be foolhardy to abandon. Secularisation was an intellectual contest and the result of more general processes, although these easily admit contradiction and qualification. Some people consciously sought to bring secularisation about, through such sects as the British National Secular Society (1866) whose pugnacious leading lights, notably Holyoake and then the Northamptonshire MP Charles Bradlaugh, combined freethinking with political radicalism. Atheism was confined to a handful of mainly London-based radical republicans who as keen ideologists were irrelevant to a country whose politics were pragmatic rather than ideological.[111] In imperial France such activity usually took place under cover of the masonic lodges until the advent of the Third Republic when they moved to the heart of government. In Imperial Germany there was a League of German Free-Religious Parishes, which exchanged lectures for sermons, and, from 1881 onwards, the more militant German Freethinkers League of Ludwig Büchner. But neither the ethical, scientific and theological challenges to religion considered at the start of this chapter nor the advent of freethinking sectarians was as important as the vaster impersonal developments which 'disenchanted' the world, deracinated traditional communities, eradicated or gave rise to social classes, transformed Churches and sects into denominations, and, the universal fact of mortality apart, diminished the incidence of crises to which religion alone had the most compelling answers. These immense themes will concern us in these concluding passages.

Politics played a significant role in whether people adhered to the Churches or rejected them, and, more subtly, contributed to what proved to be evanescent religious revivals. As has been remarked already, the mid-nineteenth century saw a *return* to Catholicism of the wealthier Voltairean French bourgeoisie, who were the most educated part of the population, while, towards the close of the century and beyond, Catholicism was en vogue among many French intellectuals.[112] The French Church's ties to this 'Party of Order' resulted in a corresponding intensification of radical and republican anticlericalism. The insurrectionary Paris Commune in 1871 provided the 'clericalist' right with twenty-four martyrs, including the archbishop of Paris, whom the communards shot as an easily identifiable symbol of 'reaction', while the 'Bloody Week' that followed created a far greater number of left-wing martyrs. In effect, politics gave a considerable fillip to the vitality of religion in France, although at the expense of providing republicans with an easy target called 'clericalism'. In a more complicated way, political conflict also contributed to temporary revivals in the fortunes of a British Nonconformism, which by becoming both institutionalised and respectable had progressively cut itself off from further expansion among the upper–lower social classes it had once attracted, classes which in any event were disappearing as domestic outwork was replaced by the factories. As we shall see Nonconformity became more like a Church, while the Church of England adopted many of the Evangelical energies of Nonconformity.

In Britain, unlike much of Europe and Latin America, the confessional state was incrementally dismantled without giving overt foes of religion much cause for celebration. As the Nonconformist Society for the Liberation of the Church from State Patronage and Control explained: 'The dominant force in favour of disestablishment is a religious force; it may be safely assumed, therefore, that in putting an end to the political ascendancy of a particular Church, care will be taken, possibly at the expense of some logical consistency, to do nothing that will be prejudicial to the religious interests of the nation.'[113] With one eye to the United States Nonconformists argued that, while government and society should profess a general adhesion to religion, the state should not support one Church at the expense of another. That, of course, begged several questions regarding those who professed non-Christian or no religion, as well as regarding, for example, the temperance or Sunday-observance legislation that Nonconformists were otherwise so keen on.

From the mid-nineteenth century, pressure groups, of which the Liberation Society was among the most notable, mobilised support for the piecemeal but steady dismantling of establishment as part of a broader liberal and radical assault on the vestiges of 'aristocratic' privilege. This close association between liberalism and Nonconformity led to a defensive reliance upon the Conservative Party, and hence the liberal Nonconformist slur that the Church of England was the 'Tory Party at prayer', whereas it had been increasingly scrupulous in maintaining an at times difficult distinction between its national 'moral' engagements and involvement in political factionalism.

It would be tedious to follow each and every conflict between Nonconformists and the Church of England and their respective political champions. The exercise of civic responsibility was progressively divorced from a particular religion privileged by the state even though that religion still retains much pomp and circumstance. The key stages included the deconfessionalisation of the rites of passage, opening Oxford and Cambridge to Dissenters, the abolition of both compulsory church rates and religious oaths for public office, the disestablishment of the Church in Ireland and Wales (the latter achieved only in 1914), and, most contentious of all, the role of religion in education. Nonconformists sought to end state subsidies for Church of England schools, preferring a non-denominational state system; what they got in the 1870 Education Act was far less, namely a dual system of Church and non-denominational 'Board' schools, with a parental right to exempt children from religious instruction on grounds of conscience. This compromise continued to dissatisfy Nonconformists well into the twentieth century. On some of these questions the Church fought back, with the aid of its own Church Defence Institution (1859), notably against the 'conscience clause' in education, and over the issue of burial according to Nonconformist rites in Anglican graveyards. On other questions, such as the abolition of compulsory church rates (1868) or the admission of Nonconformists to the ancient universities as either undergraduates or fellows (1871 and 1882), the Church of England gave ground relatively smoothly. While Nonconformism was being transformed from a sect into a denomination, the Church of England, regardless of its claim to monopoly, was metamorphosing into a denomination in a context characterised more and more by religious pluralism. In the long term, both lost out to a state that increasingly acted as an impartial umpire in these conflicts, and which, bit by unco-ordinated bit, progressively usurped social functions that they lacked the resources to perform, and by virtue of doing so further promoted both de-facto disestablishment and secularisation.[114]

Contrary to many pessimistic predictions, loss of religious faith did not result in the wholesale de-moralisation of society. On the contrary, in Victorian Britain morality – meaning an interlocking series of individual–social virtues and stigmas – itself became a form of 'surrogate religion' to which the vast majority of respectable people (of whatever class) subscribed, even if few followed Matthew Arnold's rather fey view of religion as 'morality tinged with emotion'. Visiting Cambridge in May 1873 George Eliot toured the gardens of Trinity with her academic admirer Fred Myers:

> she stirred somewhat beyond her wont, and taking as her text the three words which have been used so often as the inspiring trumpet-calls of men – the words, God, Immortality, Duty, – pronounced with terrible earnestness, how inconceivable was the first, how unbelievable the second, and yet how peremptory and absolute the third. Never, perhaps, have sterner accents affirmed the sovereignty of impersonal and unrecompensing law.[115]

Leslie Stephen struck a lighter, but similar, note in an 1876 letter to a friend: 'I now believe in nothing, to put it shortly; but I do not the less believe in morality etc., etc., I mean to live and die like a gentleman if possible.'[116] The moral canon included not just those virtues that critics of the Victorians like to parody as hypocritical and self-servingly 'bourgeois' – for example, abstinence, cleanliness, punctuality, self-help and thrift – but decency, honesty, integrity, good manners and service to others, virtues to which many poor people, regimented or not, subscribed too. The Englishman's home was not just his castle but his (or her) temple; the foundation of private and public morality.[117] We can push this argument a little further, for there were those like Newman who recognised where the over-emphasis upon morality was tending. Christian support for such moral campaigns as the prevention of (mainly working-class) cruelty to animals, Sabbatarianism and temperance not only alienated workers who *had* to shop on Sundays since they were not paid until late on Saturday or who spotted the obvious hypocrisies of household wine cellars, fox-hunting and servants who worked on the Sabbath, but in themselves represented the diversion of religion from otherworldly concerns to what amounted to social policy. From whichever angle one views these developments, God was being left out.[118]

It would be incorrect to assume that the churches were evenly distributed across the European countryside or that towns were necessarily epicentres of irreligion. For historical reasons, relatively dense parochial networks covered northern Italy, Portugal and Spain, while the southern parts of those countries were characterised by a combination of anticlericalism and superstition, the former reflecting the close relationship between the Churches and a social order based on latifundist agriculture. In France, huge belts of the countryside, in the centre and south, had never recovered from the de-Christianising holocaust of the French Revolution, while everywhere in Europe coastal areas, marsh and moors had a very light ecclesiastical presence, with single parishes in northwestern Scotland the size of Church provinces.[119]

The phenomenal growth of towns and cities presented a particular challenge to ecclesiastical logistics, even assuming that most countries were not like France, which under article 69 of the Napoleonic Organic Statutes picked up the tab not only for clerical salaries but also for church building, and under republican regimes was reluctant to encourage this. Everywhere there were usually too many churches in the historic city centres and too few in the rapidly expanding peripheries. Some parishes in working-class districts of Berlin or Paris had over 120,000 parishioners where ten or twelve thousand was already deemed hopeless. Of course, this was not a failing unique to the Churches. Every feature of the infrastructure, from cemeteries to sewers and street lighting, that made urban life civilised was often inadequate.[120]

It is far from axiomatic that incredible rates of urban growth created a race of Godless proletarians – not for nothing was Glasgow, whose population doubled every twenty years in the nineteenth century, known as 'Gospel City', while church attendance was extraordinarily low in rural Mecklenburg.[121] But leaving aside cities where ethnicity and sectarianism may have reinforced religious convictions, and that was not true of, say, Lille in northern France, there is considerable evidence, some of it dubious, that in many places working-class people were alienated from the Churches, even assuming they had the opportunity to come in contact with them. Charles Dickens caught this well in his fictional Coketown, the setting for his novel *Hard Times*:

> First, the perplexing mystery of the place was, Who belonged to the eighteen denominations? Because, whoever did, the labouring people did not. It was very strange to walk through the streets on a Sunday morning, and note how few of *them* the barbarous jangling of bells that was driving the sick and nervous mad, called away from their quarter, from their own close rooms, from the corners of their streets, where they lounged listlessly, gazing at all the church and chapel going, as at a thing with which they had no manner of concern. Nor was it merely the stranger who noticed this, because there was a native organisation in Coketown itself, whose members were to be heard of in the House of Commons every session, indignantly petitioning for acts of parliament that should make these people religious by main force.[122]

One should not assume that the clergy automatically connected with people in the countryside. In her *Scenes from Clerical Life*, serialised in 1857, George Eliot contrasted the unfortunate curate Amos Barton, whose combination of learning and prolixity prevented him from communicating with the lower-class imagination, with the Reverend Martin Cleves:

> Mr Cleves has the wonderful art of preaching sermons which the wheelwright and the blacksmith can understand; not because he talks condescending twaddle, but because he can call a spade a spade, and knows how to disencumber ideas of their wordy frippery ... He gets together the working men in his parish on a Monday evening, and gives them a sort of conversational

lecture on useful practical matters, telling them stories, or reading some selected passages from an agreeable book, and com-
menting on them; and if you were to ask the first labourer or
artisan in Tripplegate what sort of man the parson was, he
would say, – 'a uncommon knowin', sensible, free-spoken gentleman; very kind an' good-natur'd too'.[123]

Predominantly young migrants, some hailing from irreligious country-
sides, found themselves in fluid environments where there was no squire
to bolster clerical authority. Where there was constant upward, down-
ward or spatial mobility, as there was in the cities, a sustained relationship with a Church was difficult; where people inhabited homogeneous
working-class ghettos they could be bullied or persuaded into other
allegiances. What free time they had on Sundays was devoted to rest and
recreations that busy-body Sabbatarians tried to obstruct, although later
in the century less puritanical churches were surprisingly adroit in finding vicars who doubled up as footballers and prize-fighters. The
Churches' identification with middle-class respectability was one issue
that alienated the workers, although that did not lessen their enthusiasm
for sending their children to Sunday Schools or participation whenever
Churches demonstrated their practical uses. Workers' lack of suitable
attire made church attendance shameful when social distinctions
extended to such things as rented pews, while the ill-attired and noxious
were penned in towards the back or in separate galleries lest they give
olfactory offence.[124] Some argue that the imagination of the nineteenth-
century urban worker had shrunk to the point where he or she could
not easily accommodate stories about kings, wise men, lambs and
shepherds, let alone what one English labourer called 'cherrybims'. If
country folk could still find something in common with a religion that
revolved around semi-nomadic desert tribes, the inhabitants of cities
found few exemplars in sacred scriptures whose most memorable cities
were Sodom and Gomorrah.[125] As a man prosecuted by Sabbatarian
zealots for advertising his fish, muffins and crumpets on a Sunday
objected in court at Hammersmith, he and his co-accused were 'not
living in the times of Adam and Eve, but of civilisation'.[126] Country life
may have been subject to such catastrophes as drought and flood or
livestock plagues and crop-flattening storms, but these ceased to afflict
factory workers or machines that rarely stopped. A magistrate in
Besançon in eastern France encapsulated this when he wrote in 1857:

The agricultural areas are essentially moral and religious. The man who owes his fortune to the marvellous workings of machines, whose mind is constantly turned towards material things, more easily forgets his origin; the man of the fields cannot forget his creator; in his distress, when the weather is bad or his harvest threatened, he prays to Heaven for help . . . The worker in a factory only sees the action of matter, the agricultural worker relates everything to the action of a divinity.

This might suggest that workers fell prey to materialist versions of socialism, exchanging one religion for another. Actually, the speed with which socialism extricated itself from Christianity varied considerably according to local national circumstances or regions within individual nations. The transitions within individuals were very fluid, with rejection of God and hatred of the established Churches going together with continued belief in Christian moral values. Flaubert's account in his *Sentimental Education* of a meeting at the radical Club d'Intelligence in the wake of the Revolution of 1848 illustrates the general problem. In this episode, a radical priest had tried to speak about agronomy to a socially mixed audience, but had not been given a hearing:

Then a patriot in a smock climbed on to the platform. He was a man of the people, with broad shoulders, a plump, gentle face, and long black hair. He cast an almost voluptuous glance round the audience, flung back his head, and finally, stretching out his arms, said:

'Brethren, you have rejected Ducretot [the priest], and you have done well; but you did not do this out of impiety, for we are all pious men.'

Several members of the audience were listening open-mouthed, like children in a catechism class, in ecstatic attitudes.

'Nor did you do it because he is a priest, for we too are priests! The workman is a priest, like the founder of Socialism, the Master of us all, Jesus Christ!'

The time had come to inaugurate the reign of God. The Gospel led straight to 1789. After the abolition of slavery would come the abolition of the proletariat. The age of hatred was past; the age of love was about to begin.

'Christianity is the keystone and the foundation of the new edifice . . .'

'Are you making fun of us?' cried the traveller in wines. 'Who's landed us with this blasted priest?'

This interruption shocked the audience to the core. Nearly all of them climbed on to the benches, and, shaking their fists, yelled: 'Atheist! Aristocrat! Swine!' while the chairman's bell rang without stopping and there were shouts of 'Order! Order!'[127]

Devotees of 'scientific' socialism regard Christian Socialism as an archaism and its adherents as irrelevant woolly-minded mavericks, representative of a transitional phase that would inexorably, or *ideally*, be swept away by the marching cadres of the scientific sort. This is difficult to reconcile with the view of a leading historian of French socialism that 'During the 1830s and 1840s, virtually everyone who considered himself a socialist claimed to be inspired by Christianity or even by Catholicism itself. The Gospels were everywhere, and Jesus, it seemed, was the founding father of revolutionary change.'[128] While everyone knows that British socialism exhibited religious currents, it is less well known that this was the case in France too. There were several reasons why this was so.[129]

The failure of insurrections in 1834 and 1839 led some on the French left to re-evaluate the conspiratorial and violent legacy of 1789, turning to Christianity as a means of transforming the moral outlook of individuals before they set to work transforming society itself. Unlike the esoteric sects of Fourier or Saint-Simon, Christianity was something that even the most intellectually challenged person knew about and, by their own lights, understood. It required no esoteric knowledge of highfalutin German philosophy or British political economy, and its utopia involved a transformation of human values rather than the ridiculous prospect of turning the seas into lemonade.

In the wake of Romanticism, religion had also become modish. Reason had discredited itself through a franco-French holocaust; people wanted to believe. Leftists like Louis Blanc regarded Voltaireanism as 'dangerous and puerile', and – horror of horrors for progressives everywhere – argued that irreligion might be hopelessly out of date: 'A chaque époque son oeuvre! Celle de notre temps est de raviver le sentiment religieux.' Theorists such as Blanc, Cabet, Considérant and Philippe Buchez emphasised equality and fraternity at the expense of liberty, and took every opportunity to write Jesus Christ into the socialist script. Their lead was followed by the workers' press, with the Communist paper *Travail* claiming that 'communisme est le véritable christianisme appliqué aux relations de la vie'. Worker–poets identified Christianity as the original source of socialist virtues, and the early Christians as prototypical of incipient socialist organisation.

Socialist enthusiasm for Christianity was also a response to profound changes within Christianity itself. So as to undo the legacy of the Revolution, the French Church had had to rediscover the gentler Christocentric faith of cardinal de Bérulle in the early seventeenth century, downplaying the more recent sternly theocentric emphasis evident in its teachings during the eighteenth century. Out went fear, and in came love. This doubly appealed since, as we have seen, both Rousseau in theory and the Jacobins in practice tried to enforce their civil religions through fear and far worse. Lamennais popularised an egalitarian version of Christocentric Christianity, in which 'the people' were associated with a caring God and Christ while the rich and powerful consorted with their ally the devil. Equality, justice and plenty were not endlessly deferred to an afterlife, but were attainable in this life through faith in Jesus Christ. A new generation of priests, often from modest circumstances, preached this gentler Gospel to parishioners who were much like themselves, doing so with the aid of such works as Thomas à Kempis's *Imitation of Christ* which stressed the virtues of the common man. They were joined in this endeavour by lay primary school teachers who, following a law of 1833, were responsible for religious instruction in classrooms that once again had a crucifix on the wall. Unaware of doctrinal orthodoxy, these lay teachers helped disseminate an egalitarian version of Christianity that was simultaneously being propagated by Buchez, Lamennais and their acolytes. The fact that these doctrines were being taught by laymen and renegades rather than a Church that underwrote an unjust society contributed to their success, and for that matter to their enduring presence within a socialist tradition temporarily tantalised by the pseudo-omniscience of Marxist materialism.[130]

It is well known that the British socialist tradition has been constantly enriched by Nonconformism, Anglicanism and Catholicism, with Christianity, and a number of minority religions, being as important to many of Labour's leaders and adherents as they are to their counterparts among Conservatives and Liberal Democrats.[131]

Unlike some of the continental socialist movements, no rift opened in Britain between organised labour and Christianity, although the established Church was sometimes seen as having betrayed the social ideals of the latter. By the 1890s the Church had assumed the characteristics of a chameleon, being conservative in the countryside but socialist in the deprived areas of the big cities. Methodist chapels had for long been enabling working-class people to hone their civic and organisational abilities prior to translating these (and much of the accompanying rhetoric) into trade unionism and politics. In Britain, socialism did not displace Christianity; on the contrary, it was indelibly shaped by it. Whatever setbacks the Christian Churches experienced in urban Britain, these cannot be attributed to the growth of socialism among the working classes.

On the continent, the Churches were overwhelmingly identified with conservatism, with Germany's largest Protestant Church, the Old Prussian Union, actively involved in the struggle against socialism. In Britain both liberalism and labour were inextricably involved with different shades of religious dissent. Whereas many British socialists came from religious backgrounds, their German counterparts were products of an environment where church attendance was already low. By the early twentieth century, some 10 to 15 per cent of working-class Protestant Londoners still attended church on Sundays, the figure for such bastions of socialism as South Wales or Yorkshire being considerably higher. By contrast, in Godless Berlin, only 1 per cent of people in equivalent working-class parishes attended church on Sundays in 1869, and that percentage had halved again by the outbreak of the First World War, a dismal record that could be replicated for Hamburg and the industrial parts of Saxony.[132]

This does not mean that there were not tensions between Churches and the labour movement in Britain. Liberalism and Nonconformity were so enmeshed that inevitably, while it was regarded as normal to 'preach' liberalism, preaching socialism was regarded as more controversial. For some people, politics itself became a sufficient and then an overriding commitment that gradually displaced their religious allegiances; others followed their continental comrades in adopting an explicitly secular view, although more often than not this was based on Darwin and Huxley rather than Marx and Engels. But in Britain these influences had to compete against colourful and pluralist religious traditions, whether the Nonconformist chapels in South Wales, the synagogues of London's East End, or, last but not least, the occasional Anglican clergyman committed to the marriage of Christianity and socialism in some urban rookery.

Conversion to what was unabashedly described as 'the Religion of Socialism' complemented rather than challenged a convert's egalitarian notions of Christianity. A new recruit to the Independent Labour Party in 1894 wrote: 'Here I saw the way to that Kingdom of God on earth for which I had prayed and worked so long. My joy was beyond words, because the revelation of life which I had seen in Jesus of Nazareth became clearer and more real to me every day. I began to see why Jesus pitied the rich and said the poor in spirit possessed the Kingdom of God ... I realised that the incoming of the Socialist ideal into my life had revolutionised my relationships with mankind.'[133] Some thought that socialism had helped reconcile politics and religion 'since their object-matter is the same' and 'politics are henceforth merged with morals'. This era of religious incandescence was relatively brief. The rise of a single party machine out of a looser federation of sects meant that the machine, or the state it sought to capture as the only imaginable way of doing good, began to be conceived as an end in itself. Penetrating local government or the state to pursue reformist ends, recruiting members to swell the apparat and raising money to fight elections displaced wider goals. The reduction of socialism to economics and politics, which would then simultaneously benefit and be implemented by an academic and technocratic careerist 'expertocracy', meant a quiet drift of people whose concerns were to do with the moral regeneration of the individual and society into a separate Ethical movement. As socialism assumed all the characteristics of an established Church of the working classes and their middle-class sympathisers, it necessarily joined the traditional Churches in facing the secularising challenge of rising living standards and the proliferation of recreational activities, shopping, sport, the pub and newspapers, which served to undermine the totalising pretensions of both religion and politics.[134]

Not all socialists were Marxists, for anarcho-syndicalism had greater purchase in the French trades unions and in Italy or Spain, but the great continental European socialist movements were influenced by the Marxist canon in ways that remind intelligent commentators of the relationship between nineteenth-century Christians and the Bible: 'some accepted the book in the spirit of fundamentalism, some in the spirit of the higher criticism, some with heretical reservations; others respected without believing, others neither respected nor believed, but often quoted significant passages all the same'.[135]

The largest European socialist party was the German Social Democratic Party. By 1910 this had some 720,000 members, or more than the socialist parties of Austria, Belgium, Denmark, France, Great Britain, Italy, the Netherlands, Norway, Sweden and Switzerland combined. It was much more than a political party, more like a way of life. Based on a fusion of two parties, the Social Democrats were subject to anti-socialist laws between 1878 and 1890 which reduced legal activity to the parliamentary party and its voters, while banning all party organisations, activism and publicity. Some of the leaders went into permanent exile. About fifteen hundred Social Democrats were sentenced to a total of eight hundred years' imprisonment, a level of repression that paled into insignificance beside the bloodbath that followed the Paris Commune or the later persecution of organised labour under the Third Reich.

Repression provided fertile ground for the messianic doctrine of Marxism, which from the late 1870s became the official creed of the Social Democratic Party's (SPD) leaders, and displaced both anarchism and those who, like Ferdinand Lassalle, believed in co-operation with the Bismarckian state against the bourgeoisie.[136] Paradoxically, the marxification of the Party was one of the factors that contributed to a diminution of anticlerical and atheist ardour that were more evident in the 1860s and 1870s than later. Although the Party's 1875 'Gotha programme' had declared religion to be a private matter, in practice leading Social Democrats believed that 'Religion is the most powerful enemy of socialism . . . religion is the main bastion of antisocialism, of reaction, [and] the breeding ground of all social evil'. In Berlin Johann Most sponsored an aggressive exodus of socialists from the Churches, or 'Kirchenaustrittsbewegung', while opponents of socialism tried to revitalise Christianity among the workers through such initiatives as the ill-starred Christian Social movement of the antisemitic court preacher Adolf Stoecker. Neither movement was very successful. In 1878 Most persuaded a few hundred workers to leave the Churches; a year later this trickle had become the intermittent drip of a few dozen. Stoecker, as we shall see in a later chapter, failed abysmally in recruiting Berlin workers to his Christian Social platform, and turned instead to the (Christian) lower-middle class. In 1883 the SPD abandoned its aggressive campaign against the Churches, in favour of defending its own worldview. As Guido Weiss warned the comrades, by attacking the Churches: 'You are galvanising a corpse, and in the end the Church will have the advantage.'[137]

This newfound socialist moderation on the subject of religion had tactical and theoretical causes. When Bismarck abandoned the 'culture war' on Catholicism, he refocused his sights on the Social Democrats as 'Reichsfeinde' with similarly alien allegiances to the Catholics, a development which led the Social Democrats to tone down their anti-Catholic rhetoric so as to ingratiate themselves with the Catholic Centre Party. Unsurprisingly, it was also becoming apparent that militant atheism was unattractive to potential voters, should the SPD seek to break out of its working-class ghettos. In the countryside, socialism went hand in hand with traditional religious allegiances, and without those votes socialists would never gain power. But there was also an important theoretical development. The ascendancy of younger Marxist intellectuals like Eduard Bernstein or Karl Kautsky meant the Party gradually imbibed the Marxist belief that religion would simply disappear when the socio-economic conditions that had given rise to it were overcome. Put differently, religion was so ephemeral that it was not worth fighting. As Engels wrote: 'The only service that can be rendered to God today is to declare atheism a compulsory article of faith.' The SPD confined itself to attacking the political role of the Churches as part of the Establishment, and their influence on elementary schools, rather than directly challenging religion.

Social Democracy was not merely a political party together with a closely allied and subordinate trades union movement, but a way of life, consisting of a self-contained subculture that thrived in working-class quarters of big cities. As in most ghettos, including the one to which many Catholic workers belonged, exclusion was self-reinforcing. The Social Democrats were regarded as 'enemies of the Reich' with dubious international affiliations; they regarded themselves as the gravediggers of the established order. Accounts of discussions among ordinary members suggest that they thought that after the 'Last Judgement' anxiety about the availability of potatoes would be superseded by the pleasure of champagne on tap.

Since workers were also part of the wider society, whether through schools, the military, the Churches or their workplace, the Party sought to counteract these influences through a socialist parallel universe, with its own cultural, recreational and sporting clubs, newspapers, welfare organisations and, once they were legalised, public festivals. The Churches might have been envious of a movement that included separate co-operative stores, health insurance, charities, cycling, bowling, gymnastic and singing clubs, choirs, libraries, festivals, celebrating 18 March 1871 or May Day, and at life's end socialist cremation. The birth of the

Paris Commune was commemorated as a rival to Sedan Day which celebrated Prussia's triumph over the French. Although they clung, against the realities of the German economy, to a belief in capitalism's imminent demise and to a rhetorical romantic revolutionism, the emphasis was increasingly on organisation for organisation's sake and the realities of incremental reformism through participation in municipal government. Some argue that this, and those aspects of the dominant culture that seeped into that of the socialists, effectively integrated them into the wider society that rejected them. Be that as it may, the movement gave workers' lives structure and ultimate meaning that reminded some of the religion that Social Democracy affected to despise. As one scion of a Berlin socialist household recalled:

> In the solidaristic identification of the individual with the whole, they built the powerful organisations and communities which, like great religions, placed people under their spell. They gave them a view of the world, a country and a home. Here people did not only take part in politics: they also sang and drank, celebrated and made friendships. What was impossible else where was possible here: you could be a human being.

In their prison cells, several socialist leaders reflected on the nature of utopia, a fashionable literary genre that also thrived among people staring at the walls of a cell. The most famous such product was Bebel's *Die Frau und der Sozialismus* (1879), written during two stints in prison in 1872–4 and 1877–8. In addition to its egalitarian and statist economic musings, Bebel's book imagined that in his future society idleness would be replaced by a fervour to work; many crimes would disappear; literary taste would be cleansed; and life would be happy and carefree. This anthropological optimism accounts for why his book became the socialist Bible.[138]

Some socialists made the connection between religion and socialism explicit. 'Beloved fellow citizens!' wrote a Marxist autodidact, 'the tendencies of socialism contain the building blocks for a new religion ... Until now, religion was a question for the proletariat. Now, by contrast, the question of the proletariat is becoming a religion.'

Outside such totalitarian environments it was usual to find more variegated allegiances based on apparent contradiction. In the Erzgebirge, where workers had pictures of Luther next to those of the Virgin Mary, they also had August Bebel beside the king of Saxony, leading a pastor to comment: 'In the soul of the people, it is the same as it is on the wall; they bring together harmlessly things that are most opposed.'[139] This was what respectively Martin Rade and Alfred Levenstein discovered in two small surveys of working-class religious beliefs and practices which they conducted in 1898 and 1912. Levenstein found that just over half of his miners, metal and textile workers did not believe in God (13 per cent said they did) but that only a handful had gone to the trouble of disaffiliating from the state Churches. Their party did not demand this and, besides, most of them did not want to offend other family members who were religious, or feared damage to their children's future prospects. Pastor Rade discovered a near universal contempt for the Churches and scepticism towards parts of the Bible. By contrast, there was unanimous respect for Jesus as a 'true workers' friend', with one claiming that were Jesus alive 'today he would certainly be a Social Democrat, maybe even a leader and a Reichstag deputy'. In other words, Jesus was a proto-revolutionary or secular reformer.[140]

The claim that Social Democracy was a surrogate religion was made at the time by such opponents as the German Jesuit who in 1878 wrote: 'Because Man must have a religion, socialism has become the religion of atheistic workers particularly in Protestant regions.' Protestant critics accused the socialists of trying to establish 'a heaven on earth' through the fire and sword once used by the Anabaptists in sixteenth-century Münster. However this was not something simply imputed to socialists by their opponents, but a claim they frequently made themselves. Closing the 1890 party congress in Halle, one of the Party founding fathers, Wilhelm Liebknecht, said:

> Wenn wir unter dem Sozialistengesetz freudig das schwerste Opfer gebracht haben, uns die Familie und die Existenz zerstören liessen, uns auf Jahre trennten von Frau und Kind, blos um der Sache zu dienen, so war das auch Religion, aber nicht die Religion des Pfaffenthums, sondern die Religion des Menschenthums. Es war der Glaube an den Sieg des Guten und der Idee; die unerschütterliche Überzeugung, der felsenfeste Glaube, dass das Recht siegen und dass das Unrecht zu Falle kommen muss. Diese Religion wird uns niemals abhanden kommen, denn sie ist eins mit dem Sozialismus.

Socialism resembled a religion in several respects and for various reasons. Even those socialists who rejected religion in favour of Darwinism and Marxism depended on the Christian heritage for such concepts as 'heaven' or 'salvation', not to speak of the most powerful rhetoric that lay to hand. They hardly had a monopoly of that, for scientific materialists everywhere tended to sound like members of proselytising religious sects. As the atheist Liebknecht unhelpfully explained: 'I would say, provided the word religion is not misconstrued, that socialism is at the same time a religion and science – rooted in the head and the heart.'[141] Rhetoric reliant on the religious heritage may also have made the SPD less objectionable to such new constituencies as 'women' or Catholic 'peasants' in southern and western Germany. But, apart from these contextual or instrumental uses of religious words and images, Social Democracy catered to human needs and fulfilled functions normally associated with a religion. The language and visual imagery of socialism was saturated with angels and happy people marching into the warm rays of the 'world-historical sunrise'.

Exposure to the fundamental tenets of the faith led workers to remark: 'I saw the world with entirely different eyes.' Socialism gave the most insecure, marginal and vulnerable that most valuable thing of all: hope that the future would turn out for the good since it charted a path through the ambient chaos and darkness towards a warmly reassuring light. It converted aspirations and feelings, whether of envy or fellowship, into what purported to be scientifically grounded knowledge, in the process enabling workers to controvert the bourgeoisie's monopoly of learning with a narrow range of stock formulae. It afforded the individual's life higher meaning, moral worth, while providing an ersatz community consisting of the dedicated and truly informed. It simplified moral complexities into a world of easy allegiances; one could hate or resent with good conscience since one had surrendered to the higher necessities of a movement that transcended delicacies of conscience. Finally, socialism promised reality-defying leaps from the 'world of necessity to that of freedom' that, coolly considered, were as improbable as a belief in feeding thousands with loaves and fishes or walking on water. The end of the existing world would come not in the form of a divine apocalypse but as a result of laws immanent in the productive process, though an apocalypse it would be all the same. It was called a revolutionary 'Last Judgement'. As society evolved towards the revolutionary end-state, a 'new man' would arise to populate the post-apocalyptic age. This vision owed very little to 'science' and much to religious eschatology.[142]

Readers may object that socialism came in different guises and tempers. So did Protestantism. Just as liberal bourgeois Protestants had abandoned the more dramatically eschatological aspects of their faith, through their accommodations with modern science and criticism, so some socialists abandoned an emphasis upon the revolutionary apocalypse that was supposed to inaugurate utopia, in favour of a modern appreciation for incremental, practical reforms, to be achieved by working with the grain of the existing system. In 1891 Georg von Vollmar amused delegates to a socialist convention when he mocked the prophetic certainty of some of his fellow SPD leaders in and outside Germany:

> The point in time when that (the great crash-bang-wallop) will be, has – since prophecy has now become fashionable in the party – (applause) recently been established by those in London as being the year 1898. I don't know the day or month. But I do know people in the party, for whom this date is far too distant, and who think it could be 1893, perhaps even 1892 (applause).[143]

Going to buy the Party newspaper was like entering sacred ground, with people putting on their Sunday best to do it. Socialist meetings followed a liturgy that unconsciously mimicked that of the Churches, with choral singing of alternative words to the tune of Christian hymns, together with cheers and toasts to socialism. Celebrations of the early socialist leader Ferdinand Lassalle's birthday on Palm Sunday were not complete without a portrait of the leader surrounded with leafy greenery and banners inscribed with such sayings as 'The workers are the rock on which the Church of the present shall be founded.' Speeches referred to Lassalle as 'the new messiah of the people'. Down to 1890 when restrictions on political demonstrations were lifted, socialists used funerals as a means of impressing the scale of their support on the public. While these took on more secular characteristics, it is noteworthy that at the graveside the assembled comrades felt obliged to reaffirm their 'confession of faith'.

If the European working classes, and middle-class fellow travellers, took to the religion of socialism in prodigious numbers, people higher in the social scale adopted a number of creeds that have evinced greater durability. This was especially true of Protestant northern Germany where middle-class alienation from the Churches seems to have set in remarkably early, that is before 1848, and people turned to the arts as well as commerce for consolation and meaning. Concerned Protestant clergy routinely came down on the well-educated professional middle classes and the wealthier commercial bourgeoisie for failing in their religious duties. Once, Christianity had constituted a common bond between the highest and the lowest, regardless of the different levels at which they apprehended the same stories. In the early modern period, humanistic culture was confined to court life and made little impression on the world beyond. By the nineteenth century this had been augmented by the specialised scholarship of universities, which divided fragments of knowledge among rival faculties, to be further dissected by a specialising professoriate that revelled in wilful obscurity.[144] History, natural sciences and political economy edged aside theology, although philosophy would follow in due course. Beginning with the demi-education that went with the layabout life of students, religious indifferentism spread to the urban bourgeoisie, who moreover were as mobile in their way as the new industrial proletarians, and hence not embedded in ecclesiastical structures for any length of time. While the urban middle class moved their dwellings to places that reflected their status and discovered the cultural diversity of modern urban life, the intellectual scope of the Churches contracted to a dialogue of the like-minded who by dint of their modest circumstances were unable to leave their place of birth. Protestant pastors operated within a relatively narrow circle of lower-middle-class bureaucrats and shopkeepers who were committed to parish life, who were active on parish councils, and who had very limited cultural or intellectual horizons. By contrast, those higher up the social scale, like architects, doctors and lawyers, found other diversions, such as private clubs and reading-rooms, commercial associations, concerts and theatre, and hardly ever visited a church.[145]

However, alienation from formal religious observance did not mean that the urban bourgeoisie were lacking in religiosity, a word which originally meant the individual's subjective religious experience, but which mutated into a diffuse emotional piety. This occurred especially wherever liberal Protestantism simultaneously invested such worldly activities as work, politics, science or the arts with transcendental significance, as cultural Protestantism attempted to reconcile faith with the culture of the times.[146] Cultivation of the self through education and exposure to art, literature and music as means of moral and spiritual improvement could easily become a quasi-religious vocation, with such geniuses as Goethe, Schiller or Beethoven representing the quasi-divine apogee of human perfection around whom cults accreted. Goethe said as much when he wrote:

> He who possesses art and knowledge,
> Possesses religion also;
> He who possesses neither one nor the other,
> Let him have religion instead.[147]

Never ranked as the ultimate art form by either Kant or Hegel, music came to be regarded as the purest expression of the sublime. Music consoled and music transcended, claimed the artists, and as the public increasingly expected once they had been disciplined into thinking that a concert hall was not primarily a venue for business deals or marriage market but a church: 'One goes to the Conservatoire with religious devotion as the pious go to the temple of the Lord,' as a French writer put it in 1846. Music was especially suitable as a means of reaching for the sublime, especially when what is called musical idealism resulted in symphony orchestras performing an almost hallowed repertory of dead masters, such as Haydn, Mozart or Beethoven, in austere concert halls where audiences of the earnest were expected to behave, keep quiet and applaud in the right places, all in marked contrast to the febrile social whirl that eclipsed the music in Europe's metropolitan opera houses.[148]

Hector Berlioz and, more especially, Richard Wagner were composers (and prolific authors) who had an extraordinarily elevated view of the transformative potential of their art, and disdain for both crass commercialism (never incompatible with Wagner's remorseless quest for money, best symbolised by his wife Cosima hauling off bags of coins when banknotes were not forthcoming) and the mediocrity of contemporary public taste that was over-tantalised by flashy performers whose technique triumphed over substance. Wagner the man and his music offered the frisson of being avant-garde, dangerous and slightly subversive, elements essential to the romance of modernistic success as the artist himself became a cause adopted by the cognoscenti in their self-satisfied fight with uncomprehending philistines. Obsessive contemporary interest in Wagner's odious, if scarcely unique, views on Jews has rather overshadowed what he signified in the broader evolution of art galleries, concert halls and opera houses into temples where modern man glimpses the sublime, or his influences upon a modernist tradition that relies upon evoking myths that resonate in obscure regions of our psyches. The mystical transports of Wagner's brooding, fractured and swirling chords lifted audiences into a realm of deep emotions and myth. It seemed to open profounder and more human vistas than that of the prevailing desiccated dogmas of Comtean Positivism or reductive Darwinian science, the musical medium through which this emotional piety was expressed being inherently unsusceptible to the Straussian critiques that had challenged a religion based on controvertible historical texts. Music could and did substitute for religious experience in a twofold manoeuvre. At Easter enthusiasts went to performances of Bach's operatic *St Matthew Passion*, perhaps in a concert hall rather than a sacred setting, but then made a 'pilgrimage' to experience Wagner's *Tristan und Isolde* or *Parsifal*. Opera became a sacramental event that transformed an audience who arrived as atomised products of a dehumanised society into a church-like community transported into sacred realms through music-drama that evoked the rites of some half-grasped myth. Wagner's art provided a religious experience for people who could no longer believe in God, in which sacred meaning derives from the music itself, and which described the ideal of this-worldly redemption through the sacrifices made by the characters. Art had replaced religion in the sense of giving higher meaning to a world that was increasingly disenchanted, temporarily giving striking form and purpose to mythic incarnations of the human self to audiences all too aware of the ambient chaos and meaninglessness of the Godless condition.[149]

Wagner saw himself as a cultural messiah whose 'holy gift' would cleanse and transform not just opera audiences but society at large. Cosima encouraged the atmosphere of a cult that surrounded the irascible 'Master'. The cult spread through such devices as the national subscription societies founded to finance his festival house at Bayreuth. According to Wagner, art preserved a kernel of religious experience, to which churches and their paraphernalia had become irrelevant; as he wrote, music provided 'the essence of Religion free from all dogmatic fictions', giving modern society a soul and 'a new religion', as well as a new task for art itself.[150]

Much of this must seem speculative. A quick glance at late-nineteenth-century Birmingham, Leeds and Manchester, places uncharitably identified with brass-tacked philistinism, may counter this last impression. All three cities had concert series or music festivals which were attended by the urban prominenti, who positively glistened and glowed amid the plush seats and soft gas lighting. Behaviour and dress were informally codified, with opportunities for applause narrowly circumscribed.

Increasingly, gossip and sociability was left outside, or stilled inside by an insistent 'Hush!' by audiences who were being trained to think that music had no other function than the aesthetic, by among others the professional music critics attached to provincial newspapers. The famous conductor evolved into a quasi-dictatorial figure, while the repertoire became correspondingly narrower and more demanding, including Wagner in the 1870s, and Grieg and Dvořák a decade later. Correspondingly large claims were made for the power of music by audiences who were increasingly referred to as 'apostles of music' or 'initiates in the divine art', both terms indicative of the degree to which music had achieved autonomy from religion while, in a neo-Romantic sort of way, performing many of its collective and individual functions. As Charles Hallé himself had it: 'The art which I profess has been a sort of religion for me. It has certain influences beyond those of any other art.'[151]

Such cities became the hubs of a civic religion in which they themselves fulfilled part of the divine purpose. It took a clergyman to encapsulate this, but the sentiment was more widespread. George Dawson was a Nonconformist minister in late-Victorian Birmingham, for whom 'a city . . . was a society, established by the divine will, as the family, the State, and the Church are established, for common life and common purpose and common action'. Like the nation in miniature, the city was a surrogate Church: 'This then was the new corporation, the new Church, in which they might meet until they came into union again – a Church in which there was no bond, nor text, nor articles – a large Church, one of the greatest institutions yet established.'[152] Service on the new municipal administrations was a religious as well as a moral obligation, and one prestigious enough to attract leading businessmen, accustomed to handling huge sums of money, who were elected to office by a democratised electorate that did not have to pay for the ensuing municipal extravaganzas that were then funded by enormous borrowing. Such religious visions of the improved city inspired the great urban reformers of Victorian Britain, notably Joseph Chamberlain, the driving force behind the transformation of Birmingham. Interpreting Dawson's eleventh Commandment, 'Thou shalt keep a balance-sheet,' rather literally, Chamberlain municipalised urban utilities in a manner that made them more cost-effective in the eyes of ratepayers, and then ploughed back the prodigious profits into leasehold shops and offices, as well as a new Italianate Council House and City Museum and Art Gallery. A gleaming Victorian Venice had obliterated what Pugin had once described as 'the most hateful of all hateful', eradicating any industrial–philistine connotations, although Chamberlain's legacy is not readily identifiable today amid some of the worst modernist architecture in Europe.

The monumentally refashioned civic centres of Birmingham, Leeds or Manchester – nowadays surrendered by a craven bourgeoisie to nightly scenes that would have overtaxed the capacities of Breughel – were formerly the arena for a rich civic culture that expressed municipal Liberalism's quasi-religious sense of urban community. Royal visits to Birmingham, Manchester and Leeds in the 1850s were paradoxically the apogee of bourgeois self-celebration, in which councillors wore splendid robes and triumphal arches were emblazoned with the arms of the cities. Other civic rituals were organised around the commencement of the judicial assizes, the inauguration of municipal buildings, the unveiling of statues and the funerals of local notables. These occasions were designed to celebrate the city, to make clear where municipal power lay, and to invest its holders with the illusion of permanence. On each occasion, the Mayor and Corporation were the centre of attention, with other local worthies precisely positioned to reflect their respective prominence. The 'centipedic' funerals of important men involved casts of thousands, that of Sir Edward Baines – owner of the *Leeds Mercury* – in 1890 closed shops and factories, as a procession half a mile long trudged and trundled from his mansion at Burley to the Leeds Town Hall where the bell tolled and the flag flew at half-mast. All gone now, into the silent funeral of a once great provincial culture.

CHAPTER 7

New Men and Sacred Violence in Late-Nineteenth-Century Russia

I 'NEW MEN'

In the east a form of political religion was developing in which 'sacred violence' was intrinsic to men who considered themselves to be 'just' murderers on the ground that their terror allegedly struck only at those guilty of oppression. Paradoxically, such figures emerged at a time when social reform seemed a distinct possibility.

War is often the forcing house of domestic liberalisation and modernisation. The ancien régime in Prussia was compelled to undertake various internal reforms following its defeats by Napoleon. Defeat by the French, British and Ottoman Turks in the Crimean War also compelled tsar Alexander II of Russia, who came to the imperial throne in early 1855, to introduce movement into a society that had been immobilised, as if entombed in lead, by Nicholas I.

The scale of Alexander's undertaking was so breathtaking that even exiled opponents of the regime, such as the leading liberal Alexander Herzen, praised the Tsar Liberator. Serfdom was abolished in 1861, ending the institution of 'baptised property' that most isolated Russia from enlightened Europe, although slavery, and then racial segregation, lingered in parts of the no less civilised US into the 1960s.

While it was relatively easy to emancipate the twenty-one million serfs owned by the state and the royal family, liberation of the twenty-two millions who were the property of thirty-three thousand private land-owners was a more complicated affair. This was because of the tangled tenurial relations that the custom-conscious serfs were liberated into, and the complexity of the compensation arrangements for landlords that the government felt obliged to put in place. Three years later the authorities conceded elected local government in the provinces and councils in the major towns. Trial by jury and an independent and irremovable judiciary followed. Together with juries which, by virtue of gentlemanly indulgence or guilt, often sympathised with the perpetrators of what were crimes, these measures ensured that those convicted of murder or treason, for which in Britain or France they would have been executed, paradoxically received far more lenient treatment in Europe's most grim autocracy. Universal military conscription was introduced, with six years' service replacing the standard twenty-five years formerly inflicted on generations of superfluous village simpletons. Jews were effectively entitled to reside in Russia proper, with converts to Orthodoxy occasionally able to achieve prominent positions in government and society. Among Jews, Alexander II was known as 'the good emperor'. Finally, censorship was relaxed, and preliminary censorship abolished altogether, which indirectly contributed to the formation of a critical intelligentsia.[1]

The location of radical dissent shifted from noble army officers, such as the Decembrists, who sought to capture the state from within, to a more socially heterogeneous student population that was part of the newly emergent 'intelligentsia', a term that became current in Russia in the 1860s. The usual perils of mindless expansion of education, however limited in this context, were soon there for some to see. All levels of education were expanded and the numbers of university students increased. The student body of St Petersburg University trebled between 1855 and 1861. Modest levels of tuition fees were waived for the poorest students, and Jews and women were admitted for the first time. At the universities, young noblemen who on idealistic grounds forsook state service under Nicholas I after 1825 mixed with the sons of clergy and minor officials, or with those whose origins were even further down in the social depths. Intoxicated with ill-digested abstract ideas and often seething with social resentment, the intelligentsia became progressively detached from conventional society. Its bureaucracies and professions could not absorb or satisfy people whose heady idealism ill suited them to these severely technical occupations in a society where individuality was not encouraged. The more advanced sections of the intelligentsia often described themselves as 'new men' to conceal their alienation from those above and below them with a term that suggested baptism into a new moral mode of being whose corollary was sometimes the rejection of moral discernment in general.[2]

The 'new man' had a name and definable characteristics in fiction before he could be said to have existed in reality. Rarely can literary criticism have exerted such a deleterious effect, beside which the solipsistic jargon of contemporary structuralism (upon whose doorstep multiple ills are sometimes unfairly laid) amounts to venial sin.[3]

'New men' were products of literary conflicts with serious social implications. The 'new man' appeared in the context of the inter-generational struggle waged within the Russian literary intelligentsia in the 1860s. The fault line ran through those who were part of the gentry Establishment, or at least, like Dostoevsky, could be sure of being reabsorbed into it should they abandon their juvenile political radicalism, and those extremists who were excluded and hence compelled to grub a modest living in criticism, journalism, translating and tutoring. Effectively they amounted to an academic or literary proletariat. A younger generation of influential literary cum social critics, such as Dobrolyubov and Chernyshevsky, whom Turgenev dismissed as 'literary Robespierres', despised such amiably superfluous fictional slovens as Goncharov's Oblomov and the older generation of liberal gentry writers, for whom the sovereign moral intelligence of the artist and his ability to 'discover' autonomous and plausible fictional characters was paramount.

Part of the conflict was about the nature and purposes of the novelist's art. Neither the mature Dostoevsky, who was no liberal, nor Turgenev, to take two outstanding examples, knew whether they loved or hated the characters they created, nor how their individual destinies would end, with Raskolnikov, the protagonist of the new amorality in Dostoevsky's *Crime and Punishment*, shooting himself in the authorial notes that preceded Dostoevsky's final option for Raskolnikov's slightly unreal religious conversion at the hands of Sonia Marmeladova. That indeterminacy to how things can snake this way or that is partly what made these men great writers, whose work speaks to us long after their radical critics have slipped into oblivion.

The radical critics were responsible for a series of extra-literary encroachments on the absolute freedom of the artist, where the latter's prime 'duty' was to conform his or her creative work to a series of ideological agendas. This resembled, albeit from an opposite political perspective, the desire of the late-eighteenth-century writer Bogdanovich to put all writers in civil service uniforms, and to give them ranks according to their degree of usefulness to the state.[4] No serious creative artist could possibly go along with constraints that were worse than those of the government's own negative censorship, which while banning certain themes did not demand conformity to a set of socio-political objectives.[5] In the view of the radical critics, literature was to be saturated with, and subordinate to, political creeds that sought to change the world, with their new positive heroes being the fictional anticipation of the 'new men' who would ceaselessly strive to bring about universal human emancipation. Emblematic fiction was designed to help these new moral personalities constitute themselves, rather in the manner of adolescents who try to model themselves on characters in a book or film, or, having become students, upon posters of Che Guevara.

The 'new man', as constituted in these critics' own indifferent novels, was an activist, a totally politicised type of new moral personality, the forerunner of Bolshevik 'leather men in leather jackets', for in important respects the Bolsheviks ignored the reverence Marx and Engels themselves paid to absolute quality in high art, in favour of the indigenous Russian radical tradition of the 'pre-Marxist materialists' whom we are discussing.

The 'new man' was a monolithic personality, a tyro of enormous will, a little poorly digested utilitarian knowledge, no capacity for self-doubt and blinkered singularity of purpose. He was incapable of relating to the complexities of another human being beyond whatever ideological stereotype he had already imposed upon them. In the eyes of Herzen, who attacked such 'new men' in an article entitled 'The Superfluous Men and the Men with a Grudge', they had the roughness, rudeness and ruthlessness of ambitious and unsuccessful mediocrities, although they were themselves notoriously touchy. When Chernyshevsky met Herzen in London in 1859, the latter felt that this boorish 'Daniel on the Neva' gazed at him as 'on the fine skeleton of a mammoth, as at an interesting bone that had been dug up, and belonged with a different sun and different trees'.[6] Translated into fictional characters, the 'new men' lacked identifying marks of humanity, or the flaws that might make their actions vaguely interesting, except of course, when Dostoevsky or Turgenev got to grips with them. Such 'new men' had all the plausibility of religious saints; indeed, the literature that celebrated them, whose lineal descendant was Soviet socialist realism, was little more than a form of political hagiography, except that hairshirts and loincloths had been exchanged for uniforms and leather coats and jackets, the latter with their dual glamour of animality and perversion.[7]

The critics responsible for the outline of the 'new men' were themselves invariably myopic, sallow, sickly, bookish types, of whom Nicholas Chernyshevsky was the prototype.[8] Of Chernyshevsky's influence there can be little doubt. As one of his greatest admirers put it shortly after the turn of the nineteenth century:

> Under his [Chernyshevsky's] influence hundreds of people became revolutionaries ... For example, he fascinated my brother and he fascinated me. He ploughed me up more profoundly than anyone else. When did you read *What is to be Done?* ... I myself tried to read it when I was about fourteen. It was no use, a superficial reading. And then, after my brother's execution, knowing that Chernyshevsky's novel was one of his favourite books, I really undertook to read it, and I sat over it not for several days but for several weeks. Only then did I understand its depth ... It's a thing which supplies energy for a whole lifetime. An ungifted work could not have that kind of influence.

This was Lenin talking to a fellow revolutionary in a Swiss café. Exploring Chernyshevsky's main work it is not difficult to see why he should have exerted such an attraction on this admirer. Part of that appeal was that of all prison literature, although in this case one has to imagine the four walls and bars to invest this 'gospel' of Russian radicalism with spurious romantic poignancy. *What is to be Done?* was published in the spring of 1863, despite the fact that Chernyshevsky had been in solitary confinement in the Petropavlovsk fortress in St Petersburg since December 1862, in itself striking testimony to the inefficiency of the tsarist censors.

Chernyshevsky's life was devastated as well as deformed by ideological fanaticism, perhaps an appropriate fate for this scion of a long line of priests from provincial Saratov. In 1864, following his arrest for revolutionary conspiracy, Chernyshevsky was subjected to mock execution, with a wooden sword being broken over his head to symbolise civil degradation, and was then sentenced to fourteen years' penal servitude to be followed by permanent exile. After spending the years 1864–71 in a prison in trans-Baikal, he was despatched in 1872 to a desolate town called Viliuisk, where he remained until 1883. During that entire period he saw his wife and son once, for other lives were devastated by fanaticism too. Chernyshevsky spent his last years under close surveillance in

Astrakhan; he died in Saratov, after the authorities had finally released him, in June 1889.[9]

What is to be Done? was a radical's rejoinder to Turgenev's *Fathers and Sons*, with its alleged slanders against the 'new men' who as the 'new people' comprise the subject of Chernyshevksy's own tale. They have become 'people' because the proto-feminist Chernyshevsky had much to say about 'new women'. The 'novel', for early on the narrator concedes 'I haven't a drop of literary talent in me,' is a modern rationalist's answer to the old-fashioned agonies of a ménage à trois.

It begins with an alleged suicide that particularly distresses the young man and woman who are the other angles of the love triangle Chernyshevsky describes. The background to the 'suicide' is as follows. A medical student Lopukhov marries Vera Pavlovna, the daughter of a caretaker and his harpy pawnbroker consort. Lopukhov marries Vera to deliver her from her awful family circumstances. The couple live as brother and sister rather than man and wife, merely interrupting their respective reading and sewing sessions to rendezvous for tea in the middle of their flat. Vera opens what becomes a highly successful dress-making co-operative, run on Owenite lines, which miraculously transforms troubled girls into paragons of industrial virtue. To underline his point, Chernyshevsky informs his readers that the only decoration in Lopukhov's study–bedroom is a portrait done in the presence of the great British socialist himself. Refusing to allow her husband even to kiss her hand, Vera transfers her unassuaged affections to Kirsanov, another former medical student who is her husband's best friend. Lopukhov duly enacts the hoax suicide to oblige Vera and Kirsanov who live as husband and wife. The relationships drawn in the novel reject the sort of intense emotions that such situations usually entail; everyone chooses to play by the rules of 'let's be friends'. The trio also represent the normal types of 'new people'. Rather awkwardly, Chernyshevsky intrudes into the story the more advanced version of the 'new man' – in the form of Rakhmetov, the man of unalloyed will, who brings Vera the intelligence that Lopukhov is not dead but living abroad. He convinces Vera and Kirsanov that their guilt regarding his (fake) suicide is irrational.

The aristocratic radical Rakhmetov combines being a physical fitness fanatic (who eats nothing but raw beef) with the capacity to devour book after book, his life consisting of 'Calisthenics, hard labour and books'.[10] At one point he takes to sleeping on a bed of nails simply to establish that he can, although the result is blood all over his nightshirt and floor. Having inherited prodigious wealth, Rakhmetov proceeds to give it away or to use it to subsidise poor students. Every minute of his day is usefully employed. He suffers no fools gladly, but pursues interesting people at any hour of day or night, for he has utter disdain for social convention. The only time he entertains the notion of love is rapidly quashed as he rebuffs the woman concerned with a gruff 'Love is not for me.' No sooner has this titan entered the novel than it is time for him to disappear, criss-crossing Europe in Chernyshevsky's thinly veiled version of a professional revolutionary career. Lopukhov reappears as the foreigner Beaumont. He rescues another girl from destructive family circumstances, and he, his second wife, Vera and Kirsanov live happily ever after.

Given that the book was written in prison, and would have to evade censorship, dreams are used to convey its explicit political message. Vera has four dreams, which are like escalators to her progressive enlightenment. Her protracted and vivid fourth dream is used to muse on mankind's own progression to the total stasis of a richly described Fourierist utopia. Here nothing, as the pop song goes, ever happens, or at least nothing that might make life bearable by way of depth or variety. Heaven is like a Russian version of California. Blandly beautiful people, although California has its share of gnarled specimens too, populate the communities Chernyshevsky describes: 'This is a lovely, joyful people, theirs is a life of elegance and light. Their humble homes reveal inside a wealth of refinement and mastery in the art of leisure; furniture and furnishings delight the eye in every detail. Aesthetically alive and appealing themselves, these people live in and for love and beauty.'

Vera is transported into a future that revolves around several aluminium, steel and glass replicas of London's contemporary Crystal Palace exhibition halls: 'Glass and steel, steel and glass, and that is all'. Once parched deserts have been rolled back by the intelligent application of human diligence; even changes in climate have been brought under mankind's control. As in many utopias, and socialist realist posters, there are few old people; instead, everywhere abounds with children and cheery youths, while only machines puff about in the fields. There is human labour, but this has been reduced to the point where its chief value is to create the desire for endless leisure. Food is served in vast communal dining-halls, with aluminium tables bedecked with flowers and crystal vases. Nights are spent beneath 'light – sunny, white and bright without harshness – electric of course' dancing and singing: 'Here there is neither the fear nor the memory of need, no thought but that of the good, of labour free and rich in satisfaction and none but the same in sight.'[11] Those not enjoying these hedonistic nocturnal pursuits beaver away in lecture halls, libraries and museums. Given the briefest glimpse of the future, Vera concludes:

> No, the world has yet to see true celebration, to produce the proper people for it. Only those we have just observed may drain the cup of pleasure to the dregs. In the full bloom of vitality they are full of grace, their features bold and striking. Handsome one and all, they are blessed with a life of liberty and labour – what fortune, what tremendous fortune.[12]

However banal Chernyshevsky's utopian imaginings may have been, *What is to be Done?* had two important effects on the future of Russian radicalism. It provided models of human conduct, or what we might call 'identities', regarding how individual radicals should behave, and how they should interact among themselves and towards people outside the sect. Resembling a religious conversion, the neophyte became a member of a likeminded sectarian group, to which his or her behaviour was obliged to conform. Put differently, this meant the creation of a parallel radical morality, some of whose characteristics were unimpeachable enough, such as recognition of the autonomy of women, other aspects utterly appalling in the sense that the revolutionary ends justified the corrupt means, provided inordinate will-power had been demonstrated. Secondly, however risible Chernyshevsky's vision of rosaceous beings amid their crystal palaces and glistening cornfields, by imagining the future, he contributed to making it happen. As we saw, Lenin (and his terrorist elder brother shared this feeling) regarded Chernyshevsky's execrable book as one of his life's inspirations.[13]

II 'THE GOSPEL OF THE REVOLVER' (AND THE BOMB)

The flurry of reforms with which we began stopped short of a national parliament. Alexander II dismissed this with an elegantly curt: 'surtout, pas d'Assemblée de notables!'[14] In radical circles there was alarm that these reforms might lead to a constitutional monarchy, thwarting their desire for violent social transformation or, in some cases, their psychopathic visions of a cleansing revolutionary bloodbath. Among such people, incremental reform lacked the sinister glamour of the peasant's axe, the terrorist's gun or the devastating explosion, and the feeling of omnipotence that came from striking fear in the hearts of the powerful.[15] Radicals, whose murderous activities and even more sanguinary rhetoric provoked reaction, therefore bore some moral responsibility for the polarised atmosphere that was uncongenial to the emergence of a more liberal rather than a totalitarian Russia. Others were not blameless.

The government overreacted to sporadic disturbances by peasants who, thinking they could simply usurp land, vented their anger against those who they imagined were frustrating the tsar's noble intentions. Forty-one peasants were shot and seventy wounded in a minor (and passive) demonstration in Kazan province that was suppressed by troops. Simultaneously, in early 1861 Russian troops fired on Polish nationalist demonstrators in Warsaw, these unconnected events encouraging revolutionaries to imagine that the time was ripe to activate their inchoate conspiracy, for nationalist revolt on the peripheries of empire was supposed to coincide with full-scale uprisings by the Russian peasantry. In early 1862 a series of mysterious fires burned down entire areas of St Petersburg, leaving many wondering whether they were the inevitable risk that went with wooden houses or evidence of revolutionary incendiarism.

Minuscule radical sects issued revolutionary paperwork that was heroic in its ambition. Manifestos and proclamations, inciting agitation among the peasants and mutiny in the army, were issued in the name of a shadowy organisation called Land and Freedom. This was the first revolutionary organisation in Russia to be based on the western European model of co-option into small cells. It was also a classic example of revolutionary disconnection from those in whose name revolution would be made. For in reality the peasants had little or no contact with the tiny revolutionary intelligentsia, a term that encompassed all those with modest education in a land of mass illiteracy, while Polish nationalists, who in 1863 essayed a major rising, found that even their Russian revolutionary friends were infected by Greater Russian chauvinism. By early 1864, Land and Freedom had collapsed, but the example of a cell-based revolutionary organisation lived on.

Shortly after the demise of Land and Freedom, a new group called Organisation came into being, consisting of approximately fifty members and with an inner core of dedicated assassins called Hell. Their aim was regicide. It was from Hell that Dmitri Karakozov hailed, who in the spring of 1866 tried to shoot Alexander II as the tsar finished his daily walk in a St Petersburg public park and was about to mount his carriage. A hatter's apprentice managed to jog the assassin's arm just as he aimed, so that the bullet flew past the tsar's head. When Karakozov was restrained, the tsar bravely decided to interrogate him, bravely because Karakozov still had a vial of acid (which he should already have used to disfigure his own face) and strychnine (which he would have used to kill himself after the successful assassination) about his person.

'Who are you?' asked the tsar.

'A Russian,' answered Karakozov

'What do you want?'

'Nothing, nothing,' said the failed assassin.

Following this botched assassination, the government went cool on its earlier reforming zeal, without implementing more repressive policies with the requisite rigour. That equivocal stance partly explains why otherwise decent, liberal-minded people proved extraordinarily indulgent about what were essentially criminal acts, provided their radical perpetrators could camouflage them with a higher moral–political purpose. Of course, some liberal-minded people were not immune either to the vicarious thrill of violence committed by 'people's criminals' in the name of 'people's justice', a pathology by no means unique to nineteenth-century Russia, since remote salivation over violence seems to be a more general inheritance.

People's Justice was the title of a manifesto issued on behalf of the committee of a new revolutionary organisation called People's Justice that in reality consisted of a psychotic confidence trickster and autodidact philosopher called Sergei Nechaev, who having falsely claimed to have escaped from Petropavlovsk fortress wormed his way into the willing confidences of the anarchist Bakunin in Geneva. We know quite a bit about this arch-terrorist.

Until 1861 Nechaev's family had been serfs. He grew up with his grandparents, for his mother had died young, before being returned to his father and his second wife. The father worked as a part-time waiter in the homes of the rich, something that clearly demeaned the son. Nechaev followed his grandfather's trade of sign painting. Having educated himself, although probably not to read Kant in German, Nechaev managed to get a post teaching 'the word of God' in a St Petersburg parish school. A photograph shows a slight, raffishly dressed young man, with the lean, bearded countenance of an American outlaw, for he was more like Jesse James than a bespectacled revolutionary swot.

Nechaev fell under the influence of an older Russian Jacobin and in turn brought his own malign intelligence to bear on the capital's population of gullible students. Insofar as Nechaev had a strategy, it was to multiply the ranks of agitators by engineering expulsions of students from the university; these cadres would then direct a peasant uprising that Nechaev seemed to believe would erupt on or about 19 February 1870, when emancipated serfs would have to cough up for the land they had received in 1861. Nechaev fled Russia after the authorities began arresting students. He had long since taken the precaution of mastering elementary French.[16]

In Switzerland, Nechaev was warmly welcomed by the veteran Bakunin, who wrote: 'They are magnificent, these young fanatics. Believers without God and heroes without phrases!' He and Nechaev co-authored a number of manifestos destined for consumption in Russia. Nechaev may well have intended to radicalise the recipients of his pamphlets through the underhand method of having them arrested for receiving seditious literature from abroad. The *Revolutionary Catechism* may have been such a joint enterprise. It outlined the optimum structure of revolutionary organisations and the need to forge contacts with the criminal classes, and then sought to specify the inhuman qualities that should ideally characterise the dedicated revolutionary. The *Catechism* idealised a mythical being who was part revolutionary, part monk. He was a 'doomed man'. The debt to Chernyshevsky's 'new man' was striking:

> He has no personal interests or activities, no private feelings, attachments, or property, not even a name. He is absorbed by one single aim, thought, passion – revolution ... Moved by sober passion for revolution he should stifle in himself all considerations of kinship, love, friendship, and even honour.
>
> In the depths of his being, not only in words, but in deed, he has broken every tie with the civil order and with the entire educated world, with all laws, conventions, generally accepted conditions, and with the morality of this world. He is its implacable enemy, and if he continues to live in it, that is only the more certainly to destroy it.[17]

This single-minded suppression of things that make us human, including intellectual curiosity, moral discernment and feeling for others, was accompanied by murderous prescriptions for the future division of society. This was brutal, crude and schematic. There would be those who would be killed immediately, those whose temporary reprieve might provoke mass revolt, influential people and liberals whose stupidity could be exploited, other revolutionaries who could be propelled into self-destruction, and, finally, the remnant, and it was inevitably going to be modest after this bloodbath by categories, of those still deemed ideologically sound. Any methods were legitimate: 'Poison, the knife, the noose . . . The revolution sanctifies everything in this battle.' Bakunin went along with this, provided, as he was to discover, such amoral methods were not turned against him.

Equipped with this *Catechism*, and a certificate of membership number 2771 in the Russian section of a non-existent World Revolutionary Alliance, Nechaev returned to Moscow. He formed a revolutionary cell, whose members included impressionable students and Ivan Pryzhov, the dipsomaniac author of *The History of Taverns* and a self-pitying tract called *I have had a Dog's Life*. This was almost too true since in the depths of despair Pryzhov tried to drown himself and his hound Leperello, but both were dragged alive from a pond. Trust was not paramount among the revolutionary group. Short of funds, they left a copy of the *Revolutionary Catechism* in the home of a supporter, disguised themselves as police officers, and then tried to extort money from the victim for possession of seditious literature. The quest for money led them to ultimate crimes. On 16 November 1869 Nechaev informed members of his cell that they had to kill the student Ivan Ivanov, another of their number, solely it seems because Ivanov had a mind of his own and was unhappy about how money he had given to Nechaev was being used. More generally, Ivanov was exercised about being treated as 'merely a blind tool in someone else's hands'. When Pryzhov objected that his alcohol-sodden eyes could not see in the dark and that he had hurt his leg, Nechaev replied that they would carry him to the scene of the intended crime.

Ivanov was lured to the grounds of the Petrovsky Academy of Agriculture where the gang rather clumsily pinned their victim down so as to strangle him. Although Ivanov was already dead, Nechaev insisted on firing a shot into his head, perhaps in a fury that the victim had sunk his teeth into one of the assassin's hand. Weighed down with bricks, Ivanov's corpse was thrown into an icy pond. After the murder, the assassins gathered in an apartment, whose floor was soon awash with water and blood. Clearly in an excitable state, Nechaev sent a bullet flying past Pryzhov's drunken head. He escaped to Switzerland, where he returned the sanctuary provided by Bakunin with an obliging threat to murder the Swiss publisher who was hounding him for the late delivery of a translation of the first volume of Marx's *Kapital*. Bakunin's heart was probably not in the task since he numbered Marx as among the worst of the 'Yids and Germans' he hated.

During his sojourn in Geneva, Nechaev tried to use his combined amorality and charm to prevail upon the young heiress daughter of Herzen, who had recently died. It was then, in the summer of 1870, that Bakunin felt moved to warn a family with whom Nechaev had also entered into contact that the erstwhile 'young eagle' was a very dangerous man. This warning was all the more remarkable since it was designed to revoke earlier letters of the 'warmest' recommendation that Bakunin had supplied on his protégé's behalf. Bakunin acknowledged that Nechaev was the most 'persecuted' man in Russia and that he was 'one of the most active and energetic men I have ever met', a singular compliment from the most indefatigable of European anarchists. But then the doubts came thick and fast:

> When it is a question of serving what he calls the cause, he does not hesitate; nothing stops him, and he is as merciless with himself as with all the others. This is the principal quality which attracted me, and which impelled me to seek an alliance with him for a good while. Some people assert that he is simply a crook – but this is a lie! He is a devoted fanatic, but at the same time a very dangerous fanatic whose alliance cannot but be harmful for everybody.

The revolutionary secret committee had been decimated by arrests, leaving the fugitive Nechaev to refound his own clandestine organisation abroad. Bakunin detested the spirit that informed this enterprise: 'one must take as the foundation the tactics of Machiavelli and totally adopt the system of the Jesuits, violence as the body, falsehood as the soul'. Bakunin warned his friends that Nechaev believed in deceiving and exploiting honest dupes, insinuating himself into their confidence, and then using any means, up to and including blackmail, to bend them to his ferocious will. He would stop at nothing:

> If you have presented him to a friend, his first concern will be to sow discord between both of you by gossip and intrigue – in

a word, to cause a quarrel. Your friend has a wife, a daughter; he will try to seduce them, to make them pregnant, in order to tear them away from official morality and to throw them into a forced revolutionary protest against society.

Bakunin testified to his personal experience of betrayal at the hands of Nechaev, who had stolen his letters in order to compromise the older man. He continued:

He is a fanatic, and fanaticism carries him away to the point of becoming an accomplished Jesuit, at moments, he simply becomes stupid. The majority of his lies are woven out of whole cloth. He plays at Jesuitism as others play at revolution. In spite of his relative naïveté he is very dangerous, because each day there are acts, abuses of confidence, treacheries, against which it is all the more difficult to guard oneself because one hardly suspects their possibility.

Bakunin recommended that the family lock up its daughters since Nechaev was hell bent on seducing and corrupting young girls, the example of Natalia Herzen being fresh in his mind. He also urged another person, whose address Nechaev had somehow got his hands on, to move at once.[18]

Meanwhile, Nechaev's accomplices were rapidly apprehended, confessing their crimes to interrogators who applied the mildest of psychological pressures rather than thumbscrews. After further adventures, Nechaev was extradited in 1872 from Switzerland, where he had tried to organise bank robberies that qualified him as a criminal rather than political refugee. He was sentenced in 1873 to twenty years' hard labour in Siberia. The trial took place amid the hysteria generated by the Paris Commune. The tsar personally intervened to have him confined in the altogether more rigorous Petropavlovsk fortress, whence he had allegedly escaped earlier in his revolutionary career. After many years of confinement, the remorseless Nechaev managed to suborn his guards, with a view to having him sprung by the People's Will, the terrorist organisation that emerged from the ranks of disillusioned Populists. Discovery of this plot led him to be secreted deeper within the fortress prison, where in 1882 he died of scurvy, the date coinciding with that of the murder for which he had been convicted a decade earlier.

This squalid episode became the kernel in a great novelist's reckoning with the modern Russian revolutionary tradition, a reckoning all the more devastating because the author had experience of life within the conspiratorial Pale. For in December 1849, after being convicted for his role in the radical Petrashevsky Circle, Dostoevsky was subjected to a terrifying mock execution, and then despatched to four years' penal servitude in Siberia. There, among the lowest of the low, he experienced the epiphany that convinced him that Christ was mysteriously present in the peasant soul. In exile in Semipalatinsk he would lie on the grass on warm nights, marvelling at the Creator of the millions of stars in the night sky.[19] From there, in 1854, he wrote the famous letter in which he described himself as 'a child of the century, of unbelief and doubt', a struggle not only played out in all his major novels, but in the subsequent evolution of his own rather complex political positions.

Between 1867 and 1871 Dostoevsky and his wife settled in Dresden. Circumstances seemed to militate against this being a period of intense creativity. A newly born daughter died aged three months; a second infant daughter was constantly ill. His wife, without the benefit of either a maid or nanny, was exhausted and painfully thin. In winter, German stoves never seemed to generate enough heat, so the couple were perpetually cold. Frequent epileptic fits left Dostoevsky dazed for up to a week at a time: 'They used to pass after three days, while now they may take six. Especially at night, by candlelight, an indefinite hypochondriac melancholy, and as if a red, bloody shade (not colour) upon everything. Almost impossible to work during those days.'[20] His permanently irascible mood was compounded by his dislike of the Germans (and English tourists) in whose midst he had paradoxically settled: 'It's all trashy people, that is, in general. And my God, what trash there is!'[21]

His solution to chronic indebtedness – 'I'm absolutely in a horrible position now (Mister Micawber). I don't even have a kopeck' – was to rob Peter to pay Paul, or, more desperately, to pawn his valuables so as to right all his financial problems at the roulette wheels of German spa towns.[22] Like many compulsive gamblers, he began each foray confident in a foolproof system, but then lost everything betting on desperate hunches. Every trip to 'Roulettenburg' resulted in disastrous losses as the small white ball ineluctably rattled into the wrong slot. Serial losses eventually tempered his addiction.

Dostoevsky could control excess that would destroy lesser people. He was above all a professional writer, fluent, self-disciplined, well read, and equipped with an exceptional memory and acute powers of observation.

He settled into a routine in the couple's ever more modest Dresden lodgings, or as he had it: 'I live boringly and too regularly.'[23] He rose at one o'clock, worked for a few hours, walked and read the Russian newspapers in a reading-room, then returned for dinner. After a second walk, he took tea at ten, and then worked until five or six in the morning. His working notebooks testify to his extraordinarily meticulous artistry and to a lifetime of demanding reading.

A major breakthrough in Dostoevsky's work, which would be elaborated in his subsequent 'fat books', was the publication in 1864 of the relatively short *Notes from Underground*. The psychological deformation of the narrator, a forty-year-old former government clerk who in earlier life behaves in an erratic, sadistic and vengeful fashion towards others, can be attributed, not just to the disparity between his pretensions and status, but also to his too rapid and uncritical ingestion of radical ideas that, by ruling his head, had incapacitated the dormant dictates of his heart. The ways in which bookish unreality contributes to an inhuman 'malice of the brain' is explored again and again in this novel, whose first part is also a reckoning with the utopian world of Chernyshevsky. Dostoevsky would develop these themes in novels that were polyphonies of characters, and one of which would take as its starting point the Nechaev case.[24]

Dostoevsky began working on *The Possessed* in February 1870. It was a 'rich idea', more 'burning' even than *Crime and Punishment*, which he had written in the interim, and one likely to make him some money too. Tempting fate, he added: 'Never have I worked with such enjoyment and such ease.'[25] What may have been intended as a satirical pamphlet grew by leaps and bounds into an enormously complex novel. By August 1870, when he had hoped to deliver the manuscript, Dostoevsky decided to scrap most of what he had done, destroying almost a year's work. Enviously he remarked in a letter: 'Would you believe that I know for certain that if I had two or three years of support for that novel, the way Turgenev, Goncharov, and Tolstoy do, I would write the sort of thing that people would be talking about 100 years later.'[26] But, as he also acknowledged, it was never just a question of lacking the means and peace of mind to work. He compared himself to Victor Hugo, another writer whose 'poetic impulse' outran his 'means of execution' and who similarly tried to cram too many novels and stories into one.[27]

In his correspondence, Dostoevsky provided us with a detailed account of the genesis of the story: 'I did not and do not know either

Nechaev or Ivanov or the circumstances of that murder except from the newspapers.' He had also been visited by his brother-in-law who was a student at the Petrovsky Academy where the Ivanov murder would later happen. But this was merely the incident around which he structured a much more complicated book, in which the crimes of an amoralist that he had *imagined* in *Crime and Punishment* now had a ghastly basis in contemporary fact. As he wrote Dostoevsky daringly upped the stakes, even though this deranged the structure of the book. While he originally intended to make the Nechaev character his central focus, by the summer of 1870 he had decided that 'I don't think that those pathetic monstrosities are worthy of literature.'[28]

If there was a fundamental problem with the novel, it stemmed from this shift of focus from the villain to Stavrogin, a sort of early nineteenth-century Byronic anti-hero whom Dostoevsky never quite managed to get right in a book whose other characters are personifications of ideas that had unfolded sequentially between the 1840s and 1860s. By October 1870 he was still dissatisfied with *The Possessed*, although he acknowledged that it was 'entertaining': 'The idea is bold and big. The whole problem is just that I keep taking topics that are beyond me. The poet in me always outweighs the artist, and that's bad.'[29] In October 1870 Dostoevsky gave a detailed account of what his novel was primarily about. Apart from the immediate stimulus of the Nechaev affair, he had been deeply affronted by those deracinated liberals who had welcomed Russian defeat in the Crimean War:

> The fact also showed us that the disease that had gripped civilized Russians was much stronger than we ourselves imagined, and that the matter did not end with the Belinskys, Kraevskys, and the like. But at that point there occurred what the apostle Luke testifies to: there were devils sitting in a man, and their name was Legion, and they asked Him: 'Command us to enter into the swine,' and He allowed them to. The devils entered into the herd of swine, and the whole herd threw itself into the sea from a steep place and they all drowned. And when the local inhabitants came running to see what had happened, they saw a formerly possessed man already dressed and in his right mind and sitting at the feet of Jesus, and those who had seen it told them how a man possessed had been healed. That's exactly the way it happened with us. The devils went out of Russian man and entered a herd of swine, that

is, the Nechaevs, Serno-Solovieches, and so on. They have drowned or are sure to, but the healed man that the devils came out of is sitting at the feet of Jesus. That's exactly how it had to be. Russia has vomited up that garbage she was fed on and, of course, there's nothing Russian left in these vomited-up scoundrels. And note, dear friend: whoever loses his people and his national roots loses both his paternal faith and God. Well, if you want to know, that's exactly what the theme of my novel is. It's called *The Possessed*, and it's a description of how those devils entered a herd of swine.[30]

The Possessed was set in a muddy, wind-swept provincial town that was possibly modelled on Tver, although there is virtually no physical description of the setting. Nothing is what it seems and values are inverted; there is endless talk, but little by way of communication, in a novel that is hysterical and unsettling. The action alternates between the salons of grand stone houses and the dark squalor of wooden hovels by the river, the two worlds linked by the leading revolutionary conspirator, Peter Verhovensky, whose ramifying plots take him back and forth in a frenzy of mendacity and murder. There is something serpentine in the first extended description of him:

> He talked quickly, hurriedly, but at the same time with assurance, and was never at a loss for a word. In spite of his hurried manner his ideas were in perfect order, distinct and definite – and this was particularly striking. His articulation was wonderfully clear. His words pattered out like smooth, big grains, always well chosen, and at your service. At first this attracted one, but afterwards it became repulsive, just because of this over-distinct articulation, this string of ever-ready words. One somehow began to imagine that he must have a tongue of special shape, somehow exceptionally long and thin, extremely red with a very sharp everlastingly active little tip.[31]

As gradually becomes apparent, Verhovensky is not simply treacherous but completely insane and given to outbursts of childlike petulance against anyone who stands in his way. A modern parallel would be Osama bin Laden lying down to weep and wail when one of his subordinates failed to shoot a leading British journalist. Verhovensky's master plan contains every revolutionary strategy being essayed by the radical sects of the time, up to and including the use of pseudo-tsars to awaken the peasants from their slumbers:

'Listen. First of all we'll make an upheaval,' Verhovensky went on in desperate haste, continually clutching at Stavrogin's sleeve. 'I've already told you. We shall penetrate to the peasantry. Do you know that we are tremendously powerful already? Our party does not consist only of those who commit murder and arson, fire off pistols in the traditional fashion, or bite colonels. They are only a hindrance. I don't accept anything without discipline. I am a scoundrel, of course, and not a socialist. Ha Ha! Listen. I've reckoned them all up: a teacher who laughs with children at their God and at their cradle is on our side. The lawyer who defends an educated murderer because he is more cultured than his victims and could not help murdering them to get money is one of us. The schoolboys who murder a peasant for the sake of sensation are ours. The juries who acquit every criminal are ours. The prosecutor who trembles at a trial for fear he should not seem advanced enough is ours, ours . . . On all sides we see vanity puffed up out of all proportion: brutal, monstrous appetites . . . Do you know how many people we shall catch by little, ready-made ideas? . . . Listen, I've seen a child of six years of age leading home his drunken mother, whilst she swore at him with foul words. Do you suppose I am glad of that? When it's in our hands, maybe we'll mend things . . . if need be, we'll drive them for forty years into the wilderness . . . But one or two generations of vice are essential now; monstrous, abject vice by which a man is transformed into a loathsome, cruel, egoistic reptile. That's what we need! And more, a little "fresh" blood that we may get accustomed to it . . . We will proclaim destruction . . . Why is it, why is it that idea has such a fascination? But we must have a little exercise; we must. We'll set fires going . . . We'll set legends going. Every scurvy "group" will be of use. Out of these very groups I'll pick fellows so keen they'll not shrink from shooting, and be grateful for the honour of a job, too. Well, and there will be an upheaval! There's going to be such an upset as the world has never seen before . . . Russia will be overwhelmed with darkness, the earth will weep for its old gods . . . Well, then we shall bring forward . . . whom?'

'Whom?'

'Ivan the Tsarevitch.'

'Who-m?'

'Ivan the Tsarevitch. You! You!'

Stavrogin thought a minute.

'A pretender?' he asked suddenly, looking with intense surprise at his frantic companion. 'Ah! So that's your plan at last!'[32]

Verhovensky's band of five revolutionaries, who co-opt the fugitive convict Fedka, seek to demoralise and destabilise the province, in anticipation of an illusory general uprising, the imaginary revolution that tantalised a fantasist such as Nechaev. Their would-be ideologist is a donkey-eared, mournful man called Shigalov, whose manifesto is contained within a notebook crammed with tiny writing. 'I am perplexed by my own data,' he says at one point, 'and my conclusion is a direct contradiction of the original idea with which I start. Starting from unlimited freedom, I arrive at unlimited despotism. I will add, however, that there can be no solution of the social problem but mine.'[33] Other emblematic characters are introduced either by the narrator or by Stavrogin, whose own casual flirtations with ideas have become his disciples' deepest commitments. We meet the atheist Kirillov, whose determination to kill himself to prove the absolute power of human will and the absence of God results in his spirit of self-sacrifice being abused by Verhovensky to conceal a brutal murder. Kirillov is an enthusiastic exponent of the 'new man': '"God is the pain of the fear of death. He who will conquer pain and terror will become himself a god. Then there will be a new life, a new man; everything will be new . . . then they will divide history into two parts: from the gorilla to the annihilation of God, and from the annihilation of God to . . ." "To the gorilla?"'[34] The serf's son Shatov, whom Stavrogin persuades to abandon the revolutionary sect, espouses a Russian messianic nationalism, and doubts about God, worthy of Dostoevsky himself.

The revolutionaries' plots are facilitated by the credulous indulgence the local literary and political 'establishment' shows to the younger generation. Verhovensky's schemes are aided and abetted by governor Lembke's ambitious consort Yulia Mihailovna, who seeks to patronise the younger generation, so as to promote her own advancement through the espousal of what might be called 'tactical chic'. At the same time Verhovensky succeeds in driving the governor mad, by persuading this rather benign Russo-German official to take draconian measures over a minor workers' disturbance while filling his head with visions of disorder and upheaval that Verhovensky is covertly seeking to bring about. Gradually, the delicate fabric of this society disintegrates. There is a perceptible increase in boorishness, lying, public drunkenness and vulgar speech, together with open expressions of cynical disrespect towards public figures on the part of a raucous rabble that becomes more omnipresent in 'democratised' elite settings. This culminates in a literary charity fête that degenerates into an unseemly slanging match and a costume ball that comes to a premature end as the guests realise that half the town is on fire.

The literary fête was the culmination of Dostoevsky's reckoning with his own generation of liberal writers whose posturings in some way conduced to a climate of indulgence towards maniacs like Nechaev. One of his friends had the insight that many of the characters in The Possessed were 'Turgenev's heroes in their old age'.[35] Dostoevsky had fallen out badly with Turgenev in Baden-Baden. He resented owing Turgenev money, just as he resented the leisure to perfect and polish his work that Turgenev's wealth bestowed upon him while Dostoevsky wrote to keep the wolf away. He disliked his creditor's aloof aristocratic manner, and in particular a kiss that never quite connected with one's cheek, not to speak of Turgenev's enthusiasm for all things German. In The Possessed Turgenev is savagely caricatured as the literary celebrity Karmazinov. He drones on at great length at the fête, unaware that the revolutionaries have rigged the event to end in disaster by inviting drunken hoi-polloi and inserting captain Lebyadkin, a notorious drunk and amateur poet, into a programme that was supposed to guarantee decorum. Dostoevsky's narrator tries to get the drift of Karmazinov's pretentious babble:

> The great European philosopher, the great man of science, the inventor, the martyr – all these who labour and are heavily laden, are to the great Russian genius no more than so many cooks in his kitchen. He is the master and they come to him, cap in hand, awaiting orders. It is true he jeers superciliously at Russia too, and there is nothing he likes better than exhibiting the bankruptcy of Russia in every relation before the great minds of Europe, but as regards himself, no, he is at a higher level than all the great minds of Europe; they are only material for his jests. He takes another man's idea, tacks on to it its antithesis,

and the epigram is made. There is no such thing as crime; there is no such thing as justice, there are no just men; atheism, Darwinism, the Moscow bells . . . But alas, he no longer believes in the Moscow bells; Rome, laurels . . . But he has no belief in laurels even . . . We have a conventional attack of Byronic spleen, a grimace from Heine, something of Petchorin – and the machine goes rolling, whistling, at full speed. 'But you may praise me, you may praise me, that I like extremely; it's only in a manner of speaking that I lay down the pen; I shall bore you three hundred times more, you'll grow weary of reading me . . .'

The culpability of the fathers was personified by Verhovensky's father Stefan Trofimovich, who has earlier acted as tutor to the young Stavrogin. Trofimovich was a promising liberal scholar, with vast ambition but little application or talent, who had gone to seed in a demeaning relationship with a richer patroness. Having belatedly realised that the younger nihilists were dangerously iconoclastic and deeply stupid, Trofimovich attempts to defend his conception of the sublime: 'I maintain that Shakespeare and Raphael are more precious than the emancipation of the serfs, more precious than Nationalism, more precious than Socialism, more precious than the young generation, more precious than chemistry, more precious than almost all humanity because they are the fruit, the real fruit of all humanity and perhaps the highest fruit that can be.'

The final speaker, a maniac professor of literature who perpetually beats the air with his fist, mounts the stage to inveigh against Russia past and present before mass pandemonium brings the afternoon to a close. That night the wooden houses along the river are engulfed by fire. The general conflagration does not conceal the fact that in a house that has also burned down despite its isolation from the general conflagration, captain Lebyadkin and his much abused sister have been murdered.

In due course Verhovensky persuades his quintet to murder Shatov, whom he falsely accuses of preparing to betray the group, simply on the ground that Shatov wishes to leave it. Shatov is lured to a park, where he is to hand over a printing machine, and is wrestled to the ground where Verhovensky shoots him. In echoes of the murder of Ivanov, Shatov's corpse is weighted with stones and thrown in a pond. Some of the gang fail to exhibit Verhovensky's steely revolutionary resolve and emit animalistic noises as they try to distance themselves from the crime. Nor does Kirillov go quietly into reason's dark night in accordance with his plan to prove there is no God other than man. Verhovensky's deal with him is that he should pen a false confession to having murdered Shatov before killing himself, the intention being to throw the authorities off the quintet's trail. But the reasonable suicide degenerates into a messy affair, with Verhovensky stiffening Kirillov's resolve at gunpoint, and receiving a bite in the hand when the 'man–God' turns all too ferally human shortly before he dies. Kirillov's suicide turns out to be otiose as the authorities quickly unravel the plot and arrest the quartet (for Verhovensky flees), who confess their crimes at the first opportunity. Meanwhile, Stepan Trofimovich, the ageing radical, has embarked on a bid for freedom from his patroness. This journey on foot represents his first encounter with the peasant people he has spent his fifty or so years invoking, people who regard him as if he has fallen from another planet. He dies of a fever, not quite reconciled to the Christian faith, and with his patroness holding his hand. The novel ends with Stavrogin hanging himself in an attic, having failed to alight upon whatever faith he was seeking.[36]

Major events in Europe seemed to confirm Dostoevsky's views on the pernicious futility of revolutionary idealism. He wrote *The Possessed* precisely when Europe was horrified by the Paris Commune:

> For the whole 19th century that movement has either been dreaming of paradise on earth (beginning with the phalanstery) or when it comes to the least bit of action ('48, '49–now) – demonstrates a humiliating inability to say anything positive. In essence it's all the same old Rousseau and the dream of recreating the world anew through reason and knowledge (positivism). Really, there seem to be sufficient facts to show their inability to say a new word is not an accidental phenomenon. They chop off heads – why? Exclusively because that's easiest of all . . . They wish for the happiness of man and are still at Rousseau's same definitions of the word 'happiness', that is, at a fantasy that is not justified even by knowledge. The burning of Paris is a monstrosity: 'It didn't succeed, so let the world perish, because the Commune is higher than the happiness of the world and of France.' But after all, to them (and to lots of people) that madness doesn't seem a monstrosity, but, on the contrary, beauty. And so the aesthetic idea in new humanity has been muddled.[37]

Viscous blood on a muddy pavement or the vivid orange blast of an explosion could be beautiful, carnage and destruction acts of creation.

III WORSHIPPING THE PEASANT FLEECE

Like Stepan Trofimovich, many of the revolutionaries paid lip-service to 'the people', the vast majority of whom, unlike the revolutionaries themselves, were peasants who knew how to deliver a new being, whether bovine, equine or human, and how to grow or make things; believed in God, tempered with much superstition; and revered the tsar as the Lord's anointed. A new radical movement, temporarily disillusioned with the fruits of nihilist terrorism, opted for agitation among those below rather than the assassination of those at the top. Populism was born of a sense of guilt, and resembled worship of 'the people' rather than prostration before such malign cult leaders as the fictional Verhovensky or the real-life Nechaev. Turgenev once described Populism as worship of the peasant sheepskin coat. This was probably too cynical, although middle-class credulity towards indigenous 'noble savages' certainly invites parody.

The Populists who in the early 1870s embarked on a crusade or pilgrimage to the people were moved by a vast outpouring of Christian love, albeit a love that simultaneously expiated the emotional burdens of being born relatively privileged. As one pilgrim said at the time: 'It was rather some sort of crusading procession, distinguished by the totally infectious and all-embracing character of a religious movement. People sought not only the attainment of a definite practical goal, but at the same time the satisfaction of a deep need for personal moral purification.' Products of an increasingly alienated and differentiated urban society, Populists sought personal and social redemption through their own reintegration in a rural idyll based on the values and virtues of the 'narod' (nation). In their eyes, the peasants represented a more integrated, rooted type of human being than the alienated cogs to which western-style industrialisation and urbanisation were reducing factory workers, and for that matter the intelligentsia itself with its mechanical Positivism and utilitarianism.[38]

The nature of the communion between intellectuals and the people had ambivalences. The former's earliest interest in the latter was often ethnographic, an approach that Populism could never entirely shed, like a well-meaning colonist celebrating the docile nobility of primitive tribes. The idealised, recruiting-poster version of Populism was best described by the anarchist prince Kropotkin in his memoirs:

> In what way could they be useful to the masses? Gradually, they came to the idea that the only way was to settle among the people, and to live the people's life. Young men came to the villages as doctors, doctor's helpers, village scribes, even as agricultural labourers, blacksmiths, woodcutters ... Girls passed teacher's examinations, learned midwifery or nursing, and went by the hundreds to the villages, devoting themselves to the poorest part of the population. These people went without any idea of social reconstruction in mind, or any thought of revolution. They simply wanted to teach the mass of the peasants to read, to instruct them in other things, to give them medical help, and in this way to aid in raising them from their darkness and misery, and to learn at the same time what were their popular ideals of a better social life.

Many Populists set out to serve 'the people' by submerging themselves in the peasant mass as midwives, nurses and teachers, albeit often subsidised by their wealthy and well-placed parents. Some went to toil with the Volga boatmen, whom they probably knew only from Repin's painting *Haulers on the Volga*.[39] Some Populists disdained and ignored the people's beliefs and customs, as Dostoevsky wrote: 'Instead of living the life of the people, the young people, without knowing about them, on the contrary, deeply despising their principles, for instance their faith, are going to the people – not to study the people, but to teach them, to teach them haughtily, with contempt for them – a purely aristocratic lordly undertaking!'[40] Others adopted more complex strategies. Notorious bandit chieftains, such as Stenka Razin or Yemelian Pugachev, were recast as 'primitive rebels', an indulgence that romantic Stalinists would subsequently apply to, say, Jesse James or Sicilian mafiosi. Since the peasants were religious in a primitive sort of way, some Populists endeavoured to create a new religion, a sort of hybrid of radical politics and socialised Christianity. So as to spread this new gospel, Jewish Populists converted to Christianity. However, the gospel recast as revolution invariably ran into the peasants' simple faith in the inherent benevolence of the tsar, and their obdurate refusal to allow simple Christian precepts to be twisted this way or that by young students masquerading as 'the people'. Peasants who knew about the injunction to render unto Caesar rejected Populist calls for tax boycotts. They used the student radicals' cheap tracts as cigarette or lavatory paper.

Peasant responses to the radical message were best symbolised by the story of the two young former artillery officers who in the autumn of 1873, and folksily attired, tried to engage a peasant driving a sled: 'We started to tell him that one should not pay taxes, that officials are robbers, and that the Bible preaches the need for a revolution. The peasant urged on his horse, we hastened our step. He put it into a trot, but we kept running, shouting about taxes and revolution ... until we could not breathe.'[41]

About a thousand young Populists embarked on a 'Pilgrimage to the People', by setting up home among the not so gnarled objects of their earnest solicitations. There were some not inconsiderable handicaps, inevitable in this forerunner of late-twentieth-century 'Revolutionary Campus Parties'. Many of the young women involved had never made a bed or brewed tea, having had servants to perform these functions. The only thing they were truly skilled at was high-flown talk. Many of them were rebelling against the constraints of their own severely patriarchal Orthodox or Jewish families.[42] Some Populist grouplets went in for a confessional–therapeutic self-analysis, foreshadowing latterday hippy communes or Bolshevik self-criticism sessions. Those who tried to deskill themselves, by abandoning careers as doctors for joinery, encountered total incomprehension among peasants who knew the value of medical expertise. In some places, the pilgrims encountered not gritty sons and daughters of toil but people who were beginning to wear city clothes and were equipped with other accoutrements of modern urban life, many of them thanks to the entrepreneurship of former peasants who had transformed their villages into minor manufacturing centres. In fact social differentiation had advanced so rapidly in recent times that it was difficult to speak of 'the people', when the reality consisted of a richly diverse rural society, in which the more well-to-do former peasants employed others. Some Populists came to loathe the people they had attempted to understand, an experience common among those who tried to propagandise among the various religious sectarians, one group of whom fell into a trance, dancing and shouting, 'He has come! He is here! He is with us!' when a Populist tried to interest them in socialism. Such negative impressions were compounded whenever peasants handed over to the authorities Populists whose agitation was explicit.[43]

What seems as harmless as a nineteenth-century Anglican Oxbridge student mission to the slums of Bermondsey or Rotherhithe in south-east London was rendered dangerous by the clumsy response of the tsarist authorities who sent hundreds of young Populists to jail or Siberia. Mass arrests of Populists certainly created martyrs, but the conditions of their confinement or exile were so mild – partly owing to the victims' age and rank – that the prisons themselves became breeding grounds for the next generation of terrorists. That is not, of course, a retrospective argument for more stringent conditions. New leaders emerged in the late 1870s, their credibility boosted by their success in springing prince Peter Kropotkin from the prison where he was awaiting trial. Land and Freedom was refounded in the late 1870s. Never numbering more than three to four hundred members and fellow travellers, Land and Freedom acknowledged the Populist ideal of peaceful agitation among the peasantry, but the improbability of this triggering general revolution increasingly inclined them to mindless acts of terrorism. Violence was a way of circumventing the frustrations the Populists had experienced in their efforts to radicalise an uncomprehending peasantry or industrial workers perplexingly preoccupied with upping their wages.

The responses of a government that exhibited signs of panic aided and abetted them. A minor demonstration outside Our Lady of Kazan cathedral in the capital, involving a handful of workers and a larger number of revolutionaries, resulted in unnecessarily harsh sentences for some of those arrested. In the south, members of Land and Freedom acted in ways that indicated a certain moral slippage worthy of Nechaev. In 1876 revolutionary conspirators decided to murder one of their own whom they suspected of being a police informer. Despite being clubbed half to death and having acid poured on his face, the victim survived to testify against his assailants. Those who organised this attack were not deterred from pressing ahead with a venture that relied upon gross deception. Disgruntled peasants in the neighbourhood of Kiev were given forged documents, allegedly from the tsar, encouraging them to murder the nobility and government officials. This fantastic scheme was nipped in the bud by the authorities. Again, the tsarist government managed to squander any moral capital when general Fyodor Trepov, the newly appointed governor of St Petersburg, ordered the flogging of a political prisoner who had had the effrontery to challenge him over some minor disciplinary dispute. This breach of the gentlemanly arrangements that had hitherto characterised treatment of upper-class political prisoners became a licence for acts of terrorism, and an alibi for the much wider body of educated and respectable opinion that routinely excused such activities. One of the very first victims was general Trepov himself, who in 1878 narrowly escaped death when a young woman called at his offices and shot him in the side at close range. It was indicative of the degeneration of public opinion that the subsequent trial managed to dilate at greater length on the sins of the victim of this assassination attempt rather than on probing the defence account of the character or motives of the would-be assassin, who incredibly enough was acquitted. By signalling that smart opinion, masquerading as society, approved of attempted murder, this trial opened the floodgates to further acts of terror, notably the 1878 stabbing of the head of the secret police force. Each assassination of progressively prominent targets, including a cousin of prince Kropotkin who was governor of Kharkov, emboldened them to go for the ultimate target. A second attack on Alexander II was made in April 1879 when an assassin fired four rounds at the tsar, who managed to escape unharmed. In the summer of that year, Land and Freedom held a 'congress' (there were twenty-one attenders) at which those who advocated violence broke away to form the People's Will, while those who were faithful to the original Populist agenda decamped to form Black Partition, one of the direct ancestors of the Bolsheviks, although the latter owed much in spirit to the rival conspiratorial organisation.

Rather grandly, the People's Will claimed to be a branch of a Russian Social Revolutionary Party, and to have an Executive Committee that steered the People's Will. In fact, such a party did not exist, and the thirty or so members of the mysterious Executive Committee were all there were of People's Will itself. Many of the cardinal tenets of previous revolutionary movements were quietly dropped by the leaders of People's Will. There was no mention of either the peasants or of oppressed non-Russian nationalities. In other respects, the People's Will anticipated the centralised discipline of Lenin's Bolsheviks, it being no coincidence that he explicitly recommended People's Will as a model of conspiratorial organisation. It demanded total and lifelong dedication among its adherents. People's Will practised infiltration of otherwise innocuous organisations. It sought out prestigious fellow travellers among the artistic and intellectual elite, seeking to win them over through calls for elections and a constitutional assembly. It abandoned the Populist emphasis upon the peasant base, in favour of seeking to capture power. There was a newfound emphasis on the role of the Party, which 'should take upon itself the task of overthrowing the regime, rather than waiting for the moment when the people undertake it by themselves'.

Terrorism was supposed to be a means of subverting public confidence in the stability and strength of the tsarist government, but in practice it was always liable to become an end in itself, as fanatic bombers, resembling the explosives-laden professor in Joseph Conrad's *Secret Agent*, went about their dastardly deeds. Both the quest to kill Alexander II, and there were seven attempts before the last succeeded in 1881, and the obsession with the most technologically 'progressive' means, involving dynamite or nitro-glycerine, gradually obliterated the more political aspects of the People's Will programme. The destructive energy released by explosives, that is human body parts and things being punctured, ripped apart and hurled through the air, became an end in itself. As later terrorists have realised too, potential targets are at their most vulnerable when they are on the move. Apparently harmless husband-and-wife teams rented houses or secured licences to open businesses. Assassins were recruited to dig tunnels under the railway lines that carried the imperial train. The first such attempt resulted in the imperial train chugging unharmed over a massive bomb that failed to explode. The second, a month later, which involved digging a much longer tunnel, successfully derailed what turned out to be the wrong train, although fortunately no one was harmed. Failure with trains resulted in the adoption of the terrorists' plan B.

Despite the discovery by the police of drawings of the layout of the Winter Palace, with an 'X' helpfully indicating the tsar's dining-room, nothing was done by the authorities to check workmen entering the palace (where they often dossed down at night in the cellars) to conduct refurbishment. In this way, small quantities of explosives were smuggled in to make a very big bomb. On the evening of 5 February 1880 this exploded in the cellars, causing mayhem in the ground-floor guardroom situated immediately beneath the tsar's dining-room. Eleven soldiers were killed and fifty-six wounded, a tragedy that in turn rippled through the lives of their families and dependants. Alexander II was elsewhere and his dining-room was unaffected by the blast. Three further assassination attempts that spring and summer came to nothing. Meanwhile, the police authorities began to gather significant intelligence about the

Executive Committee and People's Will, largely through the skilful interrogation of prisoners who, rather than having their fingers broken, were convinced by talk of imminent reform. Signs that the government was inclining towards some advisory form of elected assembly quickened the resolve of the terrorists to commit regicide so as to stymie even limited reform.

In December 1880 another apparently innocuous couple rented a basement where they set up a cheese shop, although, as customers noted, they knew little of cheese. Since the shop stood on the route the tsar took from the Winter Palace to the Hippodrome where he routinely inspected troops, at night teams of terrorists moved in to tunnel beneath the street. The plan was for the tsar to be blown up by a huge mine under his customary route. If this failed, then teams of bomb-throwers would flock to finish him off with nitro-glycerine bombs that had to be hurled within a range of one metre. The bomb-throwers would die too.[44] The last line of attack was a final lone assassin armed with a knife. Incredibly, when the constant nocturnal comings and goings in the cheese shop led the police to despatch an officer masquerading as a sanitary inspector, the latter did not check the contents of what the proprietor claimed were barrels of cheese, although this did not normally come in such containers. At lunchtime on 1 March 1881, Alexander II set off to the Hippodrome, relieved it seems by his decision that morning to concede an elected advisory assembly. He took a route that bypassed the street with the sinister cheese shop in the basement. He spent forty minutes inspecting troops, before deciding, on the spur of the moment, to call on a cousin, via a route that took him to where three of the bomb-throwers had dispersed. The first bomb missed the tsar; its thrower was seized by the police. Alexander alighted to repeat his earlier foolhardy attempt to interview a captured failed assassin. As the tsar turned away from their desultory exchange of words, another assassin threw a bomb which exploded at his feet. The tsar cried, 'Help me, help me,' and 'Cold, cold.' He died fifty minutes later; his assassin died later that night.

The 'new men' had a vision of Russian society that was markedly at variance with that society's complex reality, which included a widespread and keen appreciation of the supernatural. The Russian 'soul' may have originated as a (German) Romantic cliché, suggesting spiritual values allegedly lost in the materialistic west, but it also conveyed the existence of something beyond mere psychology.[45] Pagan superstition permeated all levels of society, ranging from peasants who worshipped several natural gods in addition to the God of the Orthodox Church to gentlefolk and nobles with their ability to fuse Orthodoxy (or Lutheranism), a certain fashionable Voltairean scepticism, and belief in soothsaying and talismans.[46] That is like saying, in an elaborate way, that Sloane Rangers, among others, often combine Anglican upbringings with faith in horoscopes and magic crystals.

The nineteenth century was a time of revival in the Russian Church, as it recovered its spiritual vitality. This was reflected in missionary work to indigenous peoples on both sides of the Bering Straits, and a renaissance of the monasteries that had been decimated by the westernising reforms of Elizabeth and Catherine the Great. One feature of this revival, namely the figure of the spiritual elder, who took on some of the wider social role of the stylites of late antiquity, has a direct bearing on our story.[47]

Dostoevsky had returned to Russia in 1871, becoming – despite continued police surveillance – editor of an ultra-conservative journal and increasingly lionised by the imperial family and Orthodox authorities. He felt himself to be maligned and misunderstood by the radical intelligentsia, writing, 'People are trying with all their might to wipe me off the face of the earth for the fact that I preach God and national roots.'[48] But he had since discovered that 'the conservative part of our society is as rotten as any other; so many swine have joined its ranks'. While the heads of would-be revolutionaries swam with shallowly lethal imported solutions, the dinosaurs and dullards of the right were obsessed with policing, neglecting a moral malaise that Dostoevsky felt was promoting social breakdown in town and countryside, crime, drunkenness and the disintegration of the family. His often stridently nationalistic journalism, peppered with invective against Germans, Jews and Poles, did not reflect his core Christian convictions, nor his refusal to confuse Christianity with the mere defence of an immobilised ecclesiastical–political hierarchy and status quo.[49]

The complexities of these views emerge from his last great novel. Dostoevsky set *The Brothers Karamazov* in a provincial town, called Skotoprigonyevsk, whose order (such as it was) was being disturbed, not simply by what a modern sociologist might call the 'dysfunctional' Karamazov family, but by the swirl of ill-digested ideas stemming from the western European Englightenment, whose effect is to undermine traditional faith without providing an alternative. Reflecting his continued interest in inter-generational struggles, Dostoevsky explores a case of parricide, it being ambiguous (at least for the public in the novel) whether the degenerately sybaritic patriarch Fyodor Karamazov has been murdered by his sensualist elder son Mitia over a disputed inheritance or a young woman, or by an illegitimate lackey who has been infected by the intellectualised amoralism of the middle son Ivan by Fyodor's second marriage.

Provocatively, Dostoevsky interrupted the fast flow of a sophisticated crime story by according the relative stillness of an Orthodox monastery (in which the youngest Karamazov brother is a monk) as much space as the courtroom drama with its extended exploration of the relationship between lawyers, morality and truth, on which theme the book ends. Fashionable opinion, parodied in the book, was that monks were 'parasites, pleasure-seekers, sensualists, and insolent vagabonds'. Dostoevsky knew otherwise. His childhood had been spent in a deeply religious household, and every year he accompanied his parents on their pilgrimage to the St Sergius Trinity monastery outside Moscow.[50] He also repaired to the famous monastery of Optina Pustyn' to recover from the death of his three-year-old son.

At the heart of the novel is the elder Zosima, whose odyssey is recounted shortly after his death. In his youth Zosima had been an army officer, given over to carefree pursuits. A beautiful young woman whom he loved had married an older man. Zosima challenged her husband to a duel. On the eve of the duel, Zosima struck his orderly twice in the face, something he had not done before with such ferocity. During the night he repents of striking the servant: 'how did I deserve that another man, just like me, the image and likeness of God, should serve me?' He falls on the ground in front of the servant and begs his forgiveness. Despite running the risk of social ostracism, Zosima then deliberately shot wide during the duel with his rival:

'Gentlemen,' I cried suddenly from the bottom of my heart, 'look at the divine gifts around us: the clear sky, the fresh air, the tender grass, the birds, nature is beautiful and sinless, and we, we alone, are godless and foolish, and do not understand that life is paradise, for we need only wish to understand, and it will come at once in all its beauty, and we shall embrace each other and weep . . .'[51]

This passage, whose words inevitably forfeit their force in translation, gets very near to Dostoevsky's own experience of Christianity. Zosima resigns his commission and enters a monastery. According to Zosima, 'in their [the monks'] solitude they keep the image of Christ fair and undistorted, in the purity of God's truth, from the time of the ancient fathers, apostles, and martyrs, and when the need arises they will reveal it to the wavering truth of the world. This is a great thought. This star will shine forth from the East.'

This ideal, at whose core was the jettisoning of 'superfluous and unnecessary needs', is contrasted with the atomised spiritual death that Dostoevsky saw in the world around him:

The world has proclaimed freedom, especially of late, but what do we see in this freedom of theirs: only slavery and suicide! For the world says: 'You have needs, therefore satisfy them, for you have the same rights as the noblest and richest men. Do not be afraid to satisfy them, but even increase them' – this is the current teaching of the world. And in this they see freedom. But what comes of this right to increase one's needs? For the rich, isolation and spiritual suicide; for the poor, envy and murder, for they have been given rights, but have not yet been shown any way of satisfying their needs . . . Taking freedom to mean the increase and prompt satisfaction of needs, they distort their own nature, for they generate many meaningless and foolish desires, habits, and the most absurd fancies in themselves. They live only for mutual envy, for pleasure-seeking and self-display . . . We see the same thing in those who are not rich, while the poor, so far, simply drown their unsatisfied needs and envy in drink. But soon they will get drunk on blood instead of wine, for they are being led to that . . . They have succeeded in amassing more and more things, but have less and less joy.

Dostoevsky's own contrasting ideal is spoken as one of Zosima's homilies, and illustrated by an encounter between Zosima the monk and his former orderly, who, now a settled married man, gives the wandering Zosima fifty kopecks for the monastery. This example of 'a great human communion' becomes Dostoevsky's vision of the future:

> I dream of seeing our future, and seem to see it clearly already: for it will come to pass that even the most corrupt of our rich men will finally be ashamed of his riches before the poor man, and the poor man, seeing his humility, will understand and yield to him in joy, and will respond with kindness to his gracious shame. Believe me, it will finally be so: things are heading that way. Equality is only in man's spiritual dignity, and only among us will that be understood.

Anticipating derision from more secular-minded proponents of social justice, Dostoevsky counters with the argument that 'They hope to make a just order for themselves, but, having rejected Christ, they will end by drenching the earth with blood, for blood calls to blood, and he who draws the sword will perish by the sword. And were it not for Christ's covenant, they would annihilate one another down to the last two men on earth.'

Of course, Dostoevsky did not entirely neglect the question of how such precepts might be converted into practice or social and political structures. What he envisaged was a theocracy worthy of Joseph de Maistre, although with socialistic undertones that would have appalled the French ideologue. Earlier in the *Brothers Karamazov*, the monks had been exposed to Ivan Karamazov's semi-scholarly ruminations on Church and state relations. Ivan argues that the pagan Roman state had incorporated the Church, investing the latter with characteristics that owed little or nothing to the Church as an eternal transcendental community. This reflected Dostoevsky's deep-seated antipathy towards the Roman Catholic Church, a theme he treated at some length in Ivan's story of the Grand Inquisitor.

Instead of the Church imperial, Dostoevsky argued that 'every earthly state must eventually be wholly transformed into the Church and become nothing but the Church, rejecting whichever of its aims are incompatible with those of the Church'.[52] The Church would absorb the whole of society, while shedding those hierarchical and 'romanising' accretions it had assumed through its own absorption by the imperial

Constantinian state. In these altered circumstances, excommunication would be the gravest social sanction, more efficacious than the punishments of the time. Dostoevsky returned to these reflections in the account of Zosima's life and teachings: 'There can be no judge of a criminal on earth until the judge knows that he, too, is a criminal, exactly the same as the one who stands before him, and that he is perhaps most guilty for the crime of the one standing before him.'[53] The reawakening of a residual faith in the criminal would make Russia's stringent penal system superfluous and might even reduce crime.

Where this could tend in a broader sense is tantalisingly left to the final scenes in the novel. One of its sub-plots concerns a poor child called Illyusha in whose fate, as the victim of cruel children, the younger Karamazov brother, the monk Alyosha, has taken a growing interest. When Illyusha sickens with tuberculosis, Alyosha persuades the other boys to include him in their fellowship. They bring the dying boy such gifts as a toy cannon. When Illyusha finally dies, his father collapses in crazed grief. The mother is mad already. By contrast, the twelve boys and Alyosha seem to grow in dignity, as Alyosha gathers them around the stone under which the father had wanted to bury Illyusha: 'And even though we may be involved with the most important affairs, achieve distinction or fall into some great misfortune – all the same, let us never forget how good we once felt here, all together, united by such good and kind feelings as made us, too, for the time that we loved the poor boy, perhaps better than we actually are.'[54] Regardless of whether one regards such scenes as saccharine or sincere, the implicit political message was clear enough. Responding to an admirer in the same letter we cited above, Dostoevsky remarked: 'a new intelligentsia is being restored to life and is on the march, and it wants to be with the people. And the first sign of an inseparable contact with the people is respect and love for what the people in all their entirety love and respect more and above anything else in the world – that is, their God, and their faith'. The prophet was wrong, because the new intelligentsia was in fact inspired by hate, and its militant atheism would destroy the Orthodox Church and send the remaining faithful underground for several generations.[55] Across western Europe at this time the Church was being challenged by the state and its liberal allies, which in some countries resulted in formal separation, the themes to which we turn next.

CHAPTER 8

Rendering Unto Caesar: Church versus State, State versus Church

The nineteenth century commenced with the near universality of the confessional state under which one religion, or Christian denomination, was privileged by the state, while other denominations and religions were tolerated at best. By the century's close, these arrangements had been abandoned, or modified, almost beyond recognition. This was done either to accommodate dissenters and religious minorities, or as a result of sustained assaults from liberal and radical anticlericals, either acting alone as in the French Third Republic or, as in Bismarck's Germany, in temporary alliance with the far from liberal wielder of state power. These clashes, many of which endured for decades, largely established the formal framework within which state and Church, or, to be more punctilious, faith groups, operate in Europe to this day. People nowadays may be unaware how France, Germany, Italy or Spain resolved these issues; at the time they were being resolved, people followed these events with avidity. Yet the consequences are important for understanding how we choose to live now; on an optimistic reading, these developments have enabled Europe's Churches to rediscover their spiritual and social mission within a free market of opinion, while states have been liberated from the sometimes deleterious influences that over-mighty religions exert on semi-formed states elsewhere.[1]

British experience during the Victorian era reminds us that the separation of government and religion (though not of Church and state, whose formal union continues to this day) was not always the result of laicising aggression on the part of liberal anticlericals, even though the latter typified continental European and Latin American experience. The impetus behind disestablishment in the British Isles came from those seeking to make society *more* religious, aided and abetted by those who sought to strengthen the Church of England by discarding its abuse-ridden accretions, rather than from militant secularists or devotees of state power. Opponents of establishment wanted to strip one denomination of its privileges, but they were also keen to use the state to protect Britain from 'popery', to maintain Sunday observance, and to close the sluices through which torrents of beer and gin poured down the gullets of the lower classes.

No British political party espoused either anticlericalism or the confessional politics to be found on the continent; and churchmen were agreed that, as one London vicar said, they 'should think it most wrong to pervert the pulpit into a platform, whence to denounce one political party and uphold another'. Where else in Europe could one imagine a bishop telling a working men's meeting (in Swansea), 'my advice to you is this: Think for yourselves, and mind when you vote that it is according to your conscience'? In practice these honourable attempts to eschew partisan loyalties were progressively abandoned towards the close of the nineteenth century as the identification of Liberalism with Nonconformity and the cause of disestablishment meant the emergence of the Church of England as the Tory Party at prayer.[2]

Both major political parties undertook piecemeal reforms, whose cumulative effect was to dismantle the single-creed state that the century began with, gradually removing those features that discriminated against, or disadvantaged, Protestant Dissenters, Roman Catholics and Jews. The state's establishment of a permanent vehicle for Church reform, the Ecclesiastical Commission of 1836, and the passage of the Irish Temporalities Act three years earlier, contributed to the rise within Anglicanism of an anti-Erastian movement known as Tractarianism, part of whose rationale was to stress the apostolic roots of the Church of England rather than treating it as something cobbled together by the state during the Reformation to facilitate a royal divorce. Having started their journey as convinced opponents of Roman Catholicism, many of the leading lights of the Oxford Movement, the epicentre of Tractarianism being Britain's premier university, left a Church whose spiritual purity was being sullied by subordination to an increasingly pluralist state, and headed for Rome.

Thenceforth, the Anglican Church would be pulled in three different directions, by Evangelical Low, High and latitudinarian Broad churchmen. At about this time, the established Presbyterian Church of Scotland was rocked by the 'Great Disruption', a protracted clash between the authority of the Church's ruling General Assembly and local congregations and a state that supported the right of patrons to make appointments to the ministry, a battle that English wits attributed to a surfeit of oatmeal porridge. The result was that in 1843 a third of so-called Non-Intrusionist ministers decamped from the General Assembly to form the Free Church of Scotland. The established Church of Scotland continued as the Church of a scant majority. The most glaring disjunction between a Church's privileged status and its following, amounting to one in fourteen of the population, was that of the Church of Ireland which Gladstone's Liberal government disestablished in January 1871.

It was characteristic of the peculiarity of British conditions that the greatest nineteenth-century leader of a Liberal Party that derived support from Scottish Presbyterians, English and Welsh Nonconformists and Irish Roman Catholics was a High Church Tractarian, who to his dying day regarded the seventeenth-century archbishop Laud as a martyr. Such idiosyncrasies are integral to the British way. Like his Tory predecessor Peel, Gladstone thought that the best way to bolster the Church of England was to discard its most indefensible aspects. 'I am convinced', he wrote to his eldest son, 'that the only hope of making it possible for her to discharge her high office as stewardess of divine truth, is to deal tenderly and gently with all the points at which her external privileges grate upon the feelings and interests of that unhappily large portion of the community who have almost ceased in any sense to care for her.' Not the least of Gladstone's achievements was surgically to remove the diseased limb of the Church of Ireland establishment, without this leading to removal of the equally anomalous Welsh establishment (a measure only taken in the First World War) or general disestablishment of the Church of England itself.[3]

Periodically, vaster developments on the continent intruded into these British debates, in the form of what English Protestants dubbed 'papal aggression', as when pope Pius IX sought to restore an English Catholic hierarchy in 1850, a development that led the newly appointed cardinal Wiseman of Westminster to gush triumphantly – 'from out of the Flaminian Gate' – to the effect that 'Catholic England has been restored to its orbit in the ecclesiastical firmament, from which its light had long vanished'.

Protestant Englishmen, accustomed to putting a torch to effigies of Guy Fawkes every 5 November, shuddered at the prospect of rampant baroque churches looming up alongside the delicate tracery of their beloved neo-gothic. The ensuing furore, which resulted in effigies of Wiseman and Pius being burned along with Guy Fawkes that bonfire night, inclined the Whig leader lord John Russell, who had been a lifelong supporter of religious toleration, to pander to mounting Protestant fears of 'popery' by introducing Britain's last venture in discrimination against a (tolerated) religious minority. This was the 1851 Ecclesiastical Titles Act which prohibited Catholic prelates from using territorial titles on pain of a £100 fine.[4] Since its author had also taken a sideswipe at Tractarian pseudo-Catholics, one of its fiercest critics was Gladstone, who not only delivered a major speech opposing this legislation, attempting to reverse, as it did, 'the profound tendencies of the age towards religious liberty', but abolished this reversion to penal legislation when prime minister twenty years later.[5]

That Gladstone was an enthusiastic admirer of the liberal Catholic German theologian Ignaz Döllinger, and became a fiery critic of Pius IX, reminds us of the interconnectedness of the epic culture wars on the continent. These wars were partly fought in the ramifying journals and newspapers of liberals and their papalist or ultramontane opponents. The press followed these conflicts in minute detail, while cartoonists reduced complex issues to crude and sometimes vicious stereotypes, for it was far easier to depict a freemason or Jew than a liberal, or a Jesuit rather than a moderate lay Catholic. The nineteenth century may have been the apogee of rival nation states, but it was also one in which divisions between anticlericals and ultramontanes, and those who for whatever reasons sympathised with them, ran through nations and across borders, agitating a pan-European interested public.[6]

At the eye of the storm was one old man, convinced that the Catholic Church was under siege from a satanic conspiracy of anticlericals, freemasons and liberals, whose menace had become global. It would be over-ambitious to give more than the barest indication of the sheer scale of events. Colombia had been the first independent Spanish republic to be recognised by the Holy See in 1835; since 1843 Catholicism had been acknowledged as the official state religion. However, successive liberal governments introduced anticlerical measures, annulling tithes and abolishing sanctuary, while a new constitution in 1853 introduced Latin America's first separation of Church and state. Under general José Maria Obando, civil marriage was made mandatory, cemeteries were secularised and Colombia's diplomatic representatives were recalled from Rome. The Church found its rights curtailed too during the 1860s and 1870s in Guatemala, Nicaragua and El Salvador, as well as Bolivia, Brazil, Chile, Ecuador, Mexico, Peru and Venezuela.

Nearer home, by the last third of the nineteenth century, there were acute tensions between Church and state in overwhelmingly Catholic Austria–Hungary, Belgium, France, Italy, Portugal and Spain; in Switzerland, the Netherlands and Germany where Catholics were substantial minorities; and finally in the parts of partitioned Poland administered by Prussia and Russia. While the conflict in each country was shaped by its separate experiences and history, important common denominators emerge. We turn first to Italy.[7]

Inherited hostilities between the Piedmontese state and the papacy were writ larger following the proclamation of the Kingdom of Italy in 1861. The status of Rome poisoned relations between the Church and an Italian nation state, belief in whose legitimacy was thinly spread among the population. The pope regarded his patrimony as crucial to the fulfilment of the Church's spiritual mission; the Italian state viewed national unification as incomplete without Rome as Italy's capital.

The state needed the support of the Church, if only to deepen the legitimacy of the liberal regime among people as yet unpersuaded by the benefits of abandoning the legacy of particularism in favour of what was tantamount to rule by the northern Piedmontese. Hence it proclaimed that 'The Roman Catholic religion is the only religion of the state. The other cults that now exist are tolerated insofar as they conform with the law.' A Catholic editor, Giacomo Margottis, coined the motto 'neither elected nor electors', which served to undermine the legitimacy of both government and state, although Catholics sat as deputies in the Italian parliament once the oath of allegiance had been amended to make this possible. The state responded by confiscating ecclesiastical property, subjecting clergy and seminarians to military conscription, and invalidating church weddings unless accompanied by civil marriage by the state. By 1873 it had abolished all university theology faculties throughout the country. In Italy, as elsewhere, the state's right to review, or veto, ecclesiastical appointments was especially contentious. By 1864, nearly half the dioceses of Italy were without bishops. Ten bishops went on trial after incurring the wrath of the state, forty-three went into exile, and a further sixteen had been prevented from taking up their posts. These assaults resulted in a commensurately belligerent response from the burgeoning Catholic press, whose most aptly militant representative was the Jesuit *La Civiltà Cattolica* that had commenced publication in 1850. This was the Holy See's equivalent of the semi-official newspapers that proliferated in the aftermath of the 1848 revolutions, a useful instrument whose contents could be denied whenever they proved inexpedient.[8] In keeping with the view that the laity were soldiers of an army whose officers were the clergy and whose commander was the pope, a number of lay organisations were founded, including a youth organisation in 1868 and six years later the Opera dei Congressi, which was modelled on Belgian and German national associations of Catholics.[9]

The situation of the pope went from bad to worse, although he was sometimes collusive in this process, since rhetorical moderation, sensitivity and subtlety were alien to him. In September 1864, the Minghetti government concluded a Convention with Napoleon III that regulated the future of the patrimony of St Peter without any reference to the pope himself. Throughout Europe, liberalism seemed to be in the ascendant, seeping gradually into the Church itself in the form of Lamennais and his disciples. At an 1863 congress in Belgian Malines, the prominent liberal Catholic Montalembert said that the Church accepted the principles of 1789 and would thrive in the atmosphere of 'modern liberty, democratic liberty'. That autumn Döllinger defended the right of the new critical scholarship to pursue the truth, regardless of dogmatic authority – the one exception to this rule being that critical scholarship's own implicit assumptions.

These attacks, together with the encroachments of the Italian state, prompted Pius to issue a comprehensive condemnation of contemporary errors, the eightieth of the eighty errors listed in his 1864 Syllabus (or catalogue) being that the pope should reconcile himself with progress, liberalism and modern civilisation. In that bald formulation, the eightieth article lost any connection with its original context, which was a papal condemnation of secularising trends in the Piedmontese educational system, a specific context Pius did not deign to retain so as to pre-empt liberal outrage. The Pope's declaration of Infallibility led to much mockery. Cartoonists on liberal papers had a field day with such images as the pope betting on the lottery, while the ticket vendor exclaimed: 'For God's sake don't do it! You are infallible, so you will win every time and bust our lottery.'[10]

What is not often stressed, in the customary identification of the Syllabus with its final jarring assertion, is that in article 39 the pope denounced the doctrine that 'the State, as being the origin and source of all rights, is endowed with a certain right not circumscribed by any limits'. The Moloch-like expansion of the modern state into areas where it had hitherto acknowledged limits was one of the two most important aspects of these nineteenth-century conflicts, and Catholics were not slow to draw attention to this as they sought to limit state authority. One unfortunate consequence of this battle was that the Church itself took on many of the authoritarian, bureaucratic and centralising features of the states it was being persecuted by. In the eyes of many Catholics, an authoritarian pope became the ultimate defender of liberty against states that liberals were pushing in a highly illiberal direction. This was the immediate background to the Declaration of Papal Infallibility, the cynosure of international liberal animadversion.[11]

In the summer of 1868 Pius summoned the first General Council of the Church for three hundred years. Over seven hundred Catholic bishops convened in St Peter's on 8 December 1869. Difficulties in understanding the variant national pronunciations of Latin, the lingua franca of the Council, were compounded by acoustics that lifted speech into an incoherent babble echoing from the roof of the north transept.[12] It took until the following May to promulgate a constitution containing fundamental statements of faith, which was finally issued with over five hundred amendments. A separate constitution on the Church proved more contentious, because of chapters on the primacy and infallibility of the pope. The Council divided into a Majority, who supported the notion of papal infallibility, and a Minority of roughly 150, who regarded this doctrine as either inopportune or untrue. Supposedly confidential discussions were leaked to the press, while caucuses acquired assiduous publicists, notably the polyglot liberal Catholic peer lord Acton, who supported the dissenting Minority, and the French ultramontane polemicist Louis Veuillot, who took up the cause of the conservative Majority. A leaked draft designed to clarify relations between Church and state was hurriedly retracted, and never resurrected, once governments had voiced their alarm. Over a long hot Roman summer the Council debated the issue of infallibility, which was voted through on 18 July 1870 as thunder cracked over St Peter's. Fifty-five dissenters slipped away from Rome, leaving a majority of 533 to approve the declaration against two bishops who voted against. The Council declared that 'the Roman Pontiff, when he speaks ex cathedra, that is ... by virtue of his supreme Apostolic authority, he defines a doctrine regarding faith or morals to be held by the universal Church ... is possessed of that infallibility with which the divine Redeemer willed that his Church should be endowed for defining doctrine regarding faith and morals'. In a famous pamphlet, William Gladstone wrote: 'With this decree the claims of [the thirteenth-century] Innocent III over mankind have been resurrected in the nineteenth century – like some mummy picked out of its dusty sarcophagus.' The distinctive individualism of European civilisation, in its ascendant liberal, Protestant form, was threatened with being 'politically debased to the Mahometan and Oriental model'.[13]

The following day France declared war on Prussia, and the last French troops evacuated Rome to fight the invading Teutons. An emissary from Victor Emmanuel explained to the pope the need for Italy to occupy his territory to forestall a republican revolution or to pre-empt disorder. 'Nice words, but ugly deeds,' replied the seventy-eight-year-old pontiff. Following the defeat of France at Sedan, Italian troops under general Rafaelle Cadorna launched an assault on Rome, which they took after a brief morning battle. After a rigged election, Rome and its environs were incorporated into the Italian kingdom. Announcing his future role as martyr–pontiff, Pius said: 'I surrender to violence. From this moment I am the prisoner of King Victor Emmanuel.' Everyone connected with the invasion and occupation was excommunicated. On various occasions Pius likened the Italian sovereign to Goliath, Holofernes and Sennacherib.[14]

Meanwhile, the Italian monarch occupied the Quirinal Palace and monasteries were converted into government ministries. The War Ministry moved into the convent of the Twelve Apostles, and a Carmelite nunnery at Regina Coeli became Rome's main prison. Ancient monastic libraries were subsumed into the Victor Emmanuel Library. Cardinals found it expedient to erase coats of arms from their carriages and to slip in or out of the Vatican in mufti as Roman anticlericalism lost its few remaining inhibitions.

For the next fifty-eight years, no pope set foot outside the walls of the Vatican once he had been elected. The May 1871 Law of Guarantees was intended to soften the blow by treating the pope as a sovereign, and affording him a large tax-free annuity to maintain his greatly reduced state. Pius rejected this deal, for, as he acidly observed, little faith could be put in Italian governments of which there had been nine in ten years. Paradoxically, although he continued to lament the acts of state piracy that had stripped him of his temporal dominions, the pope benefited in terms of a significant increase in his spiritual authority, this being partly attributable to his charisma, but also to his status as a victim of secular power. Propaganda on behalf of the poor martyred pope clearly did its work, at least judging from an 1877 letter to him from a concerned Parisian woman: 'Permit your humble daughter, Holy Father, to offer You a little underclothing intended for your personal use: I have heard harrowing details of the deprivations of Your Holiness in this regard! And I am happy to alleviate your distress!' Looking to the example of Pius VII, the pope thought he just had to wait on the course of events to regain his patrimony; as yet, in 2005, there has been no movement.[15]

Elsewhere, Church and state relations took the form of the pattern we have noticed in France: a revival of Church influence after 1848, followed by attempts to undo this by those who were suspicious of Church encroachments on the territory of the state. The 1848 revolutions led the rulers of Austria to revive the close association between Church and Habsburg monarchy, conceding a Concordat in 1855 that granted the Church far more privileges than it had enjoyed in the Josephist past. This outraged both liberals and members of religious minorities within the Empire, and liberals and Protestants elsewhere. The revival of the alliance between throne and altar meant that liberals construed curbs on the former as indirect, but related, challenges to the absolutism of the latter. Once they had achieved power in the wake of the Austro-Prussian War, Austrian liberals sought to dismantle the privileges the Church had gained under the Concordat, which was unilaterally abrogated in 1870 on the ground that the declaration of papal infallibility had so altered the character of one of the contracting parties that the agreement should be considered null and void. Besides, the Concordat was not reconcilable with the new liberal Austrian constitution, or new laws that sanctioned civil marriage and toleration of what could be taught in schools. Clergy who persisted in such quaint customs as describing children of couples who had undergone civil marriage as 'illegitimate' in their records found themselves harried by the courts. When the bishop of Brixen in the Tyrol refused to hand over records relevant to a woman seeking a divorce from a man who had fled to the USA, the police raided his diocesan office, and the bishop received a hefty fine. When Rudigier, bishop of Linz, declined to hand over marriage documents to the civil authorities, he was cited before a court whose authority he refused to recognise, and then arrested and tried. A liberal satirical weekly crowed that the law was not 'simply made for artisan youths'.[16] They crowed too soon, for among the legacies of these conflicts in Austria were the demise of a liberal politics that failed to find a mass base, and the rise of a militant political Catholicism that did not scruple to blame Vienna's Jews for their tribulations at the hands of liberals.

II 'THE STRUGGLE FOR CIVILISATIONS'

As in Austria, conservative Prussian governments during the 1850s regarded religion as a source of social stability. This was reflected in the 1848–50 Prussian constitution that granted the Catholic Church extensive rights and separate representation alongside Protestants within the Ministry of Education and Religious Affairs. This did not mean that Catholics were proportionately represented in the civil service, army officer corps or professoriat, which continued to be overwhelmingly Protestant, even in predominantly Catholic areas like the Prussian Rhine provinces which nonetheless were largely administered by Protestants. In 1852 Catholic deputies in the Prussian parliament formed their own caucus, known from 1859 onwards as the Centre Party so as to lose any explicit reference to confession, sometimes making common cause with the liberal opposition when the issues at stake were constitutional, fiscal or military. The coolness of the clergy was among the reasons why this party disintegrated within a decade.

Prussia's stunning military victories in 1864, 1866 and 1870 were enveloped in nationalistic fervour and Protestant triumphalism, the two increasingly hard to tell apart. The successive defeats of Austria in 1866 and France in 1870, resulting in the establishment of the North German Confederation followed by the German Empire, were viewed as victories for 'Germandom', Protestantism and German philosophical idealism. Some Catholic politicians, many of them Prussians, were as fervid about Prussia's triumphs as the next man. However, those whose loyalties were to the more intimate dynastic states were cool towards the chauvinism and militarism that characterised German unification, and sympathised with the 'reluctant Germans', or 'must-be Prussians', be they Alsatians, Danes, Lithuanians or Poles, who were then subjected to conquest and germanisation by the self-consciously steely Sparta on the Spree. These particularist Catholics were bundled together with non-German Catholic minorities and dubbed 'enemies of the Reich'. Cosmopolitan dual allegiances, or what might be called multiple identities, be they Jewish, Marxist or in this case Roman, were portrayed as inherently sinister. In addition to blurring the civil and spiritual spheres, Catholicism seemed to have little or no respect for national boundaries at a time when in some countries these were being defined for the first time.[17]

The papal secretary of state Antonelli was said to have exclaimed, 'the world is collapsing,' when he heard news of the Prussian victory over Austria. In confessional terms, a predominantly Protestant power had rudely extruded a venerable Catholic Empire from influence in Germany, and German Catholics had exchanged approximate parity for being a minority of a third of the population. This made the political representation of Catholic interests urgent.

The Centre Party was refounded in 1870, to defend religious freedoms; it was then given tremendous focus and impetus by the Kulturkampf. Many lay Catholic politicians were unsympathetic to the hard-line infallibilist and ultramontane direction of their Church, a view shared by the majority of German bishops who had opposed the Vatican Council's declaration. The crisis facing the papacy led them into what was clearly a misjudgement. In March 1871 they struck out an assurance in their version of the Reichstag's congratulatory address to the Crown, to the effect that the new German Empire would *not* intervene in the affairs of foreign states. This was construed as an attempt by Catholics to inveigle the emperor into using force to restore the temporalities of the pope. This lapse of tactical judgement confirmed the dominant Protestant version of the national story, whereby since the Middle Ages 'German' potency had been sapped by diversions to the south, while it also offended German liberals who sympathised with the national aspirations of their Italian confrères. When the Centre Party tried to extend the Basic Rights enshrined in the 1850 Prussian Constitution to the new constitution of the Reich, both liberal parties voted this measure down as an act of spite against their Catholic opponents. The cause of freedom took a back seat to that of consolidating the new nation.

Bismarck may or may not have been keen on separating Church and state; if he was, then rolling back the privileges that the Catholic Church had achieved since 1850 may have been a question of attacking the weaker of the two faiths first. What is clear is that his detestation of 'political Catholicism' drew its potency from several sources. Catholic deputies had co-operated with liberals in the Prussian parliament in opposing him. Memories of this collaboration festered in a man whose grudges were like those of characters in medieval Scandinavian sagas. At a time when Bismarck was engaged in nation- and state-building, Rome claimed that the rights of the Church trumped those of the state, and the Centre Party appeared to be the natural rallying point for every group disaffected from the new Empire. Under enormous stress during the daytime, Bismarck literally dreamed of a disintegrating map of the new Germany whenever before dawn he snatched his shallow dyspeptic's sleep.[18]

The most worrying disaffected group appeared to be the Prussian Poles, who after 1867 found themselves part of Germany, as opposed to Prussia, for the first time. Traditional Prussian policy in Prussian Poland had been based on isolating a patriotic nobility that was wedded to romantic insurrectionism, while respecting the Poles' language and religion and hoping that material betterment might incline the peasant majority to Prussian dynastic rule. But as the Prussian administration became more conscious of being German, the Polish leadership responded by mobilising a peasant base, principally through the strategy of 'Organic Work', a series of measures designed to modernise the structure of Polish society preparatory to regaining national independence. Although the control the Polish Catholic Church allegedly exercised over the Polish masses was one of the grounds for launching the Kulturkampf, by alienating the Polish Catholic Church the Kulturkampf played a major role in the transformation of Polish nationalism from an aristocratic into a mass phenomenon.[19] Ironically, during the 1860s the Catholic Church in Prussian Poland had been apathetic or hostile towards Polish nationalism, with archbishop Ledóchowski of Gnesen-Posen banning priests from involvement in Organic Work, and prohibiting the singing of patriotic hymns in churches. In 1870 Bismarck described the archbishop – whose spoken Polish was poor – as 'an excellent man who keeps the Poles in order for me and on whom I can rely'.

But the culture wars that raged across Europe were never simply concerned with the juridical rights of Church and state, or the anodyne-sounding administrative and legal measures used to adjust this relationship in the state's favour. They reminded some contemporaries of a war of religions, with anticlerical liberalism and the Positivist scientism that often accompanied it standing in for sixteenth-century Protestantism, a Protestantism that many liberals often construed as their historical precursor, and certainly part of their wider identity.

As in the Wars of Religion, there were similar paranoias about foreign meddling in domestic politics; in the predominantly Calvinist Netherlands, Catholics were still referred to as the 'Spanish–Roman party' to conjure up memories of the fearsome duke of Alba. To fanatical liberals, these culture wars were a struggle between the bringers of modern, scientific light and those still atavistically mired in medieval darkness and superstition, variously known to liberal opponents as the 'black gang' or 'plague' because of clerical clothing. Catholics responded by regarding themselves as victims, which they certainly were, not just of liberalism, which was hard to put a face to, but of what they more narrowly construed as a Jewish–masonic–satanic conspiracy.[20] Part of the trick of conveying what this was about involves defying the stereotypical antimonies that the contestants imposed upon these conflicts, for, as mention of Catholic newspapers and political parties already indicates, the Catholic Church can hardly be construed as being uniformly hostile to modern civilisation since it cleverly exploited many of its instruments.

The term Kulturkampf, or struggle for civilisation, was coined in 1872 by the Progressive deputy, pathologist and popular science writer Rudolf Virchow, whom we encountered earlier as a leading example of scientific hubris.[21] The Kulturkampf could not have been waged without pervasive liberal and Protestant anti-Catholicism that ranged from crude expressions of prejudice to stealthier institutionalised discrimination. Most German liberals were Protestants, some of their leaders being sons of pastors or former theology students. The main liberal political party, the National Liberals, had fifty-one Catholic deputies in the Reichstag between 1867 and 1917, in contrast to 569 Protestants. This disproportion was replicated in virtually every state assembly, in the civil service and among the learned professions.[22] Of the ninety most senior positions in the German Reich, Catholics occupied eight in the quarter century before the First World War. The only Catholic in the Ministry of the Interior was a messenger; there was one Catholic in the Finance Ministry, two in the Ministry of Education and Religious Affairs; and only five among the forty-nine senior officials in the Foreign Ministry.[23]

Catholics were also excluded on more symbolic levels, insofar as there was little or nothing for them to identify with in the publicly celebrated myths that brought Protestants together. Hermann the Cheruskan and Luther had revolted against the Roman Empire or the Rome of the popes; the battle of Leipzig, Sedan Day and the 1871 peace of Versailles were partly commemorated as victories over Catholic France. Monumental statues were a favoured form of nineteenth-century provocation. In 1875 Catholics were explicitly excluded from the inauguration in the Teutoburger Forest of the monument to Hermann, fabled liquidator of a first-century Roman legion.[24]

A number of venerable anti-Catholic stereotypes resurfaced under the guise of Progress rather than Providence. Much of this derived from the Enlightenment copybook of clerical concupiscence, although not even Voltaire managed to blame the Jesuits for allegedly poisoning a cardinal, or the sudden death of a popular lion in Berlin's zoo. In liberal Protestant eyes, Catholics personified economic backwardness and cultural obscurantism, while Protestantism was synonymous with 'Kultur', an identification partly made to reinvigorate Protestantism among a bourgeoisie that no longer attended church. Modern people made their own rational choices; priests exercised an unnatural suasion over old crones and children, many of them country folk, who composed the majority of Catholics.

In Belgium, where there were similarly acute conflicts, as late as 1936 a liberal historian could write that liberal 'Brussels had no intention of being trodden underfoot by thousands of clogs', this being a reference to the clog-shod Catholic farmers who flooded into the capital city to protest against liberal policies. This suspicion of priestly dominance of credulous peasants was why leading German National Liberals opposed the introduction of universal manhood suffrage, for it would enable the Jesuits to herd their dim and docile flocks through the polls, just as they and O'Connell had allegedly done in Ireland or the Polish clergy might do in Prussian Poland.[25] Although there were no more than two hundred Jesuits in Germany, cartoons by Wilhelm Busch – the Protestant and antisemitic father of the modern comic strip – ensured that everyone knew the grinning, treacherous and wily face of 'Father Filucius' (from the French 'filou').[26]

Prejudice was accompanied by the customary demographic paranoia. The Catholic population was believed to be increasing at an alarming rate, allegedly through conversions and mixed marriages, although many Protestants credulously assumed that the peasants of Prussian Poland bred like rabbits. In fact, the only area to register a striking increase in the Catholic population was Upper Silesia, where this was attributable to migration into its industrial hellholes, rather than to a religiously inspired lack of sexual continence, while conversions to Rome were outnumbered by those of Catholics to Protestantism. More than half of the children of mixed marriages were brought up as Protestants rather than Catholics.[27] Liberals regarded schools where clerics had influence as places where the impressionable were subjected to divided loyalties and Roman superstition; in Prussian Poland the clergy were helping to promote Polish as the language of instruction, a strategy which surreptitiously tilted the ethnic balance of these territories by turning little Germans into tiny Polish speakers. Charitable institutions were attacked for promoting dependence and sloth or subtracting productive resources from the national economy. Something as harmless as the opening of a Dominican convent in Berlin's Moabit seemed sinister when it coincided with the discovery, in a Carmelite convent in Cracow, of Barbara Ubryk, a nun who had been confined for breaking her vow of chastity, and who after over twenty years had become 'a naked, barbarised, half-insane female'. The Moabit Dominican house was repeatedly stormed by an outraged urban mob.[28] Convents and monasteries were castigated as cold citadels of cruelty or hot debaucheries, in wilful ignorance that they played a leading role in the nation's charitable, educational and hospital provision, as no less a personage than the minister of war acknowledged in 1875 when during this moment of national emergency he said: 'without the Sisters of Mercy I can't wage war'. Of the 914 religious foundations, with over eight thousand members, 623 and their five thousand members were involved in caring for the sick and infirm. Many western industrial cities, including Düsseldorf, Duisburg and Essen, would have had no hospital arrangements whatsoever without the dedication of nursing orders. So far from living a life of genteel contemplation, female religious active in hospitals toiled 250 day and 180 night shifts in a single year, naturally without material recompense.[29]

Protestant purpose and sobriety, later conveniently identified as an 'ethic' by the Protestant Max Weber, was contrasted with a drunken lackadaisical mob of priest-ridden peasants, who bestirred themselves only to gawp at hocus-pocus involving relics and shrouds perpetrated by their evil clerical masters. Germany's academic finest took a dim view of an elderly Italian's claims to infallibility, rarely extending that critical stance to the authoritarian hierarchism that characterised their own academic profession. Even in the late nineteenth century, only 13 per cent of Prussian academics were Roman Catholics, percentages that further declined in medicine, science and technology.[30] Impeccably liberal academics deplored the papacy's treatment of one of their own, the excommunicate scholar Döllinger, while disdaining the credulous stupidity of the Catholic masses, although as liberals they were not especially keen on the masses in general. Germany's great historian steam-engines, Baumgarten, Droysen, Mommsen, Sybel and Treitschke, many of them admirers of amoral power, indulged themselves as armchair generals, warning: 'Just as they vanquished Paris, the German people will also subdue the Vatican.' Heinrich von Sybel added: 'We must do to the clericals in cassocks what we have done to the clericals in white officers' uniforms.'[31] Their very notion of historical progress, attributing 'religious freedom' to the Reformation, 'intellectual freedom' to the Enlightenment and 'the state's freedom' to the present, implicitly denied the notion that there had been any 'progress' in religion since the sixteenth century. Progress was something achieved *despite* religion, an unhistorical stance that overlooked how Christian monotheism had separated God from the world and hence encouraged man to make it intelligible, but also what might be called the palaeo-liberal religious origins of many essential limitations on secular power that the modern world has inherited from much earlier clashes of Church and state.[32]

Liberal rhetorical violence was directed not just towards the Catholic Church but towards the Catholics in general, for unlike modern progressives they abhorred diversity, or what is now called multiculturalism. This reflected their frustration with the confessional, cultural and ethnic heterogeneity of the newly founded nation state, a diversity which subverted their desire for that spiritual unity which would enable the Protestant German nation state to achieve yet higher cultural goals.[33] This led liberals on to treacherous terrain. Since Rome's indoctrinated army could allegedly be prevailed upon to vote this way or that, liberals were more than prepared to allow Caesar his due, insofar as state coercion would expedite their goal of a modern unified polity based upon their values. They discovered a newfound respect for eighteenth-century absolutism, which had forged a primitive unity by destroying intermediary corporate and feudal powers. On to essentially traditional ideas about subordinating the Church to the state, liberals grafted the more modern, egalitarian notion that the state alone could guarantee the autonomy of the individual in a society of equals. Stripped of abuses and subjected to the rule of law, the state could be used to pursue liberal goals, becoming what one historian described as 'the magic spear which heals as well as wounds'.

One of the more influential and, at least in terms of literary accomplishment, the most talented of Germany's nineteenth-century historians, Heinrich von Treitschke, expressed this disarming trust in the benevolence of the state with characteristic trenchancy when he wrote: 'For us the state is not, as it is for the Americans, a power to be contained so that the will of the individual may remain uninhibited, but rather a cultural power from which we expect positive achievements in all areas of national life.'[34] Prominent Catholic politicians rejected this dubious doctrine: 'That is a political science I completely and decidedly reject. The state is the protector of existing right, it is not the sole creator of right.'[35] Perhaps above all, liberal enthusiasm for harassing Catholics reflected their guilt at having surrendered so many of their earlier principles in order to collaborate with that whiskery bruiser Bismarck. They could pretend to a certain residual militancy, while basking in the power of the state, as it sought to deliver the individual from the clutch of antiquated intermediary corporations, failing to notice that the state had an iron grip itself.

In July 1871 Bismarck merged the Catholic and Protestant sections of the Ministry of Education and Religious Affairs, transferring the Catholic head of the former and appointing a Protestant to lead the combined section. The transferred official had been both a Centre Party deputy and, so Bismarck alleged, involved in dealings with disaffected Polish aristocrats. The formal measures of the Kulturkampf began with the December 1871 imperial 'pulpit law' which made it illegal for the clergy to criticise the Reich and its constitution from the pulpit. One National Liberal, Eduard Lasker, who was Jewish, and only twelve of the forty-seven Progressive liberal deputies voted against a measure that interfered so egregiously with free speech.[36] In early 1872 the Prussian School Supervision Law removed all clergy from the schools inspectorate, in order to diminish clerical influence while boosting that of the liberals' creatures among the teachers. In Prussian Poland, this measure was designed to curtail the 'polonising' influence of the Catholic clergy in the schools.[37]

In May 1872 Bismarck appointed Cardinal Gustav von Hohenlohe as ambassador to the Vatican, anticipating that the pope would find this pupil of Döllinger, brother of a notorious Bavarian anticlerical and foe of the Jesuits, unacceptable. Pius IX did. In the Reichstag Bismarck vowed, 'Have no fear, we are not going to Canossa,' a provocative reference to the medieval emperor Henry IV who in 1077 had had to do penance to the pope at Canossa. So-called alien Polish priests and journalists (that is those from Austrian Galicia) were expelled from Prussian-controlled Poland. In July 1872, the houses of the Jesuit order and its unnamed 'confederates' were closed and the order's foreign members expelled from the country. Only the socialists, eight Progressives and two prominent Jewish National Liberals sprang to the Society's defence. By Christmas, diplomatic relations between Berlin and the Vatican had been severed, following Pius IX's condemnation of persecution designed 'to put the laws of the worldly power before the most sacred laws of God and the Church'.

In May 1873 the new minister of education and religious affairs, Adalbert Falk, introduced the 'May Laws' to the Prussian parliament. Candidates for ordination must be German citizens and graduates of state grammar schools and theology faculties at state universities; moreover they had to pass 'cultural examinations' in history, literature and philosophy, after they had completed their theological training, examinations designed to test patriotic commitment. This had implicitly grave consequences for the Polish clergy of Prussian Poland. A second law gave the state the right to veto all Church appointments; there were penalties for bishops who simply left the posts vacant rather than submit to government dictation. The third law dealt with the general issues raised by incidents like that in the West Prussian diocese of Ermland, where a chaplain had been dismissed from his teaching post by his bishop, for refusing to read to his pupils a pastoral letter explaining the dogma of papal infallibility. Since teachers were also state officials, the government refused to dismiss the chaplain and compelled pupils to attend his classes on pain of expulsion from the school. Under the new legislation, a Royal Tribunal for Ecclesiastical Affairs consisting of twelve judges would hear appeals from episcopal decisions. They could institute such proceedings without the plaintiff's consent and they could dismiss bishops whom they found against. Finally, a fourth law made it easier for Prussian subjects to abandon their tax-paying Church allegiances. The ponderously named Law for the Administration of Vacant Bishoprics and Parishes of May 1874 allowed the authorities to take control of dioceses where the incumbent had been dismissed or imprisoned for infractions of the earlier Kulturkampf laws. The Catholic press was disbarred from running lucrative government announcements. A new Press Law, whose target groups went beyond the Catholic media, permitted the confiscation of newspapers, books and pamphlets on grounds of suspected violation, while editors, publishers, printers and distributors faced draconian fines and up to a year's imprisonment. Prussia introduced compulsory civil marriage, extended a year later to the Reich as a whole. Separate laws were addressed to the use of Polish in schools. Polish-speaking teachers were transferred to German-speaking areas, while German was imposed as the sole language of instruction, first for classes on religion and then for everything else. The Official Language Law of 28 August 1876 made German the sole medium of intercourse for Poles dealing with the German-speaking bureaucracy and the courts, while bilingual signs and many Polish place names disappeared.[38]

In April 1875 Prussia legislated to cut state subsidies to the Catholic clergy, while that summer a Congregations Law sought to dissolve or suppress religious orders. An Imperial Expatriation Law enabled the state to banish priests to such remote spots as the island of Rügen or to expel them from the country. Simultaneously, the Prussian diet promulgated the Old Catholic Law, which allocated this anti-infallibilist sect, in which Catholic academics who thought the papacy guilty of dangerous innovations were prominent, a share of existing Church resources. Government attempts to promote a professorial sect that made much noise but which had few adherents were largely attributable to its potential to divide the Roman camp. The Old Catholics' resistance to absolutist papal innovations was somewhat queered in the eyes of the traditional faithful by their enthusiasm for abolishing clerical celibacy and for a married clergy. The foolishness of academics and intellectuals was also amply displayed in Old Catholic confidence that 'If twelve simpletons [the Apostles] could regenerate the world, what can we not do – we who have science on our side?'[39]

'The struggle for civilisation' stands at a midway stage between the sort of Erastian checks that the absolutist states had sought to impose on the Church and the ideologically motivated assaults it was subjected to by the totalitarianisms of the twentieth century. Although historians have emphasised that there were genuine limitations in the nineteenth century on the exercise of state power – not the least being that imperial Germany practised the rule of law and was unwilling to elaborate the administrative structures necessary to state persecution – there can be no doubt that Catholic clergy and their sympathisers were subjected to harassment, hardship and petty-minded vexations.

This began with fines which the courts levied whenever a bishop filled an ecclesiastical vacancy without the state's approval. These sums quickly mounted so that the archbishops of both Cologne and Gnesen-Posen owed almost thirty thousand thalers, the Prussian currency until it was replaced by the mark in 1875. When the bishops refused to pay these fines, their salaries or property were distrained and the proceeds put to paying off the penalties. Lay Catholic sympathisers either underbid so as to return the confiscated property to the bishops on the cheap – it seems improbable that the possessions of the bishop of Trier were worth only fifty thalers – or bid far too much so as to liquidate the fines entirely, as when a cheap plaster bust of Pius IX went for a fortune or the modest carriage of the bishop of Ermland achieved 770 thalers at auction, that being exactly what he owed in fines.[40]

Refusal to pay these fines resulted in imprisonment, the fate of five of Prussia's twelve Catholic bishops before the conflict concluded in 1887. Those who went on the run were the objects of wanted posters customarily used to track down wilder game: 'Dr theol. Paulus Melchers, formerly Archbishop of Cologne, born in Münster and last known to be living in Cologne, 64 years of age, 1.70 metres tall, with blond hair and eyebrows, open forehead, brown eyes, slightly bent nose, normal mouth, pointed chin, elongated face, pale complexion and slender build'.[41]

Of course, the terms of imprisonment were relatively mild, given the social standing of those involved, and given that the kaiser was sometimes keen not to see aristocratic prelates treated like common felons. Liberals, democratic in this if in not much else, wanted the bishops confined in cells alongside burglars and footpads, arguing that their favoured treatment 'did not deserve the name imprisonment'. The bishops were held in fortress confinement, enjoying exclusive suites of rooms, exercise, peace and quiet, flowers from well-wishers and brought-in food. When they were old and frail, like the octogenarian Marwitz of Culm, his inability to negotiate steep prison stairs meant that he was not incarcerated at all, although two bishops are said to have died as a result of the stress they were subjected to. By contrast, mere priests who violated the May Laws forfeited their salaries and hence could not pay fines – their modest boots, clocks, walking sticks and umbrellas not making a dent in these when they came to auction. Neither eliciting deference nor able to pull strings, these unfortunates – perhaps as many as eighteen hundred in Prussia alone – were subjected to the normal Spartan version of the contemporary carceral regime: a board bed, little warmth, bullying warders, and a diet of bread and water served in what looked like a dog's bowl. Even though they were not imprisoned, monks and nuns, accustomed to a tranquil and useful life, found being turfed on to the streets or out of the country a bewildering and distressing experience. The English Jesuit poet Gerard Manley Hopkins wrote one of his greatest poems about five Franciscan nuns, exiled by the Falk laws, who were drowned in a storm off the English coast when the appropriately named *Deutschland* went down in early December 1875:

> Loathed for a love men knew in them,
> Banned by the land of their birth,
> Rhine refused them. Thames would ruin them;
> Surf, snow, river and earth
> Gnashed: but thou art above, thou Orion of light;
> Thy unchancelling poising palms were weighing the worth,
> Thou martyr-master: in thy sight
> Storm flakes were scroll-leaved flowers, lily showers-sweet
> Heaven was strew with them.[42]

Of course, the authorities of imperial Germany were not the Gestapo. Not all Protestants were comfortable with persecution of their fellow Christians, and some feared that what could be done to Catholics might be done to them too, for pastor Niemöller's oft-cited Nazi-era dictum 'first they came for' had local precedent. In 1873, for example, the *Allgemeine Evangelisch-Lutherische Kirchenzeitung* fulminated against Prussian 'idolatry of the state' (Staatsvergötterung). Nor were arch-conservatives sympathetic to the Kulturkampf, fearing that the advance of liberalism would undermine their rights of ecclesiastical patronage and secularise the schools, resulting in the end of life as they knew it. A distinguished minority of liberals from both the National and Progressive camps wondered where their patriotic colleagues had buried civil liberties.

The modest reach of the nineteenth-century state, whose budgets were about 2 per cent of what they are today, meant that the laws were patchily and poorly enforced. German officialdom was scrupulous in its respect for legal norms, observing such quaint restrictions as the ban on authorities entering private homes during the long hours of winter darkness. The Pulpit Law was virtually unenforceable, especially where what had allegedly been said was open to interpretation by auditors more sympathetic to the priest than policemen. The volume of cases brought against priests who were repeat offenders meant that the courts drowned in a sea of paperwork awaiting scribbled authorisations, initialling and the official stamps without which no document could be considered properly Prussian. Wherever they enjoyed popular support, intrepid priests managed to keep several steps ahead of plodding policemen, using disguises or submerging into the urban population. Sometimes, wise and timid bailiffs and policemen put their own safety first before enforcing the laws in predominantly Catholic areas. Ecclesiastical geography multiplied the state's problems. Diocesan boundaries were not necessarily coterminous with the writ of the Prussian state. Catholics could exploit the separate jurisdictions of the German federal states, or indeed of neighbouring countries, for some archdioceses had their seats in Austria–Hungary. Exiled bishops were adept at using proxies to run their dioceses. Military barracks were not always within marching or riding distance of places whose lone gendarmes were intimidated by a large Catholic presence. If the state attempted to solve the problem represented by non-compliant Roman Catholic officials by dismissing them – a course urged upon Bismarck by leading liberals – they could do little about popular support for the plucky Catholic clergy. Bishops and priests released after serving prison sentences were treated as returning conquering heroes by kneeling crowds that lined their route. Every opportunity was taken to celebrate the anniversaries of Pius IX, the particular target of liberal Protestant animosities.[43]

Instead of limited arrests and prosecutions leading to a victory of state over Church, the clumsy enforcement of the Kulturkampf legislation resembled pushing a stick into a hornets' nest. For Catholic Germany (and Catholic Poland) mounted an impressive counter-campaign of civil disobedience and passive resistance that sometimes tipped over into riot and violence. Unlike victims of liberalism in Italy, Germany's Catholic community participated robustly in the political system to defend themselves. During the Kulturkampf the Centre Party's vote doubled, and their representation in the Reichstag rose from sixty-three seats in 1871 to ninety-three by 1877. Capable Centre Party leaders, such as Mallinckrodt or Windthorst, used their parliamentary platform to inveigh against the anti-Catholic legislation, despite the efforts of the president of the Reichstag to ignore their presence whenever they rose to speak. Despite being slight and virtually blind, Windthorst routinely got the better of

Bismarck in debate, where the latter seemed blustering, bullying and tetchy. Centre Party leaders repeatedly exposed the hypocrisy of their liberal opponents by championing freedoms that the latter preferred to overlook. They were also steadfast in opposing Bismarck's draconian Anti-Socialist Law, seeing parallels between their own fate and attempts to stigmatise an entire class. Although secular liberal Jews were enthusiastic supporters of the Kulturkampf, the Centre Party leadership resisted attempts by individual Protestant and Catholic antisemitic demagogues to lure them on board platforms allegedly based on supra-confessional, or just 'Christian', values that thinly camouflaged antisemitism.[44] Of course, not all Catholics were so fastidious, with no less a personage than Ketteler, bishop of Mainz, convinced that the Kulturkampf was the brainchild of a 'masonic–Jewish conspiracy', for where passions were so engaged it was not surprising that people groped for conspiratorial explanation.[45]

Burgeoning extra-parliamentary associations, notably the Mainz Association, which mutated into the general Catholic Assembly after it was proscribed in 1876, organised huge public demonstrations. The authorities and their liberal accomplices were exercised by the social composition of Catholic resistance since it often emanated from aristocrats (of whom the liberal bourgeoisie disapproved), women (whom they regarded as superstitious simpletons) and peasants 'with blank, stupid faces' who liked to combine demonstrating with inebriation. Intricate arrangements were developed to compensate for the deprivation of state subsidies. Catholics began to boycott days of public celebration, notably by refusing to display flags on Sedan Day which commemorated victory over France, which the socialists boycotted too. Old Catholic clergy and laity, as well as orthodox 'state priests', who took an oath of allegiance to the Prussian authorities, were exposed to ecclesiastical sanction – excommunication and a broken candle tossed into their church – and social ostracism by hostile neighbours. Policemen were sometimes met with showers of stones. In Prussian Poland, the Catholic Church swung its support behind the nationalist movement, with priests moving into key positions in the organisational network that underpinned that movement for the first time. The Kulturkampf managed the considerable feat of temporarily uniting ultramontane and secular liberal Poles behind the common cause. Worse, from Bismarck's perspective, it provided the noble and clerical leaders of Polish nationalism with something like an army of followers, who responded to rhetoric that told them they were like 'redskins' being subjected to 'a national political war of extermination'. Thanks to Bismarck's clumsy assault on their religion, intermediary ethnic groups that had hitherto held aloof from Polish nationalist politics, such as the Kashubians in West Prussia or Polish-speakers in Upper Silesia, began to identify with the Polish national cause.

The principal architects of the Kulturkampf received death threats, with Bismarck narrowly evading assassination when a young Catholic butcher's boy Eduard Kuhlmann shot the chancellor in the hand as he journeyed to the spa of Bad Kissingen. In what was widely recognised as an all-time nadir in the tone of parliamentary debate, the chancellor insinuated that the Centre Party was implicated in this attempt to assassinate him:

> When I asked him [the assassin Kuhlmann] 'If you did not know me, why did you want to kill me?' the man answered: 'Because of the Church laws in Germany. And then he added: 'You have insulted my fraction.' (Great laughter) I said, 'Which then is your fraction?' To that he said to me before witnesses: 'The Centre Fraction in the Reichstag.' (Laughter. Pfiu! From the Centre) Yes, gentlemen (turning towards the Centre), you may repudiate the man as much as you like! He still hangs on your coattails.

The Kulturkampf was gradually defused through diplomacy rather than abruptly terminated. That process continued from Falk's resignation in 1879 until the Peace Bills of the mid-1880s. Bismarck had achieved the rebalancing of relations between Church and state that had been his goal from the start. Having launched an assault against the Social Democrats, it was time to patch matters up with the Catholics, not with the aid of either the Centre Party or the old guard in the German Church, but through the Vatican, which might be deployed against democratic Catholicism. Mortality facilitated these developments; Pius IX's long, fulminating pontificate ended in 1878. When he heard of the pope's death, Bismarck exclaimed, 'We must drink to that,' and ordered a noble wine. Few deals could be made with a pope who had publicly dubbed the German chancellor 'a modern Attila', 'Satan in a helmet', 'the great sorcerer' and the 'boa constrictor' of contemporary diplomacy.[46]

The new pope was count Luigi Domenico Pecci, cardinal archbishop of Perugia, who took the name Leo XIII. He had had some diplomatic experience as a nuncio to Belgium, and was known to regard the Syllabus of Errors with reserve. Without consulting the Centre Party, he authorised talks with German diplomats to explore ways out of the Kulturkampf. Princes of the Church mistrusted democratically elected Catholic politicians, with their propensity to make compromises with the Church's enemies on issues that were not narrowly religious: far better to revert to the high-level diplomacy of the era of absolutism. This was a game Bismarck was only too willing to play. Bribes from the government's 'reptile fund' rewarded the more politique curial cardinals, while in bishop Georg Kopp of Fulda, who was elevated to the Prussian upper chamber, Bismarck found a tractable Catholic bishop. Kopp was fully prepared to relay to Bismarck confidential discussions among Prussia's bishops and instructions from Rome. Another useful fault line Bismarck exploited involved retaining, or sharpening, repressive measures against Prussia's Polish Catholics, so as to divide his Catholic opponents on ethnic lines. In other words, in the 1880s the Catholic camp was divided in ways that had not been true of the 1870s.

Having no personal investment in the German struggle, in February 1880 Leo conceded the need to inform the state about ecclesiastical appointments, and that the state had the right to approve candidates. Windthorst remarked that he had been shot in the back by the papacy. Bismarck in turn alighted upon the strategy of seeking parliamentary approval for successive Discretionary Relief Bills. In essence, these were designed to retain state subordination of the Catholic Church, while leaving it up to the government whether or not to enforce the Kulturkampf laws. This adroit step prevented the pope from deriving any credit for improving the position of German Catholics, while warning the latter of the cost of continued non-cooperation. Most damagingly, it meant that the Centre Party voted against measures that appeared to alleviate the lot of their co-religionists, at a time when papal pressure to accommodate Bismarck took the bizarre form of encouraging the Centre Party to vote for a prolongation of the military budget.

The chancellor also skilfully played to the pope's desire to be an international peacemaker. In the autumn of 1885, Bismarck invited Leo to arbitrate a dispute between Germany and Spain over the Caroline Islands, negotiations followed by the dispensing of honours all round. Bismarck, so recently denounced by Pius IX as 'Satan in a helmet', metamorphosed into a Knight of the Order of Christ. Two Peace Bills, in 1886 and 1887, abolished the requirement that trainee priests be compulsorily saturated in national cultural values, although the effect was spoiled by continued state regulation of seminaries. The Second Peace Bill allowed most religious orders to return to Germany, although the Jesuits were conspicuously omitted. The government made minimal concessions in rewording the laws on the state's veto of ecclesiastical appointments. When a senior curial official visited Berlin in March 1887 to participate in the emperor's jubilee, he slipped easily into the company of those responsible for waging the Kulturkampf while virtually ignoring the leaders of the Centre Party who had borne the brunt of that fight.

III RALLYING TO THE REPUBLIC

Relations between Church and state in France were governed by the 1801 Concordat, with a subsequent accretion of custom as to how these relationships were negotiated in practice. The Church was viewed as an 'accomplice' of Napoleon III's repressive Second Empire, an association all the more bitterly resented because of the more liberal stance the Church had briefly adopted in the late 1840s. However, in the general chaos that followed the Empire's collapse, the clergy were the sole nationwide pressure group to survive. Bismarck cunningly insisted that the election of a new National Assembly would have to precede conclusion of the war, calculating that a republican France would be weaker than a monarchy. This Assembly, elected in early 1871, was predominantly Catholic and royalist.

The political ascendancy of the right, whose sole unifying focus was conservative Catholicism, was extended long beyond its expiry date, by a spasm of revolutionary violence that seemed to signify a return to the Jacobinism of 1793. The Paris Commune was an attempt to realise a nationwide federation of autonomous communes after elections to the National Assembly had revealed that much of rural France was profoundly conservative. When government forces attempted to retrieve cannons from the heights of Montmartre, a Parisian mob killed their commander and a passing general in civilian clothes. The Commune announced the formation of a Committee of Public Safety, closed opposition newspapers and declared the separation of Church and state. Half of the capital's churches and convents were turned into political meeting places or munition dumps. Approximately 120 hostages were taken to deter the troops of the provisional government at Versailles from shooting prisoners of their own. On 24 May, as government troops advanced into the burning city, archbishop Darboy of Paris and other clerical hostages were taken from the prison of La Roquette and shot against a wall. Over the following two days another fifty clerics were shot and bayoneted. Between 21 and 28 May 1871 the Versaillais forces repressed the Commune, either shooting communards on the spot or after appearances before perfunctory drumhead tribunals. In nineteenth-century Europe's largest domestic massacre of civilians, twenty thousand former Communards were killed, and thousands more were deported overseas.

The issue of what sort of state France should become was resolved through the intransigence of the principal candidate for the throne, the 'miracle' grandson of Charles X who styled himself Henry V, but was better known as the comte de Chambord. The rival liberal Orléanistes compromised on his candidacy, calculating that since he was childless, and a halfwit who had never learned to tie his own shoelaces, it would only be a matter of time before their man, the comte de Paris, came to the throne. Things went awry for the monarchist cause when on 5 July 1871 Chambord threw down the gauntlet in a manifesto from his exile, in which he insisted upon the tricolour being replaced by the white banner of the Bourbons, rejecting such ingenious compromises as having the tricolour on its reverse side. Already indicating a certain distance from the Bourbons, Pius IX acidly remarked: 'Henry IV said Paris was worth a Mass, Henry V finds France not worth a serviette.'

While Chambord mulishly stuck to this course, government passed from Thiers to marshal de MacMahon – his erstwhile co-conqueror of the Commune, who then continued in power until early 1879. Down to 1876, the apprehensions of voters regarding another Commune, and the rhetorical intemperance of left republicans, meant that the right dominated the Chamber, and hence that the Catholic Church rejoiced in a continuation of official favour. The papal nuncio exerted considerable influence in the choice of bishops. Clerics were exempted from military conscription in July 1872 and the Ministry of War licensed military chaplains. Three years later, the Catholic Church was authorised to establish its own universities with degree-awarding powers. There was a modest rise in the annual state 'budget des cultes' through which the salaries of bishops and some other clergy were defrayed. Anticlericals were incensed by MacMahon's attempts to put France back on the path of 'moral order', deviation from which, according to clericals, had resulted in defeat at the hands of the Prussians and the bloodbath of the Commune. This latest crime was added to the original sin of the Revolution, in a dark catalogue of waywardness that required ever greater acts of national expiation.

In this context, who or what occupied the public sphere intensely mattered. While commemoration of 14 July and such republican symbols as Marianne were banned, the forces of ultramontane conservative Catholicism seemed to be conniving in the diffusion of new Catholic cults, whose mass appeal had been greatly facilitated by the advent of cheap rail transport. The lines between politics and religion were being blurred, although clericalists hardly disguised their belief that the authority of the Church should count in temporal as well as spiritual affairs, determining standards of public and private life.[47] Fifty deputies took part in an expiatory festival at Paray-le-Monial, where in the late seventeenth century Christ had reappeared, to a Visatandine nun, revealing His bleeding heart crowned with thorns.

Acting in belated response to the nun's vow, senior clerics campaigned to build a Church of the Sacred Heart on the heights of Montmartre, the site of the martyrdom of Saint-Denis, where a chapel had stood until erased by earlier revolutionaries in 1793. This imposing Romano-Byzantine pastiche in brilliant white (still the fifth largest tourist attraction in Paris) was regarded as an attempt to expiate the revolutionary tradition recently so grimly active on the city plain below. Attempts to insert an homage to the Sacred Heart itself into the text of the law granting permission to acquire the hilltop site caused an uproar in anticlerical republican circles.[48]

MacMahon's presidency limped along until 1879, although republicans had secured a majority in the Chamber in elections three years earlier. One of the republicans' first initiatives was to remove degree-awarding powers from Catholic universities; next they tried to undermine the minister of war for his refusal to allow honour guards to participate in secular funerals of distinguished public figures. From 1871 the Catholic bishops had clumsily sought French intervention on behalf of the pope regarding the loss of the papal patrimony, the only result of which was to drive Italy deeper into the arms of Bismarck's Germany. As the Italian statesman Luzzatti crisply remarked: 'Clericalism generates solitude.'[49] In 1876 French Catholics returned to the fray by seeking government condemnation of Italian anticlerical legislation, urging it to 'use all

The formal and legal unification of Ita[ly]
was less than inspiring so cults w[ere]
established to venerate the hero[es of]
the Risorgimento as well as othe[r]
figures from 'Italian' h[istory]

Out of this apparent chaos Dostoevsky created some of the most devastating fictional accounts of the revolutionary fanaticism.

Revolutionary sectarians insinuate themselves into the life of a provincial town so as to destroy it. They turn a literary soiree into a farce while the town burns down outside the windows.

Out of this apparent chaos Dostoevsky created some of the most devastating fictional accounts of the revolutionary fanaticism.

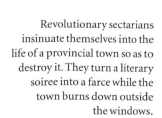

Revolutionary sectarians insinuate themselves into the life of a provincial town so as to destroy it. They turn a literary soiree into a farce while the town burns down outside the windows.

places or munition dumps. Approximately 120 hostages were taken to deter the troops of the provisional government at Versailles from shooting prisoners of their own. On 24 May, as government troops advanced into the burning city, archbishop Darboy of Paris and other clerical hostages were taken from the prison of La Roquette and shot against a wall. Over the following two days another fifty clerics were shot and bayoneted. Between 21 and 28 May 1871 the Versaillais forces repressed the Commune, either shooting communards on the spot or after appearances before perfunctory drumhead tribunals. In nineteenth-century Europe's largest domestic massacre of civilians, twenty thousand former Communards were killed, and thousands more were deported overseas.

The issue of what sort of state France should become was resolved through the intransigence of the principal candidate for the throne, the 'miracle' grandson of Charles X who styled himself Henry V, but was better known as the comte de Chambord. The rival liberal Orléanistes compromised on his candidacy, calculating that since he was childless, and a halfwit who had never learned to tie his own shoelaces, it would only be a matter of time before their man, the comte de Paris, came to the throne. Things went awry for the monarchist cause when on 5 July 1871 Chambord threw down the gauntlet in a manifesto from his exile, in which he insisted upon the tricolour being replaced by the white banner of the Bourbons, rejecting such ingenious compromises as having the tricolour on its reverse side. Already indicating a certain distance from the Bourbons, Pius IX acidly remarked: 'Henry IV said Paris was worth a Mass, Henry V finds France not worth a serviette.'

While Chambord mulishly stuck to this course, government passed from Thiers to marshal de MacMahon – his erstwhile co-conqueror of the Commune, who then continued in power until early 1879. Down to 1876, the apprehensions of voters regarding another Commune, and the rhetorical intemperance of left republicans, meant that the right dominated the Chamber, and hence that the Catholic Church rejoiced in a continuation of official favour. The papal nuncio exerted considerable influence in the choice of bishops. Clerics were exempted from military conscription in July 1872 and the Ministry of War licensed military chaplains. Three years later, the Catholic Church was authorised to establish its own universities with degree-awarding powers. There was a modest rise in the annual state 'budget des cultes' through which the salaries of bishops and some other clergy were defrayed. Anticlericals were incensed by MacMahon's attempts to put France back on the path of 'moral order', deviation from which, according to clericals, had resulted in defeat at the hands of the Prussians and the bloodbath of the Commune. This latest crime was added to the original sin of the Revolution, in a dark catalogue of waywardness that required ever greater acts of national expiation.

In this context, who or what occupied the public sphere intensely mattered. While commemoration of 14 July and such republican symbols as Marianne were banned, the forces of ultramontane conservative Catholicism seemed to be conniving in the diffusion of new Catholic cults, whose mass appeal had been greatly facilitated by the advent of cheap rail transport. The lines between politics and religion were being blurred, although clericalists hardly disguised their belief that the authority of the Church should count in temporal as well as spiritual affairs, determining standards of public and private life.[47] Fifty deputies took part in an expiatory festival at Paray-le-Monial, where in the late seventeenth century Christ had reappeared, to a Visatandine nun, revealing His bleeding heart crowned with thorns.

Acting in belated response to the nun's vow, senior clerics campaigned to build a Church of the Sacred Heart on the heights of Montmartre, the site of the martyrdom of Saint-Denis, where a chapel had stood until erased by earlier revolutionaries in 1793. This imposing Romano-Byzantine pastiche in brilliant white (still the fifth largest tourist attraction in Paris) was regarded as an attempt to expiate the revolutionary tradition recently so grimly active on the city plain below. Attempts to insert an homage to the Sacred Heart itself into the text of the law granting permission to acquire the hilltop site caused an uproar in anticlerical republican circles.[48]

MacMahon's presidency limped along until 1879, although republicans had secured a majority in the Chamber in elections three years earlier. One of the republicans' first initiatives was to remove degree-awarding powers from Catholic universities; next they tried to undermine the minister of war for his refusal to allow honour guards to participate in secular funerals of distinguished public figures. From 1871 the Catholic bishops had clumsily sought French intervention on behalf of the pope regarding the loss of the papal patrimony, the only result of which was to drive Italy deeper into the arms of Bismarck's Germany. As the Italian statesman Luzzatti crisply remarked: 'Clericalism generates solitude.'[49] In 1876 French Catholics returned to the fray by seeking government condemnation of Italian anticlerical legislation, urging it to 'use all

The formal and legal unification of Italy was less than inspiring so cults were established to venerate the heroes of the Risorgimento as well as other key figures from 'Italian' history

The SPD was Europe's largest Marxist party, although it took the path of reform rather than revolution to the red dawn of socialist imagining, in this case represented by the 8 hour day.

An evangelical missionary receives a less than respectful reception from the denizens of the sort of slum 'rookery' immortalised in the novels of Dickens.

A missionary from the London City Mission
is respectfully received by coalmen.
Everywhere enlightened Protestants and
Catholics tried to soften the harsher effects
of industrialisation and urbanisation.

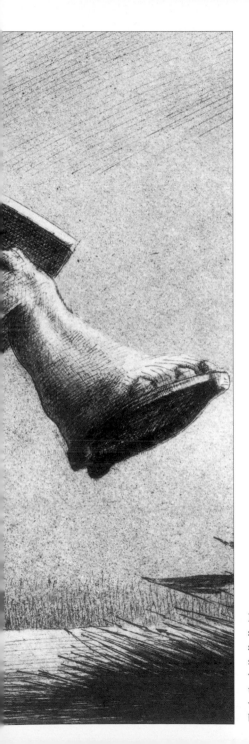

By the late nineteenth century
some people regarded the
strange gods of the nation,
state and race as objects of
worship, and during the
twentieth century Europe
was twice nearly destroyed
by the god of war.

Significant numbers of French Catholic clergy served their country in the Great War, a sacrifice that helped overcome the worst tensions between Church and State. In northern France several major church buildings were severely damaged in the war.

methods to compel respect for the independence of the Holy See'. Since that presumably included war, the left republican Léon Gambetta exploded: 'Clericalism, there is the enemy.' Other republicans spoke of 'maniacs drunk with holy water'. Clerics were blamed for the downfall of the moderate Simon ministry, whose successor was traduced as 'the government of the priests' or the 'ministry of the curés'. Between 1877 and 1879 republicans gained majorities in the Chamber and Senate. Completely isolated, MacMahon resigned when the republicans extended their purges of officials to senior army commanders whom as a matter of honour this rather dense soldier was loth to see go. The republicans were to be in power for the next twenty years, largely because of their very human unwillingness to allow examination of their deepest assumptions regarding the past, present and future.

Republicans formed a broad and fractious movement that could be rallied around a few core beliefs derived from the republican phase of the Revolution, or at least a heavily mythologised version of it. These beliefs were regarded as synonymous with being 'French', a convenient way of insinuating that anyone who held other views was disloyal. Republicans believed in popular sovereignty, provided this was informed by the exercise of critical reason, which largely explains their obsession with education as the universal panacea for society's ills. They thought that society and its institutions could be perfected in accordance with the principles of progress, science and rationality. They believed that the values of the Revolution were universally valid, and hence sought to impose them at home and export them abroad, increasingly through the medium of overseas imperialism since export opportunities were limited in a Europe where France had been eclipsed as a major power. Neither of these last two assumptions consorted altogether easily with their belief in individual liberty or other people's sovereignty, for where did it leave their domestic opponents or those foreigners upon whom these values were imposed? They were intensely and militantly patriotic, since something had to fill the affective void left by the Revolution's destruction of France's historic institutions. Finally, they managed to convert the catastrophe of the Revolution into a stirring and soft-focused myth, largely by downplaying, editing out or explaining away its most sanguinary 'episodes', like the Terror, as deviations from the noble idea, a process in which the great historians of the Republic, some of whom achieved high office, were thoroughly collusive, and which has obvious echoes of subsequent events in Russia, although there historians tended to be shot.[50]

The different groupings within this movement were a reflection of the relative importance they ascribed to the talismanic words liberty, equality and fraternity. Some regarded liberty as being synonymous with the rule of law and 'order'; others thought liberty meant guaranteeing equality of outcomes, although that rarely meant reducing social and economic inequalities. Further rifts opened up regarding the exercise of political power in a country where many people were hostile or sceptical towards the revolutionary tradition. Pragmatists, or, as their opponents had it, 'opportunists', thought that it was necessary to reassure people by acting with moderation, others were self-righteous purists who wished to forge ahead with anticlerical and secularising measures. These guardians of republican virtues were the barking dogs into whose jaws 'opportunists' were more than prepared to throw clerical bones, for they too were clear where the ultimate enemy of the Republic lay.[51]

Republicans focused on education as the battleground for their show-down with the Church. Successive nineteenth-century French regimes had been happy to leave primary education in clerical hands, because regular clergy were cheap and their main task was to discipline and moralise the poor who had grown accustomed to freedom in the turbu-lence of the revolutionary years. That priority gradually changed as economic diversification put a new emphasis upon more advanced skills. Control of secondary education was more contentious, because of its role in producing France's elites. The dominance of the Napoleonic University meant that state secondary schools were characterised by Voltairean scepticism. Down to the 1850s, the Church managed to dis-guise a handful of secondary schools as minor seminaries, until the Falloux Law enabled them to open Catholic secondary schools for boys. Some of these were socially exclusive, with plenty of particules among the names of their pupils; all offered an education that combined academic excellence, especially in the classics, with manly games, all rather remi-niscent of the regime in English public schools.

The very existence of Catholic educational establishments undermined national unity, which required a universal subscription to the values and verities of patriotism, progress and science. These values were gradually elaborated into a republican civil religion. The 14 July was adopted as a national holiday in 1880, with the storming of the Bastille being reinter-preted as deliverance from the stranglehold of superstition. The Marseil-laise not only ceased to be prohibited, but became one of the world's most evocative national anthems. As in Germany where Catholics tended to remain aloof from the noisy patriotism of Sedan Day, so French Catholics ostentatiously boycotted the 14 July celebrations.[52] Although they lacked the legislative support that existed in Bismarck's Germany, anticlerical local authorities harassed clergy as public nuisances or vagrants when they rang church bells or took collections, while encouraging secular festivities and processions, and above all ostentatiously secular public funerals. Notorious anticlericals, such as Hérold the prefect who had stripped schools of crucifixes, received civic obsequies, as did Léon Gambetta, when in 1882 he went with 'not a priest, not a whisper of a prayer' to his grave. At a cost to the Republic of twenty thousand francs, in 1885 Victor Hugo received extravagant interment in the Panthéon, which until recently had been the Church of Sainte-Geneviève, patron saint of Paris. Hugo's elaborate coffin spent the night on an immense catafalque under the Arc de Triomphe that was both illuminated and swathed in black. Catholic newspapers described the 'Babylonian' scenes that took place in the surrounding darkness as whores, with crêpe-draped pudenda signifying mourning, came out for the night shift. The following day, the funeral began with a twenty-one-gun salute. Two million people turned out to watch the passage of Hugo's pauper's hearse through the wide boulevards of Haussmann's Paris, a nice touch by a man who left little of his fortune to the poor.[53]

Public spaces began to fill up with the republican equivalent of religious kitsch, as crucifixes and other Catholic symbols were removed. In July 1880 the Republic rescinded the law compelling observance of Sunday as a day of rest that had been introduced by the Bourbons in 1814, and military chaplaincies were abolished. By contrast, places where irreligion allegedly flourished, such as bars, cafés and cabarets, no longer required official licences. In 1881 cemeteries were no longer obliged to set aside separate areas for Catholics, Protestants, suicides and Jews. Nuns were expelled from state hospitals in the capital, while seminarians had to do one year's military service. In 1884 the Republic reinstituted civil divorce, which had been repealed during the Restoration, and did away with the public prayers prescribed for the opening of each parliamentary session. In 1889 the Eiffel Tower, the highpoint of the Universal Exhibition, appeared on the Paris skyline as the iron symbol of the progressive challenge to the ultramontanes' Sacré Coeur. The road to the church was named in honour of fanaticism's quondam victim the chevalier de la Barre.[54]

It is easy to see why the republican governments of the Third Republic in the late 1870s and early 1880s should have focused legislative laicisation on the nation's schools. Some felt that the issue was a diversionary trick. Both Catholic polemicists and Marxist socialists claimed that this confrontation between Church and state over education was an attempt to deflect attention from the republicans' unwillingness to engage in more fundamental social and economic reforms. Léon Gambetta once remarked that 'to govern France you need violent words and moderate actions': the trick was to pander to the myth of Revolution, while allaying fear of it among the propertied classes. Since he also averred that 'there is no social question', it is possible that anticlericalism was exploited to rally the radical left, while leaving their reforming socio-economic agenda aside. In such a climate everything and anything could be laid at the door of the Catholic Church, with military defeat being blamed upon Jesuit instructors who had reared a generation of feeble incompetents easily massacred by the efficiently patriotic products of steely Prussian schoolmasters, a charge that the Vichy authorities would repay with interest against the Republic's own left-wing teachers in 1940.

The Republic's laicising laws, already prefigured in a programmatic speech at Romans by Gambetta in 1878, reflected the combined influences of freethinkers, freemasons, Positivists and Protestants in the governing class that alternated in cabinets that came and went with bewildering speed. They were not introduced to guarantee equality between denominations, nor indeed aggressively to return, as in Bismarck's Germany, to some hypothetical status quo ante, although they shared Bismarck's obsessive concern with national unity. Rather laicisation meant the state actively seeking to diminish the role of religion, while it promoted a rival worldview.[55]

The prime mover of the Republic's educational reforms was Jules Ferry, who was minister of public instruction in three ministries before heading a government of his own. Ferry and his principal lieutenants, the Protestant pastors Henri Buisson and Félix Pécaut and the teacher Jules Steeg, saw education as a means of creating national unity through a 'religion of the fatherland' so as to reverse the national humiliation of Sedan.[56] Ferry was a freemason and Positivist from the lost province of Lorraine: the men in his family were Voltairean freethinkers, his sister a pious cripple who prayed for his salvation, and his wife's family wealthy Protestants. Something of this schizophrenic background was reflected in his high-minded espousal of the Comtean religion of Progress and Humanity:

> When humanity appears to us, no longer as a fallen race, stricken
> with Original Sin ... but as an endless procession striding
> on towards the light; then, we feel ourselves part of the great
> Being which cannot perish, Humanity, continually redeemed.
> Developing, improving; then we have won our liberty, for we
> are free from the fear of death.

Ferry's lieutenants had a high regard for Protestantism, not simply for its own sake, but as a halfway house to 'a religious, scientific and liberal spirit', or to a secular religion divorced from traditional Christianity. Having dispensed with all dogma and religious hierarchy, they were liable to slip into a hazy humanist faith while discovering God at work in social and political movements in which they were involved.[57] Ferry appointed Buisson director of elementary education, Steeg inspector general of schools and Pécaut director of the teachers' training college for women at Sèvres.[58]

Education was seen as the great cure-all, a fallacy single-mindedly pursued by politicians reluctant to address less populist causes. It would forge the unity of will necessary to recover the territories annexed by the German Reich. It would give women equality with men and enable the poor to progress. Schools run by religious orders were divisive, and raised the spectre of two 'youths' – the 'deux jeunesses' as the historian Lavisse called them in 1880 – one of which was a hatchery for a Catholic counter-elite, ready and waiting to supplant the Republic from its bastions in the army and professions. Since religious orders were heavily involved in teaching, as a way of living down the Enlightenment lie that they were contemplative layabouts, republican animosities focused on them. There was more.

Religious orders were international, a fact that could be used to question their ultimate loyalties by a regime that was bent on creating a homogeneous nation state. As Gambetta had it, they were 'a multi-coloured militia without a fatherland'. Moreover, their vows of poverty, chastity and obedience implicitly questioned a society whose dominant concerns were with making money, leaving it to one's offspring and all the while employing the faculty of critical reasoning.[59] Religious orders wanted to control and suppress individual personality, whereas republicans were wedded to the idea of freeing its potentialities. The former 'tend to annihilate the individual, to destroy his will and initiative, to bend him under an absolute authority in the face of which the human personality itself is effaced', claimed one of the architects of the laicising laws, who had himself been educated by religious.[60]

Finally, although republicans were keen on the rights of individuals, they were hostile to those of intermediary corporations, especially if they were venerable, which seemed to obstruct expansion of the state's power. One of the reasons for allowing religious orders to run schools was that they were cheap at the price. While the state was prepared to leave religious orders running many of France's hospitals, the importance republicans attached to education meant that they were prepared to fund an education budget that rose from forty-six million francs in the late 1870s to three hundred million on the eve of the First World War.

Ferry's 1879 education law prevented members of unauthorised religious orders from teaching in either state or private schools despite their having been tolerated in this capacity for several decades. Not only did this measure extrude clergy from teaching in state schools, but it also threatened to close schools run exclusively by the Church. Although this measure had passed through the cabinet – half of whose members were Protestants – it encountered difficulties in the Senate. The Chamber retaliated by calling upon the government to dissolve the hated Jesuits, who were told to quit their houses within three months, while the other named orders were given six months to seek government authorisation. To Ferry Jesuit houses were 'schools of counter-revolution'; to his colleague Paul Bert all religious orders were akin to the phylloxera that was ravaging the nation's vines. Attempts by president Freycinet, pope Leo XIII and cardinal Lavigerie to find a compromise formula, under which the orders could stay, in return for a declaration of non-hostility towards the Republic, failed once the legitimist press had made these negotiations public.[61]

Since two thousand barristers protested that the authorities were acting illegally by avoiding the courts, a view shared by over four hundred magistrates who resigned rather than enforce these expulsions, the Jesuits and members of other proscribed orders decided to stay put. This shifted the onus on to the authorities, who were reduced to dawn raids and picking locks in order to get at the defiant religious and their lay supporters. Near Tarascon, it required an infantry regiment assisted by artillery and dragoons to break into the monastery of Frigolet, boldly defended by thirty-seven Premonstratensian fathers. Government agents, equipped with the paraphernalia of burglars, simultaneously raided eleven religious houses in the capital. Across France, some ten thousand monks were summarily evicted from 261 houses.

The dissolution of unauthorised congregations was followed by the removal of the title of university from the Catholic faculties that had won this right in 1875 and the closure of theology faculties at the state universities. Bishops were removed from the Higher Council of Education, which they had been able to join under the 1850 Falloux Law. Ferry and his associates subscribed to the view that the Church exercised a malign and mysterious influence over the 'weaker' sex: 'He who holds the female holds everything. She can make life intolerable for the husband, if he flouts a religion in which she believes. That is why the Catholic Church is so zealous in keeping her for itself. And it is precisely for this reason that democracy must wean women from Religion.'[62] A new law in December 1880 established the first state lycées for girls, together with a college to train their female teachers. This was followed a year later by the introduction of free compulsory state education for all those aged between six and thirteen. Catholics argued that they would effectively be paying twice for these state schools and their separate confessional arrangements, and that liberals who otherwise espoused the notion of free competition were conspicuously illiberal when it came to competition in this field. They were also vociferous in opposing Ferry's plan for 'moral and civic instruction' to usurp the place of 'moral and religious instruction'. As this weaved its way back and forth between the Chamber and Senate, Catholics pointed to the inconsistency of a liberal minority seeking to exclude the views of the majority, for they would not permit socialists to use schools to propagate the necessity of abolishing private property. When fresh elections increased republican representation in the Senate, even the compromise formula of teaching 'duties to God and towards the fatherland' was expunged from a law that permitted teaching of 'duties towards God' provided children were taught that God had multiple deistic identities. Apart from being hotly debated, each of these innovations churned up fresh controversy. Moral and civic instruction required new textbooks that would replace the catechism. One attempted to inculcate respect for the institution of marriage, with the aid of an illustration of a marriage bed with a portrait of the president of the Republic where the crucifix had traditionally been. Four of these manuals were immediately put on the Index, with the sacraments withheld from teachers, parents and pupils if they failed to destroy them. Bishops and priests who refused to obey a government ban on reading the Index found payment of their state stipends suspended. Finally in 1886 a law introduced the total laicisation of elementary teaching, on the ground that religious could not be expected to suspend their convictions in order to teach whatever the state required. Reasonable though that superficially sounds – not that liberal secular teachers have often been without convictions of their own – it signified the end of a venerable tradition based on the unity of religion, knowledge and moral instruction, with the attendant danger that 'God', 'nation', 'society', 'morality' and so forth would be taught as mutually exclusive entities with no sense in which they might be used to blunt one another's harder edges.[63]

As with the Prusso-German Kulturkampf, there were several reasons why the anticlerical campaign abated in France. Firstly, the advent of Leo XIII signified a pope prepared to abandon untenable positions, whether that of the legitimist comte de Chambord or the Jesuit presence in France. His nuncio to France from 1879 to 1882, Wladimir Czacki, immediately signalled to prominent republicans that the Church was not bound to any political party, nor automatically opposed to any authority that did not interfere with its freedoms. By contrast, he baldly informed the legitimists that their cause was lost. The Jesuits were thrown to the wolves when the unauthorised orders came under government attack. After the death of Chambord in 1883, Leo XIII promulgated the encyclical *Nobilissima Gallorum Gens* (1884), which while condemning attacks on the Church simultaneously enjoined the French bishops to avoid expressions of hostility towards the established government. He actively discouraged the army officer and social reformer Albert de Mun from forming a conservative Catholic party, on the Belgian, Dutch or German model, while discreetly encouraging the efforts of Jacques Piou to create a conservative bloc that would broadly accept the Republic. In elections in late 1885 conservative candidates did well. In May 1887 they took part in a government, in return for a promise to halt the programme of laicisation. Détente between the Church and the Republic was interrupted by the hiatus of the Boulanger affair. Mounting frustration with the Republic on both the right and the radical and socialist left led both separately to collaborate with the clownish figure of former war minister general Boulanger, who opportunistically exchanged his earlier anticlericalism for a promise not to persecute the Church in order to win support. He promised to repudiate the entire Jacobin heritage. Boulanger presented himself as a candidate in several constituencies on the platform 'Dissolution of the Chambers and Revision of the Constitution' and won large majorities. A Catholic newspaper observed: 'Boulangism is ceasing to be a farce and is becoming a force.' Deft alterations to electoral procedures and the general's reluctance to launch a coup put paid to his career, and the government was quick to remind Boulanger's clerical supporters of who was in charge, but the episode also impressed upon even Jules Ferry the political pitfalls of gratuitously alienating a sizeable part of the population through laicising policies at a time when anarchists and socialists were becoming a tangible threat.

The 'Ralliement' was a term first used by a cleric in 1886 to describe his readiness to rally to the Republic following Chambord's death. It became common currency in French journalism, before being adopted by a pope who was an avid reader of the French press. Although many senior clerics remained implacably opposed to the Republic, a significant minority adopted a more realistic approach to the republican regime. Some of them were opportunists, others pragmatic reactionaries. The major figure among them, cardinal Lavigerie, archbishop of Algiers, embodied the broader truth that, regardless of his personal political hinterland, overseas the Church and the Republic had common interests, for wherever foreigners went in the French Empire habits and surplices were as ubiquitous as képis and military uniforms. Of six thousand Catholic overseas missionaries in 1875, some 4,500 were French. French diplomats had pride of place in Constantinople or Jerusalem, because France was the power that protected Christians and the Holy Places. France had rights to appoint Catholic bishops in Alexandria and Baghdad, and its missionaries were active mapping and prospecting as well as preaching in faraway China.[64] Since the 1882 Triple Alliance of Austria, Germany and Italy had checked French prospects in Europe, at a time when neither England nor Russia were well disposed, imperial expansion became the sole means of French self-assertion, and for that it needed the co-operation of the Catholic Church. That was what informed Gambetta's famous dictum that 'anticlericalism was not for export'.[65]

Since French bishops were forbidden to assemble formally, the involvement of the pope proved crucial as a constant stimulus to the process of rallying Catholics to the Republic. In two encyclicals in 1885 and 1888, Leo XIII subtly distanced himself from the intransigent positions of his predecessor towards modern liberty and science. He gradually revealed his sophisticated understanding of relations between Church and state and his realisation that democracy was a force that had to be reckoned with. Although the Church was inherently superior by virtue of its transcendental goals, it had no right to interfere in temporal affairs, least of all at the prompting of self-important ecclesiastical journalists or lay activists who had no authority to speak for the Church. The Church should be neutral regarding forms of government, including those where the people decide. Leo and Lavigerie met three times in the Vatican in October 1890 to determine the strategy to be adopted towards the Republic. Towards the end of the month Lavigerie wrote to president Freycinet urging him to avoid any provocative actions that might undermine the imminent 'explicit adhesion of the French episcopate to the Republican form'. On 12 November 1890, Lavigerie hosted a banquet for officers of the Mediterranean fleet who were received to the blood-drenched choruses of the Marseillaise sung by children from a school run by the White Fathers. In the course of his toast, Lavigerie read a speech in which he said that when a people had expressed a preference for a form of government which in no way contradicted the life of civilised and Christian nations, then that government deserved to be obeyed. He added that 'In speaking thus, I am convinced I shall not be repudiated by the voice of anyone in authority.' The assembled company were so stunned that they failed to applaud. The archbishop invited the admiral to respond, which he did with a simple: 'I drink to his Eminence the Cardinal and to the clergy of Algiers.'

This 'toast of Algiers' infuriated French monarchists, some of whom were committed Gallicans, who argued that 'Ultramontanism exerting itself in favour of a Republic is no less dangerous than ultramontanism directed against it.' Very few French bishops endorsed this radical departure, leading Lavigerie to dismiss them as 'mitred rabbits'. The archbishop of Paris managed an ambiguous letter offering neutrality towards the Republic that was supported by sixty of his colleagues. That old hatreds died hard was evident when in September 1891 twenty thousand French working-class pilgrims descended upon Rome to celebrate the promulgation of Leo XIII's social encyclical *Rerum novarum*, an event that coincided with the anniversary of the Italian seizure of the capital. Three French youths who scribbled 'Long Live the Pope' in the visitors' book near the tomb of Victor Emmanuel II in the Pantheon were beaten up by outraged Italians and imprisoned. Ugly incidents took place at the French embassy, and the worker–pilgrims had to leave Rome by the night train. When France's minister for education and religious affairs warned the French bishops to dissociate themselves from these pilgrimages, one of their more intemperate number responded: 'We know how to behave. You speak of peace but your actions testify to a spirit of hate and persecution because freemasonry, that elder daughter of Satan, is in command.' This resulted in the bishop being tried for insulting a public official, and a fine of three thousand francs, which was immediately defrayed by a subscription organised by the right-wing press. With radicals calling for the separation of Church and state, and the majority of the French bishops adhering to their suspicions of the Republic, the pope took the unusual step of granting an interview to a cheap popular newspaper in which he said: 'I hold that all citizens should join in respect for the legally constituted authority. Each individual has the right to his personal preferences, but when it comes to acting, he can deal only with the government France has given herself. The republican is as legitimate a form of government as others.' He had admiring words for arrangements in the United States:

> I am of the opinion that all French citizens should unite in supporting the government France has given herself. A republic is as legitimate a form of government as any other. Look at the United States of America! There you have a Republic which grows stronger every day – and that in spite of unbridled liberty. And the Catholic Church there? It develops and flourishes. It has no quarrel with the State. What is good for the United States can be good for France too.[66]

This was immediately followed with an important French-language encyclical, *Au milieu des sollicitudes* (16 February 1892), in which Leo noted:

> The wisdom of the Church explains itself in the maintenance of her relations with the numerous governments which have succeeded one another in France in less than a century, each change causing violent shocks. Such a line of conduct would be the surest and most salutary for all Frenchmen in their civil relations with the republic, which is the actual government of their nation. Far be it for them to encourage the political dissensions which divide them; all their efforts should be combined to preserve and elevate the moral greatness of their native land.

He urged upon them the crucial distinction between governments 'excellent in form' and legislation that could be 'detestable'. He enjoined Catholics to accept legally constituted power, while contesting all too human legislation. In passing he spoke glancingly of 'idolatry of the State', a concept that would figure mightily in the era of totalitarianism. In subsequent responses to anxious French churchmen (some of whom had suppressed the pope's encyclical) Leo indicated that the Church's cause was being actively harmed by its identification with the defunct monarchist right and by the involvement of priests in politics. According to the pope, French Catholics should extricate themselves from the defunct monarchist cause, and avoid forming a separate political party for that would only excite their anticlerical opponents. Rather, they should seek common ground with moderate republicans in a broad-based party that would marginalise the rabidly anticlerical left.

In the long term, Leo XIII's explicit acceptance of various political forms was a highly significant contribution to the Church's reconciliation with democracy, although he remained studiedly agnostic regarding other available forms of government too. But in the literally short-term politics of France in the 1890s, where ministries came and went at high velocity, the pope failed to achieve his probable goals. The uncertain status of his political pronouncements, involving his indirect moral authority, contributed to their grudging reception on the French Catholic right. There were zealots who welcomed persecution by the state, not only as a test of their faith, but because it further discredited the regime they hoped would fall. Those of a more conspiratorial cast of mind convinced themselves that the pope must have been ill advised by figures in his entourage who had responded to the siren calls of moderate republicans. Some interpreted his words to mean that they should not seek to overthrow the Republic, which was a very minimal reading of his meaning. Others found it dishonourable and incomprehensible that they should be expected to abandon a hard-fought position, as if they were amoral politicians or journalists who could change their views at the drop of a hat. Some ruefully admitted that the shepherds were often financially dependent on the fatter sheep. A Catholic journalist summed up the dilemma of those bishops who were faced with obedience to the pope or ostracism and ruin:

> Do you think my diocese is made up of so many parishes? If so, you are mistaken. It is made up of 150 manors that provide the money for my various Church enterprises. The rest of the diocese is nothing more than a financial burden. When I visit twenty-five of these manors, I find a portrait of Prince Victor,

which I salute. In twenty-five others, I find photographs of the Prince Imperial and the Comte de Paris, set in a single frame. I bow to them twice over. In a hundred others, the family of Orléans holds undisputed allegiance and I bow three times. In all these houses, I find a help for my schools and for the poor that I find nowhere else.

Instead of reconciling Catholics to the Republic, the Ralliement deeply divided Catholic opinion, creating antagonistic factions and a proliferation of rival newspapers, without sinking deep roots among either Catholics or republicans outside the charmed circle at the top.[67] Attempts to translate the spirit of Ralliement into an enduring political presence failed, not least because the three most significant Catholic politicians failed to campaign on a common platform. Lack of a coherent message in these circles meant that the opportunist republicans triumphed at the polls in 1893, although there were signs that their anticlerical enthusiasm was abating. In March 1894 the minister of education and religious affairs, Spuller, condemned the socialist mayor of Saint-Denis who had banned Christian symbols from a funeral procession, remarking that 'it is time to fight all fanaticisms and all sectaries'. When a Radical anticlerical asked the minister to explain himself, he responded with a courageous declaration that times had changed:

> When the Republic had to struggle against a coalition of the old parties, when the Church constituted a link between those parties, I myself supported the policy the circumstances demanded . . . Where religion is concerned the country is no longer in the position it was ten or fifteen years ago . . . I maintain that the Church itself has changed and is evolving in spite of its pretension to infallibility. I believe that now, instead of acting as a link between the various monarchist parties, we can see the Church hurriedly striving to lead democracy . . . That is why . . . I think democracy should be animated by a new spirit . . . In place of a mean, pettifogging, irritating struggle (protests from the extreme left and applause from the centre), what is needed is a generous spirit of tolerance and an intellectual and moral reform (signs of approval from the centre and noises on the left).[68]

In Catholic eyes, this 'new spirit' was soon undermined when the Ribot cabinet imposed a 0.3 per cent tax upon the net proceeds of religious congregations that immediately antagonised Catholics. The cabinet of Méline between April 1896 and June 1898 saw the complete cessation of anticlerical measures, so much so that when in 1898 it came under threat from Radicals and Socialists at the elections, Leo XIII tried to galvanise Catholic support for the existing cabinet. He enjoined Catholics to vote tactically for moderate republicans wherever their own candidates stood slight chance of success. This strategy proved a spectacular failure, partly because more intransigent Catholic opinion failed to support it. In the end, the idea of integrating Catholics into a conservative bloc that would undo the Republic's anticlerical legislation – like, as an indiscreet cleric put it, boarding a train to hijack the locomotive – proved chimerical. A relatively quiet decade in relations between Church and state gave way to the venomous hatreds of the Dreyfus Affair.

The details of the Dreyfus Affair do not require much retelling; and if the tale had a villain, it was surely the French army rather than the Catholic Church. The original insinuations, regarding an Alsatian Jewish officer called captain Alfred Dreyfus, appeared in the antisemitic daily *Libre Parole*, founded in 1892 by Edouard Drumont. Earlier, this paper had damaged the Republic with revelations about the squalid connections between leading political figures and Jewish financiers in the Panama Affair. In December 1894 Dreyfus was falsely convicted of betraying military secrets to the Germans, degraded and banished for life to the penal colony on Devil's Island. His family discovered that a secret file, rather than the evidence produced in court, had been used to convict him, a conclusion that independently dawned on colonel Picquart, the antisemitic and Catholic head of Military Intelligence. He noticed that, despite Dreyfus' conviction, the flow of intelligence to the Germans was continuing, and deduced that a commandant Esterhazy was the guilty man. The army authorities refused to authorise a retrial and Picquart was transferred elsewhere. His replacement, colonel Henry, began doctoring the original evidence so as to prove Dreyfus' guilt. Mounting pressure resulted in a travesty of a trial of Esterhazy, in which he was acquitted in three minutes.

The novelist Emile Zola published a famous open letter in which he denounced the army's crime against Dreyfus, and warned that a conspiracy was abroad to destroy the Republic. Rival groups of intellectuals arrayed themselves in the pro-Dreyfusard League of the Rights of Man (1898) and the anti-Dreyfusard League for the French Fatherland (1899).

Membership of the former climbed from 269 in 1898 to 82,619 in 1907. One by-product of the affair was that the socialist left split between a reformist camp, led by Jaurès, which joined the progressive bourgeoisie in recognising the importance of defending individual human rights, and Marxists, identified with Guesde, who thought that the fate of an individual who was not even a worker was a distracting sideshow from the larger class struggle. This in turn conditioned the preparedness of these respective factions to collaborate with anticlerical republicans.[69] The army persisted in its cover-up, citing reasons of national security for denying Dreyfus' supporters access to the evidence. When in 1898 it became public that some of the prosecution evidence had been forged, the culprit Henry committed suicide and the war minister resigned. As a suicide, Henry was denied Christian interment, although many Catholics subscribed to a monument to his memory.[70] After a change of president and prime minister, the unfortunate Dreyfus was brought back to France for a retrial whose verdict reaffirmed his guilt, but on a reduced majority of judges, one of the dissenters being a Catholic, and with extenuating circumstances. Eventually, Dreyfus was given a presidential pardon, although it was not until 1906 that the second guilty verdict was quashed.

This bald recitation of the basic facts requires finer elaboration. First, several larger issues were superimposed on the unfortunate Dreyfus, and indeed upon the collateral casualties of the affair. The attack and defence of Dreyfus was part of a wider war of revenge, waged between right-wingers who sought to damage the Republic and its supporters who wished to discredit its opponents, real and imagined. The affair was also politically opportune, in that it rallied the broad republican movements to its core values, temporarily liberating the Opportunists from a tactical alliance with the Catholic ralliés, and from dependence upon the Socialist left with their more fundamentalist interpretation of equality. Since the affair revolved around great issues of principle, it reinvigorated a republican regime that was corrupt and tired, allowing its less than upright spokesmen to strike moral postures vis-à-vis a monolithic and sinister opponent. For a militarist plot to cover up the unfair conviction of Dreyfus quickly mutated into a clerical–militarist plot against the Republic, the tenuous link in this republican conspiracy theory being that many army officers had allegedly come under the malign influence of père Stanislas du Lac, chair of the governors of a Catholic school in the Rue des Postes. Now since nearly half the annual cadet intake to the military academy at St Cyr hailed from this school and others like it, minds began to connect the Jesuit du Lac with organised Catholic–nationalist disaffection in the army. After an interview with du Lac, a Dreyfusard dramatically announced: 'In this cell, there is a crucifix on the wall and, permanently open on the writing table, an annotated copy of the Army list.' The fact that Catholics were being systematically disbarred from other areas of government service, other than the army and Foreign Ministry, went unmentioned.[71]

There was no consolidated Catholic position on the Dreyfus Affair. Leo XIII clearly had reservations about Dreyfus' conviction, telling a correspondent of *Le Figaro* in March 1899: 'Happy the victim whom God recognises as just enough to join with His own Son in sacrifice.' He was well placed to know the truth of Dreyfus' innocence since the Germans, for whom Dreyfus was allegedly spying, had told him. Colonel Picquart, who took a number of risks on Dreyfus' behalf, was both an antisemite and Catholic, without whose investigations Dreyfus' lawyers would never have been able to undermine the prosecution case. Catholic abbés were among those who wrote pamphlets defending Dreyfus, and a prominent Catholic historian founded a Committee for the Defence of Right.

The French Catholic hierarchy, often not slow to vent strong opinions, adopted the line that the affair solely concerned the nation's courts, an uncharacteristic fastidiousness that could be interpreted as tacit support for the duplicity of the army authorities. A minority of clergy made no pretence of neutrality. Given that a third of antisemitic books published in France from 1870 to 1894 were written by Catholic priests, it was a small mercy that only three hundred (of France's fifty-five thousand) priests subscribed to a monument to the discredited forger and suicide Henry, as did impoverished female garment workers who considered the Jews harsh employers. The hundred-strong Assumptionist order had already blotted their copybook in republican eyes by meddling in the elections of 1898. Their daily and weekly newspapers – notably *La Croix* – had a readership of perhaps half a million. This was unfortunate since the Assumptionists openly described *La Croix* as 'the most anti-Jewish newspaper in France, the one that bears the [symbol] of Christ, a sign of horror to the Jews', and which simply reprinted cartoons and verse from *La Libre Parole*.[72] Again, it is important to note that when Leo XIII received its editor [whose by-line was 'The Monk'], he reproved him: 'Dreyfus, Dreyfus, all the time . . . and you might occasionally say some nice things about [president] Loubet.' Whatever the Assumptionists had to say, it was not said with the pope's approval. Claims that the Jesuits were at the dark core of the 'clerico-militarist' plot, rested on one inflammatory article in the Italian Jesuit organ *Civiltà Cattolica* claiming that the real judicial error was the 1791 emancipation of the Jews, and the self-aggrandising claims of father du Lac, for the reality of Jesuit influence in the army was that nine or ten of the 140 General Staff officers were former pupils of the Society, while only its chief, Raoul de Boisdeffre, had du Lac as his spiritual adviser. This was thin stuff for a clerical–militarist conspiracy.

Religious orders received further unwanted publicity in 1897 in the aftermath of the great Charity Bazaar fire. Each summer Catholic charities held a collective bazaar that became one of the highlights in the aristocratic social calendar. In May 1897 the bazaar was held on the Rue Jean-Goujon, which with the aid of cardboard had been converted into a mock-medieval street beneath a capacious awning. Apart from paying to give a pretty baroness a kiss, visitors also queued to watch films shown by a movie projector. A fire broke out, with the burning cardboard and the fiery awning collapsing and trapping people in the already narrowed street. One hundred and ten of the 116 dead turned out to be women, whose elaborate dresses had blazed instantaneously. The left made much of the fact that survivors had been dragged out by heroic former Communards, while aristocratic men with canes had jabbed and slashed their way to safety past burning women. Faure, the freemason president of the Republic, and other dignitaries attended the funeral in Notre Dame.

A Dominican preacher, Ollivier, took the opportunity to blame the fire not only upon hubristic Promethean 'science' – he claimed that the fire began with the over-heated projector – but on a France whose crimes had been punished by an 'exterminating angel'. God had wanted, he said, 'to give a terrible lesson to the pridefulness of this century, when man talks endlessly of his victory over God'. Although the press left little room for greater tastelessness in how this 'women's Agincourt' had been covered, Ollivier almost matched them when he declared: 'By the dead bodies strewn along the way, ye shall know that I am the Lord.' Anticlericals furiously denounced him, as well as Faure and other atheists and freemasons, for mingling in Notre Dame with aristocratic women 'who could not pronounce their names without making the sign of the cross' while the Dominican spat out his anti-republican poison. A year later, another Dominican took the opportunity of a college prize-giving day to call for condign measures against anyone who denigrated the army, in clear reference to the ongoing Dreyfus Affair. Each intemperate individual outburst was attributed first to entire orders and then to clergy in general.[73]

These lone fulminations were a convenient pretext for striking at the religious congregations, rather than the officer corps, which was responsible for the injustices Dreyfus had suffered. The new premier, Waldeck-Rousseau, who came to power in July 1899 in a ministry of 'republican defence', authorised a limited purge of the army, for its involvement in the nationalist Déroulède's 1898 failed coup, but then having obliterated the 'physical conspiracy' he turned on the 'moral conspiracy' that allegedly underpinned it. Coldly forbidding in appearance – he reminded contemporaries of a dead fish or an English statesman – Waldeck-Rousseau had mentally stored all those instances where the Church appeared to side with enemies of the Republic, and as a first-rate lawyer he knew best how to make them pay for this. His principal targets were the religious orders, which he thought had grown uncontrollably since the Second Empire, eclipsing the secular clergy, and pitching their black tents in ever wider swathes of education. Their international connections and Roman allegiances made them especially suspect, just as Dreyfus' 'cosmopolitan' background had convicted him of treason in the minds of the anti-republican right.

Waldeck-Rousseau immediately struck at the Assumptionists, whose journalistic and political representatives were arrested and charged with illegal association. On 24 January 1900 the order was dissolved, possibly with the tacit approval of the pope. Next, Waldeck-Rousseau prohibited bishops from relying upon members of orders either as preachers or as seminary instructors, using intra-clerical animosities to suggest that the bishops secretly supported this measure. Under a new law, which came into force on 1 July 1901, religious corporations were obliged to apply to Parliament for authorisation; if this was denied, their corporate property would be sold, and their members dispersed, in return for state pensions derived from the proceeds of the sales.

In elections in the spring of 1902, the left won a crushing second ballot against the right, winning 350 seats to 230, although on the first ballot the margin had been a mere two hundred thousand votes. Worried about his health, and positioning himself as a future president of the Republic, Waldeck-Rousseau resigned, nominating the sixty-seven-year-old radical deputy Emile Combes as his successor in an office he had not yet formally occupied after the elections. Combes was a typical provincial republican, whose advancement from municipality to department and then to the Senate was paralleled by his rise in the masonic rankings. Born in the Tarn in 1835, he was the sixth of ten children born to the wife of a tailor of religious habits. He studied theology at seminaries in Castres and Albi; his doctoral thesis was on St Thomas Aquinas. By the late 1860s Combes had abandoned any thoughts of ordination, turning to medicine and spiritualism, those alternative creeds of the scientific century. He became a freemason in June 1869, rising to a masonic 'mastership' a year later. He was attracted to freemasonry because it was both a voluntary family of the likeminded and an optimistic 'rational' religion. By contrast, he hated the Catholic Church for its arrogant claim to the sole truth and exclusive virtue. After a period as a local politician, in which he became mayor of Pons in 1876, Combes was elected to the Senate in 1885, bringing the certainty of a provincial, and the tortured mentality of a lapsed seminarian, into the complex world of national politics. He was briefly minister of education and religious affairs in a cabinet of Léon Bourgeois. He disliked materialism and Positivism, but quite what his own beliefs were is difficult to infer from his own obscure epitaph: 'In death as in life, our hearts tell us there is no eternal separation.' Bizarrely, at the age of sixty-eight Combes developed a platonic fixation with Jeanne Bibesco, a very wealthy thirty-four-year-old aristocratic Carmelite nun of Romanian extraction, with whom he maintained a long, and partially encoded, correspondence. When intelligence of this bizarre relationship reached Pius X, 'the Holy Father fell silent for the whole of two minutes, his look transfixed with a stupefied air'.[74]

Despite the fact that in 1902 the left lacked a clear mandate for radical change, Combes responded to the rebuke that his policy was obsessively focused on the destruction of the religious orders with 'I took office solely for that purpose.' At a stroke he implemented the letter of the law, closing three thousand non-authorised schools founded before 1901 and a further eleven thousand hospitals and educational establishments two years later. Waldeck-Rousseau had intended that the application for authorisation of each religious congregation should be scrutinised by both the Chamber and Senate so as to guarantee fairness as well as thoroughness. Some orders simply packed up and left, including the Jesuits and Assumptionists. The Trappists, who did not speak, received rapid authorisation.

By contrast, Combes gave either house of parliament the power to consider batches of applications, without the possibility of appeal, a procedure that reminded some of tumbrils carting groups of condemned to the guillotine. As a result of this cavalier procedure, in which Combes sometimes intervened to destroy orders he disliked, thousands of houses were closed and their occupants dispersed. The 'billions' that their liquidation would allegedly yield to fund clerical pensions proved to be mythical. By 1906 the sale of the century had yielded thirty-two million francs gross revenue, of which seventeen million stuck to the hands of the usual cast of greedy lawyers. The Grande Chartreuse was sold to a liqueur manufacturer after he had paid the liquidator an eighty-thousand-francs bribe.[75] Many former religious found themselves in dire straits since they were also prohibited from entering such alternative vocations as teaching. Fresh legislation in 1904 enabled Combes to attack the teaching role of authorised orders, so that between then and 1911 a further 1,843 schools were closed. Centuries of involvement by monastic orders in teaching had been wiped out.

Wilier anticlerical regimes conventionally sought to divide and rule by adopting a different strategy towards the Vatican, the bishops, religious orders and lower clergy. Combes managed to alienate the bishops by suspending their salaries when they protested against the demise of the religious orders, as well as by such gestures as removing crucifixes from courtrooms, or naming a battleship *Ernest Renan* after that distinguished sceptic. The investiture of bishops enabled Combes to take on the papacy. Ever since the Concordat, the French government and the papacy had waged a semantic war over the Latin formulas used in the presentation of candidates for canonical investiture, who by custom had already been vetted by the papal nuncio in Paris. The system worked well under the Third Republic since there were realists on both sides. Possessed of no corresponding subtlety, Combes dispensed with this consultative process and simply invited the pope to endorse his government's nominees. There were further provocations, such as nominating a seventy-six-year-old to the mountainous diocese of Ajaccio, doubtless mindful of the septuagenarian cleric wheezing up and down his inclined see. The pope refused to comply with this fait accompli.

Leo XIII died on 20 July 1903 at the age of ninety-three. In the ensuing conclave, the candidacy of Rampolla, his secretary of state, was blocked by informal Austrian government veto on the ground that he was regarded as too sympathetic to the French, although his close association with Leo XIII would probably have had him eliminated in the conclave's course. Despite Austria–Hungary's anachronistic but effective intervention, pressure to elect a temporal leader had waned since the popes now governed a territory the size of London's St James's Park.

Opting for a comparatively obscure figure, whose relations with the Italian state were untroubled, the cardinals' choice eventually fell upon the Venetian patriarch, Giuseppe Sarto, who took the name Pius X, pronouncing prospective excommunication upon anyone who sought to exercise the political veto in future. This was a simple and saintly man, whose brother was a postman and who lacked the reserve of his remarkable predecessor. Sarto had rarely left northern Italy. He was an anti-intellectual ecclesiastical disciplinarian, whose language skills (except for Italian and Latin) extended only to a little French. To compensate for this deficiency, he appointed the young Merry del Val, half Spanish, half English, as his polyglot secretary of state. Although elected chiefly because of his spiritual qualities, Pius X was aware that it was impossible clearly to delimit the spiritual from the temporal:

> We do not seek to hide from you that We expect to shock some people when We assert that We shall necessarily engage in politics. But anybody anxious to judge fairly must see that the Sovereign Pontiff, invested by Almighty God with the supreme magistrature, has no right to remove political affairs from the sphere of faith and morals.

Apart from the continued vexations over investiture rights, further trouble arose over the proposed visit of the French president Loubet to Rome, part of a French attempt to woo the Italian government away from the Triple Alliance with Austria–Hungary and Germany. French foreign policy collided with the Vatican's desire to maintain a united stance among Catholic nations regarding the Italian state's illegal seizure of Rome. When the visit took place in April 1904, the Italian government exploited it by making a number of anti-papal provocations, while the crowds cried: 'Viva Loubet! Viva la Francia anticlericale!' and indeed 'Evviva Combes!'

Merry del Val wrote to the Powers, dilating upon France's ingratitude for the custody of the Holy Places, and its generous representation in the College of Cardinals. He also unwisely added a sentence that suggested the papal nuncio was staying in Paris only because of the imminent fall of the Combes cabinet. Once leaked to the press, this letter was a gift to Combes, who sent the French ambassador in Rome on leave. That summer French bishops once more became the object of contention.

Conservative clergy and laity in two dioceses protested the conduct of two bishops who were regarded as friends of the republican government. One was a drug addict, who had allegedly conducted an improper correspondence with the mother superior of a Carmelite convent; the other had been photographed wearing a masonic apron in a procession, and had gone on to expel seminarians who refused to be ordained by such a compromised figure. When Rome summoned both bishops to investigate these charges, the French government stopped their salaries for having illegally left the country and protested Rome's technical breach of the Organic Articles. Receiving no satisfactory response, France broke off relations with the Holy See.

As we have seen, quarrels between successive French regimes, whether monarchical, imperial or republican, and the pope or French bishops punctuated the nineteenth century. The clash with the likes of Combes was fundamentally different since there was no common ground.[76] The idea of formally separating Church and state took time to diffuse since many republicans felt that the Concordat and Organic Articles enabled the state to control the Church whereas separation would not. This Erastian control would vanish with separation, the effect being, as one official had so graphically put it, akin to unleashing hungry lions and wolves on to the Place de la Concorde. There was also the piety of women, who though they could not vote could make life intolerable for their anticlerical fathers and husbands. The Socialist leader Jaurès was once bitterly attacked by his colleagues because his daughter had made her first communion. He responded, 'My friend, no doubt you can do what you like with your wife. I can't.' Another comrade shouted out: 'I would have strangled her!' In a volte-face characteristic of a left that was succumbing to embourgeoisement, many aspirant deputies, and their wives, recognised that a clerical education was good for their children's careers and marriage prospects, or at least a good deal better than what was on offer in the sometimes indifferent state schools.[77]

The Church was not keen on the notion of separation either. Its deep and recent history had revolved around the establishment, loss and restoration of the alliance of throne and altar, a shadow of which had limped along in the regime established by the Concordat. Separation would increase ecclesiastical dependence upon local notables, who would be expected to pay clerical stipends and maintain costly as well as glorious buildings in the absence of a state religious budget of some thirty-five million francs. That near unanimity of ecclesiastical opinion encouraged fervid anticlericals in the view that separation would shatter the fragile unity of the Church, which would break up into inimical sects once state tutelage had been removed. Parliamentary support for such a step increased throughout the decade we have been considering, culminating in October 1902 in the appointment of a twenty-three-man Commission to examine the proposition. The momentum behind this development came from Radicals, who in 1901 included separation in their electoral manifesto, and from the Socialists, who having regarded the issue as a distraction from the class struggle, decided to fall in line with their more rabidly anticlerical footsoldiers, and also finally to close a long-running saga that seemed to be preventing fundamental socio-economic reform.

The Commission, in which eighteen anticlericals were in the majority, considered a series of proposals on the separation of Church and state against a background dominated by increasingly fraught relations with the Vatican. Prime minister Combes' own proposed legislation revealed his extraordinary reluctance to relinquish the state's powers, since he included regular state authorisation of the local associations that were to administer ecclesiastical property and punitive controls on what priests could and could not do. By October, however, what Combes wanted was largely academic.

One of the most enduring features of the left is its unselfconscious projection of its own conspiratorial imaginings and corrupt modus operandi. An anticlerical Chamber hitherto much exercised by the jiggery-pokery that a lone Jesuit allegedly practised in promotions within the General Staff learned that in reality army promotions were subject to secret vetting, not by the military, but by the Grand Orient masonic lodge to which Combes belonged. Candidates for promotion were entered under two lists dubbed 'Corinth' and 'Carthage'. Those whose wives went to mass or whose children attended religious schools found themselves on the side of Carthage, and therefore languished as captains or majors in bleak provincial barracks. Those categorised as 'Corinthians' acquired ever fancier epaulettes and plum postings overseas or in Paris. Unmindful of the ironies in his choice of simile, the Radical Clemenceau denounced an 'inverted form of Jesuitism'. There were further revelations regarding how Combes' son, a senior civil servant, had rigged appointments and honours within the patronage of the Ministry of the Interior, whether these involved academic distinctions or the Légion d'Honneur. He had also prevented a secularised nun from visiting her own mother who was a postmistress and hence a state servant. In the wake of these scandalous revelations, Combes' cabinet resigned in January 1905; the only policy offered by the Rouvier cabinet that replaced it was separation of Church and state.

Following a three-month debate, on 3 July 1905 the Law was voted through the Chamber with a majority of 314 votes to 233, although only 130 deputies had included separation in their manifestos so the popular mandate to implement this vast change was slight. So too was its legality. Apart from its unilateral breach of the 1801 Concordat, which was a solemn international treaty, it also abrogated arrangements that had been intended to compensate the Church for its losses during the Revolution. Apart from the state laying hands on centuries of pious bequests from laymen, it was now taking what property the Church had legally acquired since 1801. Under the Separation Law, church buildings and property were expropriated by the state, but the buildings and seminaries were to be administered by religious associations, or 'associations cultuelles', for two to five years. If the Church refused to co-operate in forming these associations it would forfeit property whose gross value was 331 million francs. Breaking with Combes' desire to atomise the Church into myriad disconnected sects, these associations could federate together, and they would have to respect the wishes of the Church hierarchy. The state would cease paying clerical salaries, after a transition period of four years, but existing pension rights would be respected. The sticking point here was clearly the religious associations, which in the Church's optic raised the unwelcome prospect of laymen able to cut off clerical salaries or appointing only those clerics whose views corresponded with their own. What was to stop anticlericals employing priests who had broken with the Church, or demanding that such persons had a right to church buildings whose more orthodox incumbents would be put on the street? To counter this prospect, a clause in the law insisted that the religious associations should conform to the organisational norms of the Church to which they belonged, although all disputes were to be referred to the Council of State where republican lawyers were in the majority. Any impression that the republican authorities were sensitive to clerical sensibilities was dispelled in early 1906, when detailed instructions on making inventories of clerical property led to riots in staunchly Catholic areas as people took exception to government officials snooping in every cranny. In Paris, these protests provided a welcome pretext for violence on the part of royalist and nationalist groups who sought the downfall of the Republic.

Without waiting to learn what the French hierarchy thought, on 11 February 1906 Pius X promulgated the encyclical *Vehementer* which condemned separation of Church and state. By hiving off the Church as just one civil association among many, the new law denied that the state existed for other than material goals. The Church was being subjected to the state, in the form of the Council of State, in arbitrating disputes. Pius also had other legitimate grievances. If the French state could unilaterally abrogate an international treaty, what was to stop other governments following suit, which would not only send the entire edifice of Vatican diplomacy crashing down, but open the floodgates to anarchy in international affairs? Moreover, Pius correctly noted the frenetic succession of French cabinets, Combes' two years in office being what passed for longevity. What was to stop a future French regime unilaterally altering the terms of separation, just as Napoleon I had tacked on the Organic Articles to the Concordat? In August 1906 Pius promulgated a further encyclical, *Gravissimo*, which categorically rejected the religious associations as being a 'violation of the sacred rights that are indispensable to the very existence of the Church'. Sheep do not traditionally lead the shepherd and his dog. This ignored the wish of the French bishops to find a compromise formula with the state. They knew that roughly similar arrangements introduced in Prussia in 1875 had worked; the formula they sought was for the religious associations to be explicitly called 'canonico-legal associations'. The pope failed to acknowledge their wishes, issuing a further condemnatory encyclical. The clock was ticking as the time for forming religious associations was running out – after that the state could dispose of ecclesiastical property as it chose. The state, or rather its point-man in these matters, Aristide Briand, offered to extend the deadline by a year, and gave the clergy the option of making an annual declaration that they wished to hold services in church buildings. The government also expelled the papal nuncio, publishing his private papers, which included such embarrassing revelations as 'Clemenceau is a very bad man but he is bribable.' A law was passed in January 1907 that enabled the state to take over bishops' palaces, seminaries and presbyteries 'definitively'. Pius X responded with a further encyclical, appropriately entitled *Une Fois encore*, condemning the requirement of annual registration of prospective services, as if the clergy were like squatters dependent upon the goodwill of local authorities.

The Church that emerged from the separation was considerably poorer than its predecessor. The chinking sound from passing collection bags assumed real urgency since it was all the money the clergy received. Bishops no longer occupied imposing palaces – if they did not like these arrangements, Pius X offered to appoint Franciscans – and priests had uncertain tenure of their parishes, which in turn made the status of bequests and donations uncertain. Maintenance of churches of aesthetic or historical importance was taken over by bodies charged with the upkeep of monuments, the choice that resulted being between a ruin and a museum. Some communes were assiduous in maintaining church buildings; others allowed them to decay. A delinquent mayor who used tombstones to furnish a belltower with latrines – men could urinate on a stone engraved with 'Here rests the widow Doré, died 1900 aged 85, pray for her soul' – caused a national scandal. It took several decades for a body of customs to accrete as to how relations between Church and state would function in these novel circumstances.[78]

We can now leave events that coincided in time with the music of Debussy and Massenet, the paintings of Monet and Picasso, and the scholarship and science of Durkheim and Marie Curie. These struggles between Church and state, and the 'culture wars' that accompanied them, took place on a continent that had undergone huge transformations stemming from industrialisation and urbanisation. That process engendered an entirely new series of problems that the Churches had to confront too. To these we turn in the following chapter, beginning with Britain, the epicentre of the Industrial Revolution.

CHAPTER 9

The Churches and Industrial Society

I GOD AND MAMMON: VICTORIAN BRITAIN

The noise of Manchester stirring on Monday mornings reminded Thomas Carlyle of Atlantic breakers and the falls of Niagara. Visitors to Victorian Britain marvelled at the magnificent chaos of industrial society much as they would have reacted, with a mixture of surprise and wonder, to sublime ravines and waterfalls. Surveying London from a Thames steamer, on an English tour to raise much-needed lucre, Richard Wagner said: 'This is Alberich's dream come true, Nibelheim, world dominion, activity, work, everywhere the oppressive feeling of steam and fog.'[1] The artist Gustave Doré and the writer Blanchard Jerrold captured this extraordinary dynamism of the British capital in their 1872 *London: A Pilgrimage*:

> The view immediately to the west of London Bridge is a many-sided one. The whole round of modern commercial life is massed in the foreground, and the mighty dome which dominates London, swells proudly over the hum, and hiss, and plashing, and whistling, and creaking of the hastening crowds. The bales are swinging in the air; files of dingy people are passing into the steam-boats; the sleepy barges lower masts to pass the bridges; the heavy traffic between the City and the Borough is dragging over Southwark Bridge; trains glide across the railway arches into the prodigious Cannon Street shed. Factories, warehouses, mills, works; barges, wherries, skiffs, tugs, penny-boats; smoke and steam blurring all; and the heaving water churned from its bed and feverish in its ebb and flow, have a grandeur

that enlivens the imagination. A little pulse of the mighty organisation is laid bare. It is an eddy in the turbulent stream of London life. It is eminently suggestive of the activity that is behind the wharves, and landing-stages, and mills. The Seine has a holiday look: and the little, fussy steamers that load from London under the walls of the Louvre, seem to be playing at trade. But to the West and East of London Bridge, the surging life and vehement movement are swift and stern. There is no room for a holiday thought. The mills are grinding corn, by steam; the barges are unloading hastily, the passenger boats are bound on pressing errands, the train shoots over the river towards the Continent, and crosses another with the mail from India. The loiterer will inevitably be crushed or drowned. The very urchins knee-deep in mud, upon the banks, are intent on business – mudlarks prospecting for the droppings of the barges![2]

Neither Doré nor Jerrold was insensitive to the extreme deprivation that greeted them in their nighttime forays to the East End, to which they came like the first Europeans to set foot in Japan's Jeddo, although in this case they required the standard Scotland Yard escort to visit these nether regions of the capital. Doré's engravings are a remarkable record of such sights as a missionary reading the Gospels in a night shelter to the mummified rows of poor. In 1852 the exiled Alexander Herzen ventured into the thick 'opaline fog' where 'every night a hundred thousand men know not where they will lay their heads, and the police often find women and children dead of hunger besides hotels where one cannot dine for less than two pounds'.[3] The French conservative historian and philosopher Hippolyte Taine visited England for the first time in 1859, although he returned on several further occasions, before committing pen to paper. He visited Manchester, the apogee of the new civilisation and the economic doctrines that informed it:

We were coming to the iron and coal country, with signs of industrial activity everywhere. Slag-heaps like mountains, the earth deformed by excavation, and tall, flaming furnaces. Manchester: a sky turned coppery red by the setting sun; a cloud, strangely shaped resting upon the plain; and under this motionless cover a bristling of chimneys by hundreds, all tall as obelisks. Then a mass, a heap, blackish, enormous, endless rows of buildings; and you are there, at the heart of a Babel built of brick.

A walk in the town: seen close-to it is even more lugubrious. Earth and air seem impregnated with fog and soot. The factories extend their flanks of fouled brick one after another, bare, with shutterless windows, like economical and colossal prisons. The place is a great jerry-built barracks, a 'work-house' for four hundred thousand people, a hard-labour penal establishment: such are the ideas it suggests to the mind. One of the factory blocks is a rectangle six storeys high, each storey having forty windows: and inside, lit by gas-jets and deafened by the uproar of their own labour, toil thousands of workmen, penned in, regimented, hands active, feet motionless, all day and every day, mechanically serving their machines. Could there be any kind of life more outraged, more opposed to man's natural instincts?[4]

In London Taine sought out such sinks as Shadwell, noting: 'I have seen the lowest quarters of Marseilles, Antwerp and Paris: they come nowhere near this.' Shadwell's inhabitants seem to have been permanently engaged in gin-fuelled brawls, with 'black eyes, bandaged noses, cut cheeks', and that was only the female part, whose voices seemed 'thin, cracked, like that of a sick owl'.

Taine the traveller was less monomaniacal than the earnest young German Friedrich Engels, who had been sent in 1842 by his father to the Manchester branch of Ermen and Engels so as to isolate him from dangerous company. Nothing in provincial Barmen had prepared Engels for London. It reminded him of a gigantic physics experiment: 'The dissolution of mankind into monads, of which each one has a separate essence, and a separate purpose, the world of atoms, is here carried out to its utmost extreme.'[5]

Since Engels was no more a reliable guide to industrial Britain than Lenin was to tsarist Russia we shall not dwell too much on him. In contrast to Engels's reductively purposive account, Taine's notes capture the specific rhythms of English civilisation and the importance of religion in its culture. He experienced the limitless tedium of an English Sunday, under the pitiless and interminable drizzle that made even the most monumental classical buildings, darkened with grease and soot, look so drab and dreary. It was like imperial Rome, with the sun eclipsed. Since residual Puritanism ensured there was not much by way of Sunday recreation, Taine visited various Nonconformist chapels and Anglican churches. Unlike his native France, whose churches were filled with 'congregations of women, aged dyspeptics, servants, [and] working-class people', Taine was impressed by the 'respectable middle-class people very correctly dressed, and with serious, sensible faces' in the chapels, and by the affluent gentlemen and their ladies in the Anglican churches.[6] That in essence was their problem, although by the turn of the century even the latter had begun to desert the churches.

The Industrial Revolution transformed the lives of people who for thousands of years had been country folk dependent on the seasons, the soil and the climate. Beginning in Britain, and then varying in impact from country to country, the Industrial Revolution resulted in rapid and unprecedented concentrations of population and large-scale units of production, the mechanisation of time and work, the emergence of new social classes with rival claims to political power, novel forms of wealth and poverty, and liberal political economy which denied the state's claim to interfere in the autonomous workings of the market, an ideology that did not go unchallenged by conservatives and socialists who subscribed to more nostalgic visions.[7]

The Industrial Revolution occurred, at a varying pace, in societies that were overwhelmingly Christian in self-understanding, and which, since the Victorians certainly did not invent greed, had views on such vices as the worship of Mammon. Despite its otherworldly focus, Christianity has always been concerned with economic, social and political questions, whether one thinks of the morality of charging interest, the universal obligation of charity, relations between Church and state, or how to remind the rich and powerful of their Christian duty towards their poorer fellows. Its ethical codes were also not designed to cope with anything so abstract as economic laws, or with anything resembling the impersonality of the modern bureaucratic welfare state. Organically linked with traditional rural society, the Churches were confronted by the emergence of new population centres that seemed dedicated to the gods of machine and money, degrading human relations to what Carlyle dubbed the 'cash-nexus', while the poor sank into dirt, drink and depravity, forfeiting – in the eyes of some who like Engels did not look very deep – even their humanity.[8] The social evils engendered by industrialisation also seemed intimately bound up with disturbing trends in the sociology of religious observance.

The 30 March 1851 religious census shocked many people by revealing that five million people, out of a population of almost eighteen millions, routinely failed to attend Sunday worship. Worse, for the established Church, the percentage of those attending the Church of England was only 51 as against the 44 per cent who worshipped in Nonconformist chapels.[9] Shockingly, urban missionaries calculated that church attendance was much higher in Jamaica, Tonga, Habai and Vavau than in the imperial metropolis.[10]

Yet much had already been done to counteract the trends that the census uncovered, for one should not take Nonconformist or progressive criticism of a complacently inert Anglican establishment at face value. Clerical absenteeism in the Church of England had been almost halved between 1827 and 1848. The Church had also responded to dramatic shifts in population. After 1818 it no longer required a separate act of parliament to create each new parish. An enormous programme of church building was also supported by the legislature and private subscription.

In the previous century, competition between Church and (Huguenot) Dissent had given rise to such English baroque glories as Nicholas Hawksmoor's Christ Church Spitalfields and St Alfege's in Greenwich. The Victorians intensified the contest. It was so frenzied that it neglected the laws of supply and demand. In the 1840s, the Church of England consecrated eight new or restored churches *per month*. Nonconformists caught this building mania, in the process downgrading those elements of flexibility and imagination that had once enabled them to appeal to the lower classes through itinerant or open-air preaching: 'Town Missions etc., are all well in their place; but there wants something in addition, to gather up, consolidate and retain to ourselves, the effects which these means produce; and that something in the erection of places of worship. We must catch the building spirit of the age. We must build, build, build . . . We cannot multiply our persons, unless we multiply our places.'[11] The growth of Nonconformist places of worship was extraordinary. Whereas the Established Church had added over a million new sittings by 1851, the Nonconformists had built 16,689 new places of worship, accommodating a further four million people.[12] But even this rate of church and chapel building was inadequate. As the archdeacon of London said in 1899: 'The fact is that the population is increasing with such enormous rapidity that we are never able to overtake the neglect of 100 years ago.'[13]

The 1851 census revealed that the urban working class were the most conspicuous absentees. For example, only six thousand of the ninety thousand inhabitants of Bethnal Green attended services, while only six of the thirty-seven towns north of the line Gloucester to Grimsby achieved the 58 per cent national average of church attendance. This absence, which had important local exceptions, was partly because the 1818 Act that built more churches also made them dependent upon pew rents, with only a fifth of seating reserved for the poor, who were otherwise squeezed into the back, sides and galleries of churches, to minimise the risk of poor people's lice enlivening the well-to-do's cushions. Of course, pew rents were not entirely the problem, since the equally socially segregated Catholic churches of Ireland were hugely popular. So were the Nonconformist chapels of Welsh Merthyr Tydfil, the town with the second-highest church attendance, partly because the iron-works owners were English and Anglican.[14]

When the English iron-works owners were replaced by predominantly Welsh coal-mine owners, the chapels began to be segregated between those in the 'big pew' and the workers who stood at the rear. Social segregation characterised Nonconformist chapels more generally, with separate services for tradesmen, and the lower classes referred to solely by surname, rather than title, when the roll was called. In England, canting lower-middle-class Nonconformist preachers, often with a Welsh or Scots accent, and hence rendered alien by voice and culture, failed to make a favourable impression, especially when they insisted on temperance among those who liked a drink. By contrast, American Evangelists, who may have sounded brash but, as Anglo-Saxons, raised no ethnic hackles, were extremely popular among the working classes, and inspired such modernising movements as the Salvation Army.[15]

The Roman Catholic Church was more successful than any Protestant denomination in gaining a sizeable working-class following, chiefly because its priests were much closer by virtue of class, culture and ethnicity to the three-quarters of a million Irish immigrants in London and the northern industrial cities who made up the majority of Catholics in Britain. The 'foreignness' that even a prince of the Church like cardinal Manning felt by virtue of his adhesion to Rome may have played to the Catholic clergy's advantage in forging close links with its 'foreign' Irish constituency, but it was Manning's support for the striking dockworkers in 1889 which, earning him their warm applause, made him feel 'an Englishman'. The disadvantage was that the Catholic presence increased the sectarian awareness of the Protestant working class in Belfast, Cardiff, Glasgow and Liverpool. In 1848 Protestant mobs in Cardiff, then and now a city synonymous with drunken violence, attacked a Catholic church and the homes of the Irish after a navvy killed a Welshman, while in 1909 Liverpool witnessed attempts by both Catholics and Protestants to cleanse their respective neighbourhoods.[16]

Beyond these pockets of working-class sectarianism, the content and delivery of all religion was sometimes as inherently limiting as its identi-fication with middle-class respectability. When working-class people attended churches, dull or incomprehensible preaching by middle-class clergy, who routinely read their sermons with minimal gesticulation, invariably bamboozled or bored them. As a woman born in 1895 recol-lected: 'the parson, the one we had, he was above our heads you know ... You see with all these poor frozen people, and half-starved and half-asleep a lot of them, he would be saying "And of course, as Hegel said, as Kant said, and so and so said," quoting from the great scholars. What did they know? They couldn't even read or write, a lot of them.'[17]

That observation has to be balanced against the enormous popularity of the great dual-purpose battle hymns that steadied the trigger-fingers of riflemen facing Dervishes and Zulus, and of Sunday schools that provided rudimentary moral education, although that did not auto-matically contribute to adult church attendance. Protestantism did better wherever it pandered to the pugnacity of the population. In Lancashire, Anglican clergymen in clogs and rolled shirt-sleeves appealed to working-class Tories by denouncing Nonconformists as 'scurrilous, palm-singing, canting hypocrites' who would deny the worker his pints of 'British' beer. Others were equally successful with denunciations of a 'Babylonian' papacy, a line restricted nowadays to parts of Ulster.

This is not entirely to argue that where Churches spoke to 'vulgar' prejudices they did well, but it is to highlight the fact that the Church of England moved around the twin suns of Oxford and Cambridge, which even today bulk large in its career structures and collective con-sciousness. As far as the working classes were concerned, the Church spoke the wrong language, in a society where how you spoke, or where you went to school or university, was unmistakable to the many cognos-centi of all social classes. As a resident of Mansfield House, an East End outpost of Oxford's Congregationalist Mansfield College, had it: 'It is strange that some Londoners will say i when they mean a.' This mattered far more than such abstract concerns as the rights and wrongs of estab-lishment.

Few attempts were made to recruit working-class clergy, for the office was regarded as the preserve of gentlemen, the overwhelming majority of whom were graduates of Oxford and Cambridge, at a time when the working class had no secondary schooling. When attempts *were* made to involve working-class people actively, notably through the Church of England Working Men's Society, this was largely a tool in the High Church ritualists' battle with Low Church Evangelical Protestants in the rival Church Association. In other words, internal Church faction-fighting took precedence, a pattern that has been endlessly repeated with other 'issues', most of monumental irrelevance to all but insistent minorities. There would be further attempts to reach out to the working classes of the cities, but all, as we shall see, were failures.[18]

There were other ways of approaching the same set of problems. The Christian Churches and Nonconformist chapels had to respond to the multiple social evils that afflicted industrial Britain: disease, drunkenness, homelessness, hunger, insanitary or overcrowded housing, and adult and child prostitution since the age of consent for girls was thirteen for much of this period. These evils in turn raised fundamental questions regarding solutions, notably whether or not the state should be involved. In the earlier part of the century, Anglican clergy differed little from either domestic Dissenters or, as we shall see, continental Social Catholics in denying the state more than an occasional role in alleviating particular social evils, lest the state become an uncontrollable Moloch perpetually interfering where it had no business. Such interference seemed the height of folly to men who had little inkling that in the near future the secular state would all but displace them as the first and last resort of the poor.

This animadversion towards the state reflected the Anglican hierarchy's well-founded reluctance to engage in temporal 'politics' and their subscription to contemporary views on political economy: 'Society will work out its own good of a temporal nature, through the medium of private interest, much better than Government can do it for us, while the general error into which all plans of centralization naturally fall – that of treating in the same manner districts wholly different in circumstances and habits – is thus avoided' being the representative laissez-faire creed of many bishops in early Victorian Britain.[19] The major dissidents from this universal creed were old-fashioned Tory paternalists who regarded the factory-owning classes with snobbish disdain, and who feared that gross exploitation would lead to class warfare and a revolution that would spell the end of religion. To bishop Wilberforce, who described himself as a moderate Tory, liberalism was:

the Devil's creed: a heartless steam-engine, un-Christian, low
... utilitarian creed which would put down all that is really
great and high and noble: all old remembrances and customs:
merely to let up what is low and multiply such miserable com-
forts as going very fast through the air on a railroad – and for
this purpose it would overturn the Church; that is Christianity;
and worship the very devil if his horns were gold and his tail
was a steam-engine.[20]

The obvious compromise between widespread subscription to laissez-
faire and recognition of social evils was to advocate judicious, piecemeal
legislation that tackled individual abuses while restraining the potential
for promiscuous state interference, the thin end of the wedge for bureau-
cratised and secular state welfare. During the Victorian era religious
people tried to maintain their own distinctive approach to social evils,
based on a combination of evangelism and social work, tempering
laissez-faire liberalism with humanitarian interventions. The Church of
England gradually came round to the sort of evangelisation that was
more typical of Nonconformity. One of the most remarkable developments involved Evangelical Protestants of all denominational persuasions, although it has received far less attention than the later
Salvation Army.[21] Although celibate High Church and Roman Catholic
clergy distinguished themselves as 'slum priests', in areas where it was
unwise to relocate a genteel family, it has been estimated that Evangelical
Protestants were responsible for three-quarters of the religious social
work in nineteenth-century London.[22]

David Nasmith, a Glaswegian Nonconformist, founded the London
City Mission (LCM) in 1835. Nasmith was inspired by the earlier example
of Thomas Chalmers, who between 1815 and 1820 had used volunteers
to visit small subdivisions of his large and overcrowded Glasgow parish.
Nasmith took this system abroad, notably by founding the New York
City Mission in April 1830, before he returned to establish the LCM in
the British capital. He decided to use salaried missionaries rather than
volunteers, being helped in that endeavour by the wealthy brewer and
member of parliament Thomas Buxton. Following difficulties with the
Anglican bishop of London, Nasmith resigned from his own creation
after twenty-one months, unwilling to cede Anglicans formal parity on
the LCM's governing committee.[23]

The Mission allocated hundreds of domiciliary missionaries, each responsible for a very compact area, who were monitored in turn by district superintendents. For example, what became 'Mission District 13 Lewisham Road and (Gravel) Pits', was the domain of a Mr Horobin under the superintendence of a W. Shrimpton Esq., its boundaries marked by Blackheath Hill and Orchard Road, Dartmouth Row, Morden Road and the elusive Ravensbourne branch of the Thames.[24]

The four hundred or so missionaries of the 1870s were financially supported by an impressive number of donors and subscribers, not only in London but throughout the counties. For example, the burgers of sedate Cheltenham gave £130 per annum to support a missionary in Jacob's Island in London's Bermondsey, the setting for much of Dickens's *Oliver Twist*.[25] Most of the missionaries were Nonconformists; most of their backers and sponsors were members of the Church of England. After an initial period of scepticism, the Anglican bishops supported the LCM, chiefly because of its role in what the bishop of Norwich called 'macadamizing the road to the Church'.[26] According to the LCM's published accounts, receipts rose from about £2,700 in 1835 to £45,450 in 1876–7. The Committee was adorned with such names as Gurney Barclay, J. H. Buxton and Joseph Hoare, who brought their banking, business and brewing acumen to the LCM's affairs. Perhaps they thought up the idea of including a template bequest form in the LCM's literature?

The missionaries, most of whom were themselves working class, called on people at home or in their workplace, listening to and advising people on their problems, while trying to persuade them to read the Bible, to send their children to Sunday school and to attend church themselves. They could not dispense money, but they could solicit money from wealthy Christian sympathisers, or intercede, perhaps by writing a letter, with the authorities, private charities or, for this was the Victorian era, a person's relatives. They did much good work reclaiming the former barmaids, needlewomen and servants who had ended up in prostitution as an alternative to abuse and low wages. For example, in 1855 a missionary in London's Kentish Town reclaimed a twenty-one-year-old woman 'who had fallen into sin'. He found her a refuge in the Temporary House in Mornington Crescent, and then communicated with her elder married sister who lived near New York. Funds were raised to pay for the younger sister's new life with her sibling in the USA.[27]

Virtually all of the Ragged Schools established in London owed their inception to the efforts of LCM missionaries. They found suitable premises, and then formed committees of philanthropists to finance and administer them. At the end of each day, the missionary was obliged to write up his journal, some of which were then developed during retirement into fascinating autobiographical accounts, like that of Thomas Galt, a sales assistant in a London store, who resigned because he would not deceive customers with the 'bargains' offered in the annual sales, before joining the LCM. The LCM's magazine and reports also provided an important basis for statistical information on deprived areas. Long before Charles Booth surveyed the London poor, the LCM's John Garwood had published *The Million-Peopled City; or One-half of the people of London made known to the other half* (1853). The more astute social reformers did not need police escorts into the courts of the East End; instead they simply contacted the missionaries of the LCM. The great Evangelical social reformer Shaftesbury frequently recognised the help he had been given by the Mission in his inquiries into poverty in the capital, it being the LCM missionary Thomas Lupton Jackson who at their request arranged Shaftesbury's famous meeting with about four hundred thieves, one of whom, rising to speak, tellingly began his disquisition with 'My lord and gentlemen of the jury – not jury – I mean Mr Jackson'.[28]

The LCM catered to the fluctuating diversity of the capital's population. There were specialist missions to cabmen, dockworkers, firemen, policemen and sailors. They provided the cabmen with shelters where they could rest and enjoy refreshments, while enjoining them not to abuse or swear at their customers. Firemen, who lived with their families in eighteen local fire stations, were given such apposite tracts as *Remarkable Escapes from Peril*. The Tavern missionaries used pub signs as their opening gambit to publicans, sensing more hope in 'The Good Samaritan' than in 'The Man Loaded with Mischief'. There were also missions to the large floating population of foreign sailors, many of whom were Spanish-speaking, to whom George Gillman (who worked with sailors for fifty years) preached in their native tongue, after risking life and limb clambering over the gangways and planks heaving with burly stevedores that linked ships and quays in harbour. Sometimes Gillman was rebuffed from the lower decks 'with oaths peculiar to the language of the sea'. Occasionally the officers welcomed him aboard: 'Mira hombres, venga va a niendo a este culto, porque los Protestantes tienen una religion mayor que tenemos nostros en Espana,' although this kindly captain soon perished when his ship the *Daoiz* was accidently sunk by the English *Busy Bee* in Hamburg harbour. There were also (converted

Jewish) missionaries to the Jews, and resident foreigners, who were often suspected of political subversion.[29] Special campaigns were aimed at 'the system of social disturbance and moral pollution' known as socialism through a lecture series at the Birkbeck Institution, and others were launched to abolish such ancient dissipations as Bartholomew Fair.[30]

A famous illustration shows a missionary being hounded out of a London rookery by a mob of menacing men and women. It was dirty and dangerous work requiring a very special sort of person for whom bug and flea bites, or buildings that occasionally fell down, were the lesser deterrents. A missionary to Pestilentia, as Jacob's Island was known when it was an open sewer, recalled in 1871: 'Once I was laid up for seven weeks from fever [which killed his eldest child], twice I was stricken down with cholera, and once I was disabled from work by nervous disability.' Then there were the inhabitants:

> I had not been many hours at work when the report spread that I was a policeman in disguise, and I was hounded out of the place by a desperate, howling mob of thieves and outcasts. Upon my return home I was so cast down as only to be able to gain relief in tears and prayer. Next day I went very cautiously to work; but upon ascending a very steep, rickety staircase, a woman with hobnail boots came onto the landing, and with bitter oaths declared 'if I came a step higher she would kick my eyes out'; so I had to beat a retreat.

He persevered through months of abuse and violence until his ministrations to the sick and the dying won people over.

Others tried a different tack, assimilating the Churches to whatever afforded the working class excitement and leisure, regardless of the risk of vulgarising religion. Following the example of the Baptist Charles Haddon Spurgeon, a United Committee for Special Services used seven popular theatres for Sunday-evening services, drawing over twenty thousand worshippers, although most of them were clerks and shop assistants rather than the most impoverished. It is not clear whether the audiences cum congregations were attracted by curiosity and spectacle rather than a loftier search for meaning.

These encroachments into working-class areas were accompanied by more concerted campaigns, in which Christians played a prominent role, against animal cruelty, drunkenness and to enforce the sabbath. The effects were ambiguous. For every worker who took the pledge or refrained from kicking carthorses, many more objected to attempts to stop cock- or dog-fights, as well as the closure not just of drinking dens, but of shops and public museums, from which working-class people drew material and intellectual sustenance.[31] Sport provided another opportunity for Churches in working-class areas, with muscular Anglicans heavily involved (as were Jews) in East End boxing, and many football clubs having sectarian origins. These sports gradually detached themselves from the Churches, which baulked at the gambling that went with them. The religious origins of football teams have merely left a faintly unpleasant sectarian residue whenever supporters of Glasgow Rangers chant 'Get ye to hell, ye Fenian scum' when they play 'Catholic' Celtic.[32] Sport, like social work, gradually wriggled out of the clerical embrace, becoming a wholly secular activity, albeit one through which quasi-religious passions were rerouted. Although the Churches generated sporting heroes, such as the Anglican cricketer–missionary C. T. Studd, sport gradually displaced religion as the principal focus of primal emotions, a trend reflected in the bowler Harold Larwood's 'Cricket was my reason for living' or P. G. Wodehouse's rejoinder that 'Golf is only a game.'[33]

One spectacular inroad into working-class indifference was made by the Salvation Army, founded by William and Catherine Booth, which inherited and militarised the Primitive Methodist tradition of plebeian evangelicalism, their 'corybantic' trumpet blasts, tambourine rattles and cymbal tinkles disconcerting staid Anglican and Dissenting establishments alike until they came to their respective accommodations with this raucous phenomenon. The Booths, for Catherine was a talented preacher in her own right, began as itinerant revivalists in the north of England, a role that the Methodist New Connexion found difficult to accommodate. That inflexibility, and the Methodists' identification with the respectable classes, propelled the Booths into open-air preaching to rougher audiences, beginning with those attracted to a tent in a former Quaker burial ground in East London. The notion of a Salvation Army was slow to evolve among the hardcore, which consisted of the Booths' large family and their immediate acolytes, many of whom looked like bearded Conradian sea-captains.

Military metaphors were not unique to Christians in the 1860s, but it was from that decade that many of the great battle hymns stemmed, including 'Fight the Good Fight' and 'Onward Christian Soldiers'.[34] From the start the Booths welcomed, in a passive–aggressive sort of way, fracas with brewers' hired roughs, the so-called 'Skeleton Army', that resulted from efforts to evangelise the denizens of gin-palaces and pubs along the Mile End or Whitechapel Roads.

Open-air preaching on waste ground gave way to the search for permanent sites. In 1868 wealthy benefactors enabled the Booths to open the East London Christian Mission in a former meat market. This consisted of a meeting hall, tearoom and soup kitchen for the poor. The Booths then expanded their operations to such venues as the Eastern Alhambra theatre in Limehouse or the Oriental Theatre in Poplar. Since battles were part and parcel of the Booths' activities from the beginning, it is not surprising that in the late 1870s their mission was explicitly militarised, a development partly inspired by the Christian Soldiers who regularly expired on the Empire's wilder frontiers. William Booth became better known as 'General', rather than 'General Superintendent', of the Hallelujah Army, the missions became 'barracks', and its local branches 'corps' with colonels, majors and captains. A campaign to evangelise Whitby in 1877 saw the use of posters that announced: 'War! War! 200 Men and Women wanted at once to join the Hallelujah Army.' Other 'bulletins' put up during the six-month 'campaign' read: 'WE ARE RUSHING INTO WAR. The battle has begun: thousands killed and wounded, a few have been saved from death. It is a field of blood already, but what will it be?' In 1879 the rather staid-sounding *Christian Mission Magazine* became the *War Cry*. The final step was to abandon civilian clothes for a standardised plain uniform, the dark serge tunics, caps and bonnets that the Army wears today.[35] Battles there were aplenty. In 1882 Captain Tom Bull reported from Liverpool: 'The storm raged, the wind blew, rain and snow came down. Stones were thrown, a brickbat striking the head of Sergeant Fellowes, breaking his head, and causing the loss of a pint of blood. He was taken to the hospital, had his head bandaged, and came back leaping and praising God.'[36]

In keeping with a trend in the Churches in general, social work became more and more salient, for the hypocrisy of propagating the faith overseas when there was much residual darkness at home was not a point lost on many Victorians, whose capacity for rigorous self-scrutiny was extraordinary. Appalling living conditions were seen as obstacles to salvation. Drunks and rough sleepers were inveigled into night shelters, and prostitutes were offered honest employment by an organisation that was progressive in seeing sexually importunate men as part of the problem. Following the death of his wife, William Booth supervised the ghost-writing of *In Darkest England and the Way Out*, his prescriptions for the Empire's very own 'heart of darkness', with publicans standing in for ivory-traders and dockside helots for cannibalistic pygmies. Its object were the submerged tenth of unemployed who were not already catered for by asylums, the poor-house and prison. Blithely adapting virtually every nineteenth-century utopian solution to society's problems, Booth advocated City Colonies which would provide food and shelter to the very poor; Farm Colonies, consisting of smallholdings, which would turn 'the scum of Cockneydom' into worthy kibbutzim; and, last but not least, Overseas Colonies, to which the hardier poor could be transplanted. The interstices of this bold scheme were filled with subordinate schemes for citizens' advice bureaux, co-operative banks, crèches and halfway houses for discharged prisoners. Some of these minor schemes stuck, but the whole design never took off, while there were murmurings in and out of the press about how the funds donated were being administered by the autocratic and secretive general, until he was effortlessly absorbed into the British Establishment with the freedom of the City of London and an honorary doctorate from Oxford.

Nothing can be further from the truth that the Church of England somehow eschewed such social responsibilities, although Nonconformists liked to depict it as being socially negligent and solely concerned with preservation of the constitutional establishment that they wished to unravel. Paradoxically, although the Church of England was involved in ever ramifying social projects, its collective mind chose to act as if each venture into the slums was akin to a voyage of discovery.

Initially, advanced grouplets within the Church of England advocated various forms of collectivism; by the last decades of the century, such views had become general among Anglican bishops, many of whom were representative of broader fashions in intellectual opinion.

It may be that the security of tenure enjoyed by Anglican clerics gave them a lead in terms of social activism over Nonconformist ministers, who were more dependent upon the favour of classes unlikely to welcome anything that raided their wallets and who routinely equated poverty with sin. As the rhyme went: 'The pulpit's laws, the pulpit's patron give, And men who live to preach must preach to live'. Not only could influential laymen remove a preacher given to political harangues, since preachers itinerated they could blot his copybook with a future congregation.[37]

The Chartist crisis contributed to the formation of an Anglican grouplet, eventually known as Christian Socialism, and associated with the academic theologian Frederick Maurice, the barrister John Ludlow and the preacher and writer Charles Kingsley. Ludlow, who had discovered Christian Socialism in Paris, turned to Maurice in order to educate and evangelise the poor in the environs of the courts around Lincoln's Inn. This came to nothing, but in the wake of the Chartist fiasco, when Maurice had volunteered as a special constable, he put Ludlow in touch with Charles Kingsley, and the group was born. They founded a penny paper called Politics for the People, which first appeared in May 1848. A year later they began to hold meetings with London's artisans, which in turn led to the establishment of a number of associational workshops for bakers, builders, shoemakers and tailors that received capital investment and orders from well-to-do patrons and philanthropists. In 1850 they founded another paper called Christian Socialist from which the group took its name.[38] Maurice regarded the Evangelical concern with individual salvation as the religious analogue to the evils of capitalist competition. He was more impressed by the Tractarian emphasis upon communion, which in contrast to the egalitarian brotherhood of the socialists needed only to be rediscovered rather than imposed.[39] This also meant that he was cool towards interference by the state:

> Christian Socialism is to my mind, the assertion of God's order. Every attempt to hide it under a great machinery, call it Organization of Labour, Central Board, or what you like, I must protest against as hindering the gradual development of what I regard as a divine purpose, as an attempt to create a new constitution of society, when what we want is that the old constitution should exhibit its true functions and energies.[40]

He and his friends argued that the Church had to go about in the world, extending the notion of Christian charity to cover a range of disabling social and economic evils. If one will, it was Christianity by the deed. Like continental Social Catholics and Christian Socials, they were nostalgic for the lost 'brotherhood' of medieval guilds. They wished to create co-operatives which would span the nation and set both prices and wages. Judging from later Christian accommodations with such doctrines as revolutionary Marxism, the group's connections with 'socialism' seem nominal. They were sympathetic to working men rather than to Chartism, rejecting the calls for universal suffrage that were at the heart of the movement. Maurice opposed the Reform Bill, trades unions and indeed any state social reforms, including those in such fields as public health. He admired Bismarck, that great persecutor of German socialists, and thought that war was the best way of shaping national consciousness.[41] Their attempts to forge a new Christian form of political economy were correspondingly confused. They combined a detestation of laissez-faire and industrial England worthy of any aristocratic paternalist Tory, with a liberal emphasis upon popular education as the sine qua non for enfranchisement. Maybe that explains how their ideas became so pervasive within the Church later in the century, for the only immediate product of Christian Socialism was the Working Men's College that Maurice founded in 1854 in London's Red Lion Square.

Such groups seem eccentric when set beside the great Evangelical philanthropists of the Victorian era, or the gradual recognition by the highest Anglican authorities that something had to be done on the 'social question', the prelude to their eventual subscription to collectivism. As late as 1830 the Anglican bishops had regarded a public inquiry into the social evils of industrialisation as superfluous. This indifference was short-lived. Evangelical Protestants within the Church of England were as prominent in campaigns to improve conditions in British factories as they had been central to the campaign against overseas slavery. Memory of the latter was important, since, as Richard Oastler argued under the slogan 'Yorkshire Slavery', West Indian plantation-owners came off better in many comparisons with English mill-owners at least in terms of the hours they inflicted on minors.

The leading figure in promoting factory legislation was the Evangelical Tory lord Ashley, who after he succeeded his father in 1851 became earl of Shaftesbury. An Old Harrovian and graduate of Christ Church, Oxford, Ashley believed that parliament should use the power of the state to educate the poor and to improve their general circumstances. Private philanthropy should operate where intervention by the state was inappropriate. Ashley was one of those extraordinarily good men who are far harder to make flesh and blood than history's villains. The source of his remarkable reformist energy was the belief that degrading living conditions were preventing the poor from seeing the Evangelical light at a time when the Protestant basis of British society was being menaced by the fashionable creeds of 'infidels' and the sacerdotal mummery of the High Church Tractarians.[42] There was also his more visceral response to the sights, sounds and smells of Victorian poverty and to the 'Jacobins of commerce' whom he blamed for deranging the traditional mores and stability of British society. Having distinguished himself as a public Lunacy Commissioner, Ashley was 'astonished and disgusted' by reports he read in newspapers of conditions in Britain's factories and hastened to learn more. He was a tireless promoter of ameliorative legislation, and patron saint of countless charities, judging by the two hundred societies that were represented at his funeral, ranging from the Cabmen's Shelter Fund to the Watercress and Flower Girls and Railway Missions.

Ashley first concentrated upon a local problem: that of the bad employers and worse conditions in British textile factories. The 1833 Factory Act, which he boosted, banned work by children under nine and established an eight-hour day for those under thirteen. Employees aged between thirteen and eighteen were to work no more than twelve hours a day. Employers were obliged to ascertain the ages of their employees; those who claimed 'I thought he was eighteen' found themselves named and shamed in public. The introduction of a factory inspectorate provided the information indispensable to the further legislation closing loopholes in the 1833 law. Ashley was the driving force behind the Royal Commission into Children's Employment of 1840, which two years later led to the banning of all women and boys under ten below ground in the mines. Ashley explained: 'I have been bold enough to undertake this task, because I must regard the objects of it as being created, as ourselves, by the same Maker, redeemed by the same Saviour, and destined to the same immortality.' Thirteen bishops supported this measure, with the bishop of London dismissing the specious defences of the colliery-owning peers in the House of Lords.[43] The Ten-Hours' Act of 1847, which by curtailing the working day for women and children also shortened it for men, was all but Ashley's too in name, and it again enjoyed the support of the bishops. The latter sometimes regarded factory legislation as a form of 'pay-back' against the Dissenting manufacturers who financed the Nonconformist attacks on the Anglican establishment, that war of attrition that dominated the politics of the century.

Conditions in northern factories were but one of the areas to receive legislative attention in Victorian Britain, although it is worth bearing in mind that local initiatives often inspired national measures. Deleterious environmental conditions in both the provincial cities and the capital were exposed by Edwin Chadwick's 1842 *Report on the Sanitary Conditions of the Labouring Population*, as well as in the extraordinarily vivid journalism of Henry Mayhew, without whose writings we would not know much about costermongers, dustmen and mud-larks sifting scrap and old rope from the grey-brown mud of the unembanked river Thames. Time and again, Victorian social reformers ventured through the invisible wall that separated the London that produced marmalade from those that spread it, probing into the slums that were proliferating around the vast docks cut into the marshes of the East End. A journalist reported on life above the open sewer that was Jacob's Island. Any drinking or washing water was brought up in buckets and cans from where he described:

> It is not only the nose, but the stomach, that tells how heavily the air is loaded with sulphurretted hydrogen ... The water is covered with a scum almost like a cobweb, and prismatic with grease. In it float large masses of green, rotting weed, and against the posts of the bridges are swollen carcasses of dead animals, almost bursting with the gases of putrefaction. Along its shores are heaps of indescribable filth, the phosphorretted smell from which tells you of the rotting fish there, while the oyster shells are like pieces of slate, from their coating of mud and filth. In some parts the fluid is almost red as blood, from the colouring matter that pours into it from reeking leather-dressers close by.
>
> The striking peculiarity of Jacob's island consists in the wooden galleries and sleeping rooms at the back of the houses, which overhang the dark flood, and are built upon piles, so that the place has positively the air of a Flemish street, flanking a sewer instead of a canal; while the rackety bridges that span the ditches, and connect court with court, give it the appearance of the Venice drains, where channels before and behind the houses do duty for the ocean. Across some parts of the stream whole rooms have been built, so that house adjoins house; and here, with the very stench of death arising through the boards, human beings sleep night after night, until the last sleep of all comes upon them, years before its time.[44]

Chadwick's report prompted the establishment of a number of associations, including the Health of Towns Associations, the Association for Promoting Cleanliness among the Poor, and the Society for the Improvement of the Conditions of the Labouring Classes. The Health of Towns Association, established in 1844, was dominated by Evangelical aristocrats, whose concerns were primarily religious: 'The health, the tranquillity, the morality, nay, the Christianity of the people of this country are nearly concerned in the sanitary condition of these towns,' as viscount Ebrington put it.[45] Among the most active reformers were lord Ashley and bishop Blomfield of London, in whose diocese fourteen thousand people had perished in a major cholera epidemic. Blomfield was a leading proponent of the 1846 Bath and Wash Houses Act, which enabled local authorities to establish public baths supported from the local rates. Public sewers were a much larger proposition, not least because in London alone there were some three hundred local vested interests, ranging from lowly shopkeepers on a parish council to the patricians of the City of London, whose subscription to 'Saxon' micro-democracy felicitously coincided with their reluctance to levy and spend huge amounts of money. In 1848 Ashley became ex-officio president of the new General Board of Health, which during its six years' existence tried to improve local sanitary authorities, until Chadwick's autocratic manner grated on too many nerves. The 1858 'Great Stink' that had MPs retching into their handkerchiefs as they caught the fetid odours of the Thames spurred more effective legislative measures that resulted in the great arterial and branch sewers of Bazalgette which still flow beneath the capital.

Although bath-houses and sewers were partly due to the connection that religious people were increasingly prepared to make between dirt and sin, enhanced sanitation gradually displaced the power of public prayer. In 1831–2 a cholera epidemic prompted parliament to declare an official Day of Fasting and Humiliation. In 1848–9 a second epidemic led to a brief religious revival, but even the bishop of London spoke primarily in terms of improved sanitation being the path to salvation. In 1854, when a further epidemic occurred, the idea of a national day of prayer was rejected. These were signs of the changing times.[46]

The capital, like other towns, was constantly both expanding and metamorphosing, so that the conditions Dickens described in his novels sometimes did not exist by the time they were published. Jacob's Island, for example, was considerably improved after Peek, Frean & Co. opened in its midst a large biscuit factory that required fresh water. However, an improving infrastructure often served to condense the very poorest parts of the population, who needed to remain in the centre to have access to casual labour in the docks and meat, fish, fruit and vegetable markets. Construction of such prestige thoroughfares as New Oxford

Street, Shaftesbury Avenue and Victoria Street also slashed through the habitual haunts of the very poor, worsening conditions in Devil's Acre, Little Hell, Jack Ketch's Warren and Rat Castle, nicknames which all too vividly reflected conditions for those who lived there.[47] Similar problems occurred when Birmingham, Glasgow and Manchester were given improved municipal identities, although Improvement Bills did impose an obligation upon developers to report on displacements of population and the remedies they proposed.[48]

One of the causes of urban dilapidation was that no one seemed to own many of the worst tenements, although that did not stop the charging of extortionate rents for places that were tumbling down. Blomfield was a critic of excessive rents and overcrowding in city 'lodging houses' where unfortunates coughed, scratched, spat and turned as they lay head to toe in rooms that lacked ventilation.[49] In 1851 Shaftesbury promoted legislation that required such lodging houses to be licensed and inspected by the local police authorities, and enabled local government to build 'model lodging houses' on the rates, although very few authorities took up the opportunity.[50] He was a leading supporter of the Ragged Schools Union, founded in 1844, to solicit help for the ad-hoc schools that had sprung up in the previous decade to provide rudimentary education for the thirty thousand or so Artful Dodgers who combined casual work with theft and then crept into brick-kilns or building sites or under bridges and railway arches for a night's shelter. Having identified this constituency, further exploration of its problems led to the provision of dormitories, which in turn spurred the creation of reformatories for juvenile delinquents. A further outgrowth of the Ragged School movement was the promotion of emigration as a means of disposal and redemption for the children who had been educated in these schools.[51]

In 1888 the Anglican Lambeth conference discussed 'socialism', arriving at a definition so latitudinarian – 'every wise endeavour which has for its object the material and moral welfare of the poor' – that most clergy could eagerly subscribe. For some, this definition was so vague as to be useless, and not serviceable in their quest to identify moral postures partially derived from Christianity with a single political ideology.

The 1870s and 1880s saw a re-emergence of Christian Socialism, in the shape of the Guild of St Matthew based from 1877 in London's Bethnal Green, and the Christian Social Union formed at Oxford in 1889. The former grouping were inspired by the Etonian aesthete ritualist Stewart

Headlam, a Fabian balletomane who favoured the radical Liberals and the man who put up bail for Oscar Wilde. He believed that 'If you want to be a good Christian, you must be something very much like a good Socialist' and regarded the state as a 'sacred organisation' along with the Church. He also advocated nationalisation of the land, progressive income tax, universal suffrage and the abolition of hereditary peers. That was very much a minority view, and the Guild of St Matthew never attracted many followers, and conspicuously failed to attract the working classes.

By contrast, the CSU exerted a considerable influence upon the higher reaches of the Church. Its leading lights were Charles Gore, a Harrovian descendant of an Irish peer, and Brooke Foss Westcott, the former head-master of Harrow, canon of Westminster and from 1890 bishop of Durham, who until 1900 was its president. Between 1889 and 1913, sixteen of fifty-three appointees to bishoprics were members of the CSU. The CSU opposed the 'warring atoms' world of economic liberalism with its flighty vision of brotherhood and co-operation. Rather oddly it deliber-ately avoided having any concrete policy, although individual groups favoured what we nowadays call 'ethical investment' or white lists of employers who treated their workers well. The Oxford branch published a quarterly journal, the *Economic Review*, whose object was to introduce ethics to the dismal science. Members of the CSU sought to influence existing political parties in a Christian direction, and hence many of them saw no need for a separate Independent Labour Party.

Oxford also provided the impulse for the university settlement move-ment, although there had been earlier attempts to build bridges between the jeunesse dorée and the London poor in the form of visits to the slums organised by major public schools. University settlements differed from missions in that the residents lived collectively in what amounted to transposed colleges, rather than isolated amid the working class. The first, Toynbee Hall, involved graduates and undergraduates living permanently, or while on vacation, in Whitechapel. Using this as a base they involved themselves in matters affecting ordinary people by mounting campaigns or serving on local bodies. Toynbee Hall was also prominent in adult education, the aim being a University of East London. Other settlements, such as Oxford House, established boys' and men's clubs where there was no beer or betting. While attempts to foster social intercourse between the classes through tea parties tended to be strained affairs, the settlements did contribute to the creation of an informed body of knowledge regarding the poor, although, in purely spiritual terms, they probably did more for the souls (and careers) of Balliol or Keble men than they did for those in whose midst they settled.[52] What they manifestly did not do, for conditions in the East End apparently shocked each successive group of university men, was bridge the intergenerational replication of mutual incomprehension between the classes.

Attempts to assimilate Church or Chapel to the developing Labour movement were no more successful. In 1893 a former Unitarian minister called John Trevor presented a set of principles for a Labour Church to delegates from sixteen Churches who met in Manchester prior to breaking away from their respective institutional moorings:

1. That the Labour Movement is a Religious Movement.
2. That the religion of the Labour Movement is not a Class Religion, but unites members of all classes in working for the Abolition of Commercial Slavery.
3. That the Religion of the Labour Movement is not sectarian or Dogmatic, but Free Religion, leaving each man free to develop his own relations with the Power that brought him into being.
4. That the Emancipation of Labour can only be realized so far as men learn both the Economic and Moral Laws of God, and heartily endeavour to obey them.
5. That the development of Personal Character and the improvement of Social Conditions are both essential to man's emancipation from moral and social bondage.[53]

The Labour Churches were products of disillusionment with the social exclusivity of mainly Nonconformist places of worship, and of popular belief that a genuinely egalitarian religion could be separated from the involutions of theology. Largely restricted to Lancashire and Yorkshire, and making no impression in London, they rejected the formality and hierarchy of other Churches, while trying to accentuate such notions as brotherhood and fellowship. Their difficulty, especially after they became platforms for socialist political figures, lay in distinguishing their own pitch from secular economic or ethical doctrines set forth by the speakers who pulled in large audiences.

By the closing decades of the nineteenth century, the Church of England was no longer viewed as a monolithic obstruction to social reform, which was how it had routinely been regarded earlier in the century. The highest echelons of the Church had been converted to the anti-competitive nostrums that were fashionable among the progressive intelligentsia, and which were residual among a certain kind of Tory, albeit a conversion that was expressed in their customarily limp and qualified manner. An influential minority of activist clergymen went a great deal further, without much reflection on their privileged personal station, or their collective ignorance of the worlds of business, commerce and industry, generic incapacities that were more than camouflaged by their emphatic social moralism. The more they talked about industrial and urban society the less they seemed a part of it. They were emissaries from another world, although not the one that many working-class people still believed awaited them in the heaven.[54]

II 'SOCIAL CATHOLICISM'

British liberalism and socialism were inextricably bound up with religious Dissent, in marked contrast to continental Europe where these political forces were more nominally secular, and Catholicism, if not always Protestantism, tended to be identified with political conservatism. Nonetheless, the Catholic Church developed an explicit social philosophy, partly in response to the excesses of liberalism and the threat of socialism, both of which it routinely identified with freemasonry, Protestantism and the Jews, but also in recognition of radically altered social circumstances.

The first manifestations of what would be known as 'Social Catholicism' are difficult to disentangle from the age-old tradition of Christian charity. Social Catholicism reflected the view that the scale of the 'social question', which effectively meant morally degrading pauperism, was so great that it could not be remedied by traditional charity, although the Church was keen to preserve the generous individual impulses that inspired it, and was therefore wary of bureaucratising social policy. The sources of Social Catholicism were many and stemmed from across Europe, which partly accounts for the range of views that were represented within it.

The effects of industrialisation in France began to be apparent during the Restoration and the July Monarchy, although it lacked the frenetic 'take-offs' that occurred earlier in Britain and later in Germany, bringing much human desolation in their wake. Small-scale workshops under a single patron were more typical than factories, which in France often blurred into a strong rural economy that in turn has survived unrationalised (and heavily subsidised) into the twenty-first century. In 1890, around 64 per cent of the population lived in the countryside, a percentage that only declined to 56 per cent by 1911; in Britain, by contrast, in 1900 three-quarters of the population lived in towns, the balance between town and country having already tilted in favour of the former fifty years earlier. In 1896, a good 83 per cent of French businesses employed fewer than five people, with only 4 per cent employing more than fifty workers.[55] Moreover, apart from migrants to the working-class districts of Paris, or the eastern textile centre of Mulhouse, in 1881 only 15 per cent of French people lived outside the department in which they were born, so that France lacked the large industrial conurbations that typified the Industrial Revolution elsewhere. The French language may have given us the word 'deracination', to convey anomic urban dislocation, but the French themselves were still bien enraciné.[56]

Some French ultramontane Catholics, notably the polemicist Louis Veuillot, deplored any form of technological innovation, as well as what little he cared to know of industrial civilisation in general. Veuillot hated railways and steamboats for turning life's hitherto commodious pace into a blur of smoke and sparks, thereby diminishing man's space for contemplation and reflection. This was an eccentric, minority view, since Catholic bishops often blessed the new locomotives and steamships, both of which enabled senior ecclesiastics to deliberate regularly together, with Americans attending councils and conclaves; and, though the railways may have meant that pilgrims no longer felt the road under their feet or stopped to pray in different places, they transformed pilgrimages into vast occasions.[57]

While Catholics in authority often identified structural reform with revolution, individual Catholics were also prominent in attempting to mitigate the dislocation and misery that often went with the transition to industrial society. This was important since the French state was notoriously laggard in legislating against social evils. The first industrial legislation, prohibiting children under eight from working in factories, was passed in 1841, with a ten-and-a-half-hour day for women and children over eight being introduced only in 1900.

In some senses, Social Catholicism was simply a continuation and amplification of domestic missionary activity that stretched back to the seventeenth century. A Society of St Joseph was founded in Paris in 1822, with the aim of keeping young migrant workers on the straight and narrow, by providing them with decent lodgings, harmless recreation, employment and opportunities for worship. Its membership numbered a thousand employers and seven thousand workers. The listless deracination that the Society was designed to prevent was described by Lamennais, one of its earliest promoters, in a passage that has some contemporary resonance with the moral disorientation of contemporary migrants from traditional religious societies:

> It is dreadful to contemplate the condition of so many decent young people who are drawn to Paris each year ... and who find themselves witnesses of a licentiousness which unhappily is only too contagious. Without any bearings, without supervision or advice; surrounded by seductions; lost, so to speak, in this crowd of vices which press upon them and solicit them from every side; how can they fail to succumb? How can they preserve the religious sentiments, the sound morals, and the simple and regular habits, which most of them bring with them from the provinces? It is practically impossible: experience proves that only too well.[58]

Conservative exponents of Social Catholicism, who tended to romanticise the Middle Ages, usually wished to re-establish a corporate society, including guilds which had once provided artisans with dignity, status, training and rudimentary welfare. According to *Civiltà Cattolica*, the influential journal of Jesuit opinion, the guilds suppressed by the 1791 Chapelier Law during the French Revolution belonged to the natural law.[59] Conservative Social Catholics were also concerned to preserve the familial character of the artisanal workplace, their ideal being something along the lines of the draper's shop described by Balzac in his 1830 novella *At the Sign of the Cat and Racket*:

> These old houses were a school of honesty and sound morals. The masters adopted their apprentices. The young man's linen was cared for, mended, and often replaced by the mistress of the house. If an apprentice fell ill, he was the object of truly maternal attention. In a case of danger the master lavished his money in calling in the most celebrated physicians, for he was not answerable to their parents merely for the good conduct and training of the lads. If one of them, whose character was

unimpeachable, suffered misfortune, these old tradesmen knew how to value the intelligence he had displayed, and they did not hesitate to entrust the happiness of their daughters to men whom they had long trusted with their fortunes.[60]

The motives which inspired the conservative strain of Social Catholicism were as mixed as those that drive most idealisms, an observation only shocking to moral purists. Apart from nostalgia for societies that had not undergone the dissolvent experiences of either the French or British political or industrial revolutions, these Bourbon legitimists sought to use sporadic evidence of worker unrest to discredit the July Monarchy, while claiming that 'the men of the right are the real protectors of the poor'. They had a visceral dislike of liberalism. It was usually anticlerical. It reduced everything to money. It had an atomising impact on social solidarities and established hierarchies. It had no social conscience.

Some of these conservative social reformers were talented administrators whose legitimist sympathies disbarred them from public administration, leading them to find other channels through which to express their caste ethos of public service. The vicomte Alban de Villeneuve-Bargemont was a career prefect whose experience had included a two-year stint in the industrialising department du Nord before he was dismissed in 1830. He detested the sort of society he saw emerging in Britain, with what he called its 'pauperisme anglais', and had a physiocrat's concern with a thriving rural sector. In various works, produced in his enforced retirement after the July Revolution, Villeneuve-Bargemont argued that the state had a duty to create agricultural colonies, as well as to provide decent housing, education and rudimentary welfare, although he recognised the need too for worker self-organisation. His speech to the Chamber of Deputies on 22 December 1840 was the first in which a politician argued that social reform was a responsibility of government. He did not simply denounce such specific abuses as child labour, but condemned the wider impact of British-style industrial capitalism, responsible as it was for 'a portion of the population dependent on certain branches of industry [becoming] a caste by itself, condemned to unhappiness, as in England; their way of life, health and very existence are a matter of blind chance. This is a situation which no society that calls itself civilized and Christian can tolerate.'[61]

The realisation that new forms of deprivation were cyclical or systemic led socially minded conservative Catholics to think beyond traditional alms-giving whose impact would inevitably be merely palliative. Comte Armand de Melun was an aristocratic lawyer who was fortuitously introduced to a member of the Daughters of Charity religious order. Up to that point, he recalled, 'I had never visited anyone who was poor, I knew only those who had held out their hands to me in the streets . . . I had hitherto regarded it as the job of public assistance and welfare offices to get to know them and to provide relief for them.' Careful study of the problem led Melun to the conclusion that 'today we must broaden the horizon. It is not just a matter of filling some gaps, of rendering aid where the dole and the social interest have overlooked someone. One must address the task of making available to everybody the assistance that society is capable of rendering to each.' Melun established a series of 'patronages' to deal with the problems of such specific groups as apprentices, orphans and serving girls. He founded a journal which sought to study the problems of the poor in a systematic fashion, as well as a Society for Charitable Economy that endeavoured to co-ordinate disparate charitable initiatives. The object of the Society was to find a third way between cut-throat liberalism and 'scientific' socialism, and to express this in the form of legislation to be put before parliament. The French equivalent of Shaftesbury, Melun sought action on abandoned infants, begging, pawnbrokers and child labour. He was also involved in holding regular meetings for workers in churches, which combined religious and moral instruction from both priests and laymen with the provision of medical and funeral benefits based on a modest subscription. Known from 1840 onwards as the Society of St Francis Xavier, these meetings enjoyed the support and protection of archbishop Affre of Paris, who ordained one of the few priests, Auguste Ledreuille, actually of working-class origin. By 1845 some fifteen thousand Parisian workers were involved with the Society of St Francis Xavier, which opened a 'Workers House' that functioned as a labour exchange to help its clientele at times of cyclical downturn. These initiatives explain why the 1848 Revolution lacked the anticlerical outbursts that conventionally accompanied past upheavals, and why the conservative bishops initially welcomed the new Republic.

Conservatives nostalgic for a vanishing social order were not the only socially engaged Catholics. Liberal Catholics, of whom the most notable was Frédéric Ozanam, organised a network of conferences, which assumed the name Society of St Vincent de Paul, whose ends included visiting and befriending poor people in their own homes. By 1848 some eight to ten thousand people were active in 388 of these conferences.[62] Ozanam was also the prime mover behind a new daily paper called *Ere Nouvelle* which in its brief existence advocated reductions in working hours, graduated income taxes and the application of a scientifically considered charity to the plight of the disadvantaged.

The 1848 Revolution saw the emergence of a handful of socialist priests, thirty-three of whom attended a huge banquet for workers in April 1848. Emboldened with toasts to 'Jesus of Nazareth, the father of socialism', the priests announced, 'We want your emancipation, we will no longer allow the exploitation of man by man. It is time that the worker enjoyed all the fruit of his labour, and that an industrialist, only because he is a capitalist, should not fatten himself on your toil.'[63] Their disapproving ecclesiastical superiors quickly silenced such socialist priests.

The most prominent exponent of a left-wing form of Social Catholicism was the doctor Philippe Buchez, who had transferred his sympathies from Saint-Simonian socialism to Roman Catholicism after the former had degenerated into a species of pseudo-religious cult. Later he recalled that 'I was convinced that I should find in Christianity all that I had long desired, and I regretted that those who had taught me in my youth and the philosophes had sent me so far off the track in search of the truth when I had it so close to me.'[64] In the summer of 1848 he briefly became president of the Constituent Assembly, but his influence was mainly as a propagandist rather than as a politician. Buchez advocated worker co-operatives whose profit-sharing arrangements would enable them to acquire the capital necessary for them to become employers. He believed that 'this great social crisis cannot be solved till the day when the revolutionaries are Catholics and the Catholics are revolutionaries'. Buchez's influence was evident among the working men who founded a journal called *Atelier* in 1840. They implicitly rejected the idea that people had to belong to the Church to be good Christians. They also put much emphasis upon fraternity and deprecated both charity and paternalism, regarding the attainment of justice for the workers as the essential precondition for a more just, and hence more Christian, society.

During the brief existence of the Second Republic, it was the conservative strand of Social Catholicism, represented by Melun, that most influenced policy once more heady schemes for extensive nationalisation and the right to work had come to nothing. There was a profound scepticism about utopian 'solutions' to poverty; as a group of Catholic employers had it: 'Teach the masses morality and you will do more against need and pauperism than all the innovators and theoreticians with their systems and utopias ... Hunger, sickness, poverty, these are evils which are intrinsic to our nature; dreaming of their total eradication means surrendering oneself to a hopeful illusion.' In this unpropitious climate Melun sought to introduce a welter of reforms, including maternity hospitals, nurseries, orphan asylums, improved housing, mass education, vocational training, shorter working hours, savings schemes, and welfare associations for young workers. Elected to the National Assembly in May 1849, he secured the appointment of a committee to review the entire question of public provision for the poor. On the basis of its reports, the Assembly introduced a corpus of social legislation that dealt with insalubrious housing, pensions, hospitals, medical care and the provision of public baths. Much of this legislation survived the transition to the presidential regime, the conservatism of its main sponsor making it acceptable to the otherwise rabidly anti-socialist Party of Order which had been terrified by the disturbances of the June Days that followed the dissolution of the government's 'national workshops'. Almost immediately Church leaders abandoned their earlier enthusiasm for the Revolution, pronouncing that 'Democracy is the heresy of our age' and banning Catholics from subscribing to, or reading, *Ere Nouvelle*.[65]

The ecclesiastical authorities, whose influence upon the education system had been reasserted by the 1850 Falloux Law, fulsomely supported Bonaparte's December 1851 coup d'état. This alliance of mutual convenience meant the death knell for the left-leaning forms of Social Catholicism, although Napoleon's long-standing interest in pauperism, about which he published a book, meant limited opportunities for socially conscious conservative Catholics to influence his government's policy. Although Melun was personally a Bourbon legitimist, in early 1852 he was invited to dine with Napoleon, who proceeded to extol the virtues of a nationwide system of friendly societies to dispense sickness, accident and funeral insurance payments, membership of which would be compulsory for proprietors and employees alike. The unemployed were excluded since payments to them would only encourage their alleged idleness. Once Melun had successfully argued that these arrangements should be voluntary, he agreed to participate in their ramification. By 1869 nearly a million people, many of them artisans and professionals rather than workers, belonged to either approved or authorised friendly societies which were also closely connected to their local communes and church.

The Second Empire also witnessed attempts by many thinkers to study human society in an inductive scientific fashion, an approach that was partly inspired by their scepticism about general principles, theoretical models and Rousseauist utopianism. The most distinguished exponent of this social 'science' was Frédéric Le Play, for the first half of his life a professor of metallurgy at the Ecole des Mines. There he combined lecturing with officially sponsored study visits to the industrialising regions of a wide range of countries which resulted in a number of books on, for example, the South Wales copper industry or cutlery manufacture in South Yorkshire. As an entrepreneur–academic he surveyed the mineral resources of the Donets basin, and reorganised industry in the Urals mountains on behalf of the Russian tycoon Danilov, with whom he went into partnership. Le Play also took on an enormous range of public functions. Initially sympathetic to socialism, in 1848 he joined the Luxembourg Commission for the Workers, one of the earliest examples of industrial conciliation involving employers, workers and independent experts. Disillusioned with the Republic, Le Play moved to the right and became a supporter of Louis Napoleon, becoming a member of the Council of State in 1855. A year later he became one of the founders of the International Society for the Applied Study of Social Economy. During the 1850s he belonged to an impressive range of official inquiries, including into the coal industry, housing conditions, the public lottery, Sunday leisure, absentee landlordism, the Parisian baking trade, local government devolution, proof of paternity, and, last but not least, for it was a personal obsession, an investigation into the ill-effects upon the family and national economy of laws limiting a father's testamentary freedom. Partible inheritance both diminished the moral authority of family patriarchs, allowing younger sons to inherit as a matter of right, and led to a proliferation of dwarf agricultural units. He was an admirer of eighteenth-century English and Russian aristocratic primogeniture.

In the 1860s Le Play was appointed commissioner-general for public international exhibitions, at the time one of the major indices of national prestige. He ensured that awards for industrial relations, with international trades unionists encouraged to comment on the choice of winners, were introduced for the first time at these well-publicised orgies of competitive national display. In 1867 the first prize for excellence in industrial relations went to a Prussian silk and velvet mill that retained workers during slumps, provided free schooling for children, permitted married women to work from home, and provided workers with loans to enable them to purchase smallholdings which would reduce their dependence upon the factory itself. Le Play's own publishers won a prize for having a sick club and pension scheme, and for selling property to avoid having to make injurious layoffs.[66]

Le Play believed that moral considerations should always have priority over the merely economic or technical. His annual lecture courses on metallurgy were based on the view that the promoters of technological progress should be constantly aware of its widest human and social consequences, since new technologies were constantly undermining delicate inherited social customs. In the mid-1850s Le Play published a series of monographs on individual working-class families in various European countries that included details of their income and expenditure. He used this information (whose deficient methods are as obvious as the detailed results were impressive) to argue that a more flexible version of the traditional, religious, patriarchal family, where the father had the right to disinherit undeserving children, would best guarantee both order and innovation, security and freedom. He called this the 'stem' family, where, after all had competed for paternal approval, one son would inherit and remain the head of a ramified family whose breakaway members would still retain links with the new patriarch. The model of the family was to dominate industry too. Businesses and factories were to be run as extended families in which the employer assumed the role of father and the workforce that of children, Le Play's answer to the anonymity of modern industrial society.

Of course, Le Play's campaign against partible inheritance was primarily designed to shore up traditional French rural society, rather than to transpose its structures on to urban conditions. Partible inheritance was leading to de-facto birth control to limit the number of children seeking a slice of the family pie, as well as to the migration to towns and cities of younger sons from economically unviable dwarf-holdings, where they inevitably formed atomised and unstable nuclear families. Catholic 'familism' resulted in a number of legislative attempts throughout the Third Republic to penalise celibacy and childlessness, and to encourage 'familles nombreuses' with tax breaks.[67]

The shock of France's defeat by Prussia and the bloodshed of the Paris Commune gave a fillip to conservative forms of Social Catholicism. The former experience engendered a mood of national soul-searching, while the latter was like a dark red stain that required expiation. Two Catholic aristocrats, comtes Albert de Mun and René de la Tour du Pin, first met in a German internment camp at Aix-la-Chapelle in November 1870, where they read and discussed Emile Keller's *The Church, the State and Liberty*. Published in 1865, Keller's book was an ultra-orthodox defence of Pius IX's Syllabus of Errors, which was written to confound those (few) French clergy who had been taken aback by the violence of the domestic opposition to the pope's pronouncements. Keller inveighed against everything represented by the date 1789, and all that stemmed from it, including big government, high finance and industrial concentration. Here he echoed Marx's notion of progressive immiseration. The much vaunted value of freedom was nothing more than the 'freedom' of a rich minority to prosper at the expense of the burgeoning ranks of proletarians who were replacing independent peasants, artisans and shopkeepers. He condemned the money-crazed nineteenth-century bourgeoisie: 'They have betrayed and sold everything, starting with their own souls, in order to be allowed to continue consuming gold and dividends.' Only the Church, restored to its freedom, would give the workers real liberty. Keller called for men to come forward who would help re-Christianise society. These ideas became compelling once Mun and La Tour du Pin returned to Paris, where Mun witnessed the bloodshed of the Commune as a military press officer. Seeing a wounded Communard insurgent passing on a stretcher, he felt that 'Between these rebels and the legal society of which we were the defenders, it seemed that there was a chasm.' That autumn the two men sought out Maurice Maignen, a lay brother of St Vincent de Paul who ran a club in Montparnasse for young workers. They had been sent there by the military government of Paris that was investigating the causes of the recent explosion of class warfare. Gesturing towards the burned-out Tuileries, Maignen said:

> The criminals who burned Paris were not those people . . . No: the guilty men, the really guilty men, are you . . . I mean the rich, the great, the fortunate who amused themselves within those ruined walls, who pass by the people, without knowing them, without seeing them, with no feeling for their souls, their needs, or their sufferings . . . I live with them, and I can tell you on their behalf, they do not hate you, they are as ignorant of

you as you of them. Go to them with an open heart and an outstretched hand, and you will find that they understand you.

The two aristocrats and their friends formed an Association of Workingmen's Clubs to establish them in Paris, Lyons and other cities. By 1878 there were 375 such 'circles', with thirty-eight thousand worker members and eight thousand members of the upper-class committees that were an adjunct of them. There was even a branch in Belleville, the epicentre of working-class discontentment, for the clubs were a conservative Catholic response to the republican and socialist clubs that were attracting many workers. Workers administered these clubs, which in addition to common rooms had a chapel and chaplain so as to emphasise their Catholic character. Each club was also to have a committee representing the employers and upper classes, the aim being to encourage the two to bridge the chasm whose existence had inspired the whole enterprise. After the Commune, many in the Catholic upper class had a keen interest in ending such estrangement. Although the clubs were run by an upper-class oligarchy that included aristocrats, army officers and titled ladies, with the workers very much in statu pupillari, it is worth noting their role in alleviating minor iniquities, whether persuading the rich to pay their seamstresses and tailors on time, or encouraging store-owners to provide seats for shop assistants weary of standing.[68]

These workers' clubs were very much targeted at bachelor itinerant journeymen. Religion was to insulate them from metropolitan vice until such time as their savings enabled them to achieve economic independence and start a family. As army officers Mun and La Tour du Pin were not especially conversant with the lives of factory workers, who in any event were suspicious of their counter-revolutionary politics and of the paternalism that their schemes represented. The clergy were inherently sceptical about associations of laymen that seemed to bypass parochial and diocesan control.[69]

This emphasis upon keeping wayward journeymen on the straight and narrow changed when in 1873 Léon Harmel encountered the aristocratic leaders of Social Catholicism while on a pilgrimage to Notre Dame de Liesse. Photographs of Harmel show a straight-backed, carefully barbered member of the French bourgeoisie, with a great domed forehead and sensitive but penetrating dark eyes. Born in 1829, Harmel inherited his father's concern for the spiritual and material well-being of his workforce in the family woollen thread-spinning enterprise at Val des Bois in the Suippe Valley which the son took over in his mid-twenties. Harmel senior had already created a savings bank for the workers, and a relief fund guaranteeing a sick worker half of his or her salary, free medical care and, when the worst came to the worst, funeral expenses.[70] The younger Harmel shared his father's paternal regard for their workforce, while practising his own austere form of Catholicism, which led him to become celibate following the death of his wife (after she had borne him nine children) and to live in an unostentatious manner, that included giving up smoking. In 1860 he joined the Third Order of St Francis, subsequently supporting its campaigns against freemasons and Jews, whom he – and others – egregiously identified as being responsible for 'usurious' capitalism and the rampant anti-Catholicism of the Third Republic.

The Val des Bois factory employed between 375 and 678 people, which meant that it was a relatively large undertaking since in 1906 only 10 per cent of French factories employed more than five hundred workers. Harmel imported families from the devout Belgian Ardennes to act as exemplars for the de-Christianised workers of rural Champagne where his factory stood. Up to forty of his own family were involved in running the factory, being encouraged to participate in the factory council and in an extensive nexus of religious associations that spanned life in the Wooded Valley. In 1862 he built an imposing factory chapel, attendance at which was voluntary. Self-governing religious associations brought adult men, as well as women and minors, back into the Christian fold, and provided an extended network of support at such crucial junctures in family life as births, marriages and funerals. Although Harmel paid below the going rates in the industrial Nord, his workers benefited from his adherence to the letter and the spirit of industrial legislation, at a time when factory inspectors were often retired factory owners, and hence inclined to turn a blind eye to abuses.

Within the notoriously hot and dusty atmosphere of textile factories, Harmel provided washing facilities and a mandatory working temperature of 24 degrees Celsius, in contrast to competitors who were happy to have their workers sweltering in temperatures of 40 degrees Celsius. Men were deployed in tasks that were conventionally given to women, such as washing and dyeing, despite their strength being taxed by the heaviness of wet textiles. Children of both sexes were afforded a decent education and apprenticeships, while all workers benefited from co-operative and savings schemes, company housing, medical care and pension plans. Older workers were kept busy as gardeners and groundsmen into their seventies, at a time when most industrial workers were consigned to the scrap heap at forty-five or fifty when their physical strength was expended. Although none of these things were dependent upon the religious orthodoxy of the beneficiaries, Harmel did try to structure life in a Christian fashion. Families received a supplementary wage according to the number of children, which took away the need to practise crude contraception or abortion. All wages were paid to the designated family head, and moreover were dispensed bimonthly on Mondays, which encouraged employees to spend the money on food, rather than to binge-drink their pay, which had been depressingly frequent when monthly pay was doled out on Saturday evenings, with the ensuing weekend hangovers cancelling out work until Tuesdays. Although the anticlerical government had restored Sunday as a working day in 1880, Harmel forbade it in his factory, and proceeded to abandon work on Saturdays as well, without any appreciable dent in his firm's profitability during an era when French trade and industry were buffeted by a few decades of liberalisation.[71]

Harmel was a model Catholic patriarchal employer whose workforce was constantly reminded of Christian values, whether in the form of feasts and festivals, or a disciplinary system that was to be informed by the Christian spirit. Like a Catholic Robert Owen, Harmel had global ambitions for his model factory, hoping that it would become the norm not just in the industrial Nord, but in the industrialising world as a whole. He was an active member of the L'Oeuvre des Cercles Catholiques d'Ouvriers, and of its educational wing the Conseil des Etudes where he argued for his corporatist model against those of La Tour du Pin and Mun. Harmel was also instrumental in the formation of L'Association Catholique des Patrons du Nord, which brought together Catholic employers and which by 1895 had thirty thousand members in 177 enterprises. While some of these employers emulated individual features of Harmel's model factory, few of them were prepared to adopt such innovations as factory councils, while the majority introduced religion into an industrial context chiefly in order to reinforce their authoritarian grip on the workforce. Harmel was also the originator of a series of worker pilgrimages to Rome that had an important effect on Leo XIII's pronouncements on social policy, even as they enabled the pope to extend a diplomatic hand to republican France at a time of tensions with Italy. The pilgrimages began in 1885 when a hundred employers claiming to represent workers in every part of France travelled to Rome where they were granted three audiences with the pope. At the last audience he suggested they return with some workers. Two years later the same number of industrialists arrived in Rome, but with fourteen hundred workers and a large contingent of French clergy. Lottery tickets costing a franc a time were used to reduce the vast number of applicants, who benefited from discounted third-class railway fares. The resources of the Vatican were deployed to make the workers' week in Rome affordable and enjoyable, while rules were relaxed to enable men to meet the Holy Father in overalls, although black silk or wool dresses and a veil were stipulated for working women. So successful was this event that Leo XIII instructed Harmel to return in two years' time with ten thousand worker pilgrims. Seventeen trains shuttled back and forth between France and Rome for a month to make this huge descent upon the Vatican possible. At the formal audiences with the French workers, Leo XIII emphasised the dignity of labour, recognising the need for state intervention on the workers' behalf, while strongly condemning any form of class warfare.[72]

Harmel was one important influence on Leo XIII's historic pronouncement on the 'social question', but he was not alone. Albert de Mun was tireless in his capacity, from 1887 onwards, as a member of the Chamber of Deputies, in advocating industrial and social reform from within the political system. He campaigned for the legalisation of trades unions, conceded in 1884, and for laws restricting female and child labour. He was responsible for the 1898 law on compensation for industrial accidents, the 1905 law which gave assistance to the elderly, the 1906 law that restored the status of Sundays, and the 1910 law on old-age pensions. Sitting with the extreme right in parliament, he rejected both liberalism and socialism as the malign inheritance of the French Revolution. After the Socialist leader Jean Jaurès the second greatest orator in the Chamber, in 1878 Mun castigated the first principles of the Revolution:

> Freedom, gentlemen? Where is it then? I hear it spoken of everywhere, but I only see people who confiscate it for their own profit! . . . Absolute freedom of labour is the formula of the Revolution, the implementation of the Declaration of the Rights of Man in the economic order . . . It posits one's personal

interest as motivation for one's efforts. By depriving the sovereign power of the duty of protection that is the foundation of its right, by suppressing in one fell swoop every tutelary intervention, it has delivered the weak without defence to the mercy of the strong. By creating the individualism that makes the weak and the strong face each other in isolation, and by opening the door to free competition, that is to implacable war, the Revolution is like those gargantuan riverboat duels they have in America: each goes at the top speed that its engines will attain, until they explode and dump crew and passengers. You are the crew! The passengers are France!

As an alternative Mun proposed 'professional associations' that were in effect a corporate Catholic alternative to trade unions and employers' associations. In this he was influenced by his more theoretically inclined friend La Tour du Pin, who had spent time in Austria as a military attaché.

There he was impressed by an influential group of aristocratic Christian Social conservatives around baron Karl von Vogelsang, who from 1879 onwards produced the *Austrian Monthly Review for Christian Social Science*. Many of these men, like Vogelsang himself, who had emigrated to Austria from Mecklenburg after his business had failed, were converts to Catholicism. They were aided by younger clergy, one of whom became a hand on a barge on the Danube so as to study the lives of stevedores.

These Christian Socials were implacably opposed to the anomic and unjust conditions that modern liberalism was visiting upon such people as Vienna's trolley drivers, blaming their long hours, it has to be said, on Vienna's recently emancipated Jewish population, whom they eagerly identified with economic liberalism. Be that as it may, this group were partly responsible for the socially reforming legislation that conservative governments introduced between 1883 and 1888, including restrictions on working hours, industrial safety and the employment of child labour. Returned to France, La Tour du Pin elaborated a corporatist philosophy based on the belief that 'abuses of power in this world do not get corrected by freedom, but by constraint, when persuasion fails'. The political system was to be refashioned on vocational lines. The base unit would be something resembling Harmel's factory corporations, which were to be joined by similar bodies for those working in the arts and education, in the public service and in agriculture. The next rung in the hierarchy would consist of regional commissions in which employers and employees were represented, who would elect delegates to a national corporate senate. These delegates were duty bound to consult their corporate constituents constantly, one of the many points at which corporatism differed from representative parliamentary democracy.

In the twentieth century corporatism would act as a bridge between Catholic authoritarians and the Fascist extreme right, which shared their nostalgia for rural social harmony as well as amplifying their antisemitism to include Jews who were not liberal capitalists. But in the France of the 1880s the wider implications of conservative Social Catholicism were more ambiguous. Certainly, corporatism was profoundly anti-democratic, an attempt both to restore the traditional pre-1789 society based on functional orders and to dispense with the bouleversements of the emergent democratic process in favour of consensus and stasis. However, Mun's contemptuous dismissal of charity – he likened it to ambulances arriving after an accident – signified Catholic recognition that the industrial age required something more than piecemeal benevolence, while the attempt to combine the liberty represented by decentralised bodies with a limited measure of state intervention (regardless of whether that government was dominated by liberal anticlericals) also represented a subtle shift towards irreversible realities.

Industrialisation came significantly later to Germany than to Britain, Belgium or France. The first stretch of railway, from Nuremberg to Fürth, did not open until 1835, and even by the mid-nineteenth century there were only about six thousand kilometres of track. The Ruhr was still predominantly agricultural; in 1846 Krupps of Essen, which would later be synonymous with industrial gigantism, employed a rather modest 142 people.[73] This is not to say that there was widespread social distress. British competition wiped out the domestic textiles production that compensated for paltry and poor peasant holdings, while increasing numbers of journeymen found that the trades they had trained in were superfluous. Both groups flooded into cities and towns, which had neither the factory-based industries nor the welfare resources to employ or otherwise support them.

The responses of both Churches in Germany to mass distress were hesitant. Catholics were preoccupied with the political battles they were waging in many states, while Protestants tended to equate poverty with sin. The 1848 Revolution gave both a sharp jolt in the sense that the spectre of 'Communism' – a term covering many views on the left

– induced a limited awareness of what came to be called the 'social question'.

Protestant charitable associations and institutions existed in considerable profusion before the Revolution – there were 1,680 in Prussia alone in 1847 – and many of them included civil servants on their governing boards so as to keep them indirectly under state control. However, the idea of centrally co-ordinating Protestant activity in this field was first broached by Johann Heinrich Wichern, who since 1833 had run a home for delinquent juveniles in Hamburg. At the September 1848 Wittenberg assembly of Protestant churchmen, Wichern spoke of the need for a Home Mission ('Innere Mission') whose Central Committee would co-ordinate a broad effort to re-evangelise society – this would include detoxifying it of 'Communist' influences – through preaching, urban missions, tracts, domestic visits, as well as the many charitable institutions and organisations already active in Germany.[74]

Catholic social activity was much more focused on the problems of journeymen at a time of transition between the old economy and the new. Adolf Kolping, a former shoemaker who had been helped to study both classical languages and then theology, established a club for journeymen in Elberfeld in 1846. By 1855, Kolping, who was clearly a remarkable priest, had created 104 such clubs with twelve thousand members in most of Germany's towns and cities. By 1879 the clubs had nearly eighty thousand members. The clubs were partly boarding houses and partly labour exchanges, but also places where journeymen could learn to read and write, or take further education classes in civics, religion and business. They were initially funded by private donations (and later by small subscriptions) and kept costs low by having the diocesan clergy deal with administration. One of Kolping's fellow students in Munich had been a Westfalian aristocrat, Wilhelm Emmanuel freiherr von Ketteler, who abandoned a career in the civil service (over the arrest of archbishop Droste-Vischering of Cologne) to become a priest. He served as a delegate to the Frankfurt National Assembly in 1848, and became bishop of Mainz in 1850.[75]

Ketteler's interest in the 'social question' was initially secondary to his concern with the freedom of the Church vis-à-vis the state, and couched in conventional charitable and paternalistic terms. Catholic polemicists, from whom he drew his own ammunition, had little to say about the 'social question', concentrating their fire upon the pernicious effects of economic liberalism to which their only known antidote was a revival of the medieval guild system. While this may have had some relevance to the problems of artisans, it had little or nothing to offer industrial workers.[76]

This emphasis changed when the Catholic Church discovered the maxim 'my enemy's enemy is my friend'. Hitherto, most German workers had been content with the political tutelage that middle-class liberals exercised on their behalf. While the progressive liberal Hermann Schulze-Delitzsch had helped form four hundred or so workers' co-operatives, he was also of the view that workers were not ready to participate directly in the political process.[77] This view was shared by August Bebel and Wilhelm Liebknecht, but not by the radical firebrand Ferdinand Lassalle, who in 1863 formed the Allgemeiner Arbeiterverein, the first independent German workers' party. Lassalle was strongly opposed to the liberals, and rejected Schulze's schemes for autonomous workers' co-operatives in favour of the idea that these should be funded by the state. In January 1864 bishop Ketteler wrote anonymously to Lassalle, asking for his help in establishing five productive associations, for which he was prepared to put up fifty thousand florins as capital. Lassalle declined to take the anonymous benefactor up on his offer.

That April Ketteler published a book entitled *The Labour Problem and Christianity*. This argued that Christianity afforded the only true solution to the 'social question', whereby he offered an olive branch to social reformers among conservative Protestants. The bishop used Lassalle's concept of the 'iron law of wages', whereby wages tended to hover on or below the minimum necessary for subsistence, to assail the 'anti-Christian' or 'neo-pagan' liberalism which was responsible for the imposition of an industrialised form of slavery, from which in antiquity Christianity had once delivered humanity. The attacks on modern liberalism were more substantial than the bishop's positive proposals, which largely consisted of moralising generalities about the family, the importance of Christian charity and the role of education in Christian values. Only Christianity, he wrote, held the means to improve the condition of the working classes, although his proposals for doing so were on the thin side. Having devoted so much time to assailing liberalism, Ketteler appropriated the idea of producer associations, which he thought could be funded by voluntary contributions along the lines of the Peter's Pence being collected to support the beleaguered pope. This was as unrealistic as Ketteler's idea that Christian employers should join with the bishop in establishing artisanal workshops, half of whose profits should be distributed to the workforce.[78]

Ketteler's heavily qualified enthusiasm for Lassalle also led to complications. Workers in the Lower Rhineland who attempted to combine Catholicism with membership of Lassalle's socialist party found themselves refused absolution by local priests. Unsurprisingly, the workers went over the priests' heads to Ketteler, who after all had championed Lassalle against the Progressive Schulze-Delitzsch. The bishop extracted himself from this delicate position (which might have seen many Catholic workers joining a labour party on the ground that it must have embodied Catholic teaching since its founder had been cited so approvingly by a bishop) by praising the dead Lassalle at the expense of a Party whose 'evolution' he condemned. The Party was both anticlerical, to a degree that resembled religious fanaticism, and sympathetic to a Bismarckian 'Kleindeutsch' solution to the German Question that would extrude Catholic Austria and reduce German Catholics to a large minority.

Ketteler's views on the 'social question' reflected these political considerations. In November 1865 he addressed the Mainz branch of the Kolping Association, arguing that, as the absolutist Prussian state had often supported key industries, so it should support workers' associations. In December 1867 he demanded state intervention to limit hours of work and to preserve the special character of Sundays. This did not mean that he had come round to those 'statist' parts of Lassalle's programme that he had earlier rejected. On the contrary, in the last years of the 1860s a new 'Christian socialism' began to gain ground among clerics in Aachen and Essen in the Cologne diocese that was explicitly hostile not just towards liberalism but also to the increasing influence of Marx upon socialism in Germany. Marx was sufficiently troubled by this to mention it in a letter to Engels: 'I convinced myself that energetic action must be taken against the clerics, particularly in the Catholic areas. I shall work in this vein in the International. Where it appears viable, the rogues are flirting with workers' problems (e.g. Ketteler in Mainz, the clerics at the Düsseldorf Congress etc.).'

Ketteler took up the problems of industrial society in an address in the summer of 1869 to a gathering, which included many cigar workers, to celebrate the opening of a shrine church near Offenbach. In this address, Ketteler condemned the concentration of money-power and the corresponding weakening of an atomised workforce. He commended English-style trade unions and justified the right to strike for higher wages, with the caveat that without the adoption of moderation and thrift ever higher wages would simply be an excuse to indulge in more drink. The state would do little to stop this process because it derived tax revenues from the proliferation of pubs. Ketteler also denounced Sunday working and the employment of women and children which was undermining the family. He warned the workers against the fantastic schemes of the socialists, recommending that they pay heed to the respect shown to religion by their British counterparts:

> Even though the English working class was in worse shape than the German, so far as the dire consequences of modern economic philosophy are concerned, the efforts to organise the working class in England are vastly superior to our own. That is due first and foremost to the great respect shown in England toward the significance of religion in solving social problems. In Germany, on the other hand, the spokesmen of labour make a public display of their hatred for religion.[79]

In the summer of 1869 Ketteler visited various parishes in the vicinity of Frankfurt so as to report on the 'worker question' to the Fulda bishops' conference that September. At the conference he acknowledged that there was no going back from industrial society, which brought such 'blessings' as increased production. However, the problem was how to soften the impact of these changes upon the workers. There was a certain self-interest here, for in a remarkable acknowledgement of realities Ketteler claimed that it would soon be necessary to send missionaries to people who had reverted to being heathens. Partly informed by factory legislation in England, he called for laws to deal with several abuses. There should be statutory minimum ages for child workers in various sectors, together with adequate provision for their education. Young girls were not to be employed in factories at all. Laws should limit hours of work, and ensure observance of the sabbath. A factory inspectorate would improve health and safety, while workers were to be entitled to accident insurance. Workers' associations were to be legally recognised. Turning to his clerical auditors he suggested that in future some priests should be trained in political economy, and that those posted to industrial areas should be competent to act as apostles of peace between employers and workers. Ketteler's colleagues listened with polite interest, and then did nothing, although his nephew, count Ferdinand von Galen (the father of the famous bishop who opposed the Nazis), tried to introduce Germany's first social policy legislation in 1877. By contrast, enormous energy went into the simultaneous defence of the papacy, as when Pius IX was presented with a congratulatory address from Catholic Germany signed by a quarter of a million people and bound in twenty-three leather volumes, together with a gift of a million francs.

III *RERUM NOVARUM* AND AFTER

Social Catholicism was one of the influences upon both the Ralliement, discussed in Chapter 7 above, and Leo XIII's 15 March 1891 encyclical *Rerum novarum*. Both effectively recognised that the Church could not pursue its overall goal of re-Christianising society if politically it was exclusively identified with the intransigent right, and with social and economic privilege. The encyclical managed the considerable feat of condemning the more vicious characteristics of contemporary capitalism, while repeatedly excoriating the utopian 'solutions' of the socialists. It also had important things to say on the role of the state as well as private associations of citizens in achieving a more just society.

Subtitled 'rights and duties of capital and labour', *Rerum novarum* began by emphasising the importance of the 'social question': 'The momentous gravity of the state of things now obtaining fills every mind with painful apprehension; wise men are discussing it; practical men are proposing schemes; popular meetings, legislatures, and rulers of nations are all busied with it – actually there is no question which has taken deeper hold on the public mind.' Much of this discussion filtered into the encyclical, whose detailed proposals consisted of more than nostalgic pious generalities, and reflected the fact that the pope had previously indicated his concern with economic and social questions on several occasions.[80]

The pope was keenly aware of the topicality of industrial conflict, which in 1886 led to strikes and bloodshed in the industrial regions of Belgium, a country he had known as a nuncio. He may have mentioned medieval guilds and fraternities, but the encyclical was informed by industrial society in the late nineteenth century. He was cognisant of the discussions at the Catholic Congresses of Liège which were held in the wake of the Belgian disturbances from 1886 onwards, and of the private discussions of the Fribourg Union, a group of corporatist opponents of modern liberalism from Austria, Belgium, France, Italy and Switzerland who met for a week each year to discuss Catholic solutions to social questions.[81] Leo XIII had an audience with nine of its members in 1888 and two years later made its convener a cardinal. Further afield, Leo refrained from joining the Canadian bishops in condemning the American Knights of Labour, a large union whose membership and president were Catholics, not only because the union enjoyed the support of the US hierarchy, but because they indicated how Catholicism might flourish in a modern democracy. He also did nothing to impede Britain's cardinal Manning when he successfully and very visibly mediated in the 1889 London dock strike.

The encyclical steered a careful but steady course despite the passions of the day. While the pope condemned 'crafty agitators' who sought to exploit 'the poor man's envy of the rich', and dismissed socialism for its 'pleasant dreams' of an ideal equality which would in reality mean 'the levelling down of all to a like condition of misery and degradation', he also inveighed against 'the hardheartedness of employers and the greed of unchecked competition' which had enabled 'a small number of very rich men . . . to lay upon the teeming masses of the labouring poor a yoke little better than that of slavery'. The modern rich were not especially happy; rather, through greed and the quest for sensation, they risked becoming 'a void of self-restraint miserable in the midst of abundance'.

The pope constantly reiterated the importance of private property and of the family, while he categorically rejected the claim that class conflict was either endemic or inevitable. In reality the various classes were inter-dependent: 'capital cannot do without labour, nor labour without capital'.

The twentieth clause dealt with the mutual obligations of employers and employees. It is noteworthy that the former received far greater attention. Employers were to respect the dignity of labour, never forgetting that men are not machines whose powers were to be exhausted ad infinitum. To treat men in such a fashion would be 'truly shameful and inhuman', as would the exploitation of children or women in tasks for which they were unsuited and which would prejudice both their development and the well-being of the family. Employers were duty bound to ensure that workers had time for both their religious observances and a fulfilling home and family life. Wages were to be fair rather than reflections of the iron laws of free-market economics; to defraud people of wages (a not uncommon occurrence) was 'a great crime which cries out to the avenging anger of heaven'. In keeping with the encyclical's capacity to see things in a long continuum, Leo argued that wages were to be sufficiently generous as to facilitate modest saving, which would conduce to a more equitable and widespread distribution of property that would in turn benefit society. More general ownership of property would bridge the gap between rich and poor, enhance productivity and stem the tides of desperate migrants. However, these benefits of wider property ownership would be vitiated by 'excessive taxation'.

Recalling that 'civil society was renovated in every part by Christian institutions', Leo argued that the future lay in a 'return to Christian life and Christian institutions'. For over a thousand years the Church had practised charity, as even its bitterest critics grudgingly acknowledged. However, the time had come for the state to lend a helping hand with 'general laws', but without undue interference in spheres, notably the family, where it had no business. One of the functions of the state was to ensure that the workers, who made the greatest contribution to any nation's wealth, should share in the benefits, and receive decent clothing, housing and health care. However, the pope was careful to retain and encourage spaces for initiatives from individuals and associations, whether charitable, co-operative or, and here was the biggest departure, in the form of both mixed employer and employee and exclusively working-class associations and trade unions. Since some unions were working to covert political agendas, Catholics were urged to form their own unions in which the rights of religion would be respected. The state had no business in prohibiting man's natural right to private association. Leo took the opportunity to condemn those contemporary governments, notably that of France, which permitted trade unions while simultaneously prohibiting religious confraternities, societies and orders.

Although much of this seems uncontroversial nowadays, except to the most dogmatic socialist or free-marketeer, at the time it was considered highly radical. Speaking a year later, Albert de Mun recalled:

> Do you remember the tremendous surprise the encyclical caused to all who like to look on the Church as only a sort of gendarme in the service of bourgeois society, and to all the comfortably off who were scandalized when they heard the highest authority in the world sanction ideas and doctrines which hitherto they had regarded as fatally subversive?[82]

The first episcopal response to the encyclical came from Victor Doutreloux, archbishop of Liège in Belgium. This was partly because the encyclical had caused divisions between the ruling conservative Catholic Party (which dominated Belgian politics from 1880 to 1919) and the Democratic Belgium League (with a separate organisation in Flanders), both of which sought to give the workers a voice by infiltrating their views into the Catholic Party. While in some areas these conservative and democratic Catholics co-operated against the liberals and socialists, elsewhere their bitter rivalry gave their opponents victory. The conservative Catholics turned to archbishop Doutreloux for support against their democratic Catholic opponents. Both the archbishop and cardinal Goosens rejected their implorations, telling Catholic industrialists to fall in with the spirit of *Rerum novarum*. Thanks to the rearguard action fought by Catholic Party leader Charles Woeste, it was not until 1907 that the ideas of the democratic 'Young Right' made an impact on the Party. Depressed by these delays, the priest who led the Flemish branch of the Young Right formed his own Christian People's Party that succeeded in leaching votes away from the socialists. Both the Church and the Catholic Party crushed this development, with the result that the Flemish workers were lost to the socialists.[83]

The encyclical encouraged Catholics to concern themselves with social questions, while the Ralliement raised the question of how they were to engage with the political system. What is often called the 'second' Christian Democracy (to distinguish it from the 'first' of 1848) was influenced by the conservative criticisms of liberalism and socialism associated with the names Albert de Mun and Le Play, but at the same time rejected their hierarchical and paternalist view of society. They accorded the state a certain right to intervene in industrial affairs, and supported the creation of exclusively working-class unions and participation in factory decision-making. They also accepted the Republic and sometimes participated in its political life. For example, the abbés Gayraud and Lamire were elected to the Chamber of Deputies in the 1890s.[84] Other initiatives in the late 1890s included mixed unions consisting of employers and workers, and a group of Catholic industrialists who sought to moralise commerce, by restricting purchases of goods to firms which won approval in the group's annual report, incidentally and indirectly resulting in the first antisemitic boycott in modern European history. The Association of French Catholic Youth, which had been founded in 1886, decided to open its ranks to young peasants and workers in 1896, becoming the first national socially mixed Catholic organisation in French history.

Léon Harmel organised worker study groups in the Rheims area, followed by the first national Christian worker congresses, which were held in Rheims and Lyons between 1893 and 1900. These congresses insisted upon the sanctity of religion, the family, and private property, while arguing that laws should conform to the Ten Commandments and the Gospels. They also lobbied for the protection of Sundays, a ten-hour working day, the protection of small enterprises and the abolition of night work. In 1896 the congresses were renamed Congress of Christian Democracy. It was also decided to establish a political party whose allegiance would be republican and popular in orientation. While the former signified a break with legitimism, the latter did not signify an exclusive subscription to democracy. Only by isolating a single strand within this movement can it be regarded as the ancestor of post-Second World War 'Christian Democracy'.[85]

Localised and subject to the influence of myriad minor newspapers, Christian Democracy was regarded with suspicion in various quarters, sometimes for entirely justifiable reasons. Albert de Mun thought it was detaching the workers from the guiding reins of the socially conscious upper classes. Industrialists disliked its sponsorship of exclusively working-class trades unions, of which the first, formed in 1899, soon grew to over six hundred thousand members. The French hierarchy also disapproved of the anti-masonic, anti-Protestant and antisemitic enthusiasms of many Christian Democrats, as manifested in the 'France for the French' slogans that graced many of their newspapers, notably *La France Libre*. Christian Democracy was also supported by the Assumptionist organ *La Croix*, one of France's largest daily newspapers, and one of the worst exponents of the conspiracy explanation of the Third Republic. Cardinal Couillé was among those to prohibit his priests from joining Christian Democracy because of its antisemitism. The Dreyfus Affair led to the outflow of many Christian Democrats to the nationalist extreme right, while the aged pope's 1901 encyclical *Graves de communire* set limits to the flirtation of Christian Democrats not only with the left but with any one political system. Leo implicitly and obliquely endorsed the suspicions of 'many excellent men' regarding Christian Democracy:

> It seems by implication covertly to favour popular government and to disparage other methods of political administration. Secondly, it appears to belittle religion by restricting its scope to

care of the poor, as if the other sections of society were not of its concern. More than that, under the shadow of its name there might easily lurk a design to attack all legitimate power, either civil or sacred.

Leo reasserted the Church's traditional agnosticism towards political forms so long as they were in harmony with morality and justice. It condemned class warfare and fraternisation with socialists, and warned against an over-emphasis upon social justice at the expense of traditional Christian charity. Only initiatives that were firmly embedded in the Church's own hierarchy would henceforth receive his favour.[86]

Even as the hierarchy sought to rein in the trade unionist and party political elements in Christian Democracy, so its banner passed to the Catholic youth movement. A charismatic young Catholic former army officer called Marc Sangnier founded a spiritual study group which took its name from a journal called *Le Sillon* (The Furrow). An admirer described Sangnier's ability to attract people 'as the fingers of the bird-charmer attract the sparrows'; a rather disillusioned François Mauriac wrote of 'the disarranged necktie, the untidy hair, the rather coarse mouth set in a heavy face, the enormous neck, and the flabby cheeks, always badly shaven'. From 1899 onwards the Sillon brought together artisans, clerks, middle-class students and workers, as friends rather than as patrons and clients, the idea being that class differences would dissolve in Christian fellowship. Its ends were rather vague, largely consisting of an unending spiritual journey. As an 'immaterial link between souls' the Sillon had no membership dues or lists of who belonged, no formalities and no rules, so people seem to have come and gone as they chose.

It attracted wider notice when the group began to hold mass meetings, which were attended by hecklers and toughs from the markets at Les Halles, drawn to such confrontational theatrics as having Sangnier debate with an apostate priest. In 1901 the Sillon acquired a Young Guard, with boxing skills, black berets, white shirts and black ties, which only confirms that Christian fellowship was in short supply in France at the turn of the century.[87] It must be the only paramilitary outfit in modern history whose remit was 'to enforce respect for freedom of speech and debate'. To add to its confusion, the Young Guard's rituals were based on those of medieval military religious orders, whose spirit was certainly not characterised by either of the foregoing values. About ten thousand young people probably joined the various regional groups, whose aim was to produce a socially conscious Catholic elite, derived from all classes, who would go out to serve the entire unredeemed community. This elite would be selected rather than elected, for Sangnier's vision of the political future was of a meritocratic worker elite presiding over a society consisting of voluntary associations like trades unions. In the early 1900s the Sillon attempted to develop from being a Christian ginger group into a new, mould-breaking political party that would break through the anticlerical republican bloc and the bloc of Catholic anti-republicans. Its ideology seems rather confused: a self-professed elite that condemned capitalism and regarded democracy as 'the social organ-isation which tends to maximise the conscience and civic responsibility of each individual', and a Catholic organisation that extended the hand of friendship to freethinkers and Protestants.

The increasing politicisation of the Sillon led a growing number of French bishops to forbid their priests to join it. On 25 August 1910 pope Pius X wrote to the French hierarchy condemning Sangnier's claim that Catholics only owed obedience in matters of faith and the Sillon's pretensions to exemption from ecclesiastical hierarchies. Lest anyone mistake his views, Pius added:

> This limpid and rushing stream has been captured in the course of its forward flow by the modern enemies of the Church, to form henceforth nothing more than a miserable tributary to the great modern movement of apostasy organised in all countries with the aim of establishing a universal Church that will have neither dogma, hierarchy, nor rules for spiritual life, that will put no check on man's passions, and that, under the pretext of liberty and human dignity, would bring about in the world, did it but triumph, the legal rule of trickery and force, and the oppression of the weak and of those who toil and suffer.

After a brief period of submission, Sangnier devoted himself to purely political activities, becoming a deputy immediately after the First World War.

As in the 1813–15 wars of liberation against Napoleon, so in 1870–1 the god of war had turned the tide of battle in favour of Germans of a Protestant persuasion. Bismarck's victories over Austria and France were widely regarded as triumphs for Protestantism, rather than superior generalship and weaponry. As the *Evangelische Kirchenzeitung* crowed, the war was 'a victory of the loyal subject over Revolution, of heavenly order against anarchy, of the virtuous powers over the immorality of the flesh, of hierarchical rule over popular sovereignty'. In such circles it followed that the newly founded German Reich would be based on a clear self-understanding as an emphatically Christian, Protestant German state. This was hyperbolic since the new Reich consisted of twenty-five federal states (some of which were overwhelmingly Roman Catholic in composition), while there were twenty-eight autonomous Protestant Churches, some of them very reluctant to be absorbed by Prussia's Old Union.

An attempt to achieve the ecclesiastical equivalent of national unification in October 1871 by uniting the autonomous Protestant Churches ended in disarray and disunion. Nor did the undoubted upsurge of militant patriotism translate into an equivalent upsurge in religious enthusiasm, partly, it should be said, because the Protestant triumphalism was tempered by calls for atonement and warnings that national arrogance had brought down Napoleon III.[88] Not only did Bismarck and the ascendant National Liberals refuse to accord the Protestant Churches the central position some of the pastors craved. Worse, during the Kulturkampf, the liberals' anticlerical animus seeped from the Roman Catholics to the Prussian–conservative–Protestant establishment, whose traditional values they wished their own individualistic creed would displace. The major flashpoints between liberals and Protestants were over the introduction of civil marriage, and attempts to prise the pastors' grip from teachers in elementary and secondary schools. There were also worrying signs of defection from the Protestant Churches which contributed to their mood of epochal decline. In the new capital, Germany's largest industrial city, only two-thirds of children born to Protestant parents were being baptised, while only a quarter of Protestant couples eligible to marry in church did so, after the introduction of civil marriage in October 1874. The Protestant Churches seemed mired in the agrarian past, at a time when they needed to win over the urban bourgeoisie and the toiling masses, a chronic failing of German conservatism in general.

One of those to be appalled by these signs of religious indifference was the Court preacher Adolf Stoecker, who had risen from a humble rural smithy to become a military chaplain during the Franco-Prussian War. His solid face, immaculately groomed whiskers and piggy eyes suggest a certain Teutonic determination. Rather coarsely, Bismarck observed that 'his gob is like a sword'. Stoecker was vehemently opposed to the Social Democrats, continuing to regard them as an unpatriotic, revolutionary Party long after such a description disregarded the reformist facts. However, his main animus was directed at 'Manchester liberalism', and the Jews he held responsible for it, a claim that was untroubled by the likes of Adam Smith. Liberal individualism was undermining a God-given ethical and political order; while the rapacious capitalism that accompanied it was responsible for the advent of revolutionary socialism. Jews, he claimed, were over-represented among prominent liberals and socialists.

Stoecker was not, however, simply an antisemitic cum anti-socialist agitator. He was convinced that 'Germany's misfortune is the impotence of the Evangelical spirit'. Rather than shoring up the decrepit alliance of throne and altar, he wanted to make the 'people's Church' truly independent of the state, so that it could then exercise powerful moral leadership over both state and nation. The Church, in turn, should concentrate on consolidating its activist core, largely through charitable work for the Inner Mission network, whose example would then draw in the far larger number of nominal Protestants in the population. This was ambitious, given the rather paltry results Stoecker achieved when he turned from running Berlin's City Mission and his duties at Court to active politics.

On 3 January 1878 Stoecker held a meeting in a pub called the Eiskeller to recruit working-class socialist Berliners to a new Christian Social Workers' Party.[89] After a stuttering performance by a renegade socialist, Stoecker gave an impassioned speech in which he attacked liberalism and socialism, while calling for comprehensive social reform and enjoining the workers to turn to Christianity. Johannes Most, a fiery Social Democrat orator, immediately retorted: 'The days of Christianity are numbered and one can only respond to the priests with the cry: make your peace with heaven, your hour has run its course.'[90] Stoecker essayed a few further meetings, which invariably concluded with rival renditions of the Internationale and the Lutheran hymn 'Ein' feste Burg ist unser Gott'.

Stoecker drew up the programme of the Christian Social Workers' Party with the aid of professor Adolph Wagner. Article 1 declared that the Party 'is founded on the Christian faith and upon love of King and Country'. It advocated national workers' co-operatives, compulsory arbitration of industrial disputes, comprehensive and compulsory welfare arrangements, the reintroduction of laws against usury, and progressive income and inheritance taxes, as well as the eradication of all 'coarseness' from entertainment and the cultivation of family life in the Christian spirit.[91]

When Stoecker's Party did conspicuously badly in the July 1878 Reichstag elections, winning a mere 1,422 votes, or less than the sum total of the Party's membership, he shifted his attentions from workers to artisans, shopkeepers and small farmers outside the ambit of the traditional conservatives. In September 1879 he was elected to the Prussian House of Deputies, and two years later to the Reichstag, while his Christian Socials (the word Workers was quietly dropped) became a populist adjunct to the Conservative Party.

Stoecker sought to appeal to this social constituency by attacking the Jews as, to adapt the leading Borussian historian Treitschke's contemporary aspersion, the architects of their misfortune.[92] But the message also appealed to other constituencies. Like Treitschke, Stoecker did much to make antisemitism respectable, especially since the students whose minds he poisoned would go on to become civil servants, doctors, lawyers, judges, professors and so forth. Antisemitism became institutionally embedded in such lobby groups as the Agrarian League or the DHV which represented commercial employees. With malicious subtlety Stoecker spoke on the theme of 'Our demands on modern Judaism', parodying the Jews' own emancipatory demands, while enjoining the Jews to exercise more equality, modesty and tolerance towards a Christian society which, having lost their own faith, they allegedly wished to subvert. His attacks on the wealthiest and most influential Jews, notably Bismarck's banker Gerson Bleichröder, irritated the ruling elites.[93] Bismarck regarded Stoecker as a nuisance whose politics were driven by obscure ecclesio-political urges. 'I have nothing against Stoecker,' he wrote to crown prince Wilhelm; 'in my eyes he has only one failing as a politician, that he is a priest, and as a priest, that he pursues politics.' That did not inhibit the chancellor from offering Stoecker tacit support in the 1881 Berlin elections since the Christian Socials and their antisemitic allies promised to weaken support in the capital for the Progressive liberals. Stoecker was closely connected to such notorious racial antisemites as Wilhelm Marr (an atheist), Bernhard Förster (mobilising signatories for Marr's 1880 antisemitic petition), Otto Glagau, Ernst Henrici and Max Liebermann von Sonnenberg. The concerns of these racial antisemites began to figure amid Stoecker's cultural, economic and political reasons for opposing the emancipation of the Jews, up to and including talk of 'parasites' contaminating German blood or a sinister credulity towards tales of blood libel. Leading Protestants, as well as the Catholic leader Windthorst, denounced Stoecker's antisemitic demagoguery, which in some places resulted in anti-Jewish riots.

Stoecker's oft-rehearsed role in the dismal history of modern German Protestant antisemitism (which was far more consequential to the electoral basis of Nazism than the better publicised failings of the Roman Catholic Church) has largely occluded his indirect contribution to the expectation that, for reasons of Christian humanity as well as to emasculate the socialists, the state should guarantee certain minimal rights to the most distressed sectors of society. An extraordinarily advanced welfare policy, whatever its many limitations, was the sugared analogue of the stick represented by the 1878–90 Anti-Socialist Laws. An Evangelical Christian from Stoecker's milieu was one of the most important advisers to Bismarck when he introduced the social insurance legislation of the 1880s, including the Sickness Insurance Law of 1883, the Accident Insurance Law of 1884, and the Old Age and Disability Insurance Law of 1889. Bismarck himself referred to this legislation as 'practical Christianity' and Stoecker regarded it as the implementation of Christian Social policy.

Relations between Stoecker and traditional conservatives cooled once the latter realised that the passions he was arousing were inherently unstable. In 1890 the Higher Consistory of the Grand Duchy of Hessen had to admonish young clergy to refrain from aiding and abetting antisemitic candidates in elections. Stoecker was stirring up expectations that no government could satisfy, something that applied to many of the other noisy nationalist pressure groups that proliferated in that era. His supporters were also destabilising the traditional elite domination of conservative party politics. His Christian Social organisation, which had become indispensable to the mobilisation of electoral support for the conservatives, began to dominate conservative party congresses, successfully inserting an explicitly antisemitic statement into the 1892 Tivoli conservative programme, against the wishes of the notable elites who had hitherto controlled party affairs.[94]

The accession of kaiser Wilhelm II in February 1890 seemed to Stoecker an opportune moment to revive his reforming social agenda. This had become urgent since in that year Bismarck's anti-socialist legislation was due to expire, while the Ruhr coalfields witnessed a viciously fought miners' strike.

In May 1890 Stoecker summoned eight hundred Protestant pastors to an Evangelical–Social Congress. The Congress discussed virtually every aspect of the social question in debates that were impressively informed but which appalled traditional conservatives who wanted no reform at all. Three major groupings evolved in the wider context of 'Pastors' Socialism'. First, there were older Christian Socials, including Stoecker, who wanted a populist conservative, but non-governmental, movement of social reform based on virulent anti-socialism. Secondly, there were Social Liberals, like the historian Adolf von Harnack, who desired a sober discussion of social realities and of how the Christian ethic might humanise modern industrial society. Finally, there was a group of Young Christian Socials, exemplified by the pastors Paul Göhre, author of a bestseller about his three months as a factory hand, and Friedrich Naumann, who sought an accommodation with the revisionist wing of the Social Democrats. The latter were in the process of abandoning the Party's infantile Marxist revolutionism in order to come to terms with the economic realities of the 1890s while seeking to widen the Party's base beyond working-class ghettos.

In 1894, following a survey of a thousand rural pastors, the Young Christian Social Paul Göhre and Max Weber sharply criticised conditions in the agrarian east of Germany, thereby endangering the old operational alliance of landowner and pastor. The emperor, whose views on industrial relations were increasingly being shaped by Karl Freiherr von Stumm-Halberg and the higher consistory of the Protestant Church in Berlin, banned clergy and theologians from any further interventions in the field of social policy. They had a point since the Young Christian Socials were compromising the political neutrality of the Churches through their amateurish and biased interventions in politics and attempted arrogation of the role of umpire in social conflicts, although one should equally acknowledge that the Church authorities themselves were as correspondingly political in the sense of being vehemently anti-socialist defenders of the status quo.

Having already been dismissed from his Court position, Stoecker was expelled from the conservative party in February 1896 over the so-called Scheiterhaufenbrief or 'funeral pyre letter'. A year before, the Social Democrats had made public a highly embarrassing letter that Stoecker had written to the editor of the conservative *Kreuzzeitung* in 1888, whose gist was the need to sow the fires of discord between Bismarck and Wilhelm so that the latter would blow up like a bonfire and dismiss the chancellor, as indeed occurred when the German pilot was unceremoniously dropped two years later. But by 1895, when the letter was published, the cult of the former chancellor was in full swing, and Stoecker's stock was low. Having decided to abandon his initial flirtation with reform, Wilhelm leaked a letter that announced: 'Christian Socialism is nonsense and leads to presumptuousness and impatience. The clerical gentlemen should concern themselves with the souls of their parishioners, and leave politics alone, since it doesn't concern them.' Stoecker attempted to form an independent Christian Social Party in Frankfurt, but it was not a success. Naumann and forty-four of his clerical associates left the Church to form a separate National Social Association, and to engage fully in politics, which although a pastor himself he thought no longer had nothing to do with religion.[95]

Outsiders, who are routinely deaf to the nuances of religion in Germany, are often perplexed as to how Nazism could have taken root in a Christian nation, without over-troubling themselves with the question whether one part of that proposition is true. The story of Stoecker shows the extent to which Protestantism had become polluted with antisemitism and chauvinism, at the expense of traditional Christian values. But that is only half of the story, for nominal Protestants were hardly impressed by Adolf Stoecker. By the end of the nineteenth century, the Protestant middle classes in Germany had largely distanced themselves from the Churches, viewing them coolly as survivals from a world that had passed. They were no longer even necessary to the maintenance of external social respectability, which could just as easily be accrued from attendance at a classical concert or public lecture. Enormous credulity was shown towards a vulgar scientism; theology, once among the most topical of subjects, only sparked any interest when it touched on history or philosophy. Of course, that does not mean that their very being was not deeply influenced by residual Christian values. They believed, passionately, in the absolute value of the individual, in the vital role of individual conscience, in moral responsibility and in a sense of duty,

whether to family, society or their country. The inner space they culti-
vated so assiduously and earnestly may have been increasingly informed
by art or science, but an inner space it remained, a notion meaningless
to outright materialists. Their sense of patriotic duty was also shaped by
a religious exaltation of the German nation, into which fed the influences
of the 'national' reformer Luther, an idealist Prussian–Protestant vener-
ation of the state, vulgar anti-Catholicism and a militarism as informed
by Christianity as that of late-Victorian England: for after 1914 'Gott mit
uns' proved as much a rallying cry as 'Onward Christian Soldiers'.

A militant materialism may have characterised the leading lights of
the Social Democratic Party, but attempts to induce the rank and file
actively to renounce the Churches were spectacularly unsuccessful, partly
because this would result in domestic trouble with wives who were often
conventionally religious. Again, the world of socialism was not so free
of the grasp of the Churches as it pretended. The guiding vision of the
collapse of capitalism and the advent of a classless, ideal society owed a
great deal to Christian eschatology. As Friedrich Naumann recognised,
the power of socialism was in no small measure due to the fact that 'this
doctrine is in a position to create a mood, which is similar to the mood
in many religious sects, which put all their hopes in a great day of wrath
and joy, and which bravely winds its way through daily life, because the
morning star of the thousand year Reich is already in the heavens'. Aside
from the ultimate vision, the comrades' world was informed by a high
sense of moral purpose and self-sacrifice, by absolute adhesion to a set
of incontrovertible dogmas, as relayed by the Party prophets with the
aid of sacred screeds, and by a radical intolerance of any heretical, let
alone opposed, point of view. Miners' choirs and the like were secular
surrogates; the Internationale was sung to the tune of a well-known
Christmas hymn. The Party did especially well in overwhelmingly Protestant regions, achieving 55 per cent of the 1912 poll in Saxony, 40.4 per
cent in Schleswig-Holstein, and almost 50 per cent in Brandenburg.
Whatever the Protestant Churches were failing to supply to the workers
by way of community, meaning and ultimate purpose was being provided by the living witness of an avowedly atheist political party. How
much more susceptible might they, and their fellow countrymen, be if
that party was truly indistinguishable from a religion?

If the record of nineteenth-century German Protestantism in the field
of social policy is unimpressive, as it was almost bound to be given Protestantism's involvements with the conservative political Establishment,

what of the Roman Catholics? Industrialisation and urbanisation threatened the homogeneity of Catholic Germany by fostering solidarities between workers, whatever their confessional or political backgrounds. Moreover, the desire of Catholics for equality and parity of esteem in a society dominated by Protestants, could also lead to working-class Catholics demanding the same from the wealthier and more powerful members of their own community. On a theoretical level, there were two kinds of Catholic response to the social evils attendant upon industrialisation. One was to hark back to the supposed harmonies of medieval society through an updated form of corporatism, which would steer a middle course between liberal individualism and socialist collectivism, or between the 'power of money without religion' and 'power of workers without religion' as Catholic contemporaries put it. The other approach was to accept current realities, smoothing their harder edges through a combination of state intervention and the legalisation of workers' associations and the right to strike. Although the former tendency remained a powerful undercurrent in some quarters, in practice the latter, with its implicit acceptance of the market (albeit with its inevitable excesses curbed by Catholic moral philosophy, the state and powerful subsidiary associations), eventually set the pace.[96]

In 1877 a nephew of bishop Ketteler, count Maximilian Gereon Galen, introduced in the Reichstag a petition that combined such detailed measures as protection of the right to work and Sundays as a time of rest, with neo-medieval corporatist solutions to the atomistic individualism of modern industrial society. More significantly, the Catholics rose to the challenge that Social Democracy represented to their urban working-class constituency. In 1879 Franz Brandts, a reform-minded textile manufacturer in Mönchengladbach, and the priest Franz Hitze formed Worker Welfare, an attempt to copy Léon Harmel's French fusion of paternalism and piety. This was explicitly designed to combat the influence of the Social Democrats upon Catholic workers. So too were the associations of Catholic workers that proliferated during the 1880s in the industrial regions of the Prussian Rhineland provinces and Silesia. In 1889 there were 168 of these associations, by 1906 some 656 with 114,613 members. Each association was led by a priest, an arrangement that ensured they were closely tied to the interests and outlook of the Church. Their goal was to neutralise 'class' consciousness by emphasising the ethical–professional aspects of each craft. In the 1890s the local branches came together in larger regional associations for each point of the compass.

These regional groupings developed their own workers' press, the *Westdeutsche Arbeiterzeitung* achieveing a circulation of two hundred thousand.

Parallel with these workers' associations, the Volksverein für das katholische Deutschland was designed to promote parity of representation for Catholics in both state and society in the wake of the Kulturkampf. It was open to Catholics of all social classes, with the membership set at a token one mark so as to encourage the poorest. Membership grew from an initial one hundred thousand to eight hundred thousand by the eve of the First World War. It published a newspaper and pamphlets that discussed current issues from a Catholic perspective, while its seminars and meetings helped train future generations of Catholic leaders. Its importance lay in democratising the political culture of German Catholicism as well as expanding its horizons beyond the Church–state conflicts of the Kulturkampf era.[97]

The nationwide miners' strike in 1889 saw the formation of trade unions, whose wider orientation both socialists and non-socialist workers sought to dominate. When the Catholic miners effectively lost this battle, they established their own confessional union. Since Catholic workers were too weak to combat socialist influence, in 1894 they joined with Protestant workers to form the first inter-confessional trade union founded by August Brust in Essen. These unions were anti-socialist, nationalist, monarchist and conservative, and both pastors and priests gave them their support. The fact that they could and did resort to strikes and were increasingly led by laymen appalled those of a more traditional cast of mind. Integral Catholics based in Berlin and Trier spent the next decade opposing inter-confessional unions and any workers' representation that transcended branches for each specific craft. Their vision was of workers loyal to their employers and obedient to their priests. The fact that the Christian trade unions were under lay, working-class, rather than clerical, control, and that they could and did resort to strikes, bulked as large in integralist criticisms as the unions' retreat from the Church's insistence upon an essentially moral message. To that end, integralists supported the creation of Craft Associations within the existing Catholic Workers' Associations, thereby attempting to ensure the continued influence of clergy and employers. A bitter 'trade union dispute' broke out between the two types of worker representation, with the Catholic hierarchy largely ranged on the side of the Craft Associations.[98] Almost despite itself, the Catholic Church clung on to a significant working-class membership, with about 350,000 workers belonging to the Christian trade unions. The numbers involved in exclusively Protestant trade unions were about fifty thousand. That the Catholic trade unions constituted a mere 14 per cent of the total membership of socialist unions, who also included eight hundred thousand Catholics in their ranks, suggests the scale of the problem they faced. Nonetheless, despite the continued adhesion of the Catholic community to its Church and the practice of a rather kitschy form of religiosity, it is striking that in many respects German Catholics had negotiated the journey to a modern, pluralistic world rather better than their Protestant neighbours, whose failure to adapt was symbolised by the career of Adolf Stoecker. His rabble-rousing fusion of Christianity and antisemitism was one harbinger of what was to come, though there were worshippers of strange gods whose tidings would win followings in the aftermath of the Great War, the source of the Durkheimian 'effervescence' out of which Fascism and Nazism would flow.

CHAPTER 10

Apocalypse 1914

Recognition of the social and political utility of religion was a familiar refrain in modern French history; as the example of Thiers suggests, this was compatible with an anticlerical contempt for the Church. Among such cynics, Paris was certainly worth a mass. By the turn of the century, however, more sinister doctrines were on the loose, in which even formal subscription to the tenets of Christianity was abandoned, a development that sections of the Church chose to overlook.

In 1906 a book was published in Paris entitled *The Dilemma of Marc Sangnier*. It consisted of a collection of polemics directed at the charismatic leader of the Sillon movement who, readers will recall, had sought to reconcile Christianity with democracy and social reform. This need not detain us here. However, the book's dedication read: 'To the Roman Church, to the Church of Order'. This was startling since its author, the thirty-eight-year-old Charles Maurras, was an atheist admirer of ancient Hellas, a neo-royalist and a Comtean Positivist to boot. The dedication of the book was like the offer of a handshake. It had some precedent in the life of Auguste Comte himself. In the year of his death, 1857, Comte had despatched one of his disciples to the Gesù, the Jesuit headquarters in Rome, to offer the Order's Superior an alliance against Deism, Protestantism 'and the other forms of modern anarchy' that his own Religion of Humanity was supposed to counteract. Since the Jesuit host had never heard of Auguste Comte, and confused him with a French economist, Charles Comte, there was no meeting of minds, especially as Comte's representative wanted Catholics to 'progress' from 'special worship of the Virgin' to the worship of Humanity itself.

Charles Maurras was born in April 1868 in the fishing port of Martigues in the Bouche-de-Rhône. Even after he had immersed himself in the frenetic world of journalism under Paris's leaden skies, Maurras' nostalgia for the harsh light of the south was intense; in that respect he resembles the deracinated Algerian Albert Camus. Maurras' father, who died in 1874, was a tax collector with no known religious beliefs; his mother was a pious royalist. The boy's hopes for a career as a naval officer died when at the age of fourteen he became deaf. In 1885 the seventeen-year-old Maurras moved, with his mother and younger brother, to Paris where he began contributing to conservative and Catholic journals, despite the fact that he had already lost his religious faith, apparently because 'the Good cannot conceive of Evil, nor perfection produce imperfection'. During this time he developed his lifelong interest in Provençal literature and his fascination with France's historic regions. As this already suggests, Maurras' literary preoccupations fed directly into his political convictions.

There was only one cultural tradition that counted. It had been born in Greece during the Hellenic period and then translated to western Europe by the Roman Empire, where the Catholic Church sustained it. Its apogee had been the France of the seventeenth century, that is of Bossuet, Corneille, Descartes, La Fontaine and Racine. In other words it was classicism, whose harmony and order contrasted unfavourably with the decadent Romantic solipsism that followed, in which every foreign goose – Shakespeare, Goethe, Kant, Tolstoy, Wagner and Ibsen – was regarded as a swan.[1] There was a political–theological version of this tale of woe. The ancien régime, which Maurras idealised out of all recognition, had been destroyed by alien ideas imported from England and Switzerland by Voltaire, Montesquieu and Rousseau. They were all victims, especially Maurras' bête noire Rousseau, of the malady of Protestant individualism that had mutated into the anarchy and subjectivism of both the Revolution and the nineteenth-century Romantic movement as a whole. Maurras did not care for either Germans or Jews, which probably accounts for one of the more creative leaps in his thinking. Protestantism was nothing more than a Teutonic version of an anarchic 'Jewish spirit' that had been disciplined by the Church of Rome, but whose wild prophetic mode constantly threatened further revolutionary eruptions: 'The fathers of the revolution are in Geneva, in Wittenberg, and in more ancient times in Jerusalem; they derive from the Jewish spirit and from varieties of an independent Christianity which were rampant in Eastern deserts and Teutonic forests, in the various focal points of barbarism.' This was a very novel slant on the democracy of the Teutonic forests which generations of Oxford history students had imbibed from poor bishop Stubbs. Bizarrely, Maurras was arguing that Catholicism was to be admired as a bulwark against the very anarchy and subversion he detected in Christianity itself. But then any leap of fancy was permissible in the name of the goddess that was France.[2]

Maurras identified an influential confederacy of Protestants, freemasons, 'metics' (the Athenian term for resident foreigners with lesser political rights) and Jews, a veritable 'anti-France' responsible for ruining the 'true' France through their dominance of the educational, financial, intellectual and political Establishment of the Republic.[3] The solution was the product of Maurras' home thoughts from abroad. In 1896 he attended the Olympic Games in his capacity of freelance journalist. An antique bust, which an Athenian museum claimed resembled Christ, forced Maurras to seek the afternoon sun. As darkness fell, he identified the suffering God with the onset of the long night of the modern age. Contemplating the chaos of Greek politics, and the success of athletes from the two monarchies Britain and Germany, his thoughts clouded over as they drifted to the turbulence abroad in France. He returned home at the height of the Dreyfus Affair, when the League for the Defence of the Rights of Man, which supported revision of Dreyfus' case, found itself facing the Ligue de la Patrie Française seeking to maintain the injustice of the status quo.

This conflict provided Maurras with his moment. In the autumn of 1898 he published an extraordinary defence of colonel Henry, who had committed suicide in a prison cell after the exposure of his role in forging documents incriminating Dreyfus. Maurras took the view that, while it was unjust to sentence an innocent man, it would be more unconscionable to undermine the French army since this would endanger national security, the army's all-weathers argument for avoiding investigation. The Dreyfusards may have subscribed to 'fiat iustitia, ruat caelum' (let justice be done though the heavens fall), but Maurras believed in the absolute primacy of raison d'état. While shifts in the Republic's political landscape and the tenacity of Dreyfus' supporters inclined to a, disgracefully protracted, revision of his conviction, a few opponents of revision concluded that the Ligue de la Patrie Française was too cautiously conservative a vehicle for their views. Two young men, Henri Vaugeois and Maurice Pujo, founded a Comité d'Action

Française, whose platform sought recruits 'to remake France, republican and free, into a State as organized at home, as powerful abroad, as it was under the Old Regime'.[4] In 1899 they met Maurras, whom they already admired, and the journal *Revue de l'Action Française* was born. While the original founders had republican sympathies, this changed under the influence of Maurras, who in 1899 published a manifesto entitled *Dictator and King*. This began with the warning that a monarchical dictatorship would visit 'public vengeance ... [on] the ringleaders of the present troubles'. Thereafter, and in contrast to the present nanny-like 'Caesar-state' responsible for mismanaging everything from 'non-inflammable matches' to 'hare-brained education', the monarchy would restore the traditional liberties of the family, communes, municipalities, professional associations and the great historic regions of France:

> The citizen, in every sphere where he is competent and directly affected, where he is capable of knowing and therefore judging, is, at the present time, no more than a slave. Royal power will restore to him the sovereignty and freedom of action in this domain which was seized from him illegally, uselessly and to the detriment of the nation's strength.[5]

If this sounds like the stock-in-trade of modern neo-liberal conservatives, the rest of Maurras' rejection letter to the 'ridiculous republic' was more ominous. Power was to be 'handed over' to the successors of the House of Capet (he meant the Orléanist pretender who lived in Seville) 'by solemn and irrevocable covenant'. The future monarch would be liberated from 'the rivalry of parties, assemblies and electoral caprice'. 'Competent' people would assist the task of governance through local and provincial assemblies, while the representatives of economic and cultural corporations would fill the king's council. The representatives of the nation would be drawn from those who produce and work, rather than from 'that pack of scoundrels, intriguers and gossips who, under the pretext of an electoral mandate, jam the corridors of the Palais Bourbon or the Luxembourg: irrelevant to the nation, isolated from the nation, in terms of both its interests and its needs'. What Maurras had to say about the religious question deserves quotation in extenso:

> Roman Catholicism, France's traditional religion, will be restored to all the honours to which it is entitled. Only a government of illiterate lunatics could grudge it them and, for example,

ban from the Sorbonne of Louis IX and of Gerson all teaching of theology. This regime of paltry meddling will be declared closed. However it is clear that total intellectual freedom will reign on French soil ... On the firm ground of organization and direction there can be no conflict between the religious spirit and the scientific spirit. Catholic political thought rejects revolutionary ideology – which is equally abhorrent to the positivists. As for positivist political ideas, their sympathetic affinity with Catholicism is obvious. The state will have only to impose upon itself and observe the strict injunction neither to foster nor to subsidize (unlike the present inimitable republic) theories whose ultimate objective or immediate aim is the overthrow of the state: political anarchy and its theorists will therefore be carefully controlled and if any religious organizations exist with a tendency to lead towards anarchy, they too will be subject to the same supervision, which stems from natural law. The same rule will apply to religions which might tend to be detrimental to the national interest by serving the interests of foreigners.[6]

This manifesto converted Maurras' hitherto republican colleagues to what might be termed a functional neo-royalism and a functional Catholicism, in which the spiritual content of Christianity had been evaporated out, leaving a residue consisting of the structures it had acquired from the Roman Empire. This radical, yet reactionary, formula enabled it to attract a heterodox following, including the great-nephew of Danton and the grandson of Jules Favre, as well as students drawn to the combination of intellectual brilliance and street-fighting activism that characterised the Action Française. What had started off as little more than a literary coterie exchanging radical ideas over dinner at the Boeuf à la Mode spawned organisational forms. In 1905 a League was formed to raise funds for the journal, while wealthy sponsors paid for an Institute Action Française to propagate the doctrines of neo-royalism across several fields. The names of the professorial chairs which accompanied each lecture series included those of Comte (Positivism), Barrès (nationalism) and most provocatively Syllabus of Errors (theology), for the Action Française was capable of a certain malicious wit. Another wealthy sponsor set up an Action Française publishing house, the entire institutional ensemble representing a counter-*Encyclopédie*, with the highpoint yet to come in 1908 with the newspaper *Action Française*. This led to the simultaneous formation of a network of hawkers, the Camelots du Roi, to sell the paper in the streets, a proto-paramilitary force consisting of upper-class students and lower-class toughs.[7]

As the Dreyfus case ran its course, with Dreyfus cleared of all charges in 1906, the Action Française derived a second wind from the Republic's parallel attacks on the Church. The Republic's secularising crusade, and in particular the riots that erupted when it tried to make inventories of ecclesiastical property, provided the first occasion for the Action Française to participate in political violence. In some places it took charge of such riots, as when at the Church of Saint-Symphorien in Versailles the local Action Française leader, a retired artillery captain, struck the departmental prefect in charge of breaking into the barricaded church with a chair hurled from the organ loft.[8] It also marked the point at which the Action Française began to win serious support from the Catholic Church. This was hardly surprising in view of the content and timeliness of the book which Maurras had dedicated to the orderliness of the Roman Catholic Church. Its most startling sections were not those aimed at the 'Christian anarchist called Marc Sangnier', but those subtitled 'Barbarians and Romans', an allusion to an attack on the Church delivered four years earlier by the Radical politician (and prime minister in the interim) Georges Clemenceau. 'Are we to be the France of Rome or the France of the Revolution?' he had asked. This outburst had Maurras down on his knees, hands clasped in prayer to a Positivist goddess, 'the old and saintly maternal figure of historical Catholicism', declaring 'I am a Roman.' Why?

> I am Roman, because if my forefathers had not been Roman as I am, the first barbarian invasion, between the fifth and tenth centuries, would have made me today some sort of German or Norwegian. I am Roman, because, had it not been for my tutelary Romanism, the second barbarian invasion, which took place in the sixteenth century, namely the Protestant one, would have transformed me into some sort of Swiss. I am Roman from the moment that I give myself completely over to my historical, intellectual and moral being. I am Roman, because, if I were not, I would by now have almost nothing of Frenchness about me. And I experience no difficulty whatsoever in feeling Roman in this way, the interests of Roman Catholicism and those of France being nearly always identical and nowhere contradictory.

This strange tract received weaselly conditional approbation from the Jesuit Pedro Descoqs, although in no sense was he writing on behalf of his order:

> I myself have continuously repeated that these political theories are deplorably incomplete. But let it not be said a priori that, because they are distorted, they are necessarily false; that would be to run the risk of philosophical and theological error, namely the error of assuming that reason cannot apprehend certain truths of the natural order without the notion of God and the help of Revelation. I am led, then, to conclude that, if there is an essential conflict between the system of M. Maurras and Catholic doctrine in matters of dogmatic and moral theory, there is not, when the question is considered in the abstract, insurmountable opposition in the realm of practice.

It was symptomatic of Descoqs' failure to grasp the radicality of Maurras' views that he thought the latter might benefit from closer acquaintance with Maistre and the Catholic polemicist Louis Veuillot.

This qualified defence of Maurras provoked a number of contrary responses, a reminder of the near impossibility of generalising about 'the' position of 'the' Catholic Church. The influential Catholic philosopher Maurice Blondel (who in the Second World War gave over the top floor of his house in Aix to fleeing Jews) delivered a withering riposte to Descoqs' evident enthusiasm for:

> a religion that dispenses with souls and is satisfied with gestures, a Catholicism without Christianity, a submissiveness without thought, an authority without love, a Church that would rejoice at the insulting tributes paid to the virtuosity of her interpretative and repressive system, no, it is not a great deal, and, 'all things considered', it is less than nothing and worse than anything. To accept all from God except God, all from Christ except His spirit, to preserve in Catholicism only a residue that is aristocratic and soothing for the privileged and beguiling or threatening for the lower classes – is not all this, under the pretext perhaps of thinking only about religion, really a matter of pursuing only politics?

More trenchant criticism, of both Maurras and Descoqs, came from Lucien Laberthonnière, who was the superior of an Oratorian secondary school near Paris. In early 1903 his school was refused authorisation by the Chamber of Deputies and Laberthonnière's career as a schoolmaster was at an end. Rather than leave the country, he lived in an informal religious community in Paris, becoming editor in 1905 of the *Annales de Philosophie Chrétienne*. Highly versed in the history of Church–state relations, he launched the most comprehensive attack on the synthesis of what he called Etatism and Ecclesiasticism that he detected in Maurras' thought, and on the clerics who were seduced by it. He wrote: 'While one enraptures and fools himself with some sort of earthly paradise, the other enraptures and fools himself with the dream of the perfect society. Both equally are millenarian.' Maurras' instrumental use of Catholicism to bolster his authoritarian social order was profoundly unChristian, since it literally brought the Church down to earth, making it 'a party and partial, instead of universal and catholic as God wished'. Maurras was guilty of absolutising the merely political and at the same time expelling both ethics and the ongoing quest for justice from political concerns. Most disturbing was how some clerics welcomed Maurras' interventions at this time of acute crisis in relations between Church and state: 'Maurras and company can say anything they want and he completely pagan, yet these [churchmen] will pardon everything because Maurras and company tell them that they are the heirs of Caesar and that it is their prerogative to rule the world.'

These debates took place at the height of the war which the 'peasant pope' Pius X had declared in the early 1900s against 'modernism'. By this term Pius meant diverse attempts to reconcile Catholic civilisation with such 'insanities of the modern world' as democracy and science. While the pope could not afford to damage Catholicism's relationship with the US through an outright condemnation of 'Americanism', he could dissolve the Opera dei Congressi in Italy, the extensive Catholic network preparing for the day the Church reconciled itself with the Italian state. Marc Sangnier's organisation Sillon was proscribed for similar reasons. More locally, the anti-modernist campaign was directed against those Catholic scholars who, encouraged to combat Protestant biblical scholarship, themselves declined to treat all sacred texts as inerrant manifestations of the Holy Spirit.[9] Enhanced monitoring of the opinions of the clergy led to a proto-Stalinist witch-hunt organised by the integralist priest monsignor Umberto Benigni, whose Sodality of St Pius V secretly gathered incriminating materials on modernist priests, with his agents passing this on to Rome in a coded language in which

Pius X appeared as 'Michael'.[10] Diverse clerics, including English and French Jesuits, Italian Christian democrats, the Church historian Duchesne and Marc Sangnier in France, were challenged to submit or be subjected to ecclesiastical sanctions. Among those whose careers may have been blighted were the then seminarian Angelo Roncalli, who did not see his secret file until he became pope John XXIII. In this atmosphere of hyper-orthodoxy and suspicion that characterised the Catholic Church during the modernist crisis, Laberthonnière followed Sangnier on to the lengthening list of the proscribed. In the summer of 1913 he was forbidden to edit the *Annales de Philosophie Chrétienne* or to publish anything for the rest of his life. Where did this leave Maurras and the Action Française? It would be inaccurate to imagine that Maurras enjoyed anything like total support among the higher echelons of the Catholic Church. While sympathisers of the Action Française at the Vatican may have influenced senior appointments in the French Church, it was also the case that two southern bishops, one of them making amends for having taught the young Maurras philosophy, denounced him in Rome. In January 1914 five of his books were placed on the Index of prohibited writings, a fate that also befell the Maurrasian review *L'Action Française*. However, publication of this prohibition was deferred, with the specious formula 'worthy of condemnation, but not to be condemned', and it was not until 1926 that the Catholic membership of the movement was proscribed.

Nietzsche, himself a son of the Teutonic equivalent of the manse, once wrote that, 'as children of preachers, a great many German philosophers and academicians had their first view of ministers in childhood, and hence ceased to believe in God'. Paul Bötticher, who in 1854 took the name of a maiden great-aunt to become Paul de Lagarde after she adopted him at the age of twenty-seven, was the scion of a family of Protestant pastors. As it happens his father Wilhelm was a Berlin schoolmaster who taught Latin and Greek, but that anomaly does not substantially weaken Nietzsche's case.

The family home was grimly oppressive, and not simply because of the father's crepuscular orthodox piety. Wilhelm Bötticher blamed his son for the death of his wife a few days after Paul was born. Since Lagarde's childhood experiences included being bounced on the theologian Schleiermacher's knee, it was probably inevitable that theology would be his chosen subject when he enrolled at Berlin University in 1844, although he also majored in classical philology and Oriental languages, where his true gifts lay. In addition to knowing Greek, Latin and Hebrew, Lagarde mastered Armenian, Arabic, Chaldean, Coptic, Persian and Syrian, and was au fait with many modern languages too.

He broke with the 'throne and altar' conservatism and pietism of his family background. In a queer anticipation of the Dreyfus case, he discovered that his highly orthodox professor of theology, Wilhelm Hengstenberg, was ready to excuse the fabricated evidence used to convict a liberal deputy Benedikt Waldeck of high treason. Waldeck's real 'offence' had been to criticise the counter-revolutionary cultural permafrost that descended after the 1848 Revolutions.[11] His protest against an esteemed teacher was the one trace of nobility in a life otherwise characterised by a colossal grudge. Although Lagarde was a man of prodigious learning and talent, his Nietzschean impatience with institutionalised mediocrity doomed him to the humblest peripheries of Germany's hierarchical academic life. The speed with which he edited and published abstruse texts made him a target for the nation's professorial Beckmessers, although he was admired by the classicist Wilamowitz-Moellendorf, who delivered Lagarde's funeral oration, and by an English audience that largely knew this confirmed anglophile through his writings. Thomas Carlyle, to whom Lagarde bears a passing resemblance, held him in high regard.

Intemperate and vicious in controversy, even by the low lights of academia, Lagarde had the uniquely unappetising habit of publishing critical reviews of his own work, together with intemperate refutations of them. Nor did calling his academic colleagues 'an intellectual proletariat' help his case, especially as this was decades before this appellation came true.[12] Others viewed his diatribes against the 'Palestinisation of the universities, of the law, of medicine, and of the stage' with well-deserved distaste, although his criticism of the (much overrated) German education system of his time still have considerable point.

Having finally managed to secure a professorship in Göttingen at the time of the Franco-Prussian War, Lagarde immediately alienated his pro-Hanoverian colleagues by noisily and nastily championing Prussia's cause. In addition to advocating the shelling of Paris (excepting libraries from which he hoped to derive loot) he recommended the annexation of Alsace and Lorraine, as well as Luxembourg. Typically, Lagarde soon expressed diametrically opposed views. His patriotic enthusiasms waned when the German press discovered him among various academic fawners (Theodore Mommsen was another) who had earlier corresponded with the exiled emperor Napoleon III. Germany's dyspeptic 'prophet' was born.

For thirty-odd years Lagarde lambasted the joyless, smug and self-satisfied materialist and secularising culture of the German Empire, which probably explains why Nietzsche admired 50 per cent of his work. Like many academics he was unwarrantedly snobbish about the business world and feared the levelling impact of the masses, a term not simply synonymous with the working class. Beneath the frenetic noisy pace of the Empire he detected that 'The nation is bored: therefore individuals through smoking, reading, theatre-going, bar-loitering, home-gardening, and the addiction to humorous magazines try to dispel their awareness that ciphers like themselves cannot stand being alone for any length of time at all.' Germany was suffocating from a slow spiritual death. The military triumphs of 1870–1 and the ensuing decades revealed the inherent limitations of the political and economic conception of life. So-called political unification under Bismarck had merely perpetuated Germany's divisions, whether in terms of confessional conflict, incomprehensions between north and south, or the acrimonious vested interests represented in the Reichstag. Nor was Bismarck's cautiously conservative diplomacy any guarantee of peace, since his abstention from fighting Russia merely postponed the conflict that would inevitably come.

Himself symptomatic of a profound crisis in German Protestantism, Lagarde nonetheless had much to say about Germany's spiritual decline, as manifested in emptying churches, a mediocre ministry and the steady evaporation of religion from the nation's life. Schleiermacher's theologian successors could do nothing but disappoint: 'Any religion, even fetishism, is superior to the hodgepodge of insipid, cowardly sentimentality and stale, decaying reminders of Christianity which today we call Protestantism.' It was 'an episode in history, not an epoch'. Protestantism had retained much of the dogmatic tradition of Catholicism, mostly derived from the Saul who had become Paul, for Lagarde was unselfconscious about Bötticher's demise, while jettisoning the apostolic hierarchy that was Catholicism's saving grace. The Reformation was responsible for sundering Germany into countless 'caesaro-papist' petty principalities; Bismarck's unification of 'Germany' had merely perpetuated that division by shamefully excluding the Germans of Austria. The Kulturkampf, in which Lagarde was one of the few non-Catholics to support the Catholic side, was further evidence of the inherently divisive effects of the Reformation. Most astutely, Lagarde claimed that the ineffectuality of Protestantism after 1648 had meant that it could do nothing to impede Germany's cultural revival represented by Kant, Lessing and Goethe. On the contrary, Protestantism had been absorbed by it, since it 'will eat out of any hand'.

Lagarde's attitude towards Roman Catholicism was marginally less damning. There was something of the combination of admiration and hatred that he brought to bear on the Jews, whom he routinely coupled with 'Jesuitism' in the various malign internationals of his imagination. He admired Catholicism's hierarchy, doctrinal absolutism and emotional purchase on its adherents, but he loathed ultramontane 'Jesuitism' for declaring war on modern scientific rationalism and the nation state. Since the universal Catholic Church was in decline, and the territorial Protestant Churches too weak, Lagarde took upon himself the task of expounding a new 'Germanic–Christian faith', including a 'genius' Jesus, cleansed of all Pauline accretions, which would give the German nation the spiritual cohesion it lacked. Lagarde was more precise about how to clear the site than about what he intended to build. The state should expedite the interment of existing religions, by ceasing to collect Church taxes or to grant subsidies, and by closing theological faculties, while piling on such added responsibilities as confessional schools. Many Protestant Churches would dissolve under these pressures, while those who might have studied theology in the past would seek the essence of all faiths in new faculties of comparative religion. These would be the 'pathfinders' of the new national creed.

Lagarde never regarded this Germanic faith in the instrumental manner that many conservatives viewed Christianity, but as the expression of the unique soul and destiny of the German nation. Here his increasingly vicious antisemitism came into play. Lagarde subscribed to the common complaint that the emancipated Jews were agents of modernistic dissolution. His solutions began with the alternatives of enforced assimilation or expulsion, and ended with the late-life outburst: 'With trichinae and bacilli one does not negotiate, nor are trichinae and bacilli subjected to education; they are exterminated as quickly and as thoroughly as possible.' The teleology of this belated conversion to a Darwinian materialism he had hitherto eschewed has received more attention than some of the pathology's more paradoxical accompaniments. Leaving aside Lagarde's homely appreciation of the Jewish sabbath, he was impressed by the ways in which Judaism had inculcated a discipline and spirit of sacrifice that had stood the Jews well for hundreds of years. The Jews were formed between the anvil of inward moral self-discipline and the hammer of persecution. By contrast, his German contemporaries consisted of enfeebled materials imperfectly held together by a 'worthless' religion.[13]

The other aspect of Lagarde's national religion was to define Germany's God-given imperial mission. Germany's historic destiny lay in the 'Germanic' east, that nebulous swathe of territory that for centuries had been the object of German imperial longing. A huge programme of conquest and colonisation would resettle Germany's surplus urban populations in the Balkans, the Baltic and the non-German territories of the Habsburg Empire. This would implicitly deny the United States the creative waves of German immigrants that had been lost to Germany. Non-Germans, including the Jews, would be expelled to peripheral regions where they could vegetate. In other words his views were largely in line with those of the nationalist groups that lobbied and harried the German governments of the time.

Having earned the respect of among others, Carlyle, Nietzsche and Wagner during his own lifetime, Lagarde's reputation flourished, especially after it was released from experience of the man himself. Although his 'Germanic faith' came to nothing, at least in his lifetime, Lagarde had described a form of religious appetency while mercilessly caricaturing the insufficiencies of Christianity. As another admirer, the theologian Ernst Troeltsch, wrote: 'The great religious movement of modern times, the reawakened need for religions, develops outside the churches, and by and large outside theology as well.' By virtue of his background and vocation, Lagarde was more anchored in the Protestant tradition than some of his völkisch contemporaries, some of whom were content to cleanse Jesus of Jewish accretions, others to reclaim him as an Aryan superman who had somehow strayed among the Jews. A handful struck out more boldly, leaving Lagarde's brand of 'Germanic Christianity' behind. The year 1904 saw the appearance of a Teutonic Bible, collecting the sacred writings of the Germanic peoples, and 1910 a book whose title put matters more starkly: *Siegfried or Christ*. In their quest to 'find God in themselves, and not in the clouds', bands of the dedicated worshipped amid the rocks of the Externsteine or at the recently completed Hermannsdenkmal in the Teutoburger Forest. The tendencies that they, Lagarde and Charles Maurras represented were given a massive impetus by the cataclysm of the First World War and the turmoil that followed it.[14]

During the First World War the political religion of European nationalism threatened to engulf those who were responsible for maintaining a
Christianity posited on the transcendental City of God as reflected in
St Paul's words 'Our citizenship is in heaven.' This process occurred with
an extraordinary rapidity, and was hardly reflected in the initial responses
to the outbreak of European war, where there were even compensatory
grounds for hope, as in all countries civil conflicts were shelved in the
interests of a fleeting rediscovery of national community.

'I never thought to have lived to see such a return to barbarism.
Civilisation is in danger of dissolution,' wrote dean Inge of St Paul's. 'I
hate War. I detest it. It is the bankruptcy of Christian principle,' the
archbishop of York Cosmo Lang said from the pulpit of York Minster.[15]
The archbishop of Canterbury spoke about 'this thing' astir in Europe
which was 'not the work of God but the work of the devil'. A Liberal
British cabinet characterised by 'degrees of religious scepticism' and
reliant upon Scottish and Welsh Nonconformists declined calls from the
Church of England for a day of national prayer. Not much enthusiasm
for war there, even though the condemnations of an abstraction called
war would soon be abandoned.[16]

French Catholic clergy were diverted until late July 1914 by the revelations of the Caillaux Affair, in which the wife of a former finance minister
had shot the editor of Le Figaro for publishing love letters her husband
had written before he divorced his first wife. No sooner had the trial
resulted in an acquittal than on 31 July an extreme nationalist called
René Villain shot the Socialist leader Jean Jaurès, the great white hope
of socialist internationalism. A few days later bells tolled in remote
hamlets and villages warning that war had broken out.[17] Although the
Radical and Socialist cabinet of René Viviani, many of whose members
were militant anticlericals, rejected Catholic calls for national prayers,
president Raymond Poincaré went some way to appeasing the Church
when he proclaimed a 'Sacred Union'. This aspired to suspend the
country's domestic conflicts for the duration. In the Chamber the former
Communard Edouard Vaillant shook hands with the Catholic politican
Albert de Mun, who had been an officer in the army that had suppressed
the Commune. A similar sacred union was declared in Belgium.[18]

In Berlin, emperor Wilhelm II, who was also supreme bishop of the

Prussian Church, commanded his subjects to pray, decreeing both a day of prayer and a truce within the beleaguered German fortress. Henceforth he would recognise only Germans rather than social classes or political parties. Confusing the Volksgeist with the Holy Ghost, German clerics divined something miraculous abroad in this recrudescence of an elemental national community, not least because people seemed to be returning to vacant churches in significant numbers. The coming together of Germans in August 1914 was seen as nothing short of miraculous. A pastor in Hanover recalled:

> When the day of mobilisation had fully come, there were Germans all together in unity – villagers and city dwellers, conservatives and freethinkers, Social Democrats and Alsatians, [Hanoverian] Guelphs and Poles, Protestants and Catholics. Then suddenly there occurred a rushing from heaven. Like a powerful wind it swept away all party strife and fraternal bickering . . . and the Kaiser gave this unanimity the most appropriate expression; 'I see no more parties; I see only Germans'.[19]

In all belligerent countries there was a brief rise in church attendance during the initial months of war, as anxiously bewildered people sought spiritual consolation, either by attending services of intercession or by discovering inner peace within the stillness of a church. This occurred in such unexpected places as Carcassonne, notorious for its anticlerical excesses, as well as Berlin and Hamburg, where the Social Democrats were a strong presence.[20] These increased attendances soon dropped off, but, throughout Europe and beyond, the Churches were an important presence during over four years of warfare, their tone worlds apart from how Europe's clerics react to warfare now.

Everywhere clergy and theologians played a considerable part in justifying participation in the war, whether in terms of its justness and virtue, or by claiming that God was with their nation's defensive struggle. The French novelist Henri Barbusse gave the ubiquity of this Christian nationalism glib expression in his 1916 novel *Under Fire*. A delirious pilot recalls from his sickbed flying low over two strange gatherings on either side of the trenches, from which rise up – presumably through peculiarly muffled engine noise – cries of 'Gott mit uns' and 'God is with us'. Barbusse's novel was celebrated after 1918 as a pacifist tract; throughout the war he had been a consistent advocate of its ferocious prosecution as a form of socialist crusade.

For it is important to emphasise that the clergy were no more, and often significantly less, bellicose than the artistic avant-garde, academics, journalists, scientists and the wider intelligentsia. Whether one thinks of the Socialist Barbusse, the German conservative writer Ernst Jünger or the British Marxist biologist Haldane, there were many secular-minded people who positively revelled in the prospect of apocalyptic carnage. Many of these groups subscribed to materialistic creeds, such as Social Darwinism, that were no less questionable than that of a Christianity made serviceable for battle. Others traduced materialism in the name of a revival on the back of war of mind and spirit, thereby betraying their own fears that the 'aristocracy of the intellect' was being displaced by the bureaucrat, businessman and trade unionist in an age dominated by industry and technology.[21] Clerics were not alone in regarding war as an opportunity for spiritual revival. There were many writers, including Hugo von Hofmannsthal and Rainer Maria Rilke, and artists, such as Max Beckmann, Otto Dix and Franz Marc, who welcomed war as a chance to explore life's extreme edges, in the mistaken and commonplace conviction that ultimate 'truth' lay there, eager witnesses all to a 'cultural rebirth' unfolding in an age of machines and masses rather than popes and princes that left many abbreviated artistic or poetic talents in mass graves or ossuaries.[22]

The Great War was seen as a clash of civilisations and a contest of rival 'national' values and virtues which the clergy, together with the broader educated classes, helped shape. Exchanges of fire on the battle-fields took place beneath a no less vicious war of ideas, in which the big intellectual and spiritual cannons blazed with accusations, denials and counter-accusations. Historians everywhere rushed to serve up 'practical pasts'. French intellectuals of all backgrounds and persuasions were united in the belief that the war was between civilisation and barbarism, a view confirmed by the catalogue of German atrocities and oppressions on and off the battlefield. France's civilising mission bridged the gap between Catholic and republican messianisms, with the descendants of the Year II and those of Clovis united in the belief that France had a universal mission to mankind. For a brief moment, Frenchmen were exposed to the fusion of Christian and republican messianisms that characterises the United States of America.[23]

Across the Marne and Somme, where the German border lay, war proved the moral superiority of German 'heroes' over Anglo-Saxon 'shopkeepers', to employ the chief elements in the title of a book by the economic historian Werner Sombart, although there was much disdain for the frivolous French and the Russian barbarian 'culture of the horde' too. Hatred of England was born of envy, partly the product of an intense sense of betrayal at a time when putative racial or real religious affinities counted for a great deal more than they have since. In German eyes, Protestant England (for Ireland, Wales and Scotland failed to register) had bizarrely allied itself with a godless France and Orthodox Russia, a 'land of assassins and pogroms' beyond the pale of European civilisation – these two countries that had gone to war on behalf of Serbian robbers and regicides. Both Britain and France had also betrayed the white race when they brought Muslim or Hindu (not to speak of African animist) troops from their colonies to fight the Christian–German Michael. This charge came a little oddly from a country whose ruler had proclaimed himself the friend of '300 million Muslims' and whose Ottoman ally had a grim record of anti-Christian atrocities notably in Armenia and the Balkans. So too did attempts to impugn the humanitarian record of the British Empire, for imperial Germany had recently been responsible for systematic slaughter of the Herero people in South-West Africa (now Namibia) that eclipsed anything the British had done in South Africa or the Sudan.

As is usual in circumstances of total war, attempts were made to strip the enemy of all moral worth, or as Frank Lenwood had it in 1915: 'we idealize our own country and our own people, while in relation to a hostile nation we practise that kind of realism which ... involved the selection and emphasis of all the ugly and sordid facts'.[24] When in September 1914 prominent German clergy and theologians issued a statement enthusiastically supporting their country's cause, their British opposite numbers retaliated in kind. German theology had often been uncritically revered in the England of George Eliot, but it was not long before British clerics underwent 'the most painful experience of their lives to find men, whose names they have long been accustomed to revere, showing themselves so blindly and bitterly partisan in their judgements regarding the causes of the war'.[25]

British clergy contrasted the critical daring of modern German theologians towards the Holy Bible with German intellectuals' credulous divinisation of the German state. Since the Anglican Church was integral to the British state, churchmen had to stress its historical autonomy to distinguish it from conditions across the Rhine. They claimed that whereas in Britain the Church preceded the state by several centuries, retaining, beyond the Reformation, its moral autonomy and independent voice, as sometimes manifest on the episcopal benches in the House of Lords, in Germany the Lutheran Church was so subordinate to the state that it was tantamount to a pious claque in a system without effective institutional checks and balances. The German state was amorality incarnate, living witness to the cynical and unChristian doctrine that might is right. The archbishop of Canterbury drew the implications of this when he wrote: 'We believe, with an intensity beyond words, that there does exist exactly what our opponents deny, a higher law than the law of the state, a deeper allegiance than can be claimed by any earthly Sovereign, and that in personal and national conduct alike we have to follow higher and more sacred principles of honour than any state law can enforce.'[26] While British clergy were fervently patriotic, and sometimes susceptible to chauvinism, they also believed that there was a 'higher patriotism of the Bible' by which nations and individuals would be judged. They may have held the view that the British Empire had a divine mission, to spread Christianity to the four corners of the globe, but this was inherently universal, an expansion rather than contraction of God's love, and it did not confuse an *absolute* God with an evanescent history unfolding on earth. By contrast, the immanentist and Hegelian strain in German liberal Protestant theology, in which whatever one felt powerfully enough was indicative of the *developing* presence of God, meant that He was manifest in the intense emotions of August 1914, directing the movements of German armies at war. As a wartime German cleric put it: 'God is what the god-inspired people do.'[27] Ernst Troeltsch gave this its most grandiloquent expression:

> We fight not only for what we are, but also for what we will and must become ... Our faith is not just that we can and must defend our state and homeland but that our national essence contains an inexhaustible richness and value that are inexpressibly important for mankind, a value that the Lord and God of history has entrusted to our protection and development. The German faith is a faith in the inner moral and spiritual content of Germanness, the faith of the Germans in themselves, in their future, in their world mission ... This is a belief in the divine world ruler and world reason that has allowed us to become a great world nation, that will not forsake us or deny us because our spirit comes from its spirit.[28]

Other Allied clerics took a different tack. While some writers dilated on the drunkenness, insanity or immaturity of Germany, all conditions that could at least be regarded as temporary and curable, many thought there was something indelibly flawed about that country, a view that in intensified form has survived the Second World War. Avoiding the awkward common experience of Reformation, they argued that Germany had never been thoroughly Christianised at all, and that an imperfectly eradicated paganism had erupted in the heart of Europe. Here they paid particular heed to a prophecy made in 1834 by the German–Jewish poet Heinrich Heine:

> Christianity, and this is its greatest merit, has occasionally calmed the brutal German lust for battle, but it cannot destroy that savage joy. And when once that restraining talisman, the cross, is broken, then the old combatants will rage with the fury celebrated by the Norse poets. The wooden talisman is fast decaying; the day will come when it will break pathetically to pieces. Then the old stone gods will rise from unremembered ruins and rub the dust of a thousand years from their eyes, and Thor will leap to life at last and bring down his gigantic hammer on the Gothic cathedrals.

Evidence of this atavistic turn was apparent when in September 1915 German artillery pulverised Rheims cathedral. Some British authors mixed their religious metaphors in ways that seem rather opaque. Presumably Barnard Snell knew what he meant when he wrote: 'The will and conscience of mankind are against the return to Odinism with Berlin for its Mecca and the Kaiser for its prophet.'

Hunting intellectual culprits is a perennial intellectuals' game, played with interchangeable pieces: how much easier to pin everything on a Friedrich Nietzsche or William Kristol than to have to think. Both British and French clerics, and others, alighted upon not only the Kaiser but the 'unholy trinity' of general Friedrich von Bernhardi, the historian Heinrich von Treitschke and the philosopher Friedrich Nietzsche. Since Bernhardi had been put out to grass in 1909, partly because the General Staff was embarrassed by reactions to his opinions, his significance in German military circles was limited. Nonetheless, he was blamed for the cynical Machtpolitik which was pervasive among Germany's military and political elites, notwithstanding his view that 'the man who pursues moral ends with immoral means is involved in a contradiction of motives, and nullifies the object at which he aims, since he denies it by his actions'. The historian and nationalist prophet Heinrich von Treitschke was assailed for his glorification of a Prussian state at a time when most of Germany's present transgressions were being loaded on to a pointy-helmeted 'Prussianism'. Finally, and perhaps most unfairly, the philosopher who regarded 'bovine nationalism' as 'boorish self-conceit' and who had fled Bayreuth, Bismarck and the beer-halls for the gentler Italian south was held to be the 'immoralist' responsible for such outrages as the burning of the Catholic library at Louvain. When a new English edition of his collected works went on sale in Piccadilly, the bookshop drummed up custom with a sign saying, 'The Euro-Nietzschean War. Read the Devil in order to fight him better.'[29]

French Catholic clergy also blamed Treitschke and Nietzsche for Germany's amoral bellicosity, but further back they discovered rabid 'pan-germanism' in Martin Luther.[30] The Catholic philosopher Jacques Maritain attacked Luther for the 'pantheism' he detected in his exaltation of the individual conscience; the priest Pasquier used huge public lectures to assail Luther for separating salvation from morality, thereby laying the groundwork for Germany's current public amoralism.[31] The preposterous figure of Wilhelm II provided Allied clerics with multiple possibilities for outrage, much of it entirely warranted. The French alighted upon his bizarre claim before the war – condemning the conversion to Catholicism of the landgrave of Hesse – that 'the destruction [of Roman superstition] is the supreme object of my life'. The British were appalled by Wilhelm's claims to a unique relationship with God, as exemplified in a speech to his troops in which he said: 'Remember that the German people are the chosen of God. On me, on me as German Emperor, the Spirit of God has descended. I am His weapon. His sword and His visor. Woe to the disobedient! Death to cowards and unbelievers!'[32]

In a less ad-hominem way, the war was seen as a clash between the ideas of 1789 and those of 1914, between what the liberal theologian Ernst Troeltsch called 'The German Idea of Freedom', based on free self-subordination of the individual to a semi-autocratic state, and the much inferior British and French parliamentary systems that enabled pernicious interests to dominate atomised 'individuals'.[33] But in a broader sense the conflict was construed as being between Germans uniquely possessed of 'spirit' and 'inwardness' and an England seeking to turn the world into 'a loathsome department store', while the French indulged themselves with frivolity and pornography in their Sodom on the Seine.[34] A more elegant version of this was to contrast the ethics of duty espoused by Kant with the low utilitarianism of Bentham and his followers. A criticism of imperial Britain that has a more resonant ring was that British gold was taking over the world, reducing other nations to atomised satrapies. A German-dominated central European federation would allegedly guarantee the cultural diversity and independence of the nations that helped Germany to clean up the 'temple of mankind', although this generous spirit was not immediately apparent in occupied northern France.

The belief that God had chosen Germany for a divine mission conspired with the initial triumphs on the battlefields to foster the certainty that God was on Germany's side. As the theologian Alfred Uckeley declared: 'God is the God of the Germans. Our battles are God's battles. Our cause is a sacred, a wholly sacred matter. We are God's chosen among the nations. That our prayers for victory will be heard is entirely to be expected, according to the religious and moral order of the world.'[35] While some clergy were vulgarly triumphalist, others preferred to see the sudden onset of national unity and Germany's supreme struggle as an opportunity for national atonement after the materialism of the pre-war years. Like some of their predecessors in 1870–1 they were convinced that victory in war was an opportunity for the 'political, moral and religious rebirth' of a nation with whom God had a special covenant. Recent history was used to support this story. God had helped liberate Germany from Napoleon in 1813. In 1870–1 the miracle of German Unification had occurred in the wake of the Franco-Prussian War, God's verdict upon the regime of Napoleon III. Hopes that this would lead to a spiritual reformation of the German people had been disappointed by the drunken chauvinism and crass materialism of the years that followed, not to speak of active attempts by socialists and freethinkers to 'de-Christianise' the German people.[36] The theologian Karl Barth was one of the few to resist the 'hopeless muddle' of 'love of country, lust for war and Christian faith' which were characteristic of most of his clerical colleagues. The fundamental tenets of Christianity had been displaced by a 'warlike Germanic theology' which was tricked out with much talk of 'sacrifice' and other Christian values to the point where death on the field of battle was equated with Christ's sacrifice on the cross.

The importance of National Liberalism and Protestantism to the foundation of the German Reich had inhibited Catholic identification to the extent that Catholics were routinely ranged among such multifarious 'enemies of the Reich' as Alsatians and Poles. Although the end of the Kulturkampf and the dissolution of traditional Catholic enclaves eroded Catholic immunities to the national religion, their faith continued to enjoy primacy over nationality, while there was scant sympathy for the marginalisation of their Church by such temporal surrogates as race or nation, especially since many nationalist pressure groups were rabidly anti-Catholic. This makes the reaction of German Catholics to the outbreak of war in 1914 so remarkable, although few went as far as bishop Wilhelm von Keppler of Rottenburg in declaring it 'a struggle for the Kingdom of God'.

Less remarked on than the concurrent collapse of socialist internationalism, both Protestant ecumenicism and the internationalism of the Roman Catholic Church collapsed under the weight of the patriotic tide. Appeals to warring Protestants by the archbishop of Uppsala in Sweden came to naught, while those of the dying Pius X and his successor Benedict XV were ignored. Whereas German Catholic responses to the defeat of France in 1870–1 had been muted, in 1914 they construed the cause of the Central Powers as a defensive war by Austria–Hungary, Europe's pre-eminent Catholic power, and an opportunity to strengthen German Catholicism through closer association with Austria and impending territorial annexations in Catholic Belgium. A war of the spirits was as much common currency here as it was among Protestant pastors. In 1915 Michael von Faulhaber, later cardinal of Munich, declared the conflict a 'just war', a holy war against Paris, the 'the West's Babylon'. As a Catholic field chaplain explained in April 1915, German patriotic idealism was at war with the 'barbarism of the Russians, the atheism of the French, and the insatiable cupidity and mercantile spirit of the English'. British outrage at the violation of Belgian neutrality was turned aside with homely parables about minor acts of trespass on the part of a man who fled through a neighbouring garden after coming face to face with three hulking robbers.

Given the troubled relations between the Catholic Church and an aggressively laicising republican state in the decades before the war, it is unsurprising that a few right-wing French Catholics regarded the war as divine punishment for national apostasy, a view expressed by the bishop of Luçon: 'If France is invaded, it is a just punishment.' More thought that the war was an opportunity for people to expiate their sins, or that it might bring such benefits as reconciliation between the classes or an upsurge in national religious fervour. That in itself was an insight into the extent to which the thinking of the French Church was within national terms. The idea of a crusade had a special resonance in the homeland of St Bernard of Clairvaux, with several clerical writers claiming that France was engaged in one on behalf of Christian civilisation against a Germany given over to barbarism. If the French were fighting to repulse a massive foreign invasion, the British faced no such urgent menace, other than to their gentle island way of life.

Significant numbers of British clergy, and especially Nonconformist ministers, had voiced opposition to the Boer War and regarded militarism with distaste. In many cases, doubts about the war were overcome as they internalised the fate of 'little Belgium', a country whose 'rape' (a metaphor resonant among professional gentlemen) included the wanton destruction of such cultural treasures as the library at Louvain. Ironically, a decade before, Anglican clergy had been prominent supporters of the Congo Reform Association, which in the wake of revelations by consul Roger Casement had exposed the horrors of Belgian colonial rule. Casement's subsequent involvements with the Germans over Ireland led the *Manchester Guardian* to describe his devastating reports on the Congo as 'exaggerated' and the Church to reconstrue 'little Belgium' as a present victim rather than a past oppressor. In a famous *Punch* cartoon, the kaiser taunts king Albert amid the ruins of his country: 'So you see – you've lost everything.' To which Albert replies: 'Not my soul!' To this 1915 added further evidence of German atrocities and illegalities. These included the reprisal shooting of civilian hostages; the use of aerial bombardment and poisonous gas; the sinking by submarines of neutral commercial shipping; and the fate of such innocents as nurse Edith Cavell. This came very close to home. The daughter of a Norfolk country clergyman, nurse Cavell worked in a Red Cross clinic in Belgium, whose patients included German soldiers. She helped organise the escape of British troops stranded behind German lines before her betrayal by a Belgian collaborator led to her trial and execution. Although the spinsterish-looking Cavell was fifty when she was shot in 1915 as a spy, propaganda postcards depicted a rather more youthful corpse, surrounded by a pool of celestial light, and under the far from benign gaze of a member of the German firing squad. Clergy wept as they recalled this 'poor girl'.

The clergy's wartime role went further than the mobilisation of spiritual enthusiasm. In countries with volunteer armed forces, they figured in recruitment campaigns. This evidently started close to home since an estimated 30 per cent of those granted commissions in the British army were clergymen's sons. The death toll was horrendous, with thirteen bishops having lost their sons in combat by early 1916. The son of the bishop of Liverpool, Noel Chavasse, was the only British soldier to win the Victoria Cross with bar.[37] The country's theological colleges were drained of students, as were Church elementary schools whose teachers rushed to enlist. A few bishops attempted to refuse ordination to any able-bodied man of military age, that is between twenty and thirty, although this never became a matter of Church policy.

Diocesan bishops routinely had close links with what were still county-based army regiments, as they did with the local and national political Establishment. Hensley Henson, at the time dean of Durham, took regular Sunday church parades with the men of the Durham Light Infantry, a practice some soldiers affectionately recalled in their letters to the dean from the Western Front. As prominent members of their respective county communities, senior clerics such as Henson felt it their civic duty to participate in recruitment meetings, along with the lord lieutenants and other dignitaries such as local politicians. Henson recalled the response of people in a northern English mining county where Quakerism was strong as he explained the meaning of the conflict:

> The spirit of the people was beyond praise. I was profoundly impressed by the fact that the argument which seemed to be most effective was genuinely altruistic. The Germans never realised the effect in Great Britain of their perfidy in attacking Belgium, and their atrocious method of attack. The miners were little moved by the danger to Great Britain, for they were comfortably assured that Great Britain was impregnable, but the treatment of Belgium stirred a flame of moral indignation in their minds, and created a determination to come to the rescue which I can only describe as chivalrous.[38]

Henson felt a powerful moral obligation to resist Germany's 'career of cynical and violent aggression', a sentiment encouraged by the anti-British bellicosity he had observed in the German press when he visited pre-war Kiel. Yet Henson was acutely aware of the pitfalls and snares surrounding the patriotic preacher in wartime. He used the preface to a collection of his wartime sermons to explain his point of view:

It must surely be the true function of Christian preachers to keep steadily before their congregations the intrinsic wrongness of mere revenge, the sacred duty of forgiveness, the necessity of so carrying through this conflict that the fellowship of mankind shall be strengthened and exalted, not permanently obstructed ... They [wartime preachers] will not make themselves the mouthpieces of that anti-German passion which (for intelligible reasons) is running strongly among our people ... the Christian preacher ought to strive so to preach that in the retrospect of a later time, he shall be able to recall his words without shame. For the War will not last for ever. Sooner or later peace will return, and the passions of the conflict will begin to die down in the most exasperated minds. The work of the Christian preacher will again become normal. Again he will be preaching the Gospel of Love, and pressing on men the difficult morality of Christ's Law. His influence for good will not be helped if his people have associated him with the very violences of thought and speech of which they themselves are growing ashamed.[39]

Not all senior Anglican clergy exercised Henson's fastidious self-restraint. The bishop of London, Arthur Winnington-Ingram, had made his ecclesiastical career in the capital, becoming, while bishop of Stepney, 'the idol of the East End', a position customarily bestowed on boxers and gangsters. He was popular among Oxford undergraduates who were tantalised by his cockney accent and the romance he brought from the 'exotic' East End. From 1901 onwards he was senior chaplain to the London Territorial Rifle Brigade, with whom he spent two months in camp after the outbreak of war. Instructed by a general to 'put a little ginger' into his first Sunday sermon, the result was that all the reservists volunteered. Winnington-Ingram was a bluff-minded patriot, unembarrassed by national symbols, and, judging from photographs, manifestly comfortable in military uniform. On a visit to five thousand Territorials elsewhere, the bishop stood on a wagon covered with the Union Jack, insisting, 'We would all rather die, wouldn't we, than have England a German province,' an avocation that brought forth 'low growls of assent'. He conjured up the dread prospect of Oxford becoming another Louvain, while assuring the troops that the spirits of those who had fought at Crécy, Agincourt, Waterloo, Inkerman and Alma were with them. From the start Winnington-Ingram was convinced that this was 'The

Holy War', the title he gave to a sermon he delivered to soldiers in September 1914:

> But when we have said all that, this is a Holy War. We are on the side of Christianity against anti-Christ. We are on the side of the New Testament which respects the weak, and honours treaties, and dies for its friends, and looks upon war as a regrettable necessity ... It is a Holy War, and to fight in a Holy War is an honour ... Already I have seen the light in men's eyes which I have never seen before.

A year later he used the *Manchester Guardian* to cry, 'MOBILISE THE NATION FOR HOLY WAR', to which his more liberal clerical colleagues responded that the clergy should not become 'Mad Mullahs preaching a Jehad' (sic).[40] He spent Holy Week and Easter 1915 visiting the troops, chaplains and field hospitals in France. He conducted services in which the troops joined with the hymns 'When I Survey the Wondrous Cross' or 'Rock of Ages'. Some ten thousand Canadian soldiers crowded into an evening service that he held at their request.[41] The following year Winnington-Ingram led three thousand troops through a summer downpour from Trafalgar Square to the steps of St Paul's, where he preached from behind a makeshift altar of military drums. He was also the most active Anglican cleric in soliciting subscriptions to government war loans. The 'Bishop of the Battlefields' was an old-fashioned English patriot. He was far from unique in propagating the war as an apocalyptic crusade. His friend, Basil Bouchier of St Anne's Soho, announced: 'We are fighting, not so much for the honour of our country, as for the honour of God. Not only is this a Holy War, it is the holiest war that has ever been waged ... This truly is a war of ideas. Odin is ranged against Christ, and Berlin is seeking to prove its supremacy against Bethlehem.' Other clergy, such as bishop Diggle of Carlisle, regarded the clash of soldiers and technologies as mere surrogates for a much larger battle:

> in this war there move and work spirits deeper, stronger, more revolutionary than any or all of these – spirits of good and evil, powers of heaven and principalities of hell, invisible spirits of goodness and wickedness of which men are the instruments and the world the visible prize ... this present war is essentially a spiritual war; a war waged on earth but sustained on either side by invisible powers.[42]

British clergy were exempted from military service, with virtually every Anglican leader opposed to the clergy taking part in combat on the grounds that their true role was to husband the nation's spiritual resources. This prohibition was only reversed in the crisis of the German offensive in the spring of 1918 when clerical exemptions were abolished and conscription extended to men of fifty and below. A few Anglican clergy nonetheless enlisted in the armed forces, while a further six thousand more moved into civilian jobs, whether as mechanics or tax inspectors, vacated by men serving at the front. There were also approximately three and a half thousand chaplains attached to the British army by the time of the Armistice, of whom nearly two thousand were Anglican clergy. One hundred and seventy-two of these men died in the war, including eighty-eight Anglicans, while four were awarded the Victoria Cross. Many more received other major awards for bravery in battle.

The chaplains came under the chaplain general, bishop John Taylor Smith, a militant Evangelical with a background in crushing the Ashanti in Africa; his deputy in France was the former bishop of Khartoum. The chaplain service was poorly organised, recruitment often consisting of a session with Taylor Smith, who asked: 'If you had five minutes, and five minutes only, to spend with a man about to die, what would you say to him?' Rejects routinely forgot to ask the dying for the home address of their nearest relatives. In France, the chaplains, whose rank was that of captain, were forbidden to go nearer the fighting front than brigade headquarters. They would probably get in the way, and the sight of them wounded or dead would undermine the very morale that their presence was supposed to maintain. Chaplains were separated from most of the soldiers by education and social class, divisions not only perpetuated by their having batmen and private quarters but by their use of such terms as fighting 'with a straight bat' to men who preferred soccer. Their hearty compensatory bellicosity went down badly with men who were better acquainted with the physical reality of killing another human being. They came out poorly from any comparison with Roman Catholic priests, who were not only from a similar social background as the men, but had precise sacraments that did not leave them lost for words when confronted by the dying. To be fair, sometimes the tone used by chaplains was dictated by their commanding officers, who had a limited view of the function of these younger 'sky-pilots'. Major general Sir William Thwaites recalled that he used to gather the chaplains together before an engagement: 'I told them on one occasion that I wanted a bloodthirsty sermon next Sunday, and would not have any texts from the New Testament.' Some chaplains came to an accommodation with the soldiers, based on 'Tommy doesn't want religion, and I don't try to persuade him.' This does not mean that chaplains were entirely bereft of purpose. Those who organised canteens and cinema shows, or who brought cigarettes, tea and soup to the wounded in field hospitals were more popular than the grim fellow satirised by a mythical Tommy in reverend Studdert Kennedy's mocking doggerel:

> Our padre were a solemn bloke
> We called 'im dismal Jim.
> It fairly gave ye bloomin' creeps
> To sit and 'ark at 'im.

Exposure, often for the first time, to ordinary Britons, other than college porters, farm labourers and domestic servants, led the Church of England as a whole to reflect on its own endeavours. A member of the YMCA returning from the Western Front discerned an opportune moment for a wide-ranging assessment of the impact of the war on the religious life of the nation. Senior clerics readily concurred and an elaborate survey, soliciting views from generals to privates, and entitled *The Army and Religion* (1919), was born. It is an impressive document, there being few other institutions one could imagine that would follow the Churches (for it included Nonconformity too) in exposing their own major flaws in this way.

The report did not minimise the dulling and brutalising effects of a total war that reduced men, already become uniformed numbers, to mere adjuncts to deadly machines. Even among the well educated, such as a former inspector of schools, there was a resigned and fatalistic desire to exist only on the immediate surface: 'I stopped thinking, I now do just what I am told, and in between think about eating, drinking and sleeping.'[43] The report ruefully acknowledged that decades of intense domestic political conflict over religious education had translated into a general ignorance of the basic tenets of the Christian religion. The smattering of sentimental Christianity they had picked up from Sunday Schools was pitifully at variance with existential terrors they experienced every day.[44] Much of the report confirmed the contemporary quip that 'The soldier has got religion, I am not so sure that he has got Christianity.' Exposure to tremendous displays of material might and the immanence of death turned minds to an unseen power and the awakening of an elemental faith that most of the men were ill equipped to articulate in terms familiar to the Church.

Consciousness of God ebbed and flowed as troops neared the front. Soldiers fell back on fragments of religious ideas that they had learned, and often forgotten, which they fused with resentments about the moralised social order that the Church represented: 'a mosaic of kill-joyism and Balaam's ass's ears, and Noah, and mothers' meetings, and Athanasian damns, and the Archbishop of Canterbury on £15,000 a year'. The image of Christianity was personified for many by the abstemious old matron who asked a wounded soldier: 'Do they *really* give the poor men in the trenches rum to drink?'[45]

Soldiers were perplexed that nineteen centuries of Christianity had not resulted in universal peace, even though they knew that in many parishes rival Christians 'fought each other to the knife' over incomprehensible issues. They did not associate Christianity with the rough egalitarian comradeship and self-sacrifice that prevailed in the trenches: 'being helpful to your pals, doing your bit, keeping your troubles in your kit-bag, and scorning grousing'. A Scottish officer defined this religion: 'The religion of ninety per cent of the men at the front is not distinctively Christian, but a religion of patriotism and of valour, tinged with chivalry, and at the best merely coloured with sentiment and emotion borrowed from Christianity.'[46]

Several army chaplains ruefully admitted that the Church had failed to connect with entire swathes of British society, notably the urban and industrial working class, although much of the rhetoric (and effort) of the most progressive sections of the Church of England in the preceding decades had been directed to little else. As a chaplain with a Scottish regiment reported: 'The men are not hostile, only indifferent. We have been speaking a language that has lost all meaning for them, and for ourselves too.'[47] Others were more critical, condemning the Churches for their lack of vision and their 'unattractive standard of comfortable and complacent respectability, a respectability quite compatible with flagrant inconsistency and selfishness'.[48]

While German clergy, to their obvious chagrin, were excluded from combat duties, this was not the case in secularist France (or Italy) where since 1905 clergy had been subject to laicising laws governing general military service. Anticipating the consequences of these laws, the Holy See suspended canon law proscriptions against clerical participation in combat before hostilities commenced. The scale of the clerical contribution to the French war effort did much to reconcile the clericalist right and the anticlerical Republic, especially when the Republic was obliged to ditch incompetent officers who had been over-promoted because of their political conformity, while allowing talented Catholics, who had been discriminated against, to make their mark. Fourteen of the nineteen officers whose abilities in the field in late 1914 won them rapid promotion had hitherto been the subjects of insidious masonic smears.[49] The contribution of the Catholic Church, not forgetting either French Jews or Protestants, ranged from patriotic exhortation to clerical participation in combat itself. By claiming that patriotism was both God-given and as innate as the maternal instinct, clerical supporters of the war side-stepped any need to defend France's current form of government, although, as we have already mentioned, there was some overlapping of Catholic and republican messianisms. Welcoming evidence that a century of 'de-Christianisation' had been superficial, clergy invested the course of events with sacred meaning, in that respect being in tune with the outlook of many of their fellow countrymen and women, who despatched a blizzard of pious kitsch to the men at the front. The troops were more than willing to attribute their survival to postcards of the Virgin Mary and medals of the Sacred Heart as well as to horseshoes, lucky stars and rabbits' feet, expressing their gratitude for divine protection after the war in the poignant votive tablets in countless French churches. Clergy played a leading role in attributing the miraculous halting of the initial German thrust on the Marne on 8 September 1914 to the intercession of the Virgin Mary, the feast day of whose nativity it happened to be.[50] They also transfigured the suffering of French soldiers into a latterday version of Christ's Passion, an identification many religious soldiers were prepared to make too: 'The smashed marble tombs in the cemetery gaped over black holes. Christ, torn at last from the dark cross standing alone on the flooded plain, now lay on the ground, cold and livid, his arms outstretched. He was sharing the common lot of our men.' Countless postcards drew visual parallels between the passion of wounded soldiers with their arms outstretched and Calvary itself.

The French clergy abandoned the scowling apartness that had been their stance during the Third Republic. Since they were subject to conscription, their role was not confined to that of military chaplains: 32,699 French clerics, 23,418 seculars and 9,281 regulars, served in the Republic's armed forces; a further 12,554 worked in military hospitals. In terms of individual dioceses, this meant that 72 of the 220 clergy in Aix-en-Provence were mobilised, in Autun 286 out of 655, and in La Rochelle, 140 out of 300. These were often the youngest and most vigorous clergy, including those who had yet to embark fully on their clerical careers. In addition to young seminarians, some 841 Jesuits, ignoring the ban on religious congregations, joined the French forces, with many of them returning from far-flung missions overseas. Twenty per cent of them would die in battle or from their wounds. Of the French clergy who served in the armed forces, some 4,618 died in battle; over thirteen thousand received military decorations and many more citations.[51] Clergy served in combat, as stretcher-bearers – notably the Jesuit mystic Teilhard de Chardin – and nurses, or as chaplains in the field.[52] Given the progressive feminisation of religion, both in France and elsewhere, this reconnected the all-male clergy with an exclusively masculine world, and the earthy values that underpinned it, in ways that countered some of the more egregious anticlerical stereotypes based on the clergy's lascivious interest in over-credulous women.

The French military chaplaincy had been created in May 1913, with four priests appointed to each army corps. This meant one priest for every forty thousand soldiers, in contrast to the one per thousand envisaged by the US. By the outbreak of war there were about a hundred official military chaplains, a number plainly inadequate to demand. On 11 August the Catholic deputy Albert de Mun intervened with prime minister Viviani to sanction a further 250 unpaid volunteer chaplains. Following advertisements in the press, French Catholics donated the money needed to support these priests, although by November the Ministry of War had allocated them each ten francs per day. Rabbis and Protestant pastors further augmented their ranks. On the fighting front the war lessened intra-confessional tensions, as Catholics, Protestants and Jews were thrown together for the first time. As the story went, about the four men forced to share two beds: 'We draw lots: the pastor lies down with the rabbi (the Old and New Testaments together) and dogma, which I represent, lies down with free-thought'. A celebrated wartime painting by a Jewish artist was of rabbi Abraham Bloch with his Red Cross armband offering a crucifix to a dying Catholic soldier, shortly before the rabbi was himself killed, expiring, as it happened, in the arms of a Jesuit.[53]

Since these volunteers did not appear to be part of any command structure, their appearance at the front was initially greeted with amazement or indifference by the troops. This changed when fear and death became pervasive realities. They soon won their comrades' respect, and not just through the services they managed to rig up amid the ruins of so many places of worship or in caves and dug-outs adorned with makeshift altars and images of saints that the soldiers had salvaged.

The clergy were thrust into an elemental wasteland where uniforms and mud obliterated social distinctions. Some of them were clearly very brave. When some soldiers were loth to leave their trenches for an attack, the abbé Lelièvre pre-empted the need for their colonel to draw his gun by leaping into action himself, obliging the wavering soldiers to follow. Others put themselves in extreme danger in order to administer the last rites to men dying in no-man's land, or took the place of married men with families when an exceptionally perilous mission was required. Some went about with their packs filled with the tattered bundles of letters, knives or pipes which were all that the dying could leave their families as remembrances.

French clergy also paid the ultimate price in the eleven dioceses that were either turned into combat zones or subjected to a brutal German occupation. Cambrai, Lille and Rheims were totally occupied, together with parts of Arras, Beauvais, Châlons, Soissons, Nancy, Saint-Dié and Verdun. The Catholic clergy of Alsace and Lorraine also came under intense suspicion as sympathisers with the French enemy. The German authorities executed several French clergy as spies after they were found with maps, or in prohibited areas. Cathedrals and churches were not spared from wanton destruction. Notoriously, on 19 September 1914 Rheims cathedral, scene of the last royal coronation in 1825, was hit by three hundred German artillery shells. The bells melted and the roof caught fire, killing wounded German prisoners being held in the nave.[54] The chief rabbi of France joined other religious leaders when he wrote: 'The destruction of the Rheims basilica is an odious blasphemy against God, the Father of all, and reveals the absence of all religious and human feeling in its perpetrators.' Other fine buildings were shelled too; the cathedral at Soissons took about nineteen direct hits.

In Germany the clergy reacted slowly to signs of public disillusion with the war. Many joined the ultra-nationalist Fatherland Party, formed at Königsberg on 2 September 1917, to rally support for continuation of the conflict in furtherance of the most implacable war aims. When in the autumn of 1917 a small group of pastors in Berlin called for a negotiated end to the war, this was categorically rejected by the majority of their clerical colleagues who continued to offer prayers acclaiming Wilhelm II long after many realised that he had to go. German Catholic clergy rediscovered the internationality of their Church in the wake of papal intercessions for peace, but after being denounced by their French colleagues they fell back into the general belligerent line. Splits emerged within the Catholic Centre Party, between conservatives opposed to the reform of Prussia's inequitable franchise and those who supported Matthias Erzberger's calls for electoral reform and a peace based on the relinquishment of territorial annexations.

The scion of an impoverished Genoan aristocratic family, Giacomo Della Chiesa, was elected pope Benedict XV on 3 September 1914. The effects of war were discernible at the conclave. Cardinal Hartmann from Cologne encountered cardinal Mercier of Belgium. 'I hope that we shall not speak of war,' declared Hartmann. 'And I hope that we shall not speak of peace,' replied Mercier. There was worse. Cardinal Billot of France learned that two of his nephews had died in battle. Cardinal Piffl of Vienna used his diary to record not just the shifting permutations of votes, but the grim progress of the battle of Lemberg. The war cut through the respective national allegiances of Catholics everywhere, while threatening fundamentally to alter the European balance of power. Both considerations determined the Vatican's diplomatic and moral stance. Its diplomacy was an attempt to maintain the status quo of before the war. The Vatican sought to maintain the Habsburg Empire as a Catholic counterweight to Protestant Germany. It also sought to prop up the Ottoman Empire so as to prevent Russia achieving an Orthodox St Peter's at Aghia Sophia on the Bosphorus. Above all, the Vatican endeavoured to keep Italy out of the war, first because an Italo-Austrian war would destroy the Habsburg Empire, and secondly because it suspected that the Italian state would mismanage such a war and be engulfed by social revolution. An Italian victory was not good either. If Italy emerged on the winning side, it would ensure that the Vatican was not represented at any peace conference, possibly enabling it to settle the Roman Question on its own terms. Beyond the Church's worldly interests, the pope regarded the conflict as a terrible manifestation of European nationalism, the collective suicide of a great Christian civilisation.[55]

The moral pronouncements of the pope, as the pre-eminent religious leader in Europe, were a universal currency worth having. All belligerents attempted to persuade him to abandon an institutional stance of studied impartiality, thereby indirectly rescuing the Vatican from the diplomatic isolation it had experienced during the pontificate of Pius X. The Central Powers had three representatives at the Vatican, from Austro-Hungary, Bavaria and Prussia, and German Catholics, then as now, were among the Vatican's chief source of financial support, although they were already being eclipsed by America.[56] Britain and France endeavoured to make up lost ground. Although France had broken off diplomatic relations in 1905, it quickly repositioned an unofficial envoy to the Vatican. The British returned an envoy to the Vatican in December 1914. Diplomatic relations were also repaired with the Netherlands and Switzerland, which with Spain and the US constituted a potentially important 'league of neutrals'. Relations with the tsar's representative continued to be cool because of Russian policy in Catholic Poland. The Italian state quietly opened a back channel through one of Benedict's closest friends.

At various times the pope was accused of a bias towards the Central Powers, up to and including allowing an alleged German agent to operate in the Vatican, who was suspected of having helped sink two Italian battleships in their harbours, charges which had no basis in reality. All of the warring Powers were incensed by the pope's refusal to move beyond general condemnations of wartime atrocities and illegalities to the specifics of whatever outraged them. There was talk of the 'Silence of Benedict XV' long before graver charges were aimed at Eugenio Pacelli, his successor but one as Pius XII. In fact, Benedict did intervene to stop German deportations of Belgian civilians and to protest against the Turkish massacres of the Armenians; what he could not do, since all sides were flooding him with denunciations of their opponents, was to condemn this side or that. Evidence of atrocities built up in a series of coloured books, together with the perpetrators' counter-accusations.

In January 1915 the pope despatched the young diplomat Pacelli on a mission to Vienna, designed to persuade emperor Franz Joseph to relinquish the Trentino in order to keep Italy out of the war. When this initiative failed, Italy's intervention in the war on 25 May 1915 led to the relocation of the representatives of the Central Powers to Lugano in Switzerland. The German government attempted to compensate for this loss of influence by dangling before the Vatican a solution to the Roman Question, bait to which the pope refused to rise. Just as well since foreign minister Sonnino had inserted a clause into the secret Treaty of London between Italy and the Entente, in which they agreed to exclude the Vatican from any peace settlement and to follow Italy's lead on the

Roman Question. Throughout the years of war, Benedict attempted to alleviate the distress of prisoners of war through the Opera dei Prigionieri, which by the end of the war had dealt with six hundred thousand items of correspondence regarding captives. Sick prisoners of war were an especial object of papal solicitude; by January 1917 some twenty-six thousand of them had been given the chance to convalesce in Swiss sanatoria through the efforts of the Vatican. During the war the Vatican expended eighty-two million lire on humanitarian relief, whether to Lithuania, Lebanon or Syria, thereby virtually bankrupting the organisation, and helping oppressed civilians, while lobbying US president Wilson to restore peace.[57]

In May 1917 Benedict appointed the newly appointed archbishop Pacelli to the nunciature in Munich. This led to conversations with chancellor Bethmann-Hollweg in Berlin that June regarding arms controls, the establishment of international courts of arbitration, the restoration of a soverign Belgium, and postponement of the ultimate disposition of Alsace–Lorraine to later negotiations. The army high command at Bad Kreuznach and the Kaiser rejected these gambits. The next opportunity for papal intervention arose when with the Austro-Hungarians reeling from the Brusilov offensive, and the accession of the youthful emperor Karl, the Central Powers seemed amenable to a negotiated settlement. Although the Vatican failed to prevent the United States from becoming a belligerent in April 1917, the readiness of a majority in the German Reichstag (in which the Centre Party's Matthias Erzberger played a notable role) to relinquish wartime annexations seemed to warrant a further papal initiative on the side of peace. Benedict instructed Pacelli to talk with Berlin, the heads of discussion being arms controls, the establishment of international courts, restoration of Belgian sovereignty and future negotiations over the status of Alsace–Lorraine. These points were then elaborated in a general 'peace note' to the Powers issued on 15 August 1917. These included renunciation of indemnities and reparations, the evacuation and restoration of occupied territories, and observance of liberty of the seas. The British, French, Italians, Russians and Americans comprehensively rejected the papal proposals, on the ground that they appeared to favour the Germans, in whose good faith they had no trust. The German General Staff, who counted for more than civilian politicians such as Erzberger, could see no reason to withdraw unilaterally from Belgium when they had repulsed the Russian offensive, and seemed to be succeeding with unlimited submarine warfare. President Wilson's response was not encouraging either, since he effectively made peace conditional upon a change in the form of Germany's government. The famous French Dominican preacher Sertillanges denounced the pope's proposals so vociferously – 'Holy Father we don't want your peace' – in a sermon in La Madeleine that his order censured him.[58] Ironically, an Italian government that had rejected Benedict's peace proposals sought papal mediation in Vienna, once the armies of the Central Powers thrust Italy's armies 120 kilometres back to the River Piave in the offensive that led to the rout of Caporetto. When the Austrians sought to get out of the war with a separate peace, Benedict at least showed an eye for the new realities by referring them to US president Wilson, a Presbyterian from Virginia. Those new realities, which included the rise of the political religions of Communism, Fascism and National Socialism, would threaten to displace both Christianity and civilisation as we know it.

The Great War, the domestic and international civil wars, and economic dislocation that followed it, gave rise to mass despair, to which the solution appeared to be various forms of authoritarianism. In some countries authoritarian regimes were successfully supplanted by sinister movements that tapped into more atavistic levels of the human psyche, although in Italy the transition was from democracy to Fascism. These political religions threatened either to eradicate Christianity entirely, as the Bolsheviks sought to do in Russia, or perhaps worse, offered to accommodate it, within the new dispensations of Fascism and Nazism, which had themselves adopted many of the outward forms of Europe's old religion.

NOTES

Introduction

1 For the extensive literature on totalitarianism see Michael Burleigh, *The Third Reich. A New History* (London 2000) select bibliography

2 A good discussion of the history of the term is by Philippe Burrin, 'Political Religion. The Relevance of a Concept', *History & Memory* (1997) 9, pp. 321–49. Readers should also consult Jean-Pierre Sironneau, *Sécularisation et religions politiques* (Le Haye 1982) and above all the historian and religious philosopher Hans Maier, *Politische Religionen. Die totalitären Regime und das Christentum* (Freiburg 1995); Maier (ed.), *Totalitarismus und Politische Religionen. Konzepte des Diktaturvergleichs* (Paderborn 1996–2003) three volumes, and his *Wege in der Gewalt. Die modernen politischen Religionen* (Frankfurt am Main 1996–2000). The three-volume work will appear in English translation. Scholarly readers may find much related work in the journal *Totalitarian Movements and Political Religions* (London 2000–) vols. 1–5

3 The pioneer in this field was René Fülöp-Miller, *Leaders, Dreamers and Rebels. An Account of the Great Mass-Movements of History and the Wish Dreams that Inspired Them* (London 1935). There are also the many books of George L. Mosse, *The Nationalization of the Masses. Political Symbolism and Mass Movements in Germany from the Napoleonic Wars through the Third Reich* (Ithaca 1975) and *Masses and Man. Nationalist and Fascist Perceptions of Reality* (Detroit 1987). More recent work includes Simonetta Falasca-Zamponi, *Fascist Spectacle. The Aesthetics of Power in Mussolini's Italy* (Berkeley 1997)

4 See Hans Maier, *Das Doppelgesicht des Religiösen. Religion-Gewalt-Politik* (Freiburg 2004)

5 Bertrand Russell, *The Practice and Theory of Bolshevism* (London 1920) pp. 15–17

6 Ronald Clark, *The Life of Bertrand Russell* (London 1995) p. 380

7 Alexis de Tocqueville, *The Old Regime and the Revolution*, ed. François Furet and Françoise Mélonio (Chicago 1998) 1, p. 101

8 Maier, *Das Doppelgesicht des Religiösen* pp. 66–7

9 Peter Schöttler, *Lucie Varga. Les Autorités invisibles. Une Historienne autrichienne dans les années trente* (Paris 1991); Erwein Freiherr von Aretin, *Fritz Michael Gerlich. Prophet und Martyrer* (Munich 1983). Gerlich's major work was *Der Kommunismus als Lehre vom Tausendjährigen Reich* (Munich 1920); René Fülöp-Miller, *The Mind and Face of Bolshevism* (New York 1929); Waldemar Gurian, *Bolshevism. Theory and Practice* (London 1932). The best book on Gurian is Heinz Hürten, *Waldemar Gurian. Ein Zeuge der Krise unserer Welt in der ersten Hälfte des 20. Jahrhunderts* (Mainz 1972); see also the memorial issue of *The Review of*

Politics (1955); Luigi Sturzo's books are legion, including *Politics and Morality. Essays in Christian Democracy* (London 1938). There is fine biography by Gabriele De Rosa, *Luigi Sturzo* (Turin 1977); from a huge literature on Aron the best includes Robert Colquhoun, *Raymond Aron. The Philosopher in History 1905–1955* (London 1986); for Niebuhr see his 'The Religion of Communism', *Atlantic Monthly* (1931) 147

10 Eric Voegelin, *Autobiographical Reflections*, ed. Ellis Sandoz (Baton Rouge 1989)

11 The books referred to are *The History of the Race Idea. From Ray to Carus*, vol. 3 of Ellis Sandoz (ed.), *The Collected Works of Eric Voegelin* (hereafter cited as *CWEV*) (Columbia, Mo. 1998) and *Race and State*, vol. 2 of *CWEV* (Columbia, Mo. 1997)

12 Eric Voegelin, 'Gnostic Politics', *Published Essays 1940–1952*, vol. 10 of *CWEV* (Columbia, Mo. 2000) p. 240

13 Eric Voegelin, *The Political Religions*, vol. 5 of *CWEV* (Columbia, Mo. 2000) p. 67

14 Voegelin, 'Gnostic Politics' p. 230

15 Norman Cohn, *The Pursuit of the Millennium. Revolutionary Millenarians and Mystical Anarchists of the Middle Ages* (London 1957) and Alain Besançon, *The Rise of the Gulag. Intellectual Origins of Leninism* (New York 1981)

16 There is an excellent book on British commentators on totalitarianism by Markus Huttner, *Totalitarismus und säkulare Religionen* (Bonn 1999) that deserves to appear in English translation

17 Christina Scott, *A Historian and his World* (London 1991) p. 106

18 On Dawson see Stratford Caldecott and John Morrill (eds), *Eternity in Time. Christopher Dawson and the Catholic Idea of History* (Edinburgh 1997) and the marvellous biography by his daughter Christina Scott, *An Historian and his World*

19 Frederick Voigt, *Unto Caesar* (London 1938) p. 37

20 Raymond Aron, 'L'Avenir des religions séculières', *Une Histoire du XX siècle. Anthologie* (Paris 1996) pp. 153ff.

21 Roger Scruton, *Death-Devoted Heart. Sex and the Sacred in Wagner's* Tristan and Isolde (Oxford 2004) is a highly sophisticated discussion of these issues. There is also a fine book by Tristram Hunt, *Building Jerusalem. The Rise and Fall of the Victorian City* (London 2004), which illuminates the Victorian municipal gospel

22 The best books on the subject are Owen Chadwick, *The Secularization of the European Mind in the Nineteenth Century* (Cambridge 1975) and Hugh McLeod, *Secularisation in Western Europe, 1848–1914* (London 2000). The treatment the subject deserves on a European level is indicated by Maurice Cowling's monumental *Religion and Public Doctrine in Modern England* (Cambridge 1980–2001) three volumes. See also Edward Norman's powerful *Secularisation* (London 2002). Like the writings of Maurice Cowling, those of Edward Norman have been a great stimulus to my work

23 Friedrich Nietzsche, *Beyond Good and Evil*, trans. Helen Zimmern (New York 1989) p. 76

24 One of the most impressive books on this theme is Lucian Hölscher, *Weltgericht oder Revolution* (Stuttgart 1989)

25 A theme brilliantly explored by Michael André Bernstein in *Foregone Conclusions. Against Apocalyptic History* (Berkeley 1994)

26 Martin Greschat, *Das Zeitalter der Industriellen Revolution. Das Christentum vor der Moderne* (Stuttgart 1980) is the best overall European view

27 The best comparative treatment of utopianism is by Frank E. and Fritzie Manuel, *Utopian Thought in the Western World* (Cambridge 1979); there are also briefer discussions in Leszek Kolakowski's *Main Currents of Marxism. Its Origins, Growth and Dissolution* (Oxford 1978) vol. 1

28 James Billington, *Fire in the Minds of Men. Origins of the Revolutionary Faith* (New York 1980); Joseph Frank,

Dostoevsky (Princeton 1996–2002) five volumes; Franco Venturi, *Roots of Revolution. A History of the Populist and Socialist Movements in 19th Century Russia* (London 2001). Modern Islamic terrorism is best explored through Mark Juergensmeyer, *Violence and the Sacred in the Modern World* (London 1992) and *Terror in the Mind of God. The Global Rise of Religious Violence* (Berkeley 2000); Barry Cooper, *New Political Religions, or An Analysis of Modern Terrorism* (Columbia, Mo. 2004); Paul Berman, *Terror and Liberalism* (New York 2003); and John L. Esposito, *Unholy War. Terror in the Name of Islam* (Oxford 2002). The most interesting book is Roger Scruton, *The West and the Rest. Globalization and the Terrorist Threat* (London 2002). There are more specialised works on the Al Qaeda network and Osama bin Laden

29 Robert Bellah, 'Civil Religion in America' in his *Beyond Belief. Essays on Religion in a Post-Traditionalist World* (Berkeley 1970) pp. 168ff.

30 Steven Lukes, *Émile Durkheim. His Life and Work* (London 1973) p. 270

31 Jeffrey F. Meyer, *Myths in Stone. Religious Dimensions of Washington D.C.* (Berkeley 2001)

32 See Adam Curtis's artily slick *The Power of Nightmares. The Rise of the Politics of Fear*, BBC2 TV October–November 2004. For a fair and fascinating account of the US conservative scene see John Mickelthwaite and Adrian Wooldridge, *The Right Nation. Why America is Different* (London 2004)

33 Bellah, 'Civil Religion in America' p. 186

34 Cecilia Bromley-Martin, 'Being Honest about Europe's Roots?', *Inside the Vatican* (2003) 11, pp. 10–11

35 As argued by Michael Burleigh, 'There's More to German History than Hitler and the Holocaust', *Daily Telegraph* 27 October 2004 p. 22 and 'Don't let the Nazis occupy your mind', *Sunday Times* 15 October 2002 News Review p. 2 which rehearse these arguments in short compass

36 Home Office website: *www.uknationality.gov.uk/british citizen ship/homepage/What happens at a ceremony*

37 See Charles Moore's article in the *Daily Telegraph* 23 April 1999 cited by David Rogers, *Politics, Prayer and Parliament* (London 2000) pp. 111–12. For St Elmo see Donald Attwater and Catherine Rachel John (eds), *The Penguin Dictionary of Saints* (London 1995) p. 120

38 Richard Fenn, *Beyond Idols. The Shape of a Secular Society* (Oxford 2001) p. 179

39 Henri Troyat, *Gorky* (London 1989) pp. 114–15

40 Tommaso Campanella, *La Città del Sole. Dialogo poetico*, trans. with an introduction by Daniel J. Donno (Berkeley 1981) p. 11

41 John M. Headley, *Tommaso Campanella and the Transformation of the World* (Princeton 1997) for the biographical particulars

42 Isaiah Berlin, 'The Originality of Machiavelli' in *The Proper Study of Mankind. An Anthology of Essays*, ed. Henry Hardy (New York 1997) p. 281

43 Niccolò Machiavelli, *The Discourses*, ed. Bernard Crick (London 1970) I. 11–15 pp. 139–52 and II. 2, p. 278

44 Hans Otto Seitscheck, 'Frühe Verwendungen des Begriffs "Politische Religion". Campanella, Clasen, Wieland' in Hans Maier (ed.), *Totalitarismus und Politische Religionen* (Paderborn 2003) 3, pp. 109–14

45 Campanella, *La Città del Sole* p. 99

46 Chr. M. Wieland, *Betrachtungen über die gegenwärtige Lage des Vaterlandes* in F. Martini (ed.), *Meine Antworten. Aufsätze über die Französische Revolution 1789–1793* (Marbach 1983) p. 113

Chapter 1: Age of Reason, Age of Faith

1 Thomas Kselman, 'Religion and French Identity' in William R. Hutchison and Hartmut Lehmann (eds), *Many are Chosen. Divine Election and Western Nationalism* (Minneapolis 1994) p. 57

2 For these details see Bernard Fay,

Louis XVI or the End of the World (Chicago 1968) pp. 124–8

3 Alain Corbin, *Village Bells. Sound and Meaning in the Nineteenth-Century French Countryside* (London 1999) pp. 3–44

4 Paul Johnson, *A History of Christianity* (London 1976) p. 343

5 Ibid. pp. 342–3

6 Nigel Aston, *Religion and Revolution in France 1780–1804* (London 2000) pp. 34–60

7 Bernard Cousin, Monique Cubells and René Moulinas, *La Pique et la croix. L'histoire religieuse de la Révolution française* (Orne 1989) p. 23

8 Robert Darnton, 'Philosophical Sex. Pornography in Old Regime France' in Mark Micale and Robert Dietle (eds), *Enlightenment, Passion, Modernity. Historical Essays in European Thought and Culture* (Stanford 2000) pp. 92–3

9 Jean-Louis Ormières, *Politique et religion en France* (Paris 2002) p. 20; see also Olwen Hufton, 'The French Church' in William Callahan and David Higgs (eds), *Church and Society in Catholic Europe of the Eighteenth Century* (Cambridge 1979) pp. 15–18

10 Owen Chadwick, *The Popes and European Revolution* (Oxford 1981) pp. 257ff. is fundamental

11 See Mack P. Holt, *The French Wars of Religion 1562–1629* (Cambridge 1995)

12 W. R. Ward, *Christianity under the Ancien Régime 1648–1789* (Cambridge 1999) p. 109

13 John McManners, *Church and Society in Eighteenth-Century France* (Oxford 1998) 1, pp. 78–9

14 Derek Beales, 'Joseph II and the Monasteries of Austria and Hungary' in Nigel Aston (ed.), *Religious Change in Europe 1650–1914. Essays for John McManners* (Oxford 1997) pp. 160–84

15 Pascal, *Provincial Letters*, trans. A. J. Krailsheimer (London 1967) Letter V, p. 86

16 Montesquieu, *Persian Letters* trans. Christopher Betts (London 1973) letter 57, p. 122

17 See Douglas Letson and Michael Higgins, *The Jesuit Mystique* (London 1995) pp. 1–72

18 William Doyle, *Jansenism. Catholic Resistance to Authority from the Reformation to the French Revolution* (London 2000) is an excellent introduction. For the discussion of Richerism see M. G. Hutt, 'The Curés and the Third Estate. The Ideas of Reform in the Pamphlets of the French Lower Clergy in the Period 1787–1789', *Journal of Ecclesiastical History* (1957) 8, pp. 84ff.

19 Jean Mesnard, *Pascal. His Life and Works* (London 1952) pp. 66ff.

20 For a clear discussion see Julian Swann, 'The State and Political Culture' in William Doyle (ed.), *Old Regime France 1648–1788* (Oxford 2001) pp. 155–60

21 A. J. Ayer, *Voltaire* (London 1986) p. 30

22 Mona Ozouf, ' "Public Opinion" at the End of the Old Regime', *Journal of Modern History* (1988) 60, p. S10

23 See especially the classic Robert Darnton, *The Literary Underground of the Old Regime* (Cambridge, Mass. 1982)

24 Voltaire, *Philosophical Dictionary*, trans. Theodore Besterman (London 1972) p. 16

25 See especially Peter Gay, *The Enlightenment. The Rise of Modern Paganism* (New York 1966) 1, pp. 98ff.

26 Edward Gibbon, *The Decline and Fall of the Roman Empire*, ed. J. B. Bury (London 1896) 1, p. 28

27 Quotations from David Hume, *Dialogues and Natural History of Religion*, ed. J. C. A. Gaskin (Oxford 1993) pp. 134–96

28 Ibid. p. 295

29 For an excellent discussion see Robert R. Palmer, *Catholics and Unbelievers in Eighteenth-Century France* (Princeton 1947) especially pp. 77–102

30 For the details see Darrin M. McMahon, *Enemies of the Enlightenment. The French Counter-Enlightenment and the Making of Modernity* (Oxford 2001) pp. 32ff.

31 See especially Carl L. Becker, *The Heavenly City of the Eighteenth-Century Philosophers* (New Haven 1932) pp. 71–153 for this argument

32 J. C. D. Clarke (ed.), *Edmund Burke,*

Reflections on the Revolution in France (Stanford 2001) p. 92. Dr Clarke's introduction is an important and lucid one

33 On Barruel see Jacques Godechot, *The Counter-Revolution. Doctrine and Action 1789–1804* (London 1972) pp. 41ff.; Edmund Burke, *Reflections on the Revolution in France*, ed. Conor Cruise O'Brien (London 1968) pp. 211–12; see also J. G. A. Pocock, 'Edmund Burke and the Redefinition of Enthusiasm' in François Furet and Mona Ozouf (eds), *The Transformation of Political Culture 1789–1848. The French Revolution and the Creation of Modern Political Culture* (Oxford 1989) 3, especially pp. 25ff.

34 Alexis de Tocqueville, *The Old Regime and the French Revolution*, ed. François Furet and Françoise Mélino (Chicago 1998) 1, pp. 198–9 and 200–1

35 'Alphabet des sans culottes, ou premiers éléments d'éducation républicaine', cited by Roger Chartier, *The Cultural Origins of the French Revolution* (Durham, NC 1991) p. 89

36 Christopher Dawson, *The Gods of Revolution* (London 1972) p. 29

37 J. M. Roberts, 'The French Origins of the "Right"', *Transactions of the Royal Historical Society* (1973) 23, p. 44

38 On this see David A. Bell, *The Cult of the Nation in France. Inventing Nationalism 1680–1800* (Cambridge, Mass. 2001) pp. 27ff.

Chapter 2: The Church and the Revolution

1 See M. G. Hutt, 'The Role of the Curés in the Estates General of 1789', *Journal of Ecclesiastical History* (1955) 6, pp. 190–220

2 David Lloyd Dowd, *Pageant-Master of the Republic. Jacques-Louis David and the French Revolution* (Lincoln, Nebr. 1948) pp. 36–40

3 Norman Hampson, *Prelude to Terror. The Constituent Assembly and the Failure of Consensus 1789–1791* (Oxford 1988) p. 141

4 Hans Maier, *Revolution and Church. The Early History of Christian Democracy 1789–1901* (Notre Dame 1969) p. 102

5 See Timothy Tackett, *Becoming a Revolutionary. The Deputies of the French National Assembly and the Emergence of a Revolutionary Culture (1789–1790)* (Princeton 1996) for these observations

6 Munro Price, *The Fall of the French Monarchy. Louis XVI, Marie Antoinette and the Baron de Breteuil* (London 2002) pp. 56–7

7 Nigel Aston, *The End of an Élite. The French Bishops and the Coming of the Revolution 1786–1790* (Oxford 1992) p. 177

8 Nigel Aston, *Religion and Revolution in France 1780–1804* (London 2000) pp. 130–1

9 M. G. Hutt, 'The Diary of Rouph de Varicourt, Curé of Gex, Deputy in the Estates General of 1789', *Bulletin of the Institute of Historical Research* (1956) 29, pp. 252–61

10 John McManners, *The French Revolution and the Church* (London 1969) p. 26

11 François Furet, 'Night of August 4' in François Furet and Mona Ozouf (eds), *A Critical Dictionary of the French Revolution* (Cambridge, Mass. 1989) pp. 107–13

12 Philip G. Dwyer, *Talleyrand* (London 2002) p. 34

13 Paul Johnson, *A History of Christianity* (London 1976) p. 357

14 Yann Fauchois, *Religion et France révolutionnaire* (Paris 1989) p. 43

15 C. Dagens et al. (eds), *L'Eglise à l'épreuve de la Révolution* (Paris 1989) p. 74

16 Denis Diderot, *The Nun* (London 1974)

17 Marcel Reinhard, 'Religion, Révolution et Contre-Révolution', *Les Cours de Sorbonne* 1, pp. 46–7

18 William Doyle, *The Oxford History of the French Revolution* (Oxford 1989) p. 138

19 Bernard Plongeron, 'Die Zivilkonstitution des Klerus oder die Misgeschicke der nationalen Religion (1790–1791)' in Plongeron (ed.), *Aufklärung, Revolution, Restauration (1750–1830)*, Jean-Marie Mayeur et al.

(eds), *Die Geschichte des Christentums* (Freiburg 2000) 10, p. 331

20 For the emancipation of the Jews see David Vital, *A People Apart. A Political History of the Jews in Europe 1789–1939* (Oxford 1999) pp. 42ff.

21 Bernard Cousin, Monique Cubells and René Moulinas, *La Pique et la croix. L'Histoire religieuse de la Révolution française* (Orne 1989) pp. 122–4

22 Hampson, *Prelude to Terror* p. 149

23 J. M. Roberts, 'The French Origins of the "Right" ', *Transactions of the Royal Historical Society* (1973) 23, pp. 27–53

24 Timothy Tackett, 'The West in France in 1789. The Religious Factor in the Origins of the Counterrevolution', *Journal of Modern History* (1982) 54, pp. 715–45

25 For a good discussion of these issues see Jean Quéniart, *Le Clergé déchiré. Fidèle ou rebelle?* (Rennes 1988) pp. 39–41

26 Price, *Fall of the French Monarchy* pp. 152–3

27 For these images see Timothy Tackett, *La Révolution, l'Eglise, la France* (Paris 1986) pp. 180ff.

28 For the genesis of this second oath see E. Mangenot, 'La Législation du Serment de la Liberté et de l'Égalité', *Revue de Clergé Français* (1918) pp. 419–36

29 Plongeron, 'Die Zivilkonstitution' pp. 358–63; for detailed accounts of events see Mairie du Vie Arrondisement (ed.), *1792. Les Massacres de Septembre (Les Carmes, L'Abbaye, Saint-Fermin)* (Paris 1992)

30 Donald Sutherland, *The Chouans. The Social Origins of Popular Counter-Revolution in Upper Brittany 1770–1796* (Oxford 1982) pp. 240ff.

31 Ruth Graham, 'The Married Nuns before Cardinal Caprara' in Bernard Plongeron (ed.), *Pratiques religieuses dans l'Europe révolutionnaire (1770–1820)* (Chantilly 1986) pp. 321ff.

32 Michel Vovelle, *The Revolution against the Church. From Reason to the Supreme Being* (Columbus 1991) p. 80; Dawson, *Gods of Revolution* pp. 73–4 for the final quotation

Chapter 3: 'Puritans Thinking They are Spartans Run Amok in Eighteenth-Century Paris'

1 See M. O. Grenby, *The Anti-Jacobin Novel. British Conservatism and the French Revolution* (Cambridge 2001)

2 See especially William L. Pressly, *The French Revolution as Blasphemy. Johann Zoffany's Paintings of the Massacre at Paris, August 10, 1792* (Berkeley 1999) pp. 48ff.

3 For these biographical details see David Lloyd Dowd, *Pageant-Master of the Republic. Jacques-Louis David and the French Revolution* (Lincoln, Nebr. 1948)

4 Jean Starobinski, *1789. The Emblems of Reason* (Charlottesville 1982) pp. 101ff.

5 Dorothy Johnson, *Jacques-Louis David. Art in Metamorphosis* (Princeton 1993) pp. 81–2

6 Norman Hampson, *Will and Circumstance. Montesquieu, Rousseau and the French Revolution* (London 1983) pp. 204–5

7 For these details see Warren Roberts, *Revolutionary Artists. Jacques-Louis David and Jean-Louis Prieur. The Public, the Populace, and Images of the French Revolution* (Albany, NY 2000) especially pp. 288–9

8 See Helen Weston, 'The Corday–Marat Affair' in William Vaughan and Helen Weston (eds), *David's The Death of Marat* (Cambridge 2000) pp. 128–52

9 For the painting's history see Marie-Pierre Foissy-Aufrère et al., *La Mort de Bara* (Musée Calvet, Avignon 1989)

10 Jules Michelet, *Historical View of the French Revolution from its Earliest Indications to the Flight of the King in 1791*, trans. C. Cocks (London 1888) p. 393

11 For these details see Mona Ozouf, *Festivals and the French Revolution* (Cambridge, Mass. 1988) pp. 33–60

12 Dowd, *Pageant-Master of the Republic* pp. 54–72

13 Jean-Jacques Rousseau, *Politics and the Arts. Letter to M. D'Alembert on the Theatre*, trans. with notes and introduction by Allan Bloom (Ithaca 1960) pp. 125–6

14 Jean-Jacques Rousseau, *The Social Contract and Other Later Political Writings*, ed. Victor Gourevitch (Cambridge 1997) pp. 150–1

15 Rousseau, 'Considerations on the Government of Poland' in *The Social Contract and Other Later Political Writings* pp. 181–2

16 Bronislaw Baczko, *Utopian Lights. The Evolution of the Idea of Social Progress* (New York 1989) pp. 43–70

17 Lynn Hunt, *Politics, Culture, and Class in the French Revolution* (Berkeley 1984) p. 97

18 D. M. G. Sutherland, *France 1789–1815. Revolution and Counterrevolution* (London 1985) p. 210

19 For numerous examples see Ferdinand Brunot, *Histoire de la langue française des origines à nos jours* (Paris 1967) 9, part ii, pp. 623–9

20 Boyd C. Schafer, *Nationalism, Myth and Reality* (New York 1955) p. 142

21 James Leith, 'The Terror. Adding the Cultural Dimension' in Ian Germani and Robin Swales (eds), *Symbols, Myths and Images of the French Revolution* (Regina 1998) pp. 9–10

22 See especially James Leith, *Media and Revolution. Moulding a New Citizenry in France during the Terror* (Toronto 1968) pp. 64–5

23 See James Leith, 'On the Religiosity of the French Revolution' in George Levitine (ed.), *Culture and Revolution. Cultural Ramifications of the French Revolution* (College Park, Md 1989) pp. 174–9; on plans for education see R. R. Palmer, *The Improvement of Humanity. Education and the French Revolution* (Princeton 1985)

24 On this debate see Serge Bianchi, *La Révolution culturelle de l'an II* (Paris 1982) pp. 153ff.

25 Harold T. Parker, *The Cult of Antiquity and the French Revolutionaries. A Study in the Development of the French Revolutionary Spirit* (Chicago 1937) p. 141

26 Michel Vovelle, *The Revolution against the Church. From Reason to the Supreme Being* (Columbus 1991) pp. 40–2; René Pillorget, 'The Cultural Programme of the 1789 Revolution', *History* (1985) 70, pp. 388–9

27 Brunot, *Histoire de la langue française* 9, p. 650

28 Richard Cobb, *The People's Armies* (New Haven 1987) p. 471

29 Ernst Gombrich, 'The Dream of Reason. Symbolism of the French Revolution', *British Journal for Eighteenth Century Studies* (1979) 2, p. 192

30 On this calendar see Bronislaw Baczko, 'Le Calendrier républicain' in Pierre Nora (ed.), *Les Lieux de mémoire* (Paris 1984) 1, pp. 37–83; James Figuglietti, 'Gilbert Romme and the Making of the French Republican Calendar' in David G. Troyanski, Alfred Cismaru and Norwood Andrews (eds), *The French Revolution in Culture and Society* (Westport 1991) pp. 13–22, and Hans Maier, 'Über revolutionäre Feste and Zeitrechnungen' in Hans Maier and Eberhard Schmitt (eds), *Wie eine Revolution entsteht. Die französische Revolution als Kommunikationsereignis* (Paderborn 1990) pp. 99–117

31 Cited by David P. Jordan, *The Revolutionary Career of Maximilien Robespierre* (New York 1985) p. 193

32 R. R. Palmer, *Twelve who Ruled. The Year of the Terror in the French Revolution* (Princeton 1941) pp. 118–19

33 For an extremely astute account of the Revolution see S. E. Finer, *The History of Government*, vol. 3: *Empires, Monarchies and the Modern State* (Oxford 1999) pp. 1517–66

34 Michelle Vovelle, *La Mentalité révolutionnaire* (Paris 1985) p. 151

35 See the outstanding study by Patrice Higonnet, *Goodness beyond Virtue. Jacobins during the French Revolution* (Cambridge, Mass. 1998) p. 233

36 William Reddy, 'Sentimentalism and its Erasure. The Role of Emotions in the Era of the French Revolution', *Journal of Modern History* (2000) 72, p. 110

37 See especially J. L. Talmon, *The Origins of Totalitarian Democracy* (London 1952) pp. 149ff.

38 Brunot, *Histoire de la langue française* 9, p. 877
39 Jordan, *Revolutionary Career of Maximilien Robespierre* p. 175
40 For this see the suggestive comments in Barrington Moore Jnr, *Moral Purity and Persecution in History* (Princeton 2000) p. 74
41 Christoph Martin Wieland, 'Betrachtungen über die gegenwärtige Lage des Vaterlandes' in F. Martini (ed.), *Meine Antworten. Aufsätze über die Französische Revolution 1789–1793* (Marbach 1983) p. 113; see also Hans Otto Seitschek, 'Frühe Verwendungen des Begriffs "Politische Religion". Campanella, Clasen, Wieland' in Hans Maier (ed.), *Totalitarismus und Politische Religionen* (Paderborn 2003) 3, pp. 118–20
42 Alexis de Tocqueville, *The Old Regime and the French Revolution*, ed. François Furet and Françoise Mélonio (Chicago 1998) 1, p. 101
43 Lucien Jaume, *Le Discours jacobin et la démocratie* (Paris 1989) pp. 249–53
44 Palmer, *Twelve who Ruled* p. 328
45 For this story see Antoine de Baecque, *Glory and Terror. Seven Deaths under the French Revolution* (New York/London 2001) pp. 121–42. See also his essay on regeneration, 'L'Homme nouveau est arrivé. La "Régénération" du Français en 1789', *Dix-Huitième Siècle* (1988) 20, pp. 193–208. For more conventional accounts of the Terror that reduce it to a crude historiographical either–or of ideology or circumstances, see Hugh Gough, *The Terror in the French Revolution* (London 1998) and Arno Meyer, *The Furies. Violence and Terror in the French and Russian Revolutions* (Princeton 2000), a book chiefly interesting for the newfound salience the old academic left is prepared to accord religion in the historical process
46 Donald Sutherland, *The Chouans. The Social Origins of Popular Counter-Revolution in Upper Brittany 1770–1796* (Oxford 1982) p. 247
47 Marie-Paule Biron, *Les Messes clandestines pendant la Révolution* (Paris 1989) p. 78
48 Frank Tallett, 'Dechristianizing France. The Year II and the Revolutionary Experience' in Frank Tallett and Nicholas Atkin (eds), *Religion, Society and Politics in France since 1789* (London 1991) pp. 17–22
49 Claude Petitfrère, 'The Origins of the Civil War in the Vendée', *French History* (1988) 2, pp. 196–7
50 Reynald Secher, *Le Génocide franco-français: La Vendée-vengée* (Paris 1986) pp. 158–9
51 Graham Robb, *Victor Hugo* (London 1997) pp. 5–7
52 Cobb, *People's Armies* pp. 400ff.; Secher, *Le Génocide* p. 152
53 For the above see Sutherland, *Chouans* pp. 258ff.
54 Anne Bernet, *Histoire générale de la chouannerie* (Paris 2000)
55 F.-A. Aulard, *Le Culte de la raison et le culte de l'être suprême (1793–1794)* (Paris 1892) p. 314
56 Ibid. p. 316
57 John McManners, *Lectures on European History 1789–1914. Men, Machines and Freedom* (Oxford 1966) p. 48
58 E. Mangenot, 'La Première Déportation Ecclésiastique à Rochefort', *Revue du Clergé Français* (1916) 88, pp. 289ff.; John McManners, *The French Revolution and the Church* (London 1969) pp. 126–7
59 Olwen Hufton, 'The Reconstruction of a Church, 1796–1801' in Gwynne Lewis and Colin Lucas (eds), *Beyond the Terror. Essays in French Regional and Social History 1794–1815* (Cambridge 1983) pp. 21–52
60 *Revue de l'Histoire de l'Église de France*
61 Geoffrey Ellis, 'Religion according to Napoleon. The Limitations of Pragmatism' in Nigel Aston (ed.), *Religious Change in Europe 1650–1914* (Oxford 1997) pp. 234–7
62 Sutherland, *France 1789–1815* p. 355
63 William Roberts, 'Napoleon and the Concordat of 1801' in Frank Coppa (ed.), *Controversial Concordats* (Washington DC 1999) pp. 44–5
64 Colin Lucas, 'Presentation' in François Furet and Mona Ozouf (eds), *The Transformation of Political Culture*

1789–1848. The French Revolution and the Creation of Modern Political Culture (Oxford 1989) 3, pp. 349–50

65 Information from Robert Conquest

Chapter 4: The Alliance of Throne and Altar in Restoration Europe

1 Graham Robb, Victor Hugo (London 1997) pp. 31–2

2 For these details see the vivid account by T. C. W. Blanning, 'The Role of Religion in European Counter-Revolution 1789–1815' in Derek Beales and Geoffrey Best (eds), History, Society and the Churches. Essays in Honour of Owen Chadwick (Cambridge 1985) pp. 195ff.

3 James Sheehan, German History 1770–1866 (Oxford 1989) p. 392, and for Hegel's changing political views see Horst Althaus, Hegel. An Intellectual Biography (Oxford 2000)

4 For examples see R. S. Soloway, Prelates and People. Ecclesiastical Social Thought in England 1783–1852 (London 1969) pp. 34–45

5 Rosemary Ashton, The Life of Samuel Taylor Coleridge (Oxford 1996) p. 90

6 Mark Storey, Robert Southey. A Life (Oxford 1997)

7 Maurice Cranston, The Romantic Movement (Oxford 1994) p. 62

8 Friedrich Sieburg, Chateaubriand (London 1961) pp. 100–1

9 Elisabeth Fehrenbach, 'Über die Bedeutung der politischen Symbole im Nationalstaat', HZ (1971) 213, pp. 318–326; Joseph Leo Koerner, Kaspar David Friedrich and the Subject of Landscape (London 1995)

10 Novalis, Die Christenheit oder Europa, ed. Carl Paschek (Stuttgart 1984)

11 'Submission to the Powers that be: The "Paternal Exhortation" of Patriarch Antimos of Jerusalem' in Richard Clogg (ed.), The Movement for Greek Independence 1770–1821. A Collection of Documents (London 1976) pp. 57ff.

12 Richard Watson, A Defence of Revealed Religion in Two Sermons Preached in the Cathedral Church of Llandaff (London 1806) p. 400

13 Archivio Segreto del Vaticano. Fondo Particolare Pio IX, cassetta 5, busta 4 'Catechismo Sulle Rivoluzione' (1832)

14 Adrien Dansette, Religious History of Modern France. From the Revolution to the Third Republic (Freiburg 1961) 1, p. 176

15 Derek Beales and Eugenio Biagini, The Risorgimento and the Unification of Italy (second edition London 2002) p. 75

16 Raymond Grew, 'Culture and Society 1796–1896' in John Davis (ed.), Italy in the Nineteenth Century (Oxford 2000) p. 221

17 Leonid Strakhovsky, Alexander I of Russia (London 1949) p. 159

18 John McManners, Lectures on European History 1789–1914. Men, Machines and Freedom (Oxford 1966) p. 117

19 Strakhovsky, Alexander I of Russia p. 154

20 For Congress diplomacy see Alan Sked (ed.), Europe's Balance of Power 1815–1848 (London 1979)

21 H. Daniel-Rops, The Church in the Age of Revolution 1789–1870 (London 1965) p. 127

22 Alan Palmer, Alexander I (London 1974) pp. 326–7

23 Guido de Ruggiero, The History of European Liberalism (Oxford 1927) p. 85

24 For Metternich's religious views see Owen Chadwick, The Popes and European Revolution (Oxford 1981) p. 537

25 Hagen Schulze, States, Nations and Nationalism (Oxford 1994) p. 90

26 Salo Wittmayer Baron, Modern Nationalism and Religion (New York 1960) p. 33

27 Edward Norman, Church and Society in England 1770–1970. A Historical Study (Oxford 1976) p. 70

28 For the above see mainly A. D. Gilbert, Religion and Society in Industrial England. Church, Chapel and Social Change 1740–1914 (London 1976) p. 82 for the duchess's remarks

29 Eric Hobsbawm, The Age of Revolution 1789–1848 (London 1962) p. 299

30 Richard Lebrun, Joseph de Maistre. An Intellectual Militant (Kingston/Montreal 1988)

31 Jack Hayward, *After the French Revolution. Six Critics of Democracy and Nationalism* (New York 1991) p. 48

32 Richard Fargher, 'Religious Reactions in Post-Revolutionary French Literature' in Nigel Aston (ed.), *Religious Change in Europe 1650–1914. Essays for John McManners* (Oxford 1997) p. 270

33 Lebrun, *Joseph de Maistre* p. 183

34 Joseph de Maistre, *Considerations*, ed. and trans. Richard A. Lebrun (Cambridge, 1994) p. 73

35 Ibid. p. 53

36 Ibid. p. 41

37 Jack Lively (ed.), *The Works of Joseph de Maistre* (New York 1965) p. 253

38 Most obviously Isaiah Berlin, 'Introduction' to de Maistre, *Considerations* p. xxix

39 Lively, *Works of Joseph de Maistre* p. 142

40 See especially Leon Bramson, *The Political Context of Sociology* (Princeton 1961) pp. 11–24

41 J. L. Talmon, *Political Messianism. The Romantic Phase* (London 1960) p. 312

42 For the above see mainly David Klinck, *The French Counterrevolutionary Theorist Louis de Bonald (1754–1840)* (New York 1996)

43 Alec R. Vidler, *Prophecy and Papacy. A Study of Lamennais, the Church and the Revolution* (London 1954) p. 60

44 Dansette, *Religious History of Modern France* 1, pp. 194–5

45 P.-J. Béranger, 'The Coronation of Charles X' in J. H. Stewart, *The Restoration Era in France 1814–1830* (Princeton 1968)

46 C. S. Phillips, *The Church in France 1789–1848. A Study in Revival* (London 1929) 1, p. 193

47 Alfred Minke, 'Ein liberaler Triumph. Die Unabhängigkeit Belgiens' in Bernard Plongeron (ed.), *Aufklärung, Revolution, Restauration* pp. 738ff.

48 K. Jürgensen, *Lamennais und die Gestaltung des belgischen Staates* (Wiesbaden 1963)

49 Vidler, *Prophecy and the Papacy* pp. 105ff.

50 Talmon, *Political Messianism* p. 235

51 Daniel-Rops, *The Church in the Age of Revolution* p. 202

52 Vidler, *Prophecy and the Papacy* pp. 182–3

53 For this important point see Hans Maier, *Revolution und Kirche. Zur Frühgeschichte der christlichen Demokratie* (Freiburg im Breisgau 1975) pp. 170–1

54 Vidler, *Prophecy and Papacy* pp. 198–9

55 Owen Chadwick, *A History of the Popes 1830–1914* (Oxford 1998) p. 25

56 Frank Coppa, *The Modern Papacy since 1789* (London 1998) p. 59

Chapter 5: Chosen Peoples: Political Messianism and Nationalism

1 See the useful discussion in Conor Cruise O'Brien's *God Land. Reflections on Religion and Nationalism* (Cambridge, Mass. 1988) pp. 41–2

2 William R. Hutchinson and Hartmut Lehmann (eds), *Many are Chosen. Divine Election and Western Nationalism* (Minneapolis 1994)

3 Emilio Gentile, 'The Sacralisation of Politics. Definitions, Interpretations and Reflections on the Question of Secular Religion and Totalitarianism', *Totalitarian Movements and Political Religions* (2000) 1, pp. 18–55 is symptomatic of writing in this field that omits any discussion of the role of Christianity in relation to the pseudo-religious phenomena he otherwise describes so well. By contrast, David A. Bell's *The Cult of the Nation in France. Inventing Nationalism 1680–1800* (Cambridge, Mass. 2001) pp. 190ff. contains some valuable comparisons between the Counter-Reformation drive for 'hearts and minds' and that of the revolutionary state

4 The quotation from Hegel is from *Die Verfassung Deutschlands* (1802) in Hegel, *Politische Schriften*, ed. Hans Blumenberg et al. (Frankfurt am Main 1966) p. 37

5 Thomas Nipperdey, *Deutsche Geschichte 1800–1866. Bürgerwelt und starker Staat* (Munich 1998) pp. 431–2

6 Ernest Gellner, *Nationalism* (London 1995) pp. 66ff. and 76–8

7 Wolfgang Altgeld, *Katholizismus,*

Protestantismus, Judentum. Über religiös begründete Gegensätze und nationalreligiöse Ideen in der Geschichte des deutschen Nationalismus (Mainz 1992) p. 170; John McManners, *Church and State in France 1870–1914* (London 1972) p. 41 for Gambetta

8 *La Riforma* 3 October 1870 cited by Christopher Duggan, *Francesco Crispi. From Nation to Nationalism* (Oxford 2002) p. 328.

9 Wolfgang Altgeld, 'Religion, Denomination and Nationalism in Nineteenth-Century Germany' in Martin Walser Smith (ed.), *Protestants, Catholics and Jews in Germany 1800–1914* (New York 2001) p. 55

10 Elie Kedourie, *Nationalism* (fourth edition Oxford 1993) p. 1

11 For a useful summary of the latest work on these themes see Antony D. Smith, *Chosen Peoples. Sacred Sources of National Identity* (Oxford 2003) pp. 115ff.

12 Otto Dann, *Nation und Nationalismus in Deutschland 1770–1990* (Munich 1993) pp. 52–3

13 Nicholas Hope, *German and Scandinavian Protestantism 1700–1918* (Oxford 1995) pp. 217ff. is fundamental

14 Dräsecke, 'Vaterlandsfreude. Eine Dankpredigt zur Feier des Tages von Leipzig' (Bremen 1815), cited by Arlie J. Hoover, *The Gospel of Nationalism. German Patriotic Preaching from Napoleon to Versailles* (Stuttgart 1986) p. 59

15 Carlton Hayes, 'Nationalism as a Religion' in his *Essays on Nationalism* (New York 1926) pp. 93–125 and *Nationalism. A Religion* (New York 1960) p. 47 for the general themes, and Koppel Pinson, *Pietism as a Factor in the Rise of German Nationalism* (New York 1934) especially pp. 25–7 for these remarks on Pietism. But see also the caveats of Hartmut Lehmann, 'Pietism and Nationalism. The Relationship between Protestant Revivalism and National Renewal in Nineteenth-Century Germany', *Church History* (1982) 51, pp. 39ff. regarding Pinson's undifferentiated use of the term Pietism

16 David Nicholls, *Deity and Domination. Images of God and the State in the Nineteenth and Twentieth Centuries* (London 1989)

17 Michel de Certeau et al., *Une Politique de la langue. La Révolution française et les patois* (Paris 1975) p. 181

18 Hans Kohn, *The Idea of Nationalism* (New York 1945) pp. 368–9

19 Pinson, *Pietism as a Factor* p. 158

20 Elie Kedourie, *Nationalism* p. 60

21 On this see Maurice Cranston, *The Romantic Movement* (Oxford 1994) p. 24

22 Kohn, *Idea of Nationalism* p. 434; Isaiah Berlin, *Vico and Herder. Two Studies in the History of Ideas* (London 1980) is still serviceable, although the standard modern biography is Michael Zaremba, *Johann Gottfried Herder – Prediger der Humanität* (Cologne 2003)

23 Ute Schneider, 'Die Erfindung des Bösen. Der Welsche' in Gerd Krumreich and Hartmut Lehmann (eds), 'Gott mit uns'. *Nation, Religion und Gewalt im 19. und frühen 20. Jahrhundert* (Göttingen 2000) p. 48

24 Rainer Wohlfeil, *Spanien und die deutsche Erhebung* (Wiesbaden 1965) pp. 309ff.

25 As pointed out by Carlton Hayes, 'The Propagation of Nationalism' in his *Essays on Nationalism* pp. 76–7

26 Dann, *Nation und Nationalismus in Deutschland* p. 74

27 Jerry Dawson, *Friedrich Schleiermacher. The Evolution of a Nationalist* (Austin 1966) pp. 60ff. and Salo Wittmayer Baron, *Modern Nationalism and Religion* (New York 1960) pp. 136ff. are useful

28 Hasko Zimmer, *Auf dem Altar des Vaterlands. Religion und Patriotismus in der deutschen Kriegslyrik des 19. Jahrhunderts* (Frankfurt am Main 1971) pp. 56–7

29 For this see Hoover, *Gospel of Nationalism* p. 67

30 Hartmut Lehmann, 'The Germans as a Chosen People. Old Testament Themes in German Nationalism', *German Studies Review* (1991) 14, pp. 261ff.

31 Zimmer, *Auf dem Altar* p. 27

32 Hans-Ulrich Wehler, *Nationalismus* (Frankfurt am Main 2002) p. 69

33 Erich Pelzer, 'Die Wiedergeburt Deutschlands 1813 und die Dämonisierung Napoleons' in Krumreich and Lehmann (eds), 'Gott mit uns' pp. 150–1

34 Adam Zamoyski, Holy Madness. Romantics, Patriots and Revolutionaries 1776–1871 (London 1999) p. 193

35 Cranston, Romantic Movement pp. 42–3

36 Hayes, 'Nationalism as a Religion' p. 61; see also the discussion in Baron, Modern Nationalism and Religion p. 47

37 Jonathan Sperber, The European Revolutions 1848–1851 (Cambridge 1994) p. 99

38 Thomas Nipperdey, Deutsche Geschichte 1800–1866 pp. 279–81

39 Altgeld, 'Religion, Denomination and Nationalism' pp. 56–7

40 Altgeld, Katholizismus, Protestantismus, Judentum p. 172

41 Ulrich von Hehl, 'Zwei Kulturen – eine Nation? Die frühe burschenschaftliche Einheitsbewegung und das Wartburgfest', Historisches Jahrbuch (1991) 111, p. 47

42 Thomas Nipperdey, 'Verein als soziale Struktur in Deutschland im späten 18. und frühen 19. Jahrhundert' in his Geschichtswissenschaft und Vereinswesen im 19 Jahrhundert (Göttingen 1972)

43 George L. Mosse, The Nationalization of the Masses. Political Symbolism and Mass Movements in Germany from the Napoleonic Wars through the Third Reich (Ithaca 1975) pp. 81ff.

44 See Stuart Woolf, A History of Italy 1700–1860 (London 1979) pp. 247–8 for a good discussion of the variety of sects

45 See James Billington, Fire in the Minds of Men. Origins of the Revolutionary Faith (New York 1980) pp. 130ff., and J. Rath, 'The Carbonari. Their Origins, Initiation Rites, and Aims', AHR (1964) pp. 353ff.

46 Gellner, Nationalism pp. 41ff.

47 Richard Clogg (ed.), The Movement for Greek Independence 1770–1821. A Collection of Documents (London 1976) pp. 184ff.

48 For the diplomacy of the Greek war of independence see Paul Schroeder's excellent account in The Transformation of European Politics 1763–1848 (Oxford 1994) pp. 614ff.

49 There is an excellent discussion of these issues in David Brewer, The Flame of Freedom. The Greek War of Independence 1821–1833 (London 2001) pp. 104ff.

50 W. St Clair, That Greece Might Still Be Free. The Philhellenes in the War of Independence (New York 1972)

51 Mikhail Dimitriev, 'Polen' in Bernard Plongeron (ed.), Aufklärung, Revolution, Restauration (1750–1830), Jean-Marie Mayeur et al. (eds), Die Geschichte des Christentums (Freiburg 2000) 10, p. 751

52 For this discussion of the dominant modes of Polish political conduct see Norman Davies, Heart of Europe. A Short History of Poland (Oxford 1984) pp. 179ff.

53 S. Helsztynski (ed.), Adam Mickiewicz 1798–1855. Selected Poetry and Prose (Warsaw 1955) pp. 103–4

54 For these details see Monica Gardner, Adam Mickiewicz. The National Poet of Poland (London 1911)

55 S. J. Connolly, Priests and People in Pre-Famine Ireland 1780–1845 (Dublin 2001) pp. 209–13

56 For an exceptionally fine discussion of these issues see Alvin Jackson, Ireland 1798–1998 (Oxford 1999) pp. 25–6

57 Oliver MacDonagh, The Emancipist. Daniel O'Connell 1830–1847 (London 1989) p. 245

58 Edward Norman, A History of Modern Ireland (London 1971) p. 57

59 See Oliver MacDonagh, The Hereditary Bondsman. Daniel O'Connell 1775–1829 (London 1988); Jeanne Sheehy, The Rediscovery of Ireland's Past. The Celtic Revival 1830–1930 (London 1980) pp. 9ff. is an incisive and useful discussion of these emblems

60 MacDonagh, Hereditary Bondsman pp. 211ff.

61 Thomas Bartlett, The Fall and Rise of the Irish Nation. The Catholic Question 1690–1830 (Dublin 1992) p. 332

62 F. O'Ferrall, Catholic Emancipation and

the Birth of Irish Democracy 1820–1830 (Dublin 1985)

63 Marcus Tanner, Ireland's Holy Wars. The Struggle for a Nation's Soul 1500–2000 (New Haven 2001) p. 235

64 For a good discussion of Catholic political mobilisation see R. F. Foster, Modern Ireland 1600–1972 (London 1988) pp. 289ff.

65 MacDonagh, Emancipist pp. 226ff.

66 Charles Gavan Duffy, Young Ireland. A Fragment of Irish History 1840–1850 (London 1880) pp. 344–7

67 A. Griffith, Thomas Davis, the Thinker and Teacher (Dublin 1918)

68 On Young Ireland see D. George Boyce, Nationalism in Ireland (London 1982) especially pp. 154ff.

69 Woolf, A History of Italy p. 311

70 Giuseppe Mazzini, 'Foi et avenir' (1835) in his Scritti editi e inediti (Imola 1906–40) 6, pp. 263ff.

71 Giuseppe Mazzini, Life and Writings (London 1864) 1, pp. 105–6

72 Roland Sarti, Mazzini. A Life for the Religion of Politics (Westport 1997) pp. 54–5

73 Denis Mack Smith, Mazzini (New Haven 1994) p. 17

74 See J. L. Talmon, Political Messianism. The Romantic Phase (London 1960), pp. 256–61

75 Mazzini, Life and Writings pp. 124–5

76 Roland Sarti, 'Giuseppe Mazzini and his Opponents' in John Davis (ed.), Italy in the Nineteenth Century (Oxford 2000) p. 76

77 Sarti, Mazzini p. 80

78 E. E. Y. Hales, Mazzini and the Secret Societies. The Making of a Myth (London 1956) p. 141

79 Smith, Mazzini especially pp. 12ff.

80 Owen Chadwick, A History of the Popes 1830–1941 (Oxford 1998) pp. 50–1

81 H. Daniel-Rops, The Church in an Age of Revolution 1789–1870 (London 1965) p. 252

82 Chadwick, History of the Popes pp. 82ff.

83 David Kertzer, The Kidnapping of Edgardo Mortara (New York 1997)

84 See Lucy Riall, Sicily and the Unification of Italy. Liberal Policy and Local Power 1859–1866 (Oxford 1998)

85 Christopher Duggan, Francesco Crispi. From Nation to Nationalism (Oxford 2003)

86 Nelson Moe, ' "This is Africa". Ruling and Representing Southern Italy, 1860–61' in Albert Russell Ascoli and Krystyna von Henneberg (eds), Making and Remaking Italy. The Cultivation of National Identity during the Risorgimento (Oxford 2001) pp. 135ff.

87 Duggan, Francesco Crispi p. 304

88 Ibid. p. 433

89 Zamoyski, Holy Madness p. 409

90 La Riforma 10 June 1882, cited by Duggan, Francesco Crispi p. 438

Chapter 6: Century of Faiths

1 Maurice Cowling, Religion and Public Doctrine in Modern England (Cambridge 1980–2001) 2, p. 97

2 David Hempton, 'Religious Life in Industrial Britain, 1830–1914' in Sheridan Gilley and W. J. Sheils (eds), A History of Religion in Britain. Practice and Belief from Pre-Roman Times to the Present (Oxford 1994) p. 309, and see Chapter 9 below

3 David Blackbourn, The Fontana History of Modern Germany 1780–1918. The Long Nineteenth Century (London 1997) p. 285

4 Stefan Collini, Arnold (Oxford 1988) p. 94

5 Gordon Haight, George Eliot. A Biography (London 1968) p. 331

6 John Sutherland, Mrs Humphry Ward (Oxford 1990)

7 Ibid. p. 112

8 Mrs Humphry Ward, Robert Elsmere (27th ed. London 1889)

9 Ibid. p. 342

10 Ibid. p. 365

11 Ibid. p. 523

12 Ibid. p. 412

13 Ibid. pp. 578–81 for these details

14 Sutherland, Mrs Humphry Ward pp. 128–30

15 Frederick Crews, 'Dialectical Immaterialism', The American Scholar (1985) 54, p. 453

16 Graham Robb, Victor Hugo (London 1997) p. 273

17 Gustave Flaubert, *Sentimental Education* (London 1964) p. 334

18 Adrien Dansette, *Religious History of Modern France. From the Revolution to the Third Republic* (Freiburg 1961) 1, p. 265

19 Ralph Gibson, *A Social History of French Catholicism 1789–1914* (London 1989) pp. 195–9

20 Hugh McLeod, *Religion and the People of Western Europe 1789–1989* (Oxford 1997) p. 105

21 For these details see Jean-Louis Ormières, *Politique et religion en France* (Paris 2002) p. 88

22 Robb, *Victor Hugo* p. 302

23 François Furet, *Revolutionary France 1770–1880* (Oxford 1992) pp. 434–45

24 André Jardin, *Tocqueville. A Biography* (Baltimore 1998) p. 476

25 Owen Chadwick, *The Victorian Church* (London 1966–70) 1, pp. 290–1

26 J. V. Langmead Casserly, *The Retreat from Christianity in the Modern World* (London 1952) pp. 57–8

27 Lionel Trilling, *Matthew Arnold* (London 1939) pp. 208–13

28 H. Daniel-Rops, *The Church in an Age of Revolution 1789–1870* (London 1964) pp. 314–16 is damning of the low level of the Catholic response to these challenges

29 Michael Bartholomew, 'The Moral Critique of Christian Orthodoxy' in Gerald Parsons (ed.), *Religion in Victorian Britain* (Manchester 1988) 2, pp. 177–8

30 Chadwick, *Victorian Church* 1, p. 529; H. R. Murphy, 'The Ethical Revolt against Christian Orthodoxy in Early Victorian England', *AHR* (1955) 9, pp. 800–17

31 Maurice Cowling, *Religion and Public Doctrine in Modern England* (Cambridge 1980–2001) 3, pp. 75ff. and Collini, *Arnold* p. 108

32 On this theme see Lucien Hölscher, *Weltgericht oder Revolution. Protestantische und sozialistische Zukunftsvorstellungen im deutschen Kaiserreich* (Stuttgart 1989) p. 68

33 Adrian Desmond and James Moore, *Darwin* (London 1991) p. 665

34 Thomas Nipperdey, *Deutsche Geschichte 1800–1866. Bürgerwelt und starker Staat* (Munich 1998) p. 496

35 Max Weber, 'Science as a Vocation' in H. H. Gerth and C. Wright Mills (eds), *From Max Weber. Essays in Sociology* (London 1970) pp. 129–56

36 Dansette, *Religious History of Modern France* 1, p. 311

37 Chadwick, *Victorian Church* 1, p. 145

38 Ibid. p. 559

39 J. W. Burrow, 'Faith, Doubt and Unbelief' in Laurence Lerner (ed.), *The Victorians* (London 1978) p. 168

40 A. N. Wilson, *God's Funeral. A Biography of Faith and Doubt in Western Civilization* (New York 1999) pp. 194–6 is excellent on this clash and much else

41 Alec Vidler, *The Church in the Age of Revolution* (London 1971) pp. 114–15

42 Desmond and Moore, *Darwin* pp. 670–1; see also James R. Moore, 'Freethought, Secularism, Agnosticism. The Case of Charles Darwin' in Parsons (ed.), *Religion in Victorian Britain* 1, pp. 274ff.

43 Chadwick, *Victorian Church* 2, p. 23

44 W. R. Ward, *Christianity under the Ancien Régime 1648–1789* (Cambridge 1999) pp. 174–6

45 Horst Althaus, *Hegel. An Intellectual Biography* (Oxford 2000) p. 37

46 Ward, *Robert Elsmere*

47 Chadwick, *Victorian Church* 2, p. 141

48 For an excellent discussion of these processes see Martin Greschat, *Das Zeitalter der Industriellen Revolution. Das Christentum vor der Moderne* (Stuttgart 1980) pp. 76–80 and 136–9

49 James Sheehan, *German History 1770–1866* (Oxford 1989) p. 563

50 Greschat, *Das Zeitalter der Industriellen Revolution* p. 127

51 See Hans Frei, 'David Friedrich Strauss' in Ninian Smart et al. (eds), *Nineteenth-Century Religious Thought in the West* (Cambridge 1985) 1, pp. 215–60; the best account of Karl Marx's early career remains David McLellan, *Karl Marx. Life and Thought* (London 1973) pp. 32ff.

52 H. W. Wardman, *Ernest Renan. A Critical Biography* (London 1964) pp. 77–8

53 David C. J. Lee, *Ernest Renan. In the Shadow of Faith* (London 1996) pp. 198–9

54 D. G. Charlton, *Secular Religions in France 1815–1870* (Oxford 1963) pp. 96ff. For French examples

55 Langmead Casserley, *Retreat from Christianity* pp. 61–2

56 *Oeuvres de Claude-Henri de Saint-Simon* (Paris 1966) 1, p. 248

57 Leszek Kolakowski, *Main Currents in Marxism. Its Rise, Growth, and Dissolution* (Oxford 1978) 1, pp. 219–20

58 Jack Hayward, *After the French Revolution. Six Critics of Democracy and Nationalism* (New York 1991) p. 94

59 Frank E. Manuel and Fritzie P. Manuel, *Utopian Thought in the Western World* (Cambridge, Mass. 1979) p. 596

60 Frank E. Manuel, *The New World of Henri Saint-Simon* (Cambridge, Mass. 1956) pp. 312–17

61 There is an excellent discussion of Saint-Simon in Sidney Pollard, *The Idea of Progress. History and Society* (London 1968) pp. 104–14

62 Isaiah Berlin, *Freedom and its Betrayal. Six Enemies of Human Liberty* (London 2003) p. 108

63 As cogently argued by Berlin, ibid. p. 107

64 Manuel, *The New World of Henri Saint-Simon* pp. 360–1

65 Lucien Hölscher, *Die Entdeckung der Zukunft* (Frankfurt am Main 1999) pp. 96–7

66 Frank Manuel, *Prophets of Paris* (Cambridge, Mass. 1962) for the details

67 Langmead Casserley, *Retreat from Religion* p. 42

68 Mary Pickering, *Auguste Comte. An Intellectual Biography* (Cambridge 1993) 1, pp. 362ff.

69 T. R. Wright, *The Religion of Humanity. The Impact of Comtean Positivism on Victorian Britain* (Cambridge 1986) p. 14

70 Andrew Wernick, *Auguste Comte and the Religion of Humanity* (Cambridge 2001) pp. 87–97

71 Charlton, *Secular Religions in France* pp. 46ff.

72 Henri de Lubac, *The Drama of Atheist Humanism* (San Francisco 1983 originally Paris 1944) p. 216

73 Raymond Aron, *Main Currents in Sociological Thought* (New York 1965) 1, p. 123

74 De Lubac, *Drama of Atheist Humanism* p. 229

75 Edward Caird, *The Social Philosophy and Religion of Comte* (Glasgow 1885) p. 239

76 De Lubac, *Drama of Atheist Humanism* pp. 260–1

77 J. L. Talmon, *Political Messianism. The Romantic Phase* (London 1960) pp. 130–6

78 Manuel and Manuel, *Utopian Thought in the Western World* p. 652

79 Kolakowski, *Main Currents in Marxism* 1, p. 202

80 Robert Owen, 'A New View of Society' in his *A New View of Society and Other Writings*, ed. Gregory Claeys (London 1991) p. 28

81 J. F. C. Harrison, *Robert Owen and the Owenites in Britain and America. The Quest for the New Moral World* (London 1969) p. 158

82 Frank Podmore, *Robert Owen* (London 1906) two volumes.

83 Harrison, *Robert Owen and the Owenites* p. 32

84 Ibid.

85 Greschat, *Das Zeitalter der Industriellen Revolution* p. 103

86 Harrison, *Robert Owen and the Owenites* p. 212

87 Ibid. p. 133

88 *Social Hymns. For the Use of Friends of the Rational System of Society* (Manchester 1835) Nr 129

89 R. A. Soloway, *Prelates and People. Ecclesiastical Social Thought in England 1783–1852* (London 1969) p. 262

90 Edward Norman, *Church and Society in England 1770–1970. A Historical Study* (Oxford 1976) p. 169

91 Greschat, *Das Zeitalter der Industriellen Revolution* p. 37 for these statistics

92 Kolakowski, *Main Currents in Marxism* 1, p. 184

93 James Billington, *Fire in the Minds of Men. Origins of the Revolutionary Faith* (New York 1980) p. 246

94 Henry James, *The Princess*

Casamassima (London 1987 originally 1886) pp. 283–4

95 Wilhelm Weitling, *Das Evangelium des armen Sünders. Die Menschheit, wie sie ist, und wie sie sein sollte* (Hamburg 1971)

96 Kolakowski, *Main Currents of Marxism* 1, pp. 211–13

97 McLellan, *Karl Marx* pp. 156–7

98 Hölscher, *Weltgericht oder Revolution* p. 166

99 See Karl Marx and Friedrich Engels, *The Communist Manifesto*, ed. Gareth Stedman Jones (London 2002) pp. 39–49

100 John Edward Toews, *Hegelianism. The Path toward Dialectical Humanism 1805–41* (Cambridge 1980)

101 Leonard P. Wessell, *Prometheus Bound. The Mythic Structure of Karl Marx's Scientific Thinking* (Baton Rouge 1984) pp. 153–5

102 Van A. Harvey, 'Ludwig Feuerbach and Karl Marx' in Smart et al. (eds), *Nineteenth-Century Religious Thought in The West* p. 295

103 McLellan, *Karl Marx* pp. 93–8

104 Karl Löwith, *Meaning in History. The Theological Implications of the Philosophy of History* (Chicago 1949) p. 43

105 The key works here apart from Löwith, *Meaning in History* are Kolakowski, *Main Currents in Marxism* 1; Wessell, *Prometheus Bound*; E. Tuveson, 'The Millenarian Structure of the Communist Manifesto' in C. Patrides and J. Wittreich (eds), *The Apocalypse in English Renaissance Thought and Literature* (Ithaca 1984)

106 Löwith, *Meaning in History* p. 36 quoting an 1856 essay by Marx

107 Igor Halfin, *From Darkness to Light. Class, Consciousness, and Salvation in Revolutionary Russia* (Pittsburgh 2000) especially pp. 39–84

108 Hobsbawm, *Age of Revolutions* p. 271: 'The general trend of the period 1789 to 1848 was therefore one of emphatic secularisation.' This is strange since leading historians of secularisation in the subsequent period 1848 to 1914 are totally at odds as to when, where and why limited secularisation occurred in their period, with the majority preferring to push it forwards to the 1960s; similarly, his 'Religion and the Rise of Socialism' in his *Worlds of Labour. Further Studies in the History of Labour* (London 1984) pp. 22–48 follows Marx in treating all religious aspects of socialism as 'archaisms' and fails to engage with the notion that socialism itself may have been a secular religion. One suspects that anyone who knows about Argentina, China, Mexico and all the other places which he writes about with such concise confidence may have similar criticisms

109 Owen Chadwick, *The Secularization of the European Mind in the Nineteenth Century* (Cambridge 1975) p. 91; religious semantics are usefully discussed by Lucian Hölscher, 'Semantic Structures of Religious Change in Modern Germany' in Hugh McLeod and Werner Ustorf (eds), *The Decline of Christendom in Western Europe 1750–2000* (Cambridge 2003) pp. 184ff.

110 A. D. Gilbert, *Religion and Society in Industrial England. Church, Chapel and Social Change 1740–1914* (London 1976) p. 185

111 José Harris, *Private Lives, Public Spirit. A Social History of Britain 1870–1914* (London 1993) p. 158

112 Gibson, *Social History of French Catholicism* p. 194

113 Edward Norman, 'Church and State since 1800' in Sheridan Gilley and W. J. Shiels (eds), *A History of Religion in Britain* (Oxford 1994) p. 278

114 Harris, *Private Lives, Public Spirit* pp. 167–8

115 Haight, *George Eliot* p. 464

116 F. W. Maitland, *The Life and Letters of Leslie Stephen* (London 1906) p. 144

117 See especially Getrude Himmelfarb's outstanding *The De-Moralization of Society. From Victorian Virtues to Modern Values* (New York 1996) pp. 21–52. Recently many of Himmelfarb's British critics seem to have thought better of the Victorians,

117 without having the grace to concede their earlier errors

118 See the important article by Brian Harrison, 'Religion and Recreation in Nineteenth-Century England', *Past & Present* (1967) 38, pp. 124–5

119 McLeod, *Religion and the People of Western Europe 1789–1989* p. 57

120 Chadwick, *Victorian Church* 1, p. 325

121 Callum Brown, 'Did Urbanization Secularize Britain?', *Urban History Yearbook* (1988) p. 12

122 Charles Dickens, *Hard Times*, ed. with an introduction by Kate Flint (London 1995) pp. 29–30

123 George Eliot, *Scenes of Clerical Life*, ed. with an introduction by Jennifer Gribble (London 1998) pp. 27–31 and 55

124 Eileen Yeo, 'Christianity in Chartist Struggle 1832–1842', *Past & Present* (1981) 91, pp. 132–3

125 Chadwick, *Victorian Church* 2, pp. 266ff.

126 Harrison, 'Religion and Recreation' p. 110

127 Flaubert, *Sentimental Education* p. 303

128 Edward Berenson, 'A New Religion of the Left. Christianity and Social Radicalism in France 1815–1848' in François Furet and Mona Ozouf (eds), *The French Revolution and the Creation of Modern Political Culture*, vol. 3: *The Transformation of Political Culture 1789–1848* (Oxford 1989) p. 543

129 For a good introduction to God's relationship with the British Labour Party see Graham Dale, *God's Politicians. The Christian Contribution to 100 Years of Labour* (London 2000)

130 Ibid. pp. 549ff.

131 Shirley Williams, *God and Caesar. Personal Reflections on Politics and Religion* (London 2003)

132 Hugh McLeod, 'Religion in the British and German Labour Movements c. 1890–1914. A Comparison', *Bulletin of the Society for the Study of Labour History* (1986) 51, p. 30

133 Stephen Yeo, 'A New Life. The Religion of Socialism in Britain 1883–1896', *History Workshop* (1977) 4, p. 12

134 Yeo, 'Religion of Socialism' especially pp. 31ff.

135 John McManners, *European History 1789–1914. Men, Machines and Freedom* (Oxford 1966) p. 334

136 Thomas Nipperdey, *Deutsche Geschichte 1866–1918* (Munich 1998) 2, pp. 356–7

137 Hölscher, *Weltgericht oder Revolution* pp. 161–2

138 Ibid. pp. 315–17

139 Hugh McLeod, *Secularisation in Western Europe 1848–1914* (London 2000) p. 122

140 Vernon Lidtke, 'Social Class and Secularisation in Imperial Germany. The Working Classes', *Leo Baeck Institute Yearbook* (1980) 25, pp. 28–30

141 Hölscher, *Weltgericht oder Revolution* p. 184

142 Sebastian Prüfer, 'Die frühe deutsche Sozialdemokratie 1863 bis 1890 als Religion. Zur Problematik eines revitalisierten Konzepts' in Berthold Unfried and Christine Schindler (eds), *Riten, Mythen und Symbole – Die Arbeiterbewegung zwischen 'Zivilreligion' und Volkskultur* (Vienna 1999) p. 42 and Britte Emig, *Die Veredelung des Arbeiters. Sozialdemokratie als Kulturbewegung* (Frankfurt am Main 1980) especially pp. 94–103

143 Hölscher, *Weltgericht oder Revolution* pp. 189–90 and 237 for the Vollmar speech

144 For a brilliant discussion of these processes see the still useful Franz Schnabel, *Deutsche Geschichte im neunzehnten Jahrhundert* (Freiburg im Breisgau 1937) 4, pp. 568ff.

145 On this see especially Lucian Hölscher, 'Die Religion des Bürgers. Bürgerliche Frömmigkeit und Protestantische Kirche im 19. Jahrhundert', *HZ* (1990) 250, pp. 602ff.

146 Lucian Hölscher, 'Bürgerliche Religiosität im protestantischen Deutschland des 19. Jahrhunderts' in Wolfgang Schieder (ed.), *Religion und Gesellschaft im 19. Jahrhundert* (Stuttgart 1993) especially pp. 208ff.

147 Horst Althaus, *Hegel. An Intellectual Biography* (Oxford 2000) p. 206

148 For this see William Weber, 'Wagner, Wagnerism, and Musical Idealism' in David C. Large and William Weber (eds) *Wagnerism in European Politics and Culture* (Ithaca 1984) pp. 28ff.

149 See especially Roger Scruton, *Death-Devoted Heart. Sex and the Sacred in Wagner's Tristan and Isolde* (Oxford 2004) especially pp. 177ff.

150 Richard Wagner, 'Religion und Kunst' in D. Borchmeyer (ed.) *Dichtungen und Schriften* (Frankfurt 1983) 10, pp. 117–63. For a good discussion of these themes see Thomas Nipperdey, 'Religion und Gesellschaft. Deutschland um 1900', *HZ* (1988) 246, pp. 610–11 and his *Religion in Umbruch. Deutschland 1870–1918* (Munich 1988) pp. 140–3

151 For this see especially Simon Gunn, *The Public Culture of the Victorian Middle Classes. Ritual and Authority and the English Industrial City 1840–1914* (Manchester 2000) pp. 150–1

152 Hunt, *Building Jerusalem* p. 242

Chapter 7: New Men and Sacred Violence in Late-Nineteenth-Century Russia

1 Richard Pipes, *The Russian Revolution 1899–1919* (London 1990) p. 138

2 The best analysis of the intelligentsia is by Martin Malia, 'What is the Intelligentsia?' in Richard Pipes (ed.), *The Russian Intelligentsia* (New York 1961) pp. 1ff.

3 Gottfried Künzlen, *Der Neue Mensch. Eine Untersuchung zur säkularen Religionsgeschichte der Moderne* (Munich 1994) is the most interesting recent study of this concept

4 W. Gareth Jones, 'Politics' in Malcolm V. Jones and Robin Feuer Miller (eds) *The Cambridge Companion to the Russian Novel* (Cambridge 1998) p. 63

5 Pipes, *Russian Revolution* p. 140

6 Joseph Frank, *Dostoevsky. The Stir of Liberation 1860–1865* (Princeton 1986) p. 164

7 For an outstanding discussion of these questions see Rufus W. Mathewson, *The Positive Hero in Russian Literature* (Stanford 1975)

8 James Billington, *Fire in the Minds of Men. Origins of the Revolutionary Faith* (New York 1980) pp. 389ff. provides a vast quarry of information

9 See William F. Woehrlin, *Chernyshevskii. The Man and the Journalist* (Cambridge, Mass. 1971) pp. 312ff.

10 Nikolai Chzernyshevsky, *What is to be Done? Tales of the New People* (Moscow 1983) p. 311

11 Ibid. p. 407

12 Ibid. p. 408

13 Abbott Gleason, *Young Russia. The Genesis of Russian Radicalism in the 1860s* (Chicago 1983) p. 298

14 Adam B. Ulam, *Prophets and Conspirators in Pre-revolutionary Russia* (New Brunswick 1998) p. 95

15 Fyodor Dostoevsky, *Complete Letters*, ed. and trans. David A. Lowe (Ann Arbor 1990) 5, nr 742, p. 34 made precisely this last point about the young people's 'gospel of the revolver and the conviction that the government is afraid of them'

16 The best account of Nechaev's life is in Gleason, *Young Russia* pp. 339–50. See also Franco Venturi, *Roots of Revolution. A History of the Populist and Socialist Movements in 19th-Century Russia* (New York 1960)

17 Gleason, *Young Russia* p. 359

18 Joseph Frank, *Dostoevsky. The Miraculous Years 1865–1871* (Princeton 1995) pp. 439–42 for the text of this letter which was written in July 1870

19 Orlando Figes, *Natasha's Dance. A Cultural History of Russia* (London 2002) pp. 330ff.

20 Fyodor Dostoevsky, *The Notebooks for the Possessed*, ed. Edward Wasiolek (Chicago 1968) p. 29

21 Dostoevsky, *Complete Letters* 3, nr 398, p. 281

22 Ibid. nr 387 p. 246 is a brief expression of his plight. Other letters are more akin to elaborate financial accounts

23 Ibid. nr 400, p. 284

24 Fyodor Dostoevsky, *Letters from the Underworld* trans. C. J. Hogarth (London 1913)

25 Dostoevsky, *Complete Letters* 3, nr 384, p. 235

26 Ibid. nr 393, p. 268

27 Ibid. nr 425, p. 353

28 Ibid. nr 397, p. 275

29 Ibid. nr 398, p. 277

30 Ibid. nr 399, pp. 279–80

31 Dostoevsky, *The Possessed*, trans. Constance Garnett (London 1931) 1, p. 162

32 Ibid. 2, pp. 71ff.

33 Ibid. p. 55

34 Ibid. 1, p. 102

35 Dostoevsky, *Complete Letters* 3, nr 413, p. 324

36 See Frank, *Dostoevsky. The Miraculous Years 1865–1871* pp. 472ff.

37 Dostoevsky, *Complete Letters* 3, nr 428, p. 360

38 Joseph Frank, *Dostoevsky. The Mantle of the Prophet 1871–1881* (Princeton 2002) p. 80

39 Billington, *Fire in the Minds of Men* p. 404

40 Dostoevsky, *Complete Letters* 5, nr 742, p. 32

41 Ulam, *Prophets and Conspirators* p. 225

42 Anna Geifman, *Thou Shalt Kill. Revolutionary Terrorism in Russia 1894–1917* (Princeton 1993) p. 12

43 Ibid. p. 232

44 Venturi, *Roots of Revolution* p. 711

45 See Ellis Sandoz, *Political Apocalypse. A Study of Dostoevsky's Grand Inquisitor* (Baton Rouge 1971) especially pp. 40ff.

46 Figes, *Natasha's Dance* pp. 324–5

47 Timothy Ware, *The Orthodox Church* (London 1972) p. 127

48 Dostoevsky, *Complete Letters* 5, nr 915, p. 302

49 For these points see Aileen Kelly, 'Dostoevsky and the Divided Conscience' in her *Toward Another Shore. Russian Thinkers Between Necessity and Chance* (New Haven 1998) pp. 55ff., although her arguments involve leaving out many of Dostoevsky's vituperations against his radical critics

50 Malcolm V. Jones, 'Dostoevskii and Religion' in W. J. Leatherbarrow (ed.), *The Cambridge Companion to Dostoevskii* (Cambridge 2002) p. 150

51 Fyodor Dostoevsky, *The Brothers Karamazov*, trans. Richard Pevear and Larissa Volokhonsky (New York 1991) p. 299

52 Ibid. p. 62

53 Ibid. pp. 320–1

54 Ibid. p. 774

55 Dostoevsky, *Complete Letters* 5, nr 915, p. 302

Chapter 8: Rendering Unto Caesar: Church versus State, State versus Church

1 René Rémond, *Religion and Society in Modern Europe* (Oxford 1999) p. 133 and Roger Scruton, *The West and the Rest. Globalization and the Terrorist Threat* (Oxford 2002) pp. 41ff.

2 Edward Norman, *Church and Society in England 1779–1970* (Oxford 1976) pp. 100–5

3 Edward Norman, 'Church and State since 1800' in Sheridan Gilley and W. J. Sheils (eds), *A History of Religion in Britain. Practice and Belief from Pre-Roman Times to the Present* (Oxford 1994) p. 278; on Gladstone, Owen Chadwick, *The Victorian Church* (London 1970) 2, p. 430

4 Chadwick, *Victorian Church* 1, pp. 271ff. has an excellent discussion of these issues

5 Owen Chadwick, *A History of the Popes 1830–1914* (Oxford 1998) pp. 266–7; Roy Jenkins, *Gladstone* (London 1995) pp. 127–33

6 For an excellent discussion of the press see Christopher Clark, 'The New Catholicism and the European Culture Wars' in Christopher Clark and Wolfram Kaiser (eds), *Culture Wars. Secular–Catholic Conflicts in Nineteenth-Century Europe* (Cambridge 2003) pp. 23ff.

7 Winfried Becker, 'Der Kulturkampf als europäisches und als deutsches Phänomen', *Historisches Jahrbuch* (1981) 101, p. 423 is an excellent tour d'horizon by a leading German scholar

8 F. Dante, *Storia della 'Civiltà Cattolica' (1850–1891). Il laboratorio del Papa* (Rome 1990)

9 G. de Rosa, *Il movimento cattolico in Italia* (Bari 1966) for the details

10 Wolfram Kaiser ' "Clericalism – that is

our enemy!'". European Anticlericalism and the Culture Wars' in Clark and Kaiser (eds) *Culture Wars* p. 71

11 David Blackbourn, 'The Catholic Church in Europe since the French Revolution', *Comparative Studies in Society and History* (1991) 33, p. 780

12 Chadwick, *History of the Popes* pp. 196–7

13 Kaiser, 'European anticlericalism' p. 49

14 Anthony Rhodes, *The Power of Rome in the Twentieth Century. The Vatican in the Age of the Liberal Democracies 1870–1922* (London 1983) p. 32

15 Clark, 'New Catholicism' p. 22

16 Laurence Cole, 'The Counter-Reformation's Last Stand. Austria' in Clark and Kaiser (eds), *Culture Wars* p. 303

17 Margaret Lavinia Anderson, *Windthorst. A Political Biography* (Oxford 1981) p. 131

18 Otto Pflanze, *Bismarck and the Development of Germany* (Princeton 1990) 2, p. 213

19 Richard Blanke, *Prussian Poland in the German Empire (1871–1900)* (Boulder 1981) p. 17

20 Heinrich Bornkamm, 'Die Staatsidee im Kulturkampf', *HZ* (1950) 170, p. 49

21 See the seminal article by David Blackbourn, 'Progress and Piety. Liberals, Catholics and the State in Bismarck's Germany' in his *Populists and Patricians. Essays in Modern German History* (London 1987) p. 148

22 Helmut Walser Smith, *German Nationalism and Religious Conflict. Culture, Ideology, and Politics 1870–1914* (Princeton 1995) pp. 34–5

23 Ronald Ross, *Beleaguered Tower. The Dilemma of Political Catholicism in Wilhelmine Germany* (Notre Dame 1976) pp. 20–1

24 Barbara Stambolis, 'Nationalisierung trotz Ultramontanisierung oder "Alles für Deutschland. Deutschland für Christus". Mentalitätsleitende Wertorientierung deutscher Katholiken im 19. und 20. Jahrhundert', *HZ* (1999) 269, pp. 58–9

25 Winfried Becker, 'Liberale Kulturkampf-Positionen und politischer Katholizismus' in Otto

Pflanze (ed.), *Innenpolitische Probleme des Bismarck-Reiches* (Munich 1983) p. 69

26 Harald Just, 'Wilhelm Busch und die Katholiken. Kulturkampfbestimmung im Bismarck-Reich', *Geschichte und Gesellschaft* (1974) 25, pp. 71ff.

27 Ronald J. Ross, *The Failure of Bismarck's Kulturkampf. Catholicism and State Power in Imperial Germany 1871–1887* (Washington DC 1998) p. 17

28 For the details see Manuel Borutta, 'Enemies at the Gate. The Moabit Klostersturm and the Kulturkampf. Germany' in Clark and Kaiser (eds), *Culture Wars* p. 235

29 Ibid. p. 81

30 Thomas Nipperdey, *Religion im Umbruch. Deutschland 1870–1918* (Munich 1988) p. 40

31 James Sheehan, *German Liberalism in the Nineteenth Century* (Chicago 1978) p. 136

32 Marcel Gauchet, *The Disenchantment of the Modern World. A Political History of Religion* (Princeton 1997) p. 53; Becker, 'Liberale Kulturkampf-Positionen' p. 63

33 See Smith, *German Nationalism and Religious Conflict* pp. 37–41

34 Heinrich von Treitschke, 'Die Maigesetze und ihre Folgen' in his *Zehn Jahre deutscher Kämpfe* (Berlin 1897) p. 440

35 Anderson, *Windthorst* p. 170

36 Ibid. p. 152

37 Marjorie Lamberti, *State, Society and the Elementary School in Imperial Germany* (New York 1980) pp. 40ff.

38 Blanke, *Prussian Poland in the German Empire* p. 24

39 Ross, *Failure of Bismarck's Kulturkampf* p. 38

40 Ronald Ross, 'The Kulturkampf and the Limitations of Power in Bismarck's Germany', *JEH* (1995) 46, pp. 672–3

41 Blackbourn, 'Progress and Piety' p. 156

42 Gerard Manley Hopkins, *Poems and Prose*, ed. W. H. Gardner (London 1953) p. 10

43 Stambolis, 'Nationalisierung' p. 70

44 Anderson, *Windthorst* pp. 251–60 has an important discussion of this issue

45 Adolf Birke, *Bischof Ketteler und der*

deutsche Liberalismus (Mainz 1971) p. 92

46 Rhodes, *Power of Rome in the Twentieth Century* p. 85

47 On 'clericalism' see Sudhir Hazareesingh, *Political Traditions in Modern France* (Oxford 1994) pp. 99ff.

48 Raymond Jonas, *France and the Cult of the Sacred Heart* (Berkeley 2000) p. 177 and John McManners, *Church and State in France 1870–1914* (London 1972) p. 40

49 Luzzatti to Minghetti 3 September 1873 in S. Halperin, *Italy and the Vatican at War* (London 1939) p. 326

50 Hazareesingh, *Political Traditions in Modern France* pp. 65ff. has an excellent discussion of these themes

51 Robert Tombs, *France 1814–1914* (London 1996) pp. 442–3 brings the complexities of French republicanism to life with wit and style

52 Jean-Louis Ormières, *Politique et religion en France* (Paris 2002) p. 123

53 Graham Robb, *Victor Hugo* (London 1977) pp. 525–32

54 Rémond, *Religion and Society in Modern Europe* p. 146

55 See the useful discussion of laicisation in ibid. p. 144

56 On Buisson see Jacqueline Lalouette, *La République anticléricale xixe–xxe siècles* (Paris 2002) pp. 52ff.

57 Hugh McLeod, *Secularisation in Western Europe 1848–1914* (London 2000) p. 140

58 Adrien Dansette, *Religious History of Modern France. From the Revolution to the Third Republic* (Freiburg 1961) 2, p. 55

59 Becker, 'Der Kulturkampf' p. 432 citing Waldeck-Rousseau

60 Ralph Gibson, *A Social History of French Catholicism 1789–1914* (London 1989) p. 132

61 Ormières, *Politique et religion en France* p. 115

62 Rhodes, *Power of Rome* p. 114

63 Becker, 'Der Kulturkampf' p. 437

64 Rhodes, *Power of Rome* pp. 210–11

65 C. S. Phillips, *The Church in France 1848–1907* (London 1936) p. 213

66 Rhodes, *Power of Rome* p. 116

67 Alexander Sedgwick, *The Ralliement in French Politics 1890–1898* (Cambridge, Mass. 1965) is still useful

68 Phillips, *Church in France* p. 236

69 Clive Castaldo, 'Socialism and Catholicism in France. Jaurès, Guesde and the Dreyfus Affair' in Frank Tallett and Nicholas Atkin (eds), *Religion, Society and Politics in France since 1789* (London 1991) p. 141

70 Pierre Pierrard, *Les Chrétiens et l'affaire Dreyfus* (Paris 1998) pp. 102–6

71 Dansette, *Religious History of Modern France* 2, p. 180

72 Maurice Larkin, *Church and State after the Dreyfus Affair* (London 1974) p. 86

73 Michel Winock, *Nationalism, Anti-Semitism, and Fascism in France* (Stanford 1998) pp. 59–70

74 Larkin, *Church and State after the Dreyfus Affair* p. 94; and Gabriel Merle, *Émile Combes* (Paris 1995) for the biographical details

75 Gibson, *Social History of French Catholicism* p. 129

76 Merle, *Combes* p. 318

77 McManners, *Church and State in France* p. 150

78 Chadwick, *History of the Popes* p. 399

Chapter 9: The Churches and Industrial Society

1 A. N. Wilson, *The Victorians* (London 2002) p. 413

2 Gustave Doré and Blanchard Jerrold, *London. A Pilgrimage* (originally London 1872, reprinted Toronto 1970) pp. 37–8

3 Alexander Herzen, *My Past and Thoughts*, trans. Constance Garnett (Berkeley 1982) p. 447

4 *Taine's Notes on England* trans. and introduced by Edward Hyams (London 1957) p. 219

5 Friedrich Engels, *The Condition of the Working Class in England* ed. Victor Kiernan (London 1987) p. 69

6 *Taine's Notes on England* pp. 10–12

7 David Landes, *Prometheus Unbound. Technological Change and Industrial Development in Western Europe from 1750 to the Present* (second edition Cambridge 2003) p. 5

8 *Taine's Notes on England* p. 98 for his

comments on Manchester's Little
Ireland in New Town

9 For these statistics see G. Kitson Clark,
The Making of Victorian England
(London 1962) pp. 149–51

10 R. W. Vanderkiste, *Notes and
Narratives of a Six Years' Mission
Principally among the Dens of London*
(London 1859) pp. xii–xiii

11 A. D. Gilbert, *Religion and Society in
Industrial England. Church, Chapel and
Social Change 1740–1914* (London 1976)
p. 170

12 Kitson Clark, *Making of Victorian
England* p. 171

13 Kenneth Inglis, *Churches and the
Working Classes in Victorian England*
(London 1963) p. 57

14 Hugh McLeod, *Religion and the People
of Western Europe 1789–1989* (Oxford
1997) pp. 127–8

15 David Hempton, 'Religious Life in
Industrial Britain 1830–1914' in
Sheridan Gilley and W. J. Shiels (eds),
A History of Religion in Britain
(Oxford 1994) p. 310

16 Hugh McLeod, *Religion and Society in
England 1850–1914* (London 1996) p. 84

17 Ibid. p. 19

18 Inglis, *Churches and the Working
Classes in Victorian England* p. 46

19 Edward Norman. *Church and Society
in England 1770–1970. A Historical
Study* (Oxford 1976) p. 137

20 R. S. Soloway, *Prelates and People.
Ecclesiastical Social Thought in England
1783–1852* (London 1969) p. 260

21 Ibid. p. 342

22 Kathleen Heasman, *Evangelicals in
Action. An Appraisal of their Social
Work* (London 1962) p. 14

23 See Irene Howat and John Nicholls,
*Streets Paved with Gold. The Story of
the London City Mission* (London
2003) pp. 35–6 and in greater detail
Donald M. Lewis, *Lighten their
Darkness. The Evangelical Mission to
Working-Class London 1828–1860*
(Westport 1986)

24 London City Mission Archive, *The 42
Annual Report of the London City
Mission* (1877) p. 223

25 LCM Archive, *London City Mission
Magazine* (1871) 36, p. 173

26 LCM Archive, *London City Mission
Magazine* (1849) 14, p. 18

27 LCM Archive, *London City Mission
Magazine* (1855) 20, p. 225

28 John Matthias Weylland, *These Fifty
Years being the Jubilee Volume of the
London City Mission* (London 1884)
p. 156

29 Details from LCM Archive, *London
City Mission Magazine* (1859)
1 December, p. 347 and (1889) 54,
pp. 253–64 for the mission to East End
Jews

30 Weylland, *These Fifty Years* pp. 47–50

31 Brian Harrison, 'Religion and
Recreation in Nineteenth-Century
England', *Past & Present* (1967) 38,
pp. 108ff.

32 Information kindly supplied by Niall
Ferguson from his childhood
memories as a Rangers man

33 McLeod, *Religion and Society in
England* p. 200

34 Owen Chadwick, *The Victorian Church*
(London 1966–70) 2, p. 290

35 See Roy Hattersley, *Blood and Fire.
William and Catherine Booth and their
Salvation Army* (London 1999)
especially pp. 229ff.

36 Inglis, *Churches and the Working
Classes in Victorian England* p. 192

37 Ibid. pp. 299–300

38 Chadwick, *Victorian Church* 1, p. 355

39 Inglis, *Churches and the Working
Classes in Victorian England* p. 264

40 Ibid. p. 269

41 Norman, *Church and Society in
England* p. 170

42 Maurice Cowling, *Religion and Public
Doctrine in Modern England*
(Cambridge 1980–2001) 3, p. 256

43 Soloway, *Prelates and People* p. 205

44 LCM Archive, *London City Mission
Magazine* (1871) 36, p. 176

45 Tristram Hunt, *Building Jerusalem. The
Rise and Fall of the Victorian City*
(London 2004) p. 216

46 McLeod, *Religion and Society in
England* p. 215

47 Norris Pope, *Dickens and Charity*
(New York 1978) p. 234; see also
Tristram Hunt's spirited *Building
Jerusalem* pp. 292–4

48 Edwin Hodder, *The Life and Work of*

the Seventh Earl of Shaftesbury (London 1886) 2, pp. 418–19

49 Henry Mayhew, *London Labour and the London Poor*, selected and introduced by Victor Neuburg (originally 1849–50, London 1985) pp. 107–22

50 Geoffrey Best, *Mid-Victorian Britain 1851–75* (London 1975) pp. 45–7

51 Pope, *Dickens and Charity* pp. 182–3

52 Herbert Hensley Henson, *Retrospect on an Unimportant Life* (Oxford 1942) 1, p. 28

53 Inglis, *Churches and the Working Classes in Victorian England* pp. 221–2

54 Norman, *Church and Society in England* pp. 227ff.

55 Martin Greschat, *Das Zeitalter der Industriellen Revolution. Das Christentum vor der Moderne* (Stuttgart 1980) p. 153

56 Joan L. Coffey, *Léon Harmel. Entrepreneur as Catholic Social Reformer* (Notre Dame 2003) p. 71

57 Michel Lagrée, 'The Impact of Technology on Catholicism in France' in Hugh McLeod and Werner Usdorf (eds) *The Decline of Christendom in Western Europe 1750–2000* (Cambridge 2003) pp. 172–4

58 A. R. Vidler, *A Century of Social Catholicism 1820–1920* (London 1964) p. 5

59 Roger Aubert, *The Church in a Secularised Society* (New York 1978) p. 145

60 Honoré de Balzac, *At the Sign of the Cat and Racket and Other Stories* (Amsterdam 2002) p. 10

61 Paul Mismer, *Social Catholicism in Europe. From the Onset of Industrialization to the First World War* (New York 1991) p. 62

62 Jacques Gadille and Jean-Marie Mayeur (eds), *Liberalismus, Industrialisierung, Expansion Europas (1830–1914)*; Jean-Marie Mayeur et al. (eds), *Geschichte des Christentums. Religion, Politik, Kultur* (Freiburg 1996–2003) 11, p. 38

63 Vidler, *A Century of Social Catholicism* p. 48

64 Ibid. p. 14

65 Greschat, *Das Zeitalter der Industriellen Revolution* p. 117

66 Michael Z. Brooke, *Le Play. Engineer and Social Scientist. The Life and Work of Frédéric Le Play* (London 1970) pp. 64–5

67 Maria Sophia Quine, *Population Politics in Twentieth-Century Europe* (London 1996) pp. 55–8 is fashionably disapproving of Le Play as a harbinger of 'Fascist' pro-natalist policies

68 John McManners, *Church and State in France 1870–1914* (London 1972) p. 83

69 Hans Maier, *Revolution and Church. The Early History of Christian Democracy 1789–1901* (Notre Dame 1969) p. 259

70 Coffey, *Léon Harmel* p. 14

71 Ibid. especially pp. 77–92

72 Ibid. p. 167

73 Greschat, *Das Zeitalter der Industriellen Revolution* pp. 65ff.

74 Kurt Nowak, *Geschichte des Christentums in Deutschland. Religion, Politik und Gesellschaft vom Ende der Aufklärung bis zur Mitte des 20. Jahrhunderts* (Munich 1995) pp. 127–8

75 Edgar Alexander, 'Church and Society in Germany' in Joseph N. Moody (ed.), *Church and Society. Catholic Social and Political Thought and Movements 1789–1950* (New York 1953) pp. 410ff.

76 See the discussion in Fritz Vigener, *Ketteler. Ein deutsches Bischofsleben des 19. Jahrhunderts* (Munich 1924) pp. 420–7

77 James Sheehan, *German Liberalism in the Nineteenth Century* (London 1982) pp. 92–4

78 Vigener, *Ketteler* p. 461

79 Mismer, *Social Catholicism in Europe* p. 142

80 On the genesis of the encyclical see G. Antonazzi, *L'encyclica Rerum novarum. Testo autentico e redazioni preparatorii dei documenti originali* (Rome 1957)

81 Mismer, *Social Catholicism in Europe* pp. 190 and 202–8

82 Vidler, *A Century of Social Catholicism* pp. 128–9

83 Mismer, *Social Catholicism in Europe* pp. 224–5

84 André Encrevé, Jacques Gadille and

Jean-Marie Mayeur, 'Frankreich' in Mayeur et al. (eds), *Geschichte des Christentums* 11, p. 522

85 For this see Martin Conway, *Catholic Politics in Europe 1918–1945* (London 1997) p. 24

86 Leo XIII, *Graves de Communi Re* 18 January 1901, paragraphs 4ff.; McManners, *Church and State in France* pp. 98–9

87 Adrien Dansette, *Religious History of Modern France. From the Revolution to the Third Republic* (Freiburg 1961) 2, p. 274

88 Martin Greschat, 'Der deutsche Protestantismus im Kaiserreich' in Mayeur et al. (eds), *Geschichte des Christentums* 11, p. 657

89 G. Brakelmann, Martin Greschat and Werner Jochmann (eds), *Protestantismus und Politik. Werk und Wirkung Adolf Stoeckers* (Hamburg 1982)

90 Ibid. p. 28

91 Ibid. pp. 114–16 for the programme

92 Gordon Craig, *Germany 1866–1945* (Oxford 1978) p. 154

93 For an excellent discussion of Stoecker see Fritz Stern, *Gold and Iron. Bismarck, Bleichröder and the Building of the German Empire* (London 1977) pp. 510ff.

94 Ibid. p. 177

95 Greschat, *Das Zeitalter der Industriellen Revolution* pp. 218ff.

96 For the above see Thomas Nipperdey, *Deutsche Geschichte 1866–1918* (Munich 1998) 1, p. 461

97 H. W. Heitzer, *Der Volksverein für das katholische Deutschland im Kaiserreich 1890–1918* (Mainz 1979)

98 For the details see Ronald J. Ross, *Beleaguered Tower. The Dilemma of Political Catholicism in Wilhelmine Germany* (Notre Dame 1976) pp. 86–91

Chapter 10: Apocalypse 1914

1 Denis Brogan, 'Nationalist Doctrine of M. Charles Maurras' in his *French Personalities and Problems* (London 1946) p. 67

2 See Ernst Nolte, *Three Faces of Fascism* (New York 1966) p. 124

3 Michael Sutton, *Nationalism, Positivism and Catholicism. The Politics of Charles Maurras and French Catholics 1890–1914* (Cambridge 1982) pp. 52ff.

4 Eugen Weber, *Action Française. Royalism and Reaction in Twentieth-Century France* (Stanford 1962) pp. 18–19

5 Charles Maurras, 'Dictator and King' in J. S. McClelland (ed.), *The French Right from de Maistre to Maurras* (London 1970) p. 220

6 Ibid. p. 232

7 Weber, *Action Française* p. 39

8 Sutton, *Nationalism, Positivism and Catholicism* p. 94

9 Paul Johnson, *A History of Christianity* (London 1976) pp. 471ff.

10 Frank Coppa, *The Modern Papacy since 1789* (London 1998) especially pp. 140–53

11 Ina Ulrike Paul, 'Paul Anton de Lagarde' in Uwe Puschner, Walter Schmitz and Justus Ulbricht (eds), *Handbuch zur 'Völkischen Bewegung' 1871–1918* (Munich 1999) pp. 50ff.

12 For an insider's view of Lagarde's professional odyssey see Fritz Stern, *The Politics of Cultural Despair* (Berkeley 1961) pp. 7–18

13 Ina Ulrike Paul, 'Paul Anton de Lagarde' p. 69

14 On these developments see Stefanie von Schnurbein, 'Die Suche nach einer "arteigenen" Religion' in Puschner et al. (eds), *Handbuch zur 'Völkischen Bewegung'*. This conspectus replaces such older works as George L. Mosse's *The Crisis of German Ideology. Intellectual Origins of the Third Reich* (New York 1964)

15 Alan Wilkinson, *The Church of England and the First World War* (London 1978) p. 16

16 Adrian Hastings, *A History of English Christianity 1920–2000* (fourth edition London 2001) p. 54

17 Jacques Fontana, *Les Catholiques français pendant la Grande Guerre* (Paris 1990) p. 25

18 Leonard Smith, Stéphane Audoin-Rouzeau and Annette Becker, *France and the Great War 1914–1918* (Cambridge 2003) p. 27

19 Wilhelm Pressel, *Die Kriegspredigt 1914–1918 in der evangelischen Kirche Deutschlands* (Göttingen 1967) pp. 17–18

20 Hugh McLeod, *Secularisation in Western Europe 1848–1914* (London 2000) pp. 277–8

21 See Klaus Vondung, *Die Apokalypse in Deutschland* (Munich 1998) pp. 189ff.

22 Wolfgang J. Mommsen, 'Die kulturellen Eliten im Ersten Weltkrieg' in his *Bürgerliche Kultur und politische Ordnung. Künstler, Schriftsteller und Intellektuelle in der deutschen Geschichte 1830–1933* (Frankfurt am Main 2000) pp. 178–95; the visual reference is to sculptures by Ernst Barlach

23 Smith et al., *France and the Great War* p. 58

24 Frank Lenwood, *Pharisaism and War* (London 1915) p. 14

25 Arlie J. Hoover, *God, Germany and Britain in the Great War. A Study in Clerical Nationalism* (New York 1989) p. 36

26 Randall Davidson, *The Testing of a Nation* (London 1919) p. 87

27 Hoover, *God, Germany and Britain in the Great War* p. 98

28 Ernst Troeltsch, *Deutscher Glaube und deutsche Sitte in unserem grossen Kriege* (Berlin n.d.) p. 19

29 Albert Marrin, *The Last Crusade. The Church of England and the First World War* (Durham NC 1974) p. 103

30 Fontana, *Les Catholiques français* pp. 52–3. Treitschke came in for a trouncing too from Emile Durkheim; see Steven Lukes, *Émile Durkheim. His Life and Work* (London 1973) pp. 550–1

31 Martha Hanna, *The Mobilization of the Intellect. French Scholars and Writers during the Great War* (Cambridge, Mass. 1996) pp. 118–19

32 Hoover, *God, Germany and Britain in the Great War* p. 29

33 Wolfgang Mommsen, 'Die "deutsche Idee der Freiheit"' in his *Bürgerliche Kultur und politische Ordnung* pp. 133ff. See also Klaus von See, *Die Ideen von 1789 und die Ideen von 1914. Völkisches Denken in Deutschland zwischen Französischer Revolution und Erstem Weltkrieg* (Frankfurt am Main 1975)

34 Arlie J. Hoover, *The Gospel of Nationalism. German Patriotic Preaching from Napoleon to Versailles* (Stuttgart 1986) p. 125

35 Wilhelm Laible (ed.), *Deutsche Theologen über den Krieg. Stimmen aus schwerer Zeit* (Leipzig 1915) p. 51

36 Harmut Lehmann, '"God is our Old Ally". The Chosen People Theme in Late Nineteenth- and Early Twentieth-Century German Nationalism' in William R. Hutchinson and Hartmut Lehmann (eds), *Many are Chosen. Divine Election and Western Nationalism* (Minneapolis 1994) p. 87

37 Marrin, *Last Crusade* p. 187

38 Herbert Hensley Henson, *Retrospect of an Unimportant Life* (Oxford 1942) 1, p. 174

39 Ibid. p. 188

40 Alan Wilkinson, *The Church of England and the First World War* (London 1978) p. 253

41 Percy Colson, *Life of the Bishop of London. An Authorised Biography* (London 1935) pp. 18off.

42 Marrin, *Last Crusade* p. 141

43 *The Army and Religion. An Enquiry and its Bearing upon the Religious Life of the Nation* (London 1919) p. 88

44 Ibid. p. 177

45 Ibid. pp. 8–14 and 61–2

46 Ibid. p. 10

47 Ibid. p. 208

48 Ibid. p. 207

49 Maurice Larkin, 'The Catholic Church and Politics in Twentieth-Century France' in Martin Alexander (ed.), *French History since Napoleon* (London 1999) p. 155

50 Annette Becker, *War and Faith. The Religious Imagination in France 1914–1930* (Oxford 1998) p. 75

51 Fontana, *Les Catholiques français* p. 303 for these statistics

52 See Pierre Teilhard de Chardin, *Writings in Time of War* (London 1968) for the worked-up versions of his letters to his cousin

53 Becker *War and Faith* pp. 44–6

54 Jacques Le Goff, 'Reims, City of Coronation' in Pierre Nora (ed.),

Realms of Memory. The Construction of the French Past (New York 1998) 3, pp. 246–8 with photographs of the damage sustained

55 On Vatican diplomacy see John Pollard, *The Unknown Pope. Benedict XV (1914–1922) and the Pursuit of Peace* (London 1999) p. 90

56 John Pollard, 'The Papacy in Two World Wars. Benedict XV and Pius XII Compared', *Totalitarian Movements and Political Religions* (2001) 2, p. 85

57 Pollard, *Unknown Pope* p. 116

58 Jean-Marie Mayeur, 'Die katholische Kirche' in Jean-Marie Mayeur et al. (eds), *Geschichte des Christentums. Religion, Politik, Kultur* (Freiburg 1996–2003) 12, p. 390

SELECT BIBLIOGRAPHY

Works of outstanding interest are indicated with an asterisk, although this informal rule is not observed where, as in the case of, for example, Dostoevsky, Nietzsche, Novalis or Pascal, this practice seemed impertinent.

Alexander, Martin (ed.) *French History since Napoleon* (London 1999)

Altgeld, Wolfgang *Katholizismus, Protestantismus, Judentum* (Mainz 1992)

Althaus, Horst *Hegel. An Intellectual Biography* (Oxford 2000)

Anderson, Margaret Lavinia *Windthorst* (Oxford 1981)*

—— 'The Kulturkampf and the Course of German History' *Central European History* (1986) 19, pp. 82–115

Anderson, Olive 'The Growth of Christian Militarism in Mid-Victorian Britain' *English Historical Review* (1971) 86, pp. 46–72

The Army and Religion. An Enquiry and its Bearing upon the Religious Life of the Nation (London 1919)*

Arnal, Oscar *Ambivalent Alliance. The Catholic Church and the Action Française 1899–1939* (Pittsburgh 1985)

Arnold, Matthew *Culture and Anarchy. An Essay in Political and Social Criticism* (London 1893)

Ascoli, Albert Russell and Henneberg, Kystyna von (eds) *Making and Remaking Italy* (Oxford 2001)

Ashton, Rosemary *The Life of Samuel Taylor Coleridge* (Oxford 1996)

Aston, Nigel *The End of an Élite. The French Bishops and the Coming of the Revolution 1786–1790* (Oxford 1992)

—— *Religion and Revolution in France 1780–1804* (London 2000)*

—— *Christianity and Revolutionary Europe c. 1750–1830* (Cambridge 2002)*

—— (ed.) *Religious Change in Europe 1650–1914. Essays for John McManners* (Oxford 1997)

Aulard, F.-A. *Le Culte de la raison et le culte de l'être suprême* (Paris 1892)

Baczko, Bronislaw *Utopian Lights. The Evolution of the Idea of Social Progress* (New York 1989)

Baecque, Antoine de 'L'Homme Nouveau est Arrivé' *Dix-Huitième Siècle* (1988) 20, pp. 193–208

—— *La Caricature révolutionnaire* (Paris 1988)

—— *Glory and Terror. Seven Deaths under the French Revolution* (New York/London 2001)

Baker, Keith Michael (ed.) *The French Revolution and the Creation of Modern Political Culture* (Oxford 1987)*

Barbusse, Henri *Under Fire* trans. Robin Buss (London 2003)

Baron, Salo Wittmayer *Modern Nationalism and Religion* (New York 1960)

Beales, Derek and Best, Geoffrey (eds) *History, Society and the Churches* (Cambridge 1985)

—— 'The French Church and the Revolution' *Historical Journal* (2003) 46, pp. 211–18

Beales, Derek and Biagini, Eugenio *The Risorgimento and the Unification of Italy* (second edition London 2002)

Becker, Annette, *War and Faith. The Religious Imagination in France 1914–1930* (Oxford 1998)

Becker, Carl L., *The Heavenly City of the Eighteenth-Century Philosophers* (New Haven 1932)*

Becker, Winfried 'Der Kulturkampf als europäisches und als deutsches Phänomen' *Historische Zeitschrift* (1981) 101, pp. 422–46*

—— 'Liberale Kulturkampf-Positionen und politischer Katholizismus' in Otto Pflanze (ed.) *Innenpolitische Probleme des Bismarck-Reiches* (Munich 1983) pp. 47–71

—— 'Die deutsche Zentrumspartei im Bismarckreich' in Winfried Becker (ed.) *Die Minderheit als Mitte. Die deutsche Zentrumspartei in der Innenpolitik des Reiches 1871–1933* (Paderborn 1986) pp. 9–45

Bell, David *The Cult of the Nation in France. Inventing Nationalism 1680–1800* (Cambridge, Mass. 2001)

Bellah, Robert N. *Beyond Belief. Essays on Religion in a Post-Traditionalist World* (Berkeley 1970)*

—— 'The Revolution and Civil Religion' in Jerald C. Brauer (ed.) *Religion and the American Revolution* (Philadelphia 1976) online version

Berlin, Isaiah *Vico and Herder. Two Studies in the History of Ideas* (London 1980)

—— *The Proper Study of Mankind. An Anthology of Essays* ed. Henry Hardy (New York 1998)

—— *Freedom and its Betrayal. Six Enemies of Human Liberty* (London 2003)

Besier, Gerhard *Religion, Nation, Kultur. Die Geschichte der christlichen*

Kirchen in den gesellschaftlichen Umbrüchen des 19. Jahrhunderts (Neukirchen-Vluyn 1992)*

—— *Kirche, Politik und Gesellschaft im 19. Jahrhundert* (Munich 1998) 2 volumes

Bianchi, Serge *La Révolution culturelle de l'an II* (Paris 1982)

Billington, James *Fire in the Minds of Men. Origins of the Revolutionary Faith* (New York 1980)*

Biron, Marie-Paule *Les Messes clandestines pendant la Révolution* (Paris 1989)

Blackbourn, David *Populists and Patricians. Essays in Modern German History* (London 1987)*

—— 'The Catholic Church in Europe since the French Revolution' *Comparative Studies in Society and History* (1991) 33, pp. 776–90

—— *Marpingen. Apparitions of the Virgin Mary in Bismarckian Germany* (Oxford 1993)*

Blanke, Richard *Prussian Poland in the German Empire (1871–1900)* (Boulder 1981)

Blanning, Timothy *The French Revolution. Class War or Culture Clash?* (London 1998)

Blaschke, Olaf and Kuhlemann, Frank-Michael (eds) *Religion im Kaiserreich. Milieus. Mentalitäten. Krisen* (Gütersloh 1996)*

Blessing, Werner K. 'Gottesdienst als Säkularisierung? Zu Krieg, Nation und Politik im bayrischen Protestantismus des 19. Jahrhunderts' in Wolfgang Schieder (ed.) *Religion und Gesellschaft im 19. Jahrhundert* (Stuttgart 1993) pp. 216–53

Bornkamm, Heinrich 'Die Staatsidee im Kulturkampf' *Historische Zeitschrift* (1950) 170, pp. 41–72 and 273–306

Bossut, Nicole 'Aux Origines de la Déchristianisation dans la Nièvre, Fouché, Chaumette, ou les Jacobins Nivernais?' *Annales Historiques de la Révolution Française* (1986) 58, pp. 181–202

Boussoulade, Jean *Moniales et hospitalières dans la tourmente révolutionnaire* (Paris 1962)

Boyce, D. George *Nationalism in Ireland* (London 1982)

Bramson, Leon *The Political Context of Sociology* (Princeton 1961)

Brogan, Denis W. *French Personalities and Problems* (London 1946)*

Bruce, Steve *Religion in the Modern World* (Oxford 1996)

Burke, Edmund *Reflections on the Revolution in France* ed. Conor Cruise O'Brien (London 1968) and ed. with an introduction by J. C. D. Clarke (Stanford 2001)*

Burleigh, Michael 'Religion and Social Evil. The Cardinal Basil Hume Memorial Lectures' *Totalitarian Movements and Political Religions* (2002) 3, pp. 1–60

—— '"The Thin Crust of Civilisation". The Masses, Power and Political Religions' in U. Lappenküper, J. Scholtyseck and C. Studt (eds) *Masse und Macht im 19. und 20. Jahrhundert. Studien zur Schlüsselbegriffen unserer Zeit* (Munich 2003) pp. 181–99

Burrin, Philippe 'Political Religion. The Relevance of a Concept' *History & Memory* (1998) 9, pp. 321–49

Butterfield, Herbert *Christianity and History* (London 1949)

—— *Christianity in European History* (London 1952)*

Caird, Edward *The Social Philosophy and Religion of Comte* (New York 1968 reprint of 1885 Glasgow edition)*

Callahan, William and Higgs, David (eds) *Church and Society in Catholic Europe of the Eighteenth Century* (Cambridge 1979)

Campanella, Tommasso *La Città del Sole. Dialogo poetico* trans. Daniel J. Donno (Berkeley 1981)

Carter, Stephen L., *The Culture of Disbelief* (New York 1993)*

—— *God's Name in Vain. The Wrongs and Rights of Religion in Politics* (New York 2000)

Centre Vendéen de Recherches Historiques (ed.) *Christianisme et Vendée* (La Roche-sur-Yon 1999)

Chadwick, Owen *The Victorian Church* (London 1966–70) 2 volumes*

—— *The Secularization of the European Mind in the Nineteenth Century* (Cambridge 1975)*

—— *The Popes and European Revolution* (Oxford 1981)

—— *Hensley Henson. A Study in the Friction of Church and State* (Oxford 1983)

—— *A History of the Popes 1830–1914* (Oxford 1998)

Charlton, D. G. *Secular Religions in France 1815–1870* (Oxford 1963)

Chartier, Roger *The Cultural Origins of the French Revolution* (Durham, NC 1991)

Clark, Christopher and Kaiser, Wolfram (eds) *Culture Wars. Secular–Catholic Conflicts in Nineteenth-Century Europe* (Cambridge 2003)*

Clogg, Richard (ed.) *The Movement for Greek Independence 1771–1821. A Collection of Documents* (London 1976)

Cobb, Richard *The People's Armies* (New Haven 1987)

Coffey, Joan L. *Léon Harmel. Entrepreneur as Catholic Social Reformer* (Notre Dame 2003)

Collini, Stefan *Arnold* (Oxford 1988)*

—— *Public Moralists. Political Thought and Intellectual Life in Britain 1850–1930* (Oxford 1991)

—— *English Pasts. Essays in History and Culture* (Oxford 1999)

Coppa, Frank J. *The Italian Wars of Independence* (London 1992)

—— *The Modern Papacy since 1789* (London 1998)

—— (ed.) *Controversial Concordats. The Vatican's Relations with Napoleon, Mussolini and Hitler* (Washington DC 1999)

Corbin, Alain *Village Bells. Sound and Meaning in the Nineteenth-Century French Countryside* (London 1999)

Cousin, Bernard, Cubells, Monique and Moulinas, Réne *La Pique et la croix. Histoire religieuse de la Révolution française* (Orne 1989)

Cowling, Maurice *Religion and Public Doctrine in Modern England* (Cambridge 1980–2001) 3 volumes*

Cranston, Maurice *The Romantic Movement* (Oxford 1994)*

Crocker, Lester G. *Nature and Culture. Ethical Thought in the French Enlightenment* (Baltimore 1963)

Dagens, C. et al. (eds) *L'Eglise à l'épreuve de la Révolution* (Paris 1989)

Dann, Otto *Nation und Nationalismus in Deutschland 1770–1990* (Munich 1993)

Dansette, Adrien *Religious History of Modern France. From the Revolution to the Third Republic* (Freiburg 1961) 2 volumes

Darnton, Robert *The Literary Underground of the Old Regime* (Cambridge, Mass. 1982)*

—— *The Great Cat Massacre and Other Episodes in French Cultural History* (London 1984)

Davis, John (ed.) *Italy in the Nineteenth Century* (Oxford 2000)

Dawson, Christopher *The Gods of Revolution* (London 1972)

Dawson, Jerry F. *Friedrich Schleiermacher. The Evolution of a Nationalist* (Austin 1966)

Diderot, Denis *The Nun* (London 1974)

Dostoevsky, Fyodor *The Notebooks for the Possessed* ed. Edward Wasiolek (Chicago 1968)

—— *Letters* ed. and trans. David Lowe (Ann Arbor 1989) 5 volumes

—— *The Devils* trans. Michael R. Katz (Oxford 1992)

—— *A Writer's Diary 1873–1881* ed. and trans. Kenneth Lantz (London 1994) 2 volumes

—— *The Brothers Karamazov* trans. Richard Pevear and Larissa Volokhonsky (New York 1991)

Dowd, D. L. *Pageant-Master of the Republic. Jacques-Louis David and the French Revolution* (Lincoln, Nebr. 1948)

Doyle, William *The Oxford History of the French Revolution* (Oxford 1989)

—— *Jansenism* (London 2000)*

—— (ed.) *Old Regime France* (Oxford 2001)*

Düding, D. (ed.) *Öffentliche Festkultur in Deutschland von der Aufklärung bis zum Ersten Weltkrieg* (Reinbek 1988)

Duffy, Charles Gavan *Young Ireland. A Fragment of Irish History 1840–1850* (London 1880)

Duggan, Christopher *Francesco Crispi. From Nation to Nationalism* (Oxford 2002)

Durkheim, Emile *The Elementary Forms of Religious Life* ed. Mark Cladis (Oxford 2001)

Edel, Leon *Henry James. A Biography* (London 1953–63) 5 volumes

Eliot, George *Scenes from Clerical Life* ed. Jennifer Gribble (London 1998)

Fauchois, Yann 'Révolution française, religion et la logique de l'état' *Archives de Sciences Sociales des Religions* (1989) 66, pp. 9–24

—— *Religion et France révolutionnaire* (Paris 1989)

Fehér, Ferenc. 'The Cult of the Supreme Being and the Limits of the Secularization of the Political' in Ferenc Fehér (ed.) *The French Revolution and the Birth of Modernity* (Berkeley 1990) pp. 174–97

Fehrenbach, Elizabeth 'Über die Bedeutung der politischen Symbole im Nationalstaat' *Historische Zeitschrift* (1971) 213, pp. 296–397

Fenn, Richard *Beyond Idols. The Shape of a Secular Society* (Oxford 2001)

Figes, Orlando *Natasha's Dance. A Cultural History of Russia* (London 2002)*

Figuglietti, James 'Gilbert Romme and the Making of the French Republic Calendar' in David Troyansky, Alfred Cismaru and Norwood Andrews (eds) *The French Revolution in Culture and Society* (New York 1991) pp. 13–22

Foissy-Aufrère, Marie-Pierre (ed.) *La Mort de Bara* (Avignon 1989)

Frank, Joseph *Dostoevsky* (Princeton 1976–2002) 5 volumes*

Friedrich, Carl J. 'The Deification of the State' *Review of Politics* (1939) 1, pp. 18–30

Furet, François *Interpreting the French Revolution* (Cambridge 1981)

—— *Revolutionary France 1770–1880* (Oxford 1992)

—— *The French Revolution 1770–1814* (Oxford 1996)

Furet, François and Ozouf, Mona (eds) *Critical Dictionary of the French Revolution* (Cambridge, Mass. 1990)*

Gaskell, Elizabeth *Mary Barton* (London 1996)

Gauchet, Marcel *The Disenchantment of the Modern World. A Political History of Religion* (Princeton 1997)*

Gay, Peter *The Enlightenment. The Rise of Modern Paganism* (New York 1966) volumes 1–2

Gellner, Ernest *Nationalism* (London 1995)

Gennrich, Paul-Wilhelm *Gott und die Völker. Beiträge zur Auffassung vom Volk und Volkstum in der Geschichte der Theologie* (Stuttgart 1972)

Gentile, Emilio *Le religioni della politica. Fra democrazie e totalitarismi* (Rome 2001)

Germani, Ian and Swales, Robin (eds) *Symbols, Myths and Images of the French Revolution* (Regina 1998)

Gibson, Ralph *A Social History of French Catholicism* (London 1989)

Gilbert, A. D. *Religion and Society in Industrial England. Church, Chapel and Social Change 1740–1914* (London 1976)

Gilley, Sheridan and Sheils, W. J. (eds) *A History of Religion in Britain. Practice and Belief from Pre-Roman Times to the Present* (Oxford 1994)

Godechot, Jacques *The Counter-Revolution. Doctrine and Action 1789–1804* (London 1972)

Gombrich, Ernst 'The Dream of Reason. Symbolism of the French Revolution' *British Journal for Eighteenth-Century Studies* (1979) 2, pp. 187–205

Grenby, M. O. *The Anti-Jacobin Novel. British Conservatism and the French Revolution* (Cambridge 2001)

Greschat, Martin *Das Zeitalter der Industriellen Revolution. Das Christentum vor der Moderne* (Stuttgart 1980)*

Griffiths, Richard *The Reactionary Revolution. The Catholic Revival in French Literature 1870–1914* (New York 1965)

Gunn, Simon *The Public Culture of the Victorian Middle Classes. Ritual and Authority and the English Industrial City 1840–1914* (Manchester 2000)

Haight, Gordon *George Eliot. A Biography* (London 1968)

Halfin, Igor *From Darkness to Light. Class, Consciousness, and Salvation in Revolutionary Russia* (Pittsburgh 2000)

Hampson, Norman *The Enlightenment* (London 1968)

—— *Danton* (London 1978)

—— *Will and Circumstance. Montesquieu, Rousseau and the French Revolution* (London 1983)*

—— 'From Regeneration to Terror. The Ideology of the French Revolution' in Noel O'Sullivan (ed.) *Terrorism, Ideology, Revolution* (Brighton 1986) pp. 49–66

—— *Prelude to Terror. The Constituent Assembly and the Failure of Consensus 1789–1791* (Oxford 1988)

Hanna, Martha *The Mobilization of the Intellect. French Scholars and Writers during the Great War* (Cambridge, Mass. 1996)

Harris, Jennifer 'The Red Cap of Liberty' *Eighteenth-Century Studies* (1980) 14, pp. 283–312

Harris, Jośe *Private Lives, Public Spirit. A Social History of Britain 1870–1914* (Oxford 1993)

Harrison, J. F. C. *Robert Owen and the Owenites in Britain and America. The Quest for a New Moral World* (London 1969)

Hartwig, Wolfgang 'Bürgertum, Staatssymbolik und Staatsbewusstsein im Deutschen Kaiserreich 1871–1914' *Geschichte und Gesellschaft* (1990) 16, pp. 269–95

—— 'Political Religion in Modern Germany. Reflections on Nationalism, Socialism, and National Socialism' *Bulletin of the German Historical Institute, Washington DC* (2001) 28, pp. 3–27

Hayes, Carlton *Essays on Nationalism* (New York 1926)

Hayward, Jack *After the French Revolution. Six Critics of Democracy and Nationalism* (New York 1991)

Hazareesingh, Sudhir *Political Traditions in Modern France* (Oxford 1994)*

—— *The Legend of Napoleon* (London 2004)*

Heffer, Simon *Moral Desperado. A Life of Thomas Carlyle* (London 1995)*

Hehl, Ulrich von 'Zwei Kulturen-eine Nation? Die frühe burschenschaftliche Einheitsbewegung und das Wartburgfest' *Historisches Jahrbuch* (1991) 111, pp. 28–52

Hempton, David *Religion and Political Culture in Britain and Ireland* (Cambridge 1996)

Herzen, Alexander *My Past and Thoughts* trans. Constance Garnett (Berkeley 1982)

Hettling, Manfred and Nolte, Paul (eds) *Bürgerliche Feste. Symbolische Formen politischen Handelns im 19. Jahrhundert* (Göttingen 1993)

Higgonet, Patrice *Goodness beyond Virtue. Jacobins during the French Revolution* (Cambridge 1998)*

Himmelfarb, Gertrude *Victorian Minds. A Study of Intellectuals in Crisis and Ideologies in Transition* (New York 1968)

—— *The De-Moralization of Society. From Victorian Virtues to Modern Values* (New York 1996)*

Hobbes, Thomas *Leviathan* ed. John Plamenetz (London 1978)

Hobsbawm, Eric *Worlds of Labour. Further Studies in the History of Labour* (London 1984)

Hölscher, Lucian *Weltgericht oder Revolution. Protestantische und sozialistische Zukunftsvorstellungen im deutschen Kaiserreich* (Stuttgart 1989)*

—— 'Die Religion des Bürgers. Bürgerliche Frömmigkeit und Protestantische Kirche im 19. Jahrhundert' *Historische Zeitschrift* (1990) 250, pp. 595–630

Hoover, Arlie J. *The Gospel of Nationalism. German Patriotic Preaching from Napoleon to Versailles* (Stuttgart 1986)

—— *God, Germany and Britain in the Great War. A Study in Clerical Nationalism* (New York 1989)*

Hope, Nicholas *German and Scandinavian Protestantism 1700 to 1918* (Oxford 1995)

Hübinger, Gangolf 'Kulturprotestantismus, Bürgerkirche und liberaler Revisionismus im wilhelminischen Deutschland' in Wolfgang Schieder (ed.) *Religion und Gesellschaft im 19. Jahrhundert* (Stuttgart 1993) pp. 272–99

—— *Kulturprotestantismus und Politik. Zum Verhältnis von Liberalismus und Protestantismus im wilhelminischen Deutschland* (Tübingen 1994)

Hume, David *Dialogues and Natural History of Religion* ed. J. C. A. Gaskin (Oxford 1993)

Hunt, Lynn *Politics, Culture, and Class in the French Revolution* (Berkeley 1984)

Hunt, Tristram *Building Jerusalem. The Rise and Fall of the Victorian City* (London 2004)*

Hutchinson, William R. and Lehmann, Hartmut (eds) *Many are Chosen. Divine Election and Western Nationalism* (Minneapolis 1994)

Hutt, M. G. 'The Role of the Curés in the Estates General of 1789' *Journal of Ecclesiastical History* (1955) 6, pp. 190–220 and (1957) 8, pp. 74–92

—— 'The Curés and the Third Estate. The Ideas of Reform in the Pamphlets of the French Lower Clergy in the Period 1787–1789' *Journal of Ecclesiastical History* (1957) 8, pp 74–92

Im Hof, Ulrich *The Enlightenment* (Oxford 1994)

Inglis, K. S. *Churches and the Working Classes in Victorian England* (London 1963)

Jackson, Alvin *Ireland 1798–1998* (Oxford 1999)*

James, Henry *Italian Hours* (New York 1979)

—— *The Princess Casamassima* (London 1987)

Jardin, André *Tocqueville. A Biography* (Baltimore 1998)

Jaume, Lucien *Le Discours jacobin et la démocratie* (Paris 1989)

Jemolo, Arturo Carlo *Chiesa e stato in Italia negli ultimi cento anni* (Milan 1948)

Johnson, Dorothy *Jacques-Louis David. Art in Metamorphosis* (Princeton 1993)

Jones, Gareth Stedman 'How Marx covered his tracks: the hidden link between Communism and religion' *Times Literary Supplement* 7th June 2002, pp. 13–14

Jordan, David P. *The Revolutionary Career of Maximilien Robespierre* (New York 1985)*

Just, Harald 'Wilhelm Busch und die Katholiken. Kulturkampfstimmung im Bismarck-Reich' *Geschichte in Wissenschaft und Unterricht* (1974) 25, pp. 65–78

Kaiser, Jochen-Christoph 'Zur Politisierung des Verbandsprotestantismus. Die Wirkung Adolf Stoeckers auf die Herausbildung einer evangelischen Frauenbewegung um die Jahrhundertwende' in Wolfgang Schieder (ed.) *Religion und Gesellschaft im 19 Jahrhundert* (Stuttgart 1993) pp. 254–71

Kedourie, Elie *Nationalism* (fourth edition Oxford 1993)

Kennedy, Emmet 'The French Revolutionary Catechisms. Ruptures and Continuities with Classical, Christian, and Enlightenment Moralities' *Studies on Voltaire and the Eighteenth Century* (1981) 199, pp. 353–62

Kertzer, David *Ritual, Politics and Power* (New Haven 1988)

Kitson Clark, G. *The Making of Victorian England* (London 1962)

Kley, Dale K. van *The Religious Origins of the French Revolution. From Calvin to the Civil Constitution 1560–1791* (New Haven 1996)*

Klinck, David *The French Counterrevolutionary Theorist Louis de Bonald (1754–1840)* (New York 1996)

Knight, Frances *The Nineteenth-Century Church and English Society* (Cambridge 1995)

Koerner, Joseph Leo *Caspar David Friedrich and the Subject of Landscape* (London 1990)

Kohn, Hans *The Idea of Nationalism* (New York 1945)

Kolakowski, Leszek *Main Currents in Marxism. Its Rise, Growth, and Dissolution* (Oxford 1978–) 3 volumes*

—— *Religion* (London 1982)

Krumreich, Gerd and Lehmann, Hartmut (eds) *'Gott mit uns'. Nation, Religion und Gewalt im 19. und frühen 20. Jahrhundert* (Göttingen 2000)

Küenzlen, Gottfried *Der Neue Mensch. Eine Untersuchung zur säkularen Religionsgeschichte der Moderne* (Munich 1994)

Langmead Casserly, J. V. *The Retreat from Christianity in the Modern World* (London 1952)*

Lannon, Frances *Privilege, Persecution and Prophecy. The Catholic Church in Spain 1875–1975* (Oxford 1987)

Latreille, André *L'Eglise catholique et la Révolution française* (Paris 1946)

Lebrun, Richard A. *Joseph de Maistre. An Intellectual Militant* (Kingston/Montreal 1988)

Lehmann, Hartmut 'The Germans as Chosen People. Old Testament Themes in German Nationalism' *German Studies Review* (1991) 14, pp. 261–73

Leith, James *Media and Revolution. Moulding a New Citizenry in France during the Terror* (Toronto 1968)

Lenz, Max 'Nationalität und Religion' *Preussische Jahrbücher* (1907) 127, pp. 385–408

Lerou, Paule and Dartevelle, Raymond (eds) *Pratiques religieuses dans l'Europe révolutionnaire (1770–1820)* (Paris 1986)

Levitine, George *Culture and Revolution. Cultural Ramifications of the French Revolution* (College Park 1989)

Lewis, Gwynne and Lucas, Colin (eds) *Beyond the Terror. Essays in French Regional and Social History 1794–1983* (Cambridge 1983)

Lidtke, Vernon L. 'August Bebel and German Social Democracy's Relation to the Christian Churches' *Journal of the History of Ideas* (1966) 27, pp. 245–64

Lively, Jack (ed.) *The Works of Joseph de Maistre* (New York 1965)

Löwith, Karl *Meaning in History. The Theological Implications of the Philosophy of History* (Chicago 1949)

Lubac, Henri de *The Drama of Atheist Humanism* (San Francisco 1995)*

Lukes, Steven *Émile Durkheim. His Life and Work* (London 1973)

MacDonagh, Oliver *Daniel O'Connell* (London 1988–9) 2 volumes

Machiavelli, Niccolò *The Discourses* ed. Bernard Crick (London 1970)

Machin, G. I. T. *Politics and the Churches in Great Britain 1832 to 1868* (Oxford 1977)

McLeod, Hugh *Religion and Society in England 1850–1914* (London 1996)

—— *Secularisation in Western Europe 1848–1914* (London 2000)*

—— *Religion and the People of Western Europe 1789–1989* (Oxford 1996)

—— (ed.) *European Religion in the Age of Great Cities 1830–1930* (London 1995)

McLeod, Hugh and Ustorf, Werner (eds) *The Decline of Christendom in Western Europe 1750–2000* (Cambridge 2003)

McMahon, Darrin *Enemies of the Enlightenment. The French Counter-Enlightenment and the Making of Modernity* (Oxford 2001)

McManners, John *The French Revolution and the Church* (London 1969)*

—— *Church and State in France 1870–1914* (London 1972)*

—— *Church and Society in Eighteenth-Century France* (Oxford 1998) 2 volumes*

Maier, Hans *Revolution und Kirche* (fourth edition Freiburg 1975)* English
translation *Revolution and Church* (Notre Dame 1969)

—— *Katholizismus und Demokratie* (Freiburg 1983)

—— *Religion und moderne Gesellschaft* (Freiburg 1985)

—— *Politische Religionen* (Freiburg 1995)*

—— *Das Doppelgesicht der Religiösen. Religion-Gewalt-Politik* (Freiburg 2004)*

—— (ed.) *Totalitarismus und Politische Religionen. Konzepte des
Diktaturvergleichs* (Paderborn 1996–2003) 3 volumes*

—— (ed.) *Wege in der Gewalt. Die modernen politischen Religionen*
(Frankfurt am Main 2000)

Maier, Hans and Schmitt, Eberhard (eds) *Wie eine Revolution entsteht*
(Paderborn 1990)

Maistre, Joseph de *Considerations on France* ed. and trans. Richard A.
Lebrun (Cambridge 1994)

Malcolm, Noel *Aspects of Hobbes* (Oxford 2002)*

Mansfield, Paul 'Collot d'Herbois and the Dechristianisers' *Journal of
Religious History* (1986) 14, pp. 406–18

Manuel, Frank E. and Manuel, Fritzie P. *Utopian Thought in the Western
World* (Cambridge, Mass. 1979)*

Marrin, Albert *The Last Crusade. The Church of England and the First World
War* (Duke 1974)

Marx, Anthony W. *Faith in Nation. Exclusionary Origins of Nationalism*
(Oxford 2003)

Marx, Karl and Engels, Friedrich *The Communist Manifesto* introduced by
Gareth Stedman Jones (London 2002)

Mathewson, Rufus W. *The Positive Hero in Russian Literature* (Stanford 1975)

Mathiez, Albert *La Révolution et l'église* (Paris 1910)

Mayeur, Jean-Marie and Pietri, Charles and Luce, Vauchez, André and
Venard, Marc (eds) *Geschichte des Christentums. Religion, Politik, Kultur*
(Freiburg 1996–2003) 14 volumes*

Mayeur, Jean-Marie and Rebérioux, Madeleine *The Third Republic from its
Origins to the Great War 1871–1914* (Cambridge 1987)

Merle, Gabriel *Émile Combes* (Paris 1995)

Mesnard, Jean *Pascal. His Life and Work* (London 1952)

Meyer, Jeffrey *Myths in Stone. Religious Dimensions of Washington D. C.*
(Berkeley 2001)*

Micale, Mark and Dietle, Robert *Enlightenment, Passion, Modernity.
Historical Essays in European Thought and Culture* (Stanford 2000)

Mismer, Paul *Social Catholicism in Europe. From the Onset of
Industrialization to the First World War* (New York 1991)*

Mommsen, Wolfgang *Bürgerliche Kulture und politische Ordnung. Künstler,*

Schriftsteller und Intellektuelle in der deutschen Geschichte 1830–1933 (Frankfurt am Main 2000)

Montesquieu, *Persian Letters* trans. Christopher Betts (London 1973)

Morange, Jean *La Déclaration des droits de l'homme et du citoyen* (Paris 1988)

Mosse, George L. *The Crisis of German Ideology. Intellectual Origins of the Third Reich* (New York 1964)

—— *The Nationalization of the Masses. Political Symbolism and Mass Movements in Germany from the Napoleonic Wars through the Third Reich* (Ithaca 1975)

Motzkin, Gabriel 'Säkulisierung, Bürgertum und Intellektuelle in Frankreich und Deutschland während des 19. Jahrhunderts' in Jürgen Kocka (ed.) *Bürgertum im 19. Jahrhundert. Deutschland im europäischen Vergleich* (Munich 1988) pp. 141–71

Müller, H.-M. *Kulturprotestantismus. Beiträge zu einer Gestalt des modernen Christentums* (Gütersloh 1992)

Neuhaus, Richard John *The Naked Public Square. Religion and Democracy in America* (Grand Rapids 1984)*

Nicholls, David *Deity and Domination. Images of God and the State in the Nineteenth and Twentieth Centuries* (London 1989)

Nietzsche, Friedrich *Beyond Good and Evil* trans. Helen Zimmern (New York 1989)

Nipperdey, Thomas 'Nationalidee und Nationaldenkmal in Deutschland im 19. Jahrhundert' in Thomas Nipperdey *Gesellschaft, Kultur, Theorie* (Göttingen 1976) pp. 133–73

—— 'Der Kölner Dom als Nationaldenkmal' *Historische Zeitschrift* (1981) 233, pp. 595–613

—— *Religion im Umbruch. Deutschland 1870–1918* (Munich 1988)*

—— 'Religion und Gesellschaft. Deutschland um 1900' *Historische Zeitschrift* (1988) 246, pp. 591–615

—— *Deutsche Geschichte 1866–1918* (Munich 1998) 3 volumes

Norman, Edward. *A History of Modern Ireland* (London 1971)

—— *Church and Society in England 1770–1970. A Historical Study* (Oxford 1976)*

—— *Secularisation* (London 2002)

Novalis (Friedrich von Hardenberg) *Fragmente und Studien. Die Christenheit und Europa* ed. Carl Paschek (Stuttgart 1984)

Nowak, Kurt *Geschichte des Christentums in Deutschland. Religion, Politik und Gesellschaft vom Ende der Aufklärung bis zur Mitte des 20. Jahrhunderts* (Munich 1995)*

O'Brien, Conor Cruise *God Land. Reflections on Religion and Nationality* (Cambridge, Mass. 1988)

—— *The Great Melody. A Thematic Biography of Edmund Burke* (Chicago 1992)*

Ormières, Jean-Louis *Politique et religion en France* (Paris 2002)*

Outram, Dorinda *The Enlightenment* (Cambridge 1995)

Owen, Robert *A New View of Society and Other Writings* ed. Gregory Claeys (London 1991)

Ozouf, Mona *Festivals and the French Revolution* (Cambridge 1988)

—— 'Public Opinion at the End of the Old Regime' *Journal of Modern History* (1988) 60, pp. S1–S21 (Supplement)

Painter, George D. *Chateaubriand. A Biography* (New York 1978) volume 1

Palmer, Robert R. *Twelve who Ruled. The Year of Terror in the French Revolution* (Princeton 1941)

—— *Catholics and Unbelievers in Eighteenth Century France* (Princeton 1967)

—— *The Improvement of Humanity. Education and the French Revolution* (Princeton 1985)

Parker, Harold T. *The Cult of Antiquity and the French Revolutionaries. A Study in the Development of the French Revolutionary Spirit* (Chicago 1937)

Parsons, Gerald *Perspectives on Civil Religion* (Milton Keynes 2002)

Parsons, Gerald and Wolffe, John (eds) *The Church in Victorian Britain* (Manchester 1988–96) 5 volumes

Pascal, *Provincial Letters* trans. A. J. Krailsheimer (London 1967)

Payne, Stanley *Spanish Catholicism. An Historical Overview* (Madison 1984)

Pelling, Henry *The Origins of the Labour Party 1880–1900* (Oxford 1965)

Pereiro, James *Cardinal Manning. An Intellectual Biography* (Oxford 1998)

Peronnet, Michel *Les Evêques de l'ancienne France* (Paris 1977)

Petitfrère, Claude 'The Origins of the Civil War in the Vendée' *French History* (1988) 2, pp. 181–207

Phillips, C. S. *The Church in France 1789–1907* (London 1929–39) 2 volumes

Pierrard, Pierre *Les Chrétiens et l'affaire Dreyfus* (Paris 1998)

Pillarget, René 'The Cultural Programmes of the 1789 Revolution' *History* (1985) 70, pp. 386–96

Pinson, Koppel S. *Pietism as a Factor in the Rise of German Nationalism* (New York 1934)

Pipes, Richard *Russia under the Old Regime* (London 1974)

Pollard, John *The Unknown Pope. Benedict XV (1914–1922) and the Pursuit of Peace* (London 1999)

—— 'The Papacy in Two World Wars. Benedict XV and Pius XII

Compared' *Totalitarian Movements and Political Religions* (2001) 2, pp. 83–96

Portier, Philippe *Église et politique en France au xxe siècle* (Paris 1993)

Pressly, William L. *The French Revolution as Blasphemy. Johann Zoffany's Paintings of the Massacre at Paris, August 10, 1792* (Berkeley 1999)

Price, Munro *The Fall of the French Monarchy. Louis XVI, Marie Antoinette and the Baron de Breteuil* (London 2002)

Puschner, Uwe, Schmitz, Walter and Ulbricht, Justus (eds) *Handbuch zur 'Völkischen Bewegung' 1871–1918* (Munich 1999)*

Quéniart, Jean *Le Clergé déchiré. Fidèle ou rebelle?* (Rennes 1988)

Reichardt, Rolf E. *Das Blut der Freiheit. Französische Revolution und demokratische Kultur* (Frankfurt am Main 1998)

Rémond, René *Religion and Society in Modern Europe* (Oxford 1999)*

Rhodes, Anthony *The Power of Rome in the Twentieth Century. The Vatican in the Age of Liberal Democracies 1870–1922* (London 1983)*

Riall, Lucy *Sicily and the Unification of Italy. Liberal Policy and Local Power 1859–1866* (Oxford 1998)

Riley, Patrick (ed.) *The Cambridge Companion to Rousseau* (Cambridge 2001)*

Robb, Graham *Victor Hugo* (London 1997)

Roberts, J. M. 'The French Origins of the Right' *Transactions of the Royal Historical Society* (1973) 23, pp. 27–53

Roberts, Warren *Revolutionary Artists. Jacques-Louis David and Jean-Louis Prieur. The Public, the Populace and Images of the French Revolution* (Albany 2000)

Roche, Daniel *France and the Enlightenment* (Cambridge 1998)

Rogers, David *Politics, Prayer and Parliament* (London 2000)

Ross, Ronald *Beleaguered Tower. The Dilemma of Political Catholicism in Wilhelmine Germany* (Notre Dame 1976)

—— 'The Kulturkampf and the Limitations of Power in Bismarck's Germany' *Journal of Ecclesiastical History* (1995) 46, pp. 669–88

—— *The Failure of Bismarck's Kulturkampf. Catholicism and State Power in Imperial Germany 1871–1887* (Washington DC 1998)

Roth, Joseph *The Radetzky March* (London 1995 original Berlin 1932)

Rousseau, Jean-Jacques *Politics and the Arts. Letter to M. D'Alembert on the Theatre* introduction and notes by Allan Bloom (Ithaca 1960)*

—— *The Social Contract and Other Later Political Writing* ed. Victor Gourevitch (Cambridge 1997)

Ruggiero, Guido de *The History of European Liberalism* (Oxford 1927)*

Sandoz, Ellis *Political Apocalypse. A Study of Dostoevsky's Inquisitor* (Baton Rouge 1971)

—— (ed.) *Eric Voegelin's Significance for the Modern Mind* (Baton Rouge 1991)*

Sarti, Roland *Mazzini. A Life for the Religion of Politics* (Westport 1997)*

Schafer, Boyd C. *Nationalism. Myth and Reality* (New York 1955)

Schama, Simon *Citizens. A Chronicle of the French Revolution* (London 1989)*

Schieder, Wolfgang (ed.) *Religion und Gesellschaft im 19. Jahrhundert* (Stuttgart 1993)

Schulze, Hagen *States, Nations and Nationalism* (Oxford 1994)

Scott, Christina *A Historian and his World. A Life of Christopher Dawson 1889–1970* (London 1984)

Scruton, Roger *The West and the Rest. Globalization and the Terrorist Threat* (London 2002)*

—— *Death-Devoted Heart. Sex and the Sacred in Wagner's* Tristan and Isolde (Oxford 2004)*

Secher, Reynald *Le Génocide franco-française. La Vendée-Vengé* (Paris 1986)

Sheehan, James *German Liberalism in the Nineteenth Century* (Chicago 1978)*

—— *German History 1770–1866* (Oxford 1989)*

Sheehy, Jeanne *The Rediscovery of Ireland's Past. The Celtic Revival 1830–1930* (London 1980)

Sieburg, Friedrich *Chateaubriand* (London 1961)

Sigmund, Paul E. 'The Catholic Tradition and Modern Democracy' *Review of Politics* (1987) 49, pp. 530–48

Smart, Ninian (ed.) *Religion and Politics in the Modern World* (New York 1983)

Smith, Anthony D. *Chosen Peoples. Sacred Sources of National Identity* (Oxford 2003)

Smith, Denis Mack *Mazzini* (New Haven 1994)

Smith, Helmut Walser *German Nationalism and Religious Conflict. Culture, Ideology, and Politics 1870–1914* (Princeton 1995)

—— (ed.) *Protestants, Catholics and Jews in Germany 1800–1914* (Oxford 2001)

Smith, Leonard, Audoin-Rouzeau, Stéphane and Becker, Annette *France and the Great War 1914–1918* (Cambridge 2003)

Soloway, R. S. *Prelates and People. Ecclesiastical Social Thought in England 1783–1852* (London 1969)

Sorrell, Tom (ed.) *The Cambridge Companion to Hobbes* (Cambridge 1996)

Sperber, Jonathan *The European Revolutions 1848–1851* (Cambridge 1994)

Starobinski, Jean *1789. The Emblems of Reason* (Charlottesville 1982)

Stern, Fritz *The Politics of Cultural Despair. A Study in the Rise of the Germanic Ideology* (Berkeley 1961)*

Storey, Mark *Robert Southey* (Oxford 1997)

Strakhovsky, Leonid *Alexander I of Russia* (London 1949)

Strout, Cushing *The New Heavens and New Earth. Political Religion in America* (New York 1974)

Sutherland, D. M. G. *The Chouans. The Social Origins of Popular Counter-Revolution in Upper Brittany 1770–1796* (Oxford 1982)

—— *France 1789–1815. Revolution and Counterrevolution* (London 1985)

Sutherland, John *Mrs Humphry Ward* (Oxford 1990)

Sutton, Michael *Nationalism, Positivism and Catholicism. The Politics of Charles Maurras and French Catholics 1890–1914* (Cambridge 1982)*

Swenson, James *On Jean-Jacques Rousseau. Considered as One of the First Authors of the Revolution* (Stanford 2000)

Tackett, Timothy 'The West in France in 1789' *Journal of Modern History* (1982) 54, pp. 715–45

—— *Becoming a Revolutionary. The Deputies of the French National Assembly and the Emergence of a Revolutionary Political Culture* (Princeton 1996)

Taine, Hippolyte *Taine's Notes on England*, trans. and introduced by Edward Hyams (London 1957)

—— *The French Revolution* (New York 1878) 3 volumes

Taithe, Bertrand and Thornton, Tim (eds) *Prophecy. The Power of Inspired Language in History 1300–2000* (Stroud 1997)

Tallett, Frank and Atkin, Nicholas (eds) *Religion, Society and Politics in France since 1789* (London 1991)

Talmon, J. L. *The Origins of Totalitarian Democracy* (London 1952)

—— *Political Messianism. The Romantic Phase* (London 1960)*

Tanner, Marcus *Ireland's Holy Wars. The Struggle for a Nation's Soul 1500–2000* (New Haven 2001)

Tardin, André and Tudesq, André-Jean *Restoration and Reaction 1815–1848* (Cambridge 1988)

Teilhard de Chardin, Pierre *Writings in Time of War* trans. R. Hague (London 1968)

Tocqueville, Alexis de *The Old Regime and the French Revolution* ed. François Furet and Françoise Mélino (Chicago 1998) 2 volumes

Tombs, Robert *France 1814–1914* (London 1996)*

Toyanski, David G., Cismaru, Alfred and Andrews, Norwood (eds) *The French Revolution in Culture and Society* (Westport 1991)

Trilling, Lionel *Matthew Arnold* (London 1939)

Troyat, Henri *Gorky* (London 1994)

Trzeciakowski, Lech 'The Prussian State and the Catholic Church in Prussian Poland 1871–1914' *Slavic Review* (1967) 26, pp. 618–37

Ulam, Adam *Prophets and Conspirators in Pre-Revolutionary Russia* (New Brunswick 1998)

Unfried, Berthold and Schindler, Christine (eds) *Riten, Mythen und Symbole – Die Arbeiterbewegung zwischen 'Zivilreligion' und Volkskultur* (Vienna 1999)

Vaughan, William and Weston, Helen *David's The Death of Marat* (Cambridge 2000)

Venturi, Franco *Roots of Revolution. A History of the Populist and Socialist Movements in 19th Century Russia* (London 2001)

Vidler, Alec R. *Prophecy and Papacy. A Study of Lamennais, the Church and the Revolution* (London 1954)

―― *A Century of Social Catholicism 1820–1920* (London 1964)

Vigener, Fritz *Ketteler. Ein deutsches Bischofsleben des 19. Jahrhunderts* (Munich 1924)

Voegelin, Eric *Die politischen Religionen* (Munich 1996)

Voigt, Frederick *Unto Caesar* (London 1938)

Voltaire, *Philosophical Dictionary* trans. Theodore Bestermann (London 1972)

Vondung, Klaus *Die Apokalypse in Deutschland* (Munich 1998)

Vovelle, Michel *The Revolution against the Church. From Reason to the Supreme Being* (Columbus 1991)

―― *La Mentalité révolutionnaire* (Paris 1985)*

―― (ed.) *Enlightenment Portraits* (Chicago 1997)*

Walzer, Michael *The Revolution of the Saints. A Study in the Origins of Radical Politics* (London 1965)

Ward, Mrs Humphry *Robert Elsmere* (twenty-seventh edition London 1889)

Weber, Eugen *Action Française. Royalism and Reaction in Twentieth-Century France* (Stanford 1962)

Weber, Max *From Max Weber. Essays in Sociology* ed. H. H. Gerth and C. Wright Mills (London 1970)

Wehler, Hans-Ulrich *Nationalismus* (Frankfurt am Main 2002)

―― *Deutsche Gesellschaftsgeschichte 1849–1914* (Munich 1995)

Wernick, Andrew *Auguste Comte and the Religion of Humanity* (Cambridge 2001)

Wessell, Leonard P. *Prometheus Bound. The Mythic Structure of Karl Marx's Scientific Thinking* (Baton Rouge 1984)

Wilson, A. N. *Hilaire Belloc* (London 1984)

—— *God's Funeral. A Biography of Faith and Doubt in Western Civilisation* (New York 1999)*

—— *The Victorians* (London 2002)

Winiger, Josef *Ludwig Feuerbach. Denker der Menschlichkeit* (Berlin 2004)

Winkler, Heinrich-August (ed.) *Nationalismus* (Königstein/Taunus 1985)

Winock, Michel *Nationalism, Anti-Semitism, and Fascism in France* (Stanford 1998)

Wolffe, Robert L. *Gains and Losses. Novels of Faith and Doubt in Victorian England* (New York 1977)

Wright, T. R. *The Religion of Humanity. The Impact of Comtean Positivism on Victorian Britain* (Cambridge 1986)*

Zamoyski, Adam *Holy Madness. Romantics, Patriots and Revolutionaries 1776–1871* (London 1999)*

Zillessen, H. (ed.) *Volk-Nation-Vaterland. Der deutsche Protestantismus und der Nationalismus* (Gütersloh 1970)

Zimmer, Hasko *Auf dem Altar des Vaterlands. Religion und Patriotismus in der deutschen Kriegslyrik des 19. Jahrhunderts* (Frankfurt am Main 1971)

Zola, Emile, *Doctor Pascal* (Stroud 1989)

PICTURE CREDITS

1 'The Planting of a Tree of Liberty' by Le Sueur Brothers
Musée de la Ville de Paris, Musée Carnavalet, Paris/Bridgeman Art Library, London

2–3 'The Plunder of the King's Wine Cellar 1792' by Johann Zoffany
Noorfman, Maastricht/Bridgeman Art Library, London

4 Self-portrait by Jacques Louis David 1794
Louvre/Bridgeman Art Library, London

'The Death of Marat' by Jacques Louis David 1793
Musées Royaux des Beaux-Arts de Belgique, Brussels/Bridgeman Art Library, London

5 'The Death of Joseph Barra' by Jacques Louis David
Musee Calvet, Avignon/Bridgeman Art Library, London

Joseph Barra by Pierre-Michel
© Michéle Bellot/Réunion des Musées Nationaux, Paris

6 An Allegory of the Revolution with a portrait medallion of Jean-Jacques Rousseau 1794 by Nicolas Henri Jearat de Bertry
Musée de la Ville de Paris, Musée Carnavalet, Paris/Bridgeman Art Library, London

'Noyades dans la Loire par ordre du féroce Carrier' by Jean Duplessis-Bertaux (dessinateur) and Pierre-Gabriel Berthault (graveur)
Collection Musée d'Art et d'Histoire de Cholet. Cliché Patrick Pestre, Musée de Cholet. Direction de la Communication

7 'Incendie d'une chapelle en Vendée' by Marie-Felix Parmentier
*Collection Musée d'Art et d'Histoire de Cholet. Cliché Musée de Cholet.
Dépôt du Musée Tavet-Delacour de Pontoise*

8 Napoleon as a baby in Antichrist's arms. Illustration from 'Gott mit
uns' by G. Krumeich/H. Lehmann (Vanderhoeck and Ruprecht
Gottingen)

'Monk by the Sea' by Caspar David Friedrich 1809
Staatliche Museum, Berlin/Bridgeman Art Library, London

9 Sanctification of Garibaldi, 1863. Illustration from 'Modern Italy:
Images and History of a National Identity' Vol 1 (Milan 1982)

10–11 Dostoevsky's working table at Staraya Russa 1881
TopFoto

Illustration of the Ball scene in *The Devils* by N. Karasin
Russian State Library, Moscow

12 Sunrise 8 Hour day postcard from 'Weltgericht oder Revolution' by
Lucien Hölscher (Klett-Cotta, 1989)

13 'Missionary Hounded out of a Rookery'. Illustration from 'These Fifty
Years' by John Matthias Weylland

'Missionary singing to coal heavers' (1899)
London City Mission

14–15 'Der Krieg' by Alfred Kubin
© DACS 2005. *Photo courtesy AKG Images*

16 Reims Cathedral from 'Les Catholiques Français Pendant la Grande
Guerre' by Jacques Fontana (Cerf 1990)

While every effort has been made to trace the owners of copyright material
reproduced herein, the publishers would like to apologise for any omissions
and will be pleased to incorporate missing acknowledgements in any future
editions

INDEX

agitates against, 420; and German
unification, 435

Black Partition (Russian movement),
303

Blair, Tony, 9

Blanc, Louis, 261

Bleichröder, Gerson, 417

Bloch, rabbi Abraham, 455

Blomfield, Charles James, bishop of
London, 384

Blondel, Maurice, 431

Blücher, Marshal Gebbard Leberecht
von, 155

Bogdanovich, Ippolit Fyodorovich, 278

Boisdeffre, Raoul de, 355

Boisgelin de Cercé, Raymond de,
archbishop of Aix, 52, 59

Bolivar, Simon, 178

Bologna, Concordat of (1516), 29

Bolsheviks, 279, 460

Bonal, François de, bishop of Clermont,
54, 57

Bonald, Louis Gabriel Ambroise,
vicomte de: life and ideas, 124,
130–2, 205, 225; anti-liberalism,
134; *Théorie du pouvoir politique et
religieuse dans la société civile*, 130

Bonheur, Raymond, 228

Book of the New Moral World, 240

Booth, Catherine, 377–8

Booth, Charles, 375

Booth, William, 377–9; *In Darkest
England and the Way Out*, 379

Borodino, battle of (1812), 113

Bötticher, Paul *see* Lagarde, Paul de

Bötticher, Wilhelm, 433

Boulanger, Georges Ernest Jean Marie,
346–7

Bourbon dynasty: restoration, 132–3

Bourgeois, Léon Victor Auguste, 223,
357

bourgeoisie: indifference to religion,
207–8; return to Catholicism in
France, 254

Bradlaugh, Charles, 253

Brandts, Franz, 422

Brentano, Clemens, 114

Briand, Aristide, 363

Brienne, Jean de, 61

Brisson, Henri, 223

Britain: and new citizens, 15; and
religious toleration, 116; attitude to
European monarchies, 118; parish
structure, 123; and ethnic
chosenness, 148; and Catholic Irish
nationalism, 176–84; Catholic
hierarchy restored, 212, 313–14; and
honest doubt, 213–15;
nonconformism in, 254–6, 262;
moral values, 256–7; organised
labour and Christianity in, 262–3;
church attendance, 263, 312,
369–70; socialism and Christianity
in, 263–4; civic culture in, 273–5;
government and religion
separated, 311–12; and
disestablishment, 312; industrial
society, 365–8; Victorian religious
indifference, 368–9; Victorian
social problems and reforms,
372–85; urban missions, 373–5; in
First World War, 441, 447–51

British Association, 216

Browning, Robert, 202

Bruno, Giordano, 216

Brunswick Manifesto (1792), 68

Brussels Communist Correspondence
Committee, 247

Brust, August, 423

Buchez, Philippe, 261–2, 393

Büchner, Ludwig, 254

Buckland, William, 215

Buisson, Henri, 223, 342–3

Bull, Captain Tom, 378

Buonarroti, Filippo, 186, 243

Burckhardt, Jacob, 145

Burke, Edmund: on French Revolution,
43, 68, 90, 92; on religion, 121–2,
205; *Reflections*, 125

Burschenschaften, 161, 162

Burton, Frederic, 183

Busch, Wilhelm, 324

Bush, George W., 9
Buxton, J.H., 374
Buxton, Thomas, 373
Byron, George Gordon, 6th Baron, 114, 167

Cabet, Etienne, 243, 261
Cadorna, general Rafaelle, 318
Caillaux affair (1914), 438
calendar: French revolutionary, 85–7, 108
Calvinism, 46
Cambridge University: opened to Dissenters, 255
Camelots du Roi, 430
Campanella, Tommaso: life and thought, 17–21, 91; *The City of the Sun*, 17, 20
Camus, Albert, 426
Camus, Armand, 59, 62
Caprara, cardinal Giovanni Battista, conte, 109
Carbonari, 170, 186
Cardiff, 370
Carlos, Don (Spanish pretender), 176
Carlyle, Jane Welsh, 190
Carlyle, Thomas, 190, 365, 368, 434, 437
Carrier, Jean-Baptiste, 101
Casement, Sir Roger, 447
Castlereagh, Robert Stewart, viscount, 120
catechisms, secular, 82–3, 153, 286–7
Catherine II (the Great), Empress of Russia, 34, 58
Catholic Assembly (Germany), 333
Catholic Church: repressed and abused in French Revolution, 51–7, 85, 106, 112, 145; establishes Ecclesiastical Committee (1789), 57; French diocesan boundaries reorganised, 57–8; clandestine French, 95–6; separated from state in France (1795), 105–6; and Napoleon's religious settlement, 107–11, 112; survives revolutionary repression, 107; in England, 122;

and French education, 133, 340; status under Louis Philippe, 135; universalism, 144, 146–7; accused of being 'Jewish', 147; status in Germany, 147, 321–3, 327, 335, 414, 422–4, 446; and Polish independence movement, 169–70, 172; and Irish nationalism, 176–85; and Italian nationalism, 191–2, 195–6; opposes nationalism, 199; and 1848 revolution in Paris, 206–9; accepts social inequality, 206–7; supports Emperor Napoleon III, 210–11; French republican hostility to, 211; opposes French participation in Crimean War, 211; restoration of hierarchy in England, 212, 313; French bourgeoisie revives interest in, 254; and Kulturkampf, 266, 322–3; and states in 19th-century, 311–15; in Prussia and Germany, 321–2, 324–5, 328–35; popular prejudice against, 324–6; in 19th-century France, 336–52; and Dreyfus affair, 354; working class following, 370; social philosophy and reforms, 388–94, 398–9, 402–3, 408; and German reform, 406–7; and industrial labour movement, 409–11; supports Action Française, 430–3
Catholic Emancipation Act (Britain, 1828), 181
Catholic Relief Act (Britain, 1793), 179
Cavaignac, general Louis Eugène, 206
Cavell, Edith, 447
Cavour, Camillo Benso, conte, 192–5, 197
Chadwick, Edwin: *Report on the Sanitary Conditions of the Labouring Population* (1842), 382–3
Chaix, Dominique, 27
Chalmers, Thomas, 373
Chamberlain, Joseph, 274
Champ de Mars, Paris: festivals, 76, 79–80

France – *cont.*

Vienna, 118; education in, 133, 209, 340, 342–6; religious revival under Charles X, 134, 319; cultural hegemony, 150; German resentment of, 155–7, 159; territorial gains under Italian republicanism, 193; and 1848 revolution, 206–8, 393; Second Empire established (1852), 210; freemasonry in, 223, 254; and Christian Socialism, 261–2; trade unions in, 264; Church and state in 19th/20th-century, 311, 319, 336–52, 358–61; war with Prussia (1870), 318, 396; republicanism, 339–42, 347–9; secularism, 341; religious repression in, 344–7, 350–1, 357–8; women's education in, 345; differences with papacy, 359–60, 400–1; Church separated from state (1905), 362–4; social effect of industrialisation, 388–98; friendly societies in, 394–5; inheritance laws in, 396; pilgrimages to Rome, 400–1; Christian workers' congresses in, 412; and social/political utility of religion, 425; and outbreak of First World War, 438–41; and justification of First World War, 447; clergy in First World War, 454–5; *see also* French Revolution; Paris

France Libre, La (newspaper), 412
Francis I, emperor of Austria, 120
Francis I, king of France, 29
Francis I, king of Two Sicilies, 194
François de Pâris, 35
Frank, Joseph, 12
Frayssinous, Denis Antoine Luc, comte de, bishop of Hermopolis, 133
Frederick II (the Great), king of Prussia, 30, 34, 45, 148, 151
Frederick William III, king of Prussia, 120, 155, 218

Frederick William IV, king of Prussia, 218
Free Church of Scotland, 313
freemasons and freemasonry: French clerics as, 27; Maistre and, 125; in Italy, 164; in France, 223, 254, 349, 357, 361; and political discussion, 223
French language: in diplomacy, politics and culture, 117, 150–2
French Revolution: civic cults, 1; and Enlightenment ideas, 21–2, 43, 45; attitude of Church to, 46; anti-clericalism and Church sequestration, 51–4, 56–7, 85, 112, 145; outbreak, 51; clergy required to take oaths, 64–5, 106–7; as religion, 65, 81, 88, 91–2, 111; depicted, 68–76; festivals, 76–80, 86, 102–4; manners and behaviour, 83; renaming, 83–4, 98; revised calendar, 85–7, 108; anti-religious measures, 86–7; ideology, 90–1; and the Terror, 93, 97–102, 339; refugee and recusant clergy, 95–6; hostility and resistance to, 96–102; influence outside France, 112–15; Maistre on, 127–8; and nationalism, 145; destroys historic institutions, 339; *see also* France
Freycinet, Charles-Louis de Saulces de, 344, 348
Fribourg Union, 408
Friedrich, Caspar David, 115
Fries, Jakob Friedrich, 162
Froude, James Anthony, 213
'Fructidor' coup (France, 1796), 106
Fugger family (of Augsburg), 18
Fülop-Müller, René, 4

Gagarin, prince, 172
Galen, Ferdinand von, 407
Galen, Maximilian Gereon, count, 422
Galileo Galilei, 216
Gallicanism, 28
Galt, Thomas, 375

Galton, Francis, 215–16

Gambetta, Léon, 147, 223, 339, 341–3, 347

Garibaldi, Giuseppe, 145, 192–7

Garwood, John: *The Million-Peopled City*, 375

Gayraud, Hyppolyte, abbé, 411

Geffroy (locksmith), 93–5, 104

Gellner, Ernest, 148, 165

General Agency for the Defence of Religious Liberty, 139, 142

General Council of the Church (1869), 317–18

Genoa, 185–6

Gentz, Friedrich von, 120

George IV, king of Great Britain, 181

Gerlach, Ernst Ludwig and Leopold, 219

Gerlich, Fritz, 4

German Freethinkers League, 254

German Workers Educational Association, 245

Germany: Protestantism in, 146, 150, 154, 156, 218–19, 268, 270–1, 323–4, 403–4, 415–17, 420–1, 424, 435–6, 445–6; rise of nationalism in, 146, 148–9, 154–63, 320; French language in, 151–2; irregular anti-Napoleon forces, 159; student societies, 161–2; monuments, 198, 324; revisionist theology in, 218–21; free-thinking in, 254; socialism in, 263–70; atheism in, 268; religious minorities in, 311, 320–1; empire (Reich) established, 320, 415; Catholic church in, 321–3, 327, 335, 422–4, 446; Kulturkampf in, 322–3, 327–9, 333, 335–6, 414, 423, 435, 446; liberal Protestants in, 323; anti-Catholic repression in ('May Laws'), 327–36; Catholic laws relaxed, 335–6; and industrialisation, 388, 403, 406; social reform, 404–7, 422; labour movement in, 405–7; antisemitism in, 416–18; Stoecker's activities in, 416–20; Anti-Socialist Laws

(1878–90), 418–19; Lagarde criticises, 434–7; and outbreak of First World War, 438–43; accused of barbarism, 443–4; as chosen of God, 444–6

Germany in its Deepest Humiliation (pamphlet), 154

Gibbon, Edward, 40, 127

Gillman, George, 375

Gioberti, Fr Vincenzo: *Of the Moral and Civil Primacy of the Italians*, 191

Girondins, 98

Gladstone, William Ewart: reviews *Robert Elsmere*, 204; disestablishes Church of Ireland, 313; religious beliefs, 313–14; on doctrine of papal infallibility, 318

Glagau, Otto, 418

Glasgow, 258, 385

Gnosticism: Cohn on, 7; Voegelin on, 56–7

Gobel, Jean Baptiste Joseph, bishop of Paris, 87

Goethe, Johann Wolfgang von, 151, 158, 271

Göhre, Paul, 419

Golitsyn, Alexander, 119

Goncharov, Ivan Alexandrovich: *Oblomov*, 278

Goosens, Pierre-Lambert, cardinal, 411

Gore, Charles, 386

Gorki, Maxim, 17

Görres, Joseph, 114, 142

Gosse, (Sir) Edmund, 202

Gotha programme (1875), 265

Goya y Lucientes, Francisco de, 68–9; *Disasters of War*, 112

Grand National Council of Trade Unions, 239

Graves de communi (papal encyclical, 1901), 412

Gravissimo (papal encyclical, 1906), 363

Great War *see* First World War

Greece: independence movements against Ottomans, 118, 164–9; secret societies, 165–6

Grégoire, Henri, bishop of Blois, 30, 56, 83, 107
Gregory XVI, pope, 116, 136, 140–2, 172, 176, 191
Grigorios V, patriarch, 167
Guesde, Jules, 353
Guild of St Matthew, 385–6
Guizot, François Pierre Guillaume, 133, 135
Gurian, Waldemar, 4

Haeckel, Ernst Heinrich Philipp August, 216
Haldane, John Burdon Sanderson, 440
Halévy, Daniel, 7
Hallé, Sir Charles, 274
Hardy, Thomas, 202
Harmel, Léon, 398–400, 402, 412, 422
Harnack, Adolf von, 419
Hartmann, cardinal, 457
Hazlitt, William, 114
Headlam, Stewart, 216, 385–6
Hegel, Georg Wilhelm Friedrich, 113, 146, 220, 272; *Life of Jesus*, 217
Heine, Heinrich, 443
Hengstenberg, Ernst Wilhelm, 219, 434
Henrici, Ernst, 418
Henry IV, king of France, 32
Henry VIII, king of England, 28–9
Henry, colonel Hubert Joseph, 352–3, 427
Henson, Hensley, dean (later bishop) of Durham, 448–9
Herder, Johann Gottfried, 151–3
Hermann the Cheruscan (Arminius), 324
Herzen, Alexander, 276, 279, 288, 366
Herzen, Natalia, 288–9
Hitler, Adolf, 3
Hitze, Fr Franz, 422
Hoare, Joseph, 374
Hobbes, Thomas, 21
Hoche, general Lazare, 102
Hofmannsthal, Hugo von, 440
Hohenlohe, cardinal Gustav von, 327
Holocaust, 145

Holy Alliance (1815), 120
Holy Roman Empire, 148
Holyoake, George Jacob, 252–3
'honest doubt', 199, 205
Hopkins, Gerard Manley, 331
Horobin (of London City Mission), 374
How, William Walsham, bishop of Wakefield, 212
Hugo, Joseph-Léopold-Sigisbert ('Brutus'), 100, 112
Hugo, Victor, 115, 138, 206, 209–11, 291; funeral, 341
Hume, David: *Natural History of Religion*, 40–1
Huxley, Thomas Henry, 216–17, 263

Ibrahim Pasha, 169
Independent Labour Party, 264
Industrial Revolution: in Britain, 365, 368
Inge, William Ralph, dean of St Paul's, 438
Inquisition, Holy, 136
Ireland: Catholic nationalists in, 146–7, 176–85; seeks independence, 169; British palliative measures in, 183–4
Irish Catholic Association, 179–80
Irish Church Temporalities Act (1833), 181, 312
Irish Confederation, 185
Islam: Jacobinism compared with, 3; and international terrorism, 14
Italy: language and rule in, 117; nationalism and unification, 163–4, 186–97; secret societies, 164; 1848 revolutions, 191; church and state in, 196–7, 311, 315–16; history teaching and national education in, 197–8; kingdom proclaimed (1861), 315; in First World War, 458–60; rise of Fascism in, 460
Ivanov, Ivan, 287, 292

Jackson, Thomas Lupton, 375
Jacobins: civic cults, 1; compared with

La Barre, François Jean de, 30–1
Laberthonnière, Lucien, 431–3
labour conditions: in Britain, 382, 387; in France, 399–400
Lac, Stanislas du, 353–5
Lacordaire, Jean-Baptiste Henri, abbé, 140
Lafayette, Marie Joseph du Motier, marquis de, 77, 135
Lagarde, Paul de (Paul Bötticher), 1, 433–6
Lamartine, Alphonse, 115, 126, 138
Lamennais, Félicité Robert de: hostility to Napoleon's university reform, 133; career and ideas, 137–40, 143, 262; audience with pope, 141–2; abandons Church, 142–3; death, 144; supports Polish rebels, 172; criticises industrialists, 206; influence in Italy, 316; on Society of St Joseph, 390; *De la religion considérée dans ses rapports avec l'ordre politique et civil*, 138; *Paroles d'un croyant*, 142
L'Amiral (French potential assassin), 93–4
Lamire, abbé, 411
Land and Freedom (Russian movement), 284, 302–3
Lang, Cosmo, archbishop of York (then of Canterbury), 438
La Rochefoucauld, D., archbishop of Rouen, 49
Larwood, Harold, 377
Lasker, Eduard, 327
Lassalle, Ferdinand, 265, 270, 405–6
Latin America: Pentecostalism in, 122; Catholicism in, 314–15
La Tour du Pin, René de, comte, 397–8, 400, 402
Lavigerie, cardinal Charles-Martel-Allemand, archbishop of Algiers, 344, 347–8
Lavisse, Ernest, 343
Lavoisier, Antoine Laurent, 102
Law of Guarantees (1871), 318

League of Communists, 248
League of German Free-Religious Parishes, 254
League of the Just (secret society), 245–7
Lecky, William Edward Hartpole, 252
Le Coz, Claude, bishop of Rennes, 62, 96
Ledóchowski, Miechyslaw Halka, archbishop of Gnesen-Posen, 322
Ledreuille, Auguste, 392
Ledru-Rollin, Alexandre-Auguste, 211
Leeds, 273, 275
Legislative Assembly (French): and Civil Constitution, 63–4
Lelièvre, abbé, 456
Le Maître, Antoine, 35
Lenin, Vladimir Ilich: and political religion, 3; reads Campanella, 17; on Chernyshevsky, 280, 283; recommends People's Will, 303; on tsarist Russia, 367
Lenwood, Frank, 441
Leo XII, pope, 136, 138
Leo XIII, pope (Luigi Domenico Pecci): elected pope, 334–5; arbitrates in Caroline Islands dispute, 335; and Kulturkampf, 335, 346; and Ferry's education law, 344; on church and state, 347–50; and French 1898 elections, 352; and Dreyfus affair, 354; death and succession, 368–9; and Harmel and social policy, 400–1; and social-industrial questions, 408–10, 412–13; restrains Christian Democrats, 412; *see also Rerum novarum*
Leopold I, king of the Belgians, 137
Leopold II, Holy Roman Emperor, 31
Le Peletier de Saint-Fargeau, Michel, 70, 72
Le Play, Frédéric, 395–6, 411
Lessing, Gotthold Ephraim, 151
Le Tellier, Michel, 32
Levenstein, Alfred, 268
liberalism: Pius IX's hostility to, 147,

Most, Johannes, 265, 416

Mulhouse, 389

Müller, Adam, 114

Mun, Albert de, comte, 346, 397–8, 400–3, 410–12, 438, 455

music: as expression of sublime, 272–4

Mussolini, Benito, 3

Myers, Frederic William Henry, 256

Naples: secret societies, 164

Napoleon I (Bonaparte), emperor of the French: religious settlement, 106–10, 112; crowned, 110; foreign views of, 114; European alliance against, 117, 121; escapes from Elba, 118; centralises education, 133; exile on St Helena, 133; and investiture of bishops, 137; effect on German nationalism, 154–7, 159, 162; opposed by irregulars and volunteers, 159; and Italian nationalism, 163–4; creates Grand Duchy of Warsaw, 169

Napoleon III, emperor of the French (*earlier* Louis Napoleon): attempted assassination, 193; elected president of France, 208; engineers coup of 1851, 209–10, 394; becomes emperor, 210; clerical support for, 210–11; and Saint-Simon, 225; Convention on patrimony of St Peter, 316; church and state under, 336; and Melun, 394; downfall, 415; Lagarde corresponds with, 435

Nashoba, Memphis, 238

Nasmith, David, 373

Nation (Irish newspaper), 182–4

nation states: and core values, 14–15; as natural entities, 150

National Assembly (France): anticlericalism, 51–2, 54–6, 59–60, 63

National Equitable Labour Exchange, 239

National Guard (France): and revolutionary festivals, 76

National Social Association (Germany), 420

National Socialism: nihilism, 2; Voegelin on, 5; Christopher Dawson opposes, 7–8; as secular religion, 9; antisemitism, 418; spread in Christian Germany, 420; accommodates religion, 460

nationalism: effect of Christianity on, 144–5, 149–50, 153, 161; German, 146, 148–9, 154–63, 320; beginnings, 147–8; and self-dramatisation, 161; in Italy, 163; as religious surrogate, 199; in First World War, 441–50

Naumann, Friedrich, 419–21

Navarino, battle of (1827), 168

Nechaev, Serge, 285–9, 292, 295–6

Necker, Suzanne, 89

neo-Guelphism, 191

Netherlands: Catholics in, 323

Nevsky, Alexander, 120

New Catholic Association, 180

New Harmony, Indiana, 238

New Lanark, 235–7

Newman, Francis William, 213

Newman, John Henry, Cardinal, 257

'new man/woman': and rebirth, 1; in Russia, 277–9, 306

Nicholas I, tsar of Russia, 136, 168, 170–1, 276–7

Niebuhr, Reinhold, 4

Niemöller, Martin, 331

Nietzsche, Friedrich, 11, 433, 435, 437, 443–4

Nobilissima Gallorum Gens (papal encyclical, 1884), 346

nobility: Bonald's view of, 131

Nonconformity: in Britain, 254–6, 262–3, 312; buildings, 369; and church attendance, 369–70; and urban missions, 374; and social problems, 379; and Labour Churches, 387

Notre-Dame, Paris: converted to 'Temple of Reason', 87